P9-DUT-013

USED BOOK

PRICE _____

UCP BOOKSTORE

FOURTH EDITION

USSR
A Concise History

FOURTH EDITION

USSR
A Concise History

BASIL DMYTRYSHYN

CHARLES SCRIBNER'S SONS · New York

Copyright © 1984, 1978, 1971, 1965 Charles Scribner's Sons

Library of Congress Cataloging in Publication Data

Dmytryshyn, Basil, 1925-
    USSR: a concise history.

    Bibliography: p.
    Includes index.
    1. Soviet Union—History—1917-   . I. Title.
II. Title: U.S.S.R.
DK266.D57   1984   947.084   83-27126
ISBN 0-684-18083-9
ISBN 0-684-18082-0 (pbk.)

This book published simultaneously in the
United States of America and in Canada—
Copyright under the Berne Convention

All rights reserved. No part of this book
may be reproduced in any form without the
permission of Charles Scribner's Sons.

1 3 5 7 9 11 13 15 17 19 F/C 20 18 16 14 12 10 8 6 4 2
1 3 5 7 9 11 13 15 17 19 F/P 20 18 16 14 12 10 8 6 4 2

PRINTED IN THE UNITED STATES OF AMERICA

TO

Sonia and Tania

The
Soviet Union

PREFACE

The Union of Soviet Socialist Republics—USSR in brief—means different things to different people. To an impartial observer it is the world's first socialist state dominated by a single party, the Communist party. To a Communist or a Communist sympathizer, the USSR represents a "noble experiment" and an example of successful application of Marxist ideas, as elaborated by Lenin, Stalin, and Khrushchev. To most anti-Communists, however, the USSR is at best a failure—a prison of nations, and a country of slave labor camps. Most religious leaders see in it a country of religious persecution. Many intellectuals consider it a utopian ideal marred by inhuman practices. Industrialization enthusiasts think of it as an outstanding example of rapid industrialization. Military men respect it as a great military power. Space devotees see in it a pioneer of space explorations. Political leaders of underdeveloped countries have often used it as a lever against the United States. Critical observers see in the USSR a country capable of solving intricate problems of space travel but incapable of solving its agricultural, housing, and nationality problems—to name only a few. Whatever their validity, these sample illustrations show that the USSR is a protean country; that is, depending on time, place, circumstance, and above all the point of view of the observer, it stirs up passionate partisan feelings and conveys a different meaning to different observers.

Though modest in size this volume seeks to summarize, by way of a concise treatment, the main trends of development of the USSR. By its very nature this book cannot in any way pretend to be either a definitive or an exhaustive treatment. It does not present any startling revelations nor is it novel for the sake of novelty. The primary aim of this work is to provide the student of Soviet affairs with a brief, but accurate, clearly organized and dispassionate, chronological survey of domestic developments and foreign policy of the Soviet Union since 1917. The information contained in this volume is based upon primary sources (some of which are appended), which in turn are supplemented by other pertinent studies of the best scholarship to date.

It is a pleasant custom among scholars to express appreciation to all those who, in any way, have rendered help in the preparation of the work and at the same time to absolve them of all the sins committed by the author. I wish to thank my colleagues at Portland State College for relieving me of some of my teaching duties during the preparation of this work. In particular I wish to express my thanks to Professors Frederick J. Cox, John O. Dart, Jesse L. Gilmore and George C. Hoffmann who directed my attention to some of the inconsistencies in the manuscript.

I am, finally, deeply indebted to my wife, Virginia, whose keen eye, in reading and rereading the manuscript, has contributed to the shaping of every paragraph.

Basil Dmytryshyn

Champaign, Illinois
January 14, 1965

PREFACE TO THE SECOND EDITION

The purpose of this new edition is to trace events since Khrushchev's ouster late in 1964; to include, in accordance with a number of suggestions, additional documentary material; to update the selected bibliography; and, finally, to correct the typographical errors that were overlooked in the first edition.

B. D.

Portland, Oregon
February 1, 1971

PREFACE TO THE THIRD EDITION

Except for a few factual updatings, that portion of the third edition of *USSR: A Concise History* which deals with history of the Soviet Union up to Stalin's death remains the same as it was in the second edition. The basic change is in the material concerned with Khrushchev's and Brezhnev's tenures in power (1953 to present). I have thoroughly reexamined, reorganized, rewritten, and updated this part. It was essential to do so because many great events have taken place since the second edition was published in 1971. Among the most notable were the deaths of several principal characters, including Khrushchev, Mao Tse-tung, and Chou En-lai. This period also witnessed the emergence of a vocal dissent in the USSR and in Eastern Europe, several crop failures, Soviet entrenchment in certain areas in Africa, expulsion of Soviet forces from Indonesia and Egypt, detente, the Helsinki agreement, and so on. The third edition incorporates these and all other pertinent changes, and it also has new appendixes.

I would like to thank three persons who helped me in the preparation of the third edition. Miss Patricia Byrd, Portland State University Library, and Mrs. Elizabeth O'Malley, my student assistant, helped me to locate a number of pertinent facts and figures. And my wife Virginia, as she has in the past, offered many useful constructive suggestions.

Portland, Oregon

PREFACE TO THE FOURTH EDITION

The purpose of this new edition is twofold. The first seeks to update the selected bibliography and to add, as well as to delete, some documentary material. The second tries to analyze the most significant developments in Soviet domestic and foreign policy since the appearance of the third edition in early 1978. Of the many developments the following commanded interest and attention: the enormous military build-up; the staging of the 1980 Summer Olympic Games in Moscow; unrest in Poland; Soviet invasion of Afghanistan; the death of Brezhnev; the deterioration of Soviet relations with the United States; and the rise of Yuri V. Andropov as a new Soviet leader.

Portland, Oregon

CONTENTS

LIST OF ILLUSTRATIONS

LIST OF CHARTS

LIST OF MAPS

ASSR	Autonomous Soviet Socialist Republic
CC	Central Committee
CCC	Central Control Commission
CHEKA	Extraordinary Commission for Combating Counter-revolution, Speculation and Delinquency (Secret Police)
CIC	Central Inspection Commission
CM	Council of Ministers
CMEA	Council of Mutual Economic Aid (also known as COMECOM)
COMECON	Council for Mutual Economic Cooperation
Cominform	Communist Information Bureau
Comintern	Communist International
CP(b)U	Communist Party (bolshevik) of the Ukraine
CPC	Communist Party of China
CPR	Chinese People's Republic
CPSU	Communist Party of the Soviet Union
CPY	Communist Party of Yugoslavia
FPRY	Federal People's Republic of Yugoslavia
Gosplan	State Plan
kolkhoz	Collective Farm
komsomol	Communist Youth Organization
LCY	League of Communists of Yugoslavia
MGB	Ministry of State Security
MTS	Machine Tractor Station
MVD	Ministry of Internal Affairs
NEC	National Economic Council
NEP	New Economic Policy
NKVD	People's Commissariat of Internal Affairs
OGPU	Unified State Political Administration
Orgburo	Organizational Bureau
Politburo	Political Bureau
SEC	Supreme Economic Council
sovkhoz	State Farm
sovnarkom	Council of People's Commissars
SSR	Soviet Socialist Republic
VKP(b)	All-Union Communist Party (bolshevik)
YCL	Young Communist League (also known as KOMSOMOL)

🗲 I

INTRODUCTION

THE PHYSICAL SETTING

The USSR is a country of many superlatives and extremes. It is, for instance, the largest country in the world. Its area of 8,600,870 square miles represents about one-sixth of the earth's land surface. It is nearly three times the size of the continental United States, is larger than either all Latin America or all North America, and is bigger by far than China and India combined. Occupying a large area of Eastern Europe (about 42 per cent of Europe) and all of Northern Asia (about 43 per cent of Asia), the USSR has some 10,550 miles of land frontier (about twice that of the United States) and about 26,700 miles of coast line. It borders on Norway, Finland, the Baltic Sea, Poland, Czechoslovakia, Hungary, Rumania, the Black and Azov Seas, Turkey, the Caspian Sea, Iran, Afghanistan, China, Mongolia, North Korea, and the Pacific and Arctic Oceans. So vast is the territory of the USSR that it extends through eleven of the

1

world's twenty-four time zones. Needless to say, the size and the location of the USSR are extremely vital economic and military assets in the hands of its present leaders as they also were in the hands of their predecessors.

In terms of relief, the USSR can be divided into three sections: (1) *The Great Plain* that stretches west of the Yenisey River to the country's western borders in the heart of Europe, and that includes the Western Siberian Plain, the Central Asiatic Lowlands, the Ural Mountains, and the Great Russian Plain; (2) *The Uplands of North Eastern Asia* which include the Central Siberian Plateau and such Trans-Baikal mountain ranges as the Yablonovoy, Stanovoy, Dzhugdzhur, Verkhoiansk, Chersky, Kolyma, and Anadyr; and (3) *The Southern Rim of Mountains* such as the Caucasus (Mt. Elbrus, 18,468 feet), the Pamirs (24,590 feet), the Tien-Shan (Mt. Tengri Khan, 22,940 feet), the Altai (Mt. Belukha, 15,157 feet), and the Sayan (Mt. Piramida, 10,801 feet), which give the USSR the appearance of a great amphitheater facing the Arctic Ocean.

Most of the land area of the USSR lies north of the fiftieth parallel. Archangel, for instance, is only 120 miles south of the Arctic Circle. Leningrad, located on the sixtieth parallel, is in the same latitude as Stockholm, Sweden, Cape Farewell, the southern extremity of Greenland, and the northern tip of Labrador. Moscow is in the latitude of Glasgow, Scotland, and Sitka, Alaska. Kiev, the capital of the Ukrainian SSR, is in the latitude of the Aleutian Islands and the northern tip of Newfoundland; while Yalta, a resort town in Crimea on the Black Sea, is in the latitude of Portland, Oregon, Ottawa, Canada, and Milan, Italy. The most southerly point of the USSR is on the thirty-sixth parallel, which is in the latitude of Gibraltar and San Francisco, California.

The northerly location of the USSR, the lack of marine influence, the absence of protective mountains to hold back the cold air from the Arctic, and the massive character and flatness of the territory, exert an important influence on the country's climate. The latter is distinguished by its severity, astonishing uniformity, and continental nature. Because of high pressures and low temperatures, winters in the USSR are cold, long, and windy (in the western and central regions). Areas east of the Ural Mountains have lower temperatures than those of the European part of the USSR. In the Verkhoiansk-Oimiakon area of the Yakut ASSR, for instance, the temperature may drop in the coldest winter to —94° F., in contrast to a "warm" —45° F. in Moscow or —35° F. in Leningrad. The severity of this winter climate, which in some areas lasts from October to May, has a crippling effect on shipping. Many ports of the USSR on the Baltic and Caspian Seas and those on the Pacific and Arctic Oceans are inaccessible to ships from three to six months of the year. The same is true of the rivers of the Soviet Union which are frozen from six to nine months of each year.

Many of the same factors which are responsible for the severity of the winter are also responsible for the extreme conditions of the Soviet summer. Summers throughout most of the USSR are brief, dry, windy, and hot. Verkhoiansk, which, as we noted earlier, has the distinction of being one of the coldest spots in the world during the winter, has recorded a temperature as high as +93° F. in the summer, or the same as that of some regions of the south-western parts of the United States. This extreme annual range in Verkhoiansk is not unusual, for temperatures above +85° F. have been recorded in many places of the Soviet Union north of the Arctic Circle. Yakutsk, on the Lena River in North Eastern Asia, has recorded an extreme maximum of +102° F., Tomsk +95° F., Moscow +99° F., and Leningrad +97° F. The temperature in the desert of Central Asia has reached as high as +125° F. near Tashkent. The severe, frigid cold of the silent winter and the scorching heat, dust, thunder and lightning, hail, and the myriads of mosquitoes of the summer in many parts of the

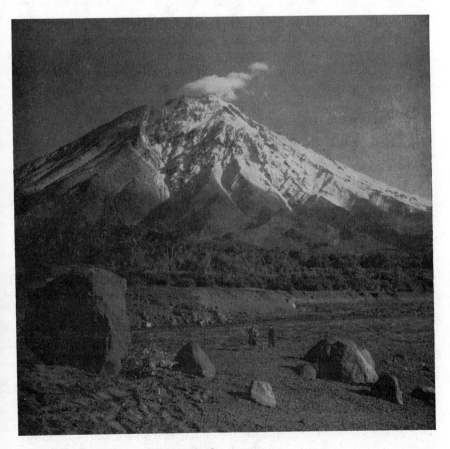

Tundra and volcano in the Kamchatka region.

USSR, and especially in Siberia, have until recently discouraged colonization as well as exploitation of natural resources.

The extreme continental climate and the northerly location of the USSR have a significant bearing on the country's soil and vegetation zones. The Arctic coast and the regions east of the Yenisey River are characterized by a phenomenon known as *permafrost,* or permanently frozen ground beneath the surface. The depth of the summer thaw of permafrost varies from eighteen inches in peat bogs to six feet, six inches in coniferous forests. The affected area is very large, covering about 3,500,000 square miles or 47 per cent of the territory of the USSR. A sizable portion of the permafrost area along the Arctic coast, (about 15 per cent of the total area of the USSR) several hundred miles in width, is known as *tundra,* an area consisting largely of water-logged bogs and marshes. The tundra is frozen during the winter and is mosquito-infested during the summer, making it thus quite uninhabitable. Because of the severity of the winter, the violence of the winds, the brevity of the summer, the dryness of the climate, the coldness of the soil, and the shallow penetration of the roots, vegetation in the tundra is practically nil. The main growth in the northern parts of the tundra is moss, while the southern part is covered with heather, blackberry, cranberry, black birch, and dwarf willow.

South of this uninhabitable area is the *taiga.* The taiga has been described as "a monotonous, dark, and mournfully silent forest with trees that grow close together, but are rarely fine specimens." Much of the taiga is semimarshy, damp and spongy forest, with spruce, fir, larch, pine, and cedar the predominant species. In its southern regions the taiga has many broad-leafed deciduous trees such as oak, linden, ash, elm, alder, and birch. Approximately one-third of all the USSR is covered by forests (coniferous and deciduous), comprising about 20 per cent of the world's forest area, and which are now, as they have been in the past, a basic resource of the country. In addition to forest, the taiga also contains vast mineral wealth.

South of the taiga is the steppe, or prairie. Covering about 14 per cent of the territory of the USSR, the steppe extends from the Ukraine across the Urals into Siberia. The chief characteristic of the steppe is the absence of trees, which is caused by climatic conditions (limited rainfall, intense evaporation, dryness of the air, and the strength of the winds). Most of the steppe consists of the richest soil in the world—the *chernozem,* or black soil, which crumbles into fine powder when dry and turns into a thick black paste when wet. The richness of the steppe soil and the mineral wealth beneath it have for centuries attracted all kinds of settlers and acted as a lure for countless invaders.

South of the steppe, roughly north and east of the Caspian Sea and extending to the Pamir Mountains, are the three desert and semidesert

NATURAL REGIONS OF THE USSR

Ice
Tundra
Taiga
Mixed forest
Steppe
Desert

MILES
0   300   600

S.H. Bryant

regions of the USSR: (1) the Ust Urt desert between the Caspian and the Aral Seas; (2) the Kyzyl Kum desert, east of the Aral Sea; and (3) the Kara Kum desert, south of the Aral Sea. These deserts cover between a fifth and a sixth of the territory of the Soviet Union. The extreme heat in summer, the lack of surface water, the swarms of locusts, and the presence of a poisonous spider called *karakurt* which spares neither man nor beast, have until now prevented these areas from being settled in appreciable numbers, except by nomads. In recent years, irrigation projects have turned fertile parts of the desert (especially the Kyzyl Kum desert) into cotton fields, and orchards of olives, figs, apricots, oranges, and lemons.

Many rivers cut their way across the immense territory of the USSR. Together with many canals (the Baltic-White Sea Canal, the Moscow-Volga Canal, the Volga-Baltic Canal and the Volga-Don Canal) the rivers

The Lenin Volga-Don Canal.

of the USSR serve now, as they have in the past, as major avenues of communication and transportation. Of some 200,000 miles of river in the USSR, about 70,000 are navigable, with Moscow being a "Port of Five Seas." The most important rivers in the European part of the USSR are the Volga, Europe's largest river (2,325 miles and a drainage area of 563,300 square miles) and its tributary, the Kama (1,200 miles); the Dnieper, historically the most important (1,410 miles long and a drainage area of 202,140 square miles); the Don (1,325 miles long); the Ural (1,000 miles long); the Pechora (1,150 miles long); the Northern Dvina (1,100 miles long); and the Western Dvina (640 miles long). In Central Asia the most important rivers are the Amu Darya (1,400 miles long) and the Syr Darya (1,300 miles long). In Northern Asia the most important rivers include the Ob, the second largest river in the USSR (3,200 miles long) and its tributary, the Irtysh (2,700 miles long); the Yenisey, the largest river in the USSR (3,500 miles long) and its tributaries, the Angara (1,200 miles long), the Stony Tunguska (1,000 miles long) and the Lower Tunguska (2,000 miles long); the Lena (3,000 miles long and a drainage area in excess of one million square miles) and its major tributary, the Aldan (1,500 miles long); and the Amur, the chief river of eastern Asia (3,000 miles long).

The usefulness of many of these rivers for transport is limited by the fact that the great majority of them either freeze over during part of each year, or empty into the Arctic Ocean, or into such lakes as the Caspian Sea (the largest lake in the world, 152,500 square miles) and the Aral Sea (26,166 square miles). Since the early 1930's, Soviet engineers have constructed on many of these rivers vast hydroelectric projects which have turned the USSR into one of the world's major producers of electric energy. The largest of these projects are: The Krasnoiarsk Dam of 5,000,000 kw. capacity on the Yenisey River; the Bratsk Dam of 4,500,000 kw. capacity on the Angara River; the Twenty-Second Party Congress Dam of 2,530,000 kw. capacity on the Volga River; the Kuibyshev Dam of 2,300,000 kw. capacity on the Volga River; and the Dnieprostroy Dam of 650,000 kw. capacity on the Dnieper River.

Within the borders of the USSR lie large quantities of fuel and raw material resources. The exact amount of these resources has not been adequately established because only some 75 per cent of the territory has been geologically studied. The USSR is almost self-sufficient with respect to raw materials. Its water resources for hydroelectric power are among the world's largest; while its coal reserves are among the greatest in the world. The most prominent coal centers are those of the Donets Basin (the Donbass), the Kuznetsk Basin (the Kuzbass), the Karaganda area (in the Kazakh SSR), the Cheremkhovo Basin (near Irkutsk), the Bureia Basin (in the Far East), and the Sub-Moscow Basin.

Soviet iron resources match those of water and coal and comprise a

PRINCIPAL INDUSTRIAL AND AGRICULTURAL
AREAS OF THE USSR

Principal industrial regions

Principal grain region

General farming

Principal fruit-growing area

Major cotton region

CITIES

Over 5 million

1-5 million

300,000-1 million

MILES

0   400   800

S.H.Bryant

Vladivostok

Khabarovsk

Amur

Chita

Irkutsk

Krasnoiarsk

Novokuznetsk

Lena

Yenisei

Ob

NEW LANDS

Novosibirsk

Omsk

Karaganda

Sverdlovsk

Magnitogorsk

Perm

Alma-Ata

Tashkent

Kazan

Gorky

Kuibyshev

Saratov

Archangel

Leningrad

Volgograd

Baku

Tula

MOSCOW

Kharkov

Donetsk

Tbilisi

Riga

Kiev

Erevan

Lvov

Odessa

MILES
0 ___ 800

0 ___ 800
KILOMETERS

MOSCOW BASIN

PECHORA BASIN

DONETS BASIN

URALS

GEORGIA

EKIBASTUZ

EASTERN SIBERIA

FAR EAST

KARAGANDA

KUZNETSK BASIN

MIDDLE ASIA

256
144
64
16

1965
1960
1913

Millions of Tons

COAL PRODUCTION
BY BASINS
IN THE
USSR

large portion of all the world's iron reserves. Though found at about 600 different locations, only about one hundred Soviet iron deposits have been exploited. The most prominent iron ore deposits of the USSR are those of the Krivoy Rog in the Ukraine, the Urals (Magnitogorsk), the Kerch Peninsula in the Crimea, the Gornaia Shoriia area of Western Siberia (near the Kuznetsk coal basin), the Caucasus (near Lake Sevan), the Kola Peninsula, Nikolaevsk (on the Amur River), and near Moscow (Tula and Kursk). The USSR also has large oil reserves. The latter are located in the Apsheron Peninsula (adjoining the city of Baku), the Emba Basin (Western Kazakh SSR), the Caucasus (Maikop and Grozny), the Pechora Basin, Sakhalin Island, the Turkmen SSR (Krasnozavodsk), the Fergana Valley and the basin of the upper Amu Darya (Uzbek SSR), and the Western Ukraine (Drohobych-Boryslav).

The USSR is a leading source of manganese (Chiatura in the Georgian SSR, Nikopol in the Ukraine, the Kazakh SSR and Eastern Siberia); has abundant copper reserves (the Kazakh SSR, the Bashkir ASSR, the Sverdlovsk and Murmansk Provinces, and the Krasnoiarsk Territory in Eastern Siberia); possesses ample deposits of lead and zinc (the Kazakh SSR, the Kuznetsk Basin, the Chita and Sverdlovsk Provinces, and the Maritime Territory in the Far East); commands vast reserves of

9

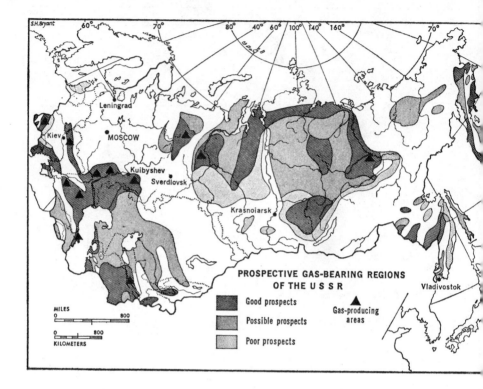

S.H.Bryant

**PROSPECTIVE GAS-BEARING REGIONS
OF THE U S S R**

Good prospects

Possible prospects

Poor prospects

Gas-producing
areas

MILES
0   800

0   800
KILOMETERS

bauxite (east of Leningrad, the Bashkir ASSR, Uzbek and Kazakh SSR's, Sverdlovsk, Tula, Novosibirsk, and Kamerovo Provinces and the Altay and Krasnoiarsk Territories); and is one of the largest nickel producing countries in the world (Krasnoiarsk Territory, the Kola Peninsula, Southern and Central Urals, and Northern Caucasus).

The USSR is one of the world's largest producers of gold (the Aldan Plateau in Eastern Siberia, the Maritime Territory in the Far East, the Kazakh SSR, the Buriat-Mongol ASSR, and the Irkutsk and Chita Provinces); has some uranium deposits (the Fergana Valley and the Tannu-Tuva area); has adequate tin resources (the Chita Province, the Maritime Territory in the Far East, the Yakut ASSR, the Kirghiz SSR, the Kazakh SSR, the Caucasus, and the east coast of Lake Ladoga); produces significant amounts of silver; claims priority in the production of platinum; is one of the world's major producers of chromium (the Urals and the Kazakh SSR); and has ample supplies of mercury, antimony, bismuth, cobalt, arsenic, and other rare metals. The USSR, finally, is rich in impor-

Soviet Kazakhstan in the vicinity of Alma-Ata.

tant industrial nonmetalic minerals such as asbestos, potassium, salts, phosphorites, borates, sodium chloride, kaolin, peat, and natural gas.

The population of the USSR matches the diversity of the country's natural resources. According to the census of January 15, 1970, the USSR had 241,748,000 people distributed among more than one hundred different nationalities. Based on their language affiliation, these diverse nationalities of the USSR belong to the following major language groups: *Slavic* (Great Russians, the dominant group, Ukrainians, and Belorussians); *Baltic* (Lithuanians and Latvians); *Romance* (Moldavians); *Finno-Ugric* (Estonians, Karelians, Veps, Komi, Mari, Mordvinians, and Udmurts); *Turkic* (Tartars, Bashkirs, Chuvash, Uzbeks, Kazakhs, Kirghiz, Turkmen, Kara-Kalpaks, and Azerbaidzhans); *Mongol* (Kalmyks and Buriat-Mongols); *Ugric* (Khanty and Mansi); *Kartvelian* (Georgians, Svan, Laz, and Adzhar); *Tungus-Manchu* (Evenki, Eveny, Ulchi, Orochi, and Udege); *Iranian* (Tadzhiks, Ossetians, and Kurds); *Dagestan* (Avars, Darghin, Laks, and Tabasarans); *Nakh* (Chechen and Ingush); and *Abkhaz-Adighe* (Kabardians, Adighe, Cherkess, Abaza, and Abkhaz).[1]

For administrative purposes these diverse nationalities of the USSR are currently grouped into the following fifteen union republics:

[1] For a complete listing of ethnic groups of the USSR, see Appendix 1.

Republic	Area in Square miles	1979 Census Population	Capital
Russian Soviet Federated Socialist Republic (RSFSR)	6,593,391	137,552,000	Moscow
Ukrainian Soviet Socialist Republic (UkSSR)	232,046	49,757,000	Kiev
Uzbek Soviet Socialist Republic	159,069	15,391,000	Tashkent
Kazakh Soviet Socialist Republic	1,064,086	14,685,000	Alma Ata
Belorussian Soviet Socialist Republic	80,154	9,559,000	Minsk
Azerbaidzhanian Soviet Socialist Republic	33,436	6,028,000	Baku
Georgian Soviet Socialist Republic	26,911	5,016,000	Tbilisi
Moldavian Soviet Socialist Republic	13,012	3,948,000	Kishinev
Tadzhik Soviet Socialist Republic	55,019	3,801,000	Dushanbe
Kirghiz Soviet Socialist Republic	76,641	3,529,000	Frunze
Lithuanian Soviet Socialist Republic	25,174	3,399,000	Vilnius
Armenian Soviet Socialist Republic	11,506	3,031,000	Erevan
Turkmenian Soviet Socialist Republic	188,417	2,759,000	Ashkhabad
Latvian Soviet Socialist Republic	24,595	2,521,000	Riga
Estonian Soviet Socialist Republic	17,413	1,466,000	Tallinn
Total	8,600,870	262,442,000	

Other administrative units include nineteen autonomous republics, nine autonomous *oblasts* (regions), 123 *krays* (territories), and ten national *okrugs* (areas). (See page 13.)

The foregoing selected samples reveal that the USSR is an extremely complicated country. It is also a rich, resourceful, and powerful country. Since the late 1920's the power of the USSR has increased appreciably as a result of a policy of forceful industrialization. Whether the peoples of the Soviet Union have been the beneficiaries or the victims of this policy is a highly debatable question among observers of the Soviet scene. This problem as well as the entire development of the USSR since 1917 can best be understood if we first examine briefly the conditions which paved the way for one of the major events in the history of the twentieth century—the Russian Revolution, the course of which made possible the emergence of the USSR.

ADMINISTRATIVE DIVISIONS OF THE USSR.

THE HISTORICAL BACKGROUND

Pre-Emancipation Russia

Technically, the USSR made its official debut on December 30, 1922, when the Russian SFSR, the Ukrainian SSR, the Belorussian SSR and the Trans-Caucasian SFSR concluded a treaty creating the union. This formality, however, was preceeded by a whole series of developments of which the Russian Revolutions of 1917 were the most significant. These revolutions—which set Russia and subsequently many parts of the world on a path of far-reaching changes—can be understood only from a knowledge of the political, economic, social, and cultural stimuli, and, above all, the conditions from which they were born. Many of these conditions, such as the autocratic form of the imperial government, the multinational nature of the empire, the relative economic backwardness of the state, the agrarian nature of the society, and the widespread illiteracy and poverty of the people, to name only a few, were products of the totality of Russian history. Some, however, such as the ideals of political liberty, equality, fraternity, and democracy of the French Revolution of 1789, and the promise of economic abundance and opportunity of the Industrial Revolution, were products of West European influences.

Students of Russian history generally agree that the ideals of the French Revolution of 1789 had a profound influence on Russia's development, as they also had on the development of many other countries. The influence of the French Revolution on Russia was neither immediate nor direct, however, but came early in the nineteenth century in two distinct and equally powerful waves. The first came via Germany in the form of an idealistic philosophy; while the second was introduced in Russia by those Russians who acquired first-hand acquaintance with West European conditions during the Napoleonic Wars of 1812–1815. Many Russian officers returned home from their victorious campaigns "with boxes crammed with books, heads full of ideas, and hearts aching over the shortcomings and backwardness of their country." Immediately upon their return these young officers and other aristocrats who shared their new and forbidden European ideas developed an intense interest in Russian history and conditions and a desire to introduce in Russia Europe's most modern institutions, methods, and ideas.

Because Russian conditions prevented open discussion of many of these issues, these aristocrats organized small secret groups of which the most important proved to be the Union of Salvation. Founded in 1816 and consisting of two branches, Northern and Southern, this organization changed its name in 1818 to Union of Welfare. The Northern Branch, with headquarters in St. Petersburg, and led by such wealthy aristocratic guardsmen as Prince Sergei P. Trubetskoi (1790–1860) and Nikita M. Muraviev (1795–1826), advocated: equality of all citizens before the law; freedom of the press; freedom of religion; social justice; advancement of education; expanded social work; promotion of economic welfare by encouraging industry, trade, and agriculture; a representative form of government; abolition of serfdom with adequate safeguards of the interests of landed aristocracy; and a federal arrangement for Russia under a constitutional monarch. The Southern Branch, with its center in the Ukraine, led by representatives of lesser nobility, of whom Colonel Pavel I. Pestel (1793–1826) was the chief spokesman, in the best Jacobin tradition advocated: replacement of the monarchy by a military dictatorship for a period of eight years to be followed by a unified, centralized, egalitarian, and democratic republic; abolition of serfdom; expropriation of landlords; abolition of all privileges based on birth, rank, or wealth; abolition of Finnish autonomy; and ruthless Russification of all territories in the Russian Empire. Such then were the ideals and demands of the first Russian revolutionary movement.

The first Russian revolutionary movement had several distinct characteristics that were to be marks of Russian revolutionaries throughout the nineteenth century. First, it was stronger in its revolutionary zeal than in its effectiveness in organization. Second, its members were drawn almost exclusively from the upper classes and had no contact with the lower strata of the society in whose name they intended to act. Third, they advocated seizure of power by a revolutionary elite to make possible the transition from autocracy to democracy. Fourth, they were Great Russian in their outlook, considered the Russian Empire a political and economic entity, and accordingly in their struggle with Tsarism directed their efforts only towards changing Russia's political, economic, and social system. This stand, in turn, caused them to ignore the struggle of non-Russian peoples against Tsarism or to consider that struggle as being something narrow, limited, and insignificant in comparison with their own "high and noble" ideals. Fifth, the leadership of the first Russian revolutionary movement from its inception demonstrated stubbornness of conviction, unwillingness to compromise, factionalism, and a conspiratorial nature. And finally, the spirit of this movement contained incredible contradictions of nobility and baseness, virtue and criminality, and love and hate.

Notwithstanding the secretiveness of the Northern and Southern Branches, government authorities knew of the existence of these organizations. They failed, however, to act decisively against them because they presented no immediate threat—their membership being pitifully small—and because Tsar Alexander I (1801–1825) was rather kindly disposed towards these young officers. Alexander's death late in 1825 precipitated a crisis known as the Decembrist Revolution. The conspirators were not prepared but moved into action as a result of the dynastic riddle. Under the law of 1797 the next in line in succession to the imperial throne of Russia (Alexander having died childless) was his younger brother Constantine. By a secret agreement with Alexander in 1822, however, Constantine had renounced his right in favor of their younger brother Nicholas. So secret was this arrangement that even Nicholas was unaware of it. Following Alexander's death, accordingly, Nicholas in St. Petersburg took the oath of allegiance to Constantine, while Constantine, who was then in Warsaw, swore allegiance to Nicholas. The confusion in the imperial family, which went on for nearly three weeks, offered the revolutionaries an opportunity to act.

The first Russian Revolution started on December 26, 1825. Irresoluteness, indecision, and lack of a clearly thought-out plan of action by its leaders proved fatal to the success of the plot. Most of the army and civilians of the capital took the oath of allegiance to Nicholas. Only a handful refused, and these marched to the Senate Square, where, joined by a few civilians, they shouted "For Constantine and for the Constitution." Leaderless, cold, and hungry the insurgents failed to act or to surrender to the loyal forces which surrounded them under the personal direction of Nicholas. When persuasion failed, the new Tsar ordered the use of force. In a few minutes the Square was cleared, and the brief defiance of governmental authority in the capital instigated by members of the Northern Branch was over. An insurrection by the Southern Branch a few days later proved no more successful than the action in the capital. Its leaders were seized by loyal troops and the expected popular rising failed to materialize.

Though a dismal failure, the Decembrist Revolution, as this insurrection is commonly known, nevertheless had several significant and far-reaching repercussions. First, it led to a thorough inquiry into the causes of the revolt, and the questioning of suspects as to the plans and the membership of the secret societies. Some 600 persons were investigated, but of this number only 121 were tried. Five of the "leaders" were sentenced to death with the remainder being sentenced to exile and forced labor. The trial of the insurgents revealed in detail the political movement led by the nobility and directed against the Romanov dynasty and autocracy. This revelation forced Nicholas I to push aside the nobles—up to then considered the backbone of Russian autocracy—and to surround himself with a bureaucracy of obedient officials regardless of their social status. The trial of the Decembrists, and their complaints about the wretched conditions of the peasants, the lack of good laws, the corruption of judges, the ignorance of the masses, and the high-handedness of officials, pointed up the evils of Russian life and urgently demonstrated the need for reforms. Some of these demands materialized in such measures as (1) organization of "His Majesty's Own Chancellery"; (2)

publication of the Code of Laws; (3) abolition of paper currency; (4) improvement of public instruction; and (5) improvement of the living conditions of state peasants. Finally, and most importantly, the Decembrist Revolution, its ideals, and the government's treatment of its leaders, served for later generations of Russian revolutionaries as a symbol of self-sacrificing struggle against autocracy.

The Decembrist Revolution was responsible for setting the tenor of the reign of Nicholas I (1825–1855) which was one of autocratic firmness and bureaucratic reaction. Russians were forbidden to travel in Europe, and Europeans were discouraged from travelling in Russia. To make certain that no alien ideas penetrated into the Empire, the government instituted a rigorous, almost absurd censorship of publications, limited educational opportunities in secondary schools to children of trusted officials and nobles, and turned university education into a preparation of upper-class youth for state service. The teaching of history of philosophy, metaphysics, and constitutional law was suspended, and instruction in logic was permitted only by professors of theology. By these and similar actions, which worsened as time went on, the imperial government of Russia further isolated its subjects from the rest of Europe and forced upon them "Autocracy, Orthodoxy, and Nationality."

Ironically this period of the most uncompromising reaction, as the reign of Nicholas I is commonly known, witnessed an exceptional literary creativeness. It was the period of the romantic poetry of Alexander S. Pushkin (1799–1837), Michael Iu. Lermontov (1814–1841), and Alexei V. Koltsov (1809–1842), and of the sultry, exuberant comedies of Nicholas V. Gogol (1809–1852). Leo N. Tolstoy (1828–1910) and Ivan S. Turgeniev (1818–1883) made their literary debuts during the reign of Nicholas I, as did such lesser known Russian writers as playwrights Alexander N. Ostrovsky (1823–1886) and Alexander S. Griboedov (1797–1829), novelist Ivan A. Goncharov (1812–1891), and poet Nikolai A. Nekrasov (1821–1878). The reign of Nicholas I saw the creative work of Vissarion G. Belinsky (1810–1848), considered by some the greatest professional literary critic in Russian history, Michael I. Glinka (1804–1857), the first Russian composer, and Alexander I. Herzen (1812–1870), one of the most important Russian novelists and a revolutionary publicist, whose *Kolokol* (The Bell), published in London, thundered against the abuses of autocracy and, in a different guise, carried on the revolutionary tradition of the Decembrists.

The reign of uncompromising reaction witnessed also a deep philosophical search for answers to Russia's future. This search manifested itself in two divergent currents of thought: Slavophilism and Westernism. The Slavophiles, inspired by the romantic nationalism then in vogue, "extolled the imaginary virtues of the truly Russian national ways," viewed the Orthodox church as a unique source of Russia's strength, were highly critical of the "decadent west," deplored the efforts of Peter the Great in behalf of Russia's modernization, opposed the constitutional form of government, and were enthusiastic about the village commune and "the voice of the people" expressed through a consultative assembly resembling the *Zemsky Sobor* (Landed Assembly) of the seventeenth century. The Slavophiles held in contempt all non-Orthodox Slavs (especially Poles), were great admirers of Great Russian supremacy, and many of them were among the most ruthless and uncompromising agents of the policy of Russification of non-Russian minorities of the Empire. Among the outstanding Slavophile representatives belong Ivan V. Kireevsky (1806–1856) and Peter V. Kireevsky (1808–1856), Ivan S. Aksakov (1823–1886) and Constantine S. Aksakov (1817–1861), Aleksei S. Khomiakov (1804–1860), Yurii F. Samarin (1819–1876), and Prince Vladimir A. Cherkassky (1824–1878).

The Westerners, in the words of a competent observer, "were primarily Russian humanitarians." They admired modern things, believed in scientific progress, favored the constitutional form of government, advocated freedom of thought and of the press, opposed serfdom, deplored the gulf in Russian society that separated the educated few from the illiterate multitude, and, above all, they favored "the education of Russian society in the ideas of a European universal culture in order to lift Russian national development to a super-national level where it would acquire world significance." The Westerners greatly admired the modernization efforts of Peter the Great, and followed with keen interest developments in Europe, be they intellectual, social, economic, artistic, literary, or revolutionary. Among the outstanding representatives of the Westerners belong Herzen, Belinsky, and Timofei N. Granovsky (1813–1855).

Both the Westerners and the Slavophiles—indeed the entire Russian society—were rocked to the foundations by the Crimean War (1853–1856). Russia's defeat in that war at the hands of France, England, Piedmont, and the Ottoman Empire, and above all the rather humiliating restrictions the victors imposed on Russia in the Treaty of Paris, dealt a heavy blow to Russia's prestige in international affairs. The defeat also destroyed the myth of Russia's gigantic strength and of its invincibility and clearly demonstrated its great backwardness. The defeat, finally, exposed the military, administrative, economic, and social ineptness of autocracy, and convinced the Tsar as well as many of his advisors that the long-overdue reforms demanded by the Decembrists and their followers, and opposed by the conservative elements of Russian society, could no longer be postponed. The realization of these reforms fell upon the new tsar, Alexander II (1855–1881). The choice was unfortunate because Alexander was unprepared, by conviction, training, or temperament, to undertake this gigantic task which was to be one of the most significant landmarks in Russian history.

The Impact of the Emancipation on Russia

The "Era of Great Reforms," as the period of Russian history from 1861 to 1874 is commonly known, commenced on March 3, 1861, with the publication of the Emancipation Statute. The most celebrated feature of this history-making document was the abolition of human bondage throughout the Russian Empire. The legal aspect of this action was admirable, but the same cannot be said of the economic side of the Emancipation Statute. The difficulty stemmed from the strong opposition to emancipation on the part of the majority of the nobles, and from the extremely complicated bondage system which had evolved in Russia through the centuries. At the time of the emancipation there were some 60,000,000 inhabitants in the European part of the Empire. Of these, about 50,000,-000 were peasants of one kind or another—about 22,000,000 were serfs of the nobility, some 20,000,000 were classified as state peasants, and the remaining 8,000,000 belonged to other categories of serf and non-serf peasantry. As the conditions of other peasants had been improved during the reign of Nicholas I, the Emancipation Statute affected primarily the serfs of the nobility. Based on their obligations, which varied in different parts of the Empire, these consisted of three basic groups: (1) *barshchina* serfs, or serfs who were tied to the village commune in which they lived and to the estate of the nobleman to whom they belonged and whose land they worked as part of their obligation, often with their own stock and implements; (2) *obrok* serfs, or serfs who were tied to the village commune and the landlord's estate but who paid their dues to their owner in kind or in money; and (3) household serfs, or serfs who had no land and were bound only to their owners.

Because the majority of the nobles disapproved the whole idea of the reform (which actually was carried through by the autocratic Tsar with the assistance of a few enlightened bureaucrats and the liberal section of public opinion), the Emancipation Statute reflected the prevailing conditions in Russia. It freed *all serfs* from their masters but granted land only to the *barshchina* and the *obrok* serfs. The amount of land each ex-serf received varied from area to area (larger portions in less productive and smaller portions in more productive regions), but averaged 6.21 acres per person. This amount equalled roughly the portions of their holdings in the open-field scattered strips they had used as serfs for their own maintenance. This amount, however, was not given to the ex-serfs as individual private owners in the usual sense of the term, but it was transferred to the village communes whose members were to receive equal portions along with the right of periodic redistribution. To complicate the matter even more the state compensated the landlords for the loss of their property and sought to recover its expenses in the form of high annual installments from the peasants known as "redemption payments." These were spread over a period of forty-nine years, with the village commune being made collectively responsible for their payment. This redemption payment system turned emancipation into the purchase of freedom on a costly installment plan.

By making them into "neither land dependents nor free men," this extremely complicated land settlement was a great disappointment to the Russian peasantry, and acted as a major reservoir of discontent and a prime cause of the deterioration of their economic conditions. Other obstacles contributing to the agricultural crisis were the high level of peasant illiteracy; use of antiquated techniques; lack of capital or even stable currency; unrealistically high taxes and redemption payments; the poor quality, low yield, and small, widely dispersed land allotments (which because of the population increase diminished from 6.21 acres in 1861 to 3.5 acres in 1900); rapid growth of rural population without a corresponding increase in opportunities; high rent and high interest rate on loans; low grain prices and thus low purchasing power of the peasantry; poor storage facilities and a costly and poorly organized transport system; and the pressure of foreign competition. All these hindrances made it difficult for the peasants to maintain their low standard of living, to say nothing of improvement. To overcome the relative (though not too critical by West European standards) shortage of land, some peasants were forced to find supplemental work, while others either rented or bought more land from the nobles.

During the first two decades following emancipation, the government did nothing to alleviate the plight of the peasantry. The first step in that direction came in May, 1881, with the establishment of a Peasant Land Bank aimed at granting the peasants credit for buying land, although the activities of the Bank did not acquire real importance until after 1905. Other measures included the reduction of redemption payments by almost 27 per cent in December, 1881; abolition of the poll tax in January, 1887; and, during the 1890's, encouragement of peasant migration from the overpopulated European parts to underpopulated Asiatic parts of the Empire. These measures, their importance notwithstanding, failed to solve the agrarian crisis or even to pacify the peasants who were obsessed with the belief that the land should belong to those who tilled it and were never reconciled to the land settlement of the 1860's.

The end of serfdom also brought the end of the predominant position of the nobility. Though they continued to enjoy preferential treatment in administrative and military appointments, the loss of a considerable part of their land, as well as the free supply of labor, spelled the beginning of a decline for them that could not be halted. There were some nobles who succeeded in turning their estates into prosperous farms. The majority of the nobility, however, being tradition-bound and unable to adjust to the new circumstances, either joined the growing revolutionary force, or went bankrupt, or was forced to sell, rent, or share-rent their holdings. The transfer of land from nobles to non-noble owners was "one of the outstanding phenomena in the economic life of Russia up to the end of the imperial regime."

By abolishing serfdom, the Emancipation Statute destroyed the entire medieval structure of Russian society. The removal of the nobleman from the performance of such duties as judge, policeman, recruiting officer, and tax collector, meant the disappearance of old and the need for the emergence of new institutions. On June 18, 1863, the Tsar approved a new University Charter, which restored university autonomy and removed most of the restrictions introduced during the reign of Nicholas I. A charter affecting the secondary schools went into effect on November 18, 1864. On January 1, 1864, the Tsar approved the *Zemstvo* Statute which created a rural self-governing institution with jurisdiction over schools, public health, food supply, roads, insurance, relief of the poor, maintenance of prisons, and other concerns of local needs. On November 20, 1864, a Judicial Statute went into effect. Considered by some scholars to be a masterpiece of legislation, the Statute separated the judicial branch from the legislative and executive branches and introduced the jury system, the office of justice of the peace, an irremovable judiciary, lawyers, oral pleading in courts, and the concept that henceforth justice was to be "equal for all subjects." A Censorship Decree of April 6, 1865, allowed considerable freedom for publishers of books, periodicals, and newspapers, holding them responsible, however, for printing "pernicious" matters. On June 16, 1870, the Municipal Statute was promulgated, granting the cities of the Empire (except those in Poland and Finland) city government. This action transformed Russian cities from mere administrative headquarters into economic and commercial centers. Finally, on January 1, 1874, the government introduced a new conscription law which replaced the concept of a large standing army with universal military service of trained reserves. The new law reduced the military service from twenty-five to six years of active service followed by fourteen years of active reserve. These and other measures moved the Russian Empire from the medieval to the modern world.

The emancipation of serfs also helped to transfer the Russian Empire from a feudal country into a relatively impressive capitalist-industrial power. A few figures will give an idea of the rate of development and change. In 1861 Russia produced 352,100 tons of pig iron; in 1900 the figure was 3,233,900 tons. In 1861 her coal output was 424,325 tons; in 1900 it was 17,809,125 tons. In 1861 her industry consumed 46,945 tons of cotton; in 1900 it used 288,900 tons. In 1861 she produced no oil; in 1900 oil production was 11,395,450 tons. In 1861 Russia had 2,200 kilometers of railroad; in 1900 there were 53,200 kilometers. In 1861 imports totalled 167,111,000 rubles, and exports 177,180,000. For 1900 the corresponding figures were 626,375,000 and 716,217,000 rubles respectively. In 1861, the free labor force was insignificant. By 1900 it numbered about 3,000,000, and was relatively organized. In 1861 Russia exported 1,354,430 tons of grain; in 1900 grain exports totalled 7,834,700 tons. These changes also affected the population, which between 1861 and 1900 rose from 73,600,000 to 132,900,000. The Emancipation, in other words, created a vast transformation which, although hindered at every step by economic and noneconomic obstacles and pressures, was rapid, productive, and constructive.

The Rebellious Generation

The emancipation of serfs and the subsequent transformation of Russian society and economy early in the 1860's gave rise to a movement known as *nihilism*. Nihilism has been defined as the philosophy and politics of young Russian radicals who sought to build a new and complete philosophy of life upon the foundations that had been laid by their predecessors in the 1840's. The nihilists thought of themselves as democrats and socialists, and accordingly as sworn enemies of aristocracy, political liberalism, and of the bourgeoisie. They were extremely hostile towards all forms of authority and everything abstract or general. They sought to destroy superstition, illusion, and falsehood; campaigned against orthodoxy, monasticism, and Christianity in general; renounced the state, church, and official Russian patriotism of "Orthodoxy, Autocracy, and Nationality," and developed a peculiar, almost sacred, love for Russia and its people. The nihilists idealized natural sciences, desiring earnestly to create a "new man," and towards that end they evolved their own ethical principles. As a haunted minority the nihilists held together and "recognized one another by dress, language, method of criticism, and general views." The most prominent nihilists were Nikolai A. Dobroliubov (1836–1861), Dimitri I. Pisarev (1840–1868), and Nikolai G. Chernyshevsky (1828–1889).

The revolt of young Russian radicals against all forms of authority assumed various forms. The earliest form was that of appeals. In 1861 the angry young men printed a number of illegal leaflets called *Velikorus* (Great Russia), in which they appealed to the educated public to end absolutist rule in Russia, seize power from the incompetent government, convene a constituent assembly to draft a constitution for Russia, and grant gratis to the peasants the land they had worked under serfdom. Another proclamation, entitled *K molodomu pokoleniiu* (To the Younger Generation), printed at the Free Press in London and smuggled into Russia late in 1861, demanded elimination of the Romanov Dynasty; the development of Russia along the principles inherent in the life of the Russian people (especially collective land tenure); the destruction, violent if need be, of all forms of opposition to this drastic transformation of

Russian society; propagation of these ideas among the people; and the formation of secret "circles of like-minded persons" to achieve these goals. Still another proclamation, *Molodaia Rossiia* (Young Russia), composed by a Moscow student in May, 1862, called for seizure of power by "the revolutionary party" which would then transform Russia into a republican and federal state with every nationality having the right to self-determination; introduce a popularly elected judiciary, just taxes, and public education for children; emancipate women; abolish monasteries, inheritance, marriage and the family; extend a welfare program to the aged and invalids; expropriate the land of landlords and distribute it to the peasant communes; socialize factories to be run by elected managers; and replace the standing army by a national guard. In the event "the ruling group" resisted the transformation of Russia from a monarchy to a "socialized republic" the proclamation promised a bloody and pitiless nation-wide revolution.

Aimed at political awakening, these appeals aroused considerable excitement among liberals as well as among the authorities, who arrested several radicals, including Chernyshevsky. Agitation for drastic changes in Russian society continued, however, and manifested itself in the form of further addresses to the public and to the Tsar (i.e., the appeal in 1862 of the Tver nobility), and above all in the organization of clandestine "circles." The earliest of these circles, organized in 1862 by radicals of St. Petersburg, was known as *Zemlia i volia* (Land and Freedom) and sought to persuade the intelligentsia to assume the leadership, join the people, expropriate the landowners, and overthrow autocracy. The society promised to terminate its activity the moment freedom of election to the national assembly had been secured. In 1865 a Moscow student, Nikolai A. Ishutin (1840–1879), organized a secret "circle" whose aim was a purely "economic revolution." The members of the circle differed over tactics. Some favored peaceful propaganda among the masses to arouse them into action, while others advocated creation of an all-powerful secret body to direct fraud, theft, liquidation of "traitors" within the society, and political assassination of high officials in order to frighten the Tsar into "decreeing a social revolution." Early in April, 1866, a member of this group, Dimitri V. Karakozov (1840–1866), attempted to assassinate the Tsar. His failure cost him his life and brought imprisonment for other members of the society.

The question of the use of terror as a political weapon, one of the basic problems of disunity among Russian radicals, assumed new dimensions thanks to the influence of Michael A. Bakunin (1814–1876), Sergei G. Nechaev (1847–1882), and Peter N. Tkachev (1844–1885). A veteran revolutionary, Bakunin formulated his program for Russia in 1868 in the *Narodnoe delo* (The People's Cause), a newspaper he published in Geneva. His program called for abolition of the state, religion, the family, and inheritance. It urged equality for women, advocated free education for children, and insisted that the land be transferred to "those who till it" (i.e., to the village communes), with factories and all the means of production being under control of the workers. Russia, in Bakunin's view, should consist of a free federation of agricultural and manufacturing associations (artels), with national minorities being granted an option of joining or not.

In 1869, Nechaev, the founder of the *Narodnaia rasprava* (The People's Justice), joined Bakunin in Geneva, and together they prepared the *Katekhizis revolutsionera* (The Catechism of the Revolutionary). Echoing some of the ideas of the extreme wing of the Ishutin "circle," this practical advice on conspiracy defined a revolutionary as "a doomed man" without private interests, affairs, sentiments, ties, property, or even a name—an individual who has severed all ties with society and "continues to inhabit it with only one purpose—to destroy it." To secure "perfect freedom and happiness"—the stated basic aim of Bakunin and Nechaev—the *Catechism* advocated absolute secrecy of the membership of the society, sought to turn every member-conspirator into a blind instrument of the leader, propagated subordination of everything to the "Cause," and insisted that everything which "promotes the success of the revolution is moral, everything which hinders it is immoral." In 1870 Bakunin parted company with Nechaev when he caught his young associate attempting to blackmail him. Their credo, however, that the entire political and social structure of Russia must be destroyed before a new and better one could be erected, exercised a profound influence on many Russian revolutionaries.

Some revolutionaries followed the teachings of Tkachev who, as an editor of *Nabad* (The Alarm) in Geneva, tried to outbid the radicalism of Bakunin and Nechaev. Tkachev subscribed to many of the ideals of Bakunin, such as expropriation of all the means of production; elimination of physical, moral, and mental inequality; universal education; transformation of the village commune into a Communist community; and gradual replacement of the centralized state by self-governing communes. Tkachev differed, however, from his contemporaries on the nature of revolutionary organization and tactics. Convinced that the peasant masses were incapable of independent revolutionary action, Tkachev assigned the leadership role to an "intellectually and morally developed" highly centralized conspiratorial minority. "The struggle," he argued, "can be conducted successfully only by combining the following conditions: centralization, severe discipline, swiftness, decisiveness, and unity of action. All concessions, all wavering, all compromises, multileadership, and decentralization of the fighting forces weaken their energy, paralyze their activity, and deprive the struggle of all chances for victory." Tkachev accordingly condemned isolated revolutionary outbreaks by small groups, rejected the federal arrangement for Russia, and placed his trust in utopian ideals of fraternity, equality, and re-education.

The main objective of many young Russian radicals in the early 1870's was not centralized terror but organized education of the masses. The followers of this trend were known as *narodniki* or populists. By birth and psychology the *narodniki* were members of the "repentant nobility," who were strongly influenced by the ideas of Herzen, Nikolai K. Mikhailovsky (1842–1904), and Peter L. Lavrov (1823–1901), the editor of a periodical, *Vpered* (Forward), published in Zurich. The *narodniki* focused their attention on the people—their misery and their grandeur. They idealized the peasant, glorified his virtues, decried his sorrows, and fought for his material welfare. Influenced by the slogan "To the People," in 1874 thousands of young men and women left their jobs and their studies in the cities, and, dressed in peasant clothes, they went to Russian villages to mingle with the people, trying to help them in every way while at the same time trying to deliver to them "the revolutionary message." That message expressed hostility towards centralized political authority; renounced the use of falsehoods as a weapon in the campaign to secure improved social institutions; rejected economic liberalism in favor of a plan to turn Russia into a land of socialism based on village communes; and tried to instill in the people confidence in themselves. The *narodniki* did not advocate the use of terror to achieve a revolution, for, influenced by Lavrov, they believed that revolutions could not be evoked artificially but rather were products of a long series of complicated historical processes and not results of individual wills. In spite of a vigorous effort, the "To the People" movement ended in a total fiasco thanks to the alertness of the police and in particular because of peasant misunderstanding and suspicion of the intention of these young enthusiasts. Hundreds of *narodniki* were arrested and brought to trial, and most of these were banished to Siberia.

The dismal failure of the young intelligentsia to penetrate peacefully the village, in order to bring a vast transformation of Russia through education of the peasant, forced again to the forefront the question of the employment of terror both as a means of self-defense and as a weapon to attain the revolutionary program. On January 24, 1878, a woman revolutionary, Vera I. Zasulich (1851–1919), shot and seriously wounded the Governor of St. Petersburg because of his alleged brutality towards an arrested member of the underground. On April 2, 1879, a terrorist shot at but missed Tsar Alexander II. These and other acts of terror caused again a split among Russian radicals. Those who approved the use of such tactics founded, in June, 1879, a new organization named *Narodnaia volia* (People's Will), while those who opposed the use of terror established a group which called itself *Chernyi peredel* (The Black Partition).

The aim of the *Narodnaia volia* was to terrorize the government and the reactionary elements of Russian society. Its followers considered themselves socialists. They viewed the state as an instrument of oppression and wanted to restore power to the people by way of a political revolution. The program of the *Narodnaia volia* advocated for Russia the establishment of national and local legislative assemblies; independence of the village commune as an economic and administrative unit; ownership of the land by those who tilled it; workers' control of the factories; absolute freedom of thought, speech, press, and assembly; universal suffrage; and replacement of standing armies by a militia. While condemning the blind campaign of destruction advocated by Nechaev and Bakunin, the *Narodnaia volia* approved terror, and favored the establishment of a nationwide network of secret organizations and the infiltration of the administrative apparatus, the army, the intelligentsia, and the young people, in order to prepare a successful rising. The most important victim of the terror of this group was Tsar Alexander II, who was assassinated on March 13, 1881. This action terminated the activity of the *Narodnaia volia* because of police reprisals and public disapproval.

The tactics of the *Narodnaia volia* were also condemned by members of the *Chernyi peredel*, whose aim was agitation among the peasants for an agrarian revolution as the first step towards a complete reconstruction of Russian society on socialist foundations. Organized by Pavel B. Axelrod (1850–1928), George V. Plekhanov (1856–1918), and Vera Zasulich, the program of the *Chernyi peredel* swore allegiance to "the principles of scientific socialism" and expressed skepticism towards political revolutions, holding that the latter had never secured economic freedom for the people nor had even guaranteed political freedom. It urged the peasants to take the land and the workers to seize the factories. Members of the *Chernyi peredel* tried to secure a foothold in Russian villages, sought to influence members of the intelligentsia, and spent considerable time and efforts on winning the attention of the rapidly swelling ranks of Russian workers. Because of the triumph of reaction following the assassination of Alexander II, the efforts of the *Chernyi peredel* were not successful, and in 1883 its leadership fled to Geneva where it founded a new organization, *Osvobozhdenie truda* (Liberation of Labor).

The program of the new group included many demands made earlier by other revolutionary groups—a democratic constitution; salaries for elected officials, the inviolability of the person and home; absolute freedom of conscience, speech, press, assembly, and association; and the replacement of the standing army by a general arming of the people. In contrast, however, to the programs of all earlier revolutionary groups, the *Osvobozhdenie truda* abandoned support for the village commune as a basic element of the future socialist society; advocated capitalism for Russia as a prerequisite for reaching "the highest stage of socialism"; and placed hope in the industrial proletariat and disciplined, closely-knit, class conscious worker's party to achieve a social revolution in Russia. This decisive shift towards Marxist lines enabled the *Osvobozhdenie truda* to establish close ties with Marxist and socialist movements in Western Europe and Germany in particular, and to lay the foundations for the rise of the Russian Social Democratic movement.

The assassination of Alexander II disrupted the activities of many secret groups and inaugurated a period of extreme reaction in Russia. The chief architect and the philosopher of that reaction was Constantine P. Pobedonostsev (1827–1907), the Procurator of the Holy Synod and the tutor of the new Tsar, Alexander III (1881–1894). Though a constitutional lawyer, Pobedonostsev denounced the parliamentary form of government, sovereignty of the people, separation of church and state, the jury system, and even universal education, and castigated everything that represented freedom. To "save" Russia from these modern "evils" Pobedonostsev revived the old reactionary formula of "Orthodoxy, Autocracy, and Nationality." In practice, this revival meant the introduction of religious censorship of sermons, forceful conversion of non-Orthodox subjects of the Empire to Orthodox Christianity, persecution of all other faiths, persecution of all non-Russian minorities through a policy known as Russification, development of extreme anti-Semitism, strict supervision of the *zemstvo* institutions, prohibition of student associations, repeal of university autonomy, exclusion from the curriculum of all classics and West European writers, exclusion from secondary schools of the lower strata of society, and increased reliance on the support of the reactionary nobility.

The Pobedonostsev-directed reaction failed to accomplish its purpose —that of saving Russian autocracy. Some persecuted minorities (Jews and Dukhobors) sought and received asylum abroad, thereby creating bad publicity for the Russian government. Other minorities (Finns, Latvians, Lithuanians, and Ukrainians) reacted to the Russification efforts of the government by developing their own sense of nationalism, which in time evolved into separatism, i.e., a desire to establish their own political independence. Many opponents of reaction joined one or another secret organization or movement. The most prominent of these movements at the turn of the century were the Social Democratic, the Socialist Revolutionary, and the Liberal.

The Russian Social Democratic movement, as we noted earlier, evolved out of the Plekhanov-founded *Osvobozhdenie truda*. Its growth, though hindered by police vigilance and internal dissensions among its spokesmen, was rather rapid thanks mainly to the accelerated industrialization program of Russia master-minded by Sergei J. Witte (1849–1915), the energetic Minister of Finance and Economy. The Social Democratic program, as adopted in 1903 by the party's second congress in London, called for socialist revolution, eradication of capitalism, and the establishment of a dictatorship of the proletariat. To make possible the attainment of these "maximum" objectives the program demanded the overthrow of the tsarist monarchy and the creation of a democratic republic whose constitution would, among other things, guarantee: the sovereignty of the people; universal, equal, and direct suffrage for all citizens irrespective of sex, national or religious affiliation; absolute freedom of conscience, speech, press, assembly, strikes, and unions; the right of self-determination for all nationalities of the Russian Empire; elective judiciary; the separation of church and state, and of school and church; free and compulsory general and professional education in native language; an eight-hour work day; confiscation of all private, church, monastery, and crown estates, and their transfer to the jurisdiction of the local government; the granting to the peasants of land of which they had been deprived by the emancipation of 1861; and replacement of the standing army by a general arming of the people.

The same congress that approved this elaborate program for Russia witnessed also a split within the Russian Social Democratic party over the question of membership. Julius O. Martov (1873–1923) and Axelrod, supported by Leon D. Trotsky (1879–1940), argued that the party should be a broad and therefore somewhat loose organization which would embrace both the working class and some segments of the intelligentsia. Vladimir I. Lenin (1870–1924) (real name Vladimir I. Ulianov) who made his appearance in the political arena in the mid-1890's, supported by Plekhanov, insisted that only individuals who actively participated in underground organizations had the right to influence party policies. In Lenin's view the party was to be an instrument of the revolution, and as such it should consist not of "fellow travellers" but of soldiers dedicated to the party's cause and ready at all times to act on the orders and instructions of the party's central leadership. Since he held that only a select group consisting of the most enlightened and the most courageous workers, under the leadership of a highly centralized body, had a chance of success, Lenin opposed the inclusion of sympathizers and "fellow travellers" within the party's framework. Lenin's views were defeated by twenty-eight to twenty-three votes after unusually heated debates. However, when the congress moved on to the election of its central organs and the editorial staff of the party's paper, Iskra (The Spark), Lenin's candidates won by two votes (nineteen against seventeen, with three abstentions). Henceforth (until October, 1952) Lenin's followers in Russia identified themselves as Bolsheviks (from bolshenstvo, or majority group), while Martov's group was labelled Mensheviks (from menshenstvo, or minority group).

Between 1903 and 1912 the cleavage between the Bolsheviks and the Mensheviks widened. Though he actually commanded the allegiance of only a minority, Lenin insisted that the election of his candidates was valid and that the central committee of the party was the supreme author-ity. The Mensheviks, who were numerically strong inside and outside Russia, refused to acknowledge Lenin's claims and the authority of the Bolshevik-dominated central committee. To Lenin the Menshevik attitude represented anarchism. The more he emphasized the idea of unity, disci-pline, and obedience, the more the Mensheviks insisted on the preserva-tion of their views and accused Lenin of trying to force upon the party his views of what the party ought to be. The controversy ended in January, 1912, when, at a conference in Prague, Lenin formally established his own party. Henceforth the Mensheviks continued to adhere to evolutionary tactics, believing that after the downfall of monarchy Russia must set up a bourgeois democratic republic as a necessary stage in the establishment of socialism, and accordingly they were willing to cooperate with the bour-geois parties in the destruction of monarchy as well as in the building of a democratic republic. The Bolsheviks under Lenin's leadership adopted revolutionary tactics, refused to cooperate with the bourgeoisie, insisted that both monarchy and the bourgeoisie were implacable enemies of the proletariat, and maintained that the monarchy must be immediately suc-ceeded by the dictatorship of the proletariat.

The chief competitor of the Bolsheviks and the Mensheviks for lead-ership in the Russian revolutionary movement was the Socialist Revolu-tionaries. Socialist Revolutionaries made their appearance in the early 1890's and represented in some ways the revival of the *narodniki* move-ment with Marxist overtones. Their program called for universal suffrage; representative institutions; civil and personal liberties; federal structure for the Russian Empire with full rights of self-determination for non-Russian minorities; a progressive tax system; labor legislation; the devel-opment in Russia of revolutionary socialism; and socialization of land without compensation with the state taking control over forests, fisheries, and all mineral resources. Though they propagated their program among the factory workers and had many followers among the intelligentsia and students, the focal point of interest of Socialist Revolutionaries was the plight of the Russian village. Widespread rural unrests in 1902–1903 in-flated the hopes of the Socialist Revolutionaries, spurred their agitation among the peasants, and produced a sizable amount of literature de-signed for peasant readers. By being able to capitalize on the deep-rooted discontent and dissatisfaction of the masses, the Socialist Revolutionaries gained a considerable following among the peasants and subsequently emerged as the strongest (numerically) political party in Russia—a posi-tion which they retained until they were dislodged by the Bolsheviks in 1918. Like their more radical populist predecessors, the Socialist Revolu-tionaries approved the use of terror, and among their eminent victims were two Ministers of Interior, Dimitri S. Sipiagin (1853–1902) and Via-cheslav K. Plehve (1846–1904) and the Grand Duke Sergei Alexandrovich (1857–1905). The most prominent Socialist Revolutionaries were Mark A. Natanson (1850–1919), Gregory A. Gershuni (1870–1908), Catherine Breshko-Breshkovskaia (1844–1934), Victor M. Chernov (1876–1952), and Yevno F. Azeff (1869–1918).

Occupying the middle position between the revolutionaries (Bolsheviks, Mensheviks, and Socialist Revolutionaries) and the supporters of autocracy were the liberals. By birth the majority of Russian liberals were nobles; by training they were professionals—lawyers, jurists, engineers, teachers, doctors, veterinarians, agronomists, and nurses—many of whom were dedicated *zemstvo* members. Russian liberals, like their European counterparts, longed for social, economic, and political reforms; favored freedom of speech, press, assembly, and conscience; and detested bureaucratic arbitrariness. At the same time, however, Russian liberals rejected revolutionary methods, were suspicious of the masses, both rural and urban, and some even preferred limited suffrage. Beyond a general agreement that autocracy must go, Russian liberals could not agree among themselves on basic issues or a program. Some advocated for Russia the English constitutional system of limited monarchy with a strong bicameral legislature. Others favored a government of responsible ministry, while some wanted only to modify the power of the Tsar. Most Russian liberals insisted that the unity of the Russian state be preserved, opposed a federal arrangement for Russia, and some, like economist Peter B. Struve (1870–1944), supported "enlightened" Russification efforts.

After 1905 Russian liberals split into two parties: Constitutional Democrats, or Cadets; and the Union of October 17, or Octobrists. The Cadets, under the leadership of historian Paul N. Miliukov (1859–1943), stood for a parliamentary constitutional monarchy, with the parliament exercising full powers in drafting the new constitution and other laws; supported many social and economic reforms; and favored the distribution among the peasants of all the land belonging to the State, the Crown, and the monasteries, and compulsory expropriation of large estates with equitable compensation for their owners. The Octobrists, led by Moscow industrialist Alexander I. Guchkov (1862–1936), disapproved of some of the "radical" positions of the Cadets because the Octobrists were satisfied with the promises Nicholas II (1894–1917) made in his October 30, 1905, Manifesto.

The Revolution of 1905 and Its Aftermath

The rise of political parties at the turn of the century and their determined efforts to remake Russia was a major sign of mounting dissatisfaction with autocracy. Other symptoms of popular discontent were: (1) an increasing number of strikes in industry for higher wages, shorter hours, and the elimination of all unfair practices; (2) widespread agrarian disturbances caused by the stagnation of agriculture, the impoverishment of the peasantry, and the general breakdown of the land settlement of the 1860's; (3) clashes between university students and authorities; and (4) a wave of political assassinations of high government officials. The most prominent victims of assassinations were: Minister of Education, N. P. Bogolepov (1847–1901), in February, 1901; Minister of Interior Sipiagin, in April, 1902; Governor of Ufa, N. M. Bogdanovich (1856–1903), in May, 1903; Governor of Finland, N. I. Bobrikov (1839–1904), in June, 1904; and Minister of Interior, Plehve, in July, 1904.

At first, government authorities replied to this increased popular discontent with the customary reprisals, unwarranted brutality, and determination to maintain intact the autocratic powers. Following Russia's involvement with Japan in the Far East in a war which the people neither supported nor understood but which inflicted upon Russia a series of military disasters, government officials relaxed the reign of terror. In November, 1904, the new Minister of Interior, Prince Peter D. Sviatopolk-Mirski (1857–1914), a bureaucrat of liberal inclinations, after some hesitation allowed a *zemstvo* conference in St. Petersburg. The members of the conference unanimously adopted an eleven-point resolution calling for freedom of thought, conscience, speech, assembly, and press; the granting of civil rights irrespective of class, nationality, or religious affiliation; equality of all citizens before the law; political amnesty; agricultural and industrial reforms; democratization and expansion of local self-government; repeal of the "state of emergency" legislation; and summoning of an elective assembly. The last provision did not receive unanimous endorsement because some delegates favored legislative power for the assembly while others were satisfied with only consultative powers.

Private and public organizations throughout the country overwhelmingly endorsed the *zemstvo* resolution; government authorities, however, took a dim view of it. Official rejection of these demands widened the existing gulf between the people and the bureaucracy and contributed heavily to a crisis commonly known as "Bloody Sunday." The latter occurred on January 22, 1905, when a peaceful procession of thousands of striking workers of the capital, headed by a priest, George A. Gapon (1870–1906), bearing a petition to the Tsar listing their grievances and wishes, was fired upon by troops, killing many and wounding hundreds.

The "Bloody Sunday" massacre had an electrifying effect on all the layers of Russian society. Working masses immediately intensified their radicalism and many industrial centers of the Empire (St. Petersburg, Moscow, Warsaw, Riga, Lodz, Odessa, and others) were hit by waves of industrial strikes during the spring and summer months, which greatly affected war production. Liberals increased their agitation for a constitutional assembly, and to coordinate their actions they organized in May, 1905, the Union of Unions. Students, too, intensified their radicalism, clashed with authorities, and forced the closing of schools until the fall of

1905. Incited by revolutionary propaganda and the developing chaos, peasants rose in many parts of the Empire against authorities and burned and looted many estates of the nobility. Encouraged by the developing nation-wide restlessness, nationalities of the Empire (Finns, Latvians, Poles, Ukrainians, Jews, and the peoples of the Caucasus) increasingly agitated for equal rights and autonomy. Revolutionary agitation affected also many members of the armed forces. The most spectacular action was the June, 1905, mutiny of the crew of the battleship *Potemkin*, which sailed without its officers to Rumania. In other words, "Bloody Sunday" opened the 1905 revolution.

Under this mounting nation-wide restlessness, on August 16, 1905, the government issued its first "major concession," an imperial decree which promised Russia an assembly to be elected by those nobles, bourgeoise, and peasants who owned property. The function of the assembly was to be purely an advisory one. This half-hearted "concession" failed to satisfy the liberals and still less the radicals. Early in October, 1905, the country was paralyzed by an effective general strike that engulfed the entire railroad network, telegraph and telephone systems, industrial enterprises, banks, schools, municipal offices, hospitals, newspapers, and many other establishments. So effective was the strike that it brought an almost complete standstill to the whole life of the country. On October 26, the strike caused the emergence of a self-styled workers' "parliament"— the Soviet of Workers' Deputies. Led by the Mensheviks, the Soviet rose in importance and popularity and began to demand a constitutional assembly, a democratic republic, political amnesty, disarming of troops and of the police and arming of workers, an eight-hour working day, civil liberties, and repeal of the "state of emergency" legislation. Since other cities of the Empire followed the example of the capital, there developed a network of Soviets throughout Russia. Under the pressure of all these developments, on October 30, 1905, Nicholas II issued a manifesto drafted by Witte, which (1) granted the people of the Empire "personal inviolability, freedom of conscience, speech, assembly, and association"; (2) promised to allow the disfranchised elements (i.e., property-less strata of society) to participate in the elections to the State *Duma*, or the legislative assembly; and (3) established as "an unbreakable rule" that no law should be promulgated without the sanction of the State Duma, which also was promised "the supervision of the legality of the actions of authorities" appointed by the Crown.

The people received the October Manifesto with mixed emotions. The majority of them greeted it with great excitement followed by noisy demonstrations and celebrations. The ultranationalist groups, however, were shocked by the "concessions" and, led by the uncompromising supporters of autocracy, they organized antiliberal, antistudent, antiminority demonstrations and pogroms in an effort to restore the status quo ante. The

Manifesto failed to satisfy the extreme radicals, who favored the abolition of monarchy, nationalization of land, and introduction of other far-reaching reforms, and who, to realize these goals, insisted on continuation of the strike and opposition to the government. They failed in their efforts because the populace seemed satisfied with the victory and unwilling to press its luck. Popular reaction against revolutionary excesses enabled the authorities to regroup their forces, terminate the activities of the St. Petersburg Soviet (November, 1905) and of the Moscow insurrectionists (December, 1905), and slowly to bring the 1905 revolution to an end by means of further concessions (especially the cancellation of the redemption payments), martial law, punitive expeditions, arrests, and executions. The gradual restoration of order also enabled the authorities to direct Imperial Russia on a period of "constitutional experiment" (1905-1917), which in the words of one observer "modified the whole life of the nation and opened the way to new and significant developments."

One of the most notable developments of the period was the transformation of Russia's absolute, autocratic regime into a constitutional system. The transformation was painful and erratic because the country lacked many needed prerequisites, such as established political parties, a literate population, the experience of self-government, and above all an atmosphere of mutual trust between the representative assembly and the government bureaucracy. Under the Fundamental Laws of April 23, 1906, the Tsar retained his historical title of Autocrat (Article 4); enjoyed the exclusive right of initiating legislation affecting the constitution; controlled the executive branch of the government; appointed all high government officials, who in turn were responsible to him only; proclaimed the state of emergency; enjoyed the exclusive right of directing foreign policy; declared war; concluded peace; negotiated treaties; enjoyed the right to pardon or revise sentences; was the official head of the church; and convoked and dissolved the legislature. No legislation could become a law without his signature. Moreover, under Article 57 of the Fundamental Laws, the Tsar enjoyed the right of promulgating emergency legislation in the intervals between sessions of the parliament by means of imperial decrees, which later had to be submitted for approval by the legislature.

But while he still enjoyed many rights, after 1905 the Tsar was no longer an absolute monarch because the constitution provided for obligatory concurrence of the two legislative chambers, the State Council and the State Duma, in legislation. One should remember, however, that Russia's parliament was not a real parliament in the western sense of the word. For one thing it was highly unrepresentative. Half of the State Council, for instance, was appointed by the Tsar, as was the Council's president; the other half was elected from among the clergy, zemstvo, nobility, and representatives of commerce, industry, and institutions of higher learning. Whether appointed or elected, all members of the State Council were well-to-do men and came almost exclusively from the central regions of Russia.

The composition of the State Duma, or the lower chamber, while more representative than the State Council, was far from perfect. The government-prepared electoral law disfranchised the bulk of the urban population (intellectuals and industrial workers), which the officials considered hostile to the government and through an intricate system of indirect voting, insured a large representation of the peasantry, which was believed to be devoted to the Crown. Contrary to the expectations of the officials, once elected the peasants aligned themselves with the left-wing parties, and together they voted for the most radical solutions of the land problem. The government's refusal to accept their radical solutions led to the dissolution of the two Dumas after very brief sessions and to the introduction on June 3, 1907, of a new electoral law. The new law divided the electorate into four groups—landowners (other than peasants), urban population, peasants, and industrial workers—and gave government authorities discretionary powers to subdivide electoral districts into smaller units on the basis of property qualifications, national origin, or residence. By these rules, which in the words of one observer violated "every canon of democratic elections," the government obtained a preponderance of conservative, nationalist, and moderate elements, and with their help introduced a number of far-reaching legislative measures.

The most notable achievement of the "constitutional period" was the agrarian reform commonly known as the Stolypin Land Reform. Set in motion between November, 1906, and May, 1911, by Premier Peter A. Stolypin (1862–1911), the reform sought to solve Russia's agrarian problem in order to place the whole economy on stable foundations. Under the terms of the Stolypin Reform, every member of the village commune was allowed to acquire title to the strips of communal land to which he had a right and to consolidate such strips into a contiguous holding. The aim of this obvious reversal of the previous governmental policy was twofold: to eliminate the village commune as an obstacle to agricultural progress; and to create in Russia an economically healthy class of small farmers—known in Russia as *kulaks*—who would act as a bulwark for the regime against every form of extremism. According to official figures, between 1907 and 1913 about 5,000,000 peasants applied for the consolidation of their holdings, and by 1915 some 7,300,000 peasant households in the European part of the Empire (or more than half of all peasant households) had settled on allotment land.

Behind the success of the Stolypin Land Reform were other vital measures. On January 1, 1907, for instance, the government cancelled all peasant redemption payments. At about the same time authorities granted the State Land Bank for Peasants broad powers in helping the peasants to buy land from the state, crown, and nobility, removed all restrictions imposed in the 1860's on peasant mobility, and inaugurated a program of massive assistance to those peasants who wanted to migrate from the overpopulated European provinces of the Empire to sparsely populated Asiatic possessions. Between 1907 and 1914 some 2,000,000 peasants settled in various parts of Asiatic Russia. Finally, with the help of the *zemstvo* institutions, the government organized a fairly efficient network of agricultural stations staffed by agricultural experts whose task was to help peasants improve their methods of cultivation. Russia's entry into World War I in August, 1914, interrupted this transformation of rural areas and left them pregnant with great explosive potentials.

In addition to the modernization efforts in rural areas, the "constitutional period" witnessed an accelerated industrial growth. Financed by foreign and domestic resources, Russian industry, after a brief interruption by the revolution of 1905, entered upon a period of prosperity and record-breaking gains which lasted until World War I. According to official figures, between 1909 and 1913 Russia's production of pig iron increased by 59 per cent; iron and steel by 50 per cent; coal by 40 per cent; and coke by 60 per cent. The period saw an extraordinary expansion of railroads; rapid growth of industrial combines as well as consumer cooperatives; steady development of mechanization; continued introduction of the latest technological innovations; and an unprecedented growth of urban population. In an effort to calm the growing industrial proletariat the government legalized the organization of labor unions, introduced health and accident insurance for workers, and either imprisoned or forced into exile the leaders of extreme groups. After 1906 the country enjoyed a relative calm and was more prosperous than it had ever been before. The calm was only temporary, for on the eve of World War I labor unrest began to gather dangerous momentum.

The modernization of the economy was accompanied by a concentrated effort to eliminate illiteracy which, according to the census of 1897, was 79 per cent. All responsible leaders recognized the urgency of the problem, and in May, 1908, both legislative chambers approved a government-sponsored education bill which provided for a gradual introduction of free, universal, compulsory education for children between eight and eleven. Because of inadequate funds and facilities (there were less than 100,000 schools in Russia in 1908) and lack of qualified personnel, the education bill envisaged the full attainment of universal education in Russia by 1922. The "constitutional period" saw also a substantial numerical increase of the secondary schools and institutions of higher learning as well as increased educational opportunities for the lower strata of society. On the eve of World War I there were about 1,700 secondary schools, followed by sixty-seven institutions of higher learning.

Finally, the "constitutional period" witnessed in Russia a phenomenal rise in newspapers and periodicals. In 1912 there were being published within the Russian Empire (excluding Finland) 2,167 different periodicals in thirty-three languages, reflecting every shade of opinion from the extreme right to the extreme left. Many of these publications encountered difficulties with the censor; some were even forced to suspend publication for a time. On the whole, however, the Russian press was enjoying the best freedom in its history. The same cannot be said of the publications of national minorities which, while allowed to appear, were subjected to arbitrary abuses by the Great Russian officialdom. In fact, the "constitutional regime" revived the old policy of Russification of border areas (Finland, Poland, and the Ukraine), supported anti-Jewish pogroms, and in innumerable other ways alienated its subject peoples thus inspiring them to work for the dissolution of the Empire.

The outbreak of World War I, and Russia's entry into it on the side of England and France, interrupted the great political, economic, and cultural transformation of Imperial Russia. Initially, the people supported the war, believing that it was one of national defense against unprovoked Austro-German aggression, and were jubilant over the successes of Russian armies against the forces of the Dual Monarchy in Galicia. A series of military disasters on the German front, which inflicted on Russia extremely heavy casualties (Tannenberg, the Masurian Lakes, and Gorlice), caused in part by inept leadership and in part by the superior organization of the enemy, greatly affected the morale of the nation. The inability of the Allies to aid Russia militarily and economically (because of the effectiveness of the German blockade) forced Russia to rely on her own inadequately developed resources and was responsible for further deterioration of morale. Repeated mobilizations of able-bodied men (some 15,000,000 were called into service during the war) produced disastrous effects on industrial and agricultural production, caused the breakdown of the transportation system, and created severe shortages of food and fuel, especially in large industrial centers. Since the authorities were unable to solve these urgent problems and unwilling to listen to constructive criticism or suggestions, early in 1917 Imperial Russia found itself on the brink of revolution.

SUGGESTED READINGS

ALSTON, PATRICK L. *Education and the State in Tsarist Russia.* Stanford: Stanford University Press, 1969.

BILLINGTON, JAMES. *Icon and the Axe. An Interpretative History of Russian Culture.* New York: Vintage, 1970.

BLACKWELL, WILLIAM L. *The Beginnings of Russian Industrialization, 1800–1860.* Princeton: Princeton University Press, 1968.

BROWER, DANIEL R. *Training of Nihilists: Education and Radicalism in Tsarist Russia.* Ithaca: Cornell University Press, 1975.

CIZEVSKIJ, DMITRIJ. *History of Nineteenth-Century Russian Literature*. Nashville: University of Tennessee Press, 1974, 2 vols.

CRANKSHAW, EDWARD. *The Shadow of the Winter Palace: The Drift to Revolution, 1825–1917*. New York: Penguin Books, 1976.

DMYTRYSHYN, BASIL. *A History of Russia*. Englewood Cliffs, N.J.: Prentice-Hall, 1977.

———. *Imperial Russia: A Source Book, 1700–1917*. 2nd ed. Hinsdale, Il.: Dryden Press, 1974.

EMMONS, TERENCE. *The Russian Landed Gentry and the Peasant Emancipation of 1861*. Cambridge: Cambridge University Press, 1968.

FIELD, DANIEL. *Rebels in the Name of the Tsar*. Boston: Houghton Mifflin, 1976.

FISCHER, GEORGE. *Russian Liberalism*. Cambridge: Harvard University Press, 1958.

FLORINSKY, MICHAEL T. *Russia: A History and an Interpretation*. Vol. 2. New York: Macmillan, 1955.

HAIMSON, LEOPOLD H. *The Russian Marxists and the Origins of Bolshevism*. Cambridge: Harvard University Press, 1955.

HARCAVE, SIDNEY. *Years of the Golden Cockerel: The Last Romanov Tsars, 1814–1917*. New York: Macmillan, 1968.

JORRE, GEORGES. *The Soviet Union: The Land and Its People*. London: Longmans, 1961.

KARPOVICH, MICHAEL. *Imperial Russia, 1801–1917*. New York: Holt, 1932.

KEEP, JOHN L. H. *The Rise of Social Democracy in Russia*. Oxford: Oxford University Press, 1963.

KORNILOV, ALEXANDER. *Modern Russian History*. New York: Knopf, 1952.

LEVIN, ALFRED. *The Second Duma*. New Haven: Yale University Press, 1940.

LYDOLPH, PAUL E. *Geography of the USSR*. New York: Wiley, 1964.

MALIA, MARTIN E. *Alexander Herzen and the Birth of Russian Socialism*. Cambridge: Harvard University Press, 1961.

MASARYK, THOMAS G. *The Spirit of Russia*. 2nd ed. Vol. 2. New York: Macmillan, 1955.

MASSIE, ROBERT K. *Nicholas and Alexandra*. New York: Dell, 1967.

MAVOR, JAMES. *An Economic History of Russia*. 2nd ed. Vol. 2. New York: Dent, 1925.

MEYER, ALFRED G. *Leninism*. Cambridge: Harvard University Press, 1957.

MILIUKOV, PAUL. *Russia and Its Crisis*. Chicago: University of Chicago Press, 1906.

MILLER, M. S. *The Economic Development of Russia, 1905–1914*. London: King, 1926.

MOSSE, W. E. *Alexander II and the Modernization of Russia*. Rev. ed. New York: Collier Books, 1962.

PARES, BERNARD. *Russia and Reform*. London: Constable, 1907.

———. *The Fall of the Russian Monarchy: A Study of the Evidence*. New York: Knopf, 1939.

PAVLOVSKY, GEORGE. *Agricultural Russia on the Eve of the Revolution*. London: Routledge, 1930.

PIPES, RICHARD. *Russia Under the Old Regime*. New York: Scribners, 1975.

———, ed. *The Russian Intelligentsia*. New York: Columbia University Press, 1961.

POMPER, PHILIP. *The Russian Revolutionary Intelligentsia*. New York: Crowell, 1970.

PUSHKAREV, SERGEI. *The Emergence of Modern Russia*. Translated by Robert H. McNeal and Tova Yedlin. New York: Holt, Rinehart and Winston, 1963.

RADKEY, OLIVER H. *Agrarian Foes of Bolshevism: Promise and Default of the Russian Socialist Revolutionaries*. New York: Columbia University Press, 1958.

ROBINSON, GEROID T. *Rural Russia Under the Old Regime*. New York: Longmans, 1949.

RUTHERFORD, WARD. *The Russian Army in World War I*. London: Gordon Cremonesi, 1975.

SETON-WATSON, HUGH. *The Decline of Imperial Russia, 1855–1914*. New York: Praeger, 1960.

———. *The Russian Empire, 1801–1917*. Oxford: Oxford University Press, 1967.

STAVROU, THEOPHANES G., ed. *Russia Under the Last Tsars*. Minneapolis: University of Minnesota Press, 1969.

THADEN, EDWARD C. *Russia Since 1801*. New York: Wiley, 1971.

TOMPKINS, STUART R. *The Russian Intelligentsia*. Norman: University of Oklahoma Press, 1957.

TREADGOLD, DONALD W. *Lenin and His Rivals*. New York: Praeger, 1955.

ULAM, ADAM B. *In the Name of the People*. New York: Viking, 1977.

VENTURI, FRANCO. *Roots of Revolution*. New York: Knopf, 1960.

VON LAUE, THEODORE H. *Sergei Witte and the Industrialization of Russia*. New York: Columbia University Press, 1963.

VUCINICH, ALEXANDER. *Science in Russian Culture, 1867–1917*. Stanford: Stanford University Press, 1970.

VUCINICH, WAYNE, ed. *The Peasant in Nineteenth-Century Russia*. Stanford: Stanford University Press, 1968.

WALKIN, JACOB. *The Rise of Democracy in Pre-Revolutionary Russia*. New York: Praeger, 1962.

WOLFE, BERTRAM D. *Three Who Made a Revolution*. New York: Dial, 1948.

YARMOLINSKY, AVRAHM. *Road to Revolution: A Century of Russian Radicalism*. New York: Collier, 1962.

✂ II

THE MARCH REVOLUTION, 1917

THE COLLAPSE OF THE MONARCHY

The revolutionary storm which had been gathering in Russia for decades exploded in March, 1917. Viewed in retrospect that explosion was one of the most important events in Russian history as well as in the history of modern times. This, however, was not the universal judgment of contemporaries, since the immediate events leading to this great political, economic, and social upheaval were neither spectacular nor extraordinary. War-weary Russia drifted into this calamity thanks to the incompetent military and political leadership which, in return for untold sacrifices and efforts, was capable of producing nothing but inefficiency and corruption at home and military defeats at the front. Rightly or wrongly the Russians believed that a change was necessary and they plunged ahead on a policy of change.

39

The elimination in December, 1916, of the hated Gregory E. Rasputin (1872–1916), who wielded a demonic influence on the imperial family, was the first sign of the approaching shift. It was followed by increasing rumors of further changes and of trouble, but trouble was neither a novelty nor an exception in Russia. Although the authorities were unable to do anything else constructive, they seem to have been determined to meet the oncoming challenge firmly. With every passing day, however, the situation was deteriorating everywhere, and most of all in Petrograd, the capital. Throughout January and February the dissatisfaction mounted. There were increased strikes in war factories, a situation hardly helpful to the war effort and least of all to soldiers in the trenches. There were also more frequent food demonstrations, some of which turned into riots. The lack of food which affected everyone and angered many, especially women shoppers, was not so much a shortage of food as the result of poor management and inadequate distribution, caused in part by the breakdown of transportation. And since the authorities did nothing to improve it, the situation went from bad to worse.

A major crisis began to develop late in February and early in March. After several postponements the Duma finally reconvened on February 27, amidst a tense atmosphere. Although the Duma consisted basically of loyal supporters of the regime, many of its members expected early ad-

Petrograd, 1917. Soldiers and citizens on their way to the Duma.

journment. There were some members, however, who were determined to remain in session come what may. In anticipation of increased demonstrations during the session of the Duma, the government strengthened the Petrograd garrison. It also intensified censorship, increased house searches, and in trying to apprehend all possible troublemakers, arrested many innocent persons. These measures, however, only heightened the existing tension. On the surface it looked as if the police and troops were in complete control of the situation, but this was only an illusion.

On March 5, the Tsar left the capital for the General Headquarters in Mogilev, leaving behind a signed but undated decree for the dissolution of the Duma. On the same day the Putilov munition factory workers struck, followed by those of other large factories in Petrograd. On March 6, streetcar conductors went on strike, forcing many disgruntled people to walk. On the following day open meetings were held on Nevski Prospekt where soapbox orators spoke of "Bread and Freedom." Although with every passing hour tension increased and the mob swelled, the demonstrations continued to be relatively orderly and the authorities still had full control of the situation.

From General Headquarters, completely unfamiliar with the seriousness of the situation, the Tsar ordered General S. S. Khabalov, commanding officer of the Petrograd garrison, to quell the disorders immediately. Fulfillment of this order became impossible, for on March 8 the unrest spread from the center of the city to the workers' quarters in the suburbs. Now the entire capital was engulfed by the turmoil. There were many street demonstrations and, except for police officials, almost everyone endorsed the manifestants, some of whom even carried banners with the slogan: "Down with Autocracy!" The regular troops still continued to obey orders, but rumors spread that the soldiers—the backbone of Russian autocracy—were favorably inclined towards the demonstrators and would not fire on them. The crowds, growing both in size and in ugly mood, applauded these rumors. This left only the police to deal with the demonstrators, and it became impossible to prevent clashes between the two. A revolution was in the making.

The inability of police authorities to control the crowds only brought more demonstrators and more spectators into the streets. Revolutionary songs and demands for "Bread and Freedom" became more frequent, resulting in more clashes with the police. By March 10 the entire city had been turned into an armed camp of soldiers, police officials, armored cars, and an unruly mob of demonstrators whose shouting was interrupted frequently by rifle and machine gun fire in the main thoroughfares. Since the situation was getting out of hand, the authorities made hasty but all-out preparations for a final showdown with the demonstrators. On the Tsar's orders the Duma was to be dissolved on March 12, and full employment of the troops was to be made to suppress the unruly mob.

The plan was ill-fated. During the night of March 11, soldiers of the Volyn Regiment of the Guard, after their return to the barracks, mutinied and agreed not to fire at crowds in the future. In the morning of March 12 they went even further. Disobeying the orders and attempts at persuasion by their officers, the soldiers poured into the streets and joined the demonstrators. Other regiments followed, and soon the entire Petrograd garrison of the imperial army ceased to exist. Drunk with this success the mob, reinforced by the defiant soldiers, moved through the streets of Petrograd unchallenged, looting, hunting down hated police officials, breaking into arsenals for arms, and into prisons to release the old inmates and to replace them with new ones. The revolution was now in full swing, and before day's end most of the government buildings were under revolutionary control. Paralyzed, the old government apparatus had ceased to function.

Out of the revolutionary turmoil slowly and quite uncertainly a new Russia began to emerge. In the afternoon of March 12 a group of members of the defunct Duma met in the Taurida Palace and elected a thirteen-man committee known as the Temporary Committee. Consisting of members of the Progressive Bloc, which had made its debut in 1915, and of representatives of leftist groups, the Committee invested itself with unlimited powers "to take in hand the reestablishment of state and public order" throughout Russia. On the same day, March 12, and in the same building, there emerged another revolutionary institution—the Petrograd Soviet of Workers' and Soldiers' Deputies. Composed of factory and workshop delegates, leaders of the revolting military units, and "representatives of democratic and socialist parties and groups," the Petrograd Soviet, reviving the goals of its 1905 predecessor, set as its task "the organization of popular forces and the struggle for the final consolidation of the people's government in Russia." To both these revolutionary bodies —the Temporary Committee and the Soviet—revolution-minded Russians began to look for guidance, advice, and leadership capable of restoring order as well as ushering in a new era of liberty and social justice. Inasmuch as the membership, the goals, and the general *Weltanschauung* of the two were vastly different, trouble between the Temporary Committee and the Soviet was unavoidable.

The appearance of these two self-appointed groups as spokesmen for the new Russia created an odd situation, inasmuch as *technically* the old regime was still in existence. Though the central government had ceased to function and one military garrison had disintegrated, the Tsar, the embodiment of the old regime, was with his army in the General Headquarters where the revolutionary developments were not immediately felt. While beneficial in one way, this divorce from the rapidly changing situation was fatal in another way. Far from the scene, Nicholas II and his closest advisers misunderstood the situation as well as underestimated

Petrograd, 1917. In the early days of the Revolution these were the first soldiers to side with the strikers and thus made the Revolution possible in Petrograd.

its seriousness. The Tsar, in particular, remained deaf to all warnings, and failed to see the "handwriting on the wall." When, for instance, at midnight of March 11 Michael V. Rodzianko (1859–1924), President of the Duma, wired the Tsar warning him of the seriousness of affairs in the capital and urging him to institute immediately far-reaching reforms to avert a catastrophe, the Tsar considered it nonsense unworthy of reply. He also remained unimpressed by Rodzianko's second warning of the morning of March 12. By the evening of that day there was no need for warnings, because the old order was dead. Abdication remained the only avenue left and Rodzianko, though a convinced monarchist, suggested it.

Action and resoluteness were not basic characteristics of Nicholas II. It is, however, very doubtful whether swift action on his part could have altered the situation. The revolution had gone too far. General Khabalov learned this when he tried to save the dying order on March 12; his special task force of some six companies simply melted away upon coming into contact with the revolutionaries. The special task force of General N. I. Ivanov dispatched from General Headquarters, also on March 12, met an identical fate. On March 13 the Tsar's train left Mogilev for Petrograd.

It never reached its destination, for it was rerouted to Pskov to the head-quarters of General Nikolai V. Ruzsky (1854–1918), commander of the Northern Front. In this ancient Russian town, all military leaders whom the Tsar consulted, including his uncle the Grand Duke Nicholas (1856–1929), urged him to abdicate in favor of his son, with the Tsar's brother, Grand Duke Michael (1878–1918), acting as regent. It was hoped that such a move would save the dynasty and prevent the spread of anarchy. An identical proposal was made by two convinced monarch-ists and spokesmen of the Temporary Committee, Guchkov and Vasili V. Shulgin (1878–1945), who had succeeded in reaching Pskov. All this pressure was too much. Repudiated by his people and deserted by his fol-lowers, the Tsar agreed and signed the abdication document. On March 16, pleading inability to part with his "beloved son," he changed his mind and abdicated in favor of his brother Michael.

But even this last attempt to save the dynasty failed. Having brought down the old Tsar, Russian revolutionaries were in no mood to accept a new one. Violent protests went up against the arrangement made at Pskov. Sensing strong antimonarchial feelings, Michael hesitated to ac-cept the crown. In this respect he was more realistic than many of his supporters, including Miliukov. On March 16, after consultation with his supporters on the Temporary Committee, the Grand Duke Michael de-clared that he was resolved "to accept the supreme power only if and when our great people, having elected by universal suffrage a Constituent Assembly to determine the form of government and lay down the funda-mental law of the new Russian State, invest me with such a power." The Russian people had no desire to make such an offer. The three hundred-year-old Romanov dynasty, which had been founded by a Michael, tech-nically expired with another Michael. In less than a week the most auto-cratic country in Europe became the most democratic "republic" in the world. The entire transition was responsible for 169 dead, 1,264 wounded, and an uncertain number of hurt feelings.

THE PROVISIONAL GOVERNMENT VS. THE SOVIET

The remarkable ease with which the monarchy collapsed stunned every-one. Although, outside Petrograd, Russian civilians and soldiers took no direct part in the overthrow of the monarchy, they followed the example set in the capital. Everywhere military units joined the revolutionaries. Everywhere, too, as soon as the news arrived, the old administration, from governors down to the last village official, disappeared without trace or struggle. Throughout Russia—in cities, villages, army units, offices, and factories—there emerged all sorts of self-appointed committees and or-ganizations, generally known as soviets. Some of these tried to maintain order; others engaged in such "extrarevolutionary activity" as raiding and looting. In many respects the downfall of the monarchy meant therefore the beginning of Russia's disintegration and administrative, political, military, and economic chaos.

To deal with this confusion, on March 16 the Temporary Committee of the Duma dissolved itself and established the Provisional Government. It was a conservative body of well-known and respected prerevolutionary public figures. They represented a solid cross section of educated Russians, but they were unfit to lead a revolutionary country in wartime. Prince George E. Lvov (1861–1925), a wealthy landowner, member of an old aristocratic family, and a veteran *zemstvo* leader, became Premier and Minister of Interior; Miliukov, historian, leader of the Cadets, and an outspoken wartime critic of the regime, Foreign Minister; Guchkov, a wealthy Moscow merchant and founder of the Octobrist Party, Minister of War; Michael B. Tereshchenko (1884–1956), a non-party philanthropist and one of the wealthiest men in Russia, Minister of Finance; Andrei I. Shingarov (1860–1918), a Cadet and *zemstvo* member, Minister of Agriculture; A. I. Manuilov, a Cadet and University of Moscow professor, Minister of Education; Alexander I. Konovalov (1875–1948), a Progressive member of the Fourth Duma, Minister of Commerce and Industry; Nikolai V. Nekrasov, (1879–?), leader of the Left Wing Cadet group, Minister of Railways; Alexander F. Kerensky (1881–1970), a lawyer, leader of a non-Marxist Labor group in the Fourth Duma, and a deputy chairman of the Petrograd Soviet, Minister of Justice; and Vladimir N. Lvov, a member of the Conservative Party, Procurator of the Holy Synod.

The task of this first Provisional Government was not enviable. Both its legality and its authority rested on shaky grounds. It had the privilege of issuing orders, but because of the lack of an administrative apparatus, it could not expect compliance. Moreover, as Kerensky rightly noted, from its predecessor the Provisional Government inherited a losing war, an acute food situation, a paralyzed transportation system, an empty treasury, and a population in a state of furious discontent and anarchic disintegration. But this was not all. Peasants demanded land, workers demanded increased benefits and rights, Russia's numerous subject peoples demanded autonomy and self-determination, soldiers demanded the end of hostilities, and Russia's allies pressed for increased war efforts. The chaos was accentuated in that most of these demands were incompatible with the basic philosophy of the new government—that of gradualness, moderation, and respectability.

In tackling these grave problems the Provisional Government would have doubtless been more successful if it had been the only organ of authority in Russia, but such was not the case. In dealing with every major issue the government had to take into account the attitude of the Petrograd Soviet. The latter, representing the victorious revolutionary mob, many professional revolutionaries, and all types of "Johnny-come-latelys," grew into an enormous and unwieldy body which did not know its mind. Like the Provisional Government, the Soviet was a product of the revolution, but unlike the former, whose outlook was liberal-conservative, the latter was politically left-oriented, deliberately "non-bourgeois and class-conscious." The basis of the Soviet was the excited, victorious, armed, and action-ready street mob. With its support, the Soviet, from its very inception on March 12, acted as if it were the governmental authority. It invited the population to rally around it, issued all kinds of proclamations and orders, and even appointed its own officials to establish "peoples' power" in Russia. Yet for many crucial weeks the Soviet had no desire to assume the responsibility inherent in political power. The explanation for this strange behavior of the spokesmen of the Soviet, among whom there was more than a usual number of hotheads, must be sought in Marxist theory. As "orthodox" interpreters of Marxism, these self-appointed spokesmen of the Soviet believed the revolution in Russia was a "bourgeois revolution"; hence, they argued, the political power must be held by bourgeois liberals of the Duma. Members of the Soviet, allegedly representing the working class, could not enter any such government, but neither were they to stand idly by. They were to organize, prepare, and see to it that the revolution was not sidetracked.

Under those odd conditions, genuine and prolonged cooperation between the two revolutionary outgrowths became impossible. This is not to say that no attempts were made in that direction. The Provisional Government itself was the product of a compromise reached between some spokesmen of the Soviet and the representatives of the Temporary Committee of the Duma on March 14. Under that compromise the Provisional Government was to exercise executive authority until a Constituent Assembly elected on the basis of universal, equal and direct suffrage could decide the future form of government in Russia. While such basic issues as war and land problems were side-stepped, under the compromise the Provisional Government obligated itself to issue complete amnesty to all political prisoners; abolish capital punishment; allow freedom of speech, press, and assembly; grant labor the right to organize and to strike; and remove all legal restrictions based on class, nationality, or religion. Since soldiers had played a decisive role in the overthrow of the monarchy and in the revolution, they were to be given political liberties insofar as these were practicable under technical limitations of the service. Under this compromise also, two high ranking spokesmen of the Soviet—Nikolai S. Chkheidze (1864–1926) and Kerensky, respectively Chairman and Vice-Chairman of the Executive Committee of the Petrograd Soviet—were to enter the first government of revolutionary Russia.

Had this agreement been allowed to go into effect unobstructed and for a reasonable period of time, Russia and the rest of the world might have been spared many troubles. But such was not the case. On the morning of March 15, after hearing a report on the compromise, a plenary session of the Soviet not only repudiated it but also passed a resolution prohibiting socialists from serving in a bourgeois cabinet. Chkheidze complied with this decision. Kerensky, however, in one of the passionate appeals for which he was famous, persuaded the assembled members of the Soviet to reverse themselves. This they did through acclamation, and Kerensky entered the government to preserve harmony between it and the Petrograd Soviet.

Ahead, however, were other hurdles and they were not as easy to surmount. In spite of its agreement to let one of its high ranking members join the Provisional Government, the relation between the latter body and the Soviet continued to be ambiguous, contradictory, cool, and even hostile. On March 16, for instance, the Soviet expressed its willingness to support the policies of the Provisional Government insofar as they corresponded to the interests of the proletariat and of the broad democratic masses. At the same time, however, it continued to interfere in governmental affairs and to issue all kinds of appeals and orders in its own right. This created a highly explosive situation which the Russians have labelled *dvoevlastie*, or dual government. Under this arrangement the Provisional Government enjoyed responsibility but had no real authority, while the Soviet had authority but no responsibility. Trouble was inevitable.

The first major crisis between the Provisional Government and the Soviet developed over control of the armed forces. Under the March 14 compromise, all soldiers were to enjoy the same political rights as other citizens. It was understood that while on duty and in war service strict discipline should be maintained, but before this agreement was published, *Izvestiia*, the official mouthpiece of the Soviet, published the now famous Order No. 1. Drawn up on March 14 at the suggestion of some of the soldiers, it was directed to all units of the armed forces. It called for the election of committees from among the lower ranks which, in turn, in all of their "political actions" were to obey the Soviet. Orders of the Temporary Committee of the Duma were to be obeyed only if these did not conflict with those of the Soviet. Moreover, these committees were to have complete control over all weapons, which under no circumstances were to be turned over to officers. While pleading for strict observance of military discipline on duty, Order No. 1 abolished saluting while off duty as well as all elaborate traditional honors to officers. The latter were forbidden to be harsh towards their men.

These instructions, which expressed a fairly accurate picture of the long-standing hostility between officers and their men, greatly accelerated the breakdown of discipline in Russia's armed forces. Attempts to mitigate the effects of Order No. 1 failed completely. Everywhere soldiers talked, debated, voted, and some tried to settle old grievances with their officers. Although there were many who continued to think along traditional lines of their duty to defend the country as well as the achievements of the revolution, there were thousands who left their units and simply went home. The appearance of national military units (Polish, Ukrainian, Georgian, Armenian, and others) responsive to native command but unwilling to listen to orders from Petrograd only deepened the existing chaos. Without discipline and leadership the seven million man Russian army, as an organized fighting unit rapidly disintegrated. Many military commanders who survived the initial storm accommodated themselves to a new situation. There were others, like Minister of War Guchkov, who openly detested the new regime that was introduced in the armed forces, and resigned in disgust because of pressure from the Soviet.

Simultaneously with the Soviet-created army crisis there developed a government-bungled foreign policy dilemma. From its inception the Provisional Government, while taking note of a need for changes in domestic affairs, had acted as if the revolution would have no effect on Russia's foreign policy. The Manifesto to the People of Russia of March 19, for example, spoke of the government's determination "to bring the war to a victorious conclusion" and to observe faithfully all alliances and agreements—both open and secret—which had been concluded between Tsarist Russia and its allies. A government circular to Russia's representatives abroad, intended to assure her allies of the continuity of Russian foreign policy, emphasized the same points. Although these and similar public declarations by Foreign Minister Miliukov were welcomed in London and Paris, they were at variance with the realities of Russian conditions. To gain some of the war objectives—the Straits and the Ukrainian inhabited regions of the Dual Monarchy—it was necessary to have a fighting force. The government had none since so many Russian soldiers had decided to go home. Miliukov's failure to realize this, as well as the fact that the revolution was the result of war weariness and a protest against Tsarist domestic and war mismanagement, was fatal to him and to the Provisional Government.

As for the Soviet, that body for a time had no clear idea about war objectives. Some of its members supported while others objected to the known war aims. It was not until March 27 that the Soviet agreed on a vague but common stand. In an "Appeal to the Peoples of the World" the Petrograd Soviet announced that "it will, by every means, resist the policy of annexations of its ruling classes," and accordingly called upon the peoples of Europe, especially of Austria and Germany, "for concerted, decisive action in favor of peace." It recommended, among other things, the overthrow of their governments and refusal "to serve as an instrument of conquest and violence in the hands of kings, landowners, and bankers —and then by our united efforts, we will stop the horrible butchery, which is disgracing humanity. . . ."

An intensified nation-wide campaign advocating that the new Russia must have a new foreign policy of peace without annexations and indemnities followed. Newspapers, demonstrations, gatherings, and committees everywhere passed resolutions demanding the government's clarification and even change of its war aims. On April 8, under this concentrated pressure the Provisional Government yielded. The aim of free Russia, stated a declaration addressed to the Russian people, was neither the domination of other peoples, nor the forcible annexation of their territories, but "the establishment of a stable peace on the basis of the self-determination of nations." The Russian people did not seek to increase their power at the expense of other peoples, but neither would they tolerate that Russia "should emerge from the great struggle humiliated, undermined in her vital strength."

This government plea for status quo failed because Miliukov made it clear that the new formula did not bind him in administering foreign affairs. The crisis deepened, and new demands were made. The fact that some members of the Provisional Government itself favored the formula of peace "without annexations and indemnities" did not help the situation. On May 1, Miliukov once again was forced to "clarify" the government's stand on foreign policy. In a note sent to various Allied governments in order to calm foreign fears, he denied that Russia was seeking a separate peace. Russia was not only remaining faithful to her obligations but would also "carry the war to decisive victory" in order to gain necessary "guarantees and sanctions."

While assuring Russia's allies, Miliukov's note inspired violent protests and demonstrations and counterdemonstrations in war-weary Russia. The Executive Committee of the Soviet branded it a new "imperialistic" declaration, while Lenin, the leader of the Bolsheviks, who had just returned to Russia from Switzerland via Germany and Sweden, published an infuriating anti-government article in the party's mouthpiece, *Pravda*. To calm the excited public the government issued a new declaration which disavowed Miliukov's interpretation. Miliukov's days as Foreign Minister were over, and he resigned on May 15.

Miliukov's resignation and that of Guchkov two days earlier led to reorganization of the Provisional Government on a coalition basis. Of the fifteen ministers, now nine were liberals and six were moderate socialists from the Soviet. The latter entered the government with full understanding that: (1) the government's policy would be directed towards a general and speedy peace without annexations and indemnities; (2) there would be further democratization of the army; (3) the food, transportation, and financial situations would be improved; (4) a new agrarian policy would be adopted; (5) the Constituent Assembly would be convened as soon as possible; and (6) Soviet ministers would be responsible to the Soviet. These conditions, which became the official policy of the coalition government ended the first phase of dual power in Russia. Once they were members of the government, moderate Soviet spokesmen began to lose ground among the urban as well as the peasant masses. The road was thus cleared for Lenin to adopt the slogan "All Power to the Soviets."

Military and foreign policy crises notwithstanding, the first cabinet of the Provisional Government accumulated an admirable record of achievements. It granted complete amnesty to political and religious prisoners, abolished capital punishment and the exile system, and reformed prisons. It removed all legal restrictions based on class, creed, or national origin. It abolished all special courts and introduced the general system of trial by jury. It guaranteed freedom of speech, press, and assembly. It reorganized food distribution. It widened the base of local administration and reformed the system of peasant administrative machinery. It strengthened the cooperative movement. It instituted the eight-hour working day and granted labor the right to organize and to strike. It reorganized the church adminstration. It inaugurated preparations for an early convocation of the Constituent Assembly whose task, among others, was to be the solution of the agrarian problem. Finally, it restored the autonomy of Finland, reorganized administration in Central Asia and the Caucasus, offered semi-independent status to Poland, and created committees to work out local autonomy for the Ukraine and Latvia.

While many of these achievements simply acknowledged *faits accomplis,* judged according to normal conditions they were nevertheless quite impressive. For revolutionary times, however, they fell short because they ignored basic wants of the masses; i.e., peasant demands for land and workers' demands for better working conditions and wages. Deprived so long by Tsarism of elementary rights, both the Russian and non-Russian peoples knew no limits to their hopes and aspirations when the revolution developed. Rightly or wrongly they demanded more rights and fewer sacrifices, more leisure and less work. The government, consisting of conservative-liberal spokesmen, moved cautiously. With shaky authority, lack of administrative apparatus, a terrible war on hand, finances in disorder, and the economy in chaos, the Provisional Government insisted on the maintenance of status quo and even postponement of some demands until the meeting of the Constituent Assembly. This was a fatal mistake. To the revolution-excited masses this attitude revealed that both at the center and at the periphery as well, government spokesmen were too slow and too conservative and above all distrustful of the masses. This attitude also placed ammunition in the hands of a more radical element which had begun to return from domestic and foreign exile. There was little ahead that was encouraging.

The revolution made possible the return of thousands of veteran revolutionaries—liberals, socialists, peasants, students, and intellectuals.

Out of a Moscow prison came Polish conspirator Felix E. Dzerzhynski (1877–1926), who later was to organize the Soviet secret police. From Siberian exile came such Bolsheviks as Jacob M. Sverdlov (1885–1919), Lev. B. Kamenev (1883–1936), and Joseph V. Stalin (1879–1953). The procession from the West included the anarchist Prince Peter Kropotkin (1842–1921), the novelist Maxim Gorky (1868–1936), and the founder of Russian Marxism, Plekhanov. After brief detention by British authorities, from New York via Canada came the versatile Trotsky and Nikolai I. Bukharin (1888–1938). From Switzerland via Germany and Sweden came a group of thirty-eight exiles, including Gregory E. Zinoviev (1883–1936), Karl B. Radek (1885–?), Anatole V. Lunacharsky (1875–1933), and Lenin, the latter the leader of the Bolshevik faction of the Russian Social Democratic Workers' Party. Lenin's return, though seemingly unimportant at the time, viewed in retrospect inaugurated a new phase of the revolution.

Lenin and his party arrived in Petrograd on April 16. At the Finland Station he was greeted by a relatively large crowd of workers, soldiers and sailors, and representatives of various revolutionary organizations. Chkheidze extended official greetings on behalf of the Petrograd Soviet by inviting Lenin to join in defense of "revolutionary democracy" against external and internal attacks. Lenin, however, had his own ideas on the revolution. After telling the assembled throngs that the Russian revolution marked the beginning of an international revolution by the toiling masses everywhere, he hurried to remold his own party, which, like all the revolutionary groups, was in a sad state. It was small numerically, had played no part in the overthrow of the monarchy, and its spokesmen in Russia were divided on tactics. Immediately after the revolution the Bolshevik mouthpiece, *Pravda*, edited by the youthful Viacheslav M. Molotov (1890–), had opposed continuation of the war, assailed the Mensheviks, and demanded all power to the Soviets. When Stalin and Kamenev, upon their return from Siberia, took over the editorship a conciliatory policy towards the Provisional Government was adopted.

Lenin ridiculed the tactics of his followers and on April 20 *Pravda* published his celebrated April Theses. His program consisted of ten points: (1) The war in which Russia was involved was an imperialistic war and any defense of it was inadmissible. Conscientious Socialists could support only a revolutionary war, provided that three conditions were fulfilled: (a) that the state power would pass into the hands of the proletariat and the poorest strata of the peasantry; (b) that all annexations be renounced; and (c) that all ties be severed with capitalist interests. Until these conditions were fulfilled, all-out propaganda must be organized everywhere, and especially in the army, in order to convince everyone that no democratic peace was possible without the overthrow of capitalism. (2) Because of the rapidly changing revolutionary situation in Russia, the party's revolutionary tactics must be flexible and capable of meeting every new situation. (3) The Provisional Government should receive no support. On the contrary its false promises should be exposed. (4) The only possible form of revolutionary government was the Soviet of Workers' Deputies. However, in view of the Bolsheviks' insignificant numbers and inadequate representation in the soviets, the party should for the time being limit its work to criticism of the government and to insistence that all power be transferred to the Soviet. (5) The party must demand not a parliamentary—that would be a step backwards—but a soviet republic without police, army, and bureaucracy. (6) All lands must be nationalized and placed under the control of local soviets, and all landed estates must be confiscated and turned into model farms under soviet supervision. (7) All banks must be merged into one national bank and placed immediately under soviet control. (8) The party's immediate task was not the introduction of socialism but only the bringing of "social production and distribution of products" under control of the soviets. (9) A party congress must be held immediately to amend the party's antiquated program and change its name from Social Democratic to Communist. (10) A new international must be organized.

Lenin's program, as well as his bitter criticism of those party members who were moderate in their demands, met considerable opposition even from his close associates. The Petrograd Party Committee rejected it by a vote of thirteen to two with one abstention. This setback did not deter Lenin from pursuing his goal. Though labelled an anarchist and a man who had long been out of touch with Russian reality, he hammered his points again and again until he won an increasing number of supporters to his way of thinking. This concentrated effort accomplished its purpose. By early May at a special Party Conference in Petrograd he picked up considerable support. Although some of his points were not accepted, the final resolutions were passed by seventy-one votes against thirty-nine, with eight abstentions. Slowly, too, the slogans of Lenin's program—"End of War," "Land to Peasants," and "Take Back the Loot" —began to penetrate down to the war-weary and land-hungry people. Lenin, though opposed to individual ownership of land, sensed their wish and capitalized on it. All-out efforts to gain a military victory, to promote patience, moderation, and postponement of vital issues, as the Provisional Government advocated, had little chance of success.

THE SUMMER CRISIS

The Provisional Government's first colossal failure occurred in its war efforts. In spite of its knowledge of the considerable demoralization of the troops, lack of supplies, and the breakdown of transportation, the government ordered preparations for a new military offensive. If victorious—and the men preparing it did not consider other possibilities—the offensive was to attain two desperately needed objectives: (1) a demonstration to the Allies that Russia was capable of military performance, but that because of great domestic problems it desired immediate negotiations for a general peace; and (2) a buildup of the government's authority and prestige and the silencing of its bitter critics at home. Intensive preparations for this great undertaking started in May. To check the disintegration of the army and to bolster its fighting spirit, trusted civilian commissars were appointed. Some leaders toyed with the idea of organizing volunteer "death brigades" and the like. These measures in turn were supplemented by a barrage of leaflets, pamphlets, resolutions, and appeals by various organizations, including the Soviet, calling upon the Russian army to defend Russia and such revolutionary gains as freedom and liberty. Immediately after his appointment as Minister of War, Kerensky toured the front where, through his eloquent persuasion and in spite of heckling and interruptions, he tried and succeeded in arousing some fighting enthusiasm.

In spite of warnings and of many technical shortcomings, the offensive began on July 1, under the supervision of General Aleksei A. Brusilov (1853–1926). The main thrust of the attack centered in Galicia against the demoralized forces of the Dual Monarchy. In its initial stages the offensive was successful. After an unusually heavy bombardment, Russian infantry broke through the battered and half-destroyed enemy lines. Casualties were heavy on both sides. The Russians captured several thousand prisoners, some equipment, and a few towns, but failed to break the enemy's resistance. Hopes placed in the military victory began to evaporate, and on July 19 the Austro-German forces launched their own counteroffensive. Russian forces panicked and fled eastward in the most disorderly fashion imaginable, perpetrating many crimes and atrocities on the defenseless civilian population. Demoralization created by war, defeats, propaganda, poor equipment, the committee system, and lack of leadership was now complete. Only the units of the Czechoslovak legion, organized in Russia from among war prisoners after the revolution had begun, showed a degree of orderliness and efficiency. Confident that Russian forces presented no threat to their security, the Germans, with their attention centered in France, did not press their advance and the front line stabilized itself east of the prewar frontier.

Simultaneously with these great military reverses at the front there developed another major political crisis at home, over the issue of self-determination in general and that of the Ukraine in particular. The collapse of the monarchy had heralded a new era not only for the Russians but for many non-Russian peoples (Finns, Estonians, Latvians, Lithuanians, Poles, Ukrainians, Georgians, and Armenians). Immediately after the collapse of the old regime, many of these nationalities organized on their respective territories their own administrations which were reluctant to take orders from Petrograd. Some of these nations demanded only autonomy within the new Russia; others insisted on complete separation. The Provisional Government found itself in a dilemma, as its spokesmen held fast to the theory that it was a successor to and trustee of the powers formerly vested in the Tsar which were to be handed over intact to the Constituent Assembly. To consent to the demands of non-Russian nationalities would have meant the acknowledgment of Russia's territorial disintegration. This the leaders of the Provisional Government, reared in the idea that Russia was indivisible, were unwilling to do, but they had no effective means to prevent this disintegration. The Soviet was of no help inasmuch as many of its members were favorably inclined towards the idea of self-determination. The government was therefore forced to adopt a stumbling middle-of-the-road policy. It agreed to grant independence to some nationalities (Poles and Finns), subject to approval by the Constituent Assembly, but it denied the same right to others. It was a policy that was bound to lead to trouble. The explosion occurred in the area the Russians least expected—the Ukraine.

To most Russians, the Ukraine, which the Tsars had acquired in the course of the seventeenth and eighteenth centuries, was the bread basket of the Empire and a major coal and metallurgical region; hence it was considered an indispensable and inseparable part of Russia. Very few were aware that although the Ukrainian population was Orthodox and spoke a language the Russians could understand, thanks to the Russification policy there had been developing and maturing for some time a national movement. When the monarchy collapsed in March, the Ukrainians, like other subject peoples, were seized with a passion for autonomy. Immediately after the revolution they organized their own revolutionary administration, the Ukrainian Central *Rada* (Council), to deal with regional matters. Initially the *Rada's* democratically-inclined petty bourgeois members did not demonstrate any serious desire for national independence. They insisted only on broad autonomy within a federated and democratic Russian republic, but the Provisional Government refused to yield to these modest demands. It argued that it lacked authority and that the matter could be disposed of only by the Constituent Assembly. The Ukrainians interpreted this as a dilatory legalistic approach to camouflage Russian imperialism, and on June 23 increased their demands in the First Universal. This document declared that while continuing to maintain their ties with Russia, the Ukrainians were embarking on a policy of exerting the right to organize their own life. A general secretariat was formed to act as a cabinet, and the organization of a Ukrainian army was begun amidst the all-out preparations for the July offensive. In view of the dismal failure of the latter, an understanding with the *Rada* became imperative. On July 12, Kerensky with his two colleagues, Tereshchenko and Irakli G. Tseretelli (1882–1960), arrived in Kiev. Their vague consent to several Ukrainian demands precipitated a crisis within the Provisional Government and four Cadet ministers resigned in protest. In the midst of this governmental crisis came the news of the great military disaster. General fear and government helplessness led to an explosion.

The call to the July uprising, as this crisis is known, was issued on July 16 by the grievance-burdened soldiers. They were immediately joined by the eager and ever-ready sailors from the nearby Kronstadt naval base, and by unemployed and hence restless workers. Although many military units decided to remain "neutral," in a very short time there emerged an angry and leaderless anti-government mob ready to loot and to shoot. On the following day, July 17, the banner-carrying demonstrators, now some 500,000 strong, demanded resignation of the Provisional Government and transfer of all power to the Soviet.

The Menshevik-dominated Central Executive Committee of the Soviet not only declined this call but branded the uprising as premature and treasonable. Tensions increased hour by hour and some government and Soviet officials were roughed up by the angry and ugly-tempered mob. Lenin and his followers watched these developments with interest. They were tempted to lead the infuriated mob but their inadequate strength called for caution. Since there was no one to give the mob positive direction, the force of the uprising subsided as rapidly as it had snowballed in the first place. Leaderless, the crowd lost enthusiasm, dispersed, and went home. The uprising, which resulted in several deaths and in a large number of wounded, was over.

The Provisional Government lost no time in re-establishing its authority. It moved along two levels. Since some Bolsheviks had had a hand in the uprising and in order to undermine their influence, Minister of Justice P. N. Pereverzev disclosed to various "neutral" regiments certain documents which seemed to implicate Lenin as a German spy. Coming as it did on the heels of the Russian defeats, this allegation caused anti-Bolshevik feeling to explode. Several regiments now placed themselves at the government's disposal. On July 19, pro-government forces raided and wrecked the plant and offices of *Pravda,* and without any difficulty occupied Party Headquarters and the Fortress of Peter and Paul. Regiments that had taken part in the uprising were disbanded and sent to the front. Simultaneously with these measures, to Kerensky's annoyance, the government published anti-Lenin allegations in the press and ordered the arrest of Lenin as well as many of his close associates, charging them with incitement to armed insurrection. Some of his associates (Trotsky and Lunacharsky) were apprehended but were later released. Lenin, protesting his innocence, went into hiding first in Petrograd and later in Finland, which was now outside of Russian jurisdiction, where he remained until autumn.

The stern government measures following the July uprising pushed aside the danger from the extreme Left, but at the same time gave encouragement to the forces of the extreme Right which had been silent since March. On July 21, in protest against the government's anticipated labor and particularly agrarian policies, Prince Lvov resigned as Premier. As there was considerable disagreement among various self-appointed leaders and spokesmen over policy and appointments, a new and prolonged government crisis developed. It ended on August 7 when a new coalition government under Kerensky's premiership emerged. It was a moderately left-oriented body. Four of the sixteen ministers were Cadets; the remainder were divided between Socialist Revolutionaries and Mensheviks. All members of the new government were released from responsibility to their party and were approved by the Executive Committee of the Petrograd Soviet. On the surface calm prevailed, but underneath the situation was deteriorating rapidly.

To check this disintegration the government summoned an All-Russian State Conference in Moscow for August 26–28. Its delegates, some 2,500 strong, represented peasants, trade unions, soviets, army committees, liberal, socialist, and bourgeois groups. Neither the extreme Right (Monarchists) nor the extreme Left (Bolsheviks) was invited, with the latter retaliating by calling a strike in Moscow. By means of such a forum the government hoped to feel out "the pulse of the country" and to achieve unity. For three days the assembled delegates made speeches, declarations, demands, and complaints. There were also charges and counter-charges. Instead of unity the conference revealed the existence of a cleavage between the proponents and the opponents of the revolution. The most forceful challenge to the revolution came from General Lavr G. Kornilov (1870–1918), the recently appointed Commander-in-Chief of the Russian armies. To the cheers of non-Socialist members Kornilov denounced the existing anarchy in the army and held the socialists responsible for it. His blunt language made him at once the hero of the Right. His star began to rise rapidly only to fall precipitously.

THE KORNILOV AFFAIR

General Kornilov was of simple Cossack origin, and throughout his life retained that simplicity. He rose to the top not through behind-the-scenes maneuvers but by his own hard work plus several fortuitous incidents. Early in the war, for instance, he was captured by the Austrians but made good his escape, an act which made his name famous. Along with his courage Kornilov was known for his resolution and integrity—attributes not necessarily appropriate for revolutionary and opportunistic times. This had been evident in his inability to handle the revolutionary garrison of Petrograd in the early stages of the revolution. Yet, unable to find anyone suitable, after the failure of the July offensive Kerensky turned to Kornilov to restore order. It was a mistake because the chaos was more political than military, and Kornilov could not handle it. He was neither a statesman nor a politician but a simple soldier who was reputed to have "the heart of a lion and the brain of a lamb."

In Kornilov's view the Soviet represented the source of all Russia's trouble. From the moment he assumed the highest military office, all of his actions were directed towards strengthening his own as well as the authority of the Provisional Government at the expense of the Soviet. He demanded and received a free hand in military operations, in naming his subordinates and in the re-establishment of military courts and the death penalty. Early in September Kornilov saw a golden opportunity to deal directly and more effectively with the Soviet. On September 3, the Germans occupied Riga, and the road to Petrograd—the center of revolutionary activity and Soviet strength—was wide open. In the face of considerable Soviet opposition, Kornilov insisted on evacuation of the capital. The government, afraid of alienating the Soviet, hesitated. To enable it to make up its mind Kornilov dispatched a cavalry corps to the capital, ostensibly to protect the government, but actually to make sure that both the government and the Soviet were ousted. Simultaneously Kerensky was approached clumsily by the former Procurator of the Holy Synod, Lvov, asking him to cooperate with Kornilov. Then followed a tragic comedy of errors.

Lvov succeeded in creating with Kerensky the impression that he was Kornilov's emissary. He urged Kerensky to transfer to Kornilov all power, resign, and place himself under Kornilov's protection. Kerensky interpreted this kind suggestion as a conspiracy, arrested Lvov and dismissed Kornilov. The latter refused to comply and appealed to the people. Using not-too-convincing old cliches, he blasted the Provisional Government for its alleged cooperation with the Germans and for inflicting ruin upon the country, and summoned all God-fearing Russian patriots to action. Convinced that there was a leaderless population and strong anti-Kerensky sentiment in Petrograd, Kornilov ordered additional troop movements to the capital. Meanwhile, sensing approaching danger, the Soviet and all other socialist organizations began to act rapidly. A Committee for Struggle Against Counter-Revolution was organized and the entire Petrograd garrison was alerted, including the ever-eager Kronstadt sailors. Petrograd workers, many of whom were now under effective Bolshevik control, were mobilized and armed. Trenches were dug, barricades were built, barbed wire was strung, some seven thousand possible Kornilov supporters were arrested, and the communication system (rail and wire) was disrupted. Without much effort the Kornilov forces sent to Petrograd were halted, isolated, and subjected to extensive propaganda and fraternization. Upon being convinced that they were helping to restore the ancient regime, even the most trusted of Kornilov's troops refused to fight. The expedition was over and had been an overwhelming failure. General Alexander M. Krymov (1871–1917), one of the main leaders of the expeditionary forces, committed suicide on September 13, and on the following day Generals Kornilov, Anton I. Denikin (1872–1947), and other rebellious officers were arrested. The government appointed a commission to gather evidence, but to the astonishment of all those who had defended the government's action the commission acted very slowly and in a spirit of forgiveness.

The immediate consequence of the Kornilov affair was the complete collapse of the military and of the government, with some ministers being dismissed summarily. The organization of a new government which would represent broad segments of Russian society proved to be a difficult task. While searching for a new government, on September 14 Kerensky organized an inner cabinet of five members. To placate the Left-wing supporters, that body enacted a number of measures close to their hearts. On September 27, against some protest, Russia was formally proclaimed a republic although it had been one in reality since March. Kornilov's army reorganization program was shelved. The State Duma, one of the last remnants of the old order, was formally dissolved. Several moderate Right-wing politicians were arrested, the General Headquarters of the Army was purged, and officers' organizations favorable to the Kornilov movement were disbanded. These measures led to further deterioration at the front. Desertion increased and no one tried to stop it. The Russian army became, in the words of an official report, "a huge crowd of tired, poorly clad, poorly fed, embittered men united by common longing for peace and general disillusionment."

The wholesale elimination of the Right-wing danger and further deterioration of general conditions was accompanied by the rise of the Left. During the crucial hours of the Kornilov crisis, Kerensky in desperation appealed to the Bolsheviks. Trotsky and other leaders, imprisoned since July, were released. Well rested and sensing the absence of leadership among the workers, peasants, soldiers, and in the restless soviets, the Bolsheviks turned their entire attention in the direction of the malcontents. In September they obtained 50 per cent of the seats in the Petrograd Soviet, whereas in July they had held barely 10 per cent. By October, supported by the Left-wing Socialist Revolutionaries, Trotsky had become the Chairman of the Petrograd Soviet. The slogan "All Power to the Soviets" now acquired a new meaning.

THE SOCIAL UPHEAVAL

The Kornilov crisis like all previous crises was a political affair. It was a struggle among a few ambitious self-appointed spokesmen in Petrograd. Although it undermined the already shaky authority of the Provisional Government and thereby helped to shorten its life span, it was not the decisive cause of its downfall. Like all previous petty squabbles, the Kornilov affair was completely overshadowed by the great social upheaval which engulfed all of Russia. In 1917 Russia was predominantly an agricultural country. About four-fifths of her population was peasant. Though strong numerically, the peasants as a group had no direct part in the overthrow of the old regime, with the exception of those who were in the army. As was everyone else, the peasants were surprised by the swift collapse of the old regime. Cautious and reserved at first, they soon became the most radical element in the country, forging far ahead of their spokesmen—the Socialist Revolutionaries.

To the Russian peasants, both in and out of the armed forces, the collapse of the old regime revived their centuries-old aspiration. That aspiration was neither the right to vote, nor a parliamentary government, nor a victorious war, nor territorial gains, but *land*. By land they understood not such schemes neatly devised by intellectuals as nationalization, or socialization, but simple partition of nearby estates. Illiterate, backward, and never reconciled to the land settlement of the 1860's, nor fully satisfied by Stolypin's efforts, the Russian peasants sincerely believed that only through the enlargement of their plots of land would they be able to improve their wretched and, even by Russian standards, miserable condition. Partition of estates thus became in the peasant mind the prime and the only objective, and towards that goal they moved like an avalanche without the slightest detour.

Peasant land hunger affected many vital areas and revealed itself in innumerable ways. In the armed forces, for instance, where the peasants formed an overwhelming majority in numbers and in losses, between March and October over one million men simply "demobilized themselves" and went home to make certain they would get their share of the land. Their departure was devastating to the morale of those who remained. With the thought of land uppermost in their minds, peasant soldiers turned deaf ears to orders, disobeyed commands, listened to propaganda, demoted their superiors, debated, and elected their own representatives. They made all possible excuses to avoid combat duty, traded or threw away their weapons, fraternized with the enemy, and constantly dreamt about land, home, and peace. Peasant soldiers, in other words, lost all stomach for war and all attempts to restore discipline or to revive the fighting spirit were futile. The disastrous July offensive confirmed this fact and the Kornilov affair only accelerated total disintegration. In their desire to get land, peasant armies "voted for peace with their legs."

The behavior of Russian soldiers reflected the prevailing attitude of Russian peasants in villages. In spite of individual instances of "boldness" during the early stages of the revolution, the peasantry as a whole remained restrained for several weeks, but this self-control was short-lived. It ended when the peasants became convinced that the old authority had ceased to exist. Peasant land hunger then became uncontrollable. The removal of local landowners and the division of their property became the cardinal objective of the peasantry, and to attain it they employed numerous devices. In some areas they tried to persuade owners of large estates that it was in their interest to dispose of their land at a nominal price. Those owners who were realists did sell and moved away, but there were many who tried to resist. Against those the peasants used the most ancient of their weapons, the burning of manors. The latter act was accompanied, as a rule, by pillage and murder and followed by partition of the land. In some areas, to gain their objective the peasants forced local landowners to release their managers, supervisors, and other help and in turn demanded prohibitive wages for their own work. Spontaneously and without any centralized guidance, through these and similar devices, by early summer the peasants had brought activity on the large estates to a standstill and thereby prepared the stage for partitioning of the land. Under the pretext that owners were incapable of managing their own affairs, local peasant land committees took over not only arable land, meadows, and forests, but also livestock, agricultural implements, furniture, and other useful articles. The Provisional Government was flooded with owners' requests for help. Its contribution was nil, as the punitive expeditionary forces, composed of peasants, sided with their brethren against the landowners. There was no effective weapon against ancient peasant determination that the land belongs to those who till it.

To a large degree the Provisional Government itself was responsible for the course of the agrarian revolution. On the one hand, the government made it known that it sympathized with peasant aspirations. On the other hand, in the midst of the revolutionary upheaval which brought about its very own existence, the government deplored such revolutionary measures as violence, pillage, force, and other extra-legal activities. Instead it insisted on legal procedures, thorough preparations, and orderly methods in settling the land problem by the Constituent Assembly whose convocation, however, it repeatedly postponed. It was a fatal policy because the peasants grew tired of waiting and, unable to get legal approval of their aspirations, they took the law into their own hands. By late summer and early fall, when the government's authority began to disappear rapidly, peasant attacks on the estates reached epidemic proportions. Chaos reigned supreme and any demagogue willing to approve of their actions—and over a hundred million peasants were interested *only* in approval—was certain of their support.

The Provisional Government was not the only institution that contributed to general agrarian confusion only to find itself out of step with the peasant revolutionary enthusiasm and determination. The Soviets of Peasant Deputies, which had emerged spontaneously in March to take care of peasant problems, like the government soon found themselves trailing behind. Like all revolutionary bodies the peasant soviets lacked cohesion and fragmented into various revolutionary groups. This became clearly evident during and following the meeting of the First All-Russian Congress of the Soviets of Peasants' Deputies held in Petrograd in May, 1917. Many of its 1,115 delegates demanded that large estates and church and state lands be divided among the peasants. The Congress, however, dominated by intellectuals elected by village soviets, went on record as reserving final settlement of the land question to the Constituent Assembly, and in endless debates wasted much time on such non-agrarian issues as "peace without annexation and indemnities," and "coalition government."

Next to the peasantry, the most revolutionary group was industrial labor. Unlike the peasantry, however, the workers—at least those of Petrograd—took an active part in the overthrow of the old regime, and on several occasions demonstrated their readiness to defend the revolutionary gains. This was not because the workers were more revolutionary than were the peasants, but rather because they were centered in industrial areas and were better organized in trade unions, factory committees, and the soviets. These organizations, jointly, from the very beginning of the revolution brought many benefits to the workers. They instituted the eight-hour working day, fought for higher wages, negotiated for improved conditions of work, discussed the problem of unemployment, insisted on factory inspection, and promoted the cultural and economic well-being of the workers. Many of these innovations were long overdue in Russia. Some, like the demand for workers' control over production and distribution, were too extreme. Under revolutionary conditions the net result of both was the furthering of the existing anarchy and chaos. Most of the benefits they gained were wiped out by galloping inflation. To make matters worse, because of increased labor and other costs and the shortage of raw materials, many industries, too many in fact, closed down during the summer. The resulting unemployment was the last thing revolutionary Russia needed. Jobless and hungry workers resorted to violence in many regions. In some places they even seized plants and made a strenuous effort to run them in order to earn their daily bread, which was becoming scarcer and more expensive with every passing day. The gov-

62   USSR: A CONCISE HISTORY

ernment, with its authority constantly declining, deplored the prevailing anarchy but took no firm action to restore industrial stability. Driven into despair many workers in such large industrial centers as Petrograd, Moscow, and the Donets Basin were in as desperate a plight as the peasants and soldiers. They were ready to listen and to follow any demagogue who would promise a change, and Lenin, the realist, did not allow this opportunity to slip away.

SUGGESTED READINGS

BROWDER, ROBERT P., and ALEXANDER F. KERENSKY, eds. *The Russian Provisional Government. Documents.* 3 vols. Stanford: Stanford University Press, 1961.
CARR, EDWARD H. *A History of Soviet Russia.* 3 vols. New York: Macmillan, 1951–1953.
CHAMBERLIN, WILLIAM H. *The Russian Revolution, 1917–1921.* 2 vols. New York: Macmillan, 1935.
CHERNOV, VICTOR M. *The Great Russian Revolution.* Translated and abridged by Philip E. Moseley. New Haven: Yale University Press, 1936.
CURTISS, JOHN S. *The Russian Revolutions of 1917.* New York: Van Nostrand, 1957.
FERRO, MARC. *The Russian Revolution of February, 1917.* Englewood Cliffs, N.J.: Prentice-Hall, 1972.
FLORINSKY, MICHAEL T. *The End of the Russian Empire.* New Haven: Yale University Press, 1931.
GILL, GRAEME JR. *Peasants and Government in the Russian Revolution.* New York: Barnes and Noble, 1979.
GOLDER, FRANK A. *Documents of Russian History, 1914–1917.* New York: Century, 1927.
GOLOVIN, N. N. *The Russian Army in the World War.* New Haven: Yale University Press, 1931.
GRONSKY, P. P., and N. J. ASTROV. *The War and the Russian Government.* New Haven: Yale University Press, 1929.
HASEGAWA, T. *The February Revolution: Petrograd, 1917.* Seattle: University of Washington Press, 1981.
HUNCHAK, TARAS, ed. *The Ukraine, 1917–1921: A Study in Revolution.* Cambridge: Harvard University Press, 1977.
KATKOV, GEORGE. *Russia, 1917: The February Revolution.* New York: Harper and Row, 1967.
KERENSKY, ALEXANDER. *The Catastrophe.* New York: Appleton-Century-Crofts, 1927.
KOHN, S., and BARON A. F. MEYENDORFF. *The Cost of the War to Russia.* New Haven: Yale University Press, 1932.
MAWDSLEY, EVAN. *The Russian Revolution and the Baltic Fleet: War and Politics February 1917–April 1918.* New York: Barnes and Noble, 1978.
MILIUKOV, PAUL N. *Russia To-day and To-morrow.* New York: Macmillan, 1922.
MOOREHEAD, ALAN. *The Russian Revolution.* New York: Harper, 1958.
PARES, SIR BERNARD. *The Fall of the Russian Monarchy.* New York: Knopf, 1939.
PIDHAINY, OLEH S. *The Formation of the Ukrainian Republic.* Toronto: New Review Books, 1966.
RADKEY, OLIVER H. *The Elections of the Russian Constituent Assembly of 1917.* Cambridge: Harvard University Press, 1950.
RESHETAR, JOHN S. JR. *The Ukrainian Revolution, 1917–1921.* Princeton: Princeton University Press, 1952.

SAUL, NORMAN E. *Sailors in Revolt: The Russian Baltic Fleet in 1917*. Lawrence: University of Kansas Press, 1978.

STONE, NORMAN. *The Eastern Front, 1914–1917*. New York: Scribners, 1975.

SUKHANOV, N. N. *The Russian Revolution, 1917: A Personal Record*. Edited, abridged and translated by Joel Carmichael. New York: Oxford University Press, 1955.

THOMPSON, JOHN M. *Revolutionary Russia, 1917*. New York: Scribners, 1981.

TROTSKY, LEON. *The History of the Russian Revolution*. 3 vols. Translated by Max Eastman. New York: Simon & Schuster, 1932.

WADE, REX A. *The Russian Search for Peace: February–October, 1917*. Stanford: Stanford University Press, 1969.

WARTH, ROBERT D. *The Allies and the Russian Revolution*. Durham: Duke University Press, 1954.

WILDMAN, ALAN K. *The End of the Russian Imperial Army: The Old Army and the Soldiers' Revolt (March–April, 1917)*. Princeton: Princeton University Press, 1980.

✂ III

THE BOLSHEVIK REVOLUTION

BACKGROUND

The Bolshevik triumph in Russia was a product of three fundamental factors: First, the Bolsheviks' ability to capitalize on the mistakes and ridicule the policy of their opponents; second, their readiness to appropriate popular policies of other parties; and third, their determination to translate to the Russian people in simple terms the meaning of "the Bolshevik program" for Russia. That program as exemplified by the April Theses was clear, concise, and easily understood by the war-weary and land-hungry masses. It called, among other things, for immediate Russian withdrawal from the unpopular and losing war; the overthrow of capitalism which it held responsible for the war; the introduction in Russia of a revolutionary government of workers and of poor peasants; and for nationalization of the economy.

64

Many Russians doubted the success of this radical program. It was ridiculed by the opposition and its wisdom was questioned even by Lenin's own close associates. Convinced, however, that his ideas echoed the feelings of the excited elements among the masses of the Russian people, Lenin remained stubbornly unmoved. His uncompromising stand and untiring reiteration of points soon began to pay dividends. Not only was he able to bring unity to his own party, but he also attracted additional followers, who, like himself, were in the mood for a complete break with the gloomy past, for total desertion of the uncertain present, and for the creation of a promised land of the future. Between March and July, 1917, according to Bolshevik sources, membership increased greatly, but even with the sizable gain in numbers it represented only a small fraction of the 150 million people of Russia.

Most Bolshevik gains resulted from the lack of realism and the disunity among the opposition. The March Revolution made possible the open appearance of many political parties. The Right was represented by the Octobrists, who wanted to preserve Russia on the basis of the 1905 October Manifesto; the Constitutional Democrats, who wished to introduce in Russia a constitutional form of government along British lines; and a group of Public Men who believed in progress to be achieved not through revolutionary methods but gradually and cautiously. The parties of the Center were heterogeneous and picturesque. Non-Marxist Socialists of Kerensky's vintage believed in a strong, orderly, and democratic Russia; the Right Wing Mensheviks adhered to orthodox interpretation of Marxism; the Right Wing Socialist Revolutionary Party, traditional defender of peasant interests, believed in a loose federal arrangement for Russia; the Left Wing Menshevik group, headed by Trotsky, flirted with various parties until July when it joined the Bolsheviks; and the United Social Democratic Internationalists, led by Martov, pursued the same tactics. Parties on the Left included the Left Wing Socialist Revolutionaries, led by Maria A. Spiridonova (1889–?), Boris D. Kamkov, and Natanson; the Bolsheviks; and the Anarchists. Because self-appointed and, in some instances, irresponsible spokesmen of these and other lesser parties sabotaged all constructive proposals and quarreled with each other and the Provisional Government with suicidal energy, they presented Lenin with limitless opportunities.

The first significant chance to exploit the differences of the opposition came to the Bolsheviks early in May. The opportunity was created by Foreign Minister Miliukov. To clarify Russia's position on war aims, as we noted earlier, Miliukov assured her allies that Russia would live up to her obligations. While well received abroad, this assurance created a grave crisis at home. It led to violent demonstrations, protests, to Miliukov's resignation, and ultimately to the formation of a new coalition government of nine liberals and six socialists. Lenin helped much to deepen the crisis by his violent attack on the Provisional Government in the Bolshevik press. On the one hand he criticized the Provisional Government for alleged subservience to British and French capital and for annexationist policies, while on the other hand he assailed the Executive Committee of the Soviet for its confidence in and support of these policies. "No class-conscious worker, no class-conscious soldier will further support the policy of 'confidence' in the Provisional Government. The policy of confidence is bankrupt. . . . We demand that there be only one power—the Soviet of Workers' and Soldiers' Deputies. The Provisional Government, the government of a handful of capitalists must give way to the Soviets."

Lenin's demand that all power be transferred to the Soviets made him and his party the center of opposition to the Provisional Government and the Central Executive Committee of the Soviet. And although the Bolsheviks were still a long way from exercising a decisive influence on national policies, in their new role they nevertheless began to attract idealists and opportunists, the naive and the realists. With their help, the Bolshevik views, ideas, and demands were spread into factories and into the armed forces. The center of Bolshevik attention was not the rank and file but the leadership of factory and military committees. It was an unspectacular but shrewd and dividend-paying policy. By June many factories and regiments in Petrograd had fallen completely under Bolshevik control. At the meeting of the First All-Russian Congress of Soviets opening in Petrograd on June 16, the Bolsheviks, headed by Lenin, presented a solid block of 105 delegates to 248 Mensheviks and 285 Socialist Revolutionaries. Although the Bolsheviks were badly outnumbered, Lenin declared on June 17, to the astonishment and ridicule of the assembled delegates, that his party was ready and willing to take power from the government. But that was not all. He also presented his listeners with a sample of his policy after seizure of power. It was simple: he would arrest and hang some one hundred of the most important capitalists and denounce all lesser ones, regardless of nationality, as enemies of the people.

While many of the delegates listened to Lenin's ingenious proposal in silence, most of the assembled soldier deputies and street mobs applauded it enthusiastically. Since it was clear that Lenin echoed their feelings, control and planned incitement of the two became now one of the prime objectives, and the Bolsheviks lost no time in undertaking it. To test their strength, within a week after Lenin's speech the Bolsheviks announced that they would hold a mass antigovernment demonstration in Petrograd. When informed of this development, the Congress of Soviets, where the Bolsheviks' influence was insignificant, voiced disapproval and forbade it. Although everything was ready, Lenin, while popular with the street mob, was still uncertain of his strength and, afraid to defy the Congress, called off the demonstration. However, not all the preparations were in vain, for on July 1, the Bolsheviks joined the official demonstration sponsored by the Congress of Soviets, whose chief task was the endorsement of the policies of the coalition government. Bolshevik placards, "All Power to the Soviets," "Down With the Ten Capitalist Ministers," and "Peace, Bread, and Freedom," which had been prohibited a week before, now overwhelmed the official banners. To his astonishment Lenin realized that his following in Petrograd was much stronger than he had ever dreamed.

The unexpected show of strength frightened the opposition and greatly inflated the Bolsheviks' own hopes. The next two weeks were filled with all sorts of rumors of additional Bolshevik demonstrations and even of real trouble. Trouble finally came on July 16. The direct cause of the crisis, as we noted earlier, was the news of the complete collapse of the Galician offensive. The sudden news of the disaster, because of the over-enthusiastic reports of earlier successes created panic in Petrograd. In the midst of rising confusion someone spread a rumor that the government intended to send many "revolutionary" regiments to the rapidly disinte-grating front. The apprehensive soldiers immediately issued a call to re-bellion and were soon joined by the Kronstadt sailors and unemployed workers. On the following day a mob 500,000 strong, consisting of work-ers, soldiers, civilians, radicals, and ordinary people, Bolshevik-incited and strongly antigovernment, demanded the resignation of the Provisional Government and transfer of all power to the Soviet.

Lenin and his associates, though they directed some of the demon-strations from their headquarters at the Kshesinski Palace hesitated to act. One of the basic reasons for this hesitation was the lack of unity and unanimity among the party chieftains on the course to be adopted. Some members suggested that the party disassociate itself completely from the demonstration and let events run their course. Others advocated caution for fear that any unsuccessful attempt to seize power would bring com-plete disaster to the party. There were those who wanted to calm the incited mob without dampening its hot revolutionary temper. There were also some who argued that the party of the revolution should neither abandon the revolution nor desert the masses in time of crisis in order not to discredit itself in the eyes of those very people on whose confidence and support Bolshevik victory depended. This hesitation led to confusion and loss of enthusiasm. Since no one issued orders to execute the well-prepared schemes (such as the seizure of power or the arrest of the Central Executive Committee of the Soviet) and no one gave the incited mob positive direction, the momentum of the upheaval subsided as rap-idly as it had snowballed in the first place. On July 19 the uprising was over and the Provisional Government lost no time in re-establishing its authority, by curtailing the activities of the Bolsheviks, by arresting some of their leaders, and by putting others to flight.

The failure of the July uprising was a shattering blow to Bolshevik expectations. Suppressed again after a brief period of free activity, the party resorted to conspiracy. To recover from the blow as well as to work out future strategy, the Sixth Party Congress met half secretly in Petrograd early in August. With Lenin and his chief lieutenants absent (in prison or in hiding), the task of reorganizing the greatly weakened forces fell upon relative anonymities. A bright future was in store for Stalin who, although a member of the Central Committee of the party, was relatively unknown either inside or outside party circles. Because his name did not arouse the anger and hatred inspired by others, Stalin was the logical man to organize the party in Lenin's absence, but under Lenin's guidance and influence.

The basic task of the Sixth Congress was the planning of the party's future. Because of the anti-Bolshevik attitude of the Central Executive Committee of the Petrograd Soviet, the delegates, at Lenin's suggestion, agreed to drop the party's famous slogan, "All Power to the Soviets!" in favor of a well-timed and well-prepared armed seizure of power. This change of tactics helped to create a lively debate, which in many ways previewed a more dramatic struggle in the twenties. Bukharin argued that because of her relative industrial backwardness Russia could not establish a successful socialist society unless there were victorious socialist revolutions in Western Europe. On the other hand, Stalin maintained that regardless of whether or not the West European proletariat was victorious, he saw no reason for Russia not to start building socialism. Paradoxically and ironically, Stalin's reasoning, which later evolved into "Socialism in One Country," was at this stage identical with that of Trotsky, whose group had formally joined the Bolsheviks and who in absentia was elected a member of the Central Committee.

A resolution of the Sixth Congress called upon Bolshevik followers to avoid any action that might lead to an open clash. With the leadership either imprisoned or in hiding and the following on the decrease everywhere, this appeal was in many respects meaningless. The events of late August and early September, however, caused unexpected changes. Thanks to the inability of the Provisional Government to deal effectively with the land problem, peasant disturbances began to reach extreme proportions throughout the country. Because of strikes or the lack of necessary material, many factories were forced to close down thus creating increased labor unrest. The July military debacle accelerated military disintegration and added much to the existing chaos. In other words, Russia found herself in a situation that was desperate and deteriorating rapidly. A strong and resolute government might have been capable of salvaging something. Unfortunately for Russia such was not the case. The Provisional Government was weak and vacillating. Because its existence depended on the good will of ambitious, irresponsible, quarreling, and often self-appointed spokesmen of various political groups, the government could neither enforce orders nor inspire confidence. Since no political party had either the sense or courage to step into the political vacuum which suddenly appeared, the Bolsheviks decided to try a comeback.

PREPARATION FOR SEIZURE OF POWER

The first significant step in the Bolshevik seizure of power was the government's decision before the Kornilov crisis to release several of Lenin's imprisoned associates. The Konilov affair brought a whole chain of consequences. Unable to defeat Kornilov alone, Kerensky and the Petrograd Soviet enlisted Bolshevik help. Some 25,000 Bolshevik-organized workers and Kronstadt sailors—the Red Guards—who had been inactive since the July revolt now received arms from the government to defend the revolution. Kornilov's forces, as we have seen, disintegrated before they reached Petrograd. The Bolsheviks, however, lost no time in exploiting to the utmost their "contribution" to the victory over Kornilov. The Provisional Government tried to deflate their strength by demanding surrender of their arms. The "defenders of the revolution," however, refused to comply. Mistrusted and deserted because there had set in throughout Russia a strong "anti-Kornilovism" sentiment, the government could not enforce its demand.

Meanwhile, because they were "in the first ranks" against Kornilov, the Bolsheviks had little difficulty in compiling an impressive record of "victories" and in gaining a following at the expense of their disunited opponents, the Mensheviks and Socialist Revolutionaries. A few days after the downfall of Kornilov, the Bolsheviks were successful in passing through the Petrograd Soviet, by 279 to 115 votes, a resolution which embodied most of their program. It called for the establishment of a Soviet republic in Russia, granting of land to peasant soviets, workers' control of industry, the annulment of all secret treaties, and immediate conclusion of peace. Shortly thereafter the Bolsheviks demanded, and won by 514 to 414, with 67 abstentions, a motion for election of a new Presidium—the all powerful policy-making body of the Central Executive Committee—of the Petrograd Soviet. When it was organized the Presidium consisted of fourteen Bolsheviks, six Socialist Revolutionaries, and three Mensheviks. Trotsky, who replaced Chkheidze as Chairman, lost no time in announcing the withdrawal of Soviet support from the Provisional Government, and demanded immediate convening of the Second All-Russian Congress of Soviets to which all power was to be transferred. Since other parts of the country followed the capital's shift to the Left, the Bolshevik insurrection against the Provisional Government was the next logical step.

Lenin foresaw this development shortly after the Kornilov crisis. From his hideaway in Finland he sensed the emerging political vacuum and urged his followers to move in by first obtaining a majority in the Petrograd and Moscow Soviets and then by seizing power. The Central Committee of the Party rejected this advice as impractical and dangerous. Lenin followed it up with two letters in which he pleaded with his lieutenants that the majority of the Russian people were with the Bolsheviks, that only the Bolsheviks had the policy to satisfy everyone, that even the international climate was favorable and that, because the time was ripe, the party should make *armed insurrection* in Petrograd and Moscow the order of the day. "History," he urged, "will not forgive us if we do not take power now."

Lenin's urgent and impatient pleas, however, failed to persuade many of his more cautious lieutenants in Russia, including Trotsky, Stalin, Kamenev, and Zinoviev. During a debate on September 28 on the armed insurrection, they all were in full agreement with Lenin's emphasis on the urgency for a revolt, but they disagreed on timing and tactics. Zinoviev and Kamenev felt that the time was not ripe. Trotsky, on the other hand, thought that Lenin's military concept of insurrection, to be undertaken by the party alone, was too narrow. He believed that to be successful the insurrection should have a broad base. Such a base he saw in the Soviets. Since the Second Congress of Soviets was scheduled to meet in Petrograd early in November, Trotsky, in his capacity as Chairman of the Presidium of the Petrograd Soviet, did everything in his power to make the rising coincide with the meeting of the Congress.

While both open and secret preparations to overthrow the Provisional Government went on, the country was sinking ever deeper into defeat and chaos. In October someone spread a rumor that, because of the German threat, the government contemplated transferring the capital from Petrograd to Moscow. The Bolshevik leadership was dismayed at such a prospect. If allowed to come about, such a move would upset their plans for the insurrection. They accordingly interpreted it as a "counter revolutionary" measure and called upon all the Leftist parties to "defend the capital of the revolution." The response was almost unanimous. The Petrograd Soviet then assumed full control of troop movements in and around the capital, and on October 26 the Executive Committee of the Petrograd Soviet appointed a Military Revolutionary Committee. Outwardly the purpose of that body was the defense of the capital. In reality, however, it was the General Staff of the Bolshevik Revolution. Trotsky, as President of the Petrograd Soviet, became the chairman of the Military Revolutionary Committee, and in that capacity he soon decreed that in military matters no order was to be executed in or around Petrograd without his or his Bolshevik assistants' countersignatures. As the real master of the garrison, Trotsky thus held in his hands all the vital threads of the insurrection which he manipulated in a masterly manner.

While Trotsky was successfully giving the conspiracy legal and moral

Lenin speaking to a crowd. Trotsky is at the right, facing the camera.

authority and a defensive appearance, Lenin tried to overcome the opposition within the party to the idea of insurrection. It was not an easy task, for his followers, although considered by many as men of action, shared their adversaries' passion for endless, hair-splitting talk. With Lenin in hiding they felt less compelled to follow his impatient suggestions, some of which they even vetoed. And though he raged and even threatened to resign from the party, he could do little. He was in hiding in Finland; they were in Petrograd and free. Early in October, to be closer to the scene of action, Lenin moved from Helsinki to Vyborg. On October 21, he secretly returned to Petrograd and two days later he attended the historic secret meeting of the Central Committee of the Party which decided in favor of insurrection.

During a ten-hour-long debate, two of Lenin's long-time associates, Kamenev and Zinoviev, afraid that an armed uprising would end in total failure, tried to persuade the Central Committee to postpone the coup d'état. They disapproved of immediate armed insurrection on two grounds: (1) they thought that Lenin underestimated the government's forces and overestimated his own; and (2) they believed that the Russian revolution should be timed to coincide with a proletarian revolution in Western Europe which they thought was imminent and indispensable to the success of the Russian revolution. Lenin brushed aside these arguments, which were later proven to be incorrect, and hammered home his own points. The time for an armed uprising was ripe, he argued, because the Bolsheviks had control of the leading soviets, because Bolshevik slogans were popular with the masses, and because the agrarian unrest had developed full momentum. Lenin's arguments won. Of the twelve members present and voting, only Kamenev and Zinoviev cast negative votes on the immediate armed uprising which was proposed for November 2, the day the Second All-Russian Congress of Soviets was to convene. Political direction of the revolution was placed in the hands of the Political Bureau (Politburo). Lenin, Trotsky, Stalin, Gregory Y. Sokolnikov (1888–?), Andrei Bubnov (1883–?), Kamenev, and Zinoviev were selected the first members of this body which subsequently became all-powerful.

The fateful decision in favor of armed insurrection was followed by vacillation as well as by intensive preparation. Since party discipline was loose, many rank-and-file members opposed the decision of the Central Committee, on the same grounds as Kamenev and Zinoviev. On October 29 the Central Committee held another meeting during which the previous decision in favor of the uprising was reaffirmed. Thereupon Kamenev resigned from the Central Committee and two days later, in Maxim Gorky's paper, *Novaia Zhizn* (New Life), he and Zinoviev made public the open secret; i.e., that the Bolsheviks were preparing for an armed uprising on the eve of the opening of the Second All-Russian Congress of Soviets.

The news of the impending Bolshevik insurrection gave rise to all kinds of rumors and speculations, threats and counterthreats, charges and denials. Lenin branded his two longtime but indiscreet lieutenants "traitors to the revolution" and demanded their expulsion from the party. Asked at a meeting of the Petrograd Soviet to comment on rumors of the impending uprising, Trotsky denied the existence of any preparations. To dampen hot tempers that suddenly flared, the non-Bolshevik Executive Committee of the All-Russian Congress of Soviets postponed the meeting of the Congress from November 2 to 7, halted all forms of demonstrations, and demanded that no arms be issued to anyone without its consent. The Bolsheviks, and especially Trotsky, welcomed the postponement as it gave them an additional week to prepare. To make sure that the garrison obeyed his orders, Trotsky appointed trusted commissars to each detachment in and around Petrograd, and officers failing to obey the commissars' orders were either removed or arrested. On November 5, Bolshevik-controlled regiments were ordered to occupy strategic points in the capital. The showdown had come.

The Provisional Government, except for issuing self-assuring statements about its own strength, did nothing to frustrate the impending armed uprising until the evening of November 5, when a cabinet meeting declared a state of emergency. All military units within the city were placed under the command of Colonel Polkovnikov, the military commander of the Petrograd garrison. Trotsky's Military Revolutionary Committee was declared illegal, and an order was issued for his arrest as well as that of other Bolshevik leaders who were free on bail. Bolshevik newspapers were ordered closed, and to enforce these measures loyal troops were ordered in from outside the capital.

The government's showdown with the Bolsheviks came too late. After repeated postponements, vacillation, indecision, and irresolution, the Provisional Government had lost all respect and authority. Only a handful of loyal troops expressed willingness to come to its rescue. The sailors of the cruiser *Aurora,* anchored in the Neva River, refused to obey the order to put out to sea and placed themselves at Trotsky's disposal. Challenged by the government, the Military Revolutionary Committee decided to move fast. It issued arms to its sympathizers throughout the city and ordered its forces to reoccupy the offices of Bolshevik papers which earlier had been taken by government troops. Bolshevik units also seized control of bridges and main thoroughfares in the capital. Railway stations, the State Bank, the central post office and all other key points were occupied without any opposition during the night of November 6–7. Deserted by everyone, Kerensky escaped from the capital to seek in vain for support outside. No attempt was made to stop him as he drove in an open car through the streets of a Petrograd controlled by Bolshevik soldiers. At 10:00 A.M. on November 7, the Revolutionary Military Committee announced the overthrow of the Provisional Government. The people of Russia were assured of "the immediate proposal of a democratic peace, the abolition of landed proprietorship, workers' control over production, and the creation of a Soviet Government." During the night of November 7, after a brief exchange of fire, Bolshevik forces occupied the Winter Palace—the seat of the Provisional Government. Except for two who escaped, all remaining ministers of the Provisional Government were arrested and were sent to the Fortress of Peter and Paul to join their tsarist counterparts. The days of the Provisional Government were over; the Soviet period of Russian history had begun. The transition, all-important not only in Russian but in world history, was responsible for some twenty dead and a few wounded.

THE FIRST PHASE OF THE REMAKING OF RUSSIA

The ease and speed with which the Bolsheviks seized power in Petrograd surprised everyone. Even Lenin admitted that to pass so suddenly from persecution and underground living to a position of power made him slightly dizzy. He lost no time, however, in consolidating his authority. On the same day that the mild and bloodless coup d'état was executed, the postponed meeting of the Second All-Russian Congress of Soviets took place. Out of some 650 delegates, about whose election or even party affiliation no reliable information is available, 390 were registered as Bolsheviks, 80 as Mensheviks, and some 150 as Socialist Revolutionaries. The opening session of the Congress was stormy, and factional strife among the non-Bolshevik delegates prevented them from forming a solid opposition to the Bolshevik armed seizure of power. The Bolsheviks outmaneuvered their disunited and quarreling opponents in the election of the Presidium of the Second All-Russian Congress of Soviets. The new body had fourteen Bolsheviks, seven Left Socialist Revolutionaries, four Mensheviks (who refused however to assume their positions), and one representative from the Ukraine. Some members of the opposition, in protest against Bolshevik machinations and the alleged disrespect for proper procedures, withdrew from the Congress. This was a fatal and foolish move because it left the Bolsheviks, who stood for the "proletariat," and their temporary allies, the Left Socialist Revolutionaries, who posed as the sole representatives of the peasantry, in full control of the Congress, thereby simplifying the Bolshevik task.

The Second Congress of Soviets, under Lenin's guidance, performed three functions. It approved the decree on peace, it adopted a decree on land, and it elected the first Soviet government. Lenin, whose victorious appearance at the Congress stirred much excitement, was the principal speaker on behalf of all three proposals. The decree on peace, which was passed unanimously, called upon all belligerents to start immediate negotiations for a just and democratic peace without annexations and indemnities. On its part, the Congress expressed willingness to consider any other peace proposals, provided they be made speedily and be clear and free of "all ambiguity and secrecy." The decree announced Russian determination to abolish secret diplomacy, publish at once all secret treaties entered into by previous regimes, and annul all agreements which aimed at "securing advantages and privileges for the Russian landlords and capitalists." The Congress appealed at once to all belligerents to conclude immediately an armistice for a period of not less than three months. It also made a particular appeal to "the class conscious workers" of England, France, and Germany to support Soviet Russia's peace move.

The land decree consisted of two parts. The first abolished landed proprietorship without compensation. All landed estates, monastery and church lands, with all their livestock, buildings, and implements, were ordered taken over by local land committees and soviets, pending the meeting of the Constituent Assembly. The instruction on the land, which formed the second part of the decree, abolished forever the right of private property in land. Henceforth land could neither be purchased, sold, leased, mortgaged, nor otherwise alienated. All land was to become the property of the whole people and be used by those who worked on it.

All mineral wealth was to "be reserved for the exclusive use of the state." Lands with highly developed forms of cultivation were not to be divided, but were to be transformed into model farms to be cultivated either by the state or by the communes. The employment of hired labor was prohibited. The land was to be subject to periodic reapportionment "in accordance with the growth of population and the increase in productiveness and efficiency of agriculture."

The Congress entrusted execution of the decrees on land and peace to the Council of People's Commissars, known by its Russian abbreviation SOVNARKOM. Lenin became chairman of the Council. Other members included: Interior, Aleksei I. Rykov (1881–1938); Agriculture, Vladimir P. Miliutin (1884–?); Labor, A. G. Shliapnikov (1884–?); Military and Naval Affairs, Vladimir A. Antonov-Ovseenko (1884–1938), Nikolai V. Krylenko (1885–1938), and Pavel E. Dybenko (1889–1938); Trade and Industry, Viktor P. Nogin (1878–1924); Public Instruction, Lunacharsky; Finance, Ivan I. Skvortsov-Stepanov (1870–1928); Foreign Affairs, Trotsky; Justice, G. I. Lomov-Oppokov; Food Supply, I. A. Teodorovich; Post and Telegraph, N. P. Glebov-Avilov; and Nationalities, Stalin. Before its adjournment on November 10, the Congress elected the All-Russian Central Executive Committee of 101 members (62 Bolsheviks and 39 Left Socialist Revolutionaries) and approved November 25 as the election date for the Constituent Assembly.

Passing of resolutions was one thing; forcing compliance with them was another. The Bolsheviks had won only in Petrograd. Their authority did not extend outside the capital. Since Russia had disintegrated following the March revolution into countless autonomous units, each region, each province, each district, each city, each village, and each local soviet had to be won over separately. This was not an easy task because the Bolsheviks commanded no real popularity. The speed of extension of their control varied, therefore, from area to area. In some places it was bloodless and easy, and in others bloody and difficult. The success or setback depended in large measure on the Bolshevik ability to win over or infiltrate the leadership of the local soviet. Moscow was brought under Bolshevik control by November 15, but only after heavy fighting. Fighting also took place in Kazan, Kharkov, Kiev, Smolensk, Saratov, Voronezh, and in many other cities and towns. In November the Bolsheviks seized control in fifteen main provincial towns. In December an additional thirteen were added, and January, 1918, saw fifteen more towns brought under Bolshevik control.

Next to the cities, the Bolsheviks centered their attention on winning over the army—or whatever remained of it—in order to prevent it from becoming an organized opposition force. This proved a relatively easy task because the Russian army, following the introduction of committees after the March revolution, had ceased to exist as an organized fighting unit. Following the Kornilov affair late in the summer of 1917, the discipline and morale of the army sank even deeper. The bulk of the enlisted personnel, demoralized and sullen, showed no desire to support the hopeless cause of the Provisional Government and simply went home. Those who remained, and especially those around Petrograd, fell under the influence of the Bolsheviks. Under these conditions, various army commanders (those who survived and adjusted themselves to the new circumstances) threw in their lot with the new regime. General Nicholas N. Dukhonin (1876–1917), the Commander-in-Chief, was an exception. At first he cooperated with the Bolsheviks. When on November 20, 1917, he was ordered to inaugurate peace talks with the German High Command, Dukhonin, pressed by the Allies, refused to comply. For his insubordination he was dismissed and replaced by Ensign Krylenko, whose special task force arrived at the army headquarters in Mogilev on December 3. Dukhonin was immediately arrested and, although Krylenko spoke out strongly against lynching, a mob of soldiers, sailors, and peasants, aroused by vengeful orators, dragged Dukhonin out on the railroad platform and beat him to death. One counterrevolution by a general was over. Another was still a thing to come.

The extension of Bolshevik influence over the army and major Russian cities was greatly helped by their control of transportation and communication lines, especially railroads. Russian railroad workers, even before the revolution, were well organized and among the best paid. Following the downfall of the monarchy, railroad workers on several occasions had come to the rescue of the revolution. They developed among themselves very strong soviet institutions as well as a feeling of solidarity with other workers. For that reason, perhaps, the Bolsheviks concentrated their agitation among railroad workers, especially during and after the Kornilov affair. The dividends of this policy were soon evident. By the end of 1917, the Bolsheviks controlled many key railroad lines around Moscow, Kiev, and Petrograd. By 1918, as employees of the Trans-Siberian Railroad, Bolshevik agitators had moved across the great Siberian stretches, even before that area fell under complete Bolshevik control. Their domination of railroad lines during the subsequent Civil War was one of the most decisive factors contributing to the Bolshevik victory.

Meanwhile the new regime of inexperienced and doctrinaire, but lucky, individuals began to introduce far-reaching cultural, social, economic, and political changes in Russia. On November 9, all newspapers which, in the view of the new regime, incited the people to open resistance or disobedience or spread confusion by distortion of facts, were ordered closed. The decree promised that these repressive measures were only temporary and would become inoperative "as soon as the new regime takes firm foot." A decree of November 23 abolished all classes, class distinctions, privileges, organizations, institutions, ranks, and civil grades.

Every Russian became a citizen of the republic. Class institutions also lost all their properties. On November 27 a decree on workers' control conferred upon workers' committees in each factory and shop the right "to supervise production, fix the minimum of output, and determine the cost of production." Business secrecy was declared illegal and the committees were given the right to examine all books and business correspondence. On December 7 all existing legal institutions in Russia (district courts, courts of appeal, the Senate, commercial courts, justices of the peace, magistrates, and the procurator's office) were abolished. Local judges henceforth were to be elected on the basis of direct democratic vote and were to be guided in their decisions by "revolutionary conscience and revolutionary conception of right." On December 11 the members of the Cadet party were declared counterrevolutionaries and made "liable to arrest and trial by revolutionary tribunals." On December 14 the Supreme Economic Council, which for over a decade was to be the central organ for the regulation of the economic life of the Soviet state, was established. On December 27 all banks were declared a state monopoly. All existing private joint stock banks and banking offices, with all their assets and liabilities, were merged into the State Bank. Gold, in coin and in bars, deposited in the bank vaults was ordered confiscated and transferred to the state's general gold fund. On December 20, to suppress any evidence of opposition, the government established "the all-Russian Commission for Suppression of Counter-Revolution, Sabotage, and Speculation," the first secret political police, popularly known as the CHEKA. A decree of December 29 abolished all titles and ranks in the army and annulled all preferences and insignia. The Russian army was to consist of "free and equal-to-one-another citizens." After December 31, church marriage was declared a private affair and only civil marriage was legally binding. Marriage procedures were greatly modified and liberalized, as was divorce. Marriage was annulled by the petition of both parties, or even one of them. Illegitimate children were given the same rights and were held to the same obligations as legitimate. A decree of January 5, 1918, abolished the old institutions of local government. Henceforth local affairs were to be administered by a network of soviets arranged in a hierarchal order. Each soviet was declared to be autonomous, but each lower soviet was to conform with the directions of the soviets on higher levels. The net result of these and other drastic measures was the destruction of many institutions of the old regime and hence further deepening of economic, administrative, cultural, and political chaos in Russia. While many of these measures were eventually amended or discarded, many had come to stay.

These measures generated little enthusiasm for the new regime. With every day the food situation—the spark that had ignited the revolution—deteriorated and the approaching winter promised no relief. By early

December, 1917, bread rations had diminished to one-eighth of a pound per day, forcing the people as well as the government to varied measures of procurement. The countryside was invaded by armed gangs and thousands of individuals to forage or barter goods, jewels, and the like for grain and potatoes. Next to food the fuel crisis became most acute, and there was no relief in sight, as the fuel-producing regions were not under Bolshevik control. In spite of all-out austerity efforts, factories were closed, streetcar service was sharply curtailed, and theaters and restaurants were deprived of light. The new regime helped by some of its actions to create a situation which bred intrigue, conspiracy, extortion, and in general demoralization and dissatisfaction. It was in such an atmosphere that the long-postponed Constituent Assembly met in the middle of January, 1918.

THE THREE DILEMMAS: THE CONSTITUENT ASSEMBLY, THE NATIONALITY PROBLEM, AND PEACE

The Constituent Assembly was one of the most difficult dilemmas for the new regime. Before they came to power the Bolsheviks, like all the revolutionary and liberal parties, were pledged to support the Constituent Assembly, and in fact one of their chief slogans had been: "Speedy convocation of the Constituent Assembly." Their persistent demand was matched only by the Provisional Government's repeated postponement. The Provisional Government had finally set November 25 as the election date, but it did not live to see it come to pass. The Bolsheviks did not interfere with the elections, which, but for a few districts, were held as scheduled, but they were not pleased with the outcome. Of some 41,700,000 votes, Socialist Revolutionaries (Russian and Ukrainian) polled 17,100,000 votes; Bolsheviks 9,800,000; Cadets 2,000,000; and Mensheviks 1,360,000. When the Constituent Assembly met, out of 703 deputies, 380 were regular Socialist Revolutionaries, 39 Left Socialist Revolutionaries, 168 Bolsheviks, 18 Mensheviks, 17 Cadets, 4 Popular Socialists, and 77 minority representatives. The nation had spoken its mind, but Lenin was determined to hold his power.

Lenin neutralized the Constituent Assembly in several ways. Since the elections had been held under the system of proportional representation (i.e., ballots were cast not for individuals but for party lists drawn prior to the Bolshevik seizure of power) Lenin empowered the soviets to recall the delegates to the Constituent Assembly. When this procedure proved to be not overly effective, many leaders of the opposition were arrested by the government, as were members of the election commission, and the commission itself was ordered disbanded. Though official statements denied rumors of the impending dissolution of the Constituent

Assembly, that action appeared imminent unless of course the Assembly approved "Soviet power, Soviet revolution, and its policies in questions of peace, land, and workers' control."

The Constituent Assembly met in a tense atmosphere on January 18, 1918, in the Taurida Palace. In addition to deputies, some of whom were wanted by Bolshevik authorities, the Palace was packed with armed soldiers and sailors. Because rumors had spread that the Assembly might be besieged, many deputies provided themselves with food and candles. Chernov, a Socialist Revolutionary, was elected the Assembly's president by a vote of 244 to 151. After the customary speeches, the Assembly rejected 237 to 138 the Bolshevik-sponsored "Declaration of the Rights of the Toiling and Exploited People," which was nothing but a summary of legislative changes introduced in Russia up to that time. The setback was only temporary. After a recess, Bolshevik deputies announced their departure from the Assembly. They were followed by Left Socialist Revolutionaries. The remaining deputies were left at the mercy of the pro-Bolshevik Lettish guards and sailors. Though interfered with, this Assembly rejected the Bolshevik dictatorship and approved four important resolutions: it approved an armistice with the Germans; it passed a land decree; it declared Russia a republic; and it called for the convocation of an international socialist conference. At five o'clock on the morning of January 19, 1918, under pressure from the sailors, the assembly adjourned for twelve hours. It never reconvened, for on the same day it was dissolved by the Central Executive Committee on Lenin's orders.

The dissolution of the Constituent Assembly, or as Lenin put it, "a complete and frank liquidation of the idea of democracy by the idea of dictatorship," marked a significant victory for the Bolsheviks for two reasons. First, the resistance-free action pointed out that now, as earlier, personnel changes in Petrograd were made by a handful of self-appointed leaders. The bulk of the population—ignorant of democratic methods and tradition, confused by the multiplicity of political parties and the complicated system of proportional representation, bewildered by promises, charges and countercharges, and above all tired of war—cared little about political strife and was only anxious to be left alone in order to digest the fruits of the revolution. Secondly, the dissolution of the Constituent Assembly removed for the new regime, without undue strain, a serious technical obstacle in the drive to consolidate its power. By the end of January, 1918, it became evident that there was no organized force in Central Russia capable of challenging the Bolshevik power. The new regime, however, had other great problems to settle. One of the most difficult was the nationality problem.

The nationality problem placed the new regime in the most embarrassing dilemma thus far. In theory, Lenin and some of his close associates, to deepen the crisis, had conceded as early as 1903 that minorities of the Russian Empire had the right to self-determination, including separation. Unconditional recognition of the struggle for freedom of self-determination, Lenin argued, however, did not at all obligate the Bolsheviks "to support every demand for national self-determination." As far as they were concerned the fundamental task centered not in the realization of self-determination of nations or peoples, but of the proletariat of every nationality. Accordingly, they agreed to support the creation of a new state only in exceptional cases. "We would be very poor revolutionaries," wrote Lenin in 1913, "if, in a great liberating war of the proletariat for socialism, we were unable to utilize *every* national movement against *separate* negative forms of imperialism in order to sharpen and broaden the crisis." On another occasion he frankly stated that when "we demand freedom of separation for the Mongols, the Persians, the Egyptians, etc., —and for *all* subjugated and unequal nations without exceptions, it is not that *we favor their separation* but *only* that we stand for a *free, willing* unity and merger, and not for a forceful one." Thanks to this dialectic, it became possible to read into Lenin's words at once his support for and opposition to self-determination. The Seventh Party Conference of April, 1917, in spite of some opposition, endorsed this view. Thereafter, to embarrass the Provisional Government in its inability and unwillingness to solve the nationality problem, and in order to attract non-Russians to their ranks, the Bolsheviks posed as the staunchest supporters of the idea of national self-determination. This policy reached a climax on November 15, 1917, i.e., a week after the Bolshevik coup d'état, in "The Declaration of the Rights of the Peoples of Russia." This solemn document proclaimed (1) the equality and sovereignty of the peoples of Russia; (2) the right of the peoples of Russia to free self-determination, even to the point of separation and formation of independent states; (3) the free development of national minorities and ethnic groups inhabiting the territory of Russia; and (4) the abolition of any and all national privileges and disabilities. The Bolshevik advent to power, in other words, formalized Russia's territorial disintegration.

The Ukraine and Finland were the first countries to experience Bolshevik dialectical interpretation of the right of self-determination. On November 19, 1917, or shortly after the Bolshevik seizure of power, the Ukrainian *Rada* proclaimed the establishment of a Ukrainian People's Republic. This change, however, did not imply separation from the Russian republic. It was rather a first step towards making Russia a federation of free and equal peoples. Pending the convocation of the Ukrainian Constituent Assembly set for January 9, 1918, the *Rada* assumed full authority over the territory considered ethnically Ukrainian. In this capacity it abolished without compensation the ownership of landed estates; introduced an eight-hour working day; pledged itself to the speedy conclusion of peace; abolished the death penalty; reaffirmed freedom of speech, press, religion, assembly, unions, strikes, and other liberties gained by the March revolution.

The Bolsheviks answered the *Rada*'s challenge by calling a Congress of Workers', Soldiers', and Peasants' Deputies for December 15, 1917, in Kiev. However, when they were able to control only from sixty to eighty delegates out of more than 2,000, the Bolshevik delegation accused the Congress of misrepresentation of "the will of the masses" and bolted to Kharkov where it declared itself the legitimate and the only power in the Ukraine. On December 24, 1917, the Ukraine was proclaimed a Soviet Socialist Republic (UkSSR). *Pravda* extended greetings to the newly-created republic two days before its formal inception. The Council of Peoples Commissars extended official recognition to the UkSSR on December 29, 1917, and promised the "brotherly republic complete and all possible support in its struggle" with the *Rada*.

One form of this aid was an ultimatum which had been presented to the *Rada* on December 16. This document recognized the Ukrainian right to full separation from Russia unconditionally and without limitations, but charged the *Rada* with perpetrating unprecedented treason to the revolution by its alleged persecution of Ukrainian soviets, by its alleged support of "counterrevolutionary forces" and of various Tsarist generals, and by its refusal to allow Bolshevik troops to cross Ukrainian territory. The *Rada* rejected Bolshevik charges, arguing that it was impossible "to recognize simultaneously the right of the people to self-determination, including separation, and at the same time to infringe roughly on that right by imposing on the people in question a certain type of government." Lenin replied to this argument with Bolshevik invasion of the Ukraine. Ukrainian resistance collapsed and Bolshevik forces occupied a number of Ukrainian cities, including Kiev. On January 22, 1918, a few days before Kiev fell, the *Rada* proclaimed a Ukrainian People's Republic as an independent sovereign state, thereby severing completely the ties with Russia.

Bolshevik practical application of self-determination for Finland resembled the pattern pursued in the Ukraine. Following the Bolshevik coup d'état, the Finnish Diet declared itself vested with the supreme power in Finland. With no objections being raised, the Diet on December 5 went a step further and formally proclaimed Finland an independent state with Per Svinhufvud as Premier. On December 31, 1917, Svinhufvud secured from the Soviet government the first formal recognition of Finland. At the same time, however, to defend "the revolutionary democracy" in Finland there were organized Red Guards as the first step to the dictatorship of the proletariat. Assisted by Russian Bolsheviks these elements began to challenge the non-socialist Finnish government of Svinhufvud. Its overthrow on January 28, 1918, plunged Finland into civil war. With Bolshevik blessing, a Finnish Socialist Workers' Republic was

proclaimed in the south of Finland. This was followed by wholesale introduction of the Bolshevik program and methods, culminating on March 1,
1918, in a treaty of "friendship and brotherhood" with Soviet Russia. The
north of Finland fell under control of Finnish anti-Bolshevik forces led by
General Gustav C. Mannerheim. By the middle of February, 1918, Mannerheim's forces cleared north and central Finland of Bolsheviks. The
clearing process was accelerated after Mannerheim was reinforced by a
German contingent under General von der Goltz. By early May, 1918, all
of Finland was cleared of Red Guards, the Red regime collapsed, its
leaders fled to Soviet Russia, and the Finnish civil war as well as the
Finnish-Russian union of 1809 came to an abrupt end.

Developments in Estonia followed largely the same pattern. On November 28, 1917, the Estonian National Council proclaimed the political
independence of Estonia. In January, 1918, however, the Bolsheviks challenged this act, and plunged the country into a bitter civil war which
ended with German occupation. Events in Latvia and Lithuania differed
slightly. The Latvian National Council assumed authority in Latvia on
November 16, 1917, while Lithuania declared its independence from Russia on December 11, 1917. Because of strong German interests in the
Baltic region, between 1915 and 1917 both states were occupied by German forces. The question of Poland offered the least difficulty (for both
the Provisional Government and the Bolsheviks) since Polish-inhabited
areas were already occupied by the Germans and the Austrians. Because
of this situation, independence of Poland was strongly advocated by the
Bolsheviks. With the Bolshevik seizure of power, centrifugal forces in the
Caucasus increased their demands for separation. At first, on April 22,
1918, a Trans-Caucasion Federal Republic was proclaimed, but age-old
rivalry among the three nations involved (Armenia, Azerbaidzhan, and
Georgia) disrupted the federation. Georgia established its independence
on May 22, 1918; Armenia on May 26, 1918; and Azerbaidzhan on May
28, 1918. Shortly thereafter all three states entered into relations with the
Germans and subsequently were drawn into the whirlpool of bitter civil
war.

The Bolsheviks discovered that next to the nationality problem, peace
was the most difficult issue to resolve. The problem of bringing about the
long promised peace acquired new meaning for the Bolsheviks after their
seizure of power, when it became apparent that without peace they could
not hope to reorganize Russia and the rest of the world according to the
projections of Marx and Lenin. Peace therefore became the prime objective of the new regime, and to achieve it several approaches were ex-
plored. On November 8, 1917, as noted earlier, the Bolshevik-controlled
Second All-Russian Congress of Soviets unanimously approved the Decree on Peace calling for an immediate armistice based on the principle of

self-determination and repudiation of the idea of annexations and indemnities. Class conscious workers everywhere were asked to support these efforts. Because no one expected the Bolsheviks to remain in power any appreciable length of time, these peace efforts generated little enthusiasm. Trotsky, now as People's Commissar for Foreign Affairs, on November 21 notified the Ambassadors of the Allied Powers (and through the ambassadors of neutral countries he also informed the governments of the Central Powers) to regard the Decree on Peace "as a formal offer for an immediate armistice on all fronts and the immediate initiation of peace negotiations." To discredit as well as to force the major powers into negotiations, the Soviet government published secret agreements concluded between the tsarist government and the Western Powers.

Meanwhile, on November 20, 1917, the Soviet government ordered army headquarters to propose to the Central Powers unilaterally and without delay the end of hostilities. Because General Dukhonin, under Allied pressure, refused to carry out this order he was relieved of his command and shortly thereafter was lynched. The new Commander-in-Chief, Krylenko, directed the army units to make their own armistice agreements with the enemy on a local basis. The first such agreement was concluded on November 27. By December 1, 1917, military operations had been halted all along the Eastern Front, and a week later a thirty days' armistice was signed between Germany and Soviet Russia. On December 22, 1917, the first peace congress of World War I was under way at Brest-Litovsk, an ancient town on the Bug River, then the headquarters of the German Eastern Front.

The German delegation was led by Foreign Minister Baron Richard von Kühlman and General Max Hoffmann. Austria-Hungary was represented by its Foreign Minister, Count Ottokar von Czernin. Prime Minister V. Radoslavov of Bulgaria represented his country. The Turkish delegation was led by Grand Vizier Talaat Pasha. The Soviet delegation was at first headed by an old Bolshevik, Adolf A. Joffe (1883–1927), but on January 9, 1918, he was replaced by Trotsky. Other members of the Soviet delegation included a worker, a sailor, and a peasant, who were brought to the conference table to dramatize the change taking place in Russia.

In spite of endless talk the negotiators made no progress in their discussions. The German delegation tried to use the peace talks as a cover for deployment of troops to the Western Front. The Bolshevik delegation on the other hand used peace talks as a means of spreading revolutionary doctrine. The main point of disagreement centered on the question of self-determination. The Bolsheviks understood the principle of self-determination (a means of destroying multinational and colonial powers) as being the right of the proletariat of a given nation, and only that part of the proletariat friendly to the Bolshevik regime, to emerge victorious and represent the people. The Germans on the other hand held that any people, and above all any group of people friendly to Germany, had the right to self-determination. The Ukraine had the unfortunate distinction of being caught between these two extreme interpretations.

The Ukrainians, as noted earlier, were not overly enthusiastic at the Bolshevik triumph and above all at the latter's attempt to speak on behalf of all the peoples of the former tsarist empire. On December 22, 1917, the *Rada* government expressed its willingness to participate in the peace conference at Brest-Litovsk on the basis of no annexations and no indemnities without the direct consent of the peoples concerned. On January 7, 1918, with little preparation, the Ukrainian delegation arrived at Brest-Litovsk. Its presence there from the very beginning was controversial and perplexing. For the Austrians, whose internal and external difficulties demanded immediate peace with a minimum loss of territory, the Ukrainians were an annoyance. Ukrainian demands for Galicia, Bukovina, and the Kholm region outraged the Austrians. Later, however, the Austrians modified their attitude in return for the promise of much-needed Ukrainian grain. Trotsky at first recognized the Ukrainians, but he soon reversed himself upon realizing the danger of a separate treaty between the Ukraine and the Central Powers. He recognized that such a move might not only force him to sign a separate treaty too, but also that it would put the Central Powers in a position to obtain food and other vital necessities and thus to emasculate the danger of the Allied blockade.

Trotsky's fear of a separate treaty between the Ukraine and the Central Powers and his employment of various delaying tactics did not escape the notice of the Germans. From the very beginning, General Hoffmann, who received the Ukrainians "with pleasure," encouraged them to talk about their plans and hopes, gained their confidence and their respect, and entered into negotiations with them. On February 9, 1918, these talks, which Trotsky was unable to control and which seriously menaced his position, culminated in a separate treaty. In return for recognition and support, the Ukrainians pledged to place their surplus of foodstuffs and agricultural products (estimated to be some 1,000,000 tons) at the disposal of the Central Powers.

Since negotiations with the Ukrainians had proceeded smoothly, the Germans felt no need to negotiate with Trotsky. As early as January 18, Hoffmann suggested to Trotsky future boundaries for Soviet Russia. This suggestion evoked a lively debate within the Bolshevik party. Many party members, headed by Bukharin, demanded that the party suspend negotiations with the Central Powers and reply with a revolutionary war. Lenin, aware of the Soviet weakness and therefore desirous of gaining a "breathing spell" for the new regime until victorious revolutions swept all of

Europe, favored acceptance of the German-suggested boundaries. Trotsky advanced his celebrated formula of "No War, No Peace." On January 21, 1918, a party conference in Petrograd considered the matter and voted 32 for Bukharin's idea, 15 for Lenin's, and 16 for Trotsky's. On January 24, however, the party's Central Committee approved Trotsky's proposal by a vote of nine to seven. On February 10, 1918, Trotsky announced his formula to the Germans and dramatically departed from Brest-Litovsk.

The German High Command denounced the armistice on February 16. Two days later, in the name of "humanity" but for the sake of security, conquest, and acquisition of food supplies which the Ukrainians had promised them, the Germans resumed military operations all along the Eastern Front, in order to prevent the Bolsheviks from gaining control there. The Germans encountered no resistance in occupying their sphere of influence, which they then held until the end of the war. The question of acceptance or rejection by the Bolsheviks of German demands now emerged again. On February 18, after considerable maneuvering, Lenin's urge to accept German terms won by seven to four votes (with four abstentions) in the Central Committee. A message to this effect was sent immediately to Berlin. When the German reply arrived on February 23, its content was harsher than their earlier demands. Lenin insisted however that, harsh or not, there was no other alternative and German demands must be accepted. His will prevailed. The final vote in the Central Executive Committee of the Soviet was 116 to 85 with 26 abstentions. On March 3, 1918, Sokolnikov, who had replaced Trotsky as head of the Soviet delegation, signed the treaty at Brest-Litovsk.

The Treaty of Brest-Litovsk—a complicated document—has been viewed by some scholars as one of the most unfortunate peace treaties in history. By its terms Germany and Soviet Russia extended to each other diplomatic recognition, agreed to exchange war prisoners, pledged to discontinue hostile propaganda against each other, and agreed to develop economic relations. The Soviet government also agreed to recognize that Georgia, the Ukraine, and Finland were independent but under German influence. Poland, Lithuania, Latvia, and Estonia fell under more direct German control. The Bolsheviks evacuated the Aaland Islands in the Baltic; the Turks occupied Kars, Ardahan, and Batum; and the Romanians were allowed to occupy Bessarabia. The total area thus affected consisted of some 1,300,000 sq. miles, and about 62,000,000 people. Before the revolution this area contained some 32 per cent of Russia's arable lands, 26 per cent of her railroads, 33 per cent of her factories, and 75 per cent of her coal and iron mines. Judged by sheer numbers it was a heavy loss. Yet it ought to be remembered that the authority of the Bolshevik regime did not extend over the areas it agreed to acknowledge as being under German influence.

Area of German influence

NORWAY

SWEDEN

Stockholm

FINLAND

Murmansk

Archangel

Petrograd

ESTONIA

Baltic Sea

LATVIA
(Livonia)

(Courland)

Riga

Volga

MOSCOW

LITHUANIA

Smolensk

RUSSIA

Danzig

Vistula

GERMANY

Berlin

Warsaw

Brest-Litovsk

Don

POLAND

Cracow

Kiev

Dnieper

Kharkov

Donets

Prague

Lvov

UKRAINE

Vienna

Budapest

Odessa

AUSTRIA·HUNGARY

CRIMEA

Danube

ROMANIA

Belgrade

Bucharest

Black Sea

SERBIA

BULGARIA

Montenegro

Sofia

TURKEY

ITALY

ALBANIA

GREECE

S.H.Bryant

| 0 | 100 | 300 |

MILES

**TERRITORIAL CHANGES IN
EASTERN EUROPE
MADE BY THE
TREATY OF BREST·LITOVSK, March 191**

Signing of the Treaty of Brest-Litovsk, while repulsive to Russian Communists and non-Communists alike, provided Lenin with a territorial base on which to introduce unhindered further revolutionary experiments. One of the first moves was the transfer of the capital from Petrograd to Moscow. To protect the revolutionary experiment from external threats, on January 28, 1918, a Red Army was ordered organized. The new army was open to all "class-conscious" citizens of Russia aged eighteen and over. On April 22 military training became compulsory for all peasants and workers. The bourgeoisie was excluded from this duty, although some 50,000 former tsarist officers were drafted to train the new Red Army. The Bolsheviks immediately restored the death penalty for deserters, terminated election of officers, and greatly curtailed the power of army committees. Each army unit was given a political commissar—usually a high party functionary who was charged with indoctrination and supervision of army personnel. Under the supervision of these commissars, the Red Army was elevated into a significant pillar of the new regime. By August 1, 1919, the Red Army numbered 300,000; by January, 1920, over 5,000,000.

On February 5, the Church was ordered separated from the state, and freedom of worship was officially introduced. The same decree abolished religious and judicial oaths and separated the schools from the Church. The teaching of religious doctrines in schools was prohibited, and all church properties were nationalized. A decree of February 14 introduced in Russia the Gregorian, or West European Calendar. A decree of February 8 confiscated the capital stock of private banks, annulled all bank shares, and discontinued all dividend payments. On February 19 the Land Law, replacing all earlier decrees, was published. The new law abolished all property rights in the land, which was ordered confiscated without compensation and placed at the disposal of those who tilled it by their own labor. All mineral resources became state property. On April 22, all foreign trade was nationalized and all export and import agreements not authorized by the state were forbidden. On April 27, inheritance, whether by law or by will, was abolished and the state became the sole recipient of all property after the death of the owner. On June 11 the government ordered the organization of "Committees of the Village Poor," which were to help with food supplies for the cities and to carry the class warfare into the rural areas. To silence criticism of some of its policies, the government on June 14 ordered the expulsion of Socialist Revolutionaries and Mensheviks from the soviets. On June 28 all large-scale industrial and commercial enterprises (mines, mills, factories, and the like) were nationalized for the purpose of "combating the economic disorganization and the breakdown of the food supply and of establishing more firmly the dictatorship of the working class and the village poor." Finally, on July 10, 1918, these and other legislative measures introduced by the Soviet government thus far were reiterated in the first Soviet constitution.

Adopted by the Fifth All-Russian Congress of Soviets this document proclaimed Russia "a republic of Soviets of Workers', Soldiers', and Peasants' Deputies" and named it the Russian Soviet Federated Socialist Republic, the RSFSR. The constitution declared socialism to be the state program not only in Russia but throughout the world as well. It abolished the exploitation of man by man, social classes, and private ownership of land; declared natural resources to be national property; confirmed the confiscation of all banks; separated the Church from the state and the school from the Church; guaranteed the freedom of religious and antireligious propaganda; proclaimed the duty of all citizens to work on the principle "He who does not work, neither shall he eat"; authorized complete disarming of the wealthy and arming of the workers; and granted only to the workers "the honor of bearing arms in defense of the revolution."

To insure genuine liberty for the workers, the constitution offered workers and poorer peasants "a complete, universal, and free education," transferred to them "all the technical and material resources necessary for the publication of newspapers, pamphlets, books, and other printed matter," and guaranteed their unobstructed circulation throughout the country. The workers, in addition, were granted complete freedom of assembly and the right to organize, and "all premises convenient for public gathering, together with lighting, heating, and furniture" were placed at their disposal. Although it openly favored workers, the constitution declared the equality of all citizens before the law, irrespective of race or nationality, granted "the right of asylum to all foreigners persecuted for political and religious offenses," and extended all rights enjoyed by Russian citizens to foreigners living in Russia provided "they belonged to the working class or to the peasantry working without hired labor."

Under the first Soviet constitution the basic political unit was the village and city soviet. Members of these soviets were elected by show of hands by all men and women over eighteen who earned their living by productive work useful to society. The constitution denied the right of franchise to persons employing hired labor for the sake of profit; to those who lived on income not deriving from their own work; to private businessmen; to monks and priests of all religious denominations; to agents and employees of the former police force; to members of the Romanov family; and to all lunatics and criminals. Above the village and the city, the soviet structure was based on the principle of indirect elections; that is, each local soviet elected deputies to the soviet above it up to the All-

Russian Congress of Soviets. To make certain that the urban proletariat predominated at this "supreme authority," the constitution stipulated that urban areas should have a five to one advantage over rural districts (one city deputy represented 25,000 voters; one rural deputy represented 125,000).

Under the 1918 constitution the supreme authority belonged to the Congress of Soviets which convened twice a year. Between the short sessions of the Congress, the constitution designated the Central Executive Committee as "the supreme legislative, administrative, and controlling body." Elected by and responsible to the Congress, the Central Executive Committee (consisting of some 200 persons, who at the same time were high party functionaries) was responsible for general direction of the government, unified and coordinated all legislative and administrative work, and examined and ratified all drafts and decrees submitted to it by the executive branch of the government, the Council of Peoples' Commissars, commonly known as the *Sovnarkom*. It is imperative to remember that at all of these levels, constitutional rights notwithstanding, the party exercised full control of the state apparatus and thus ruled the country. Before the ink was dry on these and other Bolshevik innovations in their remaking of Russia, they were challenged by foreign intervention and civil war.

SUGGESTED READINGS

ADAMS, ARTHUR E. *Bolsheviks in the Ukraine: The Second Campaign, 1918–1919*. New Haven: Yale University Press, 1963.

BORYS, JURIJ. *The Sovietization of Ukraine, 1917–1923*. Toronto: University of Toronto Press, 1982.

BROWDER, ROBERT P., and ALEXANDER F. KERENSKY, eds. *The Russian Provisional Government. Documents*. 3 vols. Stanford: Stanford University Press, 1961.

BUNYAN, JAMES, and H. H. FISHER. *The Bolshevik Revolution, 1917–1918. Documents and Materials*. Stanford: Stanford University Press, 1934.

CARR, EDWARD HALLETT. *A History of Soviet Russia: The Bolshevik Revolution, 1917–1923*. New York: Macmillan, 1952.

CHAMBERLIN, WILLIAM HENRY. *The Russian Revolution, 1917–1921*. 2 vols. New York: Macmillan, 1935.

DANIELS, ROBERT V. *Red October. The Bolshevik Revolution of 1917*. New York: Scribners, 1967.

DEBO, RICHARD K. *Revolution and Survival: The Foreign Policy of Soviet Russia, 1917–1918*. Toronto: University of Toronto Press, 1979.

DEUTSCHER, ISAAC. *The Prophet Armed: Trotsky, 1879–1921*. New York: Oxford University Press, 1954.

FEDYSHYN, OLEH S. *Germany's Drive to the East and the Ukrainian Revolution, 1917–1918*. New Brunswick: Rutgers University Press, 1971.

FERRO, MARC. *October, 1917: A Social History of the Russian Revolution*. Tr. by Norman Stone. Boston: Routledge & Kegan Paul, 1980.

KEEP, JOHN L. H. *The Russian Revolution: A Study in Mass Mobilization*. New York: Norton, 1976.

KENNAN, GEORGE F. *Russia Leaves the War*. Princeton: Princeton University Press, 1956.

LEGGETT, GEORGE. *The Cheka. Lenin's Secret Police*. New York: Oxford University Press, 1981.

MOOREHEAD, ALAN. *The Russian Revolution*. New York: Harper, 1958.

PIDHAINY, OLEH S. *The Formation of the Ukrainian Republic*. Toronto: New Review Books, 1966.

PIPES, RICHARD. *The Formation of the Soviet Union: Communism and Nationalism, 1917–1923*. Cambridge: Harvard University Press, 1954.

———, ed. *Revolutionary Russia: A Symposium*. Cambridge: Harvard University Press, 1968.

RABINOVICH, ALEXANDER. *The Bolsheviks Come to Power. The Revolution of 1917 in Petrograd*. New York: Norton, 1976.

RABINOVICH, ALEXANDER, JANET RABINOVICH, and LADIS K. D. KRISTOF, eds. *Revolution and Politics in Russia*. Bloomington: Indiana University Press, 1972.

RADKEY, OLIVER HENRY. *The Elections to the Russian Constituent Assembly of 1917*. Cambridge: Harvard University Press, 1950.

———. *The Sickle Under the Hammer*. New York: Columbia University Press, 1963.

REED, JOHN. *Ten Days That Shook the World*. New York: International Publishers, 1919.

RESHETAR, JOHN S. JR. *The Ukrainian Revolution, 1917–1920*. Princeton: Princeton University Press, 1952.

TROTSKY, LEON. *The History of the Russian Revolution*. 3 vols. Translated by Max Eastman. New York: Simon & Schuster, 1932.

TYRKOVA-WILLIAMS, ARIADNA. *From Liberty to Brest-Litovsk. The First Year of the Russian Revolution*. London: Macmillan, 1919.

ULAM, ADAM B. *The Bolsheviks*. New York: Collier Books, 1968.

WARTH, ROBERT D. *The Allies and the Russian Revolution*. Durham: Duke University Press, 1954.

WHEELER-BENNETT, JOHN W. *The Forgotten Peace: Brest-Litovsk, March, 1918*. New York: Macmillan, 1939.

✄ I V

INTERVENTION, CIVIL WAR, AND WAR COMMUNISM

THE FIRST PHASE OF INTERVENTION

The Bolsheviks' decision to withdraw Russia from the war and their efforts to project her development along the line of Marxist-Leninist teachings were challenged by foreign intervention and civil war. There were several incentives behind foreign intervention, but immediate military considerations were the most significant. Until the Treaty of Brest-Litovsk the Allies (Russia and the Western Powers) had fought the Central Powers on several fronts (France, Italy, the Balkans, the Near East, and Eastern Europe). By this policy of dispersal the Allies were able to lessen the pressure on themselves and thus to weaken their strong adversaries. The sudden ending of hostilities all along the Eastern Front, a move which released many German divisions to be deployed elsewhere, gave the Central Powers an opportunity to improve their military position. Moreover, the Treaty of Brest-Litovsk placed under direct and indirect German control an area of some 1,300,000 square miles, rich in the natural resources and food which the German industry and population badly needed. To prevent the Germans from capitalizing on this success, and in view of the apparent Bolshevik willingness to cooperate with the Germans, the Allies worked tirelessly. When all efforts to persuade the Bolsheviks to reopen the front failed, the Allies decided to intervene.

There was yet another pressing military motive behind the Allied intervention. During the war, because of Russia's military unpreparedness, the Allies had stored vast supplies of arms and ammunition in the Russian ports of Murmansk, Archangel, and Vladivostok (Black and Baltic Sea ports were blockaded by the Germans). German occupation of the Baltic countries and their landing in Finland after the Treaty of Brest-Litovsk threatened these supplies. To prevent them from falling into German or Bolshevik hands, the Allies felt that intervention was essential. Accordingly the British landed their first contingent of troops in Murmansk early in March, 1918. They were joined later by the French and by American marines and a detachment of Czechoslovak and Serbian soldiers. The first Japanese and British units disembarked in Vladivostok on April 5, 1918. Late in June the British reinforced their troops in Murmansk, and on August 5 additional British soldiers arrived in Archangel. By the end of 1918 the Allied powers had some 15,000 troops in northern Russia. In spite of violent Bolshevik objections, between July and September, 1918, Japanese and British units in Vladivostok were reinforced by French, Italian, and American troops. Finally, to prevent unfriendly forces from gaining control of the oil fields of Baku, late in 1918 British troops occupied not only that city but also Tbilisi and Batum in the Caucasus.

Next to military considerations, economic and political considerations acted as powerful stimuli in favor of intervention. The French were eager to intervene in order to protect all or at least a large part of the investment of some 16,000,000,000 francs made by Frenchmen in Russia between 1887 and 1917, which the Soviet government had nationalized. The same consideration, in part at least, motivated the Japanese and British desire to intervene. Japanese intervention in the Far East also had imperial implications. The collapse of Imperial Russia left Japan in a powerful position to build a vast territorial empire in defenseless Eastern Siberia. For that reason the Japanese were the most outspoken advocates of "Allied" intervention and were its "natural leaders" in the Far East. Their troops occupied not only Vladivostok and Northern Sakhalin but most of Eastern Siberia east of Lake Baikal. Because they were overly eager to capitalize on Russia's misfortunes, the Japanese aroused bitter feelings, especially among the Americans, and cast dark suspicion as to their ultimate aims.

Bolshevik reaction to Allied intervention went from the original seeming unconcern to violent opposition. At first, in March, 1918, they had no objection to the presence of Allied troops in northern Russia because they were aware that Allied presence there strengthened their bargaining position with the Germans. They hoped moreover that by non-resistance—in reality they were in no position to oppose the Allies—they might obtain formal recognition of the Soviet government by the Allied powers. However, when these hopes failed to materialize and above all when it became apparent that the German threat was not as dangerous as had been believed, and that some of the Allied powers (particularly Japan) had territorial designs on Russia, the Bolsheviks decided to contest the stay of Allied troops in Russia. Late in July, 1918, Allied ambassadors left Soviet Russia—an action which the Soviets interpreted as a disruption of diplomatic relations—and on July 29, 1918, the Central Executive Committee of the Soviets passed a resolution declaring "the socialist fatherland in danger." Accordingly appeals were sent "To the Toiling Masses of France, England, America, Italy, and Japan" to stop the intervention. Henceforth, as one observer noted, the Bolshevik attitude towards the Allies became "one of active hostility." Arrests of Allied subjects in Russia and of Soviet representatives in Allied countries did not help at all in easing the tension.

Allied intervention in Russia was greatly complicated by the Czechoslovak uprising. During the war the Czech and Slovak residents of Russia, in hope of liberating their country, had organized a brigade. After the revolution the strength of this unit increased to about 45,000—additions coming from among the Czech and Slovak prisoners of war. By the end of 1917 this brigade had become the most stable army unit in Russia, and on December 16, 1917, it was placed under the French Supreme Command with the understanding that it would be transported to France. Although throughout their stay in Russia the Czechoslovaks adopted a neutral view and responded to no appeals, their presence in Soviet Russia as far as the Bolsheviks were concerned was both a danger and an annoyance. Early in March, 1918, the Bolsheviks granted the Czechoslovaks permission to leave Russia for Western Europe via Siberia, since the port of Archangel was icebound.

The long Trans-Siberian odyssey of sixty trains began late in March. On their journey the Czechoslovaks encountered several official barriers, delays, threatened change of orders and the like. It was not until the middle of May, however, that the tension thus built exploded into a real crisis. At Cheliabinsk the Czechoslovaks met a train carrying Hungarian prisoners who were being returned under the provisions of the Treaty of Brest-Litovsk. A brawl between Czechoslovak and Hungarian soldiers left one Hungarian dead and several wounded. Local Soviet investigators tried to detain some of the Czechoslovaks engaged in the affair. This attempt enraged the others with the result that the detained Czechoslovaks were released and the Soviet investigators disarmed. When informed on May 25 of this incident, Trotsky, who had become War Commissar, ordered the immediate disarming of all the Czechoslovaks. The Czechoslovaks responded by occupying Pensa, Samara and all important stations along the Cheliabinsk-Omsk-Irkutsk railroad line. The Czechoslovak occupation of the Trans-Siberian Railway to the west and the Japanese, British and American occupation to the east of Lake Baikal cleared the Trans-Siberian Railway of the Bolsheviks. The successful Czechoslovak rebellion and occupation of a vast area with no appreciable resistance, followed by increased Allied landing of reinforcements in the North and Far East, elevated the hopes of Bolshevik opponents who resented Marxist-Leninist experiments in Russia. Successful intervention in other words stimulated civil war and civil war in part invited intervention.

THE FIRST PHASE OF THE CIVIL WAR

Civil War or resistance against Bolshevism was a product of many forces and pressures. It began on a small scale in the winter of 1917–1918 with the organization in Rostov-on-the-Don of a "Don Republic," by such former Tsarist generals as Michael V. Alexeev (1857–1918), Kornilov, and Alexis M. Kaledin (1861–1918). They were joined there by Miliukov, Rodzianko, and other prominent members of the former Provisional Government. This organization was a short-lived affair. Kaledin committed suicide on February 13, and Kornilov was killed on April 13. Early in May, General Peter N. Krasnov (1869–1947), who favored cooperation with the Germans, succeeded Kaledin, and General Denikin, who favored cooperation with the Allies, succeeded Kornilov. By their joint efforts Krasnov and Denikin cleared the Don and Kuban areas of Bolsheviks early in the summer of 1918. One of Krasnov's main goals was the establishment of contacts with anti-Bolshevik groups beyond the lower Volga. Another goal was to disrupt Moscow's connections with the food and oil supplies of the Caucasus. Both objectives called for control of the city of Tsaritsin. Because Stalin played some role in organizing Bolshevik defenses here, Tsaritsin was later named Stalingrad.[1]

Maintenance of Bolshevik control of other areas proved to be more troublesome. The Czechoslovak success had electrifying effects on people dissatisfied with Bolshevik experimentations. Spontaneously throughout Russia there developed anti-Bolshevik uprisings. The opposition forces were quite picturesque. They included peasants and workers, monarchists and conservatives, moderate socialists and socialist revolutionaries, and

[1] Late in 1961, as part of the de-Stalinization process, Stalingrad was renamed Volgograd.

Russian and non-Russian peoples. Diversified also were their activities and aspirations. In Moscow as early as May, 1918, a party conference of the Right Socialist Revolutionaries expressed its determination to overthrow the Bolshevik regime and to re-enter the war on the Allied side. Many Mensheviks voiced the same sentiment. Left Socialist Revolutionaries went even further. They advocated openly an active anti-German policy and called for annulment of the Treaty of Brest-Litovsk and severance of relations with Germany. On July 6, two members of the Left Socialist Revolutionary Party, posing as members of the CHEKA, assassinated Count Wilhelm von Mirbach, the German Ambassador to Moscow. Fear of German retaliation, which did not materialize, however, and additional acts of terror threw Moscow and Petrograd into chaos. Anti-Bolshevik uprisings occurred in Yaroslav, Nizhni Novgorod, Penza, Saratov, Tambov, Riazan, and some twenty other cities in Central Russia. On August 30, the chief of the Petrograd CHEKA, Michael S. Uritsky (1873–1918), was assassinated. On the same day Lenin was shot and seriously wounded by Dora Kaplan, a member of the Socialist Revolutionary Party.

Anti-Bolshevik opposition was not confined to Central Russia. One center established itself in the North in Archangel, where Tsarist General Eugene Miller (1867–?), with Allied consent, organized a force of some 7,000 to 8,000 volunteers. Another center of opposition began to form in Western Siberia, under a moderate liberal, Peter Vologodsky, who tried to minimize the importance of the soviets. Still another center established itself in Samara on the Volga, under the leadership of Victor Chernov, a Socialist Revolutionary and onetime Minister of Agriculture in the Provisional Government. The aim of this group was re-establishment of the Constituent Assembly which the Bolsheviks had dissolved. This group also established close relations with the Czechoslovaks, and with their aid it was able to secure some gold reserves of the Russian Imperial Bank which had been stored in Kazan. On September 8, to coordinate anti-Bolshevik forces as well as to prevent the developing factional feuds from exploding, under Czechoslovak pressure an All-Russian National Conference convened at Ufa. Its participants agreed to establish at Omsk a new coalition government called the Directory.

The Bolsheviks replied to the opposition's determination to unseat them with their own resolve to stay in power. In Moscow, following the July events, they bombarded Socialist Revolutionary strongholds, arrested many members, and even executed some. Executions were carried out in a number of cities along the middle Volga. Victims included nobles, merchants, former officers, clergymen, both poor and wealthy peasants, and anyone who resisted Bolshevik rule. On July 16, 1918, to prevent liberation by his followers, former Tsar Nicholas II and his entire family were executed near Ekaterinburg, where they had been exiled for safety by the

Provisional Government. To lessen the possible German threat while preparing for the challenge of the opposition, the Bolsheviks concluded three additional agreements with the German government on August 27. In these agreements they promised to supply great quantities of oil to Germany and to pay indemnities totalling six billion gold marks.

With the German danger averted, the Bolsheviks turned their attention towards the Omsk government, whose forces earlier had occupied the strategically located city of Kazan and were then advancing westward. Under Trotsky's command, the Red Army halted this advance and shortly thereafter the Bolsheviks succeeded in improving their position along the lower Volga. Their efforts were greatly aided by the disunity of the opposition. From its formation on October 9, 1918, members of the Directory at Omsk were unable to find any grounds for agreement. They argued, debated, plotted, and conspired against each other. Although the Directory included two Socialist Revolutionaries, on the whole it was nationalist, conservative, and a vigorous opponent of the Socialist Revolutionaries, whom it strongly suspected. When the Socialist Revolutionaries realized that the conservatives had no place for their philosophy, they called upon their members to resist the policy of the Directory. On November 18, the conservatives overthrew the Directory, arrested many Socialist Revolutionary leaders, and offered the post of "Supreme Ruler" to Admiral of the Black Sea Fleet Alexander V. Kolchak (1874–1920). While the execution of the coup was admirable, its timing was deplorable for the conservative cause.

THE COMINTERN

The end of World War I on November 11, 1918, introduced a new phase in Allied intervention and Civil War in Russia. The collapse of the Central Powers had several far-reaching repercussions. First it eliminated the ever-present German threat to the Bolshevik regime. Second, it created a vast power vacuum in war-torn Central and Eastern Europe. The Bolsheviks exploited these advantages to the fullest. On November 13, the Soviet government declared the Treaty of Brest-Litovsk null and void, and ordered the Red Army to occupy areas vacated by German forces. By the end of November, 1918, Red troops had overrun most of Estoria and Latvia. On November 29, an Estonian Soviet Government and, on December 14, a Latvian Soviet Government were set up. At the beginning of February, 1919, Red Army units occupied Vilnius and advanced west as far as the border of East Prussia. Early in March, 1919, the Bolsheviks made a concentrated effort to bring about a revolution in war-torn Europe. In retrospect this effort seems perhaps naive, but it looked different at the time.

When they seized power in Petrograd, many Bolsheviks, including Lenin, anxiously expected the outbreak of revolutions in more industrialized countries. Socialism, in their view, presupposed a high degree of industrial development and a strong working class. Most of them could not visualize enduring success in Russia without a European upheaval. In 1917 and 1918 there were many signs that Europe was on the brink of a great revolution. A disastrous war had inflicted enormous losses, both human and material, on all participants. War-weary troops had mutinied in France, Italy, and Germany. Hungry and overburdened workers had gone on strike. Though wartime censorship and military rule suppressed these signs of uneasiness, everywhere the great political unrest had made itself felt.

Aware of the explosive situation, the Bolsheviks tried to capitalize on it. With the Central Powers the task was easy. During the prolonged negotiations at Brest-Litovsk they ordered wide-scale fraternization with German forces and flooded the German lines with pro-revolutionary propaganda. They were also quite successful in "brainwashing" many German and Austro-Hungarian war prisoners whom they released under the provisions of the Brest-Litovsk Treaty. Following the establishment of normal diplomatic relations with Imperial Germany, Soviet diplomats engaged in various activities traditionally reserved for professional revolutionaries and agitators. These efforts, coupled with the collapse of the Central Powers, were partly responsible for a series of Bolshevik-type upheavals (in Berlin in January, 1919, in Hungary in March, 1919, and in Bavaria in April, 1919). These revolutionary flareups, ill-prepared and inadequately led, collapsed. In view, however, of social and political unrest in the Near and Far East and the slow and uneasy social, economic and political adjustment which followed the end of hostilities in Europe, the Bolsheviks' hopes for an imminent world revolution were kept alive and high.

To promote and coordinate revolutionary efforts abroad and to protect the revolutionary experiment at home, early in March, 1919, Lenin called in Moscow what was to be the First Congress of the Third International or Comintern. It was not a well attended gathering because of poor travelling conditions. The Second Congress of 1920 had somewhat better attendance. The statute of this new organization prepared by the First and adopted by the Second Congress (July 17–August 7, 1920) defined the aim of the Comintern as: "the overthrow of capitalism, the establishment of the dictatorship of the proletariat and of the International Soviet Republic for the complete abolition of classes, and the realization of socialism—the first step to Communist Society."

With their prestige as successful revolutionaries, Russian Communists dominated the Comintern from its very inception, and allowed only those parties and groups which unconditionally subscribed to the famous twenty-one conditions to affiliate themselves·with the new organization. These conditions, among others, included: obligation to carry on actively Comintern-approved propaganda; periodic purge of "reformist," "opportunist," and "petty bourgeois" elements; organization of illegal apparatus; proper indoctrination of the armed forces and rural areas; renunciation of "social patriotism," "social pacifism," and "reformism"; denunciation of imperialism and accordingly support of colonial peoples; and rendering of "every possible assistance to Soviet Republics in their struggle against counter-revolutionary forces." The Comintern, in other words, from its very inception was designed to be an international vehicle through which Russian influence could be manifested, not only in the international workers' movement but also as a powerful arm of Soviet foreign policy.[1]

A NEW PHASE IN INTERVENTION AND CIVIL WAR

The defeat of the Central Powers had ended the official Allied justification for intervention in Russia. However, the challenge of the Comintern, the Red Army's rapid occupation of territories evacuated by German forces, and the possibility of Bolshevik-German cooperation, made it necessary to strengthen Allied troops in Russia and to establish closer contacts with anti-Bolshevik forces. As early as November, 1918, the British reinforced their contingents in the Caucasus and northern Russia, and entered Estonia. The French landed in the Ukraine, while the Japanese entrenched themselves more firmly in the Far East. The Supreme Allied Commander, Marshal Ferdinand Foch, British Secretary of War Lord Milner, Winston S. Churchill, and French Premier Georges Clemenceau were strong proponents of this course of action. British Prime Minister Lloyd George and American President Woodrow Wilson advised caution. The policy of moderation won. The Allies recalled some of their units from Russia as early as April, 1919. Others were pulled out because they mutinied, either as a result of Bolshevik agitation, or war-weariness and longing for home. No Western leader dared to overlook this dangerous and widespread attitude.

Following their decision to abandon active military intervention of their own in Russia, the Allies turned to more active military and moral support of the various anti-Bolshevik forces. East of Lake Baikal the Japanese set up Ataman Gregory M. Semenov (1890–1945) in China, and Ataman Kalmykov in Khabarovsk as their puppets. The British gave *de facto* recognition to Kolchak, whose authority nominally extended between Lake Baikal and the Ural Mountains. The British also agreed to supply the small force of General Miller in the North; the force of Gen-

---

[1] For the full text of the Constitution and Rules of the Comintern, see Appendix 24.

eral Nikolai N. Yudenich (1862–1933) in Estonia; units of Krasnov and Denikin in the Azov and Don areas; and General Baron Peter N. Wrangel (1878–1928) in the Northern Caucasus. By early 1919 all these generals had acknowledged Kolchak as the supreme ruler of Russia. The French, in accordance with their decision to establish a *cordon sanitaire* consisting of such states as Poland, Rumania, Czechoslovakia, and Yugoslavia, toyed with the idea of supporting Ukrainian aspirations for independence. In other words, the stage was being set for the second phase of the Civil War.

Opposition forces, or as they often were called, the Whites, operated under several handicaps. First, they operated on the periphery of the country, where the population was non-Russian, where the transportation network was very thin, and where the industrial base was quite inadequate. Second, the great distances between various units prevented them from closer and more efficient coordination of operations. Third, personal rivalries and ambitions plagued and hindered the execution of a plan. Fourth, by virtue of their membership, the Whites acquired a conservative, indeed in some instances almost a reactionary, stigma which they were neither able nor willing to dispel. Finally, and most decisively, the opposition had no effective, far-sighted and progressive program, either for the Russian or the non-Russian population, with which to counterchallenge Bolshevik promises. Kolchak, for instance, was negatively inclined towards the independence of the Finns and other peoples. And his land program, as revealed in his declaration of April 8, 1919, insisted on the maintenance of the status quo until convocation of a new Constituent Assembly. It was not a program to generate enthusiasm in revolutionary times.

Early in March, 1919, Kolchak moved his forces, 125,000 strong, westward across the Urals towards Moscow. In this undertaking he was backed by the British and the French, although not overenthusiastically by the latter because of his lack of a sound and realistic program. At first his progress was impressive. By March 13, his troops had occupied Perm and Ufa, and in April they reached within twenty miles of the Volga, threatening Samara and Kazan. Further advances, however, were hindered by the harassment of peasant partisans as well as by the Bolshevik counteroffensive under the direction of Michael V. Frunze (1885–1925). On June 9, Kolchak lost Ufa and fell behind the Urals. Bolsheviks pursued him persistently, and late in July they took Cheliabinsk. On November 14, they occupied Omsk, the seat of Kolchak's government. Kolchak's inability to get along with the Czechoslovaks, who controlled the Trans-Siberian Railway, hindered his advance and his retreat as well. On January 4, 1920, he abdicated his power in favor of Denikin, and sought protection from the French and the Czechoslovaks. The French General Janin turned him over to the revolutionaries. On February 7, 1920, after a summary court martial, Kolchak and his associates were executed. The White cause in Asiatic Russia came to a sudden end. Those who survived proceeded to China and other parts of the world.

After disposing of Kolchak's threat, the Bolsheviks turned their attention to Denikin, whose original base of operation was the area around the Sea of Azov, and to Yudenich, who had his headquarters in Estonia. Both forces received material and technical support from the British. Denikin, hoping to join Kolchak's armies during the height of their victories, opened an all-out offensive against the Bolsheviks along a broad front stretching from Kharkov to the Volga. When Kolchak's forces were hurled back, Denikin changed his plans and divided his force of some 160,000 for a three-frontal attack on Moscow. One army under Wrangel was to move up the Volga; General Sirodin's Don Cossacks were to advance north from Rostov; and General Vladimir Z. Mai-Maievsky (1867–1920) was ordered to clear the Ukraine of Bolsheviks and proceed north. At first Denikin's successes, like those of Kolchak, were astounding. By the end of August his forces had captured Odessa, Kherson, Nikolaev, and Kiev. Kursk fell on September 20, Voronezh on October 6, Chernigov on October 12, and Orel on October 13. White armies reached within 250 miles of Moscow.

At the height of Denikin's victories, Yudenich, with a force of 20,000 men, advanced from Estonia, and on October 11 captured the city of Yamburg on the Luga River, less than one hundred miles from Petrograd. On October 16, his force occupied Gatchina, only thirty miles from Petrograd, and a few days later they reached the outskirts of the former capital. For a moment it appeared that both capitals, Moscow and Petrograd, would fall to the Whites. Within a few days, however, the picture altered drastically. Under Trotsky's leadership, Bolshevik resistance stiffened and Yudenich was forced to retreat. On November 14, Yudenich was at his original starting point, Yamburg, and retreating. His armies crossed to Estonia, where on February 1, 1920, they were demobilized. The White cause in the Baltic area came to a sudden end. Denikin's efforts met the same fate. Outnumbered, overextended, and opposed by enraged peasants and minorities, especially Ukrainians, Denikin lost Orel on October 20, Voronezh on October 24, and Kursk on November 17. During December, 1919, the Bolsheviks occupied most of the Ukraine. Remnants of Denikin's forces retreated to Rostov-on-the-Don. In March, 1920, British ships transferred some 35,000 of Denikin's men to the Crimea, the last stronghold of the Whites. On April 4, Denikin resigned his command in favor of Wrangel and left the country. At about the same time Miller's regime collapsed in Archangel. Wrangel thus remained as the last chance for the Whites.

Wrangel's task was not enviable. From Denikin he inherited an army of depressed fighters but excellent plunderers. Their excesses, coupled

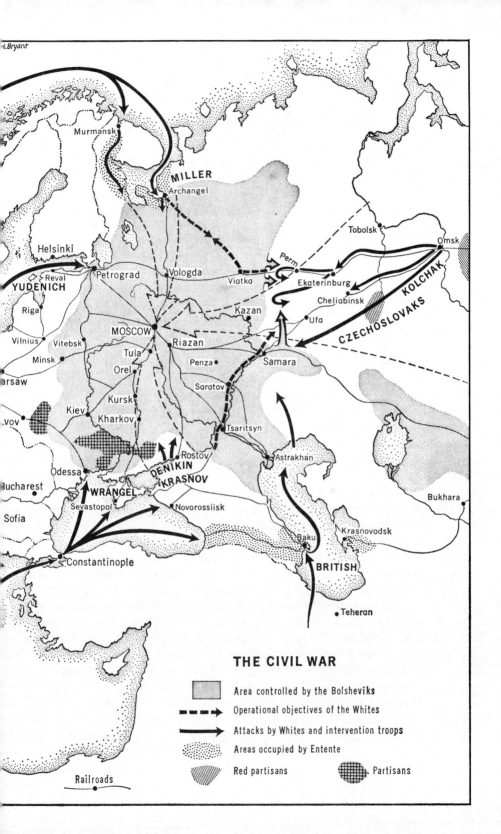

H.Bryant

Murmansk

MILLER
Archangel

Tobolsk

Omsk

Perm

Helsinki
Reval
YUDENICH
Petrograd
Vologda
Viatka
Ekaterinburg
KOLCHAK

Riga
Cheliabinsk

Kazan
Ufa
CZECHOSLOVAKS

Vilnius
MOSCOW
Riazan

Vitebsk
Minsk
Tula
Penza
Samara

Orel
Saratov

arsaw
Kursk

Kiev
Kharkov
Tsaritsyn

vov

Odessa
Rostov
Astrakhan

Bucharest
DENIKIN
KRASNOV

Bukhara

WRANGEL

Sofia
Sevastopol
Novorossiisk

Baku
Krasnovodsk

Constantinople
BRITISH

Teheran

THE CIVIL WAR

Area controlled by the Bolsheviks

Operational objectives of the Whites

Attacks by Whites and intervention troops

Areas occupied by Entente

Red partisans   Partisans

Railroads

with Denikin's support of the status quo ante bellum, generated no enthusiasm for the White cause either in Russia or abroad. By 1920 the Allies had lost all interest in Russian intervention. In January, 1920, the Supreme Allied Council ordered the end of the blockade against Soviet Russia and soon thereafter, except for the Japanese, all foreign troops left Russia. But even though he had all odds against him, Wrangel surprised many observers. He restored discipline and established order in the Crimea. He proposed a far-sighted agrarian program (two years too late), and during the height of the Polish campaign against Soviet Russia he led his 70,000-man army north into several victories over the Bolsheviks. Because of these successes, on August 12, 1920, the French offered Wrangel moral, but not material, assistance which brought little satisfaction. Like Denikin before him, Wrangel failed to win the peasant population. Moreover, freed from the Polish front by the armistice, the Bolsheviks turned their attention to him. To escape annihilation, Wrangel ordered evacuation since further resistance was hopeless. In the middle of November, 1920, some 135,000 soldiers and civilians left Russia for points unknown. The White cause was lost, and the Civil War had become history.

The last major crisis of 1920 was the Russo-Polish War. One of the main points of disagreement was the suggested boundary between Russia and Poland—the so-called Curzon Line which had been hastily proposed by the British Foreign Secretary, Lord Curzon. If adopted, the Curzon Line would have reduced Poland to a state along the Vistula Basin, with a predominantly Polish population. The Bolsheviks favored the idea, but the Poles, determined to undo the wrong of the three partitions of the eighteenth century, rejected Curzon's suggestion. In 1919, at the height of the Civil War and White successes, Polish forces occupied several regions inhabited by Lithuanians, Belorussians, and Ukrainians, but claimed by the Russians. The Bolesheviks began to challenge these gains as soon as they were able to free their forces from victorious campaigns against Kolchak, Denikin, and Yudenich. Since negotiation approaches made no headway, each side prepared to defend its claim militarily. The Poles, led by a veteran anti-Russian fighter, Joseph Pilsudski (1867–1935), entered into close political agreement with the Ukrainian anti-Russian forces of Semeon Petliura (1879–1926). In return for some minor territorial adjustments, Pilsudski offered Petliura military aid in his attempt to unseat the Bolshevik regime in the Ukraine. On April 25, 1920, the Polish army advanced into the Ukraine, and by May 6 it had reached Kiev. Because of strong anti-Polish feelings stirred up among the Ukrainians by Russian and Ukrainian agitators, the Poles made no attempt to advance beyond Kiev.

Polish advance into the Ukraine aroused a wave of religious, national and social sentiment, not only among the Ukrainians but among the Russians as well. Bolshevik appeals to all Russians to defend "Mother Russia" fell on responsive ears and pro- and anti-Communists joined hands. In May, 1920, General Mikhail N. Tukhachevsky (1893–1937) launched a counteroffensive in the north while Semeon M. Budenny's (1883–1973) cavalry forces struck at Kiev. Outnumbered, the Poles retreated all along the front back as far as Warsaw. The Bolsheviks were so excited by their victories that they created a Soviet government for Poland and were anxious to extend the benefits of their system not only to Poland but also to Germany and other countries of Western Europe as well. On July 10, Pilsudski appealed to the Allies for aid. Two days later Lord Curzon proposed a truce line along his earlier suggestion, but Moscow, victorious and marching, rejected it. A little later the French sent to Warsaw badly needed materials and a military mission headed by General Maxime Weygand. On August 14, the Poles launched their counteroffensive, outmaneuvered Tukhachevsky's force and soon the Soviet retreat degenerated into a wild rout that halted only outside Minsk. An armistice of October 12, 1920, followed by the Treaty of Riga on March 18, 1921, brought an end to that episode. By the provisions of this treaty Soviet Russia renounced its claim to the territories in question east of the Curzon Line—a situation which lasted until 1939.

Allied withdrawal from Russia, defeat of the White forces, and settlement with Poland gave the Bolsheviks an opportunity to consolidate their position in other uncertain areas. In April, 1920, following the defeat of Denikin and the British departure from the Caucasus, Bolshevik forces occupied Azerbaidzhan. Armenia was brought under Bolshevik domination in December, 1920, and in February, 1921, Georgia was forcibly returned to Moscow's control. The establishment of Bolshevik power in Central Asia resembled that in the Caucasus. Following the defeat of Kolchak and the British withdrawal, Bolshevik forces entered the vast area of Central Asia with no appreciable difficulty. By the end of 1920, Bokhara, Khiva, and Turkestan were occupied, old feudal regimes overthrown, and foundations were laid for slow introduction of the Soviet system. The Bolsheviks had occupied all Siberia west of Lake Baikal by the end of 1919, i.e., following the defeat of Kolchak. The area east of Lake Baikal, which was controlled by the Japanese, was incorporated into Soviet Russia after the Japanese withdrawal in 1922. In other words, except for Finland, Estonia, Latvia, Lithuania, parts of Poland, and Bessarabia, which the Rumanians occupied, by the end of 1921 and early 1922, the old Tsarist Empire from the Black Sea and the Baltic Sea to Kamchatka had new masters.

Bolshevik triumph and White defeat—an event of first magnitude not only in Russian but in world history—poses these two questions: Why did the Whites fail? Why did the Bolsheviks win? The Whites lost because they had neither a constructive program for Russia's future nor a plan that would satisfy the revolutionary aspirations of the masses. From the beginning to the end of the Civil War the Whites demonstrated again and again by their pronouncements and actions that they were opposed to the long-overdue changes in Russia which the revolution had introduced. They opposed, for instance, the division of landed estates among the peasants as permanent. They looked with suspicion on the improvements gained by workers. Their pro-constitutional pronouncements never satisfied the liberals. By their insistence on a Russia "united and undivided" they alienated many non-Russian peoples who aspired to gain national freedom. Finally, distances between various White resistance centers, disunity within each, and half-hearted support by the war-weary Allies contributed much to the White failure in Russia. In other words, the Whites, by their negative policies, attitudes, and mistakes, gave the Bolsheviks excellent propaganda weapons which they used masterfully to their advantage.

WAR COMMUNISM

Bolshevik ability to capitalize on the mistakes of their adversaries (in many instances there was really no need to do so) was only one of two basic factors contributing to their victory. The other was War Communism. War Communism had *four* distinct meanings or characteristics. *First,* it attempted to establish in Russia a Communist society. One form of the Bolshevik remaking of Russia found expression in the program of the Russian Communist Party (bolshevik) adopted by the Eighth Party Congress, March 18–23, 1919. This all-important document—a blueprint for Soviet society—asserted boldly that the Bolshevik revolution "began to lay the foundation of a communist society" in Russia, and as such it ushered in an "era of world-wide proletarian communist revolution." As expected, it approved "the correctness" of basic tenets of the earlier party program (1903), it assailed capitalism and imperialism (holding the latter responsible for wars), and it appealed to workers' solidarity throughout the world in order to realize the inevitable and "the final victory of the proletariat."

The party program held out great hopes for Russia's future. It promised "to liberate woman from all the burdens of antiquated methods of housekeeping, by replacing them by house-communes, public kitchens, central laundries, nurseries, and the like." It resolved to bring the government apparatus into close contact with the people "for the purpose of realizing democracy more fully and strictly in practice, by making government officials responsible to, and placing them under the control of, the masses." It pledged itself to work towards the abolition of all national privileges, extension of the fullest equality of all nationalities, recognition "of the rights of colonies and oppressed nations to political separation" in order to bring closer unity between "proletarians and semi-proletarians of different nationalities for the purpose of carrying on a general revolutionary struggle."

In the field of education the 1919 party program vowed to transform "the school from an instrument of class domination of the bourgeoisie . . into an instrument for a communist regeneration of society." The school was to be at once a conductor of communist principles as well as "of intellectual, organizational, and educational influences of the proletariat" in order to educate a generation capable of establishing communism. Education was to be free and compulsory, general and technical, with instruction in native language, free from religious influence, for both sexes to the age of seventeen. Moreover, the state was to supply all pupils with food, clothing, shoes, and all other school needs. The state was also to assist in adult education and provide libraries, lectures, and movies. The state was to aid financially those students who desired a university education. The party pledged itself in this program to "liberate" the masses from "religious superstition," but cautioned slow procedure towards that objective in order not to offend "the religious susceptibilities of believers."

In the economic sphere the program promised both to increase productive forces and "at all costs to increase the quantity of products required by the population." This goal the party hoped to achieve through a general state plan; concentration of production; and efficient, rational, and economic utilization of all material resources of the country. Trade unions were called upon to help in organizing socialized industry and establishing "a new socialist discipline," in re-educating the masses, and in similar functions. In agriculture the program recognized that "small-scale farming will continue for a considerable time," and accordingly suggested several measures designed to increase agricultural productivity. These included: (1) abolition of scattered fields; (2) supplying the peasantry with improved seeds and artificial fertilizers; (3) improvement of the breed of cattle; (4) distribution of agricultural information; (5) agricultural aid to the peasantry; (6) repair in soviet shops of peasant agricultural implements; (7) establishment of loan agencies and experiment stations; and (8) improvement of peasant lands. Alongside this, the program called for establishment of large soviet farms, aid to agricultural cooperatives, organization of state-operated farms, increase of agricultural activity, support of agricultural communes, all-out struggle against backwardness and rich peasants (kulaks), and penetration of rural areas by the party network.

The 1919 program pledged itself "to exert the greatest effort for the improvement of the housing conditions of the toiling masses," and to abolish overcrowded and unsanitary quarters by removing the old and building new ones. It advocated legislation aimed at improving working conditions of the laborer and also resolved "to abolish completely child labor and to decrease further the working hours for young persons," to introduce the premium bonus system to increase labor productivity, and to reduce the working day from an eight to a six hour maximum "without reduction in wages." That promise, however, was conditional on the general increase of productivity of labor and on the workers' pledge to spend two hours overtime without pay studying the theory of trade and industry and in administrative and military training. Finally, the program pledged development of sanitation centers to combat all kinds of infectious diseases, sanitary legislation, and free medical care and drugs to everyone.

The *second* characteristic of War Communism was its heavy contribution to economic chaos, both in industry and in agriculture. The breakdown stemmed basically from two sources. First, the Bolsheviks inherited a faltering economy, in which industrial and agricultural production and real wages were seriously declining while the cost of living and the general price index were rising. Second, immediately after their coup d'état the Bolsheviks introduced many important economic measures. They nationalized, for instance, the banks, foreign trade, and transport; annulled domestic and foreign debts; and placed industry under the workers' control. These and similar measures were not intended to ease the depressed economic situation, but rather to deprive the propertied classes of their influence, to paralyze the opposition, to consolidate Bolshevik political power, and to introduce in Russia a controlled or directed state capitalism.

Lenin called this state capitalism a "gigantic step forward." It was also a step towards accelerated economic disorganization. The leading force behind this disorganization was the system of factory committees, which by a decree of November 27, 1917, were given broad participation in the direction of industry, such as the right to supervise management, the right to determine minimum production levels, and the right to have access to all business correspondence and accounts. Intoxicated by their successes, many of these committees went beyond the legal powers granted them by the decree. They assumed not only the administration of factories but also developed the idea that factories should be run for the benefit of local workers. Since there was no effective authority to defy these syndicalist tendencies, Russian industry, already weakened by war and revolution, faltered further. Many factories were forced to close. Those continuing to operate experienced a sharp decline in workers' discipline as well as in production. Workers talked, debated, elected themselves to various posts, and resisted every attempt of the new government to coordinate and direct the economic life of the country. Their aspirations were warmly supported by Left Socialist Revolutionaries and Left Wing Bolsheviks. The latter group, in fact, favored complete and rapid nationalization of all enterprises, large and small, and firmly opposed the employment of prerevolutionary technicians and industrial experts, unless this was offset by granting greater powers of direct control over production to factory committees.

Another leading cause of accelerated economic disorganization was the territorial amputation of Russia. Between 1917 and 1920, the Soviet Russian economy lost, as a result of either fighting or permanent separation, or German, Allied, and White occupation, such vital economic regions as Finland, the Baltic states, the Ukraine, the Don and Kuban areas, the Caucasus, Central Asia, Siberia, and parts of Northern Russia. These losses reduced the Bolshevik-controlled areas to Central and part of Northern Russia. These losses, too, because of the abundance of natural resources they possessed, created an acute shortage of materials that threatened to paralyze industry. The loss of the Ukraine, for instance, meant, in prewar figures, the loss of some 72 per cent of the coal output, 75 per cent of iron ore, 68 per cent of pig iron, 25 per cent of manganese ore, 35 per cent of locomotive production, 36 per cent of flour mills, and 80 per cent of sugar refineries. Loss of the Urals, which was a fighting front in 1918–1919, meant a loss of an additional 19 per cent of pig iron output. White control of Western Siberia (1918–1919) meant complete cessation of cotton deliveries from Turkestan, while loss of the Caucasus disrupted the flow of oil from Baku and Grozny.

These losses, coupled until early 1920 with the Allied blockade, had far-reaching effects on the economy of Soviet Russia. Shortages of fuel and raw materials sharply reduced the number of operating blast furnaces, rolling mills, and textile mills. Fuel shortage and difficulties in effecting repairs, in particular, augmented the disorganization of railroads. Railroads, in fact, were threatened by a standstill—a situation which, as Lenin put it, created "difficulties for the revolution" and hope for its enemies. The Bolsheviks tried to meet the fuel crisis by converting to wood fuel on the railroads, as well as by intensifying the development of coal resources in the sub-Moscow region. These efforts, however, were only partly successful. While they contributed to military victory they also contributed to further deterioration of the equipment. By early 1920, 69 per cent of Soviet Russia's locomotives were disabled or waiting for repairs, with less than 4,000 in running order as compared with some 14,500 at the end of 1917.

The same territorial losses that paralyzed Russian industry also sharply affected the food situation. Loss of the Ukraine—the breadbasket of Imperial Russia—was felt in particular. Food shortage, the spark which had ignited the revolution, had disastrous effects on industrial productivity. Both in Moscow and in Petrograd, people were divided into various categories based on their occupation as a criterion for food distribution. Although workers were given preference, they did not receive a sufficient amount. The meager diet lowered the general productivity and the efficiency of individual workers. It also encouraged absenteeism, petty theft, speculation, and other devices to supplement the semistarvation diet. By 1920, the average productivity of the worker (as compared with prewar figures) dropped 30 to 35 per cent, and the number of workers employed in industry declined by some 50 per cent. Many industrial cities lost from one-fourth to one-third of their population; Moscow lost one-half. Some of these were drafted into the Red Army. The majority, however, moved to villages in search of food. Their quest was severely hindered by the runaway inflation, which by October, 1920, had reduced the purchasing power of the ruble to no more than 1 per cent of what it had been in October, 1917. War Communism, in other words, reduced Russia to grave economic disorganization.

The *third* distinct characteristic of War Communism was the rapid establishment of direct government control over *all* production and distribution. It might best be described as a policy of total nationalization, centralization, and mobilization. The prime motive for this development was the desire on the part of the government to insure priority for military supplies (and thus meet effectively the challenge of the opposition) and to a lesser extent to prevent sabotage. The first decisive step towards full government control came on June 28, 1918, when an order was issued for wholesale nationalization of large-scale industry. All enterprises with more than one million rubles of capital in mining, metal, textile, glass, leather, cement, timber, and the like, were placed under government control. By the end of 1918 the number of nationalized concerns reached 1,000; by the fall of 1919 some 3,000 to 4,000; and by the end of 1920 some 37,000 enterprises were listed as belonging to the state.

Initially, by a decree of August 8, 1918, the Supreme Economic Council (which had been established on December 14, 1917) and the Commissariat of Agriculture were empowered with regulation and organization of all production and management of "every enterprise of the Republic." The distribution of all commodities was entrusted exclusively to the Commissariat of Food, which had been established on May 27, 1918. On October 30, 1918, the government created a new agency, the Revolutionary War Council, and placed at its disposal "all forces and resources of the people that are needed for the defense of the Republic." A month later, on November 30, there emerged under Lenin's presidency a new institution, the Council of Defense, which in 1920 was transformed into the Council of Labor and Defense. The Council of Defense was given full powers in matters pertaining to mobilization of the forces and resources of the country in the interests of defense, and its decisions were "absolutely binding upon every department and institution, both central and local, and upon every citizen."

Government control of production and distribution and the attempt to mobilize all available resources had three important by-products. First, it led to the introduction of universal labor duty. Already the nationalization decree of June 28 had stipulated that the "entire personnel of every enterprise" was considered to be employed by the state and could not leave the establishment without authorization. Beginning with July 1, any stoppage of work or any strike was officially declared to be a betrayal of "the proletarian cause." Individuals who instigated a strike were branded "enemies of the labor movement," and were "to be handed over to the court of international proletariat." On September 3, 1918, the Commissariat of Labor decreed that in case of a shortage of manual workers, ememployment agencies had the right to assign the unemployed to any work, and that work connected with the harvesting and delivery of food products was "compulsory for all unemployed," regardless of their training or profession. Persons violating this order were to be reported to local civil authorities. This evolving trend towards universal labor duty received its fullest expression on October 31, 1918. All citizens, except persons under 16 years of age, over 50 years of age, and persons incapacitated by injury or illness, were declared subject to compulsory labor. An earlier decree of October 5 introduced labor books in place of identification cards. Other decrees established penalties for labor deserters, and stern labor discipline of a semimilitary nature.

The second major by-product of centralization and mobilization was an abnormal increase of bureaucracy. As the pace of nationalization quickened, the central administration became swollen with officials concerned with coordination, and the local administration with those concerned with management. This increase was so rapid that by mid-1920 one out of every four adults in Petrograd was said to be an official. The situation in Moscow was about the same. In industry the ratio of administrative personnel to total workers employed doubled in two years. Some administrators, in the early stages of nationalization, were hostile to the new regime; others were merely inefficient. Those who sympathized with the new system were, in the words of one observer, "rich in 'drive' and had genuine organizing capacity but were lacking in experience and in training." The net result was increased confusion. The presence of this vast bureaucracy also set the stage for a struggle between various central administrative bodies whose jurisdictions often overlapped. There were also sharp disagreements between central and local administrative units. Excited by their positions, many new administrators liberally issued orders which often contradicted those already in existence. Attempts to clear up the chaos only worsened the situation.

The third significant by-product of nationalization, centralization, and mobilization was the issuing of a whole series of decrees aimed at drastic transformation of Russia in accordance with communist principles. Thus, for instance, a decree of August 30, 1918, eliminated money as a medium for transactions between state institutions "in order to simplify and regulate the accounts of nationalized enterprises." This decree also abolished all payments in money to and from consumers and soviet organizations and institutions. In the middle of October, 1918, a plan was proposed for "wages in kind" to be introduced in Moscow, Petrograd, and other cities with a population of more than 20,000. Wages in kind were to include "living quarters, the principal manufactured and food products, and certain cultural needs." Under this plan, each factory would have a large farm operated by farm workers and specialists, and each worker's family would obtain food from that farm. Surplus, if any, was to go to the Commissariat of Food to be used elsewhere. On November 21, 1918, the government abolished all private trade. The property of all retail stores was confiscated, and permits to ship goods were revoked. The Commissariat of Food was commissioned to provide the population with articles of personal and household use through a network of state cooperatives to be established by January 1, 1919. The lapse of time between the suspension of all trade and the announced date for opening of state-run cooperatives gave the Black Market impetus to rise into a gigantic enterprise. On November 30, the government denied the right to elect or be elected officials of cooperatives to all persons who used hired labor, lived on unearned income, or had been engaged in trade during the past three years; to monks and nuns; to clergymen of all denominations (except those who supported cooperatives); and to former police officials. An earlier decree of October 30 had imposed also upon wealthier persons of cities and villages a "lump sum tax of ten billion rubles." The burden of tax was to fall on the wealthy part of the population. Wealthy peasants, in addition, were ordered to pay a "tax in kind" on their agricultural products. By these and similar decrees the Bolsheviks hastened Soviet Russia's development down a path to classless society as well as to bitter discontent.

The *fourth*, and in many ways the most distinct, characteristic of War Communism was the development of a violent struggle between the peasantry and the new regime. As Marxists, the Bolsheviks considered agriculture an integral part of socialized national economy. They believed that the state must establish rigid control over agricultural production, introduce large-scale methods of farming, and transform the peasants into agricultural workers. Because this plan generated no enthusiasm among Russian peasants, who were mainly interested in increasing their land allotments and in disposing of their produce as they saw fit, during 1917 the Bolsheviks altered their Marxist doctrines and temporarily approved some wishes of the peasants—above all the partition of landed estates. This approval was popular among the peasantry. Welcomed also was the land decree of November 8, 1917, which on the one hand declared the land state property, while on the other it affirmed the principle of equal distribution. Practical application of this decree, however, forced the peasants to part company with the new regime.

As far as the bulk of the peasantry was concerned, the land law affected the lands of the state and those of the landlord only. Bolshevik attempts to change this view met stubborn opposition. Point Five of the land law, which declared that "the land of ordinary peasants and ordinary Cossacks shall not be confiscated," provided the peasants with strong arguments. Those peasants who could not qualify as "ordinary," divided their land, livestock, and implements among their families in order to save them. Wealthy or poor, with land in their actual possession at last, the peasants showed no disposition to join in the large-scale collective farming which the Bolsheviks advocated. Nor were they willing to part with their produce at a fixed low price as the Bolsheviks began to demand. Because loss of the Ukraine, the Don, the Northern Caucasus, and Siberia reduced the Bolshevik-controlled areas of Northern and Central Russia to a condition of starvation, when all persuasions failed the Bolsheviks attempted to solve the food crisis by forcing the peasants to surrender all grain surpluses.

The first decisive step towards forcible food requisition was a decree of the Central Executive Committee on May 9, 1918. It reaffirmed previous government policy of grain monopoly and fixed prices, recognized the necessity of fighting against speculators, acknowledged the urgency of compelling peasants to surrender their surplus, and appealed to the poor to begin a merciless fight against the *kulaks*. Evaders, branded as "enemies of the people," were liable to arrest, expulsion from the village, and even confiscation of their property. The decree established rewards for information leading to the disclosure of any surplus, and granted broad powers to the Commissariat of Food, including the right to use "armed force in cases of resistance to the requisition of grain and other food products." The Commissariat was also empowered to "dismiss, remove, arrest, and turn over to the Revolutionary Tribunal" all officials who interfered with the execution of its orders.

This "food dictatorship decree," which contributed heavily to the break between the Bolsheviks and their Left Socialist Revolutionary friends, was followed by other vital measures. On May 20, 1918, the Central Executive Committee instructed local soviets to "undertake immediately the task of explaining to the poor that their interests are opposed to those of the kulaks, and of arming the poor with the purpose of establishing their dictatorship in the village." On June 11, 1918, Committees of the Village Poor were ordered created everywhere. Entrepreneurs and all wealthy peasants, who allegedly had grain surplus and other food products, were ineligible for membership in those committees. The latter were charged with distribution of food, needed articles and farming implements, and assistance to local food departments in requisitioning surplus grain from more prosperous farmers. These prerogatives gave the committees complete power in villages, and their armed status gave them added prestige.

To assist the Committees of the Village Poor, on August 6, 1918, the government organized Food Requisition Detachments. Every detachment was to consist of not less than seventy-five workers and poor peasants led by two appointed leaders, and equipped with "two or three machine guns." According to their instructions, food detachments were to obtain grain by either purchase at fixed prices or by requisition. They were also instructed to help the local population to harvest crops, to organize local Committees of the Poor, to distribute part of the requisitioned grain among the needy, and to ship the rest to the nearest government storage depot. They were to demand the surrender of firearms, to inventory all available grain stores, to uncover and confiscate hidden grain, to remain in a village until all grain surplus had been delivered, and they were not to indulge in overzealousness. In practice, however, the food requisitioning process was one of constant excesses. The detachments imposed arbitrary grain quotas upon villages, collected the assessed apportionment of grain by force, subjected whole villages to intensive house-to-house searches, inflicted heavy damage everywhere, and perpetrated all kinds of crimes.

Peasants developed several distinct forms of resistance to the activities of the Committees of the Village Poor, and especially of the Food Requisitioning Detachments, whose numbers by the end of 1918 had risen from 20,000 to 40,000 men. At first the peasants tried to evade the assigned levies by every cunning and resourceful device they could conceive. When these proved ineffective, they resorted to armed defense. Villages in the Volga Region, Western Siberia, Tambov, Saratov, and the Ukraine organized themselves against city intruders, and many officials responsible for the food collection were seized, tortured, and killed. The Bolsheviks replied with punitive expeditions. As a result tensions rose, bitterness grew, and casualties multiplied. In the end, however, the government emerged the victor. When overwhelmed, the peasant resorted to a new device: curtailment of the sown area to that sufficient only to feed his immediate family, leaving the remainder of the land uncultivated. By 1920, consequently, the sown area in Siberia had decreased by some 50 per cent, in the Caucasus by 25 per cent, and in the Ukraine, where in addition the fighting of the Civil War was rather heavy, the decline amounted to some 70 per cent to 80 per cent. This passive resistance, coupled with the continued policy of requisitioning, prepared favorable grounds for the famine which engulfed Russia from 1920 to 1922.

The policy of centralization, nationalization, bureaucratization, and requisition estranged from the government not only the peasants but the workers as well. By 1920 the workers, too, were tired of various regulations, compulsion, military discipline, and calls for additional sacrifices. Some expressed their disapproval of government policies by means of absenteeism from work, others through antigovernment resolutions, and some were brave enough to strike. These signs of disaffection occurred throughout Russia, including such Bolshevik strongholds as Petrograd and Kronstadt.

Everywhere the trend was against "the new Communist slavery" and "the bureaucratic trade unions," and in favor of "Soviets without Communists and Commissars." Because of this growing opposition it became clear that to continue War Communism as a normal system was impossible. A retreat to capitalism in the form of the New Economic Policy (NEP) became the only avenue of escape for the Bolsheviks.

Some Bolsheviks, including Lenin, retreated from War Communism gracefully, acknowledging their mistakes. There were many, however, who had difficulty in reconciling themselves to the inevitable retreat. In their view, War Communism was an attempt to realize an ideal communism. They applauded, for instance, adoption of the state-organized barter system and payments in kind instead of money transactions. They also welcomed the abolition of payment for the use of such services as the post, telegraph, railroad, water and electric supply, and the like. Finally, they approved the bitter "class war" in the villages, viewing it as an essential stage in eliminating bourgeois influence from the countryside. Not all were willing to admit that War Communism with all its excesses was not a system but a temporary expedient—an emergency method of supplying towns and armies with necessities, thus saving them from starvation and perhaps even from defeat in the darkest hours of the Civil War.

SUGGESTED READINGS

ADAMS, ARTHUR E. *Bolsheviks in the Ukraine: The Second Campaign, 1918–1919.* New Haven: Yale University Press, 1963.

BORYS, JURIJ. *The Sovietization of Ukraine, 1917–1923.* Toronto: Toronto University Press, 1982.

BRADLEY, JOHN. *Allied Intervention in Russia.* New York: Basic Books, 1968.

BRINKLEY, GEORGE A. *The Volunteer Army and the Allied Intervention in South Russia, 1917–1921.* South Bend: Notre Dame University Press, 1966.

BROWDER, ROBERT P. *Origins of Soviet-American Diplomacy.* Princeton: Princeton University Press, 1953.

BUNYAN, JAMES. *Intervention, Civil War and War Communism in Russia, April–December, 1918. Documents and Materials.* Baltimore: The Johns Hopkins Press, 1936.

———. *The Origin of Forced Labor in the Soviet State, 1917–1921.* Baltimore: The Johns Hopkins Press, 1967.

CARR, EDWARD HALLETT. *A History of Soviet Russia, 1917–1923.* Vol. 2. New York: Macmillan, 1952.

CHAMBERLIN, WILLIAM HENRY. *The Russian Revolution, 1917–1923.* Vol. 2. New York: Macmillan, 1935.

DENIKIN, ANTON. *The White Army.* London: Cape, 1930.

FISHER, HAROLD H. *The Famine in Soviet Russia, 1919–1923.* New York: Macmillan, 1927.

FOOTMAN, DAVID. *Civil War in Russia.* London: Farber & Farber, 1961.

GANKIN, OLGA HESS, and H. H. FISHER. *The Bolsheviks and the World War: The Origins of the Third International.* Stanford: Stanford University Press, 1940.

GERSON, LENNARD D. *The Secret Police in Lenin's Russia.* Philadelphia: Temple University Press, 1976.

KAZEMZADEH, FIRUZ. *The Struggle for Transcaucasia, 1917–1921.* New York: Philosophical Library, 1951.

KENEZ, PETER. *Civil War in South Russia, 1919–1920.* Berkeley: University of California Press, 1969.

KENNAN, GEORGE F. *Decision to Intervene.* Princeton: Princeton University Press, 1958.

KERENSKY, ALEXANDER. *The Catastrophe.* New York: Appleton-Century-Crofts, 1929.

LEGGETT, GEORGE. *The Cheka: Lenin's Secret Police (December 1917–February 1922).* New York: Oxford University Press, 1981.

LOCKHART, R. H. BRUCE. *British Agent.* New York: Putnam, 1933.

MORLEY, JAMES WILLIAM. *The Japanese Thrust into Siberia, 1918.* New York: Columbia University Press, 1957.

PARK, ALEXANDER. *Bolshevism in Turkestan, 1917–1921.* New York: Columbia University Press, 1957.

PILSUDSKI, JOZEF. *Year 1920 and Its Climax Battle of Warsaw During the Polish-Soviet War, 1919–1920.* London–New York: Pilsudski Institute, 1972.

PIPES, RICHARD. *The Formation of the Soviet Union: Communism and Nationalism, 1917–1923.* Cambridge: Harvard University Press, 1954.

RESHETAR, JOHN S. JR. *The Ukrainian Revolution, 1917–1921.* Princeton: Princeton University Press, 1952.

RIGBY, T. H. *Lenin's Government: Sovnarkom, 1917–1922.* New York: Cambridge University Press, 1979.

SCHAPIRO, LEONARD. *The Origin of the Communist Autocracy: Political Opposition in the Soviet State, 1917–1922.* Cambridge: Harvard University Press, 1955.

———. *The Communist Party of the Soviet Union.* New York: Random House, 1960.

TARACOUZIO, T. A. *War and Peace in Soviet Diplomacy.* New York: Macmillan, 1940.

THOMPSON, JOHN M. *Russia, Bolshevism and the Versailles Peace.* Princeton: Princeton University Press, 1966.

TROTSKY, LEON. *The History of the Russian Revolution.* 3 vols. New York: Simon & Schuster, 1932.

TUCKER, ROBERT C. *Stalin as Revolutionary, 1879–1929.* New York: Norton, 1973.

ULAM, ADAM B. *Expansion and Coexistence: The History of Soviet Foreign Policy, 1917–1967.* New York: Praeger, 1968.

ULMAN, RICHARD H. *Anglo-Russian Relations, 1917–1921.* 2 vols. Princeton: Princeton University Press, 1961–1968.

UNTERBERGER, BETTY M. *America's Siberian Expedition, 1918–1920.* Durham: Duke University Press, 1956.

VARNECK, ELENA and H. H. FISHER. *The Testimony of Kolchak and Other Siberian Materials.* Stanford: Stanford University Press, 1935.

WANDYCZ, PIOTR S. *Soviet-Polish Relations, 1917–1921.* Cambridge: Harvard University Press, 1969.

WHITE, JOHN A. *The Siberian Intervention.* Princeton: Princeton University Press, 1950.

WRANGEL, PIOTR N. *The Memoirs of General Wrangel.* London: Williams & Norgate, 1929.

✶ V

THE EXPERIMENTAL
TWENTIES

The Bolshevik military triumph over the Whites at the end of 1920 enabled them to turn their attention to other pressing problems, with which
Russia was amply supplied. Thirty-one months of disastrous participation
in World War I and forty-six months of revolutionary turmoil had produced a catastrophic situation. It has been estimated (the actual figures
can never be ascertained) that between 1914 and 1921, Russia lost some
twenty-six million people. Of that figure, about fifteen million severed
their ties with Russia by establishing independent statehood (Finland,
Estonia, Latvia, Lithuania, Poland). Some two million were actual combat casualties, and about seven million were victims of Red and White
terror, hunger, and disease. The remaining two million—nobles as well as
industrialists, doctors, teachers, scientists, and other professional people,

whose skills the country could hardly afford to lose—fled Russia during the Revolution and the Civil War.

In addition to staggering human losses, war and revolution had inflicted heavy material damage upon Russia. Hundreds of cities and villages had been destroyed. Factories and mines had ceased to produce. Transportation had broken down. Barest needs of life had become unobtainable. The peasantry produced only a fraction of the crops it formerly had. Poor harvests in 1920 and 1921 and seeming indifference of the new regime to the needs of the vast masses of its subject peoples helped to produce famine on a gigantic scale, which affected some thirty-three million and caused the death of some five million people. While Bolshevik leaders blamed much of this great tragedy on war, foreign intervention, subversion at home, and the amateurish experimentation of War Communism, the inescapable fact remained that by the end of the Civil War the Bolshevik "Promised Land" was beginning to resemble hell on earth. Signs of revolt were visible everywhere.

Within the party the restlessness took the form of a vigorous discussion of two closely related issues. The first dealt with the problem of a centralized versus a decentralized decision-making process in determining Russia's future development. The second issue was the attempt to define the precise role trade unions were to play in socialized industry. On the surface these two issues seemed trivial. In reality, however, they touched upon one of the basic elements of Leninism: *centralized leadership.* Under the stress of Civil War, Lenin had succeeded in imposing upon the party a policy of dictatorial ruthlessness and authoritarianism originating in the Politburo, the Orgburo, and the Secretariat. These three new executive organs, each consisting of five members, were approved by the Eighth Party Congress held in March, 1919. Technically these new central bodies were under the supervision of the party's Central Committee. In reality, however, they were transcendent, with full authority over party membership inside and outside Russia. As the leading organs and hence the supreme agencies of power, their decisions were absolutely and unconditionally binding on all parts of the party "regardless of their nationality composition." Strictest centralism and rigorous "outright military discipline" were declared to be essential and the highest organs of power were given complete control over the appointment, transfer, or dismissal of party members, irrespective of the position they might hold inside or outside the party.

The first formidable challenge to these centralizing and disciplinary provisions developed at the Ninth Party Congress, which met from March 29 to April 5, 1920. The challenge evolved out of the controversy over the role trade unions were to play in socialized economy and whether they were independent agents or under strict party control. The critics of Lenin's policy of centralism, who called themselves the Democratic Centralist Opposition, were an offshoot of the Left Communist Movement of early 1918. They were led by Valerian V. Osinsky (1887–?), and included such long time Bolsheviks as Shliapnikov, Timothy V. Sapronov (1886–?), and others. They strongly advocated revolutionary principles of democracy and a collective decision-making process, and violently opposed bureaucracy, expediency, centralization, and hierarchical authority in the party, the government, and industry. In defense of their position they advanced the formula that while the general leadership belonged to the party, political authority belonged to the soviets, and economic authority to the trade unions.

The supporters of centralism rejected this proposition, arguing that it was impossible to separate politics from economics. Trotsky, who was surpassed by none in his advocacy of dictatorial ruthlessness and authoritarianism during the Civil War, insisted that Soviet Russia could attain socialism only through "authoritative regulation of the economic forces and resources of the country, and the centralized distribution of labor-power in harmony with the general state plan." Accordingly, he argued that the state should have the right to mobilize civilian labor, and to transfer, assign, and dispatch it in military fashion to perform tasks economically useful for society. Lenin warmly defended Trotsky's views and shortly thereafter wrote an article entitled " 'Left-Wing' Communism: An Infantile Disorder," in which he denounced the opponents of the party's iron discipline and centralization as virtual agents of capitalism.

The defeat of the Whites and the Bolshevik defeat in Poland at the end of 1920 gave the opponents of centralism within the party additional strength for an all-out struggle against Lenin. Sensing an upsurge of anticentralist feeling, the leadership acknowledged at the Ninth Party Conference held in September, 1920, the need for more equality and democracy in the party, pledged itself to fight bureaucratism, and declared the repression of party dissenters "not permissible." The victory of the opposition was partial and short-lived, as it was soon overshadowed by renewal of the controversy over the role of trade unions in future economic development of Russia and their relation to the party and the government. Out of a multitude of suggestions on this problem, there emerged three main platforms. The first, sponsored by Trotsky and Bukharin, held that the unions were agencies of the state and that their main task should center on raising the productivity of labor. At the opposite extreme was the program of the "Workers' Opposition," sponsored by the Left Wing enthusiasts and trade unions themselves. Its spokesman was the fiery and colorful, if somewhat unstable, Madame Alexandra M. Kollontai (1872–1952). This group, citing Point 5 of the 1919 party program on economic issues, demanded that trade unions be given full control over the entire national economy. Between those two extremes was the program supported by Lenin, Zinoviev, Rykov, Kamenev, Stalin, and

Jan E. Rudzutak (1887–?), commonly known as the "platform of the ten." Their platform disapproved both the aforementioned proposals, and favored restoration of internal democracy within the unions. It also assigned to the unions the role of a link with the masses and a defender of workers' interests against bureaucratic tendencies of the state.

Early in March, 1921, the trade union issue, or more properly an acute intraparty struggle over centralism, was overshadowed by the crucial peasant problem. Up to now, except for forcing at gunpoint delivery of the assigned quota of grain, the regime had paid little or no attention to the peasantry. The peasants, as we noted in the previous chapter, resented this new form of exploitation and resorted to various forms of evasion and even armed self-defense. When they had exhausted all other media of resistance, the peasants ceased to produce. By the end of 1920, agricultural production had decreased to about one-half of the total for 1913, and the amount of cultivated land to about three-fourths. Shrinkage of production, unfavorable climatic conditions, and official indifference joined hands to bring about a gigantic tragedy—the famine. To many, Russia seemed ready for a new revolution.

Meanwhile, as the Civil War drew to a close at the end of 1920, deserters and demobilized veterans of many victorious campaigns returned home. Appalled by the unbelievable conditions in the countryside, many of them either instigated or joined rebellions. During the fall of 1920, peasant risings involving bands of tens of thousands erupted spontaneously throughout Russia, especially in agricultural areas, and increased in extent and violence throughout the winter. Now that the White danger had ceased to exist, the peasants saw no reason why they should continue to deliver oppressive exactions. From the countryside the discontent rapidly spread to cities and to the armed forces. Early in March, 1921, the massive discontent culminated in armed defiance of the Bolshevik regime at the naval base of Kronstadt, once a Bolshevik stronghold.

The Kronstadt rebellion, which formally began on March 2, 1921, was a dramatic climax to the anti-Bolshevik rural and urban unrest. The spark igniting it was the development early in 1921 of waves of strikes and demonstrations in Petrograd against food shortages and administrative overcentralization. The authorities put down these unrests forcibly as well as through concessions. The manner in which order was re-established did not please the Kronstadt sailors, who sympathized with the strikers. Inasmuch as anti-Bolshevik unrest had become a nation-wide phenomenon, the sailors, renowned for their revolutionary zeal, expected their own rebellion to succeed. Their platform, as adopted on February 28, 1921, by the crew of the battleship *Petropavlovsk*, was another indicator of envisaged success. It called for immediate re-election of the soviets by free and secret ballot. It demanded freedom of speech, press, and assembly for workers and peasants and for their political parties. It insisted that all political prisoners be released and that the privileged position of the Communist party and its armed detachments be abolished. The platform promised the peasants full rights to do as they liked with their land, and advocated the ending of discrimination in food rationing.

Sensing the danger, the authorities sent to Kronstadt Mikhail I. Kalinin (1875–1946), Chairman of the Central Executive Committee of the Soviet. It was felt that his peasant background might turn the tide. It did not. Kalinin was shouted down, and a throng of some twelve thousand men enthusiastically approved the program adopted earlier. On March 2, 1921, the defiant sailors set up a Provisional Revolutionary Committee, which they selected from among themselves. The government requested the Committee to surrender peacefully. The Committee refused to comply, but at the same time, apparently feeling that justice was on its side, it did very little to strengthen its position. To the sailors' misfortune, the expected revolt on the mainland of Russia failed to materialize. Instead, on March 7, government forces directed by Trotsky and led by Tukhachevsky began vigorous preparation for an assault which took place on March 18. Some 140 delegates to the Tenth Party Congress, which had convened on March 8, joined the soldiers in the final storming of the sailors' stronghold. The fortress fell and some fifteen thousand of its defenders who surrendered were massacred without trial. The Kronstadt rebellion against the Bolshevik regime was over, but the message carried by the revolt was not entirely lost.

KRONSTADT REPERCUSSIONS: PARTY DISCIPLINE AND NEP

Publicly, the Bolsheviks labelled the Kronstadt rebellion and the events which preceded it a work of counterrevolution. Privately, Lenin admitted quite frankly and honestly that the rebels "do not want the White Guards, and they do not want our power either." To prevent any possible future peasant-supported proletarian rebellion against the dictatorship of the proletariat—a situation for which Marxist-Leninist doctrine made no provision—Lenin masterminded, and the Tenth Party Congress approved, two far-reaching policy changes. One dealt with the strengthening of party discipline; the other officially abandoned War Communism in favor of the New Economic Policy (NEP).

The strengthening of party discipline assumed the form of two resolutions: (1) "On Party Unity," and (2) "On the Syndicalist and Anarchist Deviation in Our Party." The first resolution insisted that to maintain its monopoly of power the party must preserve "the unity and solidarity of the ranks" and "unanimity of will." These prerequisites accordingly excluded all signs of factionalism or the formation of dissident groups with separate platforms, whose objective was to "segregate and create their own group discipline." Party factionalism, the resolution went on to suggest, in practice "inevitably leads to the weakening of teamwork" and to the strengthening of the opponents of revolution. While the resolution encouraged criticism of the party's shortcomings, it made clear that "everyone who criticizes must see to it that the form of his criticism takes into account the position of the party, surrounded as it is by a ring of enemies." All factional groups with a platform within the party, such as the Workers' Opposition or Democratic Centralism groups, were ordered to dissolve or face "absolute and immediate expulsion from the Party." The Central Committee was given full disciplinary powers, including that of expulsion from the party.

The second resolution labelled the views of Workers' Opposition on trade unions as "a syndicalist and anarchist deviation," and placed the blame for it on insufficient knowledge of communist theory and on "the influence exercised upon the proletariat and on the Russian Communist party by the petty-bourgeois element." This resolution pledged to "wage an unswerving and systematic ideological struggle against these ideas," stressed that their propagation was incompatible with membership in the party, and instructed the Central Committee to enforce these decisions. Though relatively brief in content, these two resolutions enabled Lenin to gain two fundamental objectives: the strengthening of the party's monopoly on political power before relaxing economic controls in the country at large; and the establishing of a formal procedure for combating factionalism, which, in practice, as one observer aptly put it, meant that "whoever was in a position to pack the Central Committee could dispose of any minority within that body and within the Party at his leisure," by victimization, transfer, expulsion or outright liquidation. This became evident as early as the summer of 1921, when some 200,000 members were expelled from the party. Lenin's centralism, in other words, laid the foundation for Stalin's regimentation.

Far-reaching also in its implication was the Lenin-sponsored resolution on the NEP, which the Tenth Party Congress approved. Intended to appease the starving and restless peasants, this resolution called for replacement of requisitioning by a tax in kind, and abolition of restrictions on peasant trade in surplus products. On March 21, 1921, the government translated this resolution officially into a "tax in kind" decree, which technically began the dismantling of War Communism. Under the new arrangement the tax was to be progressive, was to be less than what the peasant had given through requisitions, and was "to be taken in the form of the percentage or partial deduction from the products raised in the peasant holding, taking into account the harvest, the number of consumers in the holding, and the number of cattle on hand." The new tax law promised the poorest peasants exemption from taxation, while to the industrious it offered certain privileges. It abolished collective responsibility and made each individual peasant responsible only for the tax falling on him. Once he fulfilled his obligation, the peasant could dispose of his surplus, if any, as he wished. He could deliver it to the state in return for industrial products, or he could sell it on the open market.

Because of the harvest failure of 1921, followed by a disastrous famine, the new tax in kind decree benefited neither the peasant nor the government. The chief immediate significance of the decree centered in its creation of a chain reaction effect. Abandonment of requisitioning ended the need for the Food Requisitioning Detachments, which were ordered disbanded. In May, 1922, as a further concession to the impoverished peasantry, the government limited the tax in kind to 10 per cent of production, and prohibited the seizure of livestock as a penalty for nonpayment of taxes. On May 22, 1922, the Central Executive Committee of the Soviet approved a "Fundamental Law on the Exploitation of Land by the Toilers." While preserving in theory the public ownership of land, this law gave the peasant a choice of the form of land tenure—communal, individual, associated, or mixed. It gave him also the right to treat his holding as his own, to lease it, to increase it, and even to use hired labor to cultivate it. The new Agrarian Code, which went into effect on December 1, 1922, embodied all these provisions, and while not recognizing any

Petrograd, 1922. The Red Army on review.

rights in perpetuity, implied that the rights it accorded were of indefinite duration. For the first time since the revolution, the Russian peasant was given a sense of security in existing arrangements. This confidence, in turn, acted as a strong stimulus to increased efforts and intensified production, and launched Soviet Russia on the road to economic recovery. According to official estimates, by 1925, agricultural recovery in the Northern Caucasus reached 77.5 per cent of the year 1916; in Kazakhstan the figure was 71.9 per cent; in Siberia 92.2 per cent; and in the Ukraine 96.1 per cent.

While intended only to appease the peasants, through implication the original NEP decree also exercised a profound influence on other sectors of the economy. In the first place, since the peasant could not legally dispose of his surplus, it was necessary to legalize private trade. The government accomplished this through three key decrees of March 29, of May 24, and of July 19, 1921. The revival of private trade, in turn, necessitated resumption of the use of money as the primary basis of exchange, and the appearance of brokers—commonly called Nepmen—who knew how to find buyers and sellers at the right moment, who could advise on prices, and perform like functions. Between 1921 and 1923, through a series of official decrees, the government introduced stable currency, created a new State Bank of the RSFSR, restored financial and commercial independence of cooperatives, legalized agricultural credit and loan associations, established state saving banks, and a state lottery, and in many other ways returned to the financial methods of the past.

Though not designed to do so, the NEP exerted a powerful influence on industry. This was inevitable, for if the peasant was to be encouraged to increase his production, the surplus of which could be sold on the open market, industry had to manufacture goods for him to buy. It became necessary, therefore, to undo many of the excesses of War Communism. The first step in that direction was government encouragement of industrial cooperatives. This was followed by a promise of release from nationalization or municipalization of small industrial enterprises which employed not more than ten to twenty hired workers. A decree of December 10, 1922, restored to the former owners all those enterprises which had been ordered nationalized, but which had not yet in fact been taken over by the state. A few months earlier the party had approved the idea of leasing small nationalized enterprises. While cooperatives received preferential treatment, private persons were not ruled out. Party members, however, were. By September 1, 1922, out of a total of 7,100 enterprises, some 3,800 employing 68,000 workers had been leased to cooperatives or to former owners. The aim of these and similar measures was to accord to small entrepreneurs of the countryside the same legal security and the same opportunity as had been given to the peasants. "The controlling heights," which employed over 80 per cent of the working force, the government kept firmly under its control. This included all large-scale industry, all transportation, all foreign trade, and all banking and credit facilities. By these concessions, the government gave up little, but gained a great deal of confidence. According to official estimates, industrial production, which had stood at about 18 per cent of the prewar level in 1920–1921, rose to 27 per cent in 1921–1922, and to 35 per cent in 1922–1923. By 1925–1926, the coal industry registered the largest advance, and almost reached prewar output. Iron and manganese trailed somewhat, but were not too far behind coal.

The return to private ownership and management of industrial enterprises and to a free market under the NEP also forced the return to a free labor market. It became necessary to end obligatory state service, which had been introduced during War Communism, and to dismantle much of the machinery of compulsion. Through a series of decrees during 1921 and 1922, the government removed the main restrictions on the movement of workers from one job to another, and reintroduced the wage system. While these measures helped to restore prewar normalcy, they also helped to create unemployment. Depressed conditions of the workers, in turn, provided the trade unions with an opportunity to protect workers' interests in state as well as private enterprises and thus to gain a degree of independence. They could bargain for higher wages, strike against private employers, and in theory even against the state. This independence was illusory rather than real, however, because trade unions remained under absolute control of the Communist party, which, "through its central and local organizations, as before unconditionally directs the whole ideological side of the work of the trade unions."

Though it was inevitable and greatly beneficial to the economic rehabilitation of the country, not all Bolsheviks welcomed the NEP. Opponents of Lenin's "strategic retreat" objected to the NEP on two grounds. First, they argued that the NEP represented the sacrifice of a planned economy, based on heavy industry, to the well-being of the peasants, whom they regarded as the natural enemy of socialism. Second, their Marxist indoctrination told them that a prosperous peasantry and small entrepreneurs sooner or later, by reviving capitalism, would replace socialism, thus changing the entire political superstructure. Lenin tried to assure his skeptical associates that their fears were groundless, inasmuch as the Communist party retained the monopoly of power with which to determine everything. The opposition however was not convinced and continued to regard the NEP as a betrayal of the interests of the workers and of the revolution. Throughout 1921, opponents of the NEP continually voiced their complaints against it and formed factions, notwithstanding the party's ban on such activity. In February, 1922, a group of twenty-two malcontents, former members of the Workers' Opposition, presented their grievances to the Communist International, protesting against mistreatment, persecution, "suppression of the workers' independence and initiative" and other "abnormalities." Another group, led by Alexander A. Bogdanov (1873–1928), Lenin's onetime second-in-command, and calling itself the "Workers' Truth," attacked the party and the NEP for its "state capitalism" which allowed the exploitation of workers for the benefit of "the organizer-intelligentsia." Although authorities suppressed these and similar groups critical of the NEP and "the correctness" of the party line, they continued to reappear under different names and leaders throughout most of the 1920's.

"CONCESSIONS" TO NATIONAL MINORITIES

Concession to the peasants, with all its far-reaching repercussions was only one basic characteristic of the NEP. Another was the "concession" to national minorities. In a previous chapter we noted that before the Bolshevik seizure of power, stubbornly convinced that only centralism was capable of progress and economic strength, Lenin repeatedly rejected the demands of national minorities for political independence. Territorial disintegration of the multi-national tsarist empire and the triumph of local nationalism after the downfall of monarchy, however, forced him, at least outwardly, to reverse his stand. Without abandoning centralism, Lenin and his followers, between March and November, 1917, appeared as strong opponents of the policy of Russification and staunch supporters of the principle of self-determination. By advocating such a policy, the Bolsheviks achieved two basic objectives: they deepened the existing crisis of the Provisional Government, and they won for themselves the support of Russia's subject peoples. The crowning achievement of the Bolshevik "pro-self-determination" policy was the "Declaration of the Rights of the Peoples of Russia" issued on November 15, 1917, which promised Russia's nationalities equality and sovereignty and the right to free self-determination, "even to the point of separation and the formation of an independent state." When national minorities moved to take advantage of these promises, the Bolsheviks reverted in practice to their original stand. In the course of the Civil War, with the help of local Bolshevik organizations and above all with the backing of the Red Army, Lenin offered each nationality a government consisting of his own trusted emissaries and thus reserved for himself the right to determine which nation could separate itself from Russia. Between 1918 and 1920 the Bolsheviks created on the periphery of Russia several "Soviet Socialist Republics" (Belorussian, Ukrainian, Georgian, Armenian and Azerbaidzhan), while within the RSFSR itself they carved out several "autonomous republics" (Bashkir, Volga German, and Kazakh), and a number of "autonomous regions" (Chuvash, Tartar, and Karelian). Each of the "soviet socialist republics" immediately assumed the posture of an independent state and equipped itself with such essential attributes of sovereignty as an "independent government" and a constitution. Similarly as had the government of the RSFSR, the new governments eliminated private ownership of land and all other means of production, assured the political power to the "working class," granted only to the toiling masses freedom of speech, press, and assembly, and introduced the dictatorship of the proletariat as well as all other "benefits" of the soviet system.

But while they posed as independent political entities, each of these republics expressed "complete solidarity with the existing Soviet republics" as well as readiness to enter with them "into closest political union for the common fight, for the triumph of the world communist revolution." On the basis and in pursuance of such statements, early in 1919 all republics unified their military commands, and economic, labor, financial, and railroad administrations. By the end of the Civil War, the unification process affected all major media of communication and transportation. It is essential to remember that local Bolshevik organizations never enjoyed any "autonomy," for, as a resolution on party organization approved by the Eighth Party Congress, March, 1919, stipulated, there was room for only "one unitary centralized Communist Party with a unitary Central Committee directing all the work of the party in all parts of the RSFSR." The resolution further stipulated that "decisions of the Russian Communist Party and its leading institutions" were unconditionally binding on all parts of the party "regardless of their nationality composition," and that the "Central Committees of the Ukrainian, Latvian, and Lithuanian Communists enjoy the rights of regional committees of the party and are wholly subordinated to the Central Committee of the Russian Communist Party."

Stalin, who then was responsible for the implementation of the nationality policy, revealed the Bolshevik duplicity on the self-determination principle, and the reason behind their obsession with centralism, in the following words: "We are," he said in 1920, "in favor of the secession of India, Arabia, Egypt, Morocco, and other colonies from the Entente, because secession in this case would mean the liberation of those oppressed countries from imperialism and strengthening the position of revolutions. We are against the separation of the border regions from Russia since separation would here involve imperialist servitude for the border regions, thus undermining the revolutionary power of Russia and strengthening the position of imperialism."

The natural result of this policy of expedience was the emergence of nationalist sentiment among the non-Russian peoples. The rise of this sentiment was also stimulated by the attitudes of various of Stalin's lieutenants, such as Lazar M. Kaganovich (1893–1963), Molotov, Sergei M. Kirov (1886–1934), and Gregory K. Ordzhonikidze (1886–1937), who were responsible for the implementation of party directives in various republics. As adherents to the centralist principle, these men strongly despised national minorities and considered everything non-Russian to be either reactionary or bourgeois and hence unworthy of existence. Their overzealousness in imposing centralism and the Russian language and culture on non-Russian peoples surpassed the tsarist Russification policy, lost much good will for the Bolsheviks, caused a great deal of trouble, and on occasion even drew official reprimands. Ruthless centralization of the border areas was continued nevertheless throughout the Civil War, as were all other centralist features of War Communism.

The Tenth Party Congress, which initiated the NEP, also approved a lengthy resolution on the nationality problem. Sponsored by Stalin, the resolution was full of contradicting, ambiguous clichés. On the one hand, apparently to build national ego, it described every Soviet republic as "a deadly menace to imperialism." At the same time it argued that "not a single Soviet Republic, standing alone, can regard itself as insured against economic exhaustion and military defeat by world imperialism," and accordingly called for a close political, economic, and military unity among Soviet republics. Though this new dialectic created little immediate enthusiasm among many party members, all were ordered to assist cautiously the non-Russian peoples to "catch up" with Great Russia. They were directed to help them develop administrative institutions, press, schools, theaters, and other educational and cultural institutions through which communist policy could be disseminated, in order to create a new Soviet culture: "National in form, socialist in content." This was not an easy task, for many minorities of Soviet Russia, especially in Soviet Asia, were at a very low cultural level. For some it was necessary even to devise alphabets, because their languages had never been reduced to written form. In other areas, it meant simply the establishment of schools with instruction in the native language. Determined to pose as liberators and benefactors to these peoples, party leaders quite frequently emphasized the need to accomplish the task at all cost and reminded all party members to carry out their obligations. Although there was some slowdown, the reduction of illiteracy advanced throughout the 1920's and stands as one of the noblest achievements of the NEP period.

While making concessions to minorities in the cultural field, between 1921 and 1924 the Bolsheviks introduced several vital measures which strengthened political centralism. On February 22, 1922, for instance, all Soviet Republics, which were independent in theory, delegated their rights in the sphere of foreign relations to the RSFSR. On May 9, 1922, the RSFSR deprived all republics of their rights in foreign trade. On December 30, 1922, all republics entered into a treaty designed to bring further unity to their policies, by means of a new political federation called the Union of Soviet Socialist Republics (USSR). A new constitution was ready by July 6, 1923, and it was ratified on January 31, 1924.

Like the 1918 constitution, this document was imbued with the militant spirit of the newborn dictatorship of the proletariat. Its preamble announced that since the formation of the Soviet republics the world had been divided into two camps: *the camp of capitalism,* with its alleged "national hate and inequality, colonial slavery and chauvinism, national oppression and massacres, brutalities, and imperialist war," and *the camp of socialism,* with its alleged "reciprocal confidence and peace, national liberty and equality, peaceful co-existence, and fraternal collaboration of peoples." Although in 1924 the USSR consisted of only four states (the RSFSR, the Ukrainian SSR, the Belorussian SSR, and the Transcaucasian SFSR), the constitution expressed a hope that ultimately the socialist system would extend throughout the world. In 1925 the Turkmen and Uzbek, and in 1929 the Tadzhik Autonomous Republics were elevated to full Union status within the USSR. Meanwhile the Transcaucasian SFSR was divided into the Azerbaidzhan, Armenian, and Georgian Republics. As a result of these changes, in 1929 the USSR consisted of nine republics.

In administrative structure the USSR resembled the RSFSR. At the bottom of the state administrative pyramid were the village soviets; then came city and county soviets. Above them were the soviets of territories, provinces, and autonomous and constituent republics. At the apex of the pyramid was the All-Union Congress of Soviets. In theory the Congress of Soviets was the supreme authority of the USSR. In reality it was an unwieldy assembly of some two thousand dignitaries who came to Moscow once a year to listen to the declarations of the leaders, to approve their policies, and to "elect" the All-Union Central Executive Committee to act as the supreme legislative and executive power between the brief sessions of the Congress. Constitutionally, the All-Union Central Executive Committee consisted of two houses: the Soviet of the Union, whose 371 members represented the population of the USSR, and the Soviet of Nationalities, whose members represented territorial-administrative units on the basis of five representatives for each member union republic and one for each autonomous republic. In reality, however, thanks to the policy of biased apportionment, both houses were dominated by the RSFSR. The constitution stipulated that both houses meet three times annually. Between meetings of the Central Executive Committee, the constitution designated a twenty-seven-member Presidium of the Central Executive Committee as "the supreme organ of legislative, executive, and administrative power in the USSR." In essence, though, the administrative and executive functions of the government were handled by the *Sovnarkom* of the USSR.

Under the 1924 constitution the federal government exercised complete control over foreign relations, had the exclusive right to declare war, conclude peace, ratify international treaties, contract foreign loans, and direct foreign and domestic trade. It also had the power to modify the frontiers of the USSR as well as of individual republics, and it controlled the admission of new republics into the union. The federal government established the bases and the general plan of all the national economy; defined the domains of industry; directed transport, post, and telegraphs; and organized and directed the armed forces. It approved the federal and the republics' budgets; set taxes; issued money; established general principles of exploitation and use of natural resources; controlled population movements within the union; supervised courts, education, health, weights and measures, and the rights of foreigners. The federal government likewise had the power to abrogate the acts of union republics if those acts were "contrary to the present constitution." Outside those limits, each member republic was "sovereign," exercised its "public powers independently," and even had the "right to withdraw freely from the union." On the surface this seemed a fair arrangement. In reality, however, from its inception the USSR was a very highly centralized state, led and directed by the Communist party. The latter, while not officially acknowledged in the 1924 constitution, was nevertheless the real source of power and unity.

EXPERIMENTS WITH THE FAMILY, CHURCH, AND EDUCATION

From the moment they seized power, the Bolsheviks felt they could not project Russia's development along Marxist-Leninist lines without introducing drastic changes in family, church, and education. Before the revolution the Russian family was a very conservative social institution. It was dominated by parental authority and governed by ancient customs and traditions. While they varied from place to place, many customs were obsolete and even barbaric. The customs of many non-Russian peoples, especially those in the Asiatic part of the empire, were even worse. Moslem law, for instance, approved polygamy, ignored the dignity of women, and even made possible the purchase as well as the inheritance of a wife. Throughout Imperial Russia, religion exercised a strong influence on family affairs. Church rites were obligatory for all legal marriage. Marriage between people of different faiths was prohibited. Divorce was difficult to obtain.

To weaken religious control over family affairs, as early as December 31, 1917, the Bolsheviks declared that church marriage was a private affair and that only civil marriage was legally binding. They established legal equality of the sexes, greatly liberalized marriage procedures, granted complete freedom of divorce, and gave full equality to children born in or out of wedlock. Later decrees legalized abortions and dropped incest, bigamy, and adultery from the list of criminal offenses. The Family Code of October, 1918, established the independence of all members of the family and deprived fathers of much of the authority they had previously held. To create a further rift between the old and young generation, children were instructed not only to disobey, but to report if their parents tried in any way to influence them against the policies of the new regime.

While these and other early innovations were aimed in part at freeing the individual and the family from religious influences, their fundamental objective was to destroy the patriarchal way of life, the mores of the old order, and the family—the strongholds of tradition and conservatism. Chaos and confusion of the Civil War helped greatly to undermine family life. Many parents had been killed. Families had been torn asunder. Thousands of orphans followed army units through various campaigns. Many more thousands of homeless youngsters joined bands and tramped through the country searching for food, terrorizing the population, stealing and perpetrating all kinds of crimes. In some areas the situation was so bad that authorities were forced to resort to extreme measures. Many of these homeless vagabonds subscribed to Madame Kollontai's ideas of "free love" and similar deviations.

Although the effects of these developments were unfortunate, the government introduced no change in family legislation during the years of the NEP. The new Family Code of 1926 restated the features of earlier legislation on marriage and family, except for two innovations. These were provision for adoption of homeless children, and establishment of guardianship for orphans. When compared with prerevolutionary attitudes, Russian family life showed a drastic change. In 1927, for instance, the divorce-marriage ratio was one to four. In the United States for the same year the ratio was one to six.

Next to the family, the Bolsheviks considered organized religion as the significant obstacle in their attempt to project Russia's development along Marxist-Leninist lines. Their attitude towards religion was influenced in part by Marxist ideology, which held that religion was "the opium of the people," and in part it was influenced by Russian conditions. Before the revolution the Russian Orthodox Church was an inseparable part of the state. It was headed by the tsar, but since the days of Peter the Great it had been administered in his name by the Procurator of the Holy Synod. Under those conditions, Church policy was always in perfect harmony with that of the state—a situation which many Russians resented.

Following the collapse of the monarchy, Church spokesmen tended to be liberal. But as the summer of 1917 progressed, many of them turned to the defense of the old regime in word and deed. This became evident during the meeting of the All-Russian Church Council (*Sobor*) in Moscow late in August, 1917, the first such meeting since 1681. In its composition, the *Sobor* was decidedly conservative. Many of its members, for instance, supported Kornilov's efforts to preserve military discipline—support which boded ill for the Church, inasmuch as Kornilov's efforts collapsed. The *Sobor* also proclaimed Metropolitan Tikhon of Moscow as Patriarch, the first to be installed in Russia since 1700.

One of the first acts of the new Patriarch was the disapproval of the Bolshevik seizure of power and their peace talks with the Germans. The Bolsheviks, still insecure in power and unwilling to antagonize pious Russians, did not retaliate directly against the Church. They struck indirectly, early in December, 1917, by ordering nationalization of all land, including that of the Church and monasteries. Other decrees recognized civil marriages, separated the Church from the state, deprived the Church of state subsidies, made religion a private affair, separated education from the Church, stripped the Church of its jurisdiction over marriage and divorce, and seized Church records of births and deaths. By these decrees, for which they were anathematized, the Bolsheviks dispossessed the Church of its economic power and of its control over individuals, and removed it as a possible barrier to their efforts to remake Russia along Marxist-Leninist lines.

The development of the Civil War intensified considerably the delicate nature of Church-state relations. Although they weakened it greatly, the Bolsheviks continued to view the Church as a hostile organization. All clergy were deprived of voting rights and those who resisted changing conditions were arrested. Those clergymen who actively sided with the Whites—and there were many who did—were executed. In October, 1918, Patriarch Tikhon, because of his renewed indictment of the Bolshevik regime, was placed under house arrest. Shortly thereafter the Bolsheviks ordered further confiscation of Church and monastery property, an action which netted them over seven billion rubles.

While they opposed the clergy and sought to bring an end to religion, the Bolsheviks were unwilling to provoke the devout believers and did not interfere with their worship. They hoped through education to change the people's view. This policy was explicitly outlined in the 1919 party program, which stated that in its religious policy the party was "guided by the conviction that only the realization of conscious and systematic social and economic activity of the masses will lead to the disappearance of religious prejudices." The aim of the party, the program went on to say, was "to destroy the ties between the exploiting classes and the organization of religious propaganda, at the same time helping the toiling masses actually to liberate their minds from religious superstitions, and organizing on a wide scale scientific-educational and antireligious propaganda." Party members were warned to be very careful to avoid "offending the religious susceptibilities of believers, which leads only to the strengthening of religious fanaticism."

At the close of the Civil War, when it became evident that the Bolsheviks were emerging victorious over the Whites, the Patriarch called for submission to the new regime. Shortly thereafter, however, the hostility between the Church and the new regime flared up anew as the result of misunderstanding. During the famine the Church tried to organize its own relief for the starving—an action which the Bolsheviks viewed with suspicion, being afraid that it would be used for propaganda purposes. Soon they relented, but they also asked the Church to give up its gold, jewels, and other treasures. Patriarch Tikhon interpreted this to mean that the state was openly opposing the Church, and refused to surrender the Church treasures. In his opposition he was supported by the émigré Russian church leaders. Their support, however, provided the Bolsheviks with a pretext for Tikhon's arrest in May, 1922, and for a renewed bitter attack against the Church and the clergy. In June, 1923, Tikhon was freed on condition that he disassociate himself from all anti-Communist movements. This he tried to do until his death in April, 1925. His successor, Metropolitan Peter, was arrested in December, 1925, and sent to Siberia. Early in 1926, the government also arrested Peter's successor, Metropolitan Sergei. In view of these arrests it appeared that a reconciliation between the Church and the state had become the only solution. In June, 1926, Sergei appealed to the government for recognition of the Orthodox Church, which was granted in May, 1927. Though branded by many as a surrender to the Bolsheviks, this reconciliation brought one positive result. It ended government support of the "Living Church" which had broken away from the main body in 1922, and which favored liberalization of regulations and practices of the Church as well as curbing the power of its hierarchy.

Although it was now allowed to function, the existence of the Orthodox Church in Russia was precarious. Its activities were limited, its officials suspect, and many of its buildings closed. In 1927, for instance, the authorities closed seventeen churches and thirty-four monasteries, as well as fourteen synagogues, and nine mosques. In 1928, 359 churches, forty-eight monasteries, fifty-nine synagogues, and thirty-eight mosques were closed. Moreover, the Church had to compete with the Communist party-approved antireligious propaganda spread through schools, press, and all other media of communication and education. As early as 1922, the Bolsheviks began to publish a newspaper, *Bezbozhnik* (The Atheist), in which they made a concentrated effort at attacking religion. In 1925, there was organized around *Bezbozhnik* a group which called itself The League of Militant Atheists. Headed by Emilian M. Yaroslavsky (1878–1943), the League sponsored, with the party's blessing, antireligious activities throughout the country; published books, pamphlets, and periodi-

cals; and staged antireligious parades. Though officially its membership
was small (in 1928 the League had some 130,000 members), its work
among the youth in cities made considerable headway primarily because
of official support and the greatly weakened position of the family and of
the Church.

From the outset the Bolsheviks realized that however profoundly
they weakened the influence of family and church, they could not hope to
project Russia's development along Marxist-Leninist lines without introducing drastic changes in education. Three factors seem to have strongly
influenced Boshevik determination and efforts. First, they inherited a
country whose educational system, while renowned for its academic and
scientific excellence (which compared favorably with the best available in
Western Europe), was designed for the few. Second, they inherited a
country whose population, although forced to remain outside the halls of
learning, had a deep respect as well as desire for learning—a condition
which in itself was a powerful revolutionary force. And, finally, they
inherited a country whose teachers, while approving the revolution, were
less than enthusiastic about Bolshevik policies.

The Bolshevik remaking of Russian education had two distinct
phases. First, the new regime destroyed the old system of education from
elementary through university. On February 5, 1918, the school was
ordered separated from the Church, and the teaching of religious doctrines in all state, private, and public educational institutions was prohibited. The Educational Act of October 16, 1918, replaced the Imperial
school system by a nine-year unified polytechnical school. Characteristics
of the old system, such as examinations, homework, and discipline, were
abolished. Coeducation was introduced on all levels. Administration was
entrusted to school collectives composed of teachers, students, and school
employees. Teaching of classic and modern languages was abandoned, as
was that of history. Instead, emphasis was placed on sociologically-
oriented social science and practical work. After August 8, 1918, any boy
or girl of sixteen or over had the right to enroll in a university, regardless
of his or her educational background. A decree of October 8, 1918, abolished all academic degrees. A curriculum reform of 1920 further de-
emphasized liberal education in favor of specialization in science, and in
the fall of 1922 the government annulled the autonomous status of Russian universities. By these and other decrees the new regime destroyed the
old educational system, and critics of these changes were either dismissed
or arrested. Some fled abroad, and only a few agreed to cooperate with
the new regime.

The second phase of the remaking of Russian education was the
introduction of a system which would serve the new regime. One of the
essential features of the new system was the promise to bring education to
everyone. This promise found its first expression on November 7, 1917, in

a statement issued by the People's Commissariat for Education, which called for: (1) an immediate struggle for the elimination of illiteracy through free general obligatory education; (2) training of teachers; (3) high education budget; (4) uniform schools, and (5) a wide network of adult educational institutions. The constitution of July, 1918, promised to provide "the workers and the poorer peasants with a complete, universal, and free education," while the 1919 party program vowed to transform "the school from an instrument of class domination of the bourgeoisie . . . into an instrument for a communist regeneration of society." Education, promised the party program, was to be free and compulsory, general and technical, with instruction in native language, free of religious influence, and for both sexes up to the age of seventeen. The state was to supply all pupils with food, clothing, shoes, and all other school needs. The state was to assist adult education and to aid financially those students who desired a university education.

The implementation of this program was impossible as long as civil war was in progress. With the return of normalcy under the NEP, the Bolsheviks mobilized all agencies to bring not only education but every aspect of culture into the service of the new regime. One vital agency in this effort was the People's Commissariat for Enlightenment, headed by Lunacharsky, a close associate of Lenin. Under the aegis of the Commissariat were all schools from nurseries to universities, theaters, museums, art galleries, films, radio, book publishing, libraries, and adult educational institutions. Other vital agencies through which the party transmitted its indoctrination were the trade unions, the Red Army, the *Komsomol* (Communist Youth Organization), factory schools, night schools, village reading rooms, and village teachers. Though they differed in approach, each agency had the same objective: to transform the thinking process and personal habits of the people from a religious, tradition-bound outlook to a materialistic one, and to strengthen their belief in the economic system of socialism and their faith in the leadership of the Communist party. Despite a great amount of inefficiency, the Bolsheviks made much progress in spreading their propaganda and taught some seven million illiterates the rudiments of reading and writing. It was an effort that had no historical parallel.

EXPERIMENTS IN LITERATURE, THE THEATER, AND THE CINEMA

The Bolshevik remaking of Russia left a significant imprint not only on the political, economic, and social fabric of the country, but also on every phase of the intellectual life. In literature the impact was initially a negative one, for most of the Russian writers, in common with the majority of the Russian intelligentsia, assumed a hostile attitude towards the new regime, left the country, and joined *émigré* groups in Berlin, Prague, or Paris. Included in this exodus were: Ivan A. Bunin (1870–1953), a leading writer and the first Russian to receive the Nobel Prize for literature; Alexander I. Kuprin (1870–1938), novelist; Michael Artsybashev (1878–1927), novelist; Leonid N. Andreev (1871–1919), short story writer, novelist and playwright; Ilia G. Ehrenburg (1891–1967), novelist and journalist; Dimitri S. Merezhkovsky (1865–1941), symbolist writer; Viacheslav I. Ivanov (1866–1949), symbolist poet; Aleksei N. Tolstoy (1883–1945), novelist and playwright; Boris V. Savinkov (1879–1925), radical novelist; and Marina I. Tsvetaeva (1892–1941), poetess. Of these, Ehrenburg and Tolstoy returned to Russia in 1923, and Kuprin and Tsvetaeva in the mid-thirties; all the others remained abroad.

Those writers who chose to stay in Russia following the Bolshevik coup were divided into two groups: outspoken opponents of the new regime, and apolitical supporters of the revolution. The first group included Feodor K. Teternikov (1863–1927), a leading symbolist who wrote under the pseudonym of Feodor Sologub; Nikolai S. Guimilov (1886–1921), who was executed in 1921, a poet and a founder of the anti-Symbolist movement known as *Acmeism;* Anna A. Gorenko (1880–1967), poetess who wrote under the pseudonym of Anna Akhmatova; and poet Osip E. Mandelshtam (1892–?). The supporters of the revolution included Maxim Gorky; Alexander A. Blok (1873–1924), symbolist writer; Boris N. Bugaev (1880–1934), a symbolist writer who published under the pseudonym of Andrei Bely; Valery Ia. Briusov (1873–1924), symbolist poet; Sergei A. Esenin (1895–1925), symbolist poet; Vladimir V. Maiakovsky (1893–1930), a leading Russian futurist, and for a few years unofficial poet laureate of the new regime; and Efim A. Pridvorov (1883–1945), a poet who published under the pseudonym of Demian Bedny. Several of the supporters of the new order in Russia became disillusioned with their ideal and committed suicide (Blok, Briusov, and Maiakovsky); while some went into self-imposed exile (Gorky from 1921 to 1928 and Bely from 1922 to 1923). Because of the exodus of leading writers, Russian literature, already in a state of disintegration before the revolution, declined further after the Bolshevik seizure of power.

In addition to the exodus of leading writers, the abnormal conditions of the Civil War and War Communism exercised a negative influence on the cultural life of the country. Between 1918 and 1920 the Bolsheviks succeeded in silencing not only their political opponents but uncooperative writers as well. They achieved the latter through such devices as the suspension of publication of leading literary and academic quarterlies, monthlies, weeklies, and even newspapers; nationalization of publishing houses; granting of a monopoly of publication to the State Publishing Organization, known by its Russian abbreviation as *Gosizdat;* denial to

Maxim Gorky   *Ilia Ehrenburg*

uncooperative writers and journalists of such basic needs of existence as food and fuel; and support of such groups as Futurists, Cosmists, Imaginists, and other bohemians who applauded the goals of the revolution.

Between 1918 and 1920 one of the most celebrated literary groups was centered around the journal *Proletarskaia Kultura* (Proletarian Culture), and was known by its Russian abbreviation as *Proletkult*. *Proletkult* was founded late in 1917. Its basic aim was to develop a new literature by and for the proletariat. In pursuit of that goal, studios were established in Moscow and Petrograd for the training of new writers, and many leading literary personalities, including Briusov and Bely, taught in these studios. In theory membership in the *Proletkult* was reserved exclusively to workers. In reality, however, anyone who accepted Bolshevik ideology and extolled collectivism was welcomed. Lenin and some of his close associates, preoccupied with the more pressing problems of the Civil War, initially supported the aim of the *Proletkult*. However, when its spokesmen (especially Alexander A. Malinovsky, 1873–1928) began to demand independence of party control, the *Proletkult* was placed under the supervision of the People's Commissariat for Enlightenment late in 1920, and disbanded altogether in 1923. Its demise was not tragic because the contribution of its members was significant neither in quality nor quantity.

The fading of the fortunes of the *Proletkult* coincided with the official dismantling of War Communism and the inauguration of the NEP. Though not intended, the NEP had a far reaching impact on literature. The limited restoration of capitalist economy and the resumption of private trade made possible the reappearance of private book printing and selling facilities. The return to normalcy also facilitated the appearance of such new journals as *Literaturnye Zapiski* (Literary Notes), *Krasnaia Nov* (The Red Soil) and *Pechat i Revolutsiia* (Press and Revolution). New conditions favored establishment of cultural contacts with the outside world, and those writers who until then had been deprived of an opportunity to exercise their talents were permitted to return to the literary scene. The NEP, in other words, initiated a new phase in Soviet literature.

The principal themes of Soviet literature after 1921 were the revolution, the Civil War, partisan activities, the famine, and generally the struggle between the old and new ways of life. The most prominent writer of this "revolutionary romanticism" period was Boris A. Wogau (1894–?), who wrote under the pseudonym of Boris Pilniak. His best known works include *Goly God* (The Naked Year), *Mashiny i Volki* (Machines and Wolves) and *Rossiia v Poliote* (Russia in Flight). Another noted writer of this period was Eugene I. Zamiatin (1884–1937), whose satirical fantasy *My* (We) bears a striking resemblance to Aldous Huxley's *Brave New World* and George Orwell's *1984*. Other writers worthy of attention included Isaac E. Babel (1894–?), author of *Konarmiia* (Red Cavalry) and *Evreiskie Raskazy* (Jewish Tales); and Dimitri A. Furmanov (1891–1926), whose novel *Chapaev* emerged as a major classic of Soviet literature on the Civil War.

In addition to these writers, a literary group known as the Serapion Brothers was organized in February, 1921. Among its outstanding members were Constantine A. Fedin (1892–1977), author of the novel *Goroda i Gody* (Cities and Years); Vsevolod V. Ivanov (1895–1963), author of *Bronepoezd No. 14–69* (Armored Train No. 14-69); Veniamin A. Zilberg (1902–), who wrote under the pseudonym of Kaverin; Lev N. Lunts (1901–1923), critic and author of an essay *Na Zapad* (To the West), critical of Russian literary isolation from Western Europe; Nikolai N. Nikitin (1895–1963), author of *Poliot* (The Flight), which deals with the Civil War; Nikolai S. Tikhonov (1896–), poet and writer who extolled the revolutionary romanticism of the Civil War; Michael M. Zoshchenko (1895–1958), a satirist whose collections *Uvazhaemye Grazhdane* (Esteemed Citizens) and *Nervnye Liudi* (Nervous People) reflect a fading of his optimism for the revolution. The Serapion Brothers had one thing in common: a desire to produce imaginative and nonconformist art, free of political ideology. This demand made the Serapion Brothers unpopular with party officials, and in 1923 Trotsky labelled them "Fellow Travellers"; that is, individuals who were non-Communists.

The Serapion Brothers were also bitterly assailed by such literary groupings that appeared after 1921 as "October," "Workers' Spring," "Young Guard," "Left Front," "On Guard," and the "All-Union Association of Proletarian Writers," known by its Russian abbreviation as *VAPP*, with branches in Moscow, Petrograd, and other cities. Since most members of these groupings belonged to the Communist party, they insisted that proletarian literature should have but one aim: "to serve the cause of world proletarian victory [and] to fight ruthlessly all the enemies of the Revolution."

Preoccupied with more pressing problems of domestic and foreign policy, party leaders stayed away from these literary disagreements until an explosive point was reached. In June, 1925, the Central Committee held a special session devoted to literary matters, and produced a resolution that subsequently came to be known as the "Magna Charta Libertatum" of Soviet writers. Published in all Soviet papers, this document bluntly stated that "in a classless society there is and can be no neutral art," and accordingly pledged the party's moral and material support to proletarian and peasant writers. At the same time, however, the resolution rejected demands that the party commit itself to any particular literary form, and pleaded for understanding, coexistence, and tactfulness towards other literary groups, and especially the "Fellow Travellers."

The principles of the June, 1925, resolution terminated the bitter literary feud between Communist and non-Communist writers, and governed literary life in the USSR until 1929. This period was especially fruitful to such established writers as Fedin, Kaverin, Aleksei Tolstoy, and Ehrenburg. It was also successful for such newcomers as Leonid M. Leonov (1899–), author of Barsuki (The Badgers) and Vor (The Thief); Iuri K. Olesha (1899–1960), author of a controversial novel Zavist (Envy), and Michael A. Sholokhov (1905–), author of a celebrated novel Tikhy Don (The Quiet Don). The contributions of these writers, together with those of the Serapion Brothers and other "Fellow Travellers," turned the 1920's into a highly productive period of Soviet literature.

What has been said of Soviet literature during the 1920's is to a certain extent equally true of Soviet theater. Because they recognized the value of the theater as an instrument of mass education, agitation, and propaganda following their seizure of power, the Bolsheviks nationalized all imperial and private theaters throughout the country, and placed them under the supervision of a special department at the People's Commissariat for Enlightenment headed by a veteran director Vsevolod E. Meyerhold (1874–1942). Under his direction the theater was turned into a vast laboratory in search of proletarian art. Curtains, footlights, elaborate costumes, and everything that separated the audience from the actors were banished. The change of scenery took place in full view of the spectators. Actors were trained to be athletes as well as acrobats. Pulleys and ladders —symbols of industrial age—were substituted for the conventional stage background. Mass revolutionary spectacles involving thousands of participants were staged to produce the desired effect. Those who sought new forms applauded Meyerhold's innovations, while those who preferred classic performance were shocked by his violations of old conventions and forms.

During the 1920's Soviet theaters continued to seach for new forms as well as a new repertoire. Many theaters specialized in modern plays based on experiences of the revolution or the Civil War. For a while, the Moscow Art Theater ran successfully Michael A. Bulgakov's (1891–1940) *Dni Turbinykh* (Days of the Turbines), a drama which depicted anti-Bolshevik officers as heroic and gallant defenders of their cause in the Civil War. Another successful play, a realistic presentation of Bolshevik partisans, was adapted from Ivanov's *Armored Train No. 14–69*. The repertoire of Moscow's theaters also included a number of plays based on historical subjects, such as Aleksei Tolstoy's *Tsar Feodor Ivanovich*, Merezhkovsky's *Paul I*, and Andreev's *Seven Who Were Hanged*.

During the 1920's Soviet theaters faced acute competition from the cinema. Like the legitimate theater, Soviet films displayed such features as subordination of the individual to the mass, careful reconstruction of minor details, building of productions not around single actors but ideas, and, of course, sympathy for Communist principles. Technically, Soviet films compared quite favorably with those produced in the United States or Western Europe. This achievement stemmed largely from the efforts of such producers as Sergei M. Eisenstein (1898–1948), whose best known early productions were *Stachka* (The Strike), and *Bronenosets 'Potemkin'* (The Battleship Potemkin); Vsevolod I. Pudovkhin (1893–1953), who directed the documentary *Mekhanika golovnogo mozga* (Mechanics of the Brain), and the pictures *Konets Sankt Peterburga* (The End of St. Petersburg), and *Mat'* (Mother); and Alexander P. Dovzhenko (1894–1959), who directed *Zvenihora, Arsenal,* and *Zemlia* (The Land).

It is essential to remember that the revolution created opportunities not only for the Russians to display their talents but for the non-Russians as well. The Civil War and Bolshevik adherence to centralization and Russification made conditions unfavorable for such a display for several years. The reversal came in April, 1923, when the Twelfth Party Congress ordered party members everywhere to befriend national minorities, to learn their languages, and to help them in every other way to advance. This decision led accordingly to the elevation of many native languages on a par with Russian, establishment of state publishing houses to handle publication of works in native languages, and emergence into prominence of dormant native literary and artistic talents. In Belorussia, for instance, this was a period of creative activity for poet Yanka Kupala (1882–1942) and writer Adam Babareka (1899–1937). Their counterparts in the Ukraine were poets Pavlo Tychyna (1891–   ) and Maksim Rylsky (1895–   ), and writers Mykola Kulish (1892–?) and Mykola Khvylovy (1891–1933).

The emergence of Stalin as absolute dictator in the USSR in the late

1920's, and his subsequent determination to plunge the country into a policy of rapid industrialization and collectivization terminated the most productive period of cultural creativeness in the USSR. Between 1929 and 1932, there developed under Stalin's direction a new style known as "Socialist realism." In theory the new trend, in force until Stalin's death in 1953, sought to develop "artistic works worthy of the great age of Socialism." In practice, however, the new style demanded of all writers and artists absolute conformity, and depiction of such of Stalin's favored subjects as sturdy Stakhanovites, contented cows, dedicated milkmaids, devoted pig breeders, vigilant party members, young lovers arguing by the light of the moon about problems of industrial production, enemies of Soviet power, and similar topics. Because party officials adhered strictly to these standards, from 1929 to 1953 "Socialist realism" produced, in the words of one observer, "cultural wilderness" in the USSR.

THE STRUGGLE FOR SUCCESSION

On May 26, 1922, Lenin, the founder and the unchallenged leader of Russian communism, suffered his first major paralytic stroke, lost his speech and the ability to move his right arm and leg, and accordingly was forced to relinquish active leadership of the party and of the Soviet state. Although towards the end of 1922 he partially recovered, his illness precipated among his close associates a bitter struggle for succession to his mantle. Afraid that it might endanger the system he had created, Lenin deplored the developing feud, but at the same time, except for expressing his trust in collective leadership, he did little to stop it. This is clearly evident from a brief memorandum he wrote on December 24, 1922, which has come to be known as his *Testament*. In it he tried to appraise critically all potential candidates—strongly implying that in his judgment none of them alone was capable of being the supreme leader. Trotsky, Lenin thought, was distinguished by exceptional abilities, but "his too far-reaching self-confidence and a disposition to be too much attracted by the purely administrative side of affairs" made him not fully qualified to be leader. Zinoviev and Kamenev, as events before the seizure of power had indicated, were not reliable. Piatakov was "distinguished in will and ability, but too much given over to administration and the administrative side of things to be relied on in a serious political question." Bukharin was the most valuable and favored theoretician of the party "but his theoretical views can only with the very greatest doubt be regarded as fully Marxist, for there is something scholastic in him (he never has learned, and I think never has fully understood the dialectic)." Stalin, Lenin was afraid, though powerful, did not always know "how to use that power with sufficient caution." On January 4, 1923, in a postscript to the *Testament*,

Lenin branded Stalin as "too rude" and capricious, and suggested that a way be found to replace him in the powerful position of General Secretary of the Party, with a man who would have more patience, loyalty, politeness, and attentiveness. Lenin did not live to see his suggestion fulfilled, for he died on January 21, 1924.

Publicly, Lenin's lieutenants exhibited deep sorrow over the illness and death of their leader, ordered the embalmment of his body, and deposited it with unusual pomp in a mausoleum on Red Square in Moscow, which from its inception was elevated into a national shrine. They also elevated his name and his writings to a quasi-religious worship and renamed in his memory his birthplace of Simbirsk on the Volga, Ulianovsk, and Petrograd became Leningrad.[1] Privately, however, during his illness Lenin's lieutenants had begun to maneuver for his succession. Already in 1923 two groups of pretenders could be discerned. In the first was Trotsky, a man of great learning, an inspiring orator, a gifted writer, a sound analyst and strategist, a capable organizer of the Revolution and Civil War, chief of the Red Army, and a member of the Politburo. Next to Lenin, Trotsky was probably the best known Bolshevik and, although he had joined the party only in 1917, he appeared the strongest candidate for Lenin's post. The other group of pretenders, known as the *troika* or *triumvirate,* included Zinoviev, an able orator, longtime associate of Lenin, leader of the powerful Petrograd party organization, member of the Politburo, and head of the Comintern; Kamenev, another close associate of Lenin, a spokesman of the powerful Moscow party organization and a member of the Politburo; and Stalin, an old-time Bolshevik, the party's general secretary, a member of the Politburo, the Orgburo, and the Commissariat of Workers' and Peasants' Inspection. Though the least known of the triumvirate, Stalin was the most powerful by virtue of his control of the party apparatus, which he used cautiously at first to strengthen his position and to silence the opposition.

Stalin made his first decisive move in April, 1923, when the party approved his reorganization plan. On the surface his scheme was reasonable. It called for subordination of the Politburo to the Central Committee, which was to be enlarged, and for the expansion also of the Central Control Commission, whose members would participate in the plenary sessions of the Central Committee. The approval of these changes, which were in line with Lenin's wishes, gave Stalin an opportunity to pack party and government organs with his trusted men. By these and other schemes Stalin succeeded in isolating not only Trotsky but Zinoviev and Kamenev as well.

Trotsky struck back at Stalin's maneuverings on October 8, 1923, in the form of a memorandum addressed to the Politburo, wherein he as-

---

[1] From 1700 to 1914 the city was known as St. Petersburg; from 1914 to 1924 as Petrograd; and since 1924 as Leningrad.

sailed the dictatorship of the Secretariat and hinted that a change of leadership was desirable. On October 15, a group of forty-six high party members laid before the Central Committee their criticism of Stalin's machinations. They charged that a small political machine had seized control of the party, was imposing its will, was silencing all valid criticisms, and was destroying the initiative of the rank and file. Because his men formed a majority in the Politburo and in the Central Committee, Stalin had no difficulty in branding Trotsky's criticism as a "grave political mistake" and the "Declaration of the Forty Six" as a factional move that threatened the party's unity. On December 5, 1923, to silence all the critics, the Politburo adopted a resolution which, at least on paper, embodied almost all the criticism advanced by the opposition.

On December 11, Trotsky published in *Pravda* an article entitled, "New Course," in which, while endorsing the new policy, he held that as long as the party was dominated by the all-powerful secretaries no democracy within it was ever possible. "The party," he argued, "must subordinate to itself its own apparatus without for a moment ceasing to be a centralized organization." Trotsky's defense of "intra-party democracy," however, was doomed to failure for two reasons. First, he himself was renowned for ruthless dictatorship and thus could expect little sympathy. Second, he levelled his criticism at the party apparatus which controlled the press and voting. A party conference held from January 16 to 18, 1924, overwhelmingly condemned Trotsky's views and oppositions as "petty bourgeois deviations from Leninism" and warned all the critics that neither "factionalism" nor circulation of "forbidden documents" was compatible with party membership. Trotsky thus lost the first round.

The second round he forfeited. Three days before Lenin's death, which was expected momentarily, Trotsky, who had himself been ill for some time, left Moscow to recuperate in the Caucasus. His absence provided Stalin with an excellent opportunity to identify himself as Lenin's rightful successor. On January 26, Stalin delivered a "hieratical oath of loyalty" to Lenin in which he pledged to hold high, to guard, and to strengthen the purity of party membership, the unity of the party, the dictatorship of the proletariat and the worker-peasant alliance. He elaborated on these theoretical points at some length in a series of lectures entitled "Foundations of Leninism," delivered at the Communist University in Moscow in April, 1924. To spread Leninism as interpreted by Stalin, a new journal, *Bolshevik*, was founded, opponents were purged, and some 220,000 new members were admitted into the party to strengthen Stalin's position against the "old guard." By mid-1924, through careful organization and manipulation of party members, appeals for unanimity following Lenin's death, and other devices, Stalin emerged on top. At the Thirteenth Party Congress held in May 1924, Trotsky, by declaring "My party right or wrong," went on record, publicly at least, as approving the new arrangements. In June, 1924, Stalin felt strong and confident enough to criticize the doctrinal "mistakes" of his two triumvirate companions, Zinoviev and Kamenev. To weaken their following, their supporters were assigned to distant places. To all intents and purposes the triumverate was dead.

Late in 1924, however, the struggle for succession took a new turn which again proved to be advantageous to Stalin and disastrous to his opponents. On the eve of the seventh anniversary of the revolution, Trotsky published a volume of essays entitled Lessons of October. It embodied two basic themes. The first branded as unrevolutionary the policy of the "Right," and by implication the entire NEP. The second questioned the qualifications of the two members of the triumvirate, Zinoviev and Kamenev, who had opposed the Bolshevik seizure of power in 1917, to head the party. By his charges, Trotsky drove Kamenev and Zinoviev into Stalin's arms, not as his equals but as his subordinates. With their help, Stalin mobilized the entire propaganda machinery of the party against Trotsky; and for weeks, in articles, pamphlets, and speeches, vilified him, exposed his shortcomings, his non-Bolshevik past, his disagreements with Lenin, and his past and present deviations. Before long Stalin, who led the attack, began even to question Trotsky's contribution to victory, and accordingly elevated his own importance. He also identified Trotskyism as "distrust in the leaders of Bolshevism" and a "lack of confidence in the Bolshevik party allegiance, in its monolithic nature." Since Trotskyism had become a major heresy, at the January, 1925, meeting of the Central Committee, Zinoviev and Kamenev demanded that Trotsky be expelled from the party. Stalin overruled the demand and contented himself with Trotsky's abdication from his nominal headship of the Red Army.

Trotsky's Lessons of October helped Stalin to emerge not only as undisputed party leader but as its theoretical spokesman as well. Until this time, every Bolshevik from Lenin down believed that the ultimate success of the Russian Revolution and of socialism depended on the help it received from the victorious proletariat of the industrially advanced countries of Western Europe. In spite of many disappointments, they never abandoned belief in the "permanent revolution." In fact, many felt that the more the prospects of a proletarian revolution in Western Europe receded, the more the Russian Bolsheviks had an obligation to help bring about such a revolution. The mismanagement and failure of the Comintern-supported insurrections in Germany and Bulgaria in 1923 dramatically focused Bolshevik attention to their responsibilities abroad. Trotsky, with his power slipping away, was quite critical of Zinoviev's and Stalin's apparent lack of revolutionary fire and their handling of these insurrections. He emphasized, as he had in the past, that for socialism to succeed in Russia it was necessary to make an all out effort, using Russia's resources, to ignite uprisings everywhere. For Trotsky, in other words, Russian revolution was not an end in itself but a stage in the world struggle against capitalism.

Stalin was in full agreement with Trotsky's emphasis—which was also Lenin's view—as late as April, 1924, when he asserted that the Soviet Union was not "an end in itself . . . [but] a link needed to strengthen the chain of the revolutionary movement in the countries of the West and the East." In December, 1924, however, Stalin reversed his position, branded Trotsky's "permanent revolution" as a variety of Menshevism, as "a lack of faith in the strength and capabilities of the Russian revolution, and as a negation and repudiation of Lenin's theory of the proletarian revolution." Instead, he advanced his own theory of "socialism in one country," which was simple but quite persuasive. It argued that seven years of Bolshevik rule had demonstrated that the regime could maintain itself in power without Western European aid. Moreover, Stalin stressed, the USSR possessed all the necessary prerequisites to establish a powerful socialist base by its own efforts. The achievement of this task, in turn, would greatly simplify the world revolutionary struggle, since the Soviet Union could then render any necessary assistance to the workers of other lands. Their triumph would then guarantee "the final victory of socialism in the first victorious country." The difference between Trotsky's and Stalin's positions was consequently not in the end product but in timing and temperament. Stalin's scheme called for the establishment of socialism in Russia first; Trotsky's concept had the order reversed. Stalin's dominance in the party organization, however, decided the issue in his favor.

Following the weakening of Trotsky, Stalin dropped his two former associates, Zinoviev and Kamenev, whose prestige and influence Trotsky had seriously undermined, and turned to Rykov, Michael Tomsky (1880–1936), and Bukharin, staunch backers of the NEP and of Stalin's policies. With their support he embarked on a policy of peasant "appeasement," easing their taxes and removing some restrictions on the hiring of agricultural labor. He also moved cautiously but systematically in further weakening Zinoviev's and Kamenev's positions. The effort required some maneuvering, for both were long-time leading men in the party. Zinoviev, moreover, had a powerful party organization in Leningrad and was in addition the head of the Comintern. The open clash between the former collaborators came at the Fourteenth Party Congress in December, 1925. The challenge to Stalin was doomed to failure because, except for the Leningrad delegation, the membership of the Congress was hand-picked by his supporters, who jeered and insulted all anti-Stalinists, including Lenin's widow, Nadezhda K. Krupskaia (1869–1939). The most courageous speaker was Kamenev, who led a direct attack on the Secretariat, denounced the emergence of a leader (vozhd), and openly stated that he had "reached the conclusion that Comrade Stalin cannot fulfill the role of unifier of the Bolshevik staff." For his courage Kamenev was rewarded by demotion to candidate status on the Politburo and removed from most of his government posts. Molotov, Klementii E. Voroshilov (1881–1969), Kaganovich, Kirov, Anastas I. Mikoyan (1895–1970), and others who supported Stalin were elevated to high posts.

The next challenge to Stalin's leadership came from the "United Opposition," a re-grouping which developed late in the spring of 1926. Its leaders were Trotsky, Kamenev, and Zinoviev. Having learned their lessons well, they were careful not to attack the principle of party unity or pose as a faction. They centered their attack on the party bureaucracy, to which they ascribed all the failures and faults of the regime, such as suppression of party democracy, lag in the development of industry, deplorable conditions of industrial workers, and the growing power of the kulaks. Stalin replied by replacing Zinoviev in the Politburo with Rudzutak, and by wholesale removal of Opposition followers from party and government positions. He also inaugurated a campaign aimed at discrediting the Opposition's ideas. Thus outmaneuvered by Stalin, but desirous of retaining their influence in the party, the Opposition leaders published in Pravda in the middle of October, 1926, a declaration wherein they admitted violation of party discipline, promised to discontinue factional activity, and repudiated many of their left-wing followers. After this capitulation and admission of error, Zinoviev lost his post in the Comintern and Trotsky and Kamenev lost theirs in the Politburo.

Stalin's final reckoning with the "United Opposition" came in 1927, a year that witnessed Communist failure in Britain and in China, and for which the Opposition indicted the current leadership. Early in August, 1927, Trotsky and Zinoviev were expelled from the Central Committee. Thanks to the conciliatory efforts of Ordzhonikidze, however, this order was rescinded in return for their declaration of unconditional submission to the authority of the Central Committee. The truce was short-lived, as both men insisted on the eve of the long-overdue Fifteenth Party Congress that they be allowed to present, or at least to publicize, their views. When both requests were denied, Trotsky resorted to a speech-making tour, and in a stormy meeting of the Central Committee in October, 1927, he publicly revealed the existence of Lenin's Testament—a revelation for which he and Zinoviev irretrievably lost their seats on the Central Committee. On November 14, 1927, both were expelled from the party. The Fifteenth Party Congress which met in December, 1927, authorized the expulsion of some seventy-five of their followers. Stalin's victory now was final. In the middle of January, 1928, Trotsky and his family left for Alma Ata in Central Asia, the first stop on his long journey into exile that was to end with his murder in Mexico in 1940.

Following his defeat of Trotsky, Stalin adopted many of the policies of his heretical adversary, including rapid industrialization under central planning, collectivization of agriculture in order to eliminate the influence of the *kulaks*, and generally the abandonment of the NEP. This startling about-face was not endorsed by the so-called "Rightist" group, whose spokesmen were Bukharin, Tomsky, and Rykov. Stalin destroyed this opposition by the tactics he had perfected in his duel with Trotsky; namely, manipulation of elections, call for silence and unanimity in the interests of party unity, demotions, censorship, expulsions, arrests, rowdyism, and demand of unconditional capitulation. On June 2, 1929, Nikolai M. Shvernik (1888–1970) replaced Tomsky as head of Soviet trade unions, and shortly thereafter Molotov replaced Rykov as Chairman of the *Sovnarkom*. On July 3, Bukharin was removed from control of the Comintern, accused of "collaboration with capitalist elements" and Trotskyites, and in November, 1929, was expelled from the Politburo. On November 26, 1929, Bukharin, Tomsky, and Rykov signed a declaration dictated by Stalin admitting that their views were erroneous and those of the Central Committee were correct. Celebrating his fiftieth birthday in December, 1929, Stalin was hailed as undisputed master of the Soviet Union—a *vozhd*—the position he was to hold until his death in March, 1953.

FOREIGN POLICY IN THE 1920's

Observers of Soviet affairs have offered varied interpretations of Soviet foreign policy. Some have seen in it a mere continuation of traditional tsarist objectives. Others have viewed it as a blueprint for world conquest and the establishment of world communism. Sir Winston Churchill labelled it "a riddle wrapped in a mystery inside an enigma." However defined, from the very first, one of the cardinal objectives of Soviet foreign policy has been to provide security for the territorial base of the revolution.

To defend that base the Bolsheviks enlisted all available resources of conventional and unconventional diplomacy. Immediately after seizing power, they called upon all the belligerents to end the war, went on record as favoring peace without annexations and indemnities, and appealed to class-conscious workers everywhere to come to their aid. They also repudiated all foreign debts of the tsarist regime, condemned tsarist imperialism and its oppressive policy of Russification, and outwardly championed a policy of national self-determination and equality among nations. To expose the "designs of the capitalist states" before world opinion, they published secret treaties, and late in 1917, at Brest-Litovsk, entered into peace negotiations with the Central Powers. These negotiations ended on March 3, 1918, in a treaty whereby in return for security for the territorial base of the revolution, the Bolsheviks formally withdrew a militarily humiliated, economically exhausted, and territorially amputated Russia from World War I.

To protect the revolutionary base, between 1918 and 1920 the Bolsheviks fought against German, Austro-Hungarian, English, French, American, Japanese, Czechoslovak, Polish, White Russian, and other forces led by trained officers and supplied from abroad. In this struggle for survival they saw most of their territory overrun by their opponents at one time or another. Yet, in the end they emerged triumphant. By 1921 they had beaten down all open rebellion, ruthlessly suppressed every conspiracy, and either executed, imprisoned, or forced into exile the opposition leaders. And while the Bolsheviks continued to talk constantly of the danger of foreign intervention, in reality by 1921 the new Soviet state was free from foreign intervention. Except for the rapidly diminishing Japanese threat in the Far East, by 1920 all foreign governments had lifted the blockade of Russia and withdrawn their intervening forces, thanks to lack of common policy, disunity, indecision, and general war-weariness among their own people.

But while in one way the Bolsheviks were victorious, on the other hand they were suffering defeat. In spite of tremendous propaganda efforts, by fair means and foul, and great material and human sacrifices, no other country followed the Russian example. By 1921 the Bolsheviks had been successful in imposing their system only in Russia, Belorussia, the Ukraine, the Caucasus, and the former imperial territories in Asia. They tried, but failed, to gain control in Finland, Estonia, Latvia, Lithuania, and Poland. A series of Communist-led unrests in 1919 in Hungary, Germany, Austria, and Italy also ended in failure. With these setbacks, the prophesies and high hopes for an imminent world-wide revolution began to fade. Sober, realistic thinking brought home the realization that, in spite of the great stress of World War I, the postwar world was beginning to show remarkable stability, that the bourgeois governments were in full control of the situation, that the capitalist states were in no hurry to capitulate as the Bolsheviks had anticipated, and that these states were capable of hurting as well as helping the new Soviet state. As a result of this reorientation, which was strengthened by corresponding changes of attitude abroad, early in 1921 the Bolsheviks decided to abandon aggressive militant communism and formally adopted "co-existence" as the official conventional policy towards the rest of the world.

Though the NEP formally sanctioned the period of peaceful co-existence, the first signs leading to this policy had begun in the midst of the Civil War when the Bolsheviks signed a peace treaty with Estonia on February 2, 1920. On July 12, came a treaty with Finland; on February 26, 1921, with Persia; on February 28, with Afghanistan; on March 16, with Turkey; and on March 18, with Poland. Careful scrutiny of these treaties with bordering states reveals several interesting characteristics. In all, the Bolsheviks underlined the principle of self-determination of nations. In those with Persia, Turkey, and Afghanistan they even spoke of brotherhood of nations, friendship and solidarity in the struggle against Western imperialism, and as a token gesture of their sincerity the Bolsheviks renounced tsarist power policy. To appease the appetite of new nations, in all the treaties the Bolsheviks agreed to minor frontier adjustments, renounced all rights and claims to these territories, relieved all new states from financial responsibilities of the tsarist regime, and to some they even returned national treasures which had been held in Russia. All treaties pledged to refrain from inflammatory propaganda, prohibited the stationing on either's territory of forces hostile to the other, and in the Persian treaty both sides agreed to coordinate their military efforts in suppressing hostile forces.

In signing these treaties the Bolsheviks achieved four objectives: (1) they gained *de jure* recognition from their neighbors; (2) they broke through the Allied *cordon sanitaire;* (3) they isolated or neutralized their adversaries and accordingly forced them into a predetermined line of conduct; and (4) they erected their own legal protective barrier stretching from the Arctic Ocean to the Carpathians, and from the Straits to the Himalayas. Signing of various agreements with Norway, Denmark, Italy, Austria, Hungary, and Germany had the same objective. So it was too with the Anglo-Soviet trade agreement of March 16, 1921, which among other things called for the resumption of trade, prohibited the carrying on of hostile propaganda, and forbade either country to blockade the other. In other words, by all these treaties the Bolsheviks conceded little and gained a great deal. They strengthened their security and gained the minimum safety necessary against unprovoked attacks from abroad, hence security for their institutions, experimentations, and the projection of Russia's development along Marxist-Leninist lines.

There were many leading Bolsheviks who insisted that Russia rely exclusively on her own efforts in building up an industrial base. Reality, however, dictated that the adoption of such a stand would mean a slow and painful process. Quick results in rebuilding industries, in producing needed articles, in making needed repairs, and in tapping new sources of wealth, depended on foreign capital. This could be had through loans or in return for concessions; while foreign goods could come only by trade, hence the signing of a number of trade agreements and the maneuvering to enter into normal diplomatic relations. And while the Bolsheviks realized they would have to pay in one way or another for foreign economic aid, they believed they were in a strong bargaining position. On the one hand they were convinced that postwar prosperity in Europe could not be sustained without Soviet Russia's participation. On the other hand a number of West European businessmen, hoping to reap profits, were pressing their governments to reopen trade with Soviet Russia.

In the effort to attract foreign capital as well as to gain diplomatic recognition, the Bolsheviks encountered one insurmountable obstacle: *the claims of foreign states against Russia.* There were two kinds of claims: first, prewar debts; and second, war debts and claims for reparations for the destruction and confiscation of foreign property. The Bolsheviks tried to disassociate themselves from the first category of claims by arguing that prewar debts had been contracted by a government which had no popular support. To offset the second category of claims, the Bolsheviks made their own counterclaims, far greater than those of the Allies. They argued that the Allied Powers, without formal declaration of war, had invaded Russia, plotted against its government, furnished arms to insurrectionists, and destroyed property, all in violation of the basic principles of international law.

But while the Bolsheviks demurred in theory at recognizing obligations to repay money borrowed by their predecessors, in reality by not doing so they could hardly hope to obtain the new loans needed for reconstruction. On October 29, 1921, Georgi V. Chicherin (1872–1936), People's Commissar for Foreign Affairs, offered a compromise. While refusing to admit either legal or moral liability, he expressed Soviet willingness to meet these debts—the amount to be determined in subsequent negotiations in a conference convened for that purpose. The French, who had the largest investments in Russia—some sixteen billion francs—adopted an uncompromising stand. The English, with fewer investments, although expressing contempt for the Bolsheviks, somewhat naively visualized great opportunities for export, easing unemployment at home, reopening old markets, and outdistancing their French, Italian, and German competitors. The Germans and Norwegians went so far as to send trade delegations to Moscow.

Early in 1922, Bolshevik efforts to gain diplomatic recognition and economic aid from the major powers received strong encouragement when on January 6, the Allied Supreme Council, meeting at Cannes invited Soviet Russia to attend a general European conference at Genoa. The Bolsheviks accepted the offer without hesitation, feeling that they might gain much and could lose little. They were also confident that jealousies among the great powers would pave the way to profitable bargains with individual states. When the Genoa Conference opened on April 10, 1922, it was evident from the outset that both sides were contributing to its failure. The inviting powers—Britain, France, Italy, and Belgium—hoped by means of the conference to force the Bolsheviks to recognize Russia's prerevolutionary debts and to restore private property rights of foreigners within Soviet Russia. In formulating these objectives, the West European representatives were strongly influenced by the widespread belief that Soviet Russia's economic situation was so deplorable that however much her delegates might bluff and bluster at first they would eventually yield and accept almost anything. Soviet delegates, on the other hand, viewed the purpose of the conference in an entirely different light. They hoped to gain loans with which to rebuild the economy of Soviet Russia according to their own designs, and diplomatic recognition from the major powers.

American refusal to participate in the Genoa conference deflated Bolshevik expectations, as they were firmly convinced that not Europe alone but the United States was wealthy enough to lend money on the scale necessary to rebuild Russia. This was not the first American action that had either puzzled or disappointed the Bolsheviks. On March 25, 1921, Secretary of State Charles Evans Hughes, over their protests, had excluded the Bolsheviks from participation in a Washington conference to discuss naval affairs and Pacific and Far Eastern problems. In the summer of 1921, however, in answer to Soviet appeals for aid to the famine victims, the American Relief Administration was organized under the direction of Herbert Hoover. American unwillingness to take part in the Genoa negotiations and in Russian economic recovery left the Bolsheviks too little to gain for them to make concessions to European powers. Instead they decided to use the conference as a propaganda platform from which to call for peace and total disarmament. They also utilized it to exploit differences among various powers in open and secret negotiations, which on April 16, 1922, culminated in the signing of the Soviet-German treaty at Rapallo.

In its terms, which had been in the process of negotiation for many months before the Genoa Conference, and in its many-sided implications, the Rapallo treaty was a triumph for both German and Soviet diplomacy. The two powers, outcasts of European society, re-extended to each other the *de jure* recognition which had been disrupted in November, 1918, renounced all military and civilian war claims against each other, and agreed to enter into closer economic cooperation. Needless to say, for some time thereafter, the Bolsheviks considered the Rapallo treaty a model for other treaties with Western Powers.

But although Rapallo was a great Soviet diplomatic triumph, the Genoa Conference and the subsequent Hague Conference (June 26–July 20, 1922) concerned with the problem of debts and compensations, were basically failures from the Bolshevik point of view. They failed to secure the needed loans and large-scale economic assistance for Russia's reconstruction and further industrialization. Moreover, except for Germany, no major power granted diplomatic recognition to the new Soviet state. The Bolsheviks suffered another setback at a conference on the Straits which met at Lausanne, Switzerland, from November 20, 1922, to July 24, 1923. Although they skillfully used delaying tactics, and insisted that the Straits be closed to keep the British fleet out of the Black Sea, on July 24, 1923, the final document embodied the British position. It provided freedom of navigation through the Straits for war, and merchant vessels both during war and peace. Turkey was given the right to search ships if she herself were at war. No single power could send a larger fleet through the Straits than the largest possessed by a Black Sea power. The Straits and the islands of Lemnos, Tenedos, and Imbros were to be demilitarized, with England, France, Italy, and Japan being responsible for effecting the demilitarization. Late in 1923, the Bolsheviks suffered still another resounding defeat when the Comintern-sponsored revolution in Germany ended in total failure—failure which relegated into the distant future all hopes of extending the Soviet experiment outside Russia.

In spite of these setbacks, as the year 1924 progressed, Soviet diplomacy began to pile triumph on triumph. Convinced that the Bolsheviks were firmly entrenched, amazed at Russian economic recovery under the NEP, hoping to profit from normal diplomatic and commercial relations, and in some cases swayed by pressure groups at home, the Western Powers began to extend diplomatic recognition to the Soviet government. England recognized the USSR on February 1, 1924. Italy followed suit on February 7; Norway on February 15; Austria on February 25; Sweden on March 15; Denmark on June 18; Mexico on August 4; France on October 28, 1924; and Japan on January 20, 1925. Thanks to these recognitions, in less than a year Soviet diplomacy achieved one of the basic goals it had sought desperately since 1918: it became a respectable member of the world community.

This sudden rise of the international status of the Soviet Union acted unfavorably on her relations with bordering states. As noted previously, when the Bolsheviks earlier were fighting for their very existence, Lenin was willing to grant more territory to Russia's neighbors than were "Clemenceau or Curzon," even if in so doing he violated the principle of national self-determination. As long as Bolshevik power was weak there were no controversies with border states along ethnic lines. With the consolidation of their power at home and the growth of their prestige abroad, responsible Bolshevik leaders began to clamor at major party and soviet gatherings for the revision of frontiers, and for protection of their co-nationals—demands which created ill feelings between the USSR and its neighbors.

Alongside the growth of power and international prestige, the Bolsheviks initiated in the mid-1920's an offensive for neutrality and non-aggression pacts to further strengthen the territorial base of the revolution. Officially, this offensive began with the signing of a treaty with Turkey on December 17, 1925, which was followed on April 24, 1926, by one with Germany; with Afghanistan on August 8; on September 28, 1926, with Lithuania; and on October 1, 1927, with Persia. Under Bolshevik guidance there also appeared bilateral treaties between Persia and Afghanistan, and Turkey and Afghanistan. All of these treaties with the

Near and Middle Eastern countries were negotiated and signed under the banner of struggle against British colonial imperialism and freedom for the oppressed Asian people. The treaty with Afghanistan contained, in fact, germs of an anti-British alliance of Asiatic countries under Moscow's sponsorship—an action which was not regarded with favor by the British.

Anglo-Soviet relations deteriorated for other reasons as well. The hopes which both sides had placed in the trade agreement of March 16, 1921, failed to materialize. Bolshevik inability to agree on settlement of old debts, and the Comintern-sponsored bitter anti-British propaganda contributed to the ill feelings. The Labor government's *de jure* recognition of the USSR in no way altered the uneasy truce. In fact, it indirectly contributed to its deterioration. Both Liberals and Conservatives voiced bitter disapproval of the Labor government's attempts to negotiate two treaties with the USSR, and on October 8, 1924, they were able to force its fall. In the midst of the new elections, on October 25, 1924, the British press published the famous Zinoviev Letter to British Communist leaders instructing them on how to prepare for seizure of power in England. While its authenticity has been questioned, the letter nevertheless contributed to an overwhelming Conservative victory at the polls and enabled them to refuse to honor the negotiated treaties.

Throughout the year 1925, Anglo-Soviet relations deteriorated rapidly, thanks to increased Bolshevik activity in Asia. In May, 1926, a real crisis developed when Bolshevik leaders jubilantly greeted the general strike in England as a forerunner of the socialist revolution, and publicly offered financial aid to the strikers. The British rejected Bolshevik contentions that technically the Soviet government did not take part in these and other anti-British actions. Finally, on May 12, 1927, the British government approved a police search of ARCOS, a branch of the Soviet trade delegation—a search which exposed the existence of a Soviet espionage system. This revelation, in spite of Soviet protests of diplomatic immunity of the trade delegation, led on May 26, 1927, to formal termination of the Anglo-Soviet trade agreement of March, 1921, and breaking off of diplomatic relations.

Bolshevik setbacks in relations with England in 1927 coincided with the Bolshevik defeat in China. From the first, in their quest to strengthen the territorial base of the revolution, the Bolsheviks had assigned to China a significant role. They felt that control of China's vast human and natural resources would be a key to their own security as well as to the control of most of the Asian mainland and the islands of the Southwest Pacific. They also believed that their befriending of China would be a potential blow to Western capitalism by depriving it of a source of raw materials and a vast market for finished products.

But to bring China within their sphere of influence, the Bolsheviks had to overcome a number of barriers inherited from the tsarist period.

They took far-reaching steps toward overcoming some of these by supporting the principle of national self-determination, by various appeals and
offers directed to the Asian peoples, and by letters directed to Asian
leaders. Of these documents, the Karakhan Declaration of July 25, 1919,
addressed to the Peking and Canton governments of China, contributed
the most to setting the tone of Sino-Soviet relations. Made at a time when
the Bolsheviks controlled only a very small area in Central Russia and
were struggling against great odds for their very existence, the Karakhan
Declaration was a master stroke of propaganda. To disassociate themselves in the eyes of the Chinese from the tsarist imperialist pressure and
exploitation in China, by the stroke of a pen the Bolsheviks renounced
tsarist power politics and all concessions and privileges the old regime
had enjoyed in Manchuria and on the Chinese Eastern Railway. They also
declared that the new Russia was bringing peace, freedom, and assistance
to the enslaved peoples of Asia in general and the Chinese in particular.

These promises succeeded in capturing the imagination of many Chinese intellectuals and revolutionary leaders who wished to restore order
and unity to their country. Bolshevik influence in China rose to unprecedented heights and began to climb higher when in the course of 1920 and
1921, in the wake of the departing forces of intervention, Red Armies
moved closer to the old frontiers. Now victorious, the Bolsheviks forgot
the high-sounding but expedient promises and pledges of the Karakhan
Declaration and other documents. Instead they began to exert, together
with the Japanese, great pressure on the two Chinese governments, to
exploit disagreements and disunity, and to bribe Chinese officials and
whole political groups. Soon, too, they forced the return of the Chinese
Eastern Railway under virtually the old tsarist conditions. They also
helped to organize the Communist party of China, which, as a branch of
the Comintern, was an effective tool of Moscow.

And while these developments contributed greatly to reversing pro-
Bolshevik sentiment among the Chinese, it was Bolshevik policy towards
Mongolia which brought Sino-Soviet relations almost to the breaking
point. Early in 1921, under the pretext of driving out General Baron Unger-
Sternberg, the Soviets intervened in Mongolia. With their encouragement
and help, the Mongolian People's Provisional Government was formed on
April 10, 1921, in Kiakhta. Following occupation of Mongolia, the Bolsheviks signed a treaty of friendship with that government on November 5,
1921. It called for an end to extraterritorial rights and other old privileges,
but granted the Bolsheviks the right to operate the postal and telegraph
services. Mongolia, the ancient country of nomads, began to march towards *Pax Communa* under Moscow's guidance, in spite of the
fact that for centuries the Chinese had considered Mongolia a part of
China. In December, 1921, the Bolsheviks also helped to found the Tannu-
Tuva Republic in the highly strategic and rich basin of the Yenisey River.

These Bolshevik gains at China's expense were possible because of China's utter helplessness and Bolshevik willingness to negotiate and make promises. By far the most important of these promises was an agreement of January 26, 1923, with Chinese statesman Dr. Sun Yat-sen. In return for Dr. Sun's acceptance of Chinese Communists into his Kuomintang party, the Bolsheviks promised military and organizational help, pledged not to advocate communism for China, affirmed that they had no intention of separating Outer Mongolia from China, and agreed that the future of the Chinese Eastern Railway be settled jointly. The last two points also figured prominently in the Bolshevik agreement with the Chinese government in Peking on May 31, 1924.

As realists, the Bolsheviks knew well that they could succeed in China only if the Japanese would not interfere militarily. It was necessary then to pacify Japan—a task that proved quite difficult. Because of Japanese occupation of the Primorsk Province and the island of Sakhalin, Soviet-Japanese relations were anything but cordial. The issue of Japanese fishing rights in Russian-claimed waters contributed to further misunderstanding. Finally, and most decisively, Bolshevik objectives in China, and especially in Manchuria, collided with long-standing Japanese interests there. Only after prolonged negotiations and arguments, Japan and the Soviet Union signed an agreement on January 20, 1925. This provided for the resumption of normal diplomatic as well as broad economic relations. It also stipulated that both parties were "to live in peace and amity with each other," respect each other's territorial rights, and refrain from subversion. While by this agreement Soviet diplomacy forced Japan into predetermined conduct, at the same time the agreement carried the germs of further complications in the future.

With Japan temporarily pacified, the Bolsheviks turned back towards China, where for some time their political and military aides and advisers had been penetrating in great numbers. There were sharp disagreements among top Bolshevik leaders on methods and tactics to be employed in China. Both Stalin and Trotsky wished to turn the Chinese national revolution into a Communist revolution. The death of Sun Yat-sen in March, 1925, which left China temporarily leaderless, appeared as an opportune moment to do it. In the summer of 1925, Chinese Communists attempted to seize the leadership of the Kuomintang. Their efforts, however, were frustrated when Dr. Sun's successor, Chiang Kai-shek, arrested and executed several Communist leaders in Canton in March, 1926. In his further consolidation of power in China, on April 11, 1927, Chiang disarmed the Communists in Shanghai, expelled all Bolshevik advisers, and broke the Kuomintang's ties with Moscow. To add to this disaster of the Soviets' China policy, on April 6, 1927, the Peking government, with whom the Soviets maintained official relations, approved a police raid on Soviet diplomatic establishments in Peking. A number of Embassy personnel were arrested, and documents seized implicated Soviet officials in the anti-government conspiracy. On April 10, 1927, the USSR broke off diplomatic relations with Peking. Chiang's victory over the Peking government brought only further trouble for Soviet officials in Manchuria connected with the operation of the Chinese Eastern Railway.

Soviet diplomatic reverses in England and China in 1927 and increased bitterness of the power struggle between Stalin and Trotsky were the two last major signs of the passing era of the NEP. Stalin's defeat of his rivals, his adoption of the slogan of "socialism in one country," and inauguration of the policy of industrialization and collectivization were also reflected in foreign policy. These gigantic undertakings called for additional security measures. Defense of the USSR became a sacred duty towards which the vast Comintern organization was alerted at its Sixth Congress in 1928.

Simultaneously on the conventional level, though voicing reservations, the Bolsheviks began to participate in the disarmament efforts of the League of Nations, where future Commissar for Foreign Affairs Maxim M. Litvinov (1876–1951) proposed complete and rapid disarmament to be guaranteed by a permanent system of international inspection. In 1928 also, the USSR became the first power to sign and ratify the Kellogg-Briand Pact calling for renunciation of war. On February 9, 1929, the Bolsheviks created under their own supervision an Eastern pact for the renunciation of war—the Litvinov Protocol, which was signed in Moscow by the USSR, Poland, Rumania, Estonia, and Latvia. These efforts were followed by the negotiation and signing of a series of non-aggression pacts in 1932: with Finland on January 24, 1932; with Latvia on February 8, 1932; with Estonia on April 5, 1932; with Poland on July 25, 1932; and with France on November 29, 1932. By these efforts, Soviet diplomacy tied itself to the French security system.

Striking an alliance with France was a victory for Moscow. In the Bolshevik view, France was a first-class European power which constantly threatened the security of the USSR with intervention. Although the two countries had had diplomatic relations since 1924, mutual suspicion prevented them from close cooperation. Bolshevik repudiation of tsarist debts, of which the French held a large share, contributed to further misunderstanding. While both powers had to yield on certain points to overcome these deep-rooted suspicions, the most significant factor that brought them together was the rise of Adolf Hitler in Germany.

The 1920's, in spite of numerous errors and disappointments, were on the whole years of great achievement for the Bolsheviks in their quest for security to the territorial base of the revolution. Both in Europe and in Asia, on the conventional level, they pacified their immediate adversaries. With some they signed various bilateral treaties which forced them into a predetermined line of conduct, while to other states they offered trade and other concessions. At the same time, on the unconventional level, the Bolsheviks succeeded in capturing the imagination of many underprivileged nations, offered them aid and posed as the champions of their freedom and independence. Against great odds, some of their own making and others inherited from their predecessors, and by using fair and foul means, the Bolsheviks elevated their state from obscurity and isolation to international prestige.

SUGGESTED READINGS

AVRICH, PAUL. Kronstadt, 1921. Princeton: Princeton University Press, 1970.

BABITSKY, PAUL, and JOHN RIMBERG. The Soviet Film Industry. New York: Praeger, 1955.

BATSELL, WALTER R. Soviet Rule in Russia. New York: Macmillan, 1929.

BAYKOV, ALEXANDER. The Development of the Soviet Economic System. Cambridge: Cambridge University Press, 1946.

BORKENAU, FRANZ. The Communist International. London: Faber, 1938.

BRANDT, CONRAD. Stalin's Failure in China, 1924–1927. Cambridge: Harvard University Press, 1958.

BROWN, EDWARD J. Russian Literature Since the Revolution. Revised and Enlarged Edition. Cambridge: Harvard University Press, 1982.

CARR, EDWARD H. Foundations of a Planned Economy, 1926–1929. Parts 1 and 2. New York: Macmillan, 1976.

———. The Interregnum, 1923–1924. New York: Macmillan, 1954.

———. Socialism in One Country. New York: Macmillan, 1958.

CHAMBERLIN, WILLIAM H. Soviet Russia. A Living Record and a History. Boston: Little, Brown, 1930.

CURTISS, JOHN S. The Russian Church and the Soviet State, 1917–1950. Boston: Little, Brown, 1953.

DANIELS, ROBERT V. The Conscience of the Revolution: Communist Opposition in Soviet Russia. Cambridge: Harvard University Press, 1960.

DEGRAS, JANE, ed. The Communist International, 1919–1943. Documents. 2 vols. London: Oxford University Press, 1956–1958.

———, ed. Soviet Documents on Foreign Policy, 1917–1932. 2 vols. London: Oxford University Press, 1951–1952.

DENNIS, A. L. P. The Foreign Policies of Soviet Russia. New York: Dutton, 1924.

DEUTSCHER, ISAAC. The Prophet Unarmed: Trotsky, 1921–1929. New York: Oxford University Press, 1959.

———. Stalin: A Political Biography. 2nd edition. New York: Oxford University Press, 1967.

DMYTRYSHYN, BASIL. Moscow and the Ukraine, 1918–1953. New York: Bookman, 1956.

ERLICH, ALEXANDER. The Soviet Industrialization Debate, 1924–1928. Cambridge: Harvard University Press, 1960.

EUDIN, XENIA J., and H. H. FISHER. Soviet Russia and the West, 1920–1927. A Documentary Survey. Stanford: Stanford University Press, 1957.

———. and ROBERT C. NORTH. Soviet Russia and the East, 1920–1927. A Documentary Survey. Stanford: Stanford University Press, 1957.

FISCHER, LOUIS. The Life of Lenin. New York: Harper & Row, 1964.

———. The Soviets in World Affairs. 2nd edition. 2 vols. Princeton: Princeton University Press, 1951.

FISCHER, RUTH. *Stalin and German Communism.* Cambridge: Harvard University Press, 1948.

FISHER, HAROLD H. *The Famine in Soviet Russia, 1919–1923.* New York: Macmillan, 1927.

KENNAN, GEORGE F. *Russia and the West Under Lenin and Stalin.* Boston: Little, Brown, 1960.

————. *Soviet Foreign Policy, 1917–1941.* New York: Van Nostrand, 1960.

LEYDA, J. *Kino: A History of the Russian and Soviet Film.* New York: Macmillan, 1960.

LUCKYJ, GEORGE. *Literary Politics in the Soviet Ukraine, 1917–1934.* New York: Columbia University Press, 1956.

MCKENZIE, KERMIT E. *Comintern and World Revolution.* New York: Columbia University Press, 1964.

NORTH, ROBERT C. *Moscow and Chinese Communists.* Stanford: Stanford University Press, 1953.

PAYNE, ROBERT. *The Life and Death of Lenin.* New York: Simon & Schuster, 1964.

RESHETAR, JOHN S. JR. *A Concise History of the Communist Party of the Soviet Union.* New York: Praeger, 1960.

RUBENSTEIN, ALVIN Z., ed. *The Foreign Policy of the Soviet Union.* New York: Random House, 1960.

SCHAPIRO, LEONARD. *The Communist Party of the Soviet Union.* New York: Random House, 1960.

SIMMONS, ERNEST J., ed. *Through the Glass of Soviet Literature.* New York: Columbia University Press, 1953.

SLONIM, MARC. *Modern Russian Literature.* New York: Oxford University Press, 1953.

————. *Russian Theater From the Empire to the Soviets.* New York: World, 1961.

SOLOMON, SUSAN GROSS. *The Soviet Agrarian Debate: A Controversy in Social Science, 1923–1929.* Boulder: Westview Press, 1977.

SPINKA, MATTHEW. *The Church in Soviet Russia.* New York: Oxford University Press, 1956.

STRUVE, GLEB. *Russian Literature Under Lenin and Stalin, 1917–1953.* Norman: University of Oklahoma Press, 1971.

SULLIVANT, ROBERT S. *Soviet Politics in the Ukraine, 1917–1957.* New York: Columbia University Press, 1962.

TARACOUZIO, T. A. *War and Peace in Soviet Diplomacy.* New York: Macmillan, 1940.

TIMASHEFF, N. S. *Religion in Soviet Russia, 1917–1942.* New York: Sheed & Ward, 1942.

TUCKER, ROBERT C. *Stalin as Revolutionary, 1879–1929.* New York: Norton, 1973.

ULAM, ADAM B. *Expansion and Coexistence: The History of Soviet Foreign Policy, 1917–1967.* New York: Praeger, 1968.

WHITING, ALLEN S. *Soviet Policies in China, 1917–1924.* New York: Columbia University Press, 1954.

ZAVALISHIN, VYACHESLAV. *Early Soviet Writers.* New York: Praeger, 1958.

✄ V I

THE REGIMENTED THIRTIES

THE INDUSTRIAL REVOLUTION

Stalin's triumph first over the "Left" and then the "Right" opposition had two very significant implications. First, it left him the unchallenged master of the Soviet Union—a *vozhd* surrounded by "yes men"—the position he was to hold until his death in March, 1953. Second, it ushered in a new era in Soviet history, an era to which scholars have attached different labels and interpretations. Some have described it as "The Second Revolution." Others have named it "Russia's Iron Age." There are those who labelled it "The Era of the Five Year Plans," while some have simply called it "The Stalin Era." However designated, Stalin's triumph over his rivals was fateful for the USSR and the rest of the world as well.

Stalin inaugurated his absolute one-man rule by launching the First Five Year Plan, aimed at rapid industrialization of the Soviet Union. The surprising element of this action was not the plan itself (the plan had been in preparation for several years), but the decision to launch it. Throughout his struggle with the "Left" opposition, Stalin publicly advocated a policy of prosperity, gradualness, and caution in both domestic and foreign policy. For instance, he dubbed Trotsky, Kamenev, and Zinoviev as "super-industrializers" when they suggested that in view of Russia's economic recovery during the NEP, it was possible to raise the output by slightly less than 20 per cent per year. He also dismissed the opposition-proposed hydroelectric project on the Dnieper River in the Ukraine, the famous Dnieprostroy. He is reported to have remarked that for Russia to build this dam would be similar to a peasant buying a gramophone instead of a cow. Before long, however, the Dnieprostroy became the first major achievement of Soviet planning.

What *really* caused Stalin to change his mind so abruptly is not exactly clear. Most scholars believe, though, that an immediate determinant was the food crisis which began to reach dangerous proportions in 1927 and 1928. We noted in our previous chapter that following the adoption of the NEP, Soviet Russian agriculture recovered to the prewar level as early as 1925. Further progress, however, was hindered by two factors. The first was the existence of the multitude of small farms which were capable of producing only enough to satisfy the needs of their owners. The second was the refusal of the more industrious peasants, the *kulaks*, who produced grain beyond their immediate needs, to deliver it at low prices fixed by the state. In 1927, for instance, thanks to this form of "sabotage," but above all as a result of climatic conditions, state acquisitions of grain from the peasants fell some two million tons short of the minimum required. To remedy this situation, the Central Committee of the party, late in 1927 and early in 1928, instructed all local party members to take energetic measures to extract grain from the peasants, and those members who showed any leniency were purged. As might be expected, the peasants resisted by all the devices known to them the party pressures, which in Stalin's own words included "administrative arbitrariness, violation of revolutionary law, raids on peasant houses [and] illegal searches." In view of these developments, Stalin, while triumphant over his opponents, found himself in a real dilemma. To give in to peasant demands for higher prices might have meant placing additional burdens on the town population. Refusal to yield to the peasantry, on the other hand, as one observer aptly put it, "entailed the threat of famine and unrest in the towns." The dilemma demanded a radical solution. Stalin found the answer in the First Five Year Plan.

Stalin's decision to industrialize stemmed also from his idea of "socialism in one country," and above all from his belief in the ultimate triumph of world revolution, which the successful industrialization was to promote. He made this point quite explicit in January, 1931, in a speech defending his call for increased tempo of industrialization. "Our obligations to the world proletariat," he said, "were more serious and more important" than those to the workers and peasants of the USSR.

We achieved victory not solely through the efforts of the working class of the U.S.S.R., but also thanks to the support of the working class of the world. Without this support we would have been torn to pieces long ago. It is said that our country is the shock brigade of the proletariat of all countries. This is a fitting definition. But this imposes very serious obligations upon us. Why does the international proletariat support us? How did we merit this support? By the fact that we were the first to hurl ourselves into the battle against capitalism, we were the first to establish a working-class state, we were the first to start building socialism. By the fact that we are doing work which, if successful, will change the whole world and free the entire working class. But what is needed for success? The elimination of our backwardness, the development of a high Bolshevik tempo of construction. We must march forward in such a way that the working class of the whole world, looking at us, may say: This is my vanguard, this is my shock brigade, this is my working-class state, this is my fatherland; they are promoting their cause, which is *our* cause, and they are doing this well; let us support them against the capitalists and promote the cause of the world revolution.

The bold and ambitious estimates of the First Five Year Plan rested on four premises. First, it was presupposed that during the next quinquennium there would be no serious harvest failure. Second, a substantial expansion of foreign trade and an increase in long-term credits were envisaged. Third, a sharp increase "in the qualitative indices of national economic construction," such as cost of production and crop yield, was anticipated. And finally, the plan expected "a fall in the proportionate weight of expenditure on national defense in the general economic system." None of these expectations, however, were fulfilled. The harvest of 1930 was good, but those of 1931 and 1932 were grave natural and man-made disasters. Moreover, as a result of the great world depression, prices of grain on the world market declined, and this decline in turn acted quite unfavorably on the Soviet long-term credit position. A hope for increase in the productivity of labor proved also to be a serious miscalculation. Instead of doubling, the actual increase of productivity at the end of 1932 was about 40 per cent. This then affected the estimated cost of the plan, since the expected fall of costs and of industrial wholesale prices was based on the rise of productivity of labor. Finally, the threat of war with Japan, following Japanese occupation of Manchuria in 1931–1932, forced the planners to increase defense expenditures.

These serious miscalculations, however, had little effect on the planners, whose optimism and fanaticism surpassed all limits. Speaking in November, 1929, at a mammoth rally commemorating the twelfth anniversary of the Bolshevik seizure of power, Stalin declared that the Soviet

Union was "advancing full steam ahead along the path of industrialization to Socialism, leaving behind the agelong 'Russian' backwardness," and
becoming a country of metal, automobiles, and tractors. To overcome
Russia's backwardness faster, and then "to catch up with and to overcome
the capitalist world" in industrial and economic development, the Sixteenth Party Congress, held from June 26 to July 13, 1930, adopted the
slogan "The Five Year Plan in Four Years." To help realize that goal,
appeals as well as orders were issued to all segments of the population at
home and sympathizers abroad. To those who argued that the tempo of
industrialization was too fast, early in 1931, using Marxist and nationalist
arguments and adding a few distortions of his own, Stalin replied in the
negative. "The pace must not be reduced," he declared.

On the contrary we must increase it as much as is within our powers and possibilities. This is dictated to us by our obligations to the workers and peasants of
the USSR. This is dictated to us by our obligations to the working class of the
world.

  To reduce the tempo would mean to fall behind. And those who fall behind
get beaten. But we do not want to be beaten. No, we refuse to be beaten! One
feature of the history of old Russia was the continual beating she suffered because of her backwardness. She was beaten by the Mongol Khans. She was
beaten by the Turkish beys. She was beaten by the Swedish feudal lords. She
was beaten by the Polish and Lithuanian gentry. She was beaten by the British
and French capitalists. She was beaten by the Japanese barons. All beat her—
because of her backwardness, military backwardness, cultural backwardness,
industrial backwardness, and agricultural backwardness. They beat her because
to do so was profitable and could be done with impunity. . . . Such is the law
of the exploiters—to beat the backward and the weak. It is the jungle law of
capitalism. You are backward, you are weak—therefore you are wrong; hence,
you can be beaten and enslaved. You are mighty—therefore you are right;
hence we must be wary of you. That is why we must no longer lag behind. . . .
  We are fifty or a hundred years behind the advanced countries. We must
make good this distance in ten years. Either we do it, or we shall be crushed.

On December 31, 1932, the First Five Year Plan was declared officially completed ahead of schedule, and most of its objectives fulfilled.
The reported fulfillment, however, contained many discrepancies. In
terms of ruble value (valued at 1926–1927 prices), many items showed a
marked increase. For instance, the capital goods industries registered an
increase of two and one-half times during the First Five Year Plan. The
output of machinery increased four times and that of oil doubled. The
output of electric power increased more than two and one-half times. The
production of large-scale industry showed an increase of 118 per cent.
The output of electrical equipment overfulfilled its quota, as did the
collectivization of peasant households. But the First Five Year Plan also

lagged at many points. Instead of the projected 10,000,000 tons, iron and steel attained only 6,200,000 and 5,900,000 tons respectively. The output of coal was some 10,000,000 tons short of its 75,000,000 ton target. The production of grain fell some 36,000,000 tons below the 106,000,000 ton estimate. Heavy metallurgy approached its goal by only 67.7 per cent, and consumer goods by 73.5 per cent.

This uneven performance of the First Five Year Plan gave rise to various diametrically opposed interpretations. None of these judgments seem to be valid, for, as one observer rightly noted, "the Soviet economy was planned not for the harmony of its different branches, but for one single purpose, namely the most rapid industrialization and preparation of effective national defense." This the First Five Year Plan achieved. In slightly more than four years the Soviet Union constructed seventeen new blast furnaces and modernized another twenty. It installed forty-five new open-hearth furnaces and modernized another twenty. It built fifteen new rolling mills and reconstructed twelve. It laid the foundation for two new iron and steel centers, those of Magnitogorsk in the Urals and Kuznetsk in Central Siberia. Finally, the period of the First Five Year Plan gave birth to such new industries as synthetic rubber, plastics, and aviation.

In January, 1934, the Seventeenth Party Congress formally adopted the Second Five Year Plan covering the years 1933–1937. The fundamental task of the Second Plan was "the completion of technical construction in the whole of national economy." This, in turn, meant a slight lowering of targets and paying more attention to qualitative improvements. The Second Five Year Plan, like its predecessor, assigned first priority and a high rate of investment to heavy industry. To overcome the lagging of iron and steel, the Second Plan ordered construction of 45 new blast furnaces, 164 open-hearth furnaces and 107 rolling mills. These additions, it was hoped, would allow the production of 16,000,000 tons of pig iron and 17,000,000 tons of steel in 1937. Tied to these goals was a call for considerable extension of machine tool production (milling, grinding, gear-cutting, automatic and semiautomatic machines) and development of the production of non-ferrous metals. Copper was to be developed in the Urals and in Kazakhstan (near Lake Balkash); lead in Kazakhstan, in the Altai region, in the Northern Caucasus and in the Far East; zinc in the Urals and in Siberia; aluminum in Southern Ukraine, east of Leningrad, and in the middle Urals; nickel in the Urals; tin in Kazakhstan and in the Trans-Baikal region; and magnesium in the Ukraine and in the northern Urals.

The Second Plan called also for improvement and double-tracking of the main railroad lines, which were overburdened with passengers, coal, iron, and wheat. This improvement, however, was impossible until the iron industry expanded considerably. To remove some of the pressures on the railroads, the Second Plan provided for construction of the Moscow-

S.H.Bryant

IRON AND STEEL INDUSTRY
OF THE U S S R

● Pig iron and steel ✕ Iron mining

S Steel ▬ Manganese mining

⊕ Pig iron

MILES
0   300   600

0   600
KILOMETERS

Volga Canal, widening of the old Marinsky canal system (which links the
Baltic with the Volga), improvement of river port facilities and the river
fleet, and for construction of highways linking the major cities of European Russia. The Second Five Year Plan, like its predecessor, emphasized
the need to develop untapped resources of Soviet Asia, especially the coal
and iron of the Ural-Kuznetsk complex. This emphasis had a three-fold
goal. First, it aimed at bringing industry into closer proximity to the
sources of raw material and power. Second, it sought to overcome the economic and cultural backwardness of various peoples of Soviet Asia. And
third, should this goal materialize, it would impress the multitude of
Asia's population. Finally, unlike its predecessor, the Second Five Year
Plan paid some attention to the development of light industries, housing,
bus service, and water and sanitation projects.

The official results of the Second Five Year Plan resembled in many
ways those of the First; namely, some items reached the estimated targets
while others lagged behind. Thus, for instance, steel production rose from
5,900,000 tons in 1932 to 17,600,000 tons in 1937. Rolled steel trebled in

NON-FERROUS METALLURGY
IN THE U S S R

◑ Lead and zinc mining

◉ Smelting center

▼ Copper mining

T Tin mining

output. The machine-making industry showed a threefold rise in output, while the automobile industry registered an eightfold increase. But there were many industries and products that did not fare as well. Heavy industry and pig iron, for instance, were slightly behind the assigned goal. Production of oil was 30,500,000 tons instead of the planned 46,800,000. Coal output was 128,000,000 tons instead of the projected 152,000,000. Instead of doubling, the production of cotton goods increased by 40 per cent and that of woolen goods by only 22 per cent. Notwithstanding these shortcomings, by the end of the Second Five Year Plan the Soviet Union was emerging as a strong industrial country. It possessed an increased capacity to produce iron, steel, coal, and electric power. It also had a whole range of new industries, such as aviation, tractor, locomotive, chemical, aluminum, copper, nickel, and tin. In other words, the Soviet Union at the end of the 1930's had a well-established industrial base capable of further expansion and growth.

Soviet industrialization must be viewed not only through the quantitative growth of its industry and its output capacity, but also through non-

Sam H. Bryant

Kaliningrad
Minsk
Riga
Leningrad
Archangel
Lvov
Kiev
Kaluga
Odessa
MOSCOW
Tula
Yaroslavl
Gorky
Lipetsk
Perm
Kherson
Voronezh
Sverdlovsk
Ufa
Cheliabinsk
Saratov
Kulbyshev
Krasnodar
Volgograd
Kurgan
Armavir
Orenburg
Novosibirsk
Kutaisi
Astrakhan
Orsk
Omsk
Kemerovo
Krasnoiarsk
Tbilisi
Pavlodar
Akmolinsk
Irkutsk
Baku
Karaganda
Novokuznetsk
Rubtsovsk
Ulan-Ude
Blagoveshchensk
Komsomolsk
Khabarovsk
Frunze
Alma-Ata
Tashkent
Vladivostok

MACHINE BUILDING INDUSTRIES in the U S S R

1 Kremenchug
2 Dniepropetrovsk
3 Gorlovka
4 Kharkov

○ Primary centers ◎ Diversified machinery
● Heavy machinery Ⓐ Agricultural machinery
⊖ Transport machinery
Ⓓ Electrical machinery
⊗ Machine tools

economic indices, and above all through the methods employed to produce these results. In the absence of machinery and skill and the presence of abundant manpower, the results were produced by sheer force. Workers were mobilized, directed, and regimented. Since, as we have seen, Stalin considered the industrialization program a race against time, the experts who prepared the plans for every sector of the economy and for every industry were ordered to set the quotas high. Nonfulfillment of these quotas, which in most instances bore little relation to previous performance, gave Stalin an excuse to blame someone else. Criticism of the excessive demands was impossible because this implied criticism of the party line, which was considered infallible. Stalin tolerated only those suggestions which called for increasing the output and rewarded those who overfulfilled their assigned quotas, regardless of the methods used. Those who suggested caution or who failed to exceed the plan were branded "saboteurs" and automatically invited imprisonment, exile, or even death. By these policies, Stalin intensified the totalitarian nature of the system and strengthened his absolute control over it.

LUMBERING, PAPER MILLING
and WOODWORKING in the U S S R

○ Important centers (large symbols)
⊙ Lumbering
⊕ Woodworking
Ⓜ Paper milling

Waste of material and great human sacrifices were additional by-products of the fulfillment and nonfulfillment mania. Workers built factories for which no equipment was available, and delivered equipment to plants unable to accommodate it. Many structures were built in the wrong places and had to be abandoned, while, because of poor workmanship, some collapsed before they were finished. The food supply was precarious, housing overcrowded and inadequate, and working conditions in old and new industrial centers were inhuman. Everywhere safety was neglected, barest needs were not provided for, and men and machinery were cruelly overworked. But nothing mattered so long as the plan was either fulfilled or overfulfilled. If fulfillment was really impossible, those "enterprising" officials who wanted to survive either bribed their immediate superiors or manipulated figures and falsified accounts. So long as they succeeded in "covering their tracks" by any device imaginable, no one asked embarrassing questions. When one failed to "fulfill" his part of the plan, the authorities accepted no excuse. Under those conditions, as one observer aptly put it, Soviet "planning bred a new kind of rugged individualism."

In the initial stages, industrializing efforts and propaganda succeeded in capturing the imagination of many Soviet youths. Notwithstanding all sorts of hardships and inadequacies, there appeared throughout the country "shock brigades" and other volunteer groups trying to build factories and vast public projects with bare hands. Because youthful idealism did not last long, authorities were forced to adopt and apply other measures. To stop the heavy turnover of labor and at the same time to increase its productivity, in June, 1931, Stalin proposed a six-point program aimed at remedying the difficulties that handicapped industrialization. It included: (1) organized recruitment of labor, especially from rural areas; (2) abolition of fluctuating labor and of the *uravnilovka* (leveling of wages), which he called a "leftist evil"; (3) strengthening of personal responsibility of managers; (4) training from among the working class of new technical personnel capable of mastering new techniques; (5) maximum utilization of prerevolutionary specialists and technicians; and (6) introduction of businesslike principles of management and cost accounting.

On the basis of this six-point program, in the course of the 1930's the government issued a series of laws and decrees aimed at strengthening labor discipline and the responsibility of workers and managers. A government decree of November 15, 1932, for instance, empowered local authorities to dismiss a worker and to deprive him of his factory food card and housing for one day's absenteeism from work without sufficient reason. Other decrees dealt with punctual arrival at work, producing the standard quota on schedule, striving for overfulfillment of planned goals, improving the quality of production, and taking care of socialist property. The government organized special factory colonies, whose purpose was to

Mikhail Kalinin   *Maxim Litvinov*

inculcate "labor habits" in the inmates and to raise their labor qualifications. Habitual or serious violations of government rules invited imprisonment, exile to Siberia, or even death.

This regimentation of the labor force eliminated unemployment in Soviet Russia. It also deprived the trade unions of the last remnants of their independence. Because he opposed increased exploitation of workers, on June 2, 1929, Tomsky was replaced by Shvernik as head of Soviet Trade Unions. Under his chairmanship, on June 23, 1933, the trade unions assumed many of the functions of the Commissariat of Labor and became a docile instrument of the party in exploiting the workers. To increase the productivity of labor, Stalin abolished wage equalization, recognized the difference between skilled and unskilled workers, and devised and encouraged "socialist competition" and *Stakhanovism*. The *Stakhanov* movement in particular was an enormous propaganda effort. It benefited those few workers who, for one reason or another, were able to attain striking results in their production. It was, however, detrimental to those who were just average, as their norms (not their wages) were increased, because production quotas were based not on the general average but on the average of the best. For the working people of the Soviet Union, the industrial revolution of the 1930's was a bitter experience.

THE AGRICULTURAL REVOLUTION

The industrial revolution which the Soviet Union experienced in the 1930's was accompanied by a great agricultural revolution. In fact, some scholars believe that the agricultural upheaval was more dramatic and sweeping than the industrial. For one thing it affected more people, and it also was fraught with more excesses and real horrors.

Like its industrial counterpart, the agricultural revolution, although it had been discussed during the 1920's, was ordered suddenly and without any real preparation. Most scholars believe that the major cause leading to this great upheaval was the slow rate of expansion of agricultural production during the 1920's—a rate which failed to supply the growing demands of raw materials for industry and foodstuffs for the workers. Or, to put it in another way, ten years after the revolution Russian agriculture was producing less surplus than it had before the revolution. Several factors contributed to this phenomenon. One of these was the breakup of large estates during 1917–1918, which resulted in creation of a small-scale individualistic agriculture. In 1928 there were in the Soviet Union some 25,500,000 peasant households, or an increase of some 7,000,000 in little more than a decade. Furthermore, most of these farms, both new and old, were relatively small (under thirty acres), inadequately equipped, and continued to use primitive methods of cultivation because of rooted conservativism, lack of adequate financial resources and the necessary "know-how." And although during the NEP some progress was made in removing these ills, the net effect on productivity was small and slow—too slow to satisfy the needs of both the growing city population and the growing industry. This became apparent during the harvest of 1925–1926—the year of agricultural recovery—when the marketed surplus of agriculture failed, in the words of one economist, "to recover to the prewar level, despite the recovery both of the cultivated area and of the gross harvest." According to official estimates, only 17 per cent of the total harvest yield was sent to market, and a year later the total dropped to 14 per cent, or about one-half of the prewar period. This sharp reduction of marketed grain during the 1920's affected both the export and import plans of party leaders by demonstrating that under existing conditions the envisaged large-scale industrial expansion, relying on imported machinery in exchange for agricultural surplus, was impossible.

A great deal of agricultural difficulty also stemmed from the fact that under the NEP the Soviet Union had a mixed economy: *the state-owned "socialist sector,"* which included all heavy industry, transport, banking, credit facilities, and foreign trade; and *the private ownership sector,* which predominated in small-scale industry, retail trade, and farming. Though the balance between the two sectors was quite uneven, during the NEP all responsible party leaders sought to preserve the existing cooperation as well as competition between the two. But competition also implied a degree of antagonism. Industry, making a slow recovery from ruin, sought high prices for its products but cheap prices for food and raw materials. By the same token, peasants sought low prices on industrial goods and high prices for their own produce. Moreover, once they recovered from the excesses of the Civil War and War Communism, the peasants began to press for further concessions, such as the reduction of taxes, the abolition of restrictions on hiring of farm workers, and long term leasing of land, and to the dismay of the Bolsheviks they proved to be exceedingly resourceful and productive.

Party and government leaders resisted peasant demands, for to give in would have meant to capitulate to the peasants, whom they hated and despised and whose attitudes and ambitions they considered petty-bourgeois. But so long as the outcome of the struggle for succession was undecided, unwilling to face two formidable opponents—Trotsky and the peasants—Stalin and his "right wing" associates listened to peasant demands. Both he and Bukharin rejected Trotsky's suggestion that additional levies be put on the private sector of economy to help accelerate industrialization. They feared that such a move would discourage peasant initiative, create food shortages, and upset the delicate balance between the two sectors of economy. No sooner, however, was the struggle for succession resolved than Stalin altered his stand quite suddenly.

The first sign of Stalin's changed position towards the peasants came in December, 1927, when, following his triumph over Trotsky, he instructed all local party members to take energetic measures to extract grain from the peasants. Because peasants resisted these measures by all the devices known to them, there was a great deal of "administrative arbitrariness, violation of revolutionary law, raids on peasant houses, [and] illegal searches." These actions continued until July, 1928, and those party members who showed any leniency towards the peasants were purged. The second sign of Stalin's *volte-face* came in April, 1928, at a meeting of the Central Executive Committee of the All-Union Congress of Soviets, where, without any advance warning, Stalin presented the draft of a new land law. This draft sought three objectives: (1) to deprive the peasants of their unrestricted rights to the use of land cultivated by their own labor; (2) to confine those rights to only those peasants who joined collective farms; and (3) to deprive of all rights to any land those peasants who were classified as *kulaks;* i.e., those peasants who were either industrious, or more prosperous than their neighbors, or simply those who were not enthusiastic about the policies of the Communist party. While the draft was tabled and thus failed to become law, it disclosed that Stalin had in mind rapid and forcible collectivization of the peasants in order to help industrialize the country at breakneck speed.

Stalin confirmed this point at the end of May, 1928, when he called upon party members to choose between suicide and rapid collectivization of agriculture and development of heavy industry. He again reiterated this idea at the July, 1928, meeting of the Central Committee when he stressed that while it was an "unpleasant business," since the Soviet Union had neither colonies nor ready capital to industrialize rapidly, it had to resort to exacting a "tribute" from the bulk of its population—the peasants. This frank but blunt statement was the clearest indication thus far that Stalin was parting company both with the peasants and with his former right wing associate, Bukharin.

The peasants received Stalin's decision to collectivize agriculture in order to help industrialize the country with anything but enthusiasm. From the outset therefore the drive towards collectivization turned into a ruthless and bitter war. The outcome of this struggle was never in doubt not only because the party and the government possessed all the coercive means, but also because of the nature of the soviet village itself. On the eve of collectivization there were some 25,500,000 peasant holdings. Out of that number, between 5,000,000 and 7,000,000 were classified as *bedniaks,* or poor peasants, who had neither a horse, nor a cow, nor any appreciable agricultural implements, and so were ready and willing to listen to promises of improvement. Above this destitute group were some 18,000,000 *seredniaks,* or middle peasants, who had most of the necessities of life and who desired no radical change. At the top were some 800,000 *kulaks*—industrious, and, by Soviet standards, the most productive and thus most prosperous peasants, who had the most to lose and who therefore opposed collectivization.

To overcome the *kulak* resistance to collectivization, Stalin carried the class struggle into the village by setting peasant against peasant. First he turned the *bedniaks* against the *kulaks*. The *bedniaks* were offered the *kulaks*' cattle, implements and machinery, and all-out government support in improving their living conditions in collective farms. Thus supported by local party members, the *bedniaks* unleashed a bitter civil war throughout rural areas of the USSR. The success of this upheaval encouraged Stalin to issue a call in December, 1929, to all party members to pass "from the policy of *restricting* the exploiting proclivities of the *kulaks* to the policy of *eliminating* the *kulaks* as a class." Thousands of party and *komsomol* agents, workers, police and army units were ordered to the countryside to perform this task. Their activities brought rural Russia to what one observer aptly called "pandemonium." Villages which resisted this form of "voluntary" association were surrounded by armed units and forced to surrender. Under those conditions the war against the *kulak* turned into a ruthless and chaotic war against *all* peasants. Thousands were killed, many more were arrested and millions were scattered throughout Siberia and the sub-Polar regions. All of their possessions (houses, farms, farm implements, livestock, and the like) were turned over to the collective farms. Other millions, whether they resisted or not, were forced into collective farms. The speed with which this mass collectivization drive was carried out can be best seen from the following official figures. At the end of 1928, only 1.7 per cent of all peasant households was collectivized. In October, 1929, the percentage had risen to 4.1 per cent; in January, 1930, to 21 per cent; and early in March, 1930, it stood at 58 per cent, or more than half of all the households.

The bitterness and chaos which this collectivization drive created seems to have frightened Stalin. On March 2, 1930, *Pravda* printed his now famous article entitled "Dizziness with Success," in which he placed the blame for what had happened on the overzealousness of local party officials who misunderstood party directives, became intoxicated by their initial successes, and lost all sense of proportion and "the faculty of understanding realism." Posing as a defender of peasant interests, Stalin now called his overzealous local party functionaries "opportunists," "blockheads," "lefts," and "distortionists." He admitted that force had been used in the collectivization drive, but warned that "collective farms cannot be set up by force" because to do so "would be stupid and reactionary."

Stalin's call to halt the excesses did not mean the end of collectivization. Many peasants, however, seem to have thought so, for between March and September, 1930, the percentage of collectivized households dropped from 58 per cent to 21 per cent. Following the Sixteenth Party

Congress (June 26–July 13, 1930), which formally echoed Stalin's words on the "voluntary" nature of the collectives, the drive was begun anew. In 1931 the percentage of collectivized households rose to 52.7 per cent and climbed constantly. In 1932 it stood at 61.5 per cent; in 1933 at 65.6 per cent; in 1934 at 71.4 per cent; in 1935 at 83.2 per cent; in 1936 at 90.5 per cent; and in 1938 at 93.5 per cent, with 242,400 collective farms.

The speed and ferocity with which the mass collectivization program was carried out benefited neither the state, nor the collective farms nor the peasants. Before they "joined" collectives, the peasants, in desperation, killed their cattle, pigs, and horses; destroyed their farm implements; and either burned their crops or allowed them to rot in the field. The scope of this form of peasant resistance can be seen from the following figures. Between 1928 and 1934, the number of horses dropped from 36,100,000 to 15,400,000; cattle from 66,800,000 to 33,500,000; hogs from 27,700,000 to 11,500,000; and sheep and goats from 114,600,000 to 36,500,000. Needless to say, the loss of draft animals had negative effects on the agricultural goals of the plan, with the result that agricultural production in 1933 was much lower than in 1928.

Party and government response to peasant resistance was firm and tragic in its final outcome. A joint decree of the Central Committee and of the *Sovnarkom* on January 16, 1930, established the criminal responsibility of all who destroyed their property or killed their cattle and other animals before joining collectives. A decree of February 1, 1930, empowered local authorities, in case of resistance to collectivization or destruction of the property of collective farms, to take all measures "including total confiscation of property of the *kulaks* and their deportation from a given district, territory, or region." Finally, on August 7, 1932, a Draconian law introduced the death penalty without possibility of pardon for any "theft" of property belonging to a collective farm or to the state. Strict enforcement of this decree, coupled with the forcible collection of high levies, produced a man-made famine. The areas most affected were the Ukraine and Northern Caucasus. The government officially denied the existence of famine and refused to accept outside aid. At the same time, however, it kept both regions off limits to foreign correspondents stationed in Moscow until the harvest of 1933 had been brought in. Probably no one will ever know the famine's *exact* toll of lives, but estimates (based on interpretation of the figures of the 1937–1938 census) range from 5 million to 10 million. Whatever figure is accepted, one must agree that for the rural people of the Soviet Union the agricultural revolution, especially this early period, described by one observer as "the period of licenced anarchy," was a bitter experience.

Following "the period of licensed anarchy," until 1958 agricultural organization in the Soviet Union consisted of four basic institutions: (1) *sovkhozes* or state farms; (2) *kolkhozes*, or collective farms; (3) Machine Tractor Stations (MTS); and (4) private peasant plots. With only slight modifications these units (excepting MTS's) remain the basic forms of agriculture in the Soviet Union today.

State farms, as their name implies, are entirely properties of the state. They are managed by government-appointed supervisors, who operate them with the help of hired labor and in the same spirit as is any factory in the USSR. Large in size, often exceeding 5,000 acres, these "factories in the field," have been favored by all Soviet leaders (Lenin, Stalin, and Khrushchev) for two basic reasons: first, as state owned and operated enterprises they are thought to be capable of providing the state with a high net production; and second, workers on these farms, like workers in the factories, are under relatively strong party and government control. Because Soviet leaders prefer them, state farms have enjoyed large investments and have been provided more adequately with tractors and other farm machinery. The number of state farms has also increased appreciably from 1,400 in 1927, to 4,337 in 1932, to 5,900 in 1958.

The development of state farms fell into several distinct phases. The first was during the 1920's when the government turned into model specialized farms those large estates which the peasants did not divide among themselves. Because many of these farms operated at a loss, the government later reduced their area. The second phase was roughly during the first two Five Year Plans, when, hoping to obtain a large amount of grain, Stalin ordered an increase in the number of state farms. These hopes, however, failed to materialize because the size of the farms themselves prevented efficient management, while their overspecialization precluded the application of a balanced agricultural technique. In the late 1930's, many unprofitable state farms were liquidated and those that remained were ordered to diversify their operations. During and after World War II the number of state farms rose again as a result of the emergency. The highest increase occurred in Central Asia (Kazakh SSR), in the area of the so-called "virgin lands."

Work on state farms is done by work units called brigades, headed by foremen called brigadiers. Each worker is paid on the basis of straight piece-work wages. The basic unit of cropwork measurement is the hectare (or 2.471 acres), and those workers who produce more receive more. State farms have been plagued by a high labor turnover rate, by idleness during the wintertime, and by inefficiency during the remainder of the year. To remedy these difficulties and thus to reduce the high production costs for grain, milk, meat, and other products, the government has tried many policies. Thus far, none seem to have been satisfactory.

Collective farms form the second major agricultural institution in the Soviet Union. In theory, collective farms are "voluntarily" organized farmers' cooperatives, whose members have pooled their land and capital, operate them in common, and share their "net proceeds in proportion to the quantity and quality of work they do." In reality, however, as we noted earlier, party and state officials forcibly imposed the organization of collective farms on the rural population of the USSR. Each collective farm has a charter (based on the Standard Charter of February 17, 1935), which defines the organization of the collective farm and the responsibilities of its members and officers. Economically, collective farms operate under certain handicaps. The land they use belongs to the state, and may neither be sold, leased, bought, nor given to a member who withdraws. The use of this land is determined by the national plan, which determines what, where, and in what quantity anything is to be produced. Each collective farm owns cattle, horses, simple implements, buildings, seed, fodder, and the like, but it may not dispose of this property for two reasons. First, through such disposal it would deprive itself of its means of existence; and second, without these implements, it could not fulfill the task which the plan has imposed on it. Until 1958, no collective farm owned any heavy machinery. That was supplied by the government-operated MTS's.

In theory, collective farms are democratic organizations. Under the Charter, the highest authority on a collective farm is the general meeting which elects the officers, decides on the admission of new or expulsion of old members, confirms the budget, the building program, and annual production, approves the reports of its officers, and determines the remuneration for its members. In practice, however, many of the "elected" officials, especially chairmen, have been party appointees, as have also been the members of the management board. Work on collective farms, like that on state farms, is done by work units of fifty to one hundred individuals called brigades, and by smaller units called zvena (links).

The state has always had first claim on all products of collective farms, and has always been able to take the lion's share of the production. The state collects its share in four ways. First, it receives some in the form of a tax-in-kind levy. The amount of this tax, which differs from area to area, is determined not by the actual harvest, or the area actually sown, but by a theoretical estimate of what should have been obtained from all the arable land at the disposal of a given collective farm. Another share the government receives in the form of repayment of debts, which practically all collective farms owe. The third way the state obtains much of the collective farms' production is in payment for services performed by the government-owned MTS's, although this source has declined since 1958. Finally, the state receives a substantial share from special "voluntary" commitments made by local party officials.

After all deliveries to the state have been made, each collective farm must reserve certain quantities for seed, fodder, and other needs. The remainder is then divided among the members of the collective farms as payment in kind. The share of individual members depends on the number of "labor days" credited to each. A "labor day" is a conditional unit. It may mean one, two, three, or a fraction of a calendar day, depending on the type of work done and the results achieved. A watchman may get as little as one half a "labor day" for one calendar day's work, while the chairman of the farm may collect three "labor days" for one calendar day. The obligatory minimum of "labor days"—a basic condition for remaining a member of a collective farm—was originally set at from 60 to 100 per year. During World War II that minimum was increased from 100 to 150. Should there be any surplus left after each member is paid his share, that surplus is either sold to the government or on the open market, and the money divided among the members of the collective farm.

Since the mid-1930's, the Soviet government has invested heavily in collective farms. According to official figures, in 1958 there were 78,200 collective farms. At their disposal were 1,700,000 tractors, 483,000 harvester combines, 660,000 trucks, and 277,000 skilled specialists. From the technical point of view, this heavy mechanization makes collective farms a progressive form of agricultural economy. Persistent attention of Soviet leaders to the collective farms shows, however, that mechanization alone will not produce grain, milk, meat, or vegetables, and that collectives are not as profitable as they were intended to be. Scholars have listed many reasons for the failure of the collective farm system. These include: peculiarities of the centralized system of economy; political and administrative over-supervision; vast bureaucracy; and peasant indifference. It must be remembered, however, that there are some collective farms that are prosperous.

Machine tractor stations, established on June 5, 1929, were, until 1958, the third major agricultural institution. Owned and operated by the state, the MTS's functions were manifold. They operated tractors, combines, and other complex agricultural machinery, and performed all the heavy work on collective farms from plowing, to seeding, to cultivating, to harvesting. In return for this work, the MTS's, or more properly the state, received a share of the crop. In the 1930's and the 1940's, the share was from 10 per cent to 20 per cent of the farm's grain crop. In 1953, fixed rates were introduced for different areas. The MTS's served also as a major instrument for controlling collective farms, a function which they performed in innumerable ways. Led by party members, the MTS's served finally as disseminators of party propaganda among the peasant population. In 1930, there were only 158 MTS's in the USSR; in 1935 the figure was 4,375; in 1940 the figure stood at 7,069; and in 1958 it was 7,900. In 1958, most of the MTS's were ordered to disband gradually, and to sell their assets to the collective farms.

Private peasant plots form the last major agricultural institution in the USSR. Granted to each household by the collective farm statute of 1935, these plots vary in size, depending on the nature of local economy, but legally they are not less than 0.62 and not more than 1.24 acres. Local conditions, law, and size place limits on the number of animals each plot may have. Throughout most of the European part of the USSR, each private peasant plot is allowed one cow, two calves, one sow, ten sheep or goats, an unlimited number of fowl and rabbits, and not more than twenty beehives. Though small in size, from the very beginning these plots have played a vital role in peasant lives, because peasant industriousness has turned them into a significant supplementary source of livelihood. They provide food, vegetables, eggs, and other necessities, some of which they even sell on the open market. Peasants have always treated these plots as their own, and by all devious means have tried to enlarge them. The party and the government, on the other hand, have as persistently sought a formula or a policy which would enable them to abolish these plots altogether.

CULTURAL AND SOCIAL UNIFORMITY

Stalin accompanied his vast industrial and agricultural transformation of the USSR by an excessive cultural and social regimentation. Authorities differ on the nature of this uniformity, as they do on most aspects of Soviet history, but most of them believe that these changes were an integral part of the economic planning with but one difference. Whereas, by economic planning Stalin sought to exploit the abundance of natural resources, to develop heavy industry, to strengthen the military might of the USSR, and to mechanize agriculture in order to increase its productivity, by cultural and social regimentation he aspired to exploit and control all the movements, thoughts, and ideas of every individual, in order to create a uniform, monolithic, and obedient modern totalitarian society, ruled by an "infallible" supreme leader whose word would be the ultimate law of the land. Stalin achieved these aims by "coercion" as well as by "persuasion," or the "stick and carrot" approach.

The remaking of Soviet culture and society started late in 1929, or shortly after Stalin's triumph over his opponents, and following his elevation on his fiftieth birthday to *vozhd*, "beloved leader" and "great genius" of the USSR. In 1930 he brought Soviet philosophers to submission, and Marxism-Leninism-Stalinism emerged as the only accepted philosophy in the Soviet Union. Stalin's own most notable "contribution" to this philosophy dealt with the problem of the "withering away of the state." Until Stalin changed it, the official view on this crucial theoretical issue of Marxism was that the state, which was considered by the Marxists to be a product of class struggle and an instrument of coercion, would disappear progressively with the triumph of the revolution and with the disappearance of class antagonisms. Following the revolution many demands were made to dissolve the state, and considerable literature was written on that problem. Stalin ended the controversy by announcing in 1930, in 1934, and in 1939, that the state would "wither away," not through its weakening but through development of its economic, political, and military strength to the uttermost capability in order to enable it to eliminate its external as well as internal opponents.

Next after philosophy, Stalin ordered a vast change in the writing and teaching of history. The first sign of the impending shift occurred at the end of 1931, in the form of a letter to the editors of the *Proletarskaia Revolutsiia* (Proletarian Revolution) in which Stalin made it clear that he would not tolerate any questioning of Lenin's views by any historian. This warning officially approved the sanctity of Lenin's works, and served as the first step to sanctifying Stalin's pronouncements. A more concrete measure affecting history was a decree of May 16, 1934, issued jointly by the Central Committee and the *Sovnarkom*, which declared the teaching of history in Soviet schools to be unsatisfactory, and ordered that all texts based on "abstract schematic character," "abstract definitions of social and economic formations," and "abstract sociological schemes," be replaced by a more conventional presentation with emphasis on individuals and nations. Historian Michael N. Pokrovsky (1868–1932), the chief architect of the old Marxist school, was posthumously branded a "traitor," and his works and his followers were subjected to bitter denunciation and criticism.

It is important to remember that Stalin's "new concept" of history aimed at restoring not all but a few *selected* glories and achievements of Russia's imperial past to suit the present. He ordered, for instance, the acceptance of Christianity to be viewed as an act of progress in the history of the Russian people, and many of the early princes to be presented as progressive leaders and true sons of the Russian people. Ivan the Terrible and Peter the Great were turned from despots into reformers, tireless fighters for national unity and national might, and bitter opponents of all traitors. Alexander Nevsky's victory over the Livonian knights in 1242, and Napoleon's defeat in 1812 were ordered viewed as national efforts against foreign invasion in defense of freedom. Before long Stalin elevated Generals Michael Kutuzov (1745–1813), Alexander Suvorov (1730–1800), and other heroes of the Russian past to prominence and interpreted Russian past territorial conquest in Europe and Asia not as acts of imperialism but as circumstances dictated by historical forces.

Stalin's rediscovery of the Russian past differed from prerevolutionary treatments in one significant respect: It included histories of non-Russian peoples of the USSR. But while this action was commendable in one way (histories of some peoples were written for the first time), it was distortive in another way. Russian heroes were always portrayed as superior, and non-Russians, though equally great, were *ipso facto* inferior. The same was true of all Russian literary figures and of the Russian language, which was lauded as the language of the revolutionary teachings of Marx and Engels as elaborated by Lenin and Stalin. The study of Russian became obligatory for all non-Russian minorities, and any avoidance of usage of it at home or in schools was considered a renouncement of the revolutionary method. Those who objected were branded traitors and dealt with accordingly. This form of "Soviet patriotism" was applied broadly during and after World War II.

Aware that no nation can hope to become a leading industrial and military power without a loyal, literate, and technically well-trained citizenry, Stalin paid much attention to the schools in his efforts to impose new uniformity on the Soviet people. In July, 1930, universal primary education was introduced, and in September, 1931, the Central Committee repudiated the experiment in progressive education in favor of academic education of the traditional disciplinarian type tailored to the totalitarian objectives of the Communist state. Report cards, grades, student discipline, and authority of teachers—discarded during the 1920's because of their "bourgeois origin"—were reintroduced early in the 1930's. Alongside physics, chemistry, mathematics, and biology, Soviet schools were now ordered to emphasize such "Communist virtues" as devotion to work, labor discipline, conformity, sobriety, love of country, and hatred of its enemies, and belief in the infallibility of its leaders. The new curriculum placed a twofold responsibility on the schools. First, they were to serve as the chief supplier of trustworthy and efficient functionaries to manage the new factories, to administer government agencies, to enforce party and government directives, and to develop the state's technological resources. The schools' second task was to serve as a conveyor of political indoctrination of the state's "most treasured possession, the children." The same dual responsibility was entrusted to the teachers. Each teacher was to be a fountain of knowledge as well as an effective propaganda emissary of the regime, to advertise its achievements, to promote its beliefs, to indoctrinate the young, and to disseminate the official information. Teachers who failed to qualify for those tasks were dismissed, and those who remained were upgraded both socially and financially.

Next to schools, Stalin made great efforts to bring new uniformity to the family. "Free love," "free divorce," and legalized abortions—the pride of the experimental twenties—were officially condemned as "bourgeois inventions," and the seriousness of marriage and of family stability were stressed. Two pressures operated behind the new emphasis. First was an alarming decrease of the birthrate, which, if allowed to continue unchecked, threatened to undermine both the labor supply and the national defenses. According to some estimates, between 1926 and 1937, the increase in the birthrate in the USSR was about 13,000,000 below that which had been projected by demographers. Second was the increasing problem of juvenile delinquency which resulted from the wholesale dissolution of family ties during the early stages of industrialization. Many of the delinquents were children of parents sent to forced labor camps. No one dared to show any kindness to these orphans in order not to share the fate of their parents. Most of the delinquents roved in gangs perpetrating crimes and vandalism. Some were placed in state-operated orphanages, but in many of these establishments, as one observer noted, "the authorities had lost all control and the toughest of the children reigned supreme amid dirt and violence."

To curb the nationwide lawlessness, on April 7, 1935, the government decreed that any minor over twelve years of age found guilty of "hooliganism" was "to be liable to all grades of criminal penalty," including death. Those guilty of contributing to the delinquency of minors became liable to not less than five years' imprisonment. On May 31, 1935, the government increased parental responsibility for the misdemeanors of their children. A decree of June 7, 1936, prohibited abortion except when medically authorized, made divorce more difficult, and reinstated the family as the basic unit of the social organism. The decree also provided state subsidies to large families and soon thereafter the title of "Mother Heroine" was given to women who gave birth to and reared ten children. Those mothers who bore seven children received the medal of "Mother's Glory," and those who had five or six children were awarded the medal of "Motherhood." By strengthening family ties, Stalin also strengthened the principle of collective responsibility of the family for its members, a factor which in part accounts for the heavy toll of victims during the purges.

By the end of the 1930's, the imposed changes in family and school, together with the industrial and agricultural transformations, produced an interesting shift both in thinking and in actual structure of Soviet society. Officially, the new society in 1937 was said to have consisted of workers, who comprised 36.2 per cent; peasants, who comprised 63.8 per cent; and a stratum called intelligentsia which had been recruited from both—all living in friendship among themselves. This "harmony," it was explained, stemmed from the abolition in the USSR of all classes and of private ownership of the instruments and means of production, liquidation of the capitalist system, elimination of the exploitation of man by man, and the removal of all vestiges of discrimination.

Official claims that the Soviet Union produced during the 1930's a society free of class divisions and class antagonisms did not correspond with reality, however, because the same period that witnessed the liquidation of the old classes experienced also the emergence of new social strata. Industrialization, collectivization, and Stalinization produced all kinds of party and government functionaries, technical specialists, factory man-

Mikhail Tukhachevsky *Nikolai Yezhov*

agers, artists, writers, collective farm managers, Stakhanovites, and count-less bureaucrats who received high salaries, prizes, bonuses, honoraria, and even royalties. Many of these "distinguished people" enjoyed com-fortable residences, had cars, country houses (*dachas*), and substantial bank accounts. Below this new group of Soviet "aristocrats" were ordinary workers whose membership increased greatly during the 1930's, peasants whose membership was reduced drastically, and millions of inmates of various correctional institutions and labor camps. Between the new "aris-tocracy" and the rest of the population there was a vast cleavage, which manifested itself in power and influence, as well as in the way of living.

The great cleavage between the "haves" and the "have nots" in the USSR, which the 1930's put into focus, gave rise to various interpreta-tions. Those scholars who subscribe to the Marxist definition of social classes—the exploiters and the exploited—deny the existence of class divi-sions in the USSR. In their view, everyone has an opportunity to rise on the social ladder and no group in the Soviet Union has either a class psychology or a definite status in production. Other scholars believe, how-ever, that like any other country the USSR has its own classes which differ as to their place in the national economy, their relation to the means of production, and the size of their share in the national income. There are also many scholars who maintain that during the 1930's the Soviet Union produced two main classes: First, the *obeying* class—the class that has no power over the means of production; no voice as to what should be produced, where, and in what amount; and no voice about conditions of either work or pay. The second is the *commanding* class, the class that controls the means of production, decides what is to be produced, where and how, and determines not only the distribution of the products but prices, wages, rewards and penalties as well.

Two factors seem to have been instrumental in the rise of social inequality in a "classless society." One was Stalin's replacement in 1931 of wage equalization with wages that differentiated between skilled and unskilled workers. The second, and most important cause for this inequality, was the nature of the Soviet planned and regimented economy, which, from its inception, in the absence of a market mechanism, demanded not only planned distribution of raw materials but of manpower as well. To fulfill the task assigned by each successive plan it was necessary not only to mobilize but to "freeze" a certain part of the population in industry, a certain part in agriculture, some in public service, and some in managerial work. The peasants were "frozen" on the collective farm as early as March 17, 1933, while workers could not legally find any employment without "labor booklets" after January 15, 1939. These measures enabled Stalin to distribute manpower, penalties, and rewards more easily. These measures also served effectively in recruiting a reliable bureaucracy for the regime.

To produce the new cultural and social uniformity, Stalin relied on coercion as well as persuasion. He executed thousands of people and sent millions more into oblivion. Those who remained were subjected to intensive propaganda indoctrination. All media of public communication (newspapers, radio, publishing houses, periodicals, bulletins, posters, and the like) were mobilized to publicize Stalin's goals. They recruited support for his policies, checked on the enforcement of party and government decisions, agitated for the realization of production quotas, called for liquidation of the "enemies" of the Soviet regime, publicized the achievements of the Stakhanovites and other "socialist competitors," and exposed the unsatisfactory performance of the laggards. The aim of this all-out and unprecedented propaganda effort, as one observer rightly noted, was "neither to convince nor even to persuade, but to produce a uniform pattern of public utterance in which the first trace of unorthodox thought immediately reveals itself as a jarring dissonance."

PURGES

Stalin accompanied the great industrial, agricultural, cultural, and social transformation of the Soviet Union during the 1930's by a vast purge. Scholars have sought in vain reasonable explanations of the causes which led to this odious spectacle. Some have argued that Stalin needed scapegoats to cover up his economic failures. Others have advanced the view that he sought to eliminate all possible challengers to his power, domestically based but foreign inspired. There are those who have submitted that the purge is an inherent element of the system itself, designed to terrorize every individual in order to incapacitate him of independent action. Finally, there are many who believe that Stalin's own madness was the chief cause of this abhorrent bloodbath.

Purge (the Russian word for it is *chistka*, which literally means "cleansing") was not a new phenomenon for the Soviet monolithic system. During the 1920's the party conducted four major "cleansings" of its ranks to remove the weak and the unfit. The purges of the 1930's, however, differed from previous purifications in four respects: in the number of party victims; in the number of nonparty casualties; in the spectacular "show" trials; and in the "confessions of guilt" by most of the victims.

Before the climax was reached in the late 1930's, this abominable spectacle had several "rehearsals." The first preview of things to come was early in 1928 in the Shakhty district in the Donets Basin, where the secret police (OGPU) arrested and brought to trial several non-Communist engineers. They were accused of counter-revolutionary plots, sabotage, and cooperation with Germany in order to prevent the successful execution of the First Five Year Plan. The second preview came early in 1930 in Kharkov with a "show trial" of forty-five prominent Ukrainians. They were accused of maintaining contact with Ukrainian political emigration and foreign powers (Poland and Germany), of preparing plans to organize Ukrainian peasants to resist collectivization, of planning to assassinate Stalin and his lieutenants, and of trying to separate the Ukraine from the USSR in order to restore the capitalist system of economy. The third preview trial took place in Moscow. The victim was an "Industrialists' Party" allegedly headed by Professor Leonid K. Ramzin. The defendants were accused of holding Menshevik views, of sabotaging industrial expansion, and of conspiring with France. The fourth trumped-up preview "trial" took place in 1931. Like their predecessors, the defendants, former Mensheviks headed by Professor V. Groman, an economist of the State Planning Commission, and historian N. N. Sukhanov, were accused of sabotage and conspiracy with émigré groups and foreign powers. The final preview, the "trial" of a group of engineers of the British Metropolitan-Vickers Company, took place in the Ukraine in April, 1933, at which alleged British sabotage was blamed for some of the inadequacies of the First Five Year Plan. In all of these "trials," most of the defendants received long prison terms or exile.

Simultaneously with these burlesques, Stalin ordered the "purification" of the party. Many local party members, especially those who showed any leniency towards the peasants, lost their jobs in an extensive purge, early in 1928, while others were expelled during 1929. Some were sacrificed as scapegoats following the publication of Stalin's article "Dizziness with Success," in March, 1930. Many more party members lost their jobs, and some even their lives, as the result of a purge ordered by the Central Committee on April 28, 1933. Officially the aim of this purge was "to achieve a higher ideological standard of party members, to strengthen the party organization politically, and to secure further confidence in the party on the part of millions of non-party men and women." This purge was to be conducted publicly and was to seek out "alien and hostile elements," open and secret violators of party discipline, those who had doubts of the wisdom of party decisions, opportunists, and all those who had allegedly succumbed to capitalist influence, and who did not want to fight "class enemies" and *kulaks*.

The purge officially began June 1, and ended in November, 1933. It affected the following cities and areas: Moscow, Leningrad, the Urals, Donets, Odessa, Kiev, Vinnitsia, Eastern Siberia, the Far East and Belorussia. The toll of victims was considerable. In the Ukraine alone, some 27,000 party members and candidates were expelled as "class enemies and undesirable and demoralized elements." They were replaced by new and, apparently in Stalin's view, more devoted individuals. Many of those who were purged in the Ukraine and other border regions were accused of harboring "bourgeois nationalist views"—a charge which paved the way for a turn in Stalin's nationality policy. Until this time the party officially viewed Russian great power chauvinism as the main danger to the Soviet system. Thereafter, non-Russian national deviations acquired that distinction. The road was paved for mass persecution of minorities.

The real holocaust started late in 1934 following the assassination on December 1, 1934, of Kirov, a member of the Politburo, and Stalin's chief lieutenant in Leningrad, by a young disillusioned Communist named Leonid V. Nikolaev. Officially, Stalin blamed Kirov's murder interchangeably on foreign powers, on Trotsky, on Zinoviev, and on the Right Opposition. In his famed speech before the Twentieth Party Congress in 1956, however, Khrushchev hinted that Stalin himself was the chief architect of Kirov's death. Being close to Stalin and having access to information not available to others, Khrushchev may speak with authority. Whatever the final judgment on the cause of Kirov's death, Stalin used it as an excuse for mass executions and repressions. To eliminate even the slightest legal opposition to his actions, the Central Executive Committee, on December 1, 1934, issued a decree which almost completely deprived all those accused of "terroristic acts" of any right of defense. This, in turn, paved the way for mass arrests, confessions extracted by force, and deportations or executions of thousands of persons.

The first victims of these executions were Nikolaev and his thirteen alleged accomplices who were executed on December 30, 1934. Because they implicated many of Stalin's former critics and opponents, thousands of party members were screened during the early months of 1935. Many were arrested, including Zinoviev and Kamenev, some were shot, and some were deported to Siberia. This "purification" of the party and of its auxiliaries continued throughout 1935 as did the search for new men to replace those who disappeared. Thus, Andrei A. Zhdanov (1896–1948) took over Kirov's place in Leningrad; Nikita S. Khrushchev (1894–1972) rose to prominence in the Moscow party organization; Georgi M. Malenkov (1902–) emerged as a star in the Secretariat; Andrei Ia. Vyshinsky (1883–1954) became the Chief Procurator of the USSR; and Lavrentii P. Beria (1899–1953) became a high-ranking official of the secret police (NKVD) in charge of terror.

Stalin started a new wave of "purifications" on January 14, 1936, when the Central Committee decreed that all party members must exchange their old party cards for new identification—a process which again eliminated many "passive people." Of those members who remained in the party, Stalin demanded increased vigilance in exposing hidden enemies. A new wave of denunciations, arrests, and expulsions followed, laying the groundwork for the first major spectacle which took place on August 19, 1936. Sixteen "Old Bolsheviks," including Zinoviev and Kamenev, who had been imprisoned in 1935, were arraigned for a public trial. The defendants were accused of organizing, under Trotsky's guidance, a "terrorist centre" whose aim was to carry out terrorist acts against Stalin and company. They were also blamed for Kirov's death. Some of the accused admitted, while others denied, their guilt. All sixteen were sentenced to death and were immediately executed.

Because "testimonies" of the August, 1936, trial implicated many other "founding fathers" of Russian communism, late in January, 1937, Stalin arranged the second spectacle which was better organized and more subtle than was the first. It was conducted by the new head of the NKVD, Nikolai I. Yezhov (1895–?), who replaced prisonbound Henry G. Yagoda (1891–1938). The seventeen defendants, headed by Piatakov, Radek, and Sokolnikov, were now accused of connivance with Nazi Germany and Japan to dismember the USSR, of sabotage, and of wrecking socialist construction. All seventeen defendants "confessed" their guilt. Thirteen were sentenced to death and executed. Four received long-term sentences, but their ultimate fate has never been made public.

By implicating new "conspirators," the second spectacle paved the way for further arrests and trials. This time the victims came from the Red Army. On June 11, 1937, several army commanders, including Marshal Tukhachevsky of Civil War fame, were arrested, tried, and executed.[1] Like their predecessors, they were accused of espionage on behalf of Germany and Japan, anti-party conspiracy, cooperation with Trotsky, and plotting territorial dismemberment of the USSR. Arrest of other high-ranking officers followed. According to some estimates, the Red Army lost

---

[1] Tukhachevsky and many of his codefendants were "rehabilitated" between 1956 and 1958.

35,000 men, or about half its officer corps. Of the purged officers, 30,000 were below the rank of colonel. Among the victims were 3 marshals, 13 army commanders, 57 corps commanders, 110 division commanders, 220 brigade commanders, all 11 deputy commissars of war, 75 members of the Supreme Military Council, all military district commanders, all air force, and all but one navy fleet commander. Needless to say, this wholesale elimination of the military leadership created doubts as to Soviet military capabilities.

The last major spectacle took place in March, 1938. The defendants were twenty-one former members of the Right Opposition, headed by Bukharin, Rykov, and Christian G. Rakovsky (1873–?). Also among the defendants was former head of the NKVD, Yagoda, who was accused of poisoning the writer Maxim Gorky in June, 1936, and Valerian V. Kuibyshev (1888–1935) in January, 1935. Like all their predecessors, these defendants were charged with sabotage, espionage on behalf of Germany and Japan, attempted dismemberment of the USSR, and conspiracy to kill all leaders of the USSR. Bukharin was accused, in addition, of conspiracy to kill Lenin and Stalin as early as 1918—an accusation he denied to the end. To the other charges, Bukharin and his associates "confessed," and all but three were sentenced to death and executed.[1] The three who were spared received long prison terms and their ultimate fate has never been made known.

In terms of victims, the purges of the 1930's were very costly. At the Eighteenth Party Congress in March, 1939, Stalin admitted that between 1934 and 1939 party membership dropped from 1,874,488 to 1,588,852. Not all of these, of course, were executed. Many were, however, and only some of those who perished had the benefit of public "trial." A few succeeded in committing suicide: Mykola O. Skrypnyk (1872–1933), Tomsky, and General Jan B. Gamarnik (1894–1937). The overwhelming majority were executed without due process of law. Among them were many foreign Communists who had sought political asylum in the USSR. Those top members who remained—Khrushchev, Malenkov, Molotov, Beria, Voroshilov, Mikoyan and others—were trusted, faithful, and dedicated Stalinists, his "comrades-in-arms." There is no reliable estimate of the victims of the purge who were not party members. According to some observers, they numbered in the hundreds of thousands.

Stalin accompanied the wholesale elimination of his real and imaginary opponents with the elevation of his own stature. This he accomplished by a very skillful manipulation of propaganda and a technique that may be characterized as the retroactive lie. Through all media of modern mass communication he induced everyone to attribute to him

---

[1] The New York Times, October 19, 1962, reported Bukharin's rehabilitation. No formal announcement, however, has yet been made.

wisdom and genius in everything from politics, economics, and history, to military leadership, science, art, music, and linguistics. He had his pictures constantly displayed in all public buildings and erected his statues in all prominent public places. Many cities were named for him, as were streets, mountains, collective farms, canals, and even the constitution of 1936. As an "all-knowing" and "faultless" leader, Stalin could not make mistakes or have any shortcomings. These were *ipso facto* attributed to his opponents, who were described as "wreckers," "spies," "saboteurs," and "enemies of the people." Turning of heroes of yesterday into traitors of today called for "doctoring" of pictures and complete rewriting of Russian history of the twentieth century. Stalin completed the latter task in 1938 in the form of a *Short Course on the History of the All-Union Communist Party (bolshevik)*, which until his death was the main subject of study for all Communists.

THE CONSTITUTIONAL STRUCTURE

The great industrial, agricultural and social transformation of the USSR in the 1930's, by destroying the legal order introduced during the NEP, made necessary the sanction of a new one. This came in the form of a new constitution (known as the "Stalin Constitution" until de-Stalinization in the 1950's) which, after highly publicized nation-wide discussion, was officially adopted on December 6, 1936. On the surface the new constitution (in force until 1977) was a reasonable document. It defined the USSR as a socialist state of workers and peasants who possessed all the political power. It declared that the USSR had liquidated capitalism, abolished the exploitation of man by man, and instead had established "the socialist system of economy and the socialist ownership of the instruments and means of production." All land, natural resources, water, forests, industrial enterprises, means of transportation, and "the bulk of dwelling houses in cities and industrial localities," became state property, that is henceforth they belonged to the people. The constitution recognized private property but kept it within narrow limits, inasmuch as the economic life of the USSR was determined and directed by a state plan of national economy. The latter, as noted earlier, sought an increase in public wealth, steady improvement in the material and cultural standards of the working people, and above all the strengthening of the independence of the USSR and its capacity for defense. Accordingly, the new constitution proclaimed that "Work in the USSR is a duty and a matter of honor for every able-bodied citizen, in accordance with the principle: 'He who does not work, neither shall he eat.' The principle applied in the USSR is that of socialism: 'From each according to his ability, to each according to his work.'"

In addition to the right to work, the Stalin constitution granted Soviet citizens "the right to rest and leisure," "the right to maintenance in old age and also in sickness and disability," "the right to education," free medical service, and paid vacations. The constitution accorded equal rights to men and women in all spheres of activity; insured freedom of religious worship and anti-religious propaganda; guaranteed freedom of speech, press, assembly and demonstration; freedom from arrest "except by decision of a court or with the sanction of the procurator"; and "inviolability of the homes of citizens and privacy of correspondence." Finally, the Stalin constitution guaranteed Soviet citizens the right to unite in public organizations such as trade unions, cooperatives, youth, sport, and defense organizations, and cultural, technical, and scientific societies. The most active and politically conscious citizens were allowed to "unite in the Communist Party of the Soviet Union, which is the vanguard of the working people in their struggle to build a Communist society and is the leading core of all organizations of the working people, both public and state."

The Stalin constitution made it abundantly clear that all these rights and freedoms were conditional and were guaranteed only in "conformity with the interests of the working people, and in order to develop the organizational initiative and political activity of the masses of the people." What conformed, however, was decided not by the recipient, but by the benefactor of these rights and freedoms. Since the Communist party enjoyed a complete monopoly of power, controlled everything, and acted as the guardian of the working people in the USSR, the party determined what the interests, needs, desires and aspirations of the people were. Under the Stalin constitution Soviet citizens were free to agitate for party-sponsored candidates and policies. They were free to write about the party's achievements, to take part in party-sponsored public gatherings, to speak at party-controlled public meetings, to approve the party's policies, and to acclaim the party's leaders. If they should use their rights to any other purpose they could be accused of counter-revolutionary propaganda. In other words, under the Stalin constitution Soviet citizens were free to say "yes" to everything the party did or approved, but were not allowed to say "no."

Under the Stalin constitution, the highest organ of state power and the only legislative body in the USSR was the Supreme Soviet. The Supreme Soviet was a bicameral legislature with co-equal houses: a *Soviet of the Union*, elected on the basis of population (one deputy per 300,000 people), and a *Soviet of Nationalities*, elected on a territorial basis by nationality units (twenty-five deputies from a union republic, eleven from an autonomous republic, five from an autonomous region, and one from a national area). The deputies to the Supreme Soviet were elected every four years. In reality, however, they were selected by the party leadership on the basis of their loyalty to the party or efficiency in their place of work. Since no opposition parties were allowed in the USSR, the electorate, with no other choice on election day, traditionally voted over 99 per cent for the single party-selected candidate in each electoral district. Needless to say, party members formed the overwhelming majority of every Supreme Soviet.

The Stalin constitution specified that the Supreme Soviet must meet at least twice a year. It could also convene in extraordinary sessions. The constitutional infrequency of its meetings, the enormous size of its membership (close to 1400 members), and the restricted length of its sessions (from one to seven days), were clear indications of the limited role of the Supreme Soviet in Soviet politics. The procedure of the body also became standard. As a rule the two legislative chambers met separately for the first meeting during which each selected its chairman, approved the procedure and the agenda for the session, and elected various standing commissions for preliminary preparation of legislation, such as Legislative Proposals, Budget, Foreign Affairs and Economics. The second meeting was a joint session of the two houses, attended by the all-important dignitaries, at which the government presented a report on the annual budget for the coming year or any other major current problem. Following this presentation, each house again met separately, listened to speeches of praise or criticism, and gave unanimous approval of the government's policy. Before adjournment the Supreme Soviet automatically, unanimously, and without any discussion, approved the decrees of the Presidium of the Supreme Soviet as well as the work of the *Sovnarkom*, which in 1946 was renamed the Council of Ministers.

Fifty-one out of fifty-two weeks, formal legislative power under the Stalin constitution was vested in the Presidium of the Supreme Soviet. "Elected" every four years by both houses at a joint session, this thirty-three man body—all top party members—served as collegial president and officially represented the Soviet state. The constitution granted this body broad powers. It had the right to convene and dissolve the Supreme Soviet; to issue decrees and interpret the laws of the USSR; to appoint and dismiss military commanders and Foreign Office personnel; to receive foreign dignitaries; to conclude and terminate international agreements; to order mobilization; and to declare a state of war or martial law. But although powerful constitutionally, the Presidium of the Supreme Soviet was little more than a formal instrument for promulgating some of the decisions of the party.

Another such instrument under the Stalin constitution was the Council of Ministers, the highest executive and administrative organ of state power in the USSR. It was the most important agency in the government structure for highlighting problems and planning policy, and it was the body primarily responsible for implementation of the law. Decisions and

The Organizational Structure of the Soviet Government in 1976 *

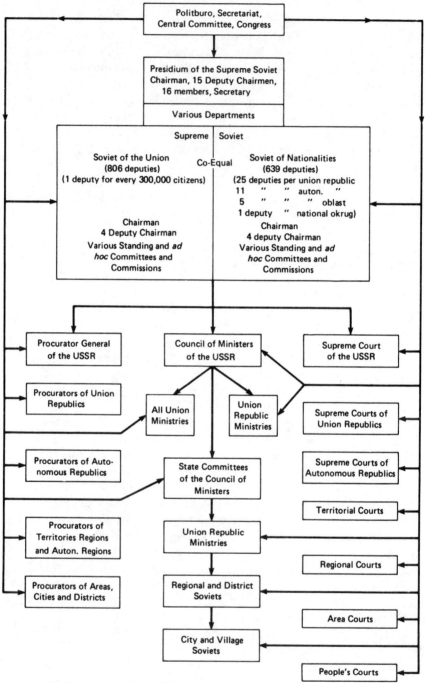

SOURCE: Basil Dmytryshyn, *A History of Russia,* © 1977, p. 545. Reprinted by permission of Prentice-Hall, Inc.

* Under the 1936 Constitution.

orders of the Council of Ministers were binding throughout the entire USSR. It was elected by the Supreme Soviet, to which it also was accountable. Between the sessions of the latter, the Council was accountable to the Presidium of the Supreme Soviet. As the highest administrative body, the Council of Ministers coordinated and directed the work of all ministries and other agencies under its jurisdiction, prepared the national economic plan and state budget, controlled the credit and monetary system, conducted foreign affairs, maintained public order, supervised the armed forces, and had the right to suspend decisions and orders of the Council of Ministers of every union republic. From its inception the Council of Ministers (as well as its predecessor, the *Sovnarkom*) also acted as a legislative agency, issuing resolutions on many problems that constitutionally belonged within the jurisdiction of the legislative branch of the government.

Under the Stalin constitution the Council of Ministers was composed of a Chairman (Premier), two First Deputy Chairmen, several Deputy Chairmen, heads of various ministries, state committees, and other agencies—individuals important because of their positions or their responsibilities. While the membership of the Council of Ministers varied (it increased or decreased as necessity demanded), all members of the Council were the highest party functionaries. The post of Premier was held by such party leaders as Stalin and Khrushchev (and temporarily by their personal selections—Molotov, Malenkov, Bulganin). The posts of Deputy Chairmen and ministers were reserved to members of the party's Politburo, Presidium, Orgburo, the Secretariat, or the Central Committee.

The functional units of the Council of Ministers were ministries, state committees, and specialized agencies whose heads were members of the Council of Ministers. There were three types of ministries in the USSR under the Stalin constitution: (1) *All Union Ministries*, which directed the branches of state administration entrusted to them throughout the territory of the USSR, either directly or through bodies appointed by them. The All-Union Ministries included railroad, transport, machinebuilding, foreign trade, electric power, and certain other key branches of the economy. (2) *Union Republic Ministries*, which, as a rule, directed the state administration entrusted to them through corresponding ministries of the union republics, and were subordinate both to the Republic Council of Ministers and to the parent ministry in Moscow. Union Republic Ministries included agriculture, communication, internal affairs, health, conservation, and similar problems. (3) The *Republic Ministries* which, though technically not a part of the Council of Ministers of the USSR, directed activities peculiar to the republic in which they existed. Republic Ministries included local industry, municipal services, social maintenance, irrigation, and like problems.

Among other high agencies of the central government were state committees and various specialized agencies. Structurally they were similar to ministries, but they were not administrative bodies. Their function was to supervise and coordinate activities of ministries, make preliminary examination of various problems and the like. The most vital of these agencies was the State Planning Committee (*Gosplan*)—the central authority supervising the USSR's planned economy. Gosplan was the economic staff of the Council of Ministers. It formulated the specific plans for implementing broad economic objectives laid down by the party and exercised direct operational control not only over its counterparts in the republics but also over the planning departments in individual ministries and state committees. However powerful, Gosplan was, like all other specialized agencies and ministries, an auxiliary of the party, called upon "to guard and defend the interests of the working class."

Under the Stalin constitution, Soviet courts performed the same function. The judicial system of the USSR consisted of four tiers of courts. At the base of the system were People's Courts. The members of these courts were elected by the voters by direct, secret ballot for a period of three years. There were no special qualifications, and any citizen of the USSR entitled to vote could be elected, provided he or she was nominated by the Communist party or one of its auxiliaries as a candidate. Above the People's Courts were the territorial, provincial, and regional courts, and the courts of autonomous regions. The autonomous republics and union republics had their own supreme courts, whose members were elected by their respective Supreme Soviets for five-year terms. The highest tribunal of the land was the Supreme Court of the USSR, whose members were elected for a term of five years by the Supreme Soviet of the USSR.

Although it was the highest tribunal, the competence of the Supreme Court of the USSR was limited. It possessed no powers of judicial review over legislation and it could not declare any law of the Supreme Soviet or of its Presidium to be unconstitutional. The chief aim of the Supreme Court of the USSR and that of other Soviet courts under the Stalin constitution was "to educate the citizens of the USSR in a spirit of devotion to the motherland and to the cause of socialism, in the spirit of an exact and unfaltering performance of Soviet laws, careful attitude toward socialist property, labor discipline, honest fulfillment of state and public duties, [and] respect towards the rules of the socialist commonwealth." In other words, the Soviet judiciary was an organ of state power under the command and guidance of the Communist party.

Closely associated with the Soviet judicial system was the Procurator General. Selected by the party and appointed by the Supreme Soviet of the USSR for a term of seven years, the Procurator was the chief legal officer of the government. In that capacity he possessed broad powers.

POLITICAL·ADMINISTRATIVE MAP OF THE USSR

Sam'l H. Bryant

Legend

	Autonomous Soviet Socialist Republics
	Autonomous Oblasts
	National Okrugs

International boundaries
Boundaries of Union Republics
"   "   " Autonomous Republics
"   "   " National Okrugs
"   "   " Autonomous Oblasts

Labels

A LITHUANIAN SSR
B LATVIAN SSR
C ESTONIAN SSR

1 DAGESTAN ASSR
2 NORTH OSETIN ASSR
3 CHECHEN-UNGUSH ASSR
4 ADZHAR ASSR
5 ABKHAZ ASSR
6 NAKHICHEVAN ASSR
7 KABARDIN-BALKAR ASSR

KORIAK NATIONAL OKRUG
CHUKO NATIONAL OKRUG
SEA OF OKHOTSK
JEWISH AUTONOMOUS OBLAST
YAKUT ASSR
KARELIAN ASSR
NENETS NATIONAL OKRUG
NOVAIA ZEMLIA
TAIMYR NATIONAL OKRUG
EVENKI NATIONAL OKRUG
KOMI ASSR
YAMAL NENETS NATIONAL OKRUG
KHANTY MANSI NATIONAL OKRUG
Lake Baikal
BURIAT ASSR
UST-ORDYN BURIAT NATIONAL OKRUG
TUVA AUTONOMOUS OBLAST
KHAKASS AUTONOMOUS OBLAST
GORNO-ALTAY AUTONOMOUS OBLAST
RUSSIAN SFSR
MOSCOW
UDMURT ASSR
BASHKIR ASSR
MARI ASSR
CHUVASH ASSR
TATAR ASSR
MORDVA ASSR
KALMYK ASSR
KAZAKH SSR
Lake Balkhash
KIRGHIZ SSR
ARAL SEA
GORNO-BADAKHSHAN AUTONOMOUS OBLAST
TADZHIK SSR
UZBEK SSR
KARA KALPAK ASSR
TURKMEN SSR
CASPIAN SEA
BELO-RUSSIAN SSR
UKRAINIAN SSR
MOLDAVIAN SSR
BLACK SEA
GEORGIAN SSR
ARMENIAN SSR
AZERBAIDZHAN SSR
"BALTIC SEA"
LATVIAN SSR

He appointed, for a term of five years, procurators of union republics, territories and provinces. Union republic procurators, in turn, appointed district and local procurators, subject to confirmation by the Procurator General. Free of local controls or influence, the agents of the Procurator General checked on abuses of administrators and on law observance by citizens of the USSR. Like the court, the procuratorial system served as an arm of the party and its officials were viewed as "watchmen of socialist legality," "leaders of the policy of the Communist party and of Soviet authority," and "champions of socialism." From its inception in 1917, the secret police, variously known as CHEKA, OGPU, NKVD, MVD, MGB and KGB performed the same function.

The 1936 constitution extended federal jurisdiction appreciably beyond that of the 1924 constitution. As outlined in Article 14 the jurisdiction of the USSR embraced: (1) representation of the USSR in international relations, conclusion, ratification and termination of treaties of the USSR with other states, and establishment of general procedure governing the relations of Union Republics with foreign states; (2) questions of war and peace; (3) admissions of new republics into the USSR; (4) control over the observance of the Constitution of the USSR and insuring conformity of the Constitutions of Union Republics with the Constitution of the USSR; (5) confirmation of alterations of boundaries between Union Republics; (6) confirmation of the formation of new territories and regions and also of new Autonomous Republics and autonomous regions within Union Republics; (7) organization of the defense of the USSR, direction of all the armed forces of the USSR, and the determination of directing principles governing the organization of the military formations of the Union Republics; (8) foreign trade on the basis of state monopoly; (9) safeguarding the security of the state; (10) determination of the national plans of the USSR; (11) approval of the consolidated state budget of the USSR, and of the report on its fulfillment, and determination of the taxes and revenues which go to the Union, the Republican, and the local budgets; (12) administration of the banks, industrial and agricultural enterprises, and trading enterprises of All-Union importance; (13) administration of transport and communications; (14) direction of the monetary and credit systems; (15) organization of state insurance; (16) contracting or granting of loans; (17) determination of the basic principles of land tenure and of the use of mineral wealth, forests and waters; (18) determination of basic principles in the spheres of education and public health; (19) organization of the uniform system of national economic statistics; (20) determination of the principles of labor legislation; (21) legislation concerning the judicial system and judicial procedure and criminal and civil codes; (22) legislation concerning union citizenship and the rights of aliens; (23) determination of the principles of legislation concerning marriage and the family; and (24) issuing of All-Union acts of amnesty. As the above-cited items indicate, the jurisdiction of the USSR was so comprehensive under the Stalin constitution that it virtually excluded the possibility of independent legislation by the Union Republics. This factor, however, did not prevent every republic's constitution from proclaiming "sovereign status" and the right "freely to secede from the USSR."

THE PARTY AND ITS AUXILIARIES

The source of all power in the USSR, constitutional provisions notwithstanding, is neither the government nor the people but the Communist party of the Soviet Union (CPSU). This power, although a living reality since 1917, was not formally acknowledged by the Soviet constitution until that of 1936. No critical observer of Soviet affairs was ever misled by this "omission," because party leaders have repeatedly stressed the supreme position of the party, and have defined it as "the vanguard of the working class and the highest form of its political organization"; "the instrument of the absolute dictatorship of the proletariat and the embodiment of its unity of will"; "the directing kernel of all organizations of the working people, both public and state"; "the personification of the unity of proletarian principles, of proletarian will and of proletarian unity"; and "the chief leader in the system of proletarian dictatorship." As the only party in the USSR, the Communist party has directed, controlled, and guided every political, economic, scientific, cultural, intellectual, sport, and social institution, and all other developments, either directly or through its members. In fact, not one important decision within the Soviet Union has been taken without the guidance of party directives.

Lenin, of course, created the party and gave it its *raison d'etat*. Stalin, however, shaped the party's organizational structure and formulated its *modus operandi*. With only slight modifications these features are as valid now as they were sixty years ago. In its organizational structure, grounded in a broad base of 414,000 primary party organizations and over 618,000 party groups in 1981, the CPSU rises like a pyramid to the single directing body at the top. In theory the party is governed by the principle of "democratic centralism," which the current party statute (1961) [1] defines as "(a) election of all leading party bodies from the lowest to the highest; (b) periodic reports of party bodies to their party organizations and to higher bodies; (c) strict party discipline and subordination of the minority to the majority; [and] (d) the unconditionally binding nature of the decisions of the higher bodies upon lower ones." The claim that final authority rests with the party members is, however,

[1] For full text of the 1961 party statute, see Appendix 36.

a myth. All life in the Soviet Union is ruled from the apex of the pyramid—the leadership of the party—and the membership of each lower body is approved by and directly responsible to its immediate superior. This cardinal rule, originally adopted by the Eighth Party Congress in 1919, has never been altered in the party statute, although the statute itself has been amended several times (Twelfth Party Conference in 1922, Fourteenth Party Congress in 1925, Seventeenth Party Congress in 1934, Eighteenth Party Congress in 1939, Nineteenth Party Congress in 1952, Twentieth Party Congress in 1956, and Twenty-second Party Congress in 1961). Since the CPSU is the guiding force in the USSR, this structural organization applies equally to soviet, trade union, cooperative, and all organizations.

The apex of all power in the USSR is the Political Bureau, or Politburo, of the Central Committee of the CPSU, which between 1952 and 1966 was known as the Presidium. Charged by the party statute with directing "the work of the Central Committee between plenary meetings," the Politburo is the supreme and the *only* policy-making body in the Soviet Union. Headed by the leader of the party, the Politburo is responsible for initiation, formulation, coordination, and execution of domestic and foreign policies. To all intents and purposes it is a law unto itself. Nominally, the members of the Politburo (full members and candidates) are elected by the party's Central Committee (CC). Actually, however, they are selected by the leader of the party on the basis of their loyalty, administrative ability, and political prowess. The Politburo is a highly secret organization, and apart from the identity of its members [1] very little is known about its formal organization or its working procedure. There are many strong indications that although all important policy questions are discussed at the Politburo's plenary sessions, they are in essence decided by the leader of the party. Since the leader's "line" is the party line, leaders of the CPSU have been elevated beyond criticism. Their views have never been questioned (or any attempts were silenced), and their statements, however crude and simple, have been treated as revelation. Until his death in January, 1924, Lenin was the undisputed party spokesman. Thereafter, Stalin dominated the party until his death in March, 1953, and subsequently, until his sudden removal on October 15, 1964, all party policies were determined by Khrushchev. After Khrushchev's removal from power all basic policies of the CPSU were decided by Brezhnev until his death on November 10, 1982, whereupon Yurii V. Andropov assumed that role.

There is some evidence to indicate that since about the middle of the 1970s the Committee on State Security or Defense [*Gosudarstvennyi Komitet Oborony*] has gained enormous decision-making power in Soviet

---

[1] For membership see Appendix 2.

The Organizational Structure of the CPSU in 1976

Membership figures are based on the Twenty-Fifth Party Congress, February–March, 1976. According to Brezhnev the CPSU had 15,694,000 members. In March, 1981 that figure was 17,400,000.

SOURCE: Basil Dmytryshyn, *A History of Russia*, © 1977, p. 549. Reprinted by permission of Prentice-Hall, Inc.

political life, including the CPSU. The Committee is headed by the General Secretary of the CC and its members include: Minister of Defense; Chief of the General Staff; Chief of the Warsaw Pact Forces; Chiefs of Soviet Ground, Naval, Air, Strategic Rocket and Air Defense Forces; Chairman of Soviet Secret Police; Chairman of the *Gosplan*; and other high party and government functionaries as problems may require. Although this Committee has no legal place within the formal structure of the party, it actually appears to be as powerful as the Politburo. While all members of this Committee are high ranking party members, most of them represent and reflect the thinking and interests of the Soviet military-industrial complex.

Another very important policy-making body is the Secretariat of the CC of the CPSU. It is headed by the General Secretary, whose position, since 1924, has been synonymous with leadership of the party. The General Secretary is currently assisted by several secretaries, whose duties and responsibilities are divided along both functional and geographic lines. Formally, all secretaries are "elected" by the CC of the CPSU, to which they are also accountable for their work. In reality, the General Secretary selects his subordinates, who are then formally approved by the CC. Under the present party statute, the Secretariat is responsible for direction of "current work, chiefly the selection of personnel and verification of the fulfillment of party decisions." This means simply that the Secretariat disseminates and explains party decisions to both party and non-party members; checks on and insures the implementation of policy by party, governmental, and other institutions; mobilizes economic and all other pressures for the implementation of party policies; allocates manpower and resources of the party; and is responsible for the trade unions, courts, police, and armed forces, health and social welfare, propaganda, publishing houses, and relations with foreign Communists.[1] The Secretariat, in other words, is the administrative head of the CPSU and provides the day-to-day direction and leadership of the party and of the world-wide Communist movement.

Still another important policy-making body in the Soviet Union is the CC of the CPSU. Technically the CC is a powerful body. According to the current party statute, the CC directs the entire work of the party in the intervals between party congresses; establishes the norms of representation at the party congresses; selects and places executive cadres; directs the work of all central government and public organizations through the party groups within them; creates and directs the work of various agencies, institutions, and enterprises of the party; appoints the editorial boards of central newspapers and journals; distributes the funds of the

---

[1] Until its abolition in October, 1952, many of the current functions of the Secretariat were within the jurisdiction of the Organizational Bureau, or Orgburo.

party; represents the CPSU in its relations with other parties; elects the party Politburo, Secretariat, and (since 1956) the Bureau for the RSFSR;[1] organizes the Central Control Commission;[2] convenes regular conferences and/or congresses of territorial party organizations; approves party organizations in the Soviet armed forces and guides their work through the Chief Political Administration; establishes rules for admitting into the CPSU Soviet citizens who formerly belonged to foreign Communist or workers' parties; issues instructions to lower party bodies on the admission of new members or candidates, or their transfer to other party organizations; keeps other party organizations informed about its work; holds plenary sessions every six months; and expels its own members or candidates from membership should they sully their honor or dignity.

In theory the CC of the CPSU is a powerful body, and its decisions and resolutions have always had the force of law. In reality, however, the CC is dominated by the leader of the party, and its chief function is the approval of his policies. The leader controls the CC through its individual members, who, while technically "elected" at each regular party congress, are in essence personally selected by him on the basis of their loyalty, administrative ability, and political prowess. The members of the CC represent the most influential element of the party, the government, trade unions, armed forces, and cultural, scientific, and other organizations.[3] Apparently to make their loyalty absolute, the current party statute calls for a compulsory turnover of "not less than one-quarter" of the membership of the CC every four years. Only the future will tell whether this new rule will be used to insure the "continuity of leadership" or to serve as a permanent purge of undesirables.

The last member of the policy-making bodies is the Party Congress. Theoretically it is the most important body of the CPSU, to which every party organ is accountable. According to the current party statute, the Congress convenes every four years to review, amend and approve the program and statute of the party; to determine the line of the party in domestic and foreign affairs; to elect members and candidates of the CC

---

[1] The RSFSR has never had its own Communist party. The Twentieth Party Congress in February, 1956, established for the RSFSR a Bureau of the CC of the CPSU, with Khrushchev as its chairman. This arrangement was approved by the two succeeding congresses. The Bureau was abolished in 1966.

[2] Under the current party statute, the Central Control Commission; (1) verifies the observance of party discipline by party members and candidates; (2) conducts purges of party members guilty of violating the program and statute of the party, party and state discipline, and party morality (such as deception, dishonesty, insincerity, slander, bureaucratism, and the like); and (3) examines all appeals and decisions of lower party organizations regarding expulsion from the party or party penalties.

[3] The Twenty-Sixth Congress of the CPSU in March, 1981, elected 319 full members and 155 candidates of the CC.

and of the Central Control Commission; [1] to hear and approve reports of the CC and other central bodies; and to decide, if need be, the question of expulsion from the party of a member or candidate member of the CC. Made up of delegates from all corners of the Soviet Union and from all walks of party life, the Congress is supposed to embody the wisdom and the will of the whole party. For the first few years of Communist rule in Russia, party congresses were held annually and they participated rather actively in policy determination. Since about 1927 they have degenerated into rubber stamp organs, and have been held irregularly for the purpose of granting automatic and unanimous approval of the principles and current policies of the self-perpetuating party leadership. The leadership controls the Congress through the members who, while technically elected at the meetings of lower party bodies, are in reality carefully selected by the central party leadership in Moscow.

Technically each union republic, except, as noted earlier, the RSFSR, has its own Communist party, presidium, secretariat, central committee, and party congress. It is to be remembered, however, that union republic Communist parties are not independent organizations, but integral parts of the CPSU which determines absolutely everything for all the republics. Each union republic Communist party acts as an instrument of the Kremlin's policies, carries out its directives, controls life in the union republic, and receives praise for successes and/or condemnation for failures. As intimate parts of the CPSU, union republic Communist parties are important reflectors of policy changes within the Soviet Union. The importance of the union republic Communist parties depends on the relative position a given republic occupies in the life of the USSR.

Below the union republic Communist parties are territorial, regional, area, and district party organizations. Within their respective jurisdictions, each of these organizations is charged with the execution of orders and policies of the central bodies of the party. At each level, too, the administrative-executive organs of the party play the decisive role. At the lowest level of party structure are primary party organizations, formerly known as cells. The primary party organizations are organized on a functional basis at the place of work—in factories, schools, collective farms, military units, offices, and such places. Three party members are required to form a primary party organization. Although it is at the lowest tier of the structural hierarchy, the primary party organization performs many vital functions. It accepts into the CPSU new members whom it is required to guide in the spirit of devotion to the party. It is required to oppose any attempts at introducing "revisionist distortions into Marxism-Leninism

---

[1] The Twenty-Sixth Congress of the CPSU elected 75 members of the CCC. According to the party statute the CCC "supervises the expeditious and proper handling of business of the central bodies of the party, and audits the accounts of the treasury and the enterprises of the CC of the CPSU."

and its dogmatic interpretation"; to organize the masses to carry out "the current tasks of communist construction," and promote competition among them for the fulfillment of production quotas; to strengthen labor discipline; to struggle against disorganization and waste; to participate actively in the economic and political life of the country; to criticize all the defects of lesser officials; and to "see to it that every communist observes in his own life" and inculcates in others the elaborate code of "moral principles" of the party. The primary party organization is also used as a scapegoat for all the failures and/or mistakes of the party leadership.

The current party statute defines the CPSU as "the tried and tested militant vanguard of the Soviet people, which unites on a voluntary basis the more advanced, the politically more conscious section of the working class, collective-farm peasantry, and intelligentsia of the USSR." The statute also acknowledges that the CPSU is "an integral part of the international communist and working-class movement," and as such it subscribes to Marxist-Leninist principles of proletarian internationalism and "actively promotes the unity of the entire international communist and workers' movement and of the fraternal ties with the great army of communists of all countries." Any soviet citizen may become a member of the CPSU if he or she accepts the party program and statutes, takes an active part in Communist construction, works in one of the party's organizations, and blindly fulfills all the decisions of the party leadership. Such was not the case in earlier times. Until 1939 applicants for party membership were divided into four groups: industrial workers of five years' standing; industrial workers of less than five years' standing, agricultural laborers, Red Army men who were formerly workers or collective farmers, and "technicians"; collective farmers, teachers in elementary schools, and members of peasant handicraft cooperatives; and other employees. In reality, however, from the inception of the party, the dominant group within it, both in numbers and in influence, has always been the intelligentsia.

Party membership has always carried with it rights and privileges as well as duties and obligations. As a member of the ruling class a party member enjoys all available material benefits, and has all existing avenues open to his advancement. He also has the right "to elect and be elected to party bodies"; to discuss questions of the party's policies at party gatherings; to introduce motions; to criticize lesser party officials; to be present at a party meeting when his "activity or conduct is discussed"; and to address questions or suggestions to higher party bodies, including the CC of the CPSU, and demand an answer. In return for these "rights" a party member is obligated to fight for communism; to set an example of the Communist attitude toward work; to raise labor productivity; to take the initiative in all that is new and progressive, and support and propagate advanced methods; to master technology and to improve his qualifications; to safeguard and increase public property; to carry out party decisions firmly and undeviatingly; to explain the policy of the party to the masses; to help strengthen the party's ties with the people; and to take an active part in the political, economic and cultural life of the country. Party members are further obligated to set an example in the fulfillment of public duty; to master Marxism-Leninism; to combat "all manifestations of bourgeois ideology"; to observe rules of "communist morality"; to be an active proponent of the ideas of socialist internationalism and Soviet patriotism among the masses; to combat survivals of "nationalism and chauvinism"; to strengthen the friendship of the peoples of the USSR; to observe party and state discipline; to be ready to denounce his own as well as the shortcomings of others; and to be sincere towards the party, hide nothing from it, be vigilant at all times and be blindly obedient. Any deviation by a party member from these prerequisites or any manifestation of factionalism or cliquishness is incompatible with retaining party membership.

Although admission requirements have altered considerably, they are still complicated because the party wants to remain an organization of the elite. To be eligible for party membership one must be conscientious, active, and devoted to the cause of communism, be at least eighteen years old, and be recommended by at least three party members. After an application for membership has been examined by a general meeting of the primary party organization, if it is recommended and then approved by a district or city committee of the party, the applicant becomes a candidate for one year. The probationary period is designed to provide candidates with an opportunity "to familiarize themselves with the Program and Statute of the CPSU . . . and [to] test their personal qualities." At the end of the probationary period a successful candidate again goes through the same procedure and screening, and only then does he become a full party member.

The party acquires many of its members from among the ranks of the All-Union Leninist Communist League of Youth, popularly known as the *Komsomol.* Founded in 1918, and organizationally patterned after the party, the *Komsomol* conducts all of its activities under the leadership of the party. It is comprised of young people between the ages of 14 and 26 and, while it does not include the whole of Soviet youth, between 1918 and 1962 the membership of the *Komsomol* has grown from 22,000 to 19,400,000. In addition to providing the party with new members, ever since its establishment the *Komsomol* has served as the party's most active assistant in every phase of activity. With its members scattered throughout the Soviet system, trade unions, industry, collective and state farms, armed forces, and such institutions the *Komsomol* has been called upon by the party to perform many urgent tasks. In the 1920's it assisted the party in the liquidation of illiteracy. During the 1930's it actively participated in industrialization and collectivization while in the 1940's it helped to defend the USSR against Nazi invasion. The *Komsomol* has always assisted the party in the training of technicians, in political indoctrination, in propagation of the party's current policies among Soviet youth, and in the struggle against juvenile delinquency. The *Komsomol* has been called upon to foster such qualities of individual character as "loyalty to the party chiefs, iron discipline, self-sacrificing bravery, ideological purity, unshakable conviction, incessant vigilance, uncompromising militancy, and hatred toward enemies." Finally, it has also been directly responsible for the guidance of the still younger party auxiliaries, the Young Pioneers (children from nine to fifteen) and the Little Octobrists (children from eight to twelve). In other words, the *Komsomol* has been the right arm of the party among Soviet youth.

In addition to normal procedure, the party has been able to acquire new members through mass recruitments. It accepted many members during the Civil War period when it was in need of wider support. Following Lenin's death in 1924 (and Stalin's rise to power), over 200,000 new members were accepted into the party ranks. Many thousands were permitted to join the party during the early stages of industrialization and collectivization as rewards for skills and accomplishments. Thousands of heroes of World War II were brought into the party ranks. The party also registered a sizeable increase in membership during the early stages of Khrushchev's rise to power. By normal and abnormal processes, heavy obligations and strict requirements notwithstanding, between 1905 and 1981 party membership has demonstrated the following growth:

GROWTH OF THE MEMBERSHIP OF THE CPSU

	Members	*Candidates*	*Total*
1905	8,500	——	8,500
1917	23,600	——	23,600
1918	115,000	——	115,000
1921	576,000	——	576,000
1922	410,430	117,924	528,354
1924	350,000	122,000	472,000
1926	639,652	440,162	1,079,814
1933	2,203,951	1,351,387	3,555,338
1934	1,826,756	874,252	2,701,008
1938	1,405,879	514,123	1,920,002
1940	1,982,743	1,417,232	3,399,975
1941	2,515,481	1,361,404	3,876,885
1945	3,965,530	1,794,839	5,760,369
1952	6,013,259	868,886	6,882,145
1956	6,795,896	419,609	7,215,505
1959	7,622,356	616,775	8,239,131
1961	8,872,516	843,489	9,716,005
1963	9,581,149	806,047	10,387,196
1965	10,811,443	946,726	11,758,169
1971	13,810,089	645,232	14,455,321
1976	——	——	15,694,000
1981	——	——	17,400,000

The numerical growth of the party has enabled it to strengthen and improve its supreme and absolute power over all aspects of life in the USSR from the highest councils of state to the lowliest private dwelling.

During the period of unprecedented growth of its membership, the party has also undergone a permanent purge. On several occasions the membership of the party has been submitted to a thorough examination from the point of view of the prevailing ideological orthodoxy, devotion to the cause of communism, and personal character and behavior. Major purges took place in 1921, 1926, 1927, 1929, 1933, 1934–1938, 1946, 1953, and 1957. Of these, as noted earlier, the most spectacular and the one with the most victims was the purge of 1934–1938. The main objective of this purge was not so much the cleansing of the party of undeserving members, but extermination of a vast majority of old Bolshevik leaders. The list of accused read like a "Who's Who" of the Russian Revolution, and included Lenin's close associates, old party members, leaders of the government, army commanders, ambassadors, and other "founding fathers" of Russian communism. They were accused of, and "confessed" their part in, murder, attempted murder, high treason, plotting with foreign powers, and "wrecking." The purge extended to every sphere of Soviet life and was carried out with ruthless thoroughness, even in the remotest corners of the land, in the armed forces, in factories, and on collective farms. Following Stalin's death, some of the more important victims were "rehabilitated." Countless thousands were less fortunate, but from their graves they cannot protest.

FOREIGN POLICY IN THE 1930's

The basic challenge facing Soviet foreign policy during the 1930's was: how to provide security for the militarily weak but rapidly industrializing territorial base of the revolution, in the face of Hitler's decision to plunge into a vast territorial conquest in Europe and the renewed Japanese efforts to build an empire at China's expense. Stalin faced this enormous challenge by ordering total mobilization of all the available resources of both conventional and unconventional diplomacy. His efforts were facilitated by the determination of many victims of aggression to resist Japanese and Nazi conquests.

The tone for unconventional diplomacy was set during the Sixth World Congress of the Communist International held in Moscow from July 17 to September 1, 1928. It was embodied in the speeches of Communist leaders who came to Moscow for the occasion, and above all in *The Programme of the Communist International* which the Congress adopted. This verbose and complex document defined itself as "the program of struggle for World Communism"—a definition which caused some observers to label it a "blueprint for world conquest." It was the most important Communist document since the publication of the *Communist Manifesto* in 1848. Perhaps for this reason it has never been withdrawn or criticized, and the principles it enunciated, with only slight modifications in details and emphasis, remain in effect to this day.

The Programme dealt at considerable length with revolutionary objectives, Communist strategy and tactics, the kind of revolutions to be fought for, and the place of the proletariat, of the anti-colonial movements, and of the Soviet Union in this struggle. *The Programme* defined the Soviet Union as "the one and only fatherland of the international proletariat," and declared that the revolutionary role of the USSR was "exceptionally great" for three reasons: (1) because the USSR was "the international driving force of revolution that impels the proletariat of all countries to seize power"; (2) because it was "The living example proving that the working class is not only capable of destroying capitalism, but of building up socialism as well"; and (3) because it was "the prototype of the fraternity of nationalities in all lands united in the World Union of Socialist Republics and of the economic unity of the toilers of all countries in a single world Socialist economic system that the world proletariat must establish when it has captured political power."

As the leader of "the citadel of world revolution," the Communist party of the USSR demanded that the international proletariat pledge its exclusive allegiance to the USSR; subordinate its local interests to those of the USSR; render assistance to make the First Five Year Plan a success; come to the defense of the USSR "by all means in its power" in case of an attack; promote proletarian revolutions everywhere and colonial revolutions in areas dominated by Western Powers; and consider Communist right wing reformists and social democrats "the most dangerous enemies of communism and of the dictatorship of the proletariat." On its part the Communist party of the Soviet Union pledged that it would not shrink "from fulfilling its international obligations and from rendering support to all the oppressed, to the labor movements in capitalist countries, to colonial movements against imperialism and to the struggle against national oppression."

Military weakness of the USSR, and its planned plunge into vast economic experimentation in the late 1920's and early 1930's, prevented Stalin from active adherence to these pledges. There was nevertheless a great deal of noisy propaganda during this period. Some of the noise was directed against armaments and alleged military preparations of the major world powers. Some of it was directed in behalf of independence of colonial peoples and the strengthening efforts of the USSR. Much energy, however, was wasted on fighting social democrats for their alleged willingness to betray the revolution. This struggle was bitter everywhere, but was fatal only in Germany where Communist obstructionist tactics teamed with those of the extreme nationalists, thereby helping to destroy the Social Democratic-led Weimar Republic—a cooperation that enabled Hitler to come to power.

Stalin greatly underestimated the significance of Hitler's rise to power. Three assumptions seem to have been responsible for his miscalculation: (1) Hitler's violent opposition to the Versailles settlement which envisaged a Franco-German war and hence improvement of the security of the USSR; (2) firm belief in the strength of the German Communist party, which polled over six million votes in the election of 1932; and (3) Soviet need for uninterrupted flow of German machinery during the initial phases of industrialization. Throughout 1933, Stalin and his associates stressed publicly their desire to continue friendly relations with Germany based on the Rapallo spirit. As late as January, 1934, during the meeting of the Seventeenth Party Congress, Stalin pleaded for friendly relations with Hitler, arguing that the existence of different political and economic systems should not serve as an obstacle to good relations between the Soviet Union and Germany. Hitler, however, ignored all of Stalin's overtures. The only "friendly" gesture was his decision to ratify, in May, 1933, a renewal of the 1926 neutrality treaty with the USSR which had been pending since 1931. Instead of cooperation, throughout 1933, Gestapo agents carried out mass exterminations of German Communists, and the Nazi press intensified its anti-Soviet campaign. Hitler's intransigence forced Stalin to turn to different tactics and emphasis.

The new tactics—commonly referred to as the period of the "Popular Front"—sought to establish friendly relations with all countries threatened by, and all movements opposed to, the rise of new German chauvinism, which was publicly proclaiming its determination to seek *Lebensraum* at the expense of its neighbors. On the surface, the new communist tactics represented a considerable departure from those set forth by the Sixth Congress of the Comintern in 1928. In reality, however, the departure was not so radical, because alongside the ultrarevolutionary methods of the unconventional diplomacy pursued by the Comintern, Stalin followed a cautious policy on the conventional level. This policy, as we noted in an earlier chapter, was responsible for such actions as Soviet entry into the disarmament negotiations sponsored by the League of Nations in 1928, signing and ratification of the Kellogg-Briand Pact in 1929, and conclusion of a series of non-aggression pacts with the Baltic states, Poland, and France in 1932, and with Italy in 1933.

The "new course" in Soviet foreign policy was nevertheless responsible for several significant developments. The first was the establishment of diplomatic relations with the United States on November 16, 1933. One of the most important factors that brought the two countries together was Japan's conquest of Manchuria in 1931–1932, and its determination to build a vast empire in the Far East. Hitler's triumph in Germany served as another motive that pressed for the need to establish the normal diplomatic contacts interrupted since the revolution. Before normal relations could be resumed, however, both governments felt a need to remove certain barriers that stood between them. Prominent among these was the question of debts, which had already been discussed but on which no agreement had been reached. In its eagerness to establish normal relations with the United States, the Soviet government promised neither to sponsor nor to permit within its jurisdiction propaganda or other activity aimed at the overthrow of the United States government. It likewise agreed to allow religious freedom and legal protection to American nationals residing in the USSR. None of these promises, however, materialized, and the relations established between the two countries continued to be, in the words of one competent observer, "troubled, distant, and devoid of real political content."

The entry of the Soviet Union into the League of Nations on September 18, 1934, was the second significant manifestation of the "new course." It was a major departure, because hitherto, or at least until 1928, Soviet leaders had repeatedly expressed their contempt for the League. The situation in 1934 was different. With Japan, Germany, and Italy "on the warpath," the League seemed to offer Stalin an effective instrument for fighting the aggressive policies of his adversaries, as well as a forum from which to dispel a widespread impression that the USSR sought to conquer the rest of the world. These two goals were pursued with considerable vigor and determination by Litvinov, Commissar for Foreign Affairs. As a permanent member of the Council, the Soviet Union became a strong supporter of the League, a firm advocate of an effective collective security system in order to avert war, and a bitter critic of the League's inability and apparent unwillingness to check Axis expansion.

The third significant manifestation of the "new course" was Soviet adherence to the French Security System in 1935. As in post-Bismarckian days, both countries were attracted to each other by the presence of the German danger. The road for the Franco-Soviet understanding was paved by the Non-Aggression Pact of November 29, 1932, by a commercial treaty of January 11, 1934, and by a close relationship between Litvinov and French Foreign Minister Louis Barthou. The Franco-Soviet rapprochement of 1935 consisted of two parts. The first was a Treaty of Mutual Assistance of May 2, 1935, by whose terms the two governments obligated themselves to assist one another in case either of them was subjected to an unprovoked attack. The second part came on May 16, 1935, in the form of a treaty signed by the Soviet Union, France, and Czechoslovakia. In its provisions, this tripartite act was identical with those of the Franco-Soviet treaty in all but one respect: it provided that the Soviet Union was obligated to come to the aid of Czechoslovakia only if France also fulfilled its obligation to Czechoslovakia. Whether or not this condition was a reflection of the growing Soviet suspicion of the West, during the subsequent Munich crisis of September, 1938, this escape clause helped the USSR to pose as the only defender of Czechoslovakia's sovereignty, and to place most of the blame on France in view of the latter's inability or unwillingess to act.

The entry of the Soviet Union into the League of Nations, but above all its joining of the French Security System, forced Stalin to alter the tactics, but not the ultimate aim of the Comintern. This formality was officially taken care of at the Seventh and last Congress of the Comintern, held in July–August, 1935, with the sanctioning of "the Popular Front." The Popular Front had two aspects. On the one hand, Communists every-where were ordered to join hands with the *leadership* of those labor unions, social democratic, bourgeois, peasant, and even right wing parties which opposed Nazi, Fascist, or Japanese aggression. At the same time, while "united at the top," the Communists were to pursue a policy of "the united front from below"; i.e., they were to try to win the rank-and-file away from its leaders.

This all-out effort to subvert, while posing as defender and champion of the interests and achievements of all people regardless of their political affiliations, was responsible for considerable increase in Communist mem-bership and in political influence, both in Europe and in Asia. In Europe classic manifestations of this policy appeared in France—where the Popu-lar Front was first tried out—and in the Spanish Civil War. In France, as early as 1934, the Communists joined hands with socialist-led trade unions against the French extreme right, dropped their opposition to French ar-maments in 1935, and were instrumental in the selection of Leon Blum as Premier of the Popular Ministry in 1936. Blum's reluctance to introduce the Communist program, however, brought an end to this cooperation period, led to Communist-organized strikes, and to his downfall in June, 1937.

The manifestation of the Popular Front in Spain was somewhat more complicated. Late in August, 1936, in answer to previous Italian and German armed intervention on behalf of General Francisco Franco, the Soviet Union intervened on behalf of Spanish republicans. Before the end of the year the USSR sent to Spain large quantities of military sup-plies and hundreds of military and political experts who, together with thousands of non-Soviet "volunteers" were able to gain control not only of military operations but of secret police, intelligence, censorship, propa-ganda, and other activities. The problem of logistics, along with French and British reluctance to help in the face of increased German and Italian support of Franco, forced the Soviet Union to abandon its operations. Throughout most of 1937, Soviet efforts in Spain were directed towards two main goals: to prolong the struggle as long as possible in order to divert German interest away from the Soviet Union; and to liquidate all the "Trotskyites" and other "anti-Stalinists" in Spain—an effort that was pursued with determined ruthlessness.

In Asia the policy of the Popular Front received classic expression in China, where it centered around the exploitation of strong anti-Japanese feelings among Chinese intellectuals. The Communists joined patriotic cries to make a vigorous effort to end the bitter civil war between Chinese Nationalists and Communists, and pleaded for a United Front against the Japanese invaders. Chiang's reluctance to listen to these "patriotic appeals" until he had disposed of the Communists, forced many of his admirers and followers into the Communist camp. Following the signing of the Anti-Comintern Pact on November 17, 1936, by Germany, Italy, and Japan, the demand for a united anti-Japanese action increased. To break his uncompromising attitude towards Communists, Chiang was kidnapped on December 12, 1936, but was released unharmed on condition that he form a United Front with the Communists against Japan. An agreement to this effect was concluded on September 22, 1937, and continued to operate fairly well until the end of 1938. As a sign of improved relations with the Communists, in August, 1937, Chiang signed a non-aggression pact with the USSR and replaced his German advisers with Soviet experts. Improved Sino-Soviet relations did not escape Japanese attention, and between 1937 and 1939 the Soviet Union and Japan, in several armed clashes, tested their military preparedness as well as their determination to resist. Both were found to exist in sufficient quantity on both sides.

The situation in Europe, however, presented a different picture. On October 3, 1935, Italian forces invaded Ethiopia, and the League, although called upon to resist, failed to cope with the aggression. On March 7, 1936, in violation of the Locarno Treaty of 1925, Hitler marched into and occupied the Rhineland. Neither England nor France nor the League made any move to stop Hitler's great gamble. These and other signs of Western irresoluteness and appeasement enabled the Nazis to execute a whole series of *faits accompli*, which greatly strengthened Germany's position and which endangered the position of other powers, including the USSR. In 1936, and again in 1937, Stalin sought to reach an agreement with Hitler, and renewed his efforts with even greater determination following German annexation of Austria on March 12, 1938. The first outward manifestation of "friendliness" was the replacement in May, 1938, of Soviet Ambassador to Berlin Jacob Surits, who was Jewish, by Alexei T. Merekalov, a Great Russian, who was instructed to improve German-Soviet relations. The second step came in July, 1938, when both governments agreed to refrain from hostile and abusive propaganda against their respective heads of state. This was later broadened to include other aspects.

The dismemberment of Czechoslovakia in September, 1938, at Munich, was a major turning point, not only for Europe but for Soviet foreign policy as well. Encouraged by Western weakness and retreat, during the summer of 1938 Hitler increased his invective against Czechoslovakia.

Alarmed by the mounting crisis and manufactured war psychosis, on September 30, 1938, Britain lost her prestige, France her honor, and Czechoslovakia much of her territory. The exclusion of the Soviet Union, however, from this classic appeasement played into Stalin's hands. Throughout the entire crisis, the Soviet government repeatedly asserted its willingness and readiness to fulfill its obligations both as a member of the League of Nations and under the provisions of the Franco-Soviet-Czechoslovak Treaty of 1935. This readiness was, however, conditional on French willingness to honor their pledge and/or on Polish or Rumanian willingness to allow Soviet troops to move across their respective territories. Since Stalin was aware that neither of these conditions was likely to materialize, scholars have questioned the sincerity of his offer. Genuine or not, Soviet pledges made a deep impression on many Czechoslovaks.

By dismembering Czechoslovakia, the Nazis lowered the resistance of Czechoslovakia's neighbors, opened the whole Danube region to German expansion, and indirectly endangered the security of the USSR. These developments made an early understanding with Germany not only urgent but imperative. Fortunately for Stalin, Hitler's actions greatly facilitated the realization of this goal. Shortly after he disposed of Czechoslovakia, Hitler directed his attention to Poland. Negotiations to resolve some of the problems between Germany and Poland started on October 24, 1938, but from the outset a deadlock developed on account of German demands, which among others included formal return of Danzig to Germany, Polish acquiescence to an extraterritorial highway and railway across the Polish Corridor, cooperation in colonial questions, and a common policy towards the Soviet Union within the framework of the Anti-Comintern Pact.

Because the Poles rejected outright the German offers to turn Poland into a German satellite, Hitler now became receptive to Stalin's feelers and made many "friendly" gestures of his own. At the end of October, 1938, he initiated talks with the Soviet Union for the conclusion of a trade agreement and further eased anti-Soviet propaganda. At the New Year's reception, Hitler broke his old precedent by cordially greeting and chatting with the Soviet Ambassador. He also departed from his usual blistering references to communism in his address to the Reichstag on January 30, 1939, and instead was bitterly critical of the Western Powers for their "hysterical, unscrupulous, tactless, and extremely malicious" press and propaganda. Stalin echoed Hitler's words on March 10, 1939, in his address to the Eighteenth Party Congress, where he too did not spare words in attacking the West and its press for spreading "vociferous lies" about "the weakness of the Red Army," "the demoralization of the Red Air Force," and "riots" in the Soviet Union. He declared that the aim of this and other suspicious uproar was "to incense the Soviet Union against Germany, to poison the atmosphere, and to provoke a conflict with Ger-

After signing the Non-Aggression Pact in Moscow, 1939 (left to right), Von Ribbentrop, Secretary Gaus (Germany), Stalin and Molotov.

many without any visible grounds." Stalin's concurrence with Hitler's contention that London and Paris were the *Weltlügenzentralen* (world centers of lies) paved half the way to a Soviet-German understanding.

The other half was prepared by the belated Franco-British firmness and unwillingness to make further concessions to Hitler in his efforts to remake the political map of Europe. On March 31, 1939, convinced belatedly that Hitler's appetite could not be satiated, the British unexpectedly extended to Poland a military guarantee and began to put out feelers to Rumania, Hungary, and the USSR for joint action against Hitler's aggression. Hitler reacted to these moves by abrogating the 1934 German-Polish treaty and the 1935 Anglo-German Naval treaty, by ordering all-out military preparations for a general attack on Poland to be launched at the end of August, 1939, and by concentrating on reaching a Nazi-Soviet understanding at all costs. Aware of Hiter's anxiety, Stalin put a high price on his friendship with the Nazis, as likewise he did on his friendship with the Western Powers. Hitler's willingness and Western unwillingness to agree to far-reaching territorial changes in Eastern Europe led to the famed Nazi-Soviet Pact of August, 1939.[1]

The Pact consisted of three parts. The first was a trade agreement signed on August 19, by which Germany granted the Soviet Union a two-year credit of 180 million German marks for the purchase of German goods. The second part was a ten year Non-Aggression Pact, signed on

[1] For the full text of the Pact, see Appendix 25.

August 23, which obligated each partner to absolute neutrality should one of them "become the object of belligerent action by a third power." The third part consisted of a secret protocol which divided Poland along the San-Vistula-Narev Rivers, and which assigned Lithuania to the German, and Estonia, Latvia, Finland, and Bessarabia to the Soviet sphere of influence. Assured of Stalin's "friendship," on September 1, 1939, Hitler ordered his armies into Poland, and World War II became a reality.

SUGGESTED READINGS

ADAMS, ARTHUR E. Stalin and His Times. New York: Holt, Rinehart & Winston, 1972.

ARMSTRONG, JOHN A. The Politics of Totalitarianism. New York: Random House, 1961.

BAUER, RAYMOND A., ALEX INKELES, and CLYDE KLUCKHOHN. How the Soviet System Works. Cambridge: Harvard University Press, 1956.

BECK, F., and W. GODIN. Russian Purge and the Extraction of Confession. New York: Viking, 1951.

BELOFF, MAX. The Foreign Policy of Soviet Russia, 1929–1941. 2 vols. New York: Oxford University Press, 1947–1949.

BRZEZINSKI, ZBIGNIEW K. The Permanent Purge: Politics of Soviet Totalitarianism. Cambridge: Harvard University Press, 1956.

BUDUROWYCZ, BOHDAN B. Polish-Soviet Relations, 1932–1939. New York: Columbia University Press, 1963.

CHAMBERLIN, WILLIAM H. Russia's Iron Age. London: Duckworth, 1935.

CONQUEST, ROBERT. The Great Terror: Stalin's Purge of the Thirties. New York: Macmillan, 1968.

———. Kolyma. The Arctic Death Camp. New York: Oxford University Press, 1979.

CURTISS, JOHN S. The Russian Church and the Soviet State, 1917–1950. Boston: Little, Brown, 1953.

DALLIN, DAVID J. The Real Soviet Russia. London: Hillis & Crater, 1947.

———, and BORIS NIKOLAEVSKY. Forced Labor in Soviet Russia. New Haven: Yale University Press, 1947.

DANIELS, ROBERT V., ed. A Documentary History of Communism. New York: Random House, 1962.

DAVIES, R. W. The Industrialization of Soviet Russia. The Socialist Offensive. The Collectivization of Soviet Agriculture. 2 vols. Cambridge: Harvard University Press, 1980.

DEUTSCHER, ISAAC. Stalin: A Political Biography. 2nd edition. New York: Oxford University Press, 1967.

DMYTRYSHYN, BASIL. Moscow and the Ukraine, 1917–1953. New York: Bookman, 1956.

DOBB, MAURICE. Soviet Economic Development Since 1917. London: Routledge & Kegan, 1948.

FAINSOD, MERLE. How Russia is Ruled. Cambridge: Harvard University Press, 1953.

———. Smolensk Under Soviet Rule. Cambridge: Harvard University Press, 1958.

FISHER, RALPH T. Pattern for Soviet Youth . . . 1918–1945. New York: Columbia University Press, 1959.

GSOVSKY, VLADIMIR. Soviet Civil Law. 2 vols. Ann Arbor: University of Michigan Press, 1948.

GUINS, GEORGE C. The Soviet Law and Soviet Society. The Hague: Nijhoff, 1954.

HAZARD, JOHN N. The Soviet System of Government. Chicago: University of Chicago Press, 1957.

HINGLEY, RONALD. Joseph Stalin: Man and Legend. New York: McGraw-Hill, 1974.

HULICKA, KAREL, and IRENE M. *Soviet Institutions, the Individual and Society.* Boston: Christopher Publishing House, 1967.

HUNT, R. N. CAREW. *The Theory and Practice of Communism.* New York: Macmillan, 1957.

JASNY, NAUM. *The Socialized Agriculture of the USSR.* Stanford: Stanford University Press, 1949.

JORAVSKY, DAVID. *The Lysenko Affair.* Cambridge: Harvard University Press, 1970.

KENNAN, GEORGE F. *Russia and the West Under Lenin and Stalin.* Boston: Little, Brown, 1961.

KULSKI, W. W. *The Soviet Regime. Communism in Practice.* Syracuse: Syracuse University Press, 1956.

LEWIN, M. *Russian Peasants and Soviet Power: A Study of Collectivization.* New York: Norton, 1975.

MCCLOSKY, HERBERT, and JOHN E. TURNER. *The Soviet Dictatorship.* New York: McGraw-Hill, 1960.

MEISEL, JAMES H., and EDWARD S. KOZERA., eds. *Materials for the Study of the Soviet System.* Ann Arbor: George Wahr, 1953.

MEDVEDEV, ROY A. *Let History Judge: The Origins and Consequences of Stalinism.* New York: Knopf, 1971.

MEDVEDEV, ZHORES A. *The Rise and Fall of T. D. Lysenko.* New York: Anchor Books, 1971.

MEYER, ALFRED G. *The Soviet Political System.* New York: Random House, 1965.

MOORE, BARRINGTON. *Soviet Politics: The Dilemma of Power.* Cambridge: Harvard University Press, 1951.

NORTH, ROBERT C. *Moscow and Chinese Communists.* Stanford: Stanford University Press, 1953.

NOVE, ALEX. *An Economic History of the USSR.* Baltimore: Penguin, 1970.

ORLOV, ALEXANDER. *The Secret History of Stalin's Crimes.* New York: Random House, 1953.

RANDALL, FRANCIS B. *Stalin's Russia.* New York: Free Press, 1965.

RESHETAR, JOHN S. JR. *A Concise History of the Communist Party of the Soviet Union.* New York: Praeger, 1960.

RUBENSTEIN, ALVIN Z., ed. *The Foreign Policy of the Soviet Union.* New York: Random House, 1960.

SCHAPIRO, LEONARD. *The Communist Party of the Soviet Union.* New York: Random House, 1960.

SOLZHENITSYN, ALEKSANDR I. *The Gulag Archipelago, 1918–1956.* 3 vols. New York: Harper & Row, 1973–1978.

STEINBERG, JULIEN, ed. *Verdict of Three Decades.* New York: Duell, Sloane, and Pearce, 1950.

TARACOUZIO, T. A. *War and Peace in Soviet Diplomacy.* New York: Macmillan, 1940.

TIMASHEFF, NICHOLAS S. *The Great Retreat.* New York: Dutton, 1946.

TOWSTER, JULIAN. *Political Power in the USSR, 1917–1947.* New York: Oxford University Press, 1948.

TUCKER, ROBERT C., and STEPHEN F. COHEN, eds. *The Great Purge Trial.* New York: Grosset & Dunlap, 1965.

———, ed. *Stalinism: Essays in Historical Interpretation.* New York: Norton, 1977.

ULAM, ADAM B. *Expansion and Coexistence: The History of Soviet Foreign Policy, 1917–1967.* New York: Praeger, 1968.

———. *Stalin: The Man and His Era.* New York: Viking, 1973.

VYSHINSKY, A. Y. *The Law and the Soviet State.* New York: Macmillan, 1948.

WEISBERG, ALEXANDER. *The Accused.* New York: Simon & Schuster, 1951.

⚔ VII

THE PATRIOTIC
FORTIES

THE "UNHOLY ALLIANCE," AUGUST 23, 1939—JUNE 22, 1941

The Nazi-Soviet Pact of August, 1939, has been variously interpreted. Hitler is reported to have considered it an essential step towards "a new distribution of the world." His critics, however, have called it "the greatest blunder of his life." In retrospect, Stalin viewed the pact as providing an opportunity to prepare his forces against German invasion. Stalin's critics, however, maintain that his prime objective in signing the pact was to bring about a war between Germany and the Western Powers that would deplete the resources of both and leave the Soviet Union in an unchallengeable position in Europe.

Whatever the motives, the "Unholy Alliance," as the pact is often called, was a turning point in the history of the world for several reasons. First, it was a revelation of the methods and possibilities of totalitarian diplomacy based on secrecy, freedom of action, rapidity of decision, and disregard for public opinion. Second, for the Communists and the Nazis alike, the pact was a supreme test of discipline which they passed with flying colors. Third, the pact disclosed Stalin's open approval and even encouragement of Hitler's immediate aggressive plans in Europe. Fourth, the pact enabled Stalin to extend the territorial base of the revolution into the heart of Europe. And, finally, the pact was *the* prelude to World War II.

The war began on September 1, 1939, when, assured of Soviet "friendship" and confident that the West would not honor its pledge, Hitler ordered his armies into Poland. On September 3, England and France formally declared war on Germany. This formality had no immediate effect on Hitler, as his war machine, brought to a high pitch of efficiency and possessing the most modern weapons, rolled victoriously over Poland. The Polish organized armed forces, though fighting heroically, could not withstand the German onslaught. They were stunned, then demoralized, and then annihilated. In less than three weeks the Polish state had ceased to exist. Its government fled, eventually to London, where it was recognized by the Allies as legitimate. These developments, in turn, brought into operation the arrangements of the Nazi-Soviet Pact.

Soviet forces entered Poland on September 17, and proceeded to occupy their assigned sphere of influence with no appreciable resistance, since the fate of the Polish army had already been decided. According to one estimate, the operation cost the Soviet Union 737 dead and 1,862 wounded, against a Polish loss of 300,000 men, most of whom were taken prisoners. The Soviets attempted to justify their aggression by pointing to the expiration of the Polish state with resultant chaos, and professing a "sacred duty" to liberate and take under Soviet protection Ukrainians and Belorussians living in Eastern Poland. The last point, which ultimately became the official version, forced Stalin to yield some territory which had been assigned to the Soviet Union by the secret protocol of the pact, but which was ethnically Polish. The new arrangement, as worked out between Stalin and German Foreign Minister von Ribbentrop late in September, 1939, assigned Lithuania to the Soviet sphere of influence and set the German-Soviet frontier along the San-Bug-Narev Rivers. Both powers also agreed to cooperate against Polish "agitation," and promised to place "no obstacles" before their respective nationals should they desire to migrate to their "fatherlands." Between 1939 and 1941, some 437,000 Germans were repatriated from Soviet Russia and about 55,000 persons went to the USSR.

The fourth partition of Poland, as this arrangement is often called, netted the Soviet Union some 76,500 square miles, and 13,000,000 inhabitants. From the outset, the Soviets treated these territories as their own. Hasty, but elaborate preparations were made for election of national assemblies, which took place on October 22, 1939. In Western Ukraine, 4,433,997, or 92.83 per cent of the eligible voters approved the selected list of candidates, while in Western Belorussia 2,672,000, or 96.7 per cent of voters participated in the election, and overwhelmingly approved the official candidates. On October 27, the newly elected national assembly of Western Ukraine formally proclaimed Soviet rule, passed a resolution requesting the Soviet government to incorporate the Western Ukraine into the USSR, confiscated without payment all movable and immovable property of the Polish nobility, the Church, and state officials, and nationalized all banks and industrial enterprises. The national assembly of Western Belorussia passed a similar resolution and took identical actions on October 29. On November 1, 1939, with pomp, fanfare, and publicity, the Supreme Soviet of the USSR granted these "requests," and Western Ukraine and Western Belorussia in less than a month and a half became integral parts of the USSR.

Following the formalities of incorporation, the new areas were given the Soviet administrative system, party, *Komsomol* and Pioneer organizations, secret police, and other "benefits" of the Soviet system. To accelerate the integration process, numerous old institutions, such as schools and cooperatives, were liquidated, as were many of their spokesmen, and new ones were introduced. The reorganization of life in the new areas was guided by trusted officials who were brought for that purpose from Soviet Russia. The peasantry was left alone throughout most of 1939, but early in 1940 a decided effort was made to introduce collective farms, state farms, and MTS's.

Soviet incorporation of the Baltic states assigned to it by the Nazi-Soviet Pact was accomplished in two stages. First was the treaty stage. On September 28, 1939, the Soviet Union forced Estonia to sign a pact of mutual assistance, which granted the USSR the right to maintain naval bases and airfields and limited garrisons on Estonian territory. On October 5, 1939, the USSR forced Latvia to make identical arrangements, and on October 10 came Lithuania's turn. With each country the Soviet Union also concluded trade agreements and promised to respect their sovereignty and their social and economic system. Lithuania, in addition, was given the city of Vilnius and vicinity, which until 1939 had been part of Poland. In June, 1940, during Hitler's vast conquest of Western Europe, Stalin introduced the second stage of the incorporation of the Baltic states —that of ultimatums. Lithuania received a Soviet ultimatum on June 12, and Latvia and Estonia on June 16, 1940. The ultimatums accused each government of anti-Soviet actions, demanded the admission of additional Soviet troops, and formation of governments "friendly" to the USSR. Without waiting for replies, Soviet forces moved in, arrested all "suspected" officials, dissolved parliaments, set up new governments, and announced new elections to be held on July 14, 1940. Under those conditions the Soviet-sponsored Working People's League received an overwhelming majority of votes. On July 21, the new parliaments "requested" that their territories be incorporated into the USSR. The Supreme Soviet of the USSR granted their requests early in August, 1940, and Lithuania, Latvia, and Estonia became Soviet Socialist Republics. These additions increased the territorial base of the revolution by 65,237 square miles and a population of 5,400,000.

Soviet attempts to bring Finland under control were not successful. Early in October, 1939, the Soviets requested that Finland sign a pact of mutual assistance, allow the establishment of military and naval bases, and agree to far-reaching territorial changes. The Finns considered these requests unreasonable and refused to surrender any part of their territory. In reply, the Soviet Union, on November 28, 1939, unilaterally renounced its 1934 non-aggression pact with Finland, severed diplomatic ties on November 29, ordered full-scale military operations on November 30, and on December 1, in anticipation of a quick victory, set up a "democratic government" for Finland in the USSR under Otto Willi Kuusinen, an old veteran of the Comintern. For three months the Finns fought an unequal duel, but fought it amazingly well, and earned the sympathy and applause of the whole world. The Soviet Union for its action was expelled from the League of Nations on December 14, 1939. Hostilities were ended by the peace treaty of March 12, 1940, through which the USSR acquired some 16,173 square miles of Finnish territory with a population of 450,000.

Hitler's preoccupation in Western Europe during May and June, 1940, enabled Stalin to strengthen the Soviet position not only in the Baltic but in the Black Sea area as well. On June 26, 1940, Molotov delivered a note to the Rumanian ambassador in Moscow, demanding the return of Bessarabia and the surrender of Northern Bukovina to the USSR. On June 27, the note was followed by an ultimatum, and on June 28, without waiting for a reply, Soviet armed forces began the occupation of both territories. The occupation of this area, which netted 21,178 square miles and 3,717,000 people, was undertaken in the name of "national liberation." New territorial gains made possible the creation of a Moldavian Soviet Socialist Republic, which "joined" the USSR.

Soviet interest in Romania and in the Balkans sharpened German suspicion, while extension of German "protection" over the Romanian oil fields in October, 1940, aroused Soviet anxiety. It was the first major clash between the "incompatible allies." Early in November, 1940, both sides tried to find a compromise, but from the outset it became apparent that the German and Soviet positions were far apart. Fresh from his victorious campaigns in Western Europe, except against England, Hitler hoped that the Soviet Union would join his "new order." To avoid future misunderstanding, and at the same time hoping to involve the USSR in a war with

England, Hitler suggested that the USSR expand towards India, the Persian Gulf, and the Arabian Sea. Molotov agreed in principle to these suggestions, but he also insisted that Germany recognize Soviet interests elsewhere. These included: (1) German recognition that Finland belonged to the Soviet sphere of influence; (2) German recognition that Bulgaria was within the Soviet sphere; (3) German guarantee of a Soviet air and naval base in the Straits; (4) German recognition of Soviet interest in the fate of Turkey, Greece, Yugoslavia, Rumania, Hungary, and Poland; (5) German recognition that the area south of Batum and Baku in the general direction of the Persian Gulf was "the center of the aspirations of the Soviet Union"; and (6) Japanese renunciation of rights to concessions for coal and oil in Northern Sakhalin. Hitler's reaction to these Soviet ambitions was an order to his military to prepare for a *blitz* campaign to "crush Soviet Russia." Preparations for "Operation Barbarossa" were ordered completed by May 15, 1941. The incompatible allies parted company.

German military preparations started at once with a vast buildup of forces along the German-Soviet frontier in Poland, and strengthening of German positions elsewhere. By mid-February, 1941, the Germans had an army of 680,000 men in Romania. Bulgaria was occupied early in March, and Yugoslavia and Greece were conquered in April, 1941. Soviet reaction to these provocative moves was two-fold. On the surface, Soviet leaders displayed considerable naïveté, sent conciliatory protests and inquiries about German moves, displayed a "friendly" attitude towards Berlin, and went out of their way to deliver punctually the German orders for food, petroleum, manganese ore, non-ferrous and other metals necessary to the success of the Barbarossa Operation. At the same time, however, the Soviets made every effort to improve their position vis-à-vis Germany. In response to the German military buildup, the Soviets strengthened their garrisons all along the German frontier, and to avoid a conflict on two fronts, on April 13, 1941, in Moscow, the USSR and Japan signed a mutual non-aggression pact. The Nazi-Soviet honeymoon came to a sudden end at dawn on June 22, 1941, when Hitler's armies rolled into the USSR.

CONVENTIONAL WARFARE, JUNE 22, 1941—MAY 7, 1945

"Operation Barbarossa" was actually a quite simple plan. Its three fundamental objectives were: the destruction of Soviet armed forces; the capture of political and industrial centers of the USSR (Moscow and Leningrad); and the occupation of coal, iron, and grain centers of the Ukraine and the Caucasus. The Germans hoped to achieve these objectives in three phases. During the first phase of the operation, both ground and air forces were to thrust deep into Soviet territory, create chaos, disrupt

On the Eastern front, 1941. Russian prisoners captured behind the German lines.

supply lines, encircle and destroy Soviet forces west of the Dvina-Dnieper line, and prevent the organization of new defenses. During the second phase, the Germans were to capture Leningrad, Moscow, and the Ukraine, in order to deprive the Soviet forces of political direction and economic strength. In the final phase the Germans were to advance to and hold firm the Volga-Archangel line.

To execute this plan, the Germans divided their forces into three groups. The first was Army Group North in East Prussia, under Field Marshal von Leeb, consisting of three panzer, three motorized, and twenty-four infantry divisions, the First Air Fleet, and Finnish forces, directed against Leningrad. The second was Army Group Centre in northern Poland, under Field Marshal von Bock, consisting of nine panzer, seven motorized, and thirty-four infantry divisions, and the Second Air Fleet. The third was Army Group South, in southern Poland and Romania, under Field Marshal von Rundstedt, consisting of five panzer, three motorized, and thirty-five infantry divisions, the Fourth Air Fleet, three Italian divisions, two Romanian armies, and Hungarian and Slovak units. Overall command of these forces was by Field Marshal von Brauchitsch.

Opposing this force were some 150 Soviet divisions grouped into three fronts. The Northwestern Front, under Marshal Voroshilov was responsible for the defense of Leningrad, Karelia, and the newly acquired Baltic states. Marshal Semeon K. Timoshenko's (1895–1970) forces of the Western Front guarded the approaches to Smolensk and Moscow. The Ukrainian Front was defended by Marshal Budenny. Little is known about Soviet orders, as the Soviet government has thus far failed to reveal fully the nature of Soviet preparedness or the actual disposition of forces.

Whatever the nature of Soviet plans, they were upset by the German "surprise attack." Actually, that attack was not a surprise. Reliable evidence indicates that between April 3 and June 18, 1941, Churchill informed Stalin several times that the Germans were regrouping their armed forces with the intent of attacking the Soviet Union. Moreover, Soviet military and naval attachés in Berlin conveyed the same warnings to their superiors in Moscow as early as May 6 and again on May 22, 1941. Finally, it should be pointed out that the terrain separating the Soviet Union from Nazi Germany, the daily contacts of officials of the two powers along the frontier, and, above all, the nature and scope of German military preparations (which involved some 2 million men and the supporting logistics for a successful campaign) made a "surprise attack" inconceivable. The legend of "surprise attack" (which has lingered in scholarly literature for too long) was embodied in Soviet propaganda to absolve Soviet leadership of all blame for the poor performance of their armed forces in the initial stages of war.

The German attack on the USSR came at dawn on June 22, 1941. It was spearheaded by the *Luftwaffe* which bombed and destroyed that part of the Soviet Air Force within its reach, and in one day's operation achieved complete air supremacy. Supported by the *Luftwaffe*, German panzers and infantry broke through Soviet defenses, and by evening were deep inside Soviet territory. Army Group North took Kaunas on June 22, reached the Dvina on June 26, occupied Riga on June 29, and by July 8 reached a new line of Soviet defensive positions south of Pskov, where the Germans encountered the first stiff resistance. Though not as spectacular as the German thrust, the Finnish offensive made remarkable progress in recovering territories Finland had been forced to yield to the Soviet Union in March, 1940.

The most spectacular of the German thrusts was that of Army Group Centre. Spearheaded by panzers and supported by the *Luftwaffe*, one German column advanced rapidly towards Vilnius, which fell on June 24, and headed for Minsk, while another column approached Minsk from Brest-Litovsk. The two columns joined on June 27, encircling large Soviet forces around Bialystok and Grodno. After fierce fighting, Soviet forces consisting of some 320,000 men, 3,000 tanks, and 2,000 heavy guns, surrendered to the Germans. By July 6, German panzers reached the Dnieper River and here, similarly as in the north, encountered signs of

The GERMAN INVASION OF RUSSIA
1941 - 1942

- - - - - - Line of deepest German penetration, 1941-1942

Borders of
U.S.S.R.
June, 1941

MILES

0   100   500

Sam¹ H. Bryant

increased Soviet resistance. The resistance, however, was not strong enough to prevent the Germans from crossing the river on July 9, taking Smolensk on July 16, and capturing an additional 300,000 prisoners. The road to Moscow was wide open.

The progress of Army Group South was slow because the front was wide and natural barriers more numerous. These factors enabled Soviet forces to withdraw in a more orderly fashion, to counterattack at times, and to prevent the Germans from breaking through and encircling them in pincer movements. Army Group South advanced along three lines. One column advanced along the Lublin-Kovel-Lutsk-Zhitomir-Kiev line. Another moved along the Przemysl-Lvov-Vinnitsia-Dnieper River line. The third column advanced from Rumania towards Odessa and Dniepropetrovsk. Distances enabled Soviet forces to escape all German encirclement attempts, except one at Uman, where early in August Soviet forces lost 103,000 men, 300 tanks, and 800 heavy guns. This loss cleared the road to Kiev and the Dnieper, and thus led to the successful conclusion of the first phase of the "Barbarossa Operation."

Execution of the second phase encountered considerable difficulty. On the one hand, Soviet land forces recovered from the initial shock and paralysis and began to offer increased resistance all along the front. Also, the Soviet Air Force recovered enough to cause harassment to the German advance. But far more important was the German inability to fix the priority of the next strategic objective of the campaign. For some five weeks, Hitler and his generals were unable to agree on what to do next. At first Hitler insisted that Leningrad should be the next primary objective in order to link up with the Finns, establish a new line of communication by sea, and clear the Baltic of the Soviet fleet. His generals, von Bock and Guderian among others, insisted that Moscow should be made the primary objective because it was the capital of the USSR, a vital communication center, and an important industrial base. They felt that the German attack on Moscow would draw most of the Soviet forces to its defense, and hence to their doom. In mid-August, however, Hitler changed his mind, relegated both Leningrad and Moscow to secondary importance, and gave priority to conquest of the Ukraine, in order to place the resources of that region at Germany's disposal.

The second phase of the "Barbarossa Operation" started accordingly with the assault on Kiev, which fell on September 19. Though many Soviet units succeeded in escaping the German pincer movement and retreated towards Kharkov, the Kiev battle netted the Germans 650,000 prisoners. Rain and mud, however, slowed the German advance, and the desired objective was not attained. An advance towards Leningrad, which started early in September, also ground to a halt at the end of the month, partly as a result of stiff Soviet defense and partly on orders from Hitler, who meanwhile developed a "new plan" of attack. The "new plan" called for reduction of Leningrad through siege and starvation, encirclement and capture of Moscow, conquest of the Crimea, and above all of the Donbass and the Caucasus in order to gain the coal and oil resources of these regions for Germany. This fantastic plan, however, failed to take into account two vital factors. The first was that both men and machines needed rest and maintenance, which they had not received since June 22. The second was that the freezing rains and snow, which had already begun affecting the morale of the men, sharply reduced the mobility of the machines and hence the superiority of the German forces and accordingly increased the importance of the superiority of Soviet manpower.

Under the new plan, the assault on Moscow was given high priority, and full scale operations started on September 30. On October 3, Orel fell to the Germans, and by October 20, around Viazma and Briansk the Germans captured some 665,000 Soviet prisoners. Thereafter, however, German progress slowed considerably. The first contributing factor was mud, which increased fuel consumption but not territorial gains. The second was the sudden drop of the temperature to 40° below zero. The third was the stubborn resistance on the part of fresh reserves from Siberia, who were provided with good equipment and winter clothing. These factors forced the Germans to give up their goal of capturing Moscow and to break off the attack with heavy losses. The failure to take Moscow was offset, in part, by gains in the Ukraine, where late in September, 1941, in the battle of the Sea of Azov, the Germans captured some 100,000 prisoners, occupied Odessa on October 16, Kharkov on October 24, Rostov-on-the-Don on November 21, and the Crimea. These gains, however, were to be only temporary, for early in December, 1941, when rains and mud halted the exhausted Germans, the Russians opened their first major counter offensive along the entire front.

The aim of the Russian winter offensive was to drive the exhausted, overextended, and nature-immobilized German forces as far back as possible and to keep them constantly off balance. Fighting was fierce and casualties were extremely heavy on both sides, not only from combat but from the severe weather as well. The least change in battle position came around Leningrad. The heaviest fighting took place around Moscow, where as early as the end of December, 1941, the Germans lost some of their advanced positions under Soviet pressure. From others they retreated voluntarily. Voluntary or under pressure, the German withdrawal cost them some 250,000 men, 1,000 tanks, and 1,500 heavy guns. For the moment it appeared that Soviet forces might even recapture Smolensk, but fierce German defense spoiled that effort. The Soviet counter offensive in the Ukraine was the most costly in terms of Soviet casualties. In the Kerch peninsula the Germans took 170,000 prisoners, Sevastopol yielded them an additional 90,000 men, and early in June, 1942, in the Donets area 240,000 Soviet soldiers surrendered. The winter offensive was extremely costly for the USSR, but it achieved an important goal. It inflicted very heavy casualties on the Germans as well, and prevented them from resting, reorganizing, and reequipping their land and air forces to launch a new offensive in 1942.

In the summer of 1942, against the advice of some of his generals, Hitler ordered a new offensive in the Ukraine. Its aim was to destroy Soviet forces in the Don area and Stalingrad and to capture the oil-rich Caucasus. For the exhausted German forces, this was a superhuman task, although initially they made considerable progress. They retook Rostov on July 23, occupied Maikop on August 8, Mozdok on the Terek River on August 25, and reached Stalingrad early in September. Lack of fuel, waning of energy, and the approach of winter, coupled with effective Russian resistance, made further German advance impossible. A disaster of first magnitude for the Germans was in the making, and it struck on November 19, 1942, in the form of a second Soviet winter offensive, which was as complete a surprise as any achieved before by the Germans.

The aim of the second Soviet offensive was simple. It sought to break through the overextended German lines along the Don River in order to cut off the retreat of German forces from Stalingrad. Soviet efforts were simplified by the panic of Hungarian, Rumanian, and Italian formations. Four days after the offensive started, the German Sixth Army of 285,000 men, commanded by General von Paulus, was encircled in Stalingrad. An immediate breakthrough might have saved this force, but Hitler refused to listen to suggestions for withdrawal. Instead he ordered a relief attack, which after an initial success was halted by December 25, 1942, and then turned into a full-scale retreat. The Sixth Army was doomed, and its survivors, consisting of 91,000 men, including twenty-four generals, capitulated on January 30, 1943. It was "the greatest defeat that a German army had ever undergone," and according to some observers was a turning point of World War II.

The Soviet offensive was stalled late in February, 1943, by a combination of two factors. The first was the effective German resistance which culminated in a tank battle at Pavlovgrad, where the Soviets lost 650 tanks, 1,000 guns, and the city of Kharkov. The second was the mud which hampered all operations. The lull in fighting enabled both sides to prepare for new blows. The Soviets brought up reinforcements along the entire front, and were able to strengthen their forces with modern American tanks, guns, and trucks received under the Lend-Lease Program. When the Germans launched their last offensive in July, 1943, the Soviet steam roller was ready to inflict heavy losses on the Germans which they could not replace. Early in August, Soviet forces retook Orel, occupied Kharkov on August 23, Novorossiisk in mid-September, Poltava and Smolensk by the end of September, Kiev in early November, and by the end of 1943 they established several bridgeheads across the Dnieper. These advances were very costly in lives, as the Germans, though greatly outnumbered and retreating, offered cunning and savage defense. These advances, however, cleared the way for a massive frontal attack all the

THE EASTERN FRONT
WORLD WAR II
1939 - 1945

1938 Boundaries

Axis and occupied areas
June 22, 1941

Russian boundary, 1941

FRONT LINES IN RUSSIA
--·--·-- 1941 ····· 1943
▲▲▲ 1942 ------ 1944

RUSSIAN AND ALLIED
DRIVES, 1941–1945

ALLIED SUPPLY
LINE FROM U.S.
AND BRITAIN

Murmansk

White
Sea

Archangel

N. Dvina

NORWAY

SWEDEN

ENMARK

FINLAND
(War with Russia,
1939 -1940)
Joined Germans
in attack on Russia
in 1941

Karelia

Leningrad

U   S   S   R

BALTIC SEA

Tikhvin

Dec.'41

Volga

Gorky

Kazan

ESTONIA

Riga

LATVIA

Kalinin

MOSCOW

Kuibyshev

"Polish
Corridor"

LITHUANIA

Vilnius

Mozhaisk

Oka

Danzig

EAST
PRUSSIA

Smolensk

BERLIN

Minsk

B E L O -

July'43

Tula

FARTHEST
GERMAN ADVANCE
1941–1942

Elbe

Oder

Torgau

Bialystok

R U S S I A

Orel

Voronezh

LLIES
ril 26,45

RUSSIA

Warsaw

Brest-Litovsk

June '44

Kursk

P O L A N D

Danube

CZECHO-
SLOVAKIA

Lvov

U   K   R   A   I   N   E

Kiev

Kharkov

Dec.'41

Stalingrad

Volga

Vienna

1939

Dnieper

Don

AUSTRIA

Budapest

HUNGARY

1940

Dniepropetrovsk

Rostov

1941

Bessarabia

Kerch

Kuban

Belgrade

ROMANIA

YUGOSLAVIA
(Taken by the
Germans, 1941)

Bucharest

Danube

1940

Sevastopol

Yalta

Novorossiisk

Mozdok

CAUCASUS   MTS.

Sofia

BLACK   SEA

Batum

Tbilisi

BULGARIA

ITALY

ALBANIA
(To Italy,
1939)

Istanbul

Erevan

GREECE

T   U   R   K   E   Y

Ankara

ALLIED SUPPLY
LINE FROM
PERSIAN GULF

IRAN

Izmir

Athens

(Taken by Germans
in 1941)

CRETE

Sam¹ H. Bryant

way from Lapland to the Black Sea which took place in 1944 in the form of ten major thrusts.

The first Soviet blow was struck in January, 1944, against Army Group North, forcing the Germans to abandon their encirclement of Leningrad. The second blow came in February and March in the Ukraine and forced the Germans to retreat to the old Polish and Romanian frontiers. The third blow came in April and May against the Crimea, while the fourth struck in the Karelian Isthmus, forcing the Finns out of the war. The fifth Soviet blow, dealt by 146 infantry divisions and 43 armored brigades, struck Army Group Centre late in June, 1944. Soviet forces overran German positions, occupied Minsk on July 3, Vilnius on July 13, and captured some 30 German divisions. This Soviet breakthrough had significant repercussions. It endangered the German hold on the entire Baltic area, and it also opened the road to the Vistula and Warsaw, which Soviet forces reached early in August, 1944. The sixth Soviet blow struck against German positions in Galicia, where Soviet forces occupied Lvov on July 25, and reached the San and Vistula Rivers and Carpathian passes early in August. The seventh Soviet blow was against Romanian and German forces along the Dniester River. The Romanians surrendered unconditionally on August 23, and shortly thereafter joined the war against Germany. The collapse of German positions in Romania opened for the Soviets the road to the Balkans and Hungary. Late in August, Soviet forces occupied Bucharest and Ploesti, and on September 16, they entered Sofia, the capital of Bulgaria. The eighth Soviet blow struck in the direction of Budapest, which Soviet forces approached early in November, and Belgrade, which they took on October 19. The ninth thrust cleared the Baltic states of German forces that had been cut off previously by the summer offensive, and the final blow hit the Petsamo region and northern Norway. By these gains and maneuvers, Soviet forces placed themselves in an advantageous position for a final assault of Germany from the East, while the Allied forces were preparing for the same from the West and the South.

The final Soviet assault against Germany began in mid-January, 1945, along a front stretching from the Baltic to the Carpathians. The attack was led by four army "fronts," the First Ukrainian Front, under Marshal Ivan S. Konev (1897–1973), north of the Carpathians; the First Belorussian Front, under Marshal Georgi K. Zhukov (1896–1974), in central Poland; the Second Belorussian Front, under Marshal Konstantine K. Rokossovsky (1896–1969), north of Warsaw; and the Third Belorussian Front, under General Ivan D. Cherniakovsky (1906–1945), in East Prussia. The combined force of the four fronts consisted of 275 infantry divisions, twenty-two armored corps, twenty-nine armored brigades, and three cavalry corps. As German defenses were now negligible, the Soviet advance was rapid. Warsaw, or what remained of it, fell on January 17, Cracow and Lodz on January 19, and Elbing in East Prussia on January 26. German resistance in East Prussia was fierce, and it was not until March 30 that

Danzig was taken by storm, and Königsberg did not surrender until April 9. Early in March, Soviet forces established bridgeheads across the Oder River for the final push against Berlin, which they surrounded by April 25, and occupied on May 2. Meanwhile, Soviet forces south of the Carpathians, under Marshals Rodion Ia. Malinovsky (1899–1969) and Feodor I. Tolbukhin (1894–1949), opened their drive and occupied Budapest on February 13, 1945, Bratislava on April 3, and Vienna on April 13. Allied advances from the west, south, and north forced the Germans to accept unconditional surrender on May 7, 1945. The war in Europe was over, but peace was not in sight.

UNCONVENTIONAL WARFARE, JUNE 22, 1941—MAY 7, 1945

The fundamental aim of the Germans' eastern campaign in June, 1941, as of their other campaigns, was to conquer, to rule, and to exploit. Like their previous campaigns too, this undertaking neglected positive political planning, and as one authority justly noted, had neither a plan for enlisting the Soviet population on the German side, nor a blueprint of political conduct except the extermination of all "undesirables." Three erroneous assumptions seem to have contributed to the German failure to prepare for the use of political warfare. First was the belief that the eastern campaign, like the previous *blitzkriegs*, would be a very brief affair and would end before the close of 1941. Second was the gross underestimation of Soviet military capabilities and willingness to resist. Third was the Nazi aim of making themselves permanent masters of the East, thus gaining space for settlement and expansion. These three factors, and especially the last one, from the outset precluded humane treatment of the conquered peoples and negated any possibility of the remaking of Eastern Europe along national lines.

Unaware at first of the real Nazi intentions, the Soviet population in most instances viewed the rapidly advancing German forces as liberators. While the welcome was more enthusiastic in the recently acquired areas of the Soviet Union (Bessarabia, Eastern Poland, and the Baltic States), everywhere the Germans came anti-Soviet sentiment burst into the open, manifesting itself in innumerable ways. At the front, it was expressed in mass surrender of Soviet soldiers. Among the peasants, anti-Soviet grievances revealed themselves in the breakup of collective farms and MTS's, and in the division of their properties. Among nationalities of the USSR, the German advance raised hopes that at last their national aspirations could be realized. Everywhere the retreat of Soviet forces was accompanied by the destruction of Stalin's statues, the abolition of Soviet institutions, emptying of prisons, and reopening of churches. The hopes of these peoples stemmed from rumors based on German propaganda, some official, but mostly unofficial, which invited Soviet soldiers to surrender, depicted Germany as a liberator, and promised self-government and private ownership of land. These hopes vanished one by one, as the Germans, intoxicated by their initial successes, began to implement their real policies.

The first to be disappointed with German promises and treatment were prisoners of war, whose numbers rose by late December, 1941, to 3,355,000, and increased by 1,653,000 in 1942. Many of these surrendered voluntarily, while others had no choice. So staggering was the number of prisoners that the Germans were not prepared to accommodate them, nor were they willing to treat them humanely. Initially, they released some, especially non-Russians, to work on farms or to clear war-damaged enterprises. Fearing, however, that freed men would join the partisans, the Germans soon abandoned this practice, and herded the prisoners into hurriedly-constructed camps. Left under the open sky without food or shelter, thousands of men perished in various epidemics. Many others died from beatings and abuse by their guards. Some were shot, others were poisoned, and some fell prey to their comrades who, in desperation to survive, turned to cannibalism. According to German figures, between 1941 and 1944, some 1,981,000 Soviet prisoners died, and 1,308,000 simply disappeared. Rumors of these abuses and cruelties cancelled the effect of surrender leaflets, stiffened Soviet military resistance, embittered the civilian population, and provided the Soviet regime with an excellent propaganda weapon. A labor shortage forced the Germans to change their policy in 1942 and bring many prisoners to Germany to work in agriculture and in industry. This, however, did not change their *Untermensch* status or exploitation and abuse. The Soviet government could not and did not attempt in any way to help, for its official attitude was that any soldier who fell into enemy hands was *ipso facto* a traitor and hence not deserving of protection from his government. Understandably, therefore, German prisoners in the Soviet Union received little or no consideration.

The second group disappointed with German occupation policies was the peasantry. Their disappointment stemmed from the widespread belief that with the coming of the Germans the *kolkhoz* system, against which they had so many grievances, would be abolished. Initially, German army units made no efforts to stop peasant division of the property of collective farms or of the MTS's. Some German officials, in fact, supported such a course of action in order to capitalize on peasant opposition to the Soviet regime. Those in authority, however, opposed peasant aspirations, for they felt that the division of land, cattle, and machinery among individual peasants was contrary to the long-range Nazi plan for colonization of Eastern Europe. They were also afraid that to sanction peasant demands would jeopardize the grain supply for the German army, which provisioned itself as it fought in the East. Mounting peasant disappointment and dissatisfaction, however, forced the Nazis to make two "concessions." The first, made in August, 1941, included abolition of the term *kolkhoz*, enlargement of private peasant plots at the expense of *kolkhoz* land, and the promise of unlimited private cattle breeding. The second "concession" came on February 15, 1942, in the form of a new agrarian law abolishing all Soviet decrees and regulations concerning collective farms, which were now designated communal economies. The change was in name only, for, as before, the peasants were forced to work under the direction of their masters, to deliver the assigned quotas of grain, and to be compensated according to a system of "labor days." German propaganda hailed the new agricultural arrangement as the dawn of a new era. Soviet peasants viewed it as a new form of exploitation. For those peasants who had dreamt so long of farming their own land, the German agricultural policy was a bitter disappointment, and many cast their lot with the partisans. Neither was the policy beneficial to the Germans. Immediately they procured most of the food required for the armies in the East, but the methods by which they did it contributed heavily to their loss of the war.

Next to mistreatment of prisoners of war and peasant exploitation, the most revolting aspect of German policy was the so-called *Ostarbeiter* program. Between 1942 and 1945, the Germans removed from the occupied areas of the USSR some 2,800,000 civilians to slave in German agriculture, mining, and industry. Except for the few volunteers in the initial stage of the program, all those sent to Germany went against their will. The Germans assigned every district a quota and rounded up their captives arbitrarily in villages, market places, and even churches. The captives were then packed into freight cars without food or sanitary facilities and shipped off to Germany. The treatment in Germany of the *Ostarbeiters* was no better. Considered *Untermenschen*, they were punished, exploited, and humiliated. Those who became ill or incapacitated, the Germans returned home to face starvation. The methods used by the Germans in procuring a labor force, which included forcible abortion of pregnant women, separation of mothers from babies, of children from families, and often burning of whole villages, spread bitterness and fear among the population. To escape this kind of treatment, many able-bodied men and women joined the partisan movement, which grew in force and intensity in proportion to German brutality. In 1944, when the collapse of the Third Reich was in sight, the Germans improved somewhat their treatment of the *Ostarbeiters*, but this "understanding" was too little and came too late.

Another German "change of heart" that came too late was Nazi support of the celebrated Vlasov movement. The founder of the movement was a well-known Soviet general, Andrei A. Vlasov (1900–1946), whom the Germans captured on July 12, 1942, and who later agreed to fight against Stalin on condition that the Germans drastically alter their policy towards Soviet peoples. From its inception the Vlasov movement encountered many difficulties. It was opposed by old Russian émigré groups, by the minorities of the Soviet Union, and by many Nazis as well.

Marshal G. K. Zhukov   *K. E. Voroshilov*

It was enthusiastically supported by some officers of the German army,
mainly because Vlasov's appeals increased the desertion of Soviet soldiers.
With the blessing of these officers, late in 1942 there was organized a
Russian committee and an army of liberation from among Soviet pris-
oners of war. But just as the movement was about to move into high gear,
Hitler, in June, 1943, vetoed its activity, for he felt that the aims of the
Vlasov movement were contrary to German goals. Discouraged by the
Nazi blindness, many of Vlasov's followers joined the partisans. Thou-
sands who could not or did not, the Germans transferred to the West, to
the Balkans, and to other theaters of operation to fight as mercenaries.

Soviet and Allied advances during 1943 and 1944, coupled with the
increasing German shortage of manpower, forced some Nazi fanatics to
change their views not only about the Vlasov movement, but other national movements as well. The "sponsor" of this new outlook was Heinrich
Himmler, the Gestapo chief, who in 1943 and 1944 launched Latvian,
Estonian, Ukrainian, Belorussian, Moslem, Turkic, and Caucasian military
formations. In September, 1944, Himmler also consented to the formation
of a Committee for the Liberation of the Peoples of Russia under Vlasov's
leadership. In 1942, these and other later innovations would have been far-
reaching. In 1944 it was an empty and hollow gesture. Vlasov and many
of his close associates were captured after the war, and on August 2, 1946,
the Soviets announced that they had been executed.

The last group disappointed with the Germans was composed of the
Soviet minorities—Estonians, Latvians, Lithuanians, Belorussians, Ukrainians, and others—who thirsted for relief and who hoped to re-establish
their independent existence with German help. Their demands were modest, but they ran contrary to German plans, which called for the division

of conquered areas of the USSR into four Reich Commissariats, the East, Ukraine, Muscovy, and Caucasus. Each Commissariat was administered by low caliber officials and presided over by true autocrats, of whom Erich Koch in the Ukraine was doubtless the most brutally bestial. It was also in the Ukraine that the clash between national aspirations and German designs burst wide open. This was inevitable, for in the preinvasion propaganda the Nazis cleverly played on Ukrainian hatred of the Kremlin, posed as defenders of the Ukraine, offered comfort and support to many nationalist spokesmen, and skillfully exploited the strong separatist tendencies of the Ukrainians. At the same time the Nazis assigned to the Ukraine a highly important role in their search for *Lebensraum*. They viewed the abundance of Ukrainian raw materials as a valuable source of supply for German industry, considered the Ukraine's fertile soil not only as a significant food base for the Third Reich, but also as an indispensable area for future German agricultural settlement, and envisaged the Ukraine's strategic location as an excellent starting point for further German economic and political penetration into Central Asia, the Near and the Middle East. Needless to say, these elaborate schemes precluded the establishment of a Ukrainian state that in any way could endanger German domination.

Between June and September, 1941, the Nazis took four steps which revealed that they had no intention of creating a Ukrainian state. First they arrested the Ukrainian nationalists who, in Lvov on June 30, 1941, proclaimed an independent Ukrainian state. Second, on August 1, 1941, they gave to Rumania some 10,000 square miles of Ukrainian territory along the Dniester River, including the city of Odessa. Third, on August 1, 1941, they transferred Galicia, or Western Ukraine, to the Government-General of Poland and banned Ukrainian political activities there. Finally, in September, 1941, Hitler appointed Koch, the most outspoken proponent of the *Herrenvolk* idea and the most violent anti-Ukrainian Nazi spokesman, to be the autocrat of the Ukraine, where for the next two years he inaugurated a real reign of terror. His abuses and atrocities disillusioned many Ukrainians, some of whom joined either nationalist-led or Communist-led partisans. Caught between the hammer and the anvil was the bulk of the terrorized and exploited population, which, as one authority rightly noted, "called down a plague on both their houses."

Of the many devices with which Soviet and non-Soviet peoples fought the Germans, once their intentions became known, the most fascinating was the partisan movement. The partisan struggle was a spontaneous development, and grew as a reaction to the German policies and above all as an answer to the behavior of German personnel. Initially, partisan groups consisted mainly of isolated Soviet army stragglers, many of whom were far from enthusiastic in their attitude towards Soviet authority. Some of these early partisan units dispersed, others surrendered, and those that were pro-Soviet inclined or inspired received little support from the bulk of the population bewildered by the far-reaching changes taking place.

The partisan movement shifted into high gear late in 1941 and early in 1942. Of the factors contributing to the increased partisan membership and activity, the following seem to have been the most significant: (1) German treatment of prisoners of war, which forced many stragglers to join the partisans; (2) German treatment of the civilian population, and especially their recruiting methods for *Ostarbeiters;* (3) German exploitation of the peasantry; (4) German "double crossing" of native nationalists; (5) the stiffening of Soviet resistance along the entire front; (6) Soviet material assistance to the partisans; and (7) German inability to liquidate partisan pockets of resistance and their liberal application of brute force and terror in the attempt to do so.

While a full study of the partisan movement still remains to be written, it presented the Germans with a "front behind the front." From their hideouts in the forests, the partisans prevented cooperation between civilian population and the occupying authorities, attacked German outposts, weakened German morale, and repeatedly disrupted German communications. Because the last activity was felt by every single unit at the front, the Germans moved to protect their overextended lines by every device possible, including commitment of regular combat forces to mopping-up operations in partisan-infested areas. This effort, however, was often more fierce and resulted in a proportionately larger number of casualties than combat at the front because of the hit and run nature of partisan tactics, and the great speed with which they operated. They appeared on the scene, completed their mission, and withdrew into their forest hideouts where it was next to impossible to ferret them out. In the spring of 1943 the Germans used front line divisions—some 100,000 strong—to clear the Briansk forest, but the results achieved did not justify the cost. The same was true of two other mass operations—the summer, 1943, offensive against Soviet partisans led by Sidor A. Kovpak (1887–   ), who crossed the Ukraine into the Carpathians, and the perpetual German offensive against the non-Soviet Ukrainian Insurgent Army organized by "Taras Bulba," whose original base of operations was in Volyn. The Germans lost against the partisans because, imbued with fantasies and intoxicated with their earlier victories, they failed to understand the aspirations of other men.

In contrast to the German policy of brutality, exploitation, and extermination, Soviet policy during the war was one of concessions, promises, and above all attempts to arouse national patriotism. These innovations were necessary in order to offset heavy losses, rumor, confusion, and panic, created by the lightning German thrust deep inside Soviet territory. The thrust was deep indeed and the losses staggering. By November, 1941, the Germans controlled an area embracing about 40 per cent of the whole Soviet population, and supplying 68 per cent of Soviet pig iron output, 58 per cent of steel, 60 per cent of aluminum, 38 per cent of the grain, 84 per cent of sugar, and 41 per cent of railroad lines. The Germans also held some 3,355,000 prisoners of war. German advances in 1942 increased considerably Soviet losses, both material and human.

It is imperative, however, to remember that Soviet losses were not *ipso facto* German gains. As they retreated the Soviets tried to evacuate all movable property (plants, machinery, tools, raw material, cattle, and even people) to new locations in the Urals and Central Asia, where everything was put back into production. Those establishments that could not be removed (houses, buildings, bridges, the Dnieprostroy Dam, and the like) the Soviets destroyed.

Just as important as the "scorched earth policy" was the upsurge of national patriotism. In part this upsurge was spontaneous. It represented an outburst of national pride and anger at the sadistic Nazi mistreatment of prisoners and peasants, their relegation of Slavs to an inferior racial status, and their unfolding of far-reaching colonization designs. In part, however, the upsurge of national patriotism was Stalin-sponsored. He gave the first signal for its rise in his first speech of the war on July 3, 1941, when he compared Hitler's early successes to those of Napoleon in "the great patriotic war of 1812." Stalin's second signal came on November 7, 1941, in his address to the troops he reviewed at Red Square, when he intoned, "Let the manly images of our great ancestors—Alexander Nevsky, Dimitri Donskoi, Kuzma Minin, Dimitri Pozharsky, Alexander Suvorov, and Mikhail Kutuzov—inspire you in this war."

Stalin's invocation of saints and warriors of Imperial Russia was immediately followed by what one observer called a "grotesquely immoderate glorification of Russia's imperial past," and in effect a large-scale rehabilitation of many prerevolutionary traditions and institutions. This rehabilitation was most immediately noticeable in the armed forces. Its first manifestation came in the form of a series of medals established by the Presidium of the Supreme Soviet, such as the Medal of the Patriotic War (May 20, 1943), Medals of Suvorov, Kutuzov, and Nevsky (July 29, 1942), and Medals of Ushakov, and Nakhimov (March 3, 1944). To revive the old imperial glamour, guard regiments and guard divisions were created in May, 1942; Cossack formations were restored later in the year; and in January, 1943, epaulettes, once scorned as symbols of a reactionary caste system in the army, were reintroduced as part of the military uniform. Saluting became obligatory and was strictly enforced, and officers were given exclusive clubs with separate messes.

Next to the armed forces, most affected by the rehabilitation of imperial tradition was the Church—the institution which had held a central place in that tradition. Following the outbreak of war, Church leaders came to the defense of their country, as had their predecessors on so many occasions. They sent messages to the faithful, reminding them of their duties, warned against cooperation with the enemy (and excom-

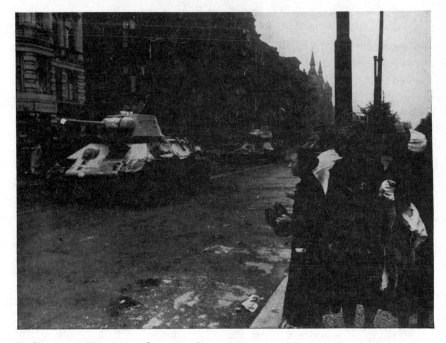

Berlin, 1945. Russian tanks enter the city.

municated those who cooperated), praised the "patriotic" work of the partisans, hailed Stalin as "the divinely appointed [sic] leader" of the nation, and collected and donated some 150 million rubles in addition to many valuables for the purchase of tanks, planes, and other equipment. On its part, the government toned down anti-religious propaganda, disbanded the League of Militant Atheists, reopened many of the closed churches, and invited Metropolitan Nikolai of Kiev to become a member of the Extraordinary State Committee for investigating crimes committed by the Nazis. The climax of this cooperation between the Orthodox Church and the Soviet state came on September 4, 1943, when Stalin received church leaders in the Kremlin and consented to the convocation of the *Sobor* and the formal election of a patriarch and a synod to assist him. The patriarch, installed in office on September 7, 1943, immediately appealed to Christians everywhere to fight Hitlerism, and through the *Journal of the Patriarchate of Moscow,* as in the imperial period, seconded many government policies. In October, 1943, the goverment created a Council for Affairs of the Orthodox Church as an adjunct to the *Sovnarkom,* allowed the restoration of organized theological instruction, relaxed rules on the religious instruction of children, and decorated many clergy for their war efforts.

To win the war it was necessary not only to rehabilitate the old traditions but to make peace with the more recent past as well. In the face of Hitler's all too real conspiracy, all bogus conspiracies of the 1930's, such as Trotskyism, Bukharinism, and the like, were discreetly dropped. Many of those who had survived the great purges were released from concentration camps and drafted into the armed forces, or assigned to other important jobs. Among the rehabilitated were scientists, writers, and many of Tukhachevsky's disciples, including Generals Rokossovsky and Tolbukhin, who soon became heroes of the victory at Stalingrad. Because the bulk of the Soviet population had little enthusiasm for the Communist party, its role was de-emphasized and the proletarian slogans replaced by such patriotic utterances as "Down with the Fascist Invader." In line with the new trend, in 1943 the *Internationale* was replaced by a new national anthem, whose first line was: "Unbreakable union of free-born republics, Great Russia has welded forever to stand."

The return to Great Russian tradition did not overlook the minorities, especially those whose efforts and sacrifices were needed in the war. On October 10, 1943, the Presidium of the Supreme Soviet established a high military decoration for Ukrainians, the Medal of Khmelnytsky. At the end of the year, the Southern Front was designated the Ukrainian Front, and the armies which operated there were renamed Ukrainian Armies. Identical changes were introduced in the central sector of the front, where Belorussian names were adopted. In February, 1944, the constitution was amended to give each Union Republic the "paper right" to have its own commissariat of armed forces and of foreign affairs. In 1944, a poem expressing love for the Ukraine even won the Stalin Prize. Outwardly these and other concessions represented a vast change and were so interpreted both at home and abroad. In reality, however, the change was negligible because Stalin neither retreated from centralism nor did he reject the total regimentation of life.

POSTWAR RECONSTRUCTION AND REHABILITATION

Four years of active Soviet participation in the greatest of all wars inflicted staggering human and material losses on the USSR. It has been estimated that the war cost the Soviet Union some 7.5 million military casualties. Of that figure, about 3 million perished in German prisoner-of-war camps; the remainder were combat casualties. No exact figures are available on the number of civilians killed, or on those who were either seriously wounded or maimed for life, or on those who chose not to return to the Soviet Union at the end of the war. Their number, however, exceeded the military casualties, and in all probability the war cost the USSR some 20 million people.

The material losses were just as staggering. According to official Soviet figures, war operations destroyed 1,710 cities, 70,000 villages, 32,000 industrial enterprises, 98,000 collective farms, 1,876 state farms, 2,890 MTS's, 7 million horses, 17 million head of cattle, 20 million hogs, 40,000 miles of railroad track, 84,000 schools, and most of the bridges, hospitals, and libraries. Officially these losses, set at 679 billion rubles (in prewar prices), were attributed to the Germans, but the Soviets' own "scorched earth policy" accounted for a good deal of the immense loss. At any rate, the close of World War II left the Soviet regime a colossal task of economic reconstruction of its land and cultural and psychological rehabilitation of its people.

Economic reconstruction became the special assignment of the Fourth Five Year Plan (1946–1950). Its announced aims were: to rebuild the war-ravaged areas of the country; to restore heavy industry and agriculture to their prewar levels, and then to surpass this level considerably; to raise the cultural and material level of the population; to overtake and surpass the scientific advances outside the USSR; and to maintain a large standing army. These ambitious goals were based on Stalin's determination (announced on February 9, 1946) to triple Soviet industrial production in order to make the USSR "ready for every eventuality." To attain that state of preparedness, Stalin proposed that by 1960 Soviet industry should produce annually up to 50 million tons of pig iron, up to 60 million tons of steel, up to 500 million tons of coal, and up to 60 million tons of oil.

To achieve this ambition, the Fourth Five Year Plan (adopted in March, 1946) allocated 250 billion rubles for capital investment, and planned to produce 19.5 million tons of pig iron, 35.4 million tons of crude oil, 250 million tons of coal, and 25.4 million tons of steel by 1950. The plan also gave high priority to the production of other strategic minerals (copper, aluminum, and nickel), as well as heavy machinery, transportation equipment, atomic energy, conventional arms, and the now famous MIG jet fighters. The plan envisaged an increase of 36 per cent in the productivity of labor, "to be achieved by making the utmost of the eight-hour working day," automation, a reduction of 17 per cent in the cost of production, a vast improvement in the quality of industrial production, a 17 per cent increase in food and consumer goods, and a 7 per cent higher harvest in 1950 than in 1940. In 1948 the planners added to these optimistic targets the construction of several huge projects for the improvement of electrical output, the communication network, and the irrigation system. These projects included: a dam on the Volga near Kuibyshev; a dam on the Volga at Stalingrad; a dam at Kakhovka on the Dnieper; an irrigation canal in Central Asia to fertilize the desert of Kara-Kum; the Volga-Don Canal; and planting of gigantic forest belts in the Ukraine and in the southern steppes to aid in drought control.

On April 17, 1951, the Soviet government announced that the Fourth Five Year Plan "has been successfully fulfilled and the most important plan goals have been considerably exceeded." Western scholars seriously questioned the validity of this claim, because the official report did not contain a single figure on actual physical output of industrial goods, but, in the words of one observer, was reduced "to long series of percentages related to some mysterious quantities which have never been publicized." Through painstaking research, however, Western scholars have concluded that at the end of 1950, Soviet production of many key raw industrial materials had exceeded their assigned quota, while the production of low priority goods lagged behind. Thus, it is believed that in 1950 the Soviet Union produced about 27.3 million tons of raw steel, 20.8 million tons of rolled steel, 264 million tons of coal, and 37.6 million tons of oil. Production of shoes, textiles, and household appliances was below the set target, as was the production of grain. The Fourth Five Year Plan, in other words, experienced the same uneven performance as its predecessors.

The recovery and progress in agriculture did not keep pace with industry. As in the past, the productivity and yield were low, while the number of people employed and production costs were high. There were good reasons for this discrepancy and lag. The war had devastated agriculture, destroying its implements, and reducing drastically the number of animals as well as people. In 1946 the Soviet Union had only 10.5 million horses, 47 million cattle, 10.4 million hogs, and 69.4 million sheep and goats. Corresponding figures for the year 1916 were 38.2 million, 58.4 million, 23 million, and 96.3 million respectively. These shortages resulted in low supplies of meat and dairy products, and they also affected power, since Soviet agriculture still depended heavily on draft animals. Moreover, as a nonpriority sector, agriculture received inadequate consideration in 1946 from the planners, who allocated only 12.3 billion rubles in contrast to 68.8 billion rubles for industry and 10 billion rubles for transport. Finally, in 1946 nature played havoc with the bold planning schemes in the form of a devastating drought, the worst since 1891–1892, which affected the Ukraine, the Volga, and other grain-producing areas of the Soviet Union. As in the past, the drought was followed by a terrible famine, the third of the Soviet period, causing thousands of casualties.[1]

Party and government authorities devised three different policies for dealing with the postwar agricultural crisis. The first was introduced on September 19, 1946, in the form of a joint resolution of the Central Committee and of the Council of Ministers, which attempted to restore some order in the rather chaotic postwar situation. The basic aim of the resolution was to recover for the collective farms the land and equipment which the peasants had appropriated for themselves during and after the war. On October 8, 1946, a special Council on Collective Farms was organized to deal with this situation, and a year later *Pravda* claimed that

[1] In December, 1963, Khrushchev publicly confirmed the occurrence of this famine, for which he held Stalin responsible.

some 14 million acres of misappropriated land had been recovered. The Council also dealt with other abuses hindering agricultural recovery, such as misuse and pilfering of the property of collective farms by local officials for personal advantage, inflated administrative staffs, and violation of numerous "democratic principles" of management of collective farms. The Council relieved many functionaries of their jobs and antagonized those peasants who were forced to give up all land in excess of the legal allotment. No information is available on whether these changes increased agricultural productivity.

The second postwar policy designed to increase agricultural productivity came in 1947 in the form of a Three Year Plan for the development of stock breeding. This new plan called for an increase by at least 50 per cent in the production of meat, lard, milk, butter, eggs, wool, and like products; a 20 per cent increase in the number of cattle, hogs, sheep, and goats; and an increase in the area sown with fodder crops. Apparently, the goals were not attained, because in April, 1949, the government reiterated these aims, and ordered that energetic measures be taken to end these discrepancies. Repeated Soviet attention to this problem in the 1950's and in the early 1960's indicates, however, that the problem is far from being solved.

The third major postwar policy in agriculture was the celebrated amalgamation of collective farms; i.e., a merging of several collectives into one gigantic farm. The aim of this policy, which was devised by Khrushchev, was threefold. First, it sought to increase agricultural productivity by a more thorough utilization of machinery; second, it sought to strengthen party control over the countryside; and, third, it sought to deprive peasants entirely of their private plots. The amalgamation experiment was first put to use in the Ukraine in 1947 on a trial basis. Because of its "success" there it became a nationwide policy in April, 1950. Officially, the Soviet press hailed the new policy as a "peaceful" and "voluntary" undertaking. In ruthlessness, however, the amalgamation almost equalled the original collectivization. Between April 5, 1950, and October, 1952, the number of collective farms was reduced from 254,000 to 97,000. There were indications that in many places these changes led to open revolts which the authorities suppressed with brutal force. This restlessness forced the party to abandon further amalgamation, at least for the time being, and, as in the past, the authorities placed the blame for the excesses on local party officials.

Peasant opposition to the amalgamation stemmed from official insistence that amalgamation be accompanied by the formation of *agrogoroda*, or farm cities of about 5,000 people. Each farm city was to provide peasants with the "luxuries" of city living, such as theaters, parks, and apartment houses. It was also hoped that the farm cities would make for greater efficiency and flexibility as well as tighter administrative control.

Under the new arrangement, peasants were to give up their private plots and be compensated by a plot in a common area, which would make peasant evasion of collective work more easily detectable by local authorities. It was this scheme of eliminating private plots that created the widespread peasant opposition and forced postponement of the whole experiment. The bitterness which this experiment generated hindered rather than improved grain production, which by 1950 was below a good prewar year in spite of the fact that the area of the USSR meanwhile had increased considerably.

On December 14, 1947, the peasants, and with them the rest of the population, were hard hit by the government's complex currency "reform." This reform sought to decrease the money in circulation, which war needs and occupation had increased. It also endeavored to curb the inflationary trend which had increased prices ten to fifteen times over the prewar level. It also aimed at eliminating from business the "speculative elements" which scarcity of goods and the abundance of money caused. To achieve these goals, the government abolished rationing, set up a state-fixed level of prices and ordered that all cash be exchanged for new currency at a rate of ten old rubles for one new ruble. By this low exchange rate, which reflected the real depreciation of the ruble, the government penalized all those who had hoarded cash as well as those who had saved their money in banks. The reform, however, had no effect on taxes, wages, and the innumerable fixed obligations to the state, which were to be paid at the same rates in the new currency.

Postwar economic recovery of the USSR was accompanied by a vast cultural and ideological "rehabilitation" of the people. The need for "rehabilitation" was obvious. To gain support of the people during the war, the regime appealed to patriotism, appeased the Church, de-emphasized Communist themes, and through innumerable other actions had instilled the hope that there was a more relaxed and more prosperous life in store for them. During the war, too, millions of Soviet civilians not only welcomed the Germans as liberators but were willing to cooperate with them. Millions of soldiers surrendered to the enemy, and additional millions moved across "foreign" territories, talked to "foreigners," and observed "foreign" ways of life. Regardless of circumstances or duration, the war exposed the Soviet people to "foreign" influences, and, in the words of the Bolshevik, the official journal of the party, deprived many of them "of the true Soviet information." The influences of the war, in other words, called for a postwar "brainwashing."

Postwar "rehabilitation" assumed different forms, the earliest of which was the development of the "elder brother" idea. The aim of this concept (inaugurated by Stalin in his celebrated victory speech of May 24, 1945, in which he singled out the Russian people as "the most outstanding nation of all the nations forming the Soviet Union," and subsequently developed further by Zhdanov) was threefold. First, it sought to depict the Great Russians as teachers, inspirers, helpers, great benefactors of freedom, cultural promoters and pioneers, and leaders of "socialist construction." Second, it sought to minimize the existence of influences other than Russian on the non-Russian minorities, such as Polish influence on the history of the Ukraine, or Islamic influence on the Turkic peoples of Central Asia. Finally, the "elder brother" concept sought to stress non-Russian solidarity with or servility to Russia and to emphasize similarities that united them rather than differences that divided them. Those who were skeptical of these aims and claims—and there were many—were *ipso facto* branded "bourgeois nationalists" and traitors. Immediately after the war, Stalin punished collectively several minorities for their cooperation with the Germans. Among those were Crimean Tartars, Kalmyks, Chechens, Estonians, Latvians, and Lithuanians, who were uprooted from their homes and scattered throughout Siberia. According to Khrushchev the Ukrainians were spared the same fate only because of their numbers.

The "elder brother" concept, of necessity, also affected the interpretation of Russian history. Russian contributions to all branches of knowledge and human endeavor were highly exaggerated. Russians were given credit for developing the steam engine, for producing the electric light, for inventing the radio, for pioneering aviation and aerodynamics, for discovering penicillin, and for priorities in innumerable other discoveries. Alongside this self-exaltation, Soviet propaganda depicted Russian history as one of constant foreign invasions (Mongol, Turkish, Tartar, Polish, Swedish, French, English, Japanese, American, and German), in which the Russians unilaterally and selflessly acted as liberators of peoples from alien yokes and as saviors of European civilization. This virtuous presentation of the Russian past (which made no mention of Russia's own vast conquests in Europe and Asia) was followed by denial of Western war efforts in World War II, and portrayal of the USSR as an innocent victim of Nazi aggression, which was allegedly encouraged by British and American "imperialists."

Another aim of such claims, many of which challenged basic and universally accepted historical facts, was to serve as a prelude to a concentrated anti-Western campaign, which moved into high gear during the summer of 1946. Through a series of decrees and official pronouncements, most of the Western authors were labelled corrupt. Western literature and art were declared decadent, antihuman, and sinister, and their reproduction was prohibited in the USSR. Those Soviet works of the past which, even through the slightest implication, pointed to Western influence on Russian development were severely criticized for alleged "servility," and their authors were branded traitors and "homeless cosmopolitans."

Viacheslav Molotov   *Andrei Gromyko*

The abnormal inflation of the superiority of the Soviet system was another major aspect of postwar rehabilitation. Stalin gave the official sanction for its development on February 9, 1946, in his analysis of victory in World War II, which, he said, meant that the Soviet social system had won, that the Soviet political system had won, that the Soviet armies had won, and that all their economic planning had won. Stalin's depiction of the victory over Germany as "the best proof" of the superiority of the Soviet system over all others meant the end of criticism in any form whatsoever of the Soviet system. Those who questioned the wisdom of this decision or who failed to demonstrate their patriotism to the satisfaction of their superiors were branded as traitors and *agent provocateurs,* as were those who disclosed "state secrets." Little or no effort was necessary to achieve the latter distinction because a decision of the Council of Ministers of the USSR of June 8, 1947, defined as state secrets all information of a military, political, and economic nature, and all information on scientific discoveries, inventions, and improvements of all kinds. By all these actions the Soviet government isolated itself and its people from the rest of the world, discouraged all social and cultural contacts with the West, including marriage of Soviet citizens with foreigners, which was prohibited on February 15, 1947, and drew around its territory an "iron curtain." The self-imposed isolation increased in intensity as time went on and was not modified until after Stalin's death, and then only on a limited scale. For Soviet minorities, for millions of former prisoners of war, and for all those who had been exposed to foreign influence during the war, the postwar "rehabilitation" was a bitter experience.

About one million Soviet citizens escaped the "rehabilitation" treatment. These were the "displaced persons" (DP's). At the end of the war there were some five million such individuals, consisting of former prisoners of war, *Ostarbeiters,* and those who had fled from the Soviet Union. Of these, about three million were in areas under Western military control, and some two million found themselves in areas under Soviet military control. At the Yalta Conference in February, 1945, Stalin, Roosevelt, and Churchill had agreed that all citizens of Allied countries should be repatriated at the end of the war. In accordance with this decision, the Soviet government established a number of repatriation missions throughout Western Europe to "assist" Soviet citizens, assembled in various DP camps managed by the United Nations Relief and Rehabilitation Administration (UNRRA), to return home. Some returned voluntarily, but hundreds of thousands refused repatriation. Ignorant of the reasons behind their unwillingness to return home, Western authorities, especially American, used force to help Soviet repatriation missions fulfill their task. Hundreds of people chose suicide rather than return home. Early in 1947, United States authorities halted forcible repatriation, but by that time some two million people had been returned to the USSR. Most of the remaining DP's, with UNRRA aid, eventually succeeded in making their homes in Australia, Canada, the United States, Latin America, and other countries of the Western world.

THE EAST EUROPEAN SATELLITE SYSTEM

The Soviet Union, as we have seen, suffered huge losses in World War II, but it also made tremendous gains. The first of these was the emergence of the USSR as one of the two great powers. This rise stemmed from the collapse of German power in Europe and that of the Japanese in Asia, and from the great weakening of English and French influence in world affairs. The second Soviet gain was territorial. The USSR acquired Southern Sakhalin and the Kurile Islands in the Far East, annexed the Tannu-Tuva Republic in Central Asia, secured from Czechoslovakia the Carpatho-Ukraine, took from Germany Königsberg and vicinity, gained from Finland the Petsamo region and Karelia, and retained all territories acquired during the period of the Nazi-Soviet Pact, namely Estonia, Latvia, Lithuania, Eastern Poland, Bessarabia, and Bukovina. The final major Soviet gain in World War II was the extension of the Russian Communist system into Poland, East Germany, Czechoslovakia, Rumania, Albania, Hungary, Bulgaria, and until 1948, Yugoslavia.

The extension of Soviet influence throughout Eastern Europe, commonly known as the creation of the satellite system, was a well-planned undertaking. It consisted of three decisive steps during the war and sev-

SOVIET TERRITORIAL GAINS IN EUROPE
1939 - 1949

U.S.S.R. in 1938

Soviet satellite states

Acquired by the U.S.S.R.
1939–1945

Communist
but not Soviet satellites

eral vital postwar moves. The first decisive step was taken early in the war in the form of organization in the USSR of National Liberation Committees for every East European country. Each committee was headed by high-ranking native Communists who had sought sanctuary in the USSR. Thus, the German National Liberation Committee was headed by Walter Ulbricht, the Czechoslovak by Klement Gottwald, the Polish by Jakub Berman and Wanda Wasilewska, the Hungarian by Matyas Rakosi, the Rumanian by Ana Pauker, and the Bulgarian by George Dimitrov. While a full study of the activity of these committees remains to be written, their aim seems to have been fourfold: they were to serve as nuclei for postwar governments "friendly" to the USSR; they were to act as recruiting agencies for military formations of East European nationals residing in the USSR; they were to be rallying points of resistance against Nazi occupation; and some were to compete with "bourgeois" governments-in-exile in London.

The second decisive Soviet step towards acquisition of a postwar sphere of influence in Eastern Europe was a concentrated diplomatic offensive. At first this offensive was directed towards the British. It started in December, 1941, during the Eden-Stalin conversations, when Stalin demanded British recognition of Soviet frontiers as of June, 1941; i.e., recognition of Soviet annexation of parts of Finland, Estonia, Latvia, Lithuania, Eastern Poland, Bessarabia, and Bukovina. Eden rejected these demands, as did Churchill during his visit to Moscow in August, 1942. The British were supported in their resistance by American officials, who felt that all boundary settlements should be postponed until the end of the war. In 1943, however, the Americans altered their position. The change came at the Teheran Conference in December, 1943, where Roosevelt sided with Stalin against Churchill's plan for invasion of the Balkans. The rejection of Churchill's scheme, which aimed at forestalling Soviet occupation of Eastern Europe, meant the division of Europe into two camps—the Western, controlled by England and the United States, and the Eastern, controlled by the USSR.

An immediate sign of postwar political realignment was Allied recognition of Soviet frontiers, based on the Curzon Line, with Poland being compensated by territories taken from East Prussia and those east of the Oder River. The Allies also tacitly recognized Estonia, Latvia, and Lithuania as parts of the USSR, and consented to the Soviet demand for Königsberg (which was renamed Kaliningrad) to be Russia's port in the Baltic. In May, 1944, the Soviets gained a further foothold in Eastern Europe when the British offered to recognize Soviet influence in Rumania in return for Soviet recognition of a similar British position in Greece. In October, 1944, the British went further and recognized the dominant Soviet influence in Rumania, Hungary, and Bulgaria, in return for a reciprocal arrangement in Yugoslavia. These diplomatic gains were greatly strengthened by armistice terms with Rumania (on September 13, 1944), Bulgaria (on October 28, 1944), and Hungary (on January 20, 1945), which granted Soviet authorities almost unrestricted political and economic rights in those countries, pending the signing of peace treaties. The Yalta Conference of February, 1945, acknowledged not only these rights but all other earlier decisions as well. To dispel growing Allied fears over the fate of Eastern Europe, however, Soviet leaders consented to allow Polish and Yugoslav representatives of the governments-in-exile to join the Communist-led governments, agreed to assist all the other liberated peoples of Eastern Europe to form broadly representative provisional governments, and pledged to establish, through free elections, governments "responsive to the will of the people." Events were soon to reveal, however, that when under Soviet influence people had strange and unusual wills.

The third decisive Soviet move towards gaining control over Eastern Europe took the form of direct negotiations with the Polish and Czechoslovak governments-in-exile. With the Czechoslovaks the task proved to be an easy one as the two countries had no outstanding differences. On the contrary, because of the German danger the Czechoslovaks had traditionally entertained strong Pan-Slavic and Russophile views. These views were further strengthened by memory of the Soviet offer of aid during the dismemberment of Czechoslovakia at Munich in September, 1938. On July 18, 1941, the two governments renewed diplomatic relations which had been interrupted since 1939, exchanged ministers, and pledged to aid and support each other in every way in the struggle against Nazi Germany. The Soviet government, in addition, "consented" to the formation of Czechoslovak military units on Soviet territory. By a special military agreement of September 27, 1941, the Soviet government recognized these units as part of the Czechoslovak armed forces, but retained for itself the right to approve appointment of the Supreme Military Commander and supervise operative and technical matters.

Meanwhile the Soviet government made additional moves aimed at attracting the Czechoslovak government to its side. In May, 1942, though not a party to it, the Soviets repudiated the Munich settlement and all policies that led to it, an action that forced the British and the French to do likewise. On December 12, 1943, the Soviet government signed with Czechoslovakia a twenty-year Treaty of Friendship, Mutual Assistance, and Post-War Collaboration. For the duration of the war, both governments promised to render each other military assistance against Nazi Germany and pledged not to enter into any negotiations or conclude any armistice or peace treaty without mutual consent. For the postwar period, both parties pledged that in the event one of them should find itself involved in a war with Germany or with any other state directly or indirectly united with Germany, the other would come to its support.

Both governments also promised not to conclude any alliance or take part in any coalition directed against the other, and agreed to maintain close and friendly relations, to develop economic cooperation on the widest possible scale, and to render each other every possible economic assistance after the war.

Following the conclusion of this treaty, which was hailed by the Soviet press as "an example of the strengthening of friendly relations of the Soviet Union with the European states," there began a gradual infiltration into the Czechoslovak government-in-exile by members of the Czechoslovak National Liberation Committee. At first, several assumed posts of unofficial observers in the Czechoslovak National Council in London. Later some were accepted into the government as Ministers-without-Portfolio or as advisors, in which capacity they served as the "eyes and ears" of Moscow. Early in 1945 when the Czechoslovak government began to prepare for its return to the homeland, several members of the National Liberation Committee obtained ministerial posts which they considered vital to their subsequent seizure of power; namely Interior, Information, and Agriculture. The stage was set for the extension of Soviet influence into Czechoslovakia.

Soviet transformation of Poland into a satellite encountered several difficulties, the foremost of which was the territorial problem. While in alliance with Nazi Germany, the Soviet Union, as we have noted, acquired some 76,500 square miles of Poland's eastern territories which were immediately incorporated into the USSR. In June, 1941, German forces occupied these territories. Polish leaders in London insisted that the Soviet government repudiate its part of the Nazi-Soviet alliance and restore the eastern territories to Poland. On July 30, 1941, the Soviet government, in an agreement which normalized Soviet-Polish relations, declared that the "Soviet-German treaties of 1939 concerning territorial changes in Poland have lost validity," but remained noncommittal as to the ultimate future of these territories. Their attitude remained unchanged until it became apparent that Germany would be defeated. Then the Soviets came forth with ethnic, cultural, linguistic, and religious claims to these territories. Polish rejection of these claims made genuine Soviet-Polish cooperation impossible.

The second problem hindering Soviet-Polish wartime cooperation was the military. In 1939, the Soviets captured some 300,000 Polish prisoners whom they scattered throughout Siberia. Following the Nazi invasion of the USSR, the Soviet government "consented" to the formation on Soviet territories of a Polish army. By a special agreement of August 14, 1941, the Soviet government recognized these forces as part of Polish armed forces subject to Polish laws and decrees, and retained for itself only the right to approve the appointment of the military commander and to supervise operative and technical matters. Early in December, 1941,

Stalin and the Polish Prime Minister, General Wladyslaw Sikorski, worked out additional details on this problem.

Trouble soon developed, however. Instead of the promised 96,000, Soviet authorities recruited only 44,000 Poles. For the remainder, they claimed lack of supplies and equipment. This was one major stumbling block. The other was Polish inquiry as to the whereabouts of several thousand missing Polish officers. Unable to satisfy the Poles, in 1942 Soviet authorities halted all further recruitment and ordered an immediate transfer of all Polish forces from the USSR to the Middle East. Relations further deteriorated because of Soviet charges that Polish diplomats were spying on behalf of Western powers. Meanwhile, the Soviet government organized new Polish army units within the framework of the Red Army, and publicly announced on March 1, 1943 the organization of a Union of Polish Patriots in Moscow to act as the "true" spokesman of Poland. In the midst of these vital developments, on April 13, 1943, the Germans announced discovery of mass graves of the missing Polish officers in the Katyn Forest near Smolensk. Polish willingness and Soviet unwillingness to submit the matter to an investigation by the International Red Cross led to the rupture of diplomatic relations between the Polish government in London and the USSR. On May 8, 1943, the Soviet government announced the formation of "Kosciuszko," a Polish division, and early in June, 1943, the Polish "Patriots" in Moscow adopted a program for Poland which called for far-reaching social and economic reforms, and which insisted that the Polish Eastern frontiers be a bridge and not an obstacle to an understanding with the USSR.

Because the Union of Polish Patriots was willing to cooperate with the Soviet Union and agree to all their demands, the Soviet government ignored the Polish government in London, and rejected its offers to restore diplomatic relations. On July 21, 1944, following the liberation of most of Eastern Poland, the "Patriots" from Moscow were joined in the city of Lublin by other Poles, and established the Polish Committee of National Liberation, which on December 31, 1944, declared itself the Provisional Government of Poland. Moscow extended recognition to the new body on January 5, 1945, and concluded with it in April, 1945, a twenty-year Treaty of Friendship. On July 6, 1945, the Western powers recognized the new coalition regime in Poland. It was a one-sided coalition because key posts—14 out of 21—were controlled by men who had received their political training in the USSR and who, in addition, could always rely on the support of the Soviet Armed Forces.

The extension of Soviet influence throughout Eastern Europe after 1945 was greatly simplified by the presence of the overwhelming Soviet military power. The Soviet army was not only the "liberator" but the absolute master of every country as well. In Poland it governed directly, and in all others its influence was indirect. But everywhere the Soviet army placed its full power behind the demands of members of the National Liberation Committees, and any opposition to these demands was called Fascist-inspired. Under these conditions no country of Eastern Europe was able to organize any effective opposition or resistance to these machinations. Those who made an attempt to do so were arrested, "tried," and executed. Soviet mastery over Eastern Europe was made easier, too, by the absence of Western military forces and the seeming indifference of Western statesmen over the fate of that area.

Next to the power of the Red Army, the extension of Soviet influence throughout Eastern Europe after 1945 was greatly aided by the skillful Communist political tactics. In every country the Communists created coalition governments which gave the appearance of representation, but which were incapable of competing for power. In Yugoslavia and Albania the coalition governments were known as the National Liberation Front; in Bulgaria it was the Fatherland Front; in Romania the National Democratic Front; in Hungary the National Independence Front; in Poland the National Unity; and in Czechoslovakia the National Front. In each of these coalition governments, the Communist party was usually the best organized, had the complete backing of the Soviet army, and succeeded at the beginning in seizing key ministries, such as Interior, Information, Defense, Justice, and Agriculture. Control of these ministries enabled the Communists to muzzle some opposition groups, appease others, and eliminate all the rest. In Czechoslovakia the final elimination of opposition took the form of the dramatic death of Jan Masaryk, son of the founder of the Czechoslovak republic; in Poland it was the flight of Stanislaw Mikolajczyk, head of the Polish Peasant Party; and in Bulgaria the execution of Nikola Petkov, leader of the Agrarian Union.

The Soviets also extended their influence throughout Eastern Europe by control of the economies of these countries. They achieved this by such means as reciprocal trade agreements, the joint stock company system (such as the Soviet-Rumanian Oil Company, or the Soviet-Hungarian Danubian Navigation Company), investments, financial loans, and similar schemes. These measures were further strengthened by the appointment of Soviet citizens to key posts in satellite countries as managers, directors, and "experts." In Moscow in January, 1949, the USSR, Bulgaria, Czechoslovakia, Hungary, Romania, and Poland (later joined by Albania) set up a Council of Mutual Economic Aid, commonly known as COMECON, or the Molotov Plan. The Plan had four major objectives: to see that the satellites aided in reconstruction of the USSR; to industrialize the East European countries; to create a Soviet-East European economic bloc; and to coordinate the economies of the satellites, who were forced to reject the Marshall Plan. This coordination placed the Soviet Union in a position where it could eliminate all other countries from trading directly

BILATERAL POLITICAL AND CULTURAL TREATIES BETWEEN THE USSR AND ITS SATELLITES

	USSR	Poland	Czechoslovakia	Hungary	Rumania	Bulgaria	East Germany
USSR		FMA 4/21/1945	FMA 12/12/1943	FMA 2/18/1948	FMA 2/4/1948	FMA 3/18/1948	
Poland	FMA 4/21/1945		FMA 3/10/1947 CC 7/4/1947	FMA 6/18/1948 CC 1/31/1948	FMA 1/26/1949 CC 2/27/1948	FMA 5/29/1948 CC 6/28/1947	F 7/6/1950 CC 1/8/1952
Czechoslovakia	FMA 12/12/1943	FMA 3/10/1947 CC 7/4/1947		FMA 4/16/1949	FMA 7/21/1948 CC 10/14/1947	FMA 4/23/1948 CC 6/20/1947	F 6/23/1950
Hungary	FMA 2/18/1948	FMA 6/18/1948 CC 1/31/1948	FMA 4/16/1949		FMA 1/24/1948 CC 11/25/1947	FMA 7/16/1948 CC 10/29/1947	F 6/26/1950
Romania	FMA 2/4/1948	FMA 1/26/1949 CC 2/27/1948	FMA 7/21/1948 CC 10/14/1947	FMA 1/24/1948 CC 11/25/1947		FMA 1/16/1948 CC 6/20/1947	F 8/22/1950 CC 9/20/1950
Bulgaria	FMA 3/18/1948	FMA 5/29/1948 CC 6/28/1947	FMA 4/23/1948 CC 6/20/1947	FMA 7/16/1948 CC 10/29/1947	FMA 1/16/1948 CC 6/20/1947		F 8/25/1950 CC 5/5/1952
East Germany		F 6/6/1950 CC 1/8/1952	F 6/23/1950	F 6/26/1950	F 8/22/1950 CC 9/20/1950	F 8/25/1950 CC 5/5/1952	

FMA = Friendship and Mutual Aid   CC = Cultural Cooperation   F = Friendship

SOURCE: Zbigniew K. Brzezinski, *The Soviet Bloc: Unity and Conflict.* Rev. ed. (New York: Praeger, 1961), p. 109.

with the satellites, and could restrict all foreign trade of these countries to the USSR.

Soviet economic influence and control of Eastern Europe manifested itself in many other ways. The most immediately noticeable was the nationalization of large industry followed by that of all lesser enterprises. Complete nationalization of industry in Bulgaria took place in December, 1947; in Romania in June, 1948; and in Hungary in December, 1949. These nationalization laws were accompanied by planned industrial expansions. Yugoslavia, in 1947, was the first of these countries to announce a Five Year Plan. Czechoslovakia announced its own in October, 1948, and Poland, Bulgaria, Hungary, and Romania followed soon after. In each country, heavy and war industries were given preference, while light and consumer industries were given lip service.

Alongside industrial expansion, each satellite country experienced a vast agricultural revolution. At first the new regimes decreed the division among peasants of all large estates of nobles, and lands belonging to the state and to the Church. Beginning with Poland on September 6, 1944, and ending with Bulgaria on March 12, 1946, expropriation decrees were issued in each of the East European countries. The purpose of this reform was fourfold: it eliminated the landlord class, which was considered "dangerous" to the new regime; it helped to reward the "faithful"; it helped to win the support of those who were economically insecure; and it paved the way for collectivization. Everywhere the agricultural reform in Eastern Europe was accompanied by excesses and deliberate stimulation of class hatred.

Between 1946 and 1948 all East European satellites adopted new constitutions patterned on the Soviet constitution. The aims of these constitutions were clear. First, they legalized the liquidation of political forces opposed to Soviet domination. In Bulgaria, Albania, Yugoslavia, and Romania, this meant formalizing the abolition of monarchies; in Hungary, that of the Regency; and in Poland and Czechoslovakia that of the nationalist republican regimes. Second, the new constitutions provided "the peoples' democracies" with a legal framework for implementation of the Communist economic, political, and social program. Each constitution empowered its government with the right to eliminate private property, to monopolize trade, to nationalize industry, and to collectivize agriculture. Each constitution vested legislative power in popularly "elected" legislative assemblies which met twice a year for a short period, and delegated their rights to steering committees known as presidiums.

After 1945 all satellite states were subjected to a strong Russification policy. The main instrument of this policy was the local Communist party and its auxiliaries, which in the last analysis were nothing but subservient branches of the Communist party of the USSR. Unconditional and blind devotion to the Soviet Union was the first prerequisite for party membership, and each new member accepted was further indoctrinated with pro-Russian attitudes. Outside the party, the Russification process was carried on through schools, theaters, newspapers, radio, and various societies organized for that purpose. Glorification of Russian achievement was emphasized everywhere, and Russian language, history, and literature were among the leading subjects in schools on all levels.

The Soviets encountered considerable opposition to the extension of their influence in every East European country, but only in Yugoslavia was this opposition successful. Commonly known as "Titoism," the Yugoslav opposition to Soviet domination developed gradually. It stemmed, among other things, from the Soviets' exaggeration of their efforts and belittling of Yugoslav military achievements; from Soviet opposition to Tito's ambitions to establish control over the Balkans; from Yugoslav resistance to Soviet attempts to establish joint companies to exploit Yugoslav resources and to plant Soviet intelligence agents in the Yugoslav army, the Yugoslav Communist party, secret police, and all other sensitive organs of the system. Soviet-Yugoslav tension remained a "family affair" for some three years. It came into the open early in 1948, when Stalin rejected the Yugoslav bid to conclude a trade treaty, ordered withdrawal of the Soviet military mission from Yugoslavia, and accused the Yugoslav Communist party of an undemocratic and unfriendly attitude. The climax came on June 28, 1948—the anniversary of Kossovo and Sarajevo—when to the astonishment of the entire world Stalin expelled Yugoslavia from the Cominform.[1] This was followed by all-out political and economic warfare, and even actual armed skirmishes. Tito resisted all Soviet and Soviet-inspired satellite pressures. His successful defiance of Stalin encouraged other satellite Communists to attempt to do likewise. Their efforts, however, were not successful, and many "Titoists" in various East European countries were executed. Titoism, or other-than-Moscow-directed movement towards communism, continued to develop, and with considerable Western help has outlived Stalin.

FOREIGN POLICY IN THE 1940'S

During the 1940's, the Soviet quest for security for the territorial base of the revolution passed through three distinct phases: an "Unholy Alliance" with Hitler against the Western Powers; a "Grand," or "Strange" Alliance with the Western Powers against the Axis; and a "Monolithic" Alliance with the satellites against the Western Powers. These alliances greatly

[1] For the full text of this document, see Appendix 29.

increased the territory as well as the military and economic might of the USSR because, in every case, the Soviets succeeded in retaining all the gains of preceding alliances.

The Nazi-Soviet Pact of August, 1939, as we noted earlier, was a quite lucrative bargain for the USSR. In less than two years the Soviets added to their territorial base parts of Finland, Estonia, Latvia, Lithuania, Eastern Poland, Bukovina, and Bessarabia, or a net gain of 179,088 square miles and some 22,567,000 people. These gains had an immense strategic value. They strengthened the Soviet position around Leningrad and in the Baltic, placed Soviet armies within striking distance of Central Europe and the Danube Basin, and improved the Soviet position in the Black Sea area. So advantageous were the new additions that the Soviets wasted no time in incorporating these areas into the USSR. Neither did they conceal their appetite for further gains. The latter factor heightened German suspicion and contributed eventually to the Nazi invasion of the USSR.

Immediately, the spectacular progress of the Nazi invasion of the USSR annulled all the Soviet gains. This same invasion, however, drew the Soviets to the side of all those opposed to the Nazi "new order" in Europe and laid the foundations for the "Grand Alliance." Churchill was the first to cast aside politics and personal feelings in the face of the Nazi menace. The day after the Nazi invasion, he offered the Soviets friendship, alliance, and "whatever help we can." On July 12, this offer was formalized in a Protocol signed by the British and Soviet governments, wherein both agreed neither "to negotiate nor conclude an armistice or treaty of peace except by mutual agreement" and "to render each other assistance and support of all kinds in the present war against Hitlerite Germany." Shortly after Churchill's commitment, convinced that the Soviet Union had the capacity to resist the Nazis, President Roosevelt extended American Lend-Lease aid to the USSR. Shipments of needed supplies began immediately and were increased considerably following the conclusion in Moscow on October 1, 1941 of an interim agreement. By the middle of 1942, the United States had sent 2,000 light and medium tanks, and 1,300 planes. During the same period, British shipments to the USSR included 2,400 tanks and 1,800 planes. Under a new Master Lend-Lease Agreement of June 11, 1942, the Soviet Union obtained tanks, planes, ships, trucks, jeeps, telephone equipment, machine tools, shoes, textiles, electric furnaces, aluminum, copper, steel, food, seeds, oil, and large quantities of other war supplies worth some thirteen billion dollars in all. Struggling for their very existence, the Soviets welcomed these supplies and pressed for more. The bulk of the shipments reached the USSR through Vladivostok, Murmansk, and Iran. Because the Iranian supply route was the safest, late in August, 1941, Soviet and British forces occupied Iran for the duration of the war.

The "Grand Alliance" was indeed a "strange alliance." From its inception it was plagued by fear, mistrust, and suspicion. Many factors contributed to this unusual atmosphere. In the early stages of the war the foremost cause of suspicion was the problem of the "Second Front." Hard-pressed by the Germans, the Soviets were extremely anxious to have opened large-scale military operations in Western Europe to relieve some of the pressure on themselves. The British and Americans sympathized with the Soviet problem, but were in no position to offer immediate relief. A full-scale invasion across the English Channel required, as events in June, 1944, were to confirm, a mammoth effort for which neither Britain nor the United States was adequately prepared. Both countries were being drained by supplies shipped to the Soviet Union under the Lend-Lease program, and both were fighting powerful enemy forces in the Pacific, China, Southeast Asia, and Africa. The Soviets seem never to have been able to understand or appreciate these other Allied engagements, and Western attempts to reach a compromise proved largely futile because the Soviets "invariably interpreted such Allied efforts in the worst possible light."

In the long run, however, Western inability to open the second front early in the war proved beneficial to the Soviets, as they were able to profit from the weakness of their Allies by extracting far-reaching political concessions. These included: Allied recognition of Soviet incorporation of parts of Finland, Estonia, Latvia, Lithuania, Eastern Poland, Bukovina, and Bessarabia; and Allied recognition of Soviet interests in Central Europe, the Balkans, the Middle and Far East. In return for these gains, the Soviets made two conciliatory gestures. On January 1, 1942, the Soviet Union joined twenty-five other states in signing the so-called Declaration of the United Nations—a broad statement of principles similar to the Atlantic Charter, and on May 22, 1943, Stalin dissolved the Comintern.

The anti-Axis coalition tried to solve the complex problems of wartime and postwar cooperation through various agreements, meetings, and conferences. Of these, the following were the most influential: The Harriman-Beaverbrook-Stalin talk in September, 1941; the Eden-Stalin talk of December, 1941; the Sikorski-Stalin talk of December, 1941; the Anglo-Soviet treaty of May 26, 1942; the Master Lend-Lease Agreement of June 11, 1942; the Churchill-Stalin talks of August, 1942; the Casablanca Conference (Churchill-Roosevelt-DeGaulle) of January, 1943; the Moscow Conference of Foreign Ministers (Molotov-Eden-Hull) of October, 1943; the Teheran Conference (Stalin-Churchill-Roosevelt) of November, 1943; the Cairo Conference (Roosevelt-Churchill-Chiang Kai-shek) of December, 1943; the Czechoslovak-Soviet Treaty of December 12, 1943; the Breton Woods Conference of July, 1944; the Dumbarton Oaks Conference of August–September, 1944; the Stalin-Churchill talk of October, 1944; the Franco-Soviet Treaty of December 10, 1944; the Yalta Conference (Stalin-Churchill-Roosevelt) of February, 1945; the San Francisco Conference of April, 1945; and the Potsdam Conference (Stalin-Truman-Churchill-Atlee) of July–August, 1945. As far as Soviet security was concerned, the most momentous of these gatherings were the Teheran, Yalta, and Potsdam Conferences.

The Teheran Conference (November 28–December 1, 1943) was the first summit meeting of the Big Three and proved to be a major triumph of Soviet diplomacy. A great share of that triumph resulted from Western, especially American, overzealousness in attempting to remove all possible obstacles responsible for Soviet suspicion of Allied action. It also stemmed from Soviet victories over the Nazis in the face of slow Western progress towards opening the Second Front. In return for Soviet agreement to join the United Nations (on condition that the executive organ of the new international body would have no power to make binding decisions), and to enter the war against Japan after the defeat of Germany, the Western Powers at Teheran passively agreed to Soviet annexation of the Baltic states; formally acknowledged Soviet incorporation of Eastern Poland, Bessarabia, and Bukovina into the USSR; compensated Poland for its losses with Silesia, Pomerania, and East Prussia (except Königsberg); abandoned Churchill's plan for invasion of the Balkans and North Italy as well as his scheme to create a Danube Federation; and by these commitments confined their interest to Western Europe. None of these commitments was definite. Each, however, laid the ground for the Yalta and Potsdam Conferences and for the postwar division of Europe into two parts—Western, under British and American influence, and Eastern, under Soviet control, with Germany a potential battleground of the future.

Problems which the Teheran Conference had failed to solve, and those which had arisen subsequently, were the subject of the second summit meeting of the war at Yalta in the Crimea, in February, 1945. At Yalta, more than at Teheran, Soviet military victories were the lever for Soviet gains. Allied forces were in control of France, the Low Countries, most of Italy, and had yet to subdue Japan, while Soviet armies were in complete control of the Baltic states, Poland, most of Slovakia, Hungary, Rumania, Bulgaria, Yugoslavia, and were massing for the final assault on Vienna and Berlin. Three problems figured prominently on the agenda of the Yalta Conference: the German, the Polish, and the Far Eastern. On the German problem, the Big Three resolved that Germany be totally disarmed; that Nazism and German militarism be totally destroyed; that those responsible for war crimes be tried and punished; that all German industry capable of military production be eliminated or controlled; that Germany make compensation in kind for the damage she had caused; that German frontiers, both eastern and western, be altered; and that Germany be divided into four zones of occupation—Soviet, British, American, and French. The same arrangement was worked out for the occupation of Austria.

The Yalta Agreement also provided a special status for Vienna and Berlin—that of joint occupation and rule by all four powers as a symbol of the Grand Alliance that won the war. The Western Powers held as self-evident that the joint occupation of Berlin by all four powers, of and by itself assumed free access to the city located in the heart of the Soviet zone. They asked no specific provisions for such free access in order not to offend the Soviets, and they also abandoned Berlin "as the most desirable objective for the forces of the Western Allies." The absence of Western forces in Berlin and of free access to the city at the time of the German collapse placed the Soviet Union in an advantageous position. To reach their respective sectors of Berlin, the Western Powers had to pass through the Soviet zone. From the start, the Soviet authorities prescribed limited air, rail, and road connections with Berlin for the Allies, and forbade any communication except by means of these routes. These restrictions prepared the ground for trouble of the first magnitude.

On the Polish problem the Big Three agreed that the Curzon Line, or Molotov-Ribbentrop Line, be the basis for the new Polish frontier in the East; that Poland be compensated at German territorial expense; that the Moscow-sponsored government for Poland be "reorganized on a broader democratic basis with the inclusion of democratic leaders from Poland itself and from Poles abroad"; and that after reorganization the government should hold "free and unfettered elections," on the basis of universal suffrage and secret ballot, as soon as possible.

The Far Eastern problem was the third major issue discussed at Yalta. The Soviets agreed to enter the war against Japan "in two or three months" after the German surrender, on three conditions: that the status quo in Outer Mongolia be preserved; that the Kurile Islands be handed over to the Soviet Union; and that Russian rights "violated" by the Russo-Japanese War of 1904–1905 be restored. These included: (1) the return of Southern Sakhalin to the USSR; (2) internationalization of Dairen; (3) lease of Port Arthur as a Soviet naval base; (4) joint Soviet-Chinese operation of the Chinese Eastern and South Manchurian Railroads; and (5) recognition of Soviet pre-eminent interests in Dairen and Manchuria. While Soviet rights in Outer Mongolia and Manchuria were conditional on Chiang Kai-shek's approval, which Roosevelt was to obtain, the Big Three agreed that Soviet claims "shall be unquestionably fulfilled after Japan has been defeated." The decisions at Yalta have been variously interpreted. However interpreted, these decisions—based in large measure on an erroneous Western estimate of the situation and on a mistaken appraisal of Soviet intentions—were a major triumph of Soviet diplomacy of World War II.

The "Big Three" at Yalta, February, 1945.

Two months after Yalta, Roosevelt met sudden death from a cerebral hemorrhage, leaving Vice-President Harry S. Truman in his vacated post. The change in American leadership had no effect on the military course of the war as Allied forces rolled victoriously over Germany, and on May 8, 1945, at Rheims, forced the Nazis to accept unconditional surrender. The change of American leadership had an important bearing on diplomatic relations, however. This became evident during the Potsdam Conference (July 17–August 2, 1945), which convened to deal with the complex problems created by the German collapse. The Potsdam Conference differed in several respects from the Teheran and Yalta meetings. First, at Potsdam the three leaders did not draw together "in the same warm, personal association in a common cause as at the two wartime meetings." Second, at Potsdam they could neither submerge nor postpone the issues that might estrange them. Third, the conferees at Potsdam met under the cloud of the first successful explosion of an atomic bomb in the proving grounds at Los Alamos, New Mexico. Finally, the chief figures met in an atmosphere of increased charges and countercharges of "bad faith" and of violations of wartime pledges. These signs indicated that while the Potsdam Conference would reach agreement on some, it would end in failure on other problems.

The Big Three addressed themselves at Potsdam to two main problems: the postwar settlement in Europe; and the achievement of military victory over Japan. In view of the Nazi collapse, the future of Germany was the main item on the agenda. The victors reaffirmed the decisions of Yalta, recognized the Four Power Zones of occupation and agreed that the aims of the Allied occupation policy in Germany were: disarmament; demilitarization; de-Nazification; trial of war criminals; democratization of German political, educational, and judicial systems; decentralization of German political institutions; and de-industrialization of German war and heavy industries. As far as it was practicable the Germans were to receive uniform treatment in all four occupation zones, and, during the period of occupation, Germany was to be treated as a single economic unit, administered by the Allied Control Council with headquarters in Berlin. The victors approved the mass transfer of German population from Poland, Czechoslovakia, Rumania, Hungary, and Yugoslavia into the four zones of occupation. They also agreed to take jointly all necessary measures "to assure that Germany never again will threaten her neighbors or the peace of the world," but stated that it was not their intent "to destroy or enslave the German people."

Several problems plagued the victors at Potsdam. These were: (1) Soviet demand that Germany pay twenty billion dollars in reparations, ten of which would go to the USSR; (2) Soviet unilateral disposition of German territories east of the Oder-Neisse Rivers; (3) Soviet high-handed rule in Rumania and Bulgaria; (4) composition of the Soviet-sponsored government in Poland; (5) Soviet bid to gain the trusteeship over Libya; and (6) Soviet insistence on a voice in the Straits. The Western Powers interpreted the Soviet *faits accompli* and demands for further expansion of Soviet influence as a threat to their safety. The Soviets, on the other hand, saw in Western reluctance to yield to their demands an anti-Soviet sign. To solve these problems, and to deal with those that might develop in the future, the Big Three agreed at Potsdam to establish the Council of Foreign Ministers consisting of the USSR, United States, Britain, and France. Their attempts to find solutions to these postwar problems form a record of failure and frustration.

The Potsdam conferees displayed considerable unanimity on the prosecution of the war against Japan. The military chiefs formulated a common course of action, while political leaders prepared the wording of an ultimatum to Japan known as the Potsdam Declaration. The latter called for immediate and unconditional Japanese surrender; restoration of Manchuria, Formosa, and the Pescadores to China; relinquishment of all Pacific Islands acquired since 1914, and all other territories "taken by violence and greed"; granting of independence to Korea; destruction of war industries; trial of war criminals; and reorganization of Japan, with Allied help, along democratic lines. Japanese rejection of those conditions led to the atomic bombing of Hiroshima on August 6, and Nagasaki on

August 9. On the latter date Soviet forces under Marshals Malinovsky and Kiril A. Meretskov (1897–   ) invaded and commenced the occupation of Southern Sakhalin, North Korea, and Manchuria. On August 14, the Japanese accepted the terms of the Potsdam Declaration, and on September 2, 1945, aboard the USS *Missouri* in Tokyo Bay, they signed the surrender papers. At last World War II was over, but peace was far from restored.

There were many signs before, during, and after the Potsdam Conference which suggested that, in spite of the terrible losses by victor and vanquished alike, genuine peace was beyond the reach of man. The end of war saw the eclipse of Nazi power in Europe and of Japanese imperialism in Asia. These eclipses created a vast power vacuum. The defeated Germans and Japanese were in no position to fill it; neither were the British, nor the French, nor the Chinese, who, although victorious, emerged from the war greatly weakened in terms of power. The task of filling this vast power vacuum fell accordingly on the United States and the Soviet Union—the two colossi—who emerged from the war as super powers in a category by themselves. Peace of the world depended on their cooperation, but events soon revealed that the two giants could not find grounds for genuine cooperation.

Literature on the development, manifestations, and objectives of the "cold war," as the period after 1945 is commonly known, is voluminous and controversial. The following constants are generally accepted as the "causes" responsible for the deterioration of East-West relations: (1) the enduring legacy of Soviet-Western suspicion; (2) the impatient Soviet quest for security which, while understandable, endangered the security of the Western Powers; (3) Soviet tendency to view the West as an enemy, once the common foe had been defeated; (4) Soviet fear of United States atomic power; (5) Soviet attempt to compensate this imbalance of power through control of large territories in Eastern Europe; (6) the rapid American dismantlement of its war machine, and withdrawal from Europe and Asia; (7) the sudden American decision in August, 1945 to end all Lend-Lease aid; (8) Soviet envy of the unprecedented American economic growth and expansion during the war, in contrast to their own vast destruction; (9) Soviet use of the chaos of war and the misery of its immediate aftermath to propagate political unrest wherever possible; (10) Soviet utilization of Italian, French, and other Communist parties to extend Soviet influence beyond their "legitimate" sphere; (11) Stalin's own xenophobia, imperial ambitions, and sense of insecurity; and (12) Soviet belief, based on Marxist-Leninist tradition, that all of Europe, indeed the whole world, must eventually fall under the sway of Moscow's spell.

After 1945 the aim of Soviet foreign policy was quite simple. It sought to retain and consolidate Soviet influence in areas the USSR had gained during World War II, and, using all possible means, to expand that influence into the regions the Western Powers considered to be theirs. In the Far East, realization of these goals proved to be relatively easy, thanks to the collapse of the Japanese empire with the resulting power vacuum, the far-reaching Anglo-American concessions at Yalta, and the weakness of Nationalist Chinese forces. Under the Yalta arrangement, as mentioned earlier, the USSR recovered everything Imperial Russia had lost to Japan in the war of 1904–1905: namely, Southern Sakhalin, control of the Chinese Eastern and South Manchurian Railroads, and the ports of Dairen and Port Arthur. Nominally, these Soviet gains were at the expense of Japan. Actually, however, they were at the expense of China, since, as one authority noted, "had Soviet Russia not claimed the fruits of Czarist imperialism, China would have recovered the position in Manchuria which she had lost fifty years ago to Russia and Japan." These Soviet gains, plus the severance of Outer Mongolia, were formally acknowledged by China in a Sino-Soviet treaty of August 15, 1945, ironically called a "Treaty of Friendship and Alliance," in return for the Soviet pledge "to render to China moral support and aid in military supplies and other material resources." This support, however, failed to materialize. Instead, Soviet forces seized and removed plants, equipment, and materiel in Manchuria as "war booty," and refused the Nationalists the right to use Dairen as a port of entry for their troops. These actions contributed greatly to the dramatic deterioration of Nationalist forces in 1947–1948, and to the remarkable Chinese Communist advances to the banks of the Yangtze and beyond. Throughout this period, the Soviet government maintained a façade of "neutrality" and "non-interference" in Chinese affairs. However, on October 2, 1949, the day following the proclamation of the Chinese People's Republic, the USSR granted diplomatic recognition to the new regime in China, and in December, 1949, Mao Tse-tung went to Moscow to negotiate a new Sino-Soviet alliance.

In the Near and Middle East after 1945, Soviet interests were most intense in Iran, Turkey, and Greece. The objective was to gain access to the Persian Gulf and control of the Straits. In Iran, Soviet interests seem to have been in a relatively strong position, guaranteed by the presence of Soviet forces in Northern Iran which had been dispatched there in 1941 to safeguard the flow of Lend-Lease supplies to the Soviet Union. Under a treaty of January 29, 1942, among Iran, the USSR and Britain, all Allied troops were to respect the territorial integrity, sovereignty, and independence of Iran and were to withdraw within six months after the end of the war. The Soviets did not observe strictly these provisions. They denied the Iranian authorities access, for instance, to Soviet-controlled areas, supported the local Communist (Tudeh) party, and refused to evacuate at the end of the war. In September, 1945, with Soviet backing, the Tudeh party requested autonomy for Persian Azerbaidzhan, and when the request was denied, an Autonomous Azerbaidzhan Republic was proclaimed under veteran Communist Ja'far Pishevari. On January 19, 1946, Iran appealed to the United Nations, charging the USSR with interference in its domestic affairs, and combined United Nations-United States pressure early in March, 1946, forced the Soviets reluctantly to evacuate their forces from northern Iran.

Soviet interest in Turkey met the same fate. As early as May 20, 1945, the Soviet government unilaterally denounced the Soviet-Turkish Treaty of Friendship and Neutrality (signed on December 17, 1925 and renewed on March 24, 1941), and demanded the cession of Kars and Ardahan, joint Russo-Turkish control of the Straits, and a new alliance of friendship along the lines of those signed with the East European countries. The Turks rejected these demands. Early in 1946, the Soviets rejected the United States' mediation proposal for a revision of the Montreaux Convention of 1936, and on August 7, 1946, announced new demands. These were: (1) that the Straits be open at all times to merchant ships of all countries; (2) that the Straits be open at all times to warships of the Black Sea powers; (3) that the warships of non-Black Sea powers be denied passage through the Straits, "except in cases specially provided for"; (4) that the Straits be operated by the Black Sea powers; and (5) that the Straits be defended jointly by the USSR and Turkey. Since neither Britain, Turkey, nor the United States favored the Soviet arrangement, the Soviets shelved the entire matter.

In Greece, Soviet interest manifested itself in the support, both direct and indirect, of the Communist-led Greek Liberation Front (EAM), and the Greek People's Liberation Army (ELAS). This support was contrary to the wartime Soviet-British understanding which made the British responsible for the liberation of Greece and for the restoration of order. A Communist regime in Greece, however, offered the Soviets a prospect of realizing complete control of the Balkans, seizing the Straits, and establishing Soviet influence in the Eastern Mediterranean. The monarchist victory at the polls resulted in a bitter civil war in December, 1946, veiled Yugoslav and Bulgarian intervention, and a United Nations investigation. Determined British resistance, American aid in the form of the Truman Doctrine, and development of the Yugoslav-Soviet dispute in June, 1948, however, spoiled Soviet efforts to turn Greece into a satellite as the first step towards seizure of the Straits.

In Eastern Europe, as we noted earlier, the Soviets were able to realize their goals with no appreciable difficulty because Soviet armed forces were in actual control of the area. In every country of Eastern Europe the Soviets installed governments in which native, but Moscow-trained, Communists were assured strategic posts. With these governments the USSR then signed long-term bilateral mutual assistance treaties and alliances (Czechoslovakia, December, 1943; Yugoslavia and Poland, April, 1945; Rumania and Hungary, February, 1948; and Bulgaria, March,

1948). These alliances were further interlocked by a dozen or more bilateral agreements among the states of Eastern Europe. All of these treaties emphasized the pledge of mutual assistance in case of direct renewed German aggression, or aggression of "any other state which would unite with Germany directly or in any other form in such a war." The Soviets also strengthened their military and political influence in Eastern Europe through various barter agreements, reparations, formation of binational stock companies, investments, direct loans, control of key industries, and wholesale export of cultural, social, economic, administrative and legal institutions. By these actions the Soviets turned the East European countries into satellites, and curbed all of their contacts with the non-Communist world. These actions, however, aroused Western suspicion and led to vigorous counter measures.

The Soviets did not accept Western opposition to their plans in Iran, Turkey, and Greece, nor Western criticism of Soviet machinations in Eastern Europe. On February 9, 1946, Stalin delivered his now-famous pre-election speech, wherein he "dropped the front of agreeable and co-operative meeting of minds," reaffirmed the basic Communist teachings on the causes and nature of capitalist wars, blamed the West for World War II, dropped the pretense that the defeat of Germany eliminated the danger of war, lauded the superiority of the Soviet system, and called for a "new mighty upsurge in the national economy" that would treble pre-war production. This gloomy outlook on relations with the non-Communist world—made a month before Churchill's famous "Iron Curtain" speech on March 5, 1946, at Fulton, Missouri—set the pattern for Soviet behavior. Thereafter, the Soviets automatically branded as a "warmonger" anyone opposed to their actions, and denounced all attempts to bring stability to the postwar world as "smoke screen for capitalist expansion." Under those conditions it was impossible to find grounds for a *modus vivendi*.

The "cold war" entered a new phase in 1947 following the announcement of the Truman Doctrine, on March 12, 1947. The aim of the Doctrine was simple. It sought to render immediate assistance to Greece and Turkey, then under Soviet pressure, in order to prevent a repetition of what had happened to various states of Eastern Europe. It was official notice that the United States would do everything possible to "contain" Soviet expansion. Soviet reaction was prompt. The Truman Doctrine was denounced as "a fresh intrusion of the USA into the affairs of other states," a violation of the United Nations Charter, and an example of the United States postwar policy of imperialism.

Soviet reaction to the Marshall Plan was even more violent. Proposed on June 5, 1947, the Marshall Plan was a coordinated, long-range program of massive assistance aimed at bolstering the economic recovery of Europe. All European countries ruined by war, including the USSR, were invited to prepare a list of their needs, and a conference was convened in

Paris late in June, 1947, to work out details. On June 29, the Soviets refused to participate in the program, withdrew from the Conference, and denounced the Marshall Plan as "The American Plan for the enthrallment of Europe"; American interference in the affairs of other countries; a "glaring example" of violation of the United Nations Charter; "an attempt to split Europe into two camps"; and a striving of American monopolies "to avert the approaching depression." Because they interpreted the Marshall Plan as an anti-Soviet act, the Soviets forced Poland and Czechoslovakia to withdraw their acceptance of American aid.

The Soviets' formal answer to the Marshall Plan was the partial resurrection, in September, 1947, of the Comintern under the label of Cominform (Communist Information Bureau, with headquarters in Belgrade, and, after the Yugoslav-Soviet dispute, in Bucharest), and organization in January, 1949, of the COMECON, with headquarters in Moscow. The aim of these organizations was manifold. They were to coordinate policies of the Communist parties; to oppose actively the Marshall Plan (in France and Italy, Communist opposition led to general strikes and considerable labor violence); to serve as instruments to enforce unquestioning adherence to the Moscow line; to promote the consolidation of Communist power in Eastern Europe; to act as avenues of intra-East European planning and integration; to serve as a vehicle for Moscow's struggle with Tito; and to be a symbol of Communist unity and cooperation, and a symbol of a permanent cold war against the West.

Of all the postwar problems, none contributed more to East-West antagonism than the German dilemma. The dilemma stemmed from what one observer rightly called "a schizophrenic attitude" of all powers towards Germany; that is, their fear of Germany's resurrection, their willingness to punish the Germans, and their eagerness to win the Germans over in view of Germany's geographic, demographic, and industrial situation. This attitude was clearest in the postwar German policy of the Soviets. At first, the Soviets favored an exploitative policy, insisted on heavy reparations, dismantled German industrial plants, sought to have a voice in the Ruhr, and did everything possible to weaken Germany industrially and to aid Soviet postwar reconstruction. Afraid, however, that a mere policy of revenge might align the Germans against the USSR, the Soviets shifted their stand. The shift came on July 10, 1946, at the Paris meeting of the Council of Foreign Ministers. The new Soviet policy on Germany, as outlined by Molotov, consisted of the following points: (1) the "spirit of revenge" ought not to be a guide in the framing of a treaty with Germany; (2) it would not be "in the interests of the world's economy and tranquility in Europe" to destroy Germany as a state, or to destroy her main industrial centers and turn her into an agricultural nation; (3) Germany ought not to be destroyed, but transformed "into a democratic and peace-loving state which, alongside of agriculture, would have its own industry and foreign trade, but which would be deprived of the economic and military potentiality to rise again as an aggressive force"; (4) Germany ought neither to be dismembered into several autonomous states nor federalized but unified along "democratic lines"; (5) the USSR was "in principle in favor of the conclusion of a peace treaty with Germany"; and (6) before concluding such a treaty, Germany must establish a single, responsible, democratic government "capable of extirpating the last vestiges of fascism," and able to fulfill all its obligations towards the Allies, especially reparations. The American answer to this Soviet bid for German support came in a speech by Secretary of State James F. Byrnes, on September 6, 1946, at Stuttgart, in which he made similar comments concerning the German economy and announced that the United States did not consider the German eastern frontiers as final. These two speeches, in the opinion of many observers, are regarded as "the unofficial funeral of the Potsdam agreement and the overt beginning of a race for Germany between the Western Powers and the USSR."

The race for Germany prevented the working out of a common policy for Germany by the Council of Foreign Ministers. Meetings of the Foreign Ministers were held in Paris (April–July, 1946), New York (November–December, 1946), Moscow (March, 1947), and London (November–December, 1947); but the sessions of all these conferences were devoted almost entirely to endless recriminations and propaganda speeches; and the meetings ended in utter failure. The sessions of the Allied Control Council in Berlin fared no better. They became more bitter, less frequent, and more fruitless. On March 20, 1948, the Soviet delegation walked out of the meeting of the Control Council, and the administrative machinery for four-power rule of Germany was at an end. On June 24, 1948, the Soviets halted all traffic to and from Berlin and put the Western Powers to the first endurance test. The West countered the Berlin blockade with the almost miraculous airlift. So effective was this countermove that the Soviets gave up after 324 days. Arrangements were worked out for the lifting of the blockade and for reconvening the Council of Foreign Ministers in Paris in May, 1949. But this meeting was no more successful than any of the preceding conferences.

Unable to find an agreement with the Soviets, the Western Powers adjusted their own differences, some of which were quite serious, and embarked on a policy which ultimately resulted in creation of a West German Federal Republic at Bonn. The Soviets, too, took steps which transferred their zone—about one-third of Germany with much of the original agricultural and industrial potential—into a satellite. As early as April, 1946, they abolished all political parties and approved only the Socialist Unity Party led by Moscow-trained men and supported by Soviet armies; nationalized coal, electric power, metallurgical, machine tool, chemical, textile, and other industries which they did not seize outright

262 USSR: A CONCISE HISTORY

and transfer to Soviet ownership; cut up the large estates; and initiated a policy of collectivization. On October 7, 1949, the zone was ready for an "advanced status"—that of a People's Republic. These actions confirmed that the division of Germany was there to stay until such time as one side should decide to capitulate to the other.

SUGGESTED READINGS

ADAMS, ARTHUR E. *Stalin and His Times*. New York: Holt, Rinehart and Winston, 1972.
ANDERS, WLADYSLAW. *Hitler's Defeat in Russia*. Chicago: Regnery, 1953.
ARMSTRONG, JOHN A. *The Politics of Totalitarianism*. New York: Random House, 1961.
————. *Soviet Partisans in World War II*. Madison: University of Wisconsin Press, 1964.
————. *Ukrainian Nationalism, 1939–1945*. 2nd ed. Littleton, Co.: Ukrainian Academic Press, 1980.
BAUER, RAYMOND A., ALEX INKELESS, and CLYDE KLUCKHOHN. *How the Soviet System Works*. Cambridge: Harvard University Press, 1956.
BELOFF, MAX. *Soviet Policy in the Far East, 1944–1951*. New York: Oxford University Press, 1953.
BERMAN, HAROLD J. *Justice in Russia*. Cambridge: Harvard University Press, 1950.
BETHEL, LORD NICHOLAS. *The Last Secret: The Delivery to Stalin of Over Two Million Russians by Britain and the United States*. New York: Basic Books, 1974.
BIALER, SEWERYN, ed. *Stalin and His Generals: Soviet Military Memoirs of World War II*. New York: Pegasus, 1969.
BRZEZINSKI, ZBIGNIEW K. *The Soviet Bloc: Unity and Conflict*. Cambridge: Harvard University Press, 1960.
CAROE, O. *Soviet Empire: The Turks of Central Asia and Stalinism*. London: Macmillan, 1967.
CLARK, ALAN. *Barbarossa. The Russian-German Conflict, 1941–1945*. New York: Morrow, 1965.
CLEMENS, DIANE S. *Yalta*. Cambridge: MIT Press, 1970.
CONQUEST, ROBERT. *Soviet Deportation of Nationalities*. New York: St. Martin's Press, 1960.
DALLIN, ALEXANDER. *German Rule in Russia, 1941–1945*. New York: Macmillan, 1957.
DAVIES, LYNN E. *The Cold War Begins: Soviet-American Conflict Over Eastern Europe*. Princeton: Princeton University Press, 1974.
DEANE, JOHN R. *The Strange Alliance*. New York: Viking, 1947.
DEDIJER, VLADIMIR. *The Battle Stalin Lost. Memoirs of Yugoslavia, 1948–1953*. New York: Grosset & Dunlap, 1972.
DJILAS, MILOVAN. *Conversations With Stalin*. New York: Harcourt, Brace, 1962.
ELLIOTT, MARK R. *Pawns of Yalta: Soviet Refugees and America's Role in Their Deportation*. Urbana: University of Illinois Press, 1982.
ERICKSON, JOHN. *The Road to Stalingrad: Stalin's War With Germany*. New York: Harper & Row, 1975.
FEIS, HERBERT. *Between War and Peace: The Potsdam Conference*. Princeton: Princeton University Press, 1960.
————. *Churchill-Roosevelt-Stalin*. Princeton: Princeton University Press, 1957.
FISCHER, GEORGE. *Soviet Opposition to Stalin*. Cambridge: Harvard University Press, 1952.
GALLAGHER, M. P. *The Soviet History of World War II*. New York: Praeger, 1963.

HARRIMAN, W. AVERELL, and ELIE ABEL. *Special Envoy to Churchill and Stalin, 1941–1946*. New York: Random House, 1975.

HART, B. H. LIDDELL, ed. *The Red Army*. New York: Harcourt, 1956.

HERRING, GEORGE C. *Aid to Russia, 1941–1946. Strategy, Diplomacy, the Origins of the Cold War*. New York: Columbia University Press, 1973.

KERN, ERICH. *Dance of Death*. New York: Scribners, 1951.

LANE, ARTHUR BLISS. *I Saw Poland Betrayed*. Indianapolis: Bobbs-Merrill, 1948.

LEACH, BARRY A. *German Strategy Against Russia, 1939–1941*. Oxford: Clarendon Press, 1973.

MACVICKER, CHARLES P. *Titoism: Pattern for International Communism*. New York: St. Martin's Press, 1957.

MAISKY, IVAN. *Memoirs of a Soviet Ambassador: The War, 1939–1943*. New York: Scribners, 1968.

MARTEL, LEON. *Lend-Lease, Loans and the Coming of the Cold War*. Boulder: Westview Press, 1979.

MASTNY, VOJTECH. *Russia's Road to the Cold War. Diplomacy, Warfare and the Politics of Communism, 1941–1945*. New York: Columbia University Press, 1979.

MEDVEDEV, ROY A. *Let History Judge: The Origins and Consequence of Stalinism*. New York: Knopf, 1971.

MIKOLAJCZYK, STANISLAW. *The Rape of Poland*. New York: Whittlesey House, 1948.

NAGY, FERENC. *The Struggle Behind the Iron Curtain*. New York: Macmillan, 1948.

NETTL, JOHN P. *The Eastern Zone and Soviet Policy in Germany*. New York: Oxford University Press, 1951.

NORTH, ROBERT C. *Moscow and the Chinese Communists*. 2nd ed. Stanford: Stanford University Press, 1967.

PAVLOV, DMITRI. *Leningrad, 1941: The Blockade*. Chicago: University of Chicago Press, 1965.

RIGBY, T. H. *Communist Party Membership in the USSR, 1917–1967*. Princeton: Princeton University Press, 1968.

RIPKA, HUBERT. *Czechoslovakia Enslaved*. London: Golancz, 1951.

ROSSI, ANGELO. *The Russo-German Alliance*. Boston: Beacon Press, 1951.

ROSTOW, W. W. *The Dynamics of Soviet Society*. New York: Norton, 1953.

ROZEK, EDWARD J. *Allied Wartime Diplomacy: A Pattern in Poland*. New York: Wiley, 1951.

RUBINSTEIN, ALVIN Z., ed. *The Foreign Policy of the Soviet Union*. New York: Random House, 1960.

SALISBURY, HARRISON E. *The 900 Days: The Siege of Leningrad*. New York: Harper & Row, 1969.

SCHAPIRO, LEONARD. *The Communist Party of the Soviet Union*. New York: Random House, 1960.

SCHWARTZ, HARRY. *The Red Phoenix. Russia Since World War II*. New York: Praeger, 1961.

SEATON, ALBERT. *The Russo-German War, 1941–1945*. New York: Praeger, 1971.

SETON-WATSON, HUGH. *The East European Revolution*. New York: Praeger, 1956.

SHTEMENKO, GENERAL S. M. *The Last Six Months*. New York: Zebra Books, 1978.

SHULMAN, MARSHALL D. *Stalin's Foreign Policy Reappraised*. Cambridge: Harvard University Press, 1963.

SLUSSER, ROBERT, ed. *Soviet Economic Policy in Postwar Germany*. New York: Praeger, 1953.

SNELL, JOHN L., ed. *The Meaning of Yalta*. Baton Rouge: Louisiana State University Press, 1956.

SOLZHENITSYN, ALEKSANDR I. *The Gulag Archipelago*. 3 volumes. New York: Harper & Row, 1973–1978.

SONTAG, RAYMOND J., and JAMES S. BEDDIE, eds. *Nazi-Soviet Relations, 1939–1941.* Washington: State Department, 1948.

STEENBERG, S. *Vlasov.* New York: Knopf, 1970.

STETTINIUS, EDWARD R. JR. *Lend-Lease. Weapon for Victory.* New York: Macmillan, 1944.

———. *Roosevelt and the Russians: The Yalta Conference.* New York: Doubleday, 1949.

TANNER, VAINO. *The Winter War: Finland Against Russia, 1939–1940.* Stanford: Stanford University Press, 1950.

TOLSTOY, NIKOLAI. *The Secret Betrayal, 1944–1947.* New York: Scribners, 1978.

ULAM, ADAM B. *Expansion and Coexistence: The History of Soviet Foreign Policy, 1917–1967.* New York: Praeger, 1968.

———. *Titoism and the Cominform.* Cambridge: Harvard University Press, 1952.

VOZNESENSKY, NICHOLAS. *Economy of the USSR During World War II.* Washington: Public Affairs Press, 1948.

WERTH, ALEXANDER. *Russia at War, 1941–1945.* New York: Dutton, 1964.

ZAWODNY, J. K. *Death in the Forest. The Story of the Katyn Forest Massacres.* South Bend: Notre Dame University Press, 1962.

ZHUKOV, GEORGII I. *The Memoirs of Marshal Zhukov.* New York: Delacorte, 1971.

ZIEMKE, EARL F. *Stalingrad to Berlin. The German Defeat in the East.* Washington: Government Printing Office, 1968.

USSR UNDER
KHRUSHCHEV, 1953–1964

THE STRUGGLE FOR STALIN'S SUCCESSION AND THE RISE OF
KHRUSHCHEV

On the night of March 1–2, 1953, Stalin is reported to have suffered a massive brain hemorrhage, losing consciousness and the power of speech. "The best medical personnel" was called to treat him "under the continuous supervision of the Central Committee and the Soviet Government," but his condition continued to deteriorate. He was officially declared dead on March 5, 1953, and was entombed with great honors on March 9, next to Lenin in the mausoleum on Red Square. At present it is not clear whether his death was timely or well timed. Whatever the final judgment on the exact time and circumstance of his death, Stalin's demise threw the struggle for succession wide open.

This struggle had begun in earnest with the official disclosure on

January 13, 1953, that nine distinguished physicians (some of whom were Jewish) had been arrested and had allegedly confessed to the murder of Zhdanov, who died under mysterious circumstances on August 31, 1948, and Alexander S. Shcherbakov (1901–1945), who had been Chief of the Main Political Administration of the Soviet Army. The announcement further alleged that some of the accused physicians were agents of American intelligence (recruited by the American Joint Distribution Committee, a Jewish charitable organization), whose mission was to liquidate a number of top Soviet military leaders and certain other public figures, thus undermining Soviet defenses.

There is some evidence indicating that the faked "doctors' plot" and the intended "trial" were to serve as a prelude to further accusations, arrests, and a massive purge similar to that of the late 1930s. It is not known who was the *real* instigator of the purge or who were its intended victims. In his secret speech at the Twentieth Congress of the CPSU in February, 1956, Khrushchev claimed that the new bloodbath was aimed at "the removal of the old Politburo members and the bringing in of less experienced persons so that these would extoll him [Stalin] in all sorts of ways." A similar view was advanced by many Western observers as early as October, 1952, i.e., immediately after the Nineteenth Congress of the CPSU announced changes in the structure and membership of the leading party organs. These changes included doubling of the membership of the CC, abolishment of the Politburo and the Orgburo, and division of the latter bodies' functions between the greatly enlarged Presidium of the CC (of twenty-five members and eleven candidates) and the Secretariat (of ten secretaries). While it is inconceivable that such vital changes would have been made without Stalin's approval, the architect of these innovations and the spokesman on their behalf before the congress was Khrushchev.

Whatever the final judgment on the *real* intentions behind the "doctors' plot" and changes in the party, the present evidence suggests that they were early manifestations of the struggle for succession. The struggle centered among four principal rivals: Malenkov, a member of the Secretariat and the Presidium of the CC, whom Stalin had selected as the main speaker at the Nineteenth Congress of the CPSU, thus unofficially designating him as the heir apparent; Molotov, a member of the Presidium of the CC and an "Old Bolshevik" of long party standing; Beria, a member of the Presidium of the CC and head of the security forces of the USSR; and Khrushchev, a rising star in the Secretariat, with a wealth of practical experience with the problems of nationality and agriculture acquired as First Secretary of the Communist Party of the Ukraine. Outwardly, Malenkov's and Beria's positions seemed to be the strongest. The future, however, was to reveal that this assumption was incorrect.

Moscow, March, 1953. Pallbearers (right to left) Beria, Malenkov, Vasily
Stalin, Molotov, Bulganin, Kaganovich and Shvernik carry Stalin's coffin.

Stalin's passing opened a new chapter in the struggle for succession.
Even before they revealed to the public the news of Stalin's death, his
lieutenants divided among themselves authority in the government and
in the party. In the government the new distribution of power was as
follows: Malenkov became the Chairman of the Council of Ministers of
the USSR, the position Stalin had held since 1941. Beria, Molotov, N. A.
Bulganin, and Kaganovich became First Deputy Chairmen. Voroshilov
replaced Shvernik as Chairman of the Presidium of the Supreme Soviet,
with Shvernik taking charge of trade unions. In the party the following
changes were made. The recently enlarged Presidium of the CC was
reduced to ten members (Malenkov, Beria, Molotov, Voroshilov, Khrushchev, Bulganin, Kaganovich, Mikoyan, M. Z. Saburov, and M. G. Pervuk-
hin) and four alternates. The Secretariat was decreased to four persons
(Malenkov, S. D. Ignatiev, P. N. Pospelov, and N. N. Shatalin). Khrushchev was released from his duties of First Secretary of the Moscow Party

Committee in order to arrange Stalin's funeral and "to concentrate on work in the CC of the CPSU." These changes introduced the era of collective leadership in the USSR.

The collective leadership accomplished three things "collectively." It belatedly issued the announcement of Stalin's death, in which it paid loveless and griefless tribute to the "wise leader," and made an appeal for "steel-like and monolithic unity of the party," "high political vigilance," "stalwartness in the struggle against external and internal foes," and "the prevention of any kind of disorder and panic." The second action of the collective leadership was the staging of Stalin's funeral with orations by Malenkov, Beria, and Molotov. Malenkov promised "peace" and a "happy life," pledged that the party and the people would continue "high political vigilance, irreconcilability and firmness in the struggle against internal and foreign enemies," and declared that the USSR had "everything needed for the construction of a complete communist society." Beria repeated the warning against "confusion and panic," and stressed the need to "intensify and sharpen the vigilance of the party and of the people against the intrigues and machinations of the enemies of the Soviet state." Molotov warned the rest of the world not to "rock the boat" because Soviet military might was formidable. The final act of the collective leadership was a wholesale removal of men who had been close to Stalin in the final hours of his life.

Collective leadership suffered its first setback on March 10, 1953, when Malenkov, apparently overeager to pose as Stalin's rightful heir, reproduced an altered photograph in *Pravda*. The picture was originally taken on February 14, 1950, on the occasion of the conclusion of the Sino-Soviet Treaty. It included many Soviet and Chinese dignitaries, but now only Stalin, Mao Tse-tung, and Malenkov appeared in it. Apparently the new collective leaders did not appreciate Malenkov's high-handed elimination of their images from the photograph. On March 14, at a special plenary session of the CC, Malenkov "requested" that he be freed "from duties as Secretary of the CC of the CPSU." The request was granted and the post went to Khrushchev, who thus became *de facto* boss of the party machine. On the following day, a vast reorganization of the government was announced, with mergers of some ministries and abolition of others. Under this reorganization Malenkov remained Chairman of the Council of Ministers, Beria took charge of all internal affairs, Bulganin of defense (with Marshals Zhukov and Vasilevsky as his first deputies), Mikoyan of domestic and foreign trade, and Molotov of foreign affairs. The new reorganization of party and government positions revealed that within the collective leadership a new *troika* had emerged consisting of Malenkov, as the head of government bureaucracy, Beria, as the head of the secret police, and Khrushchev, as the principal spokesman for the party.

Immediately, as head of the huge internal security apparatus, Beria appeared to be in the strongest position. His advantage, however, was short-lived. On April 4, 1953, came the official announcement that all the charges against the physicians involved in the "doctors' plot" were invented, that their confessions were obtained by torture, that the officials responsible for fabricating these falsehoods would be punished, and that of the nine doctors, seven who survived had been released and exonerated. This news caused the dismissal and arrest of several of Beria's subordinates. His own turn came on June 26, 1953, when he was arrested and denounced as an "adventurer," "hireling of foreign imperialist forces," a British agent since 1919, and an "enemy of the people," who had "wormed his way into a position of confidence." He was charged with "criminal anti-party and anti-state work," machinations to seize power and to eliminate the collective leadership, interference in every way with solution of the "urgent problems in agriculture," attempting to undermine the collective farms, sowing discord "among the peoples of the USSR," and with intensifying "the activity of bourgeois nationalist elements." Beria was tried on December 17, 1953, under the Kirov Law of December 1, 1934, i.e., without being present or represented by counsel. He confessed to all the charges and within twenty-four hours of the trial was shot. Subscribers to the *Bolshaia Sovetskaia Entsiklopedia* (Great Soviet Encyclopedia) were asked to remove with a razor blade Beria's photograph and the account of his life and to paste in that place an enlarged article on the Bering Sea. With Beria perished also six of his close associates who were labelled as terrorists, counterrevolutionaries, and long-time

Lavrentii Beria   *Anastas Mikoyan*

anti-Soviet conspirators. These charges against top Soviet security officials were no more credible than similar charges Beria and his officers had often fabricated for use against others. They did help, however, to undermine the position of the security organs as a state within a state— the position they had acquired under Stalin.

The decline of Malenkov's and Beria's fortunes increased those of Khrushchev. Following his appointment to the Secretariat, Khrushchev turned his attention to a thorough overhaul of the party machinery throughout the country, replacing doubtful or unreliable party secretaries with his own trusted men from the Ukrainian and Moscow party organizations he once had headed. The most notable changes occurred in the Leningrad, Armenian, Georgian, Azerbaidzhan, Uzbek, Kazakh, Moldavian, and key RSFSR party organizations. Khrushchev also reorganized local party committees and increased the number of district party secretaries, thereby strengthening his position everywhere. With the help of his appointees, on September 13, 1953, Khrushchev became the First Secretary of the CC, the position Stalin had used to emerge as absolute dictator. To all intents and purposes, this appointment eliminated the collective leadership.

As First Secretary, and hence the leader of the party, Khrushchev soon began systematically to build up his image. In April, 1954, on his sixtieth birthday, he was proclaimed a Hero of Socialist Labor, and was awarded the Order of Lenin. Before long, the party press, which he controlled, began to hail him as an "Old Bolshevik," an aide to Lenin and Stalin, and an organizer of victories during the Civil War and World War II. During 1953, and more so in 1954, Khrushchev emerged as the chief spokesman on basic domestic and foreign policies and a chief critic of all other high-ranking Soviet officials. His views were repeatedly cited by others, and eventually his word became the law of the land. He travelled extensively throughout the country, discussed all kinds of problems, and made himself known to local party officials. While paying lip service to collective leadership, everywhere Khrushchev tried to create an image of himself as the effective, colorful, powerful, and rightful successor to Stalin.

Early in 1955, the collective leadership, or what remained of it, received a further setback. This setback came about over the issue of the direction of economic development of the USSR. To appease the population following Stalin's death, his uneasy heirs agreed to pay long overdue attention to agriculture and to the production of consumer goods. Malenkov outlined the new course before the Supreme Soviet on August 8, 1953. It called for improvement in agriculture; accumulation of abundant food supplies and of raw materials for light industry; devising of greater economic incentive for collective farms; correcting and revising the peasant attitude towards private plots; tax reform; and substantial reduction of peasant "obligatory delivery quotas." Because these promises, some of which were fulfilled during 1953, sharply departed from communist orthodoxy, they were attacked by more militant party functionaries.

The issue of consumer versus heavy industry came to a head on December 21, 1954, when *Izvestia*, the government's—or Malenkov's—mouthpiece, urged editorially a build-up in consumer goods, while *Pravda*, the party's—or Khrushchev's—mouthpiece, advocated the development of heavy industry. On January 24, 1955, *Pravda's* editorial went further. It branded the emphasis on consumer goods as "utterly alien to Marxist-Leninist political economy and to the general line of the Communist Party," and stressed that "heavy industry was, is, and will be the granite foundation of all branches of the socialist economy, the cornerstone of the might of the Soviet country and of its peoples' well being." Khrushchev repeated these warnings more bluntly at the January 25, 1955 meeting of the CC where he declared that to claim priority for light industry was a "slander of the party" and a new form of anti-Leninist "right-deviation." It became obvious that there was room for only one spokesman in the USSR.

The decision came on February 8, 1955, when, in Malenkov's presence, a clerk read Malenkov's letter of resignation to the hastily convened Supreme Soviet. In this obviously artificial document, Malenkov requested that he be relieved from the post of Chairman of the Council of Ministers in order "to strengthen the leadership" of that body. Although for over twenty years he had been a high-ranking party functionary, and as a member of the Committee of State Defense had been responsible for increasing Soviet aircraft production during World War II, he now pleaded insufficient experience in state and "local work and the fact that I did not have occasion, in a ministry or some economic organ, to effect direct guidance of individual branches of national economy." As if these falsehoods were insufficient, he acknowledged his "guilt and responsibility for the unsatisfactory state of affairs which had arisen in agriculture" (which Khrushchev had mismanaged since 1949), conceded that renewed emphasis on heavy industry was the only correct "foundation" for a sound agricultural and consumer industry program, and promised to "perform in the most conscientious manner my duty and the functions which will be entrusted to me" in the future. The Supreme Soviet granted Malenkov's request and, at Khrushchev's suggestion, appointed Bulganin as Chairman of the Council of Ministers.

Malenkov's resignation signalled the end to collective leadership and the emergence of Khrushchev as undisputed and supreme dictator in the USSR. In that capacity Khrushchev further reshuffled party and government bureaucrats on all levels, doubled the membership of the Secretariat in July, 1955, and elevated some of his supporters to the Presidium of the

CC without benefit of the party congress' action. These moves, in turn, greatly strengthened his position in the CC and in the party. At the Twentieth Congress of the CPSU in February, 1956, Khrushchev was the most conspicuous spokesman. He delivered the opening address, gave the report on behalf of the CC, rudely interrupted other speakers, and, at a secret session, delivered a devastating attack on Stalin. The Congress approved Khrushchev's selection of, and considerable increase in, the membership of the CC and of its Presidium and the Secretariat. Since most of the new men were his loyal supporters, Khrushchev's influence in the policy-making bodies increased appreciably. Confident of their support, he relaxed some of the stringent rules of labor discipline, made concessions to peasants, and introduced far-reaching administrative decentralization of economic enterprises.

In June, 1957, "Old Bolsheviks" Malenkov, Molotov, Kaganovich, and Saburov made an attempt to strip Khrushchev of his powers. Taking advantage of his official visit to Finland, they convened a meeting of the Presidium of the CC and demanded his resignation. Khrushchev fought back their demands and, supposedly with the help of Marshal Zhukov, succeeded in transferring the question of his resignation to the CC where he had many allies and where, after a week of bitter struggle (June 22–29), he won. Malenkov, Molotov, Kaganovich, and Saburov were dismissed from their party and government posts, and were accused of violating the 1921 party ban on factions, obstructing policies designed to ease international tensions, resisting economic reorganization, opposing material incentives in agriculture, and conspiring to seize power in the USSR. The purge of the "anti-party" group enabled Khrushchev to consolidate his position in the Presidium of the CC, whose membership was now "pro-Khrushchev." Late in October, 1957, Khrushchev abruptly stripped Marshal Zhukov of his authority and on March 27, 1958, as an anticlimax to his victory over all of his rivals, he relieved Bulganin of his duties and assumed the post of Chairman of the Council of Ministers. From March, 1958, until October 15, 1964, no one doubted that Khrushchev, as the First Secretary of the party's CC, Chairman of the Presidium of the CC, and Chairman of the Council of Ministers of the USSR, was the supreme dictator in the USSR, and had proven to be one of Stalin's most perceptive students.

DE-STALINIZATION

The struggle for succession was accompanied by a development known as "de-Stalinization," or downgrading of Stalin. The *real* reasons for "operation cutdown" are unknown. The available evidence suggests, however, that like all things in a regimented society, the downgrading of Stalin was a well-planned undertaking, carefully timed, masterfully controlled, and doled out in tolerable, properly spaced, and gradually habituating doses. Four distinct phases may be discerned in the process: the moderate phase (March, 1953–January, 1956); the dethronement phase (February, 1956–January, 1957); the reappraisal phase (January, 1957–October, 1961); and the phase of liquidation of his memory (October, 1961–October, 1964).

One of the basic characteristics of the early phase of de-Stalinization was the heavy emphasis by his heirs on the principle of collective leadership, and criticism of one-man rule. The classic formulation of the new trend appeared in an article entitled "Collectivity is the Highest Principle of Party Leadership." Published in *Pravda* on April 16, 1953, the article stressed that the solution of all important problems of party work must be "the fruit of collective discussion"; that regardless of their experience, wisdom, and ability, individual leaders do not possess and "cannot replace the initiative and experience of a whole collective"; and that party leaders must be able to accept criticism of themselves and must show "readiness to bend their will to the will of the collective." The article did not mention Stalin's name, but the implication was obvious.

Accompanying the attack on what became known as "the cult of individual" was the campaign designed to inflate the fame of Lenin and deflate the name, stature, and reputation of Stalin. The most striking revelation in this connection was the official chronicle of the fifty years of the Communist party, published in the summer of 1953. This curious document repeated time and again that it was Lenin who founded the party, led it to victory, provided the inspiration for its success (even after his death), and authored the "collective leadership principle." Stalin, in contrast, was credited only with development of "the Marxist-Leninist theory in conformity with the new historical conditions." By omitting Stalin's name from the account of the Bolshevik revolution and the Civil War, the new "history" exploded the Stalin-created legend that he was Lenin's right-hand man before, during and after the revolution. This was indeed a radical departure, for while he was alive Stalin was credited with almost every known achievement, thanks to his "unerring foresight," "wisdom," "genius," and "infallibility." His writings, in the words of one observer, "had the force of sacred writ and were considered the irrefutable source of all judgments on any matter he ever discussed." The most ironic part of this rewriting of history was the fact that it was done by the very men Stalin had selected and elevated to the highest positions in the Soviet system.

The undermining of Stalin's reputation manifested itself in innumerable other ways. Following his funeral, references to his name declined sharply in the press as did quotations from his works. His pictures disappeared from publications and public displays, except on great ceremonial occasions. An article in the first volume of the *Bolshaia Sovetskaia Entsiklopedia,* published after his death, deprived Stalin of the exclusive authorship of the *Short History of the Communist Party.* His revolutionary activities in the Caucasus, which had been glorified by Beria in a book that went through nine editions (the last one in 1952), were officially condemned—not only because of Beria's "treachery" but also because of historical inaccuracies and falsehoods. The collective leadership suspended in 1953 the annual award of Stalin Prizes, issued amnesties to some victims of Stalin's mistreatment, reduced the population of concentration camps, posthumously rehabilitated some of the purge victims, promised to improve living standards, allowed relative freedom of movement, decreased police power, and abandoned many other harsh aspects of Stalin's rule. These carefully prepared preliminaries paved the way for the second phase of the de-Stalinization process—the dethronement of Stalin at the Twentieth Congress of the CPSU in February, 1956.

The dethronement assault was led by Mikoyan on February 16. He was followed by Khrushchev with the now famous secret speech on the night of February 24–25, 1956.[1] Labelled by some observers as perhaps the most important document ever to have come from the Communist movement, Khrushchev's de-Stalinization speech (from which foreign Communists were excluded) is remarkable for its half truths, its falsehoods, and its revelations. The list of Khrushchev's charges against Stalin is sweeping. He accused his former chief: (1) of violating collegiality in leadership and in work; (2) of practicing "brutal violence not only towards everything which opposed him, but also towards that which seemed to his capricious and despotic character, contrary to his concepts"; (3) of imposing "his concepts and demanding absolute submission to his opinion"; (4) of originating the concept "enemy of the people"; (5) of inaugurating a reign "of the most cruel repression"; (6) of violating "all norms of revolutionary legality" and ignoring all norms of party life; (7) of acting in the name of the party, its CC and its Politburo; (8) of using "extreme methods and mass repression" against anyone who dared to disagree with him; (9) of branding and liquidating many honest Communists as "enemies," spies, and wreckers; (10) of arresting and shooting (between 1934 and 1938) 70 per cent of the members of the party's CC; (11) of elevating "himself above the Party and above the nation"; (12) of deviating from all precepts of Leninism; (13) of gaining confessions "with the help of cruel and inhuman torture"; (14) of ignoring all pleas of innocent victims; (15) of causing "tremendous harm to our country and to the cause of Socialist advancement" by mass arrests of

[1] For the full text of the speech, see Appendix 35.

party, soviet, economic, and military personnel; (16) of creating uncertainty, suspicion, and distrust in the country; (17) of not preparing the country against the German invasion, in spite of repeated warnings by Soviet and foreign observers; (18) of interfering with actual military operations, of which he knew nothing, thereby causing "our army serious damage"; (19) of taking all credit for military victories of World War II, and thus belittling the heroic efforts of the Soviet peoples; (20) of ordering mass deportation of Soviet minorities accused of collaborating with the Germans; (21) of growing "more capricious, irritable, and brutal" after World War II; (22) of causing the conflict with Yugoslavia; (23) of being ignorant of conditions in the country at large; (24) of believing himself to be "the greatest leader" and the "sublime strategist of all times and nations"; and (25) of self-glorification, erecting statues of himself and naming cities, collective farms, canals, and prizes for himself.

Khrushchev's charges contained little that was new; however, coming from one of Stalin's closest comrades-in-arms, they carried considerable authority. At the same time, the indictment of Stalin was in many ways distortive and one-sided. Khrushchev, for instance, attributed the purges to Stalin, yet it was Lenin, not Stalin, who invented purges. Stalin's contribution was to make them more bloody and capricious. Khrushchev deplored Stalin's intolerence, domination, and absolutism. Yet it is doubtful whether Stalin could have acquired these traits so easily had it not been for the Leninist organization principles of the party, with the lack of respect for minority views within its membership and for majority opinion outside it. Khrushchev ridiculed Stalin's infallibility, yet failed to acknowledge that this claim was and is an inherent part of the system and of the doctrine that claims to be scientific. Finally, Khrushchev deplored Stalin's self-glorification, yet was silent on the fact that it was he and the other masters of the art of serving and surviving who glorified Stalin's name, blindly executed his will, helped to destroy all others in advancing his and their own fortunes, and thus created "the cult of individual."

Khrushchev's carefully selected audience of 1,436 high party functionaries is reported to have responded to his indictment of Stalin with "animation," "movement in the hall," "applause," and occasional "laughter." Western observers have labelled the speech the anatomy of terror, and the most damning indictment of communism to come from the lips of a Communist ruler. Whatever the ultimate judgment of this strange and awful document, perhaps without parallel in history, the indictment fully confirmed Lord Acton's immortal truism that: "Power tends to corrupt and absolute power corrupts absolutely." Khrushchev asked his listeners not to allow "this matter to get out of the Party, especially not to the press," in order not to "give ammunition to the enemy." Needless to say,

Khrushchev's address has not been published in the USSR. A special resolution of February 25, by the Twentieth Congress of the CPSU entitled "On the Cult of Individual and Its Consequences," confirmed, however, that a closed session was held, and called upon the CC to liquidate the "cult" in all of its manifestations everywhere.

The secret, however, did leak out abroad and made a deep impression on Communists and non-Communists alike. The complete text of Khrushchev's speech was published on June 4, 1956, by the U.S. State Department. Moscow took notice of this publication on June 30, 1956, in a resolution of the CC of the CPSU entitled "On Overcoming the Cult of Individual and Its Consequences." The resolution paraphrased many key passages of Khrushchev's secret speech (with no specific charges); acknowledged that the "cult of individual" had harmed Soviet society; argued that Stalin's "cult of individual" was not a natural outgrowth of the Soviet system or of Leninist norms of party life, but a result of foreign intervention, capitalist encirclement, World War II, and Stalin's own character; reasoned that any opposition to Stalin had been impossible because, as leader of the party, Stalin fought for socialism, acquired authority and popularity, and anyone who spoke out against him "would not have received the support of the people"; and pretended that "many of the facts and incorrect actions of Stalin, particularly in the area of violations of socialist legality, became known only recently, only after the death of Stalin, principally in connection with the unmasking of the Beria gang and the establishment of party control over the organs of state security." This revelation could be credible only if it were assumed that Khrushchev and his lieutenants had been asleep for the two decades preceding 1953.

On January 17, 1957, Khrushchev made an attempt to "rehabilitate" Stalin. Speaking at the Chinese Embassy in Moscow, he declared that

It is, of course, a bad thing that Stalin launched into deviations and mistakes which harmed our cause. But even when he committed mistakes and allowed the law to be broken, he did that with the full conviction that he was defending the gains of the Revolution, the cause of socialism. That was Stalin's tragedy. But in the fundamental, in the main thing—and for Marxist-Leninists the fundamental and main thing is the defense of . . . the cause of socialism and the struggle against the enemies of Marxism-Leninism—in this fundamental and main thing, I . . . would to goodness every Communist could fight as Stalin fought. The enemies of Communism have deliberately invented the word "Stalinist" and are trying to make it sound abusive. For all of us, Marxist-Leninists . . . Stalin's name is inseparable from Marxism-Leninism. Therefore, each one of us, members of the Communist Party of the Soviet Union, strives to be as faithful to the cause of Marxism-Leninism . . . as Stalin was faithful to this cause.

This reappraisal remained in force until October, 1961, when, at the Twenty-second Congress of the CPSU, Khrushchev launched the phase of liquidation of Stalin's memory. On that occasion he labelled Stalin a murderer, instigator of mass repression against Communists and army leaders, a man who seriously violated Lenin's principles and who abused power. Many hand-picked delegates to "the monolith congress" seconded Khrushchev's charges against Stalin as they also did his denunciation of Molotov and company. On October 30, 1961, the cheering delegates voted unanimously to remove Stalin's remains from the hallowed place beside Lenin in the mausoleum on Red Square for reburial alongside the Kremlin Wall, and to erase Stalin's name from the tomb. The proposal for the removal was made by I. V. Spirodonov, leader of the Leningrad party organization, and was promptly endorsed by the Moscow, Georgian, and Ukrainian delegations. Shortly after this action, the city of Stalingrad was renamed, as were other cities, streets, collective farms, mountains, canals, factories, and the like throughout the USSR and its European satellites, save Albania. These actions cleared for free and open discussion in the Soviet Union the reign of terror during the Stalin regime. Khrushchev even suggested that a monument be erected in Moscow to the victims of Stalin's purges—a proposal which was quickly endorsed by the Moscow City Soviet.

The obliteration of Stalin's name brought on two visible repercussions: a new wave of rehabilitation of Communist, but not of non-Communist, victims of Stalin's terror; and relaxation of rigid controls over intellectuals. The most notable members of the new wave of rehabilitation were Bukharin, cleared posthumously in October, 1962; Chicherin, restored to good repute in December, 1962; and A. Voznesensky (1903–1950), cleared in December, 1963. These vindications of the early 1960's, like those of the late 1950's, had one thing in common: they did not tell the truth, the whole truth, and nothing but the truth. Neither did they restore the right to draw conclusions from the moral wrong done the victims by the state. They were, in the words of one observer, "a pragmatic affair in which truth is a matter of convenience and innocence or guilt a utilitarian consideration."

REFORMS, CONCESSIONS, AND INNOVATIONS

Stalin's death opened the way for the rise of new leaders, and also made possible the introduction of many interesting innovations. The first of these was the legal reform. This reform consisted of four amnesty decrees (March 27, 1953; September 17, 1955; September 20, 1956; and November 1, 1957) by the Presidium of the Supreme Soviet and the revision of the criminal codes. Under the 1953 and 1957 amnesty decrees, all persons serving short-term sentences (up to five years) for lesser offenses were freed, as were all pregnant women, women with small children, juveniles, men over sixty, women over fifty-five, and all those who were incurably ill. The 1955 and 1956 amnesty decrees freed all those who had been sentenced in person or in absentia to ten-year imprisonment for collaboration with the enemy during World War II or for surrender to the enemy. Persons serving terms for "counterrevolutionary activity, major theft of socialist property, banditry, and premeditated murder"—and these formed a major portion of the prison population—were not affected by these decrees. The government altered the status of many of these unfortunates only in 1961 and 1962 when a number of modifications to the law went into effect. Thus, while freeing many persons, these amnesties were only limited concessions.

Revision of the criminal codes was also a limited concession. Officially, its aim was to "provide on the one hand for an increased struggle against such crimes dangerous to society as treason against homeland, espionage, sabotage, banditry, murder, and robbery; and on the other hand for reducing penalties for minor civil, economic, and administrative violations or replacing them with administrative or public pressure." In accordance with this objective, in April, 1954, the Supreme Soviet extended the death penalty to persons committing premeditated murder under "iniquitous" circumstances, and a decree early in 1955 imposed strict penalties for damage to crops on collective and state farms. At the same time Stalin's heirs placed limits on the power of the police to arrest without a warrant or to imprison without a trial, abolished crimes by analogy, reduced the maximum term of imprisonment, and annulled some of the most objectionable procedures instituted during the Stalin era. They rejected, however, as "alien", demands that the accused be presumed innocent until proven guilty, that confessions not be accepted as evidence without independent corroboration, and that defendants be represented by counsel from the beginning of the investigation.

In addition to the limited legal reforms, under Khrushchev's guidance Stalin's heirs offered minor concessions to Soviet minorities. The most notable of these concessions was the curtailment of the Russification policy introduced on a large scale after World War II, and dismissal of some of the officials responsible for its implementation. On February 19, 1954, the UkSSR—Khrushchev's former domain—with great fanfare and publicity received the Crimea from the RSFSR. The aim of this administrative transfer seems to have been twofold. It sought to meet the Ukrainians half way and thus to reduce their gravitation towards independence from Moscow. It also attempted to pose as a gift of the "elder brother" to the "younger brother" on the much publicized occasion of the tricentennial of the "unification" of Russia and the Ukraine. Another concession to minorities was the elevation of several non-Russians to the Presidium of the CC of the CPSU. Still another concession came early in 1957, when the Chechens, Ingush, Balkars, and certain other minority groups punished by Stalin for their alleged cooperation with the Germans during World War II, were rehabilitated. While these concessions modified some aspects of the Soviet nationality policy, they did not change the policy itself.

Another interesting of Khrushchev's innovations was the educational reform of 1958. Its aim was to give young Soviet people experience in factories and farms, to narrow the gap in the severe shortage of skilled manpower, and to control the white-collar jobs. Under the new system, "unanimously acclaimed" by the Soviet press, Soviet education began with an eight-year school, instead of the previous ten-year system. The first four years were devoted to general academic training. In the fifth through the eighth years, students, in addition to traditional subjects, were introduced to technical studies and practical work. Further secondary education consisted of "full-time employment in production, supplemented by correspondence study or by attendance at evening or shift classes." Entrance to the higher educational institutions was dependent on proof of having spent two or three years at work, and on the recommendation of a *komsomol*, party, or trade union organization. Those who qualified obtained their education tuition-free.

Khrushchev's rule witnessed several other interesting innovations. His regime, for instance, permitted the marriage of Soviet citizens to foreigners, adopted a more liberal tourist visa policy, opened many cities to foreign tourists, allowed some of its selected citizens to travel abroad, decreased terror and censorship, relaxed labor discipline, increased the supply of goods in the stores, and inaugurated a program aimed at improving the critical housing situation. By Western standards all of these innovations and concessions were small. By Soviet standards they were great, and for the moment at least they made the life of the average Soviet citizen a little easier and more hopeful. Because none of the concessions modified the power of the CPSU all innovations were either marginal or minimal.

SOVIET ECONOMY UNDER KHRUSHCHEV

Next to his struggle for power, Khrushchev's greatest challenge was the Soviet economy, especially its agricultural sector. The crisis of Soviet agriculture, or failure of agriculture to keep food production abreast of the rapidly growing population, stemmed from many natural causes. It

A modern collective farm showing the little fields (back of the houses) which belong to the farmers.

was, however, aggravated by such factors as official repression; peasant hostility; extremely overcentralized, authoritarian, and often inept and perverse planning; inadequate supply of work animals; poor allocation and employment of capital; lack of initiative on the collective farm itself; widespread deceit; inadequate compensation of the collective farm members for their efforts; pilferage and neglect of property; low labor incentives; inflated clerical staff; wasteful methods; and material and human losses during World War II. To raise agricultural production, as was mentioned in the previous chapter, late in the 1940's Soviet authorities experimented with crop rotation, merged collective farms, and devised a shelter-belt program, irrigation schemes, and an ambitious but unsuccessful three-year plan to increase livestock numbers. In spite of the gloomy outlook, the Fifth Five Year Plan (1951-1955) called for about a 50 per cent rise in agricultural output during the five years. This increase was to be attained by raising sharply the yields per acre and productivity per animal. It is not known whether the planners really believed this goal to be attainable. At the Nineteenth Congress of the CPSU in October, 1952, Malenkov boasted, however, that the "grain problem, formerly considered the most acute and serious problem, has been solved definitely and finally." Events soon revealed that this boast was an empty one.

Five months after Stalin's death, his successors admitted publicly (August–September, 1953) that all was not well with Soviet agriculture. It is difficult to say whether this admission was intentional, to spur the campaign, or exaggerated in the official records as a result of concealment of produce and income by the peasants. The condition of Soviet agriculture, as painted by Malenkov in his speech before the Supreme Soviet on August 8, and Khrushchev's report before the CC of the CPSU on September 3, was not bright. Both men attributed its sad condition to the historical need to develop heavy industry first, to war, to misplanning, to improper incentives, and to government failure to encourage the peasant to cultivate his private plot. Both promised to turn concentrated attention to agriculture in order to produce an "abundance of food for the population and of raw materials for light industry in two or three years." As a first step in the direction of "abundance," the government revised the tax structure, reduced by about one-half the levies of private holdings, cancelled tax arrears, granted tax deductions to peasants who purchased livestock, and reduced quotas for compulsory deliveries of animal products and vegetables. The government nullified these "concessions," however, by tightening party control of the collective farms and by raising the number of "labor days" required of collective farm members.

To relieve the acute food shortage, in February, 1954, Khrushchev laid before the CC of the CPSU a plan that sought to bring under cultivation vast areas of "virgin and idle lands" in the Urals, Siberia, and Central Asia. This plan called for the ploughing of some 32 million acres of virgin land in 1954, to be increased to some 74 million acres in 1956. The newly sown areas were to be organized into state farms devoted largely to grain production. To make it a success, machinery and people were moved to the new regions (some voluntarily, some under pressure).

The plan achieved some success in 1954, failed because of drought in 1955, scored a major triumph in 1956, and experienced difficulties in subsequent years.

In his quest to increase the food supply, in January, 1955, Khrushchev launched a "corn program"—which called for the cultivation of some 69 million acres of corn, potatoes, and root crops for fodder, in order to increase livestock production. A few months later he sent an agricultural delegation to the United States in order to learn the "secret" of corn growing, and invited American agricultural experts to visit and comment on Soviet collective farms. The observations of these groups brought further concessions to the peasant in the form of various material incentives, followed by a radical reform of the collective farm system. In March, 1956, for instance, the government made available liberal cash payments to farm workers; granted tax exemptions to farms in April, 1957; abolished the collective farms' compulsory delivery quotas to the state in July, 1957; granted the collective farms a nominal voice in the planning of their production; and in June, 1958, allowed the collective farms to purchase the equipment of the MTS's. These concessions, however, failed to produce the desired goal—the expansion of production of foodstuffs. Three factors contributed to this failure: the tightening of party controls over collective farms; official efforts to curtail peasants' use of private plots; and penalizing of those who spent too much time cultivating their plots. At a December, 1958, meeting of the CC of the CPSU it was publicly revealed that all was not well with collectivized Soviet agriculture. The CC approved, however, a plan for a vast increase of grain, meat, milk, and other products by 1965.

The dry fall of 1959 and the bitter and snowless winter that followed ruined about one-fourth of the winter grain crops. Early in the spring of 1960, the two main grain-producing areas, Ukraine and Northern Caucasus, were badly hit by black dust storms, while most of the USSR experienced late cold and rain. Climatic conditions also slowed down much of the harvest in the UkSSR, Central Asia, and Siberia. An unusual press silence about the 1960 harvest, absence of criticism of the districts that lagged behind, and an all-out effort by the government to harvest as much as possible pointed dramatically to an agricultural crisis. During 1960 the government dispatched to the "virgin lands" thousands of people from all over the USSR to help in gathering the harvest. Continuous rain and wind, however, prevented men and machinery from working to full capacity, with the result that in mid-October, 1960, millions of acres of grain were lying unthreshed in Central Asia and Siberia, while in the UkSSR the harvesting of corn was behind schedule. These developments severely affected all sectors of the economy and the projected harvest target of 152,400,000 tons for 1960 remained a planner's dream.

To deal with this crisis, Khrushchev called a meeting of the CC of the CPSU in January, 1961. It was an unusual gathering, since, in addition to some 240 members and candidates of the CC, the meeting was attended by some 2,000 carefully selected representatives of the economy, science, technology, and media, who, under party rules, had no business there. Khrushchev and the First Secretaries of all union republics admitted in their reports that there were serious shortages and shortcomings in agriculture; that grain production in 1960 was 20 million tons less than planned; that the livestock situation was no better; that the country was suffering from shortages of meat, milk, and butter; that in 1960 some 9,334,000 head of sheep had starved in the USSR; that privately owned livestock had increased at a far greater rate than that of collective or state farms; and that in view of these factors the USSR would have to postpone overtaking the United States in per capita production of dairy and meat products (originally set for 1961) by at least five years.

Khrushchev put the prime blame for the 1960 failure of the agricultural plan not on climatic conditions but on poor organization of agriculture by party and economic organs; the obsolete structure of agricultural administration; backwardness in agricultural science and machine construction; low standards of agricultural engineering; large-scale pilfering of grain before and during the harvest; and juggling of figures by officials. He cast grave doubt on the accuracy of Soviet statistics by revealing that many party officials, to gain favors in higher quarters, assumed high obligations they could not fulfill or could fulfill on paper only. Some, Khrushchev revealed, bought produce in the stores, which was then counted "by a collective farm toward fulfillment of its production" and delivered to the state. He labelled this practice a distortion, a form of speculation, and even a serious crime, and affirmed that anyone found guilty "should be expelled from the party and brought to trial for their violations of party and government resolutions." [1] Khrushchev pledged to "divert a part of capital investment" to agriculture, and insisted that people should actually get milk, meat, and other products instead of simply a promise. Later in the spring of 1961, he embarked on a tour of the country's most vital agricultural regions, where he obtained many pledges from local party officials for increased agricultural production. These pledges were extremely high and unattainable even if the harvest were to be perfect. Apparently all did not go well, because in November, 1961, Khrushchev again toured the agricultural regions of Central Asia, dismissing officials responsible for the failure of the agricultural program.

To alleviate the critical grain problem, during the summer of 1963 the Soviet government negotiated two large grain purchases. One was

[1] Between 1961 and 1964 thousands were reprimanded for "economic crimes" and about 200 were sentenced to death.

from Canada, involving 6.5 million tons; the other was from Australia, involving 1.6 million tons. Soviet officials also sought to purchase some 5 million tons of grain from the United States. American unwillingness to offer long-term credits without some genuine easing of international tensions, and insistence that at least half of the American grain be transported in United States ships (whose owners charged $10 more per ton), brought Soviet-American negotiations to an impasse which was not resolved until the end of the year. The volume of Soviet purchases of grain abroad in 1963 (together with those of all Soviet East European satellites) reflected the magnitude of the failure of Soviet collectivized agriculture to achieve "the mighty upsurge in output" which Khrushchev had predicted on numerous occasions. This magnitude was even more dramatic because of the fact that in 1963 the USSR had the largest sown area in its history—some 350 million acres.

The agricultural crisis was the basic preoccupation of the December, 1963, and the February, 1964, meetings of the CC of the CPSU. To dramatize the importance of these meetings, Khrushchev invited some 5,000 to 6,000 "guests" from all walks of Soviet life who listened to and approved his "new economic plan." It was a crash program involving expenditure of 42 billion dollars over seven years (1964–1970) to triple the chemical industry, which Khrushchev labelled "a mint from which gold flows." The bulk of the investment was to be diverted into production of agricultural chemicals. Some was to go for the production of synthetic consumer items. Because the program was silent on any attempt at removal of the built-in inefficiency of the system itself, it had no chance of success.

The crisis in agriculture was closely linked with a dilemma in industry. The dilemma revolved around the question of the relative importance to be attached to the expansion of heavy industry and the production of consumer goods. Under the Fifth Five Year Plan (1951–1955) adopted in August, 1952, the production of pig iron was to climb from 22.0 to 33.9 million tons; steel from 31.4 to 44.2 million tons; coal from 281.9 to 377.5 million tons; oil from 42.3 to 69.5 million tons; and electricity from 104.0 to 163.0 billion kilowatt hours. If realized, as planned, by 1955 these targets would have given the USSR "a level of military-economic potential more than twice as great as at the beginning of World War II." But these targets also called for great sacrifices. Uncertain of the loyalty and support of the Soviet people and fearing "disorder and panic," Stalin's heirs shifted the emphasis somewhat from heavy to consumer industry and excited the Soviet peoples' hopes with a number of vague promises.

Malenkov launched the "new course" on August 8, 1953, in his speech before the Supreme Soviet. It was not a radical shift. He stressed that armaments and heavy industry, which he called "the basis of the foundation" of the Soviet economy, must be developed "in every way." At the same time he promised that the government would give attention to consumers' needs; make available more resources for the peoples' satisfaction; press for more production as well as better quality; see that at least a minimum of essential goods was available everywhere; spend more on housing, hospitals, and schools; and try to supply cities with ample quantities of potatoes and other vegetables. In October, 1953, Soviet leaders further excited the hopes of Soviet consumers with the promise that by 1955 or 1956 Soviet industry would produce annually about 330,000 refrigerators, 500,000 vacuum cleaners, and 1,000,000 television sets. A large department store, the famous GUM (*Gosudarstvennyi Universalnyi Magazin*, or State Department Store), was opened on Red Square opposite the Kremlin, and another store specializing in children's toys across from the headquarters of the secret police. Soviet sales executives were urged to study and learn from capitalist methods of attracting, serving, and satisfying consumers.

The new course was short-lived. Late in 1954 and early in 1955, as noted earlier, a serious division developed among Stalin's heirs on the issue of consumer versus heavy industry. Khrushchev repudiated Malenkov and his consumer goods program and adopted a Stalinist policy of heavy industry. During the Sixth Five Year Plan (1956–1960), approved by the Twentieth Congress of the CPSU in February, 1956, production of pig iron was to increase from 33.3 to 53.0 million tons; steel from 45.2 to 68.3 million tons; coal from 390.1 to 593.0 million tons; oil from 70.6 to 135.0 million tons; and electricity from 166.8 to 320.0 billion kilowatt hours. Late in 1956, however, party leaders confessed that the planners

The Dnieprostroy Dam and power station in the Ukraine.

had overestimated the country's material and human resources, that the targets could not be fulfilled under existing conditions, and that the original drafts would have to be completely revised. The revised version took the form of a Seven Year Plan (1959–1965). Its declared aim was "a further mighty upsurge of all branches of the economy on the basis of priority for the expansion of heavy industry and a substantial rise in the country's economic potential so as to insure a continuous improvement in the living standards of the people." In accordance with this objective, the plan listed the following order of priorities: (1) iron and steel industry; (2) non-ferrous metal industry; (3) chemical industry; (4) fuel industry; (5) electrification; (6) machine building; (7) lumber; (8) light industry; (9) food; and (10) consumer industry. By 1965, the Seven Year Plan expected the USSR to produce 65 to 70 million tons of pig iron; 86 to 91 million tons of steel; 230 to 240 million tons of oil; 596 to 609 million tons of coal; and 500 to 520 billion kilowatt hours of electricity. To expedite the achievement of these goals, Khrushchev divided the USSR into 105 economic regions. Of these, seventy were in the RSFSR, eleven in the UkSSR, four in the Uzbek SSR, and nine in the Kazakh SSR, and the remaining eleven union republics constituted one economic region each.

The heavy investment in the military-industrial sector of the economy brought spectacular returns. On October 4, 1957, Soviet scientists successfully launched the *Sputnik,* the first man-made satellite, thus inaugurating the Space Age. On September 12, 1959, a Soviet space rocket made a direct hit on the moon, and four weeks later another rocket circled the moon and photographed its hidden surface. On May 15, 1960, the Soviets launched and later recovered a space ship weighing about 9,000 lbs., with two dogs aboard. In mid-February, 1960, they shot into space a Sputnik weighing close to 13,000 lbs., a prototype for launching a man into space, equipped with an automatic interplanetary station. In March, 1961, they launched two space ships, each weighing 9,000 lbs., carrying experimental animals and biological specimens. In addition to these impressive experiments, Soviet scientists carried out a number of less spectacular feats. During 1960, for instance, they tried four heavy rockets in the Pacific, 167 experimental rockets in the upper atmosphere, and 160 meteorological rockets; in 1961, they launched 115 research rockets with telemetering devices for the study of space and the upper layers of the atmosphere; while in 1963 they orbited seventeen earth satellites to study space. One of these satellites, dubbed *Poliot I* (Flight I), was a maneuverable space station, a prototype of vehicles needed to start interplanetary explorations. It was equipped with special guiding instruments and a system of rocket engines to make possible repeated maneuvers in various directions while orbiting the earth.

On April 12, 1961, Soviet scientists scored another first with the

Yuri Gagarin   *Marshal Rodion Malinovsky*

successful launching of Yuri A. Gagarin, a Major of the Soviet Air Force, into the first manned orbital flight around the earth aboard the space ship *Vostok I* (East I). Four months later, on August 6, Herman S. Titov, another Soviet Air Force Major, completed seventeen orbits in the space ship *Vostok II*. In mid-August, 1962, Major Andrian G. Nikolaev in *Vostok III*, dubbed "The Falcon," completed sixty-four orbits, while his travelling companion Colonel Pavel R. Popovich in *Vostok IV*, dubbed "The Golden Eagle," made forty-eight orbits. In mid-June, 1963, Lieutenant Colonel Valeri F. Bykovsky completed eighty-two orbits in "The Hawk," while his female travelling companion Lieutenant Valentina V. Tereshkova completed forty-eight orbits in "The Seagull". On October 12, 1964, the Soviets launched a three-man space ship, the *Voskhod* (Rising), which with Colonel Vladimir M. Komarov, scientist Konstantin P. Feoktistov, and physician Boris B. Yegorov aboard, completed sixteen orbits.

As technical achievements and as pure human adventure, these Soviet manned and unmanned flights were both breathtaking and history-making. Behind their success were such factors as: Soviet recognition at an early date of the importance of rocket development for the future; mobilization of all available forces and resources to attain that goal; the rich scientific tradition inherited from Imperial Russia; the systematic training of qualified scientists; creation of a favorable social climate for scientists, and assurance of a high position for them in society; development of science and technology with the same speed in peace time as in war; and obtaining help from abroad through both normal and abnormal channels. Regardless of how or at what cost they were attained, Soviet space spectaculars inaugurated the Space Age, underscored the very great challenge the West faced in this field, exerted enormous pressure on the United States to duplicate Soviet achievements, and intensified the rocket armaments race. Above all, the flights presented the Soviets with an excellent opportunity to emphasize, both at home and abroad, that these achievements were "a fresh triumph of Lenin's ideas," an embodiment of "the genius of the Soviet people," and a manifestation of "the might of socialism."

Excited by these space spectaculars, acute agricultural and consumer shortages notwithstanding, in October, 1961, the Twenty-second Congress of the CPSU unanimously approved the Khrushchev-sponsored party program. The new program—the party's third [1]—called for the building of the foundations of communism in the USSR to be completed by 1980, at which time the principle "From each according to his abilities, to each according to his needs" was to be in operation. Compared with its two predecessors, Khrushchev's program was more voluminous and more ambitious. It consisted of two parts: one dealing with ideology and foreign policy, the other with the building of a Communist society in the USSR. The latter goal was to be achieved in two stages: 1961–1970, when the USSR was to create a material and technical base of communism, surpass the United States in per capita production, and improve the living standards of the people; and 1971–1980, when the USSR was to reach the principle of distribution according to needs and "a gradual transition to a single form of public ownership."

The new party program envisaged for the USSR by 1980 an increase of the volume of industrial output "by not less than 500 per cent," and a rise in the productivity of labor "by 300 per cent to 350 per cent." It also hoped to achieve an annual output of three trillion kilowatt hours of electricity, 250 million tons of steel, substantial increases of aluminum and oil, great expansion of the chemical industry, large-scale integrated automation of production, modernized construction, modernized and expanded transport and communication systems, and a "rapid rise in the output of consumer goods." The bulk of this expansion was to take place east of the Urals in order to create there a new and powerful metallurgical base.

For agriculture the Twenty Year Plan set a two-fold aim: to produce an abundant supply of food and to eliminate in the main "the distinction between town and country." To attain these goals, Soviet agriculture was expected to achieve a high degree of mechanization. By 1980 its total

---

[1] The first program was adopted at the Second Congress in London in 1903. It called for the overthrow of Tsarism and the establishment of the dictatorship of the proletariat in Russia. The second program was adopted at the Eighth Party Congress in March, 1919. It called for the building of socialism in Russia.

volume of production was to increase by 250 per cent, grain output was to double, milk to triple, meat to quadruple, and the productivity of agricultural labor was to rise by 400 to 500 per cent. The Plan envisaged extensive irrigation projects, wide application of chemicals, an extensive network of research institutes and experimental stations, and a "scientific system of land cultivation and animal husbandry." State farms, and above all collective farms, were to remain the basic units of production, but their functions were to undergo many changes. They were to continue to supply the state with needed food and were in addition to provide peasants with a guaranteed monthly income, public catering, kindergartens, nurseries, boarding schools, clubs, hospitals, and the like. When that was achieved, collective farms were expected to turn into "amalgamated urban type communities with modern housing, communal utilities, services, and cultural and medical institutions." The Plan hoped that the extension of "the luxury of city living" to the countryside would make peasant private plots economically "obsolete" and unprofitable and that the peasants would "give them up of their own accord."

By 1980 the Plan expected living standards in the USSR to be "higher than in any capitalist country." The national income was to increase by about 400 per cent, per capita real income was to rise 250 per cent, wages of industrial workers were to increase by 250 per cent, while those of collective farmers were to quadruple. There was to be for everyone plenty of meat, fats, dairy products, fruits, vegetables, attractive clothing, footwear, and automobiles. By 1980 every Soviet family was to have "a well appointed apartment meeting the requirements of health and cultural living," and all transport facilities were to be free, as was to be water, gas and heating. The Plan promised a 30- to 36-hour working week (provided the productivity of labor rose as anticipated), increase of paid vacation to one month, an end to night shift work, and introduction of modern safety devices and hygienic measures at all enterprises. The Plan also promised to meet the medical needs of all the people, build hospitals, sanatoria, and rest homes, provide longer maternity leaves, free food, catering service at all public enterprises, and many labor-saving devices for the home. By 1980, according to the Plan, the state was expected to provide free nurseries, kindergartens, free hot lunches, free books and clothing, free education at all educational institutions, and increased old age and disability pensions. All of these promises, however, were conditional on a peaceful international situation, increased productivity, and increased sacrifices. Some Westerners observed that should all of this be achieved, Soviet leaders would be forced to erect a high wall to prevent the entry of envious outsiders.

To realize the economic goals of the Twenty Year Plan on time, Khrushchev introduced two significant measures in 1962. The first was

A kindergarten on a collective farm.

substantial price increases for food (31 per cent for beef, 34 per cent for mutton, 19 per cent for pork, 25 per cent for butter, and 31 per cent for sausage products) beginning June 1, 1962, in order to transfer to the steadily growing urban population some of the cost of increasing agricultural output. Khrushchev's second measure was a radical reorganization of the party and government structures. The new reorganization, approved by the CC of the CPSU at its November, 1962, meeting, put an end to the decentralization measures of 1957 and concentrated all economic planning in the USSR in the Supreme Economic Council. Directly below the new Council were three pivotal agencies: the *Gosplan*, responsible for long-range planning, the National Economic Council responsible for the current plan, and the National Building Agency in charge of all construction. The new reform reduced sharply the number of economic regions which had been set up in 1957, and approved formation within the party structure of two bureaus: one for agriculture and one for industry and construction. The aim of all of these changes was threefold: to strengthen party control over the economy, to increase agricultural and industrial production, and to eliminate waste, inefficiency, and corruption.

As the year 1963 progressed it became evident that these goals were very elusive. Contributing to this elusiveness were such factors as uneconomic prices, rapid industrial growth without checks and balances, the shortage of capital, badly and costly organized repair of equipment, sluggish response and even opposition to demands for a faster rise of labor productivity, dissipation of funds, lack of necessary equipment, uneconomic location of industrial plants, extremely high labor turnover in industrial enterprises, and above all bureaucratic chaos and uncertainty caused by these changes. On June 4, 1963, all of these factors culminated in an official announcement that the much vaunted Seven Year Plan had been scrapped. In mid-October, 1964, Khrushchev's associates sent him into political oblivion and put his ambitious program in a deep freeze.

THE INTELLECTUAL FERMENT IN THE USSR

Stalin's death, the ensuing struggle for succession, and de-Stalinization produced in the USSR an interesting intellectual ferment popularly known as "the thaw." The most pronounced ebullition occurred in literature. The agitation among writers, already present at the end of 1953, became a full-fledged movement early in 1954. The literary ferment, which centered around the journal *Novyi Mir* (New World), took a threefold course. It sought to dismantle Stalin's literary orthodoxy; it tried to escape the party's tutelage and its "constant preachment of propaganda"; and it attempted to reassert the right of writers to produce "sincerity" and "immediacy of expression." An outstanding example of the new course was Ehrenburg's novel *Ottepel* (The Thaw), which complained that it was difficult, if not impossible, for real art to flourish under Soviet conditions. Other works of the "thaw period" included *Seasons of the Year*, by Vera F. Panova; *The Fall of Pompeev*, by Nikolai E. Virta; and *The Daughter of a Public Prosecutor*, by Yurii Yanovsky. While these works voiced criticism of party and government bureaucrats corrupted by power, none departed significantly from the precepts of "socialist realism." Their publication nevertheless roused hopes, both in the USSR and abroad, that Soviet literature was at last to be freed from its shackles.

Criticism of the upper strata of Soviet society and, indirectly, of some aspects of Communist faith itself, while favored by the repressed writers, encountered stiff opposition from party hacks and scribblers. The clash between the two groups, mild at first, grew progressively bitter, and in April, 1954, led to expulsion from the Union of Soviet Writers—"the intellectual fountainhead of the USSR"—of several of its members. Later, writer and playwright Feodor I. Panferov was dismissed from the editorial board of the journal *Oktiabr* (October), and in August, 1954, poet

Alexander T. Tvardovsky, editor of *Novyi Mir,* was replaced by poet K. M. Simonov. By these dismissals the party achieved several objectives. It ostracized the most vocal critics of "socialist realism"; it denied them the right to attend the Second All-Union Congress of Soviet Writers, held in Moscow in December, 1954, to discuss literary problems created by new developments; it prevented the outbreak of open hostility at the Congress between the proponents and opponents of liberalization in literature; it "demonstrated" to the world the existence of complete harmony among Soviet writers; it reasserted that "socialist realism" was "the only creative trend in literature of socialist society"; and it reemphasized that, because of its subordination to politics, Soviet literature must continue to serve as the party's "active assistant in Communist education of the masses."

Early in 1956 the literary restlessness, dormant since December, 1954, was reactivated. The new agitation was sparked by Khrushchev's bitter denunciation of Stalin's criminal deeds at the Twenty-second Congress of the CPSU in February, 1956. The ensuing campaign against "the cult of individual" provided writers with a "legal" framework to renew their criticism of the party's tutelage in literature. Khrushchev's speech also led to the posthumous rehabilitation of many victims of Stalin's terror and to the return of those who had survived it. During the height of the assault on Stalin, an attempt was made by a group of Soviet writers associated with the almanac *Literaturnaia Moskva* (Literary Moscow), to organize a semi-autonomous organization of Moscow writers outside the party-controlled Union of Soviet Writers, with the aim of demolishing the foundations of "socialist realism." Other examples of the renewed effort included a novel by Daniel A. Granin, *A Personal Opinion,* serialized in *Novyi Mir,* which portrayed a "repentant" party member who had come to the realization that party bureaucrats represent the main obstacle to progress; and a novel by Vladimir D. Dudintsev, entitled *Not by Bread Alone.* Dudintsev's work created a real uproar among party officials because of its realistic portrayal of unscrupulous party members who use their positions to satisfy and expand their own ruthless ego and ambition, and because of its blunt assertion by a main character that "Someone who has learned to think can never be deprived of freedom." Still another example of the literary tumult in 1956 was the rise to prominence of poet Evgeni A. Evtushenko, whose depiction of the hard life of the people made him the *bête noire* of the die-hard champions of "socialist realism."

The real literary sensation of 1956 was *Dr. Zhivago,* a complex novel critical, sharply but indirectly, of the Soviet regime, by poet and novelist Boris L. Pasternak (1890–1960). The furor caused by *Dr. Zhivago* stemmed to a large extent from: (1) the stern and serious, although

Boris Pasternak

Evgeni Evtushenko

politely worded, refusal by the editors of *Novyi Mir* to publish the novel in the USSR; (2) Pasternak's granting of permission to an Italian pro-Communist publisher to produce it abroad; (3) the highly publicized official Soviet effort to dissuade the Italian publisher from bringing out the novel; and (4) the selection of Pasternak as the recipient of the 1958 Nobel Prize for literature. Although Pasternak declined the latter honor, his presentation of the negative aspects of Soviet life made him the target of savage criticism by party leaders, including Khrushchev, and by many members of the Union of Soviet Writers. Critics abroad, however, classed *Dr. Zhivago* with the important works of modern times.

Writers' criticism of the negative aspects of Soviet life alarmed party bureaucrats, with the result that there developed a partial curb on literary deviations from "socialist realism." In 1957, Khrushchev summoned the leading Soviet authors to his *dacha* (villa), bluntly told them that he would not tolerate their insubordination, and warned that if they rebelled against the party he would repress them with all force. Khrushchev made no attempt to return to Stalin's restrictions, but his ominous warning induced many recalcitrant writers to admit their "errors." To uphold the principles of absolute conformity, there was also established in 1958 a Union of Writers of the RSFSR, headed by a literary die-hard, Leonid Sobolev. The aim of the new group was to halt the spread of the disturbing new trend in Soviet literature, and whenever possible to emphasize positive rather than negative characteristics of Soviet life.

The latter goal, in fact, became the central theme of the Third Congress of the Union of Soviet Writers held in Moscow in May, 1959. In a special message to that body, the CC of the CPSU reminded the members that they must inspire people for communism, must educate them according to Communist principles, must develop in them high moral virtues, must become passionate propagandists of the Seven Year Plan, must bring cheerfulness, vigor, and energy into the heart of man, and accordingly must reject "bourgeois ideology and morals." Khrushchev, who addressed the gathering, repeated most of these same clichés.

In contrast to his ominous warning of 1957, however, he insisted on tolerance among writers, hinted of his willingness to relinquish some aspects of party control of literature and leave literary matters to the collective judgment of writers themselves to be solved in "a comradely fashion," and guaranteed that there would be no return to the intolerable phenomena associated with the "cult of individual." To implement these unusual grants of autonomy, the most far-reaching since the mid-1920's, the Presidium of the Union of Soviet Writers replaced Aleksei A. Surkov as its secretary with Constantin A. Fedin, and reinstated Tvardovsky and Panferov to their editorial posts (with *Novyi Mir* and *Oktiabr* respectively) from which they had been dismissed in 1954. These changes greatly enlivened Soviet literary and cultural life and turned the second half of the 1950's into a highly productive period in Soviet literature.

The obliteration of Stalin's name, as decreed by the Twenty-second Party Congress in October, 1961, resulted also in a partial relaxation of controls over intellectuals. The most outstanding proof of this was the publication in the November, 1962, issue of *Novyi Mir* of a novel *One Day in the Life of Ivan Denisovich*, by Alexander Solzhenitsyn. The novel has been described as a literary masterpiece and "the most startling work ever to have been published in the Soviet Union." Its chief significance, however, is that it is a revolutionary document. It is a tale of forced labor camps under Stalin, a stark account of the systematic attempt to degrade and brutalize a whole nation in the name of "socialism," and an indictment of Soviet society. Why Soviet officials authorized the publication of this major assault on tyranny and totalitarianism remains a mystery. The entire edition of *Novyi Mir* (95,000 copies) sold out immediately, and the issue has become a collector's item.[1]

The appearance of Solzhenitsyn's shattering work increased the demands by Soviet intellectuals for additional relaxation and forced party leaders to clarify the party's position on "ideological matters." The clarification took place at a series of conferences between party leaders and intellectuals during the first half of 1963. The most important of these conferences was the March, 1963, meeting between party spokes-

---

[1] Solzhenitsyn's novel was mentioned for a Lenin Prize, highest award a Soviet artist or scientist achieves in the USSR, but in April, 1964, *Pravda* stated definitely that the novel was not art.

men and writers and artists, and the June, 1963, session of the CC. The principal speaker on both occasions was Khrushchev, who reminded Soviet writers, artists, composers, cinematographers, and theatrical "workers," that the task of Soviet literature and art was "to produce in vivid artistic imagery the great and heroic epoch of Communist construction [and] to depict truthfully the assertion and victory of new Communist relations in our life." He cautioned the intellectuals not to spend their energies on "one-sided" presentations of such aspects of Soviet reality as "lawlessness, arbitrary reprisals and abuse of power" during "the years of the personality cult," and reprimanded Ehrenburg for presenting in his memoirs, *People, Years, Life,* "everything in gloomy colors"; film producer Sergei Gerasimov for his "misrepresentation of Soviet youth"; Evtushenko for his defense of abstractionism; and Shostakovich for his admiration of "music without melody." He warned the intellectuals, whom he termed "the smiths of human psychology," that unless they presented positive aspects of the Soviet life that the workers and peasants had achieved they could not expect the party's support. Khrushchev did not remain in power long enough to implement this advice to Soviet intellectuals. On October 15, 1964, without any advance indication, he was unceremoniously removed from power.

What has been said of Soviet literature under Khrushchev is equally true of Soviet theater and the cinema, i.e., they too rebelled against standardization of style. In theater the first sign of deviation occurred in 1954 with the staging of Leonid Zorin's *Gosti* (The Guests), a satire critical of party bureaucracy and careerism, which was condemned by the Ministry of Culture after only two Moscow performances. Khrushchev's de-Stalinization speech in February, 1956, though not concerned directly with the theater, brought new life to it, as de-Stalinization meant rehabilitation of many playwrights, decline of the popularity of the prerevolutionary Russian plays, in official vogue from 1947 to 1953, and appearance in the repertoire of foreign plays and of Soviet comedies and dramas. Among foreign plays, the most popular were *My Family* by Eduardo de Filippo, *Dangerous Corner* by John B. Priestley, and *Dial M for Murder* by Agatha Christie and Fredrick Knott. The most popular Soviet plays from 1956 to 1960 were *Alone* by Sergei Aleshin, *Eternally Alive* by Victor Rozov, and *The Factory Girl* by Volodin. The popularity of Soviet plays stemmed from their treatment of such "contemporary themes" as marriage, divorce, unrequited love, and lonely women whose husbands had sought and found new passions. Because these themes were "alien to socialist realism," they were criticized by many die-hard party scribblers.

Soviet cinema during Khrushchev's rule experienced an even greater rejuvenation than the legitimate theater. In fact, according to some observers, the period after 1954 was "the second greatest phase in the history of Russian cinema." This glowing praise stems largely from the release by Soviet producers of such films as *Three Men on a Raft* (1954); *Othello* (1955); *The Forty-First* (1956); *Don Quixote* (1957); *The Cranes Are Flying* (1957), the winner of the Grand Prix de Cannes; *A Man Is Born* (1957); *The House I Live In* (1957); *A Man's Destiny* (1959); and *Ballad of A Soldier* (1960). All of these films were worthy of the name of art, were free from schematism, were "no longer dedicated to the party, or its offshoots, but to humanity," and treated such problems as human conflict, the fate of mankind, the chaos of war, dissolution, demoralization, corruption, adultery, and other class-free elements of human life.

Khrushchev's rule also significantly affected Soviet music. The impact, however, was a negative one. A few days after Stalin's death came the death of composer and conductor Sergei S. Prokofiev (1891–1953), whose best known works include the opera *War and Peace*, the ballets *Romeo and Juliet* and *The Stone Flower*, the symphonic tale *Peter and the Wolf*, the ballet suite *The Scythian Suite*, and numerous concertos, scores for motion pictures, and other compositions. Because of Prokofiev's universal fame, Stalin never officially disgraced him. He reprimanded him, however, on several occasions for "formalism" and suppressed some of his works in the USSR. Composer Dmitri D. Shostakovich was subjected to similar harassment for his failure to comply with Stalin's musical tastes, and it was not until 1954 that his heirs reversed Stalin's policy and, in recognition of the composer's achievement, awarded Shostakovich the title of "People's Artist." But shortly after he received that award Shostakovich was assailed by the party press for deviations in his *Tenth Symphony*. The composer apologized, acknowledged the "shortcomings" in his remarkable work, and after that remained in relative silence. Another gifted composer of symphonies and ballet scores, Aram I. Khachaturian, apparently adopted the same attitude following the party's rejection of his plea in November, 1953, that it abandon the tutelage over music and allow "the composer and the librettist [to] work exactingly on their own responsibility," producing works that would be "beautiful in form" and "provocative and bold in approach."

It is essential to remember that the intellectual ferment under Khrushchev also affected many non-Russian peoples of the USSR. The ebullition among the intellectuals of Soviet minorities began in 1956, i.e., after Khrushchev's dramatic exposure of Stalin's crimes. Many writers were cleared of suspicion, others were rehabilitated posthumously, and the few of them who had survived Stalin's terror were allowed to return from exile. To pacify the growing excitement, Stalin's heirs permitted non-Russian minorities to receive foreign cultural delegations, allowed many selected groups to travel abroad to establish cultural and scientific contacts with "capitalist countries," and granted greater freedom to use native languages in the publication of literary works. In view of Stalin's bitter repression of minorities, these changes were more than a "thaw"; they represented a real spring.

To calm the intellectual storm at home and at the same time to sell Soviet achievement abroad, Stalin's heirs also launched a program of "cultural competition" with the non-Communist world. Under the program, selected groups of Soviet performers were allowed to thrill foreign audiences, while foreign entertainers were permitted to thrill Soviet audiences. The most outstanding example of the "cultural competition" in 1956 was the tour of the United States and Western Europe by violinist David F. Oistrakh; the performance of Boston and London Philharmonic Orchestras in Leningrad and Moscow in September and October, 1956; and the triumphal visit to London of the Bolshoi Ballet in October, 1956. Because of the apparent success of these exchanges, Soviet leaders decided to expand the program of cultural competition, and since 1957 the Ministry of Culture has dispatched thousands of Soviet performers to "capitalist countries" of South East Asia, the Near East, Western Europe and the Western Hemisphere, and has received thousands of foreign artists from "capitalist countries." Since the mid-1950's Soviet leaders have also sent educators, scientists, scholars, and other groups to various international conferences, and on many occasions have hosted international scientific and scholarly gatherings.

Last but not least, Khrushchev's rule witnessed a great change in the official attitude toward sports. Sports, especially soccer football, ice skating, and gymnastics, have always been popular in the USSR. The excellence of Soviet athletes, however, had been questioned because during Stalin's regime they were not allowed to compete with athletes from the "capitalist countries." Limited contacts with athletes from satellite countries were "staged" in the Soviet favor. Stalin's heirs reversed the isolation policy in sports. In 1956 Soviet athletes participated in great numbers in the Olympic Games in Melbourne, Australia, where they won thirty-seven gold, twenty-nine silver, and thirty-two bronze medals. In April, 1959, in an effort to coordinate sports activities and to increase interest in sports, the Union of Sport Societies and Organizations was organized. Increased interest in sports led to impressive results at the 1960 Olympic Games, where Soviet athletes won fifty gold, thirty-four silver, and forty bronze medals, and where they set many Olympic records. Competition with foreign athletes led to the development of such events as swimming, wrestling, boxing, tennis, skiing, rowing, basketball, and various track and field events. In all of these, Soviet athletes, who were basically professionals, revealed promise and excellence. Party leaders used the achievements of their athletes as weapons in the ideo-

Olga Korbut, member of the Soviet Olympic Team, 1972 and 1976.

logical struggle with the West, and elevated their performers to an exalted position in Soviet society similar to that of arists.

As depicted in the preceding pages, the intellectual ferment in the USSR under Khrushchev produced far-reaching changes in Soviet society. On the whole, these changes, despite occasional alarming setbacks, were beneficial to literature, the performing arts, and sports. Judged by a normal yardstick of measurement, these changes were not spectacular. Viewed, however, from the perspective of Soviet reality, they were revolutionary.

FERMENT IN EASTERN EUROPE

Stalin's death and the ensuing struggle for succession led to many vital developments not only in the USSR but in the East European satellites as well. Of the many developments in the satellite countries, the most prominent were the East Berlin uprising of June, 1953; the Polish upheaval of June–October, 1956; the Hungarian revolution of October, 1956; and the Soviet-Yugoslav rapprochement between 1953 and 1956. None of these events led to disintegration of the Stalinist system, but they shook the system to its foundations and forced Stalin's heirs to evolve a more flexible arrangement of control.

The first concussion struck in East Germany, the satellite whose regime was probably the most Soviet-dependent. As early as April, 1953, East German leaders pleaded with Moscow for urgent assistance, and requested that the USSR reconsider its capital development policy in East Germany. Early in June, 1953, East German authorities openly admitted "aberrations in the past," reduced delivery quotas and taxes for the farmers, made available state loans to private business, and promised improvement in living standards for everyone. Events soon revealed that these concessions were insufficient. On June 16, 1953, encouraged by the lack of self-assurance on the part of the authorities, construction workers in East Berlin protested against a 10 per cent increase in compulsory work quotas, and demanded "butter, not a people's army." Within hours the nonviolent protest spread to other parts of Berlin as well as to other parts of East Germany. The demonstrators were in an ugly mood, shouted down the Communist leaders who attempted to pacify them, and defied the efforts of the East German security forces called to disperse them. Unable to restore order with its own efforts, the East German regime asked Soviet authorities for protection and help. Both were granted immediately. The Soviet army intervened, quelled the uprising, and restored the East German regime to power. By June 18, the unrest in East Berlin was over, but the message it carried was not entirely lost.

The East Berlin uprising was significant for two reasons. First, it revealed the unpopularity of the East German regime with the people, and its utter dependence on Soviet military support for its existence. Second, it demonstrated an urgent need for further concessions not only in East Germany, but throughout the Soviet Empire. In East Germany the immediate concessions included dismissal of high officials who had wavered in the face of the crisis; formal acceptance of the principle of "collective leadership" of Ulbricht and Grotewohl; public acknowledgment by East German officials of error in formulating past policies; reduction of investment in heavy industry; reduction of income taxes and prices; granting of partial amnesty to minor offenders; return to East German control of enterprises managed by the USSR; and termination of reparations to the USSR. None of these concessions weakened Communist control. They did, however, promise an improvement in standards of living, and thus relieved some of the political tensions in the country.

Many East Germans did not wait for this improvement to materialize. During 1953, some 305,737 sought asylum in West Germany. By October 1, 1955, that figure rose to 2,664,000, and by the end of the 1950's it reached 4,000,000. Most of those who fled were young and skilled. No country can afford to lose the services of the best element of its population, and least of all a country whose entire life is almost totally regimented. The mass exodus of population also became bad propaganda for communism, which pictures itself as "the way of life of tomorrow." Because the bulk of the escapees fled to West Germany via Berlin, by the end of the 1950's Berlin had become the most explosive spot in international relations.

The East Berlin uprising left a deep imprint on Soviet leaders. Between July 4, and October 29, 1953, they forced the "new course" of concessions on Hungary, Romania, Bulgaria, Czechoslovakia, and Poland, in that order. Each satellite regime adopted the principle of "collective leadership," and promised (alongside continued industrialization) to improve the standard of living; to abandon the policy of economic autarky; to increase wages and to decrease prices; to give increased attention to agriculture; to slow the tempo of collectivization; to encourage private initiative in small production and trade; to curb the activity of the police; and to release those who had been imprisoned unjustly. Viewed by the normal yardstick of measurement these concessions were minor. Measured, however, by the standards of Eastern Europe these promises heralded a new era, and any attempt to alter this "liberalizing" development, as events in 1956 in Hungary and Poland demonstrated, was bound to meet with stiff resistance.

The "new course" in Eastern Europe was short-lived, however. It came to an end early in 1955, or shortly after Khrushchev forced Malenkov's resignation and advanced "the Khrushchev formula" for future Communist development and relations. That formula, designated by some as neo-Stalinism, called for an increased development of heavy industry, closer economic and military integration of the USSR and its satellites, greater emphasis on common ideological unity and uniformity, and a continued common approach in the realm of foreign policy.

A major manifestation of Khrushchev's formula was the Warsaw Pact, entitled "On Friendship, Cooperation and Mutual Aid." It was signed on May 14, 1955, by Albania, Bulgaria, Czechoslovakia, East Germany, Hungary, Romania, Poland, and the USSR. Communist China had an observer in Warsaw who announced his government's full support of the efforts of the Warsaw Pact members. Ostensibly a belated answer to the North Atlantic Treaty Organization, the Warsaw Pact, concluded for the duration of twenty years, was a political and military agreement. The members pledged to settle international disputes by peaceful means; to cooperate in all international actions aimed at insuring peace and security; to hold mutual consultations in event of a threat of war; to afford immediate assistance in case of armed aggression against one or several members of the Pact; to establish a joint command of their armed forces (Marshal Konev was designated first Supreme Commandant); to establish a political consultative committee; not to enter into any coalitions or agreements contrary to the terms of the treaty;

to strengthen economic and cultural ties among themselves without interfering in each other's internal affairs; and to invite other states to join the Pact on condition they adhere to the terms and principles of the treaty. On the surface, the Pact offered East European countries a greater independence of action than they had under Stalin. In reality, however, it formalized Moscow's control over them and tied their destinies more closely to that of the USSR.

The Soviets reinforced military and political ties with their East European satellites through increased economic integration. One of the major forms of this integration was specialization of industrial production. Under this scheme, devised late in 1954, East Germany was to specialize in the production of electrical equipment and precision instruments; Poland in ship building, mining equipment, and rolling stock; Czechoslovakia in engines, automobiles, and machine building; Hungary in diesel engines, buses, and motor trains; and Romania in oil pipes and drilling equipment. The role of the USSR was that of principal supplier of iron ore, manganese, cotton, food, and other raw materials, as well as the active source of credit and technical know-how. Plans were also worked out for the integration of foreign trade, investment, transportation, labor allocation, financial and clearing systems, and of many other fields. These arrangements made the development of each satellite economy dependent on the development of the economy of other satellites, and above all on that of the USSR. These arrangements, too, paved the way in 1956 for synchronization of East European Five Year Plans with the Sixth Five Year Plan of the USSR. As a climax to this grand achievement of economic integration, in Moscow in March, 1956, members of the Warsaw Pact set up a Joint Nuclear Research Institute, headed by a professor of the Soviet Academy of Sciences. Shortly thereafter the stress and strain of the neo-Stalinist arrangements, which appeared to end the hope for further reforms, led to violent explosions in Poland and in Hungary.

The upheaval in Poland took two distinct, but inseparable forms: a mass strike in Poznań in June, 1956; and a "revolution" in October, 1956. The immediate cause of the Poznań strike was the official ignoring of a demand by workers of the ZISPO enterprises, producers of railroad cars, for improved working conditions. This bold demand, however, was preceded by a whole series of developments, of which the following were the most significant: (1) a gradual weakening between 1953 and 1956 of the power of the secret police; (2) growing criticism within the party of the methods used by the party leadership; (3) creation in the spring of 1955 of various party discussion clubs to debate issues, develop ideas, and crystallize attitudes; (4) open criticism of Stalin after Khrushchev's de-Stalinization speech, and question of the wisdom of

Polish blind imitation of the USSR; (5) an amnesty in April, 1956, which freed some 30,000 persons; (6) public ridicule of the Polish parliament for voting unanimously on all issues; (7) public criticism by the Congress of Polish Economists early in June, 1956, of the primacy of heavy industry, and a demand that the government follow reform and not the neo-Stalinist line; and (8) official admission that the standard of living had declined between 1955 and 1956.

Encouraged by these signs of change, on June 22, 1956, a freely elected delegation of ZISPO workers left for Warsaw to demand satisfaction of their grievances. A few days later a rumor spread that the delegation had been arrested. This rumor instigated a walkout of the ZISPO workers, who were joined by others, and in a few hours the city of Poznań was turned into a seething antigovernment camp. The strikers carried placards with such slogans as: "We Want Freedom!" "We Demand Lower Prices and Higher Wages!" "Down with Phony Communism!" "Down with Dictatorship!" and "Down with the Soviet Occupation!" The strikers broke into police stations and prisons and freed many persons. Order was restored only after Polish Regular Army units arrived on the scene. According to official estimates, the Poznań strike was responsible for 38 dead and 270 wounded. Because Poznań was at the time host to an international trade fair, news of the strike leaked out immediately and became a worldwide sensation. Moscow took note of the anti-Soviet slogans, labelled the development in Poznań "foreign imperialist inspired," and warned that it would not tolerate a break in Soviet-Polish unity. At the same time, however, it offered to provide Poland with 25,000,000 dollars' worth of consumer goods to alleviate the most acute shortages.

The Poznań strike created a deep rift within the Polish Communist leadership. Some members wanted to pursue "the essentials of Stalinism, but without Stalinist methods." Others stressed the need for continued changes, for liberalism of the system, and for more personal freedom. The question was resolved on October 9, 1956, with the resignation of Hilary Minc, architect of the Stalinist economy in Poland, and the re-entry of Wladyslaw Gomulka, whom Stalin had purged in 1949. Because of mounting criticism of Soviet methods in Poland, the Kremlin viewed this change with grave concern and invited the Poles to Moscow for consultation. When the Poles declined, Khrushchev, Kaganovich, Mikoyan and Molotov arrived uninvited in Warsaw on October 19, and alerted Soviet troops for possible action. This move increased the already tense atmosphere of Polish-Soviet negotiations, the purpose of which was to convince the Soviet delegates that the changes in personnel were designed to improve Soviet-Polish relations, and that the contemplated reform aimed at strengthening the building of socialism in Poland. The negotiations were very stormy, but the Poles succeeded in convincing the Soviets that their apprehensions were unfounded. Apparently satisfied, the Soviet delegates left Warsaw on October 20, ordered the return of Soviet troops to their bases, and left Poland to march along "the Polish road to socialism." On November 18, 1956, Gomulka and his associates went to Moscow to work out a new agreement to regularize Soviet-Polish relations on the basis of "mutual respect, non-interference, and sovereignty." The Soviet government cancelled the Polish debt to the USSR in the amount of 2.4 billion rubles, and agreed to recall Marshal Rokossovsky from Poland. On their part, the Poles promised to support undeviatingly the foreign policy of the USSR and agreed to continue to allow the stationing of Soviet troops in Poland, retaining for them-selves the right, however, to control their disposition and movements.

The partial success of this relatively mild revolution in Poland ignited a violent revolt in Hungary—a satellite whose regime was renowned for its brutality. Like its Polish counterpart, the upheaval in Hungary was preceded by a whole series of developments, of which the following were the most significant: (1) the bitter feud between Imre Nagy, the proponent of the "new course," and Rakosi, who considered it an anti-party, un-Marxist and un-Leninist development; (2) the triumph of Rakosi early in 1955, following Malenkov's downfall; (3) the resumption by Rakosi of Stalinist economic policies, collectivization, purges, and reign of terror; (4) disapproval of Rakosi's neo-Stalinist policies by many Hungarian Communists who felt that his actions were an impediment not only to communism in Hungary but to proper relations with the USSR; (5) Khrushchev's de-Stalinization speech and the posthumous "rehabilitation" of many Hungarian victims of the Stalinist reign of terror; (6) organization early in 1956 of the Petofi Clubs to discuss issues, the growing ferment among the youth and intellectuals, and an open call by some party members for "an end to this present regime of gendarmes and bureaucrats"; (7) Soviet removal of Rakosi on July 18, 1956, or shortly after he publicly announced his decision to liquidate "all troublemakers"; (8) public pledge by the new party leader, Erno Gero, for improvement, his acknowledgment of inadequacies and promise to "rehabilitate" all those who had been unjustly treated; (9) mounting pressures for further changes, and Moscow's decision to reinstate Nagy to power early in October, 1956; and (10) partial success of the Polish revolution, which the Hungarians interpreted as signaling the end to Stalinism and to Stalinists.

The Hungarian upheaval started on October 23, 1956, as a peaceful demonstration on behalf of a less brutal regime for Hungary. It as-sumed a warlike character after the security forces provoked the demon-strators into violence. On October 24, Soviet tanks and armored cars

Budapest, 1956. The Russian Army occupies revolt-torn Hungary. These Russian soldiers were objecting to this picture's being taken.

joined the battle and restored order. Meanwhile Mikoyan and Suslov arrived from Moscow, removed Gero from party leadership, authorized Nagy and Janos Kadar to initiate a series of reforms, and promised to withdraw Soviet forces in the near future. On October 30, in a major policy declaration, the Soviet government further promised to re-examine its economic relations with all the satellites, to recall economic and military advisers, and to build its future relations "on the principle of full equality, respect for territorial integrity, state independence and sovereignty, and noninterference in the domestic affairs of one another." Emboldened by concessions and determined to prevent the return of a Rakosi-type dictatorship, the Hungarians immediately produced a coalition government, allowed freedom of the press, disbanded the security police, appealed to the United Nations to pressure Soviet forces out of Hungary, repudiated their association in the Warsaw Pact, and officially declared neutrality for Hungary.

Hungary's defection from the Moscow-led "socialist camp" was a severe blow to Stalin's heirs. On November 2, the Soviets decided to intervene with force to prevent Hungary from assuming a neutral development. The Soviet decision was greatly facilitated by the absorption of the American public in the Presidential election, by the Anglo-French-Israeli attack on Egypt, and by the partial disunity among the Hungarians. The intervention was swift and well-planned. On November 3, the Soviets set up a new government for Hungary under Kadar, who had broken with Nagy, to rival the Nagy government. They responded immediately to Kadar's "request" for Soviet military aid to "smash the sinister forces of reaction" and to "restore order and calm" throughout Hungary, and ordered tanks and armored cars against Budapest. For several days the Hungarians fought an unequal duel, but fought it amazingly well, and earned the sympathy and applause of the whole world. Soviet restoration of order destroyed some 4,000 buildings, killed about 2,900 Hungarians, and wounded some 13,000. The number of Soviet casualties is unknown. The restoration of order was accompanied by mass arrests, deportations to the Soviet Union, and the flight of some 200,000 Hungarians to the West. Nagy and his officials sought political asylum in the Yugoslav Embassy. On November 22, they left the embassy on a safe conduct pass given by the Kadar government, but were arrested by Soviet authorities, "tried," found guilty, and executed. Soviet methods of keeping the unwilling satellite within its system shocked world public opinion and jolted the system to its foundations.

The course of events in both Hungary and Poland was greatly influenced by the decision of Stalin's heirs to reach an understanding with Tito of Yugoslavia. What really prompted them to stage this action is not exactly clear. No one denies, however, that it was a major Soviet *volte face*, as well as a major step in the de-Stalinization process. The rapprochement with Tito was a carefully calculated undertaking, because the Soviets were uncertain of Tito's reaction and were reluctant to acknowledge their own mistake or to approve the idea of "national communism" which Titoism represented. Following his challenge of Soviet imperial unity in 1948, the Soviets had equated Tito's regime with the most despised "capitalist imperialists" and considered treasonous any sign of laxness towards him. Until Stalin's death, in the Soviet vocabulary Tito was a "lackey of the capitalists," a "bloody maniac," a "traitor," and a "fascist gangster." Meanwhile, with American economic and military aid, Tito strengthened his position, established contact with many leaders of the Third World, and emerged as a forceful spokesman of the "neutral bloc."

The Soviet rapprochement with Tito, like de-Stalinization, came piecemeal, and was doled out in tolerable, properly spaced, and gradually habituating doses. A few weeks after Stalin's death, the Soviets dropped most of the anti-Tito slogans; proposed early in June, 1953, the resumption of diplomatic relations; ordered the easing of satellite pressure against Yugoslavia's frontiers; made concessions in December, 1953, to Yugoslavia on the matter of navigation on the Danube; agreed to resume railroad traffic; and set free Yugoslav prisoners in the Soviet bloc. Early in 1954, the Soviet press broke a precedent by quoting lengthy passages from a Tito speech opposing the European Defense Community. In September, 1954, the USSR and Yugoslavia signed a barter agreement ending the Cominform blockade of Yugoslavia. This action was followed by increased cultural contacts, by warm recollection in Moscow of the tenth anniversary of the liberation of Belgrade, by Soviet admission to the Yugoslavs in private that "in 1948 Yugoslavia was unjustly treated and condemned," and by Soviet pleas to "let bygones be bygones."

Stalin's heirs were divided over the issue of excessive fraternization with Tito. Some anti-Titoists, led by Molotov, opposed concessions, fearing that they would lead to the disintegration of Soviet influence in Eastern Europe. Khrushchev, Mikoyan, Bulganin and Kaganovich favored concessions, hoping that these would bring the defector back and thus contribute to the strengthening of communism. The proponents of the rapprochement idea won, and on May 26, 1955, a Soviet delegation headed by Khrushchev arrived in Belgrade. In his airport speech, Khrushchev blamed the break in Soviet-Yugoslav relations on Beria and other dead police officials, and pleaded for resumption of friendly relations "on the basis of the teachings of Marxism-Leninism." Tito remained silent to these overtures, although in subsequent discussions he expressed willingness to cooperate but not to follow. In return, he obtained from Khrushchev a promise to dissolve the Cominform (the announcement was made on April 17, 1956), and an agreement that there exist "national roads to communism."

Following the Belgrade talks, Soviet-Yugoslav relations improved further. On September 5, 1955, the two countries signed a new trade agreement; in January, 1956, the USSR agreed to build several industrial projects in Yugoslavia; and on February 2, 1956, the USSR granted a loan of 84 million dollars (54 million in goods and 30 million in gold). In his de-Stalinization speech, Khrushchev blamed Stalin for the break with Tito, and early in June, 1956, Tito repaid Khrushchev's visit. His reception in Moscow was friendly, but his demands unacceptable. In return for his support of Soviet foreign policy, Tito insisted that the Soviets remove all anti-Titoists in the satellites, give him a greater voice in Balkan affairs, and acknowledge national communism and independence of the satellites. Khrushchev politely rejected these demands, and unrest in Poland shortly after Tito's visit to Moscow put the first chill to the new Soviet-Yugoslav friendship.

Moscow, November 7, 1959. Garrison troops parade in celebration of the forty-second anniversary of the socialist revolution.

Early in September, 1956, Khrushchev, until now Tito's chief "appeaser," warned satellite leaders against Tito's independence and informed them that the Yugoslav League of Communists was not a pure Marxist-Leninist organization. Later that month, however, he spent a week in Yugoslavia, and early in October invited Tito to Crimea, trying to persuade him to oppose national Communist movements. His efforts were futile, as were Tito's efforts to gain from Khrushchev a promise for increased liberalization of East European regimes. The October, 1956, revolutions in Poland and Hungary proved both men right: Khrushchev, that any liberalization would lead to revolt and weakening of Soviet control; and Tito, that failure to liberalize would result in revolt. Following the removal of Molotov and Malenkov from power in June, 1957, Tito sought to establish closer understanding with Khrushchev, but his unwillingness to submit to Soviet leadership brought to an end this phase of the Soviet-Yugoslav honeymoon.

SOVIET FOREIGN POLICY UNDER KHRUSHCHEV

Khrushchev inherited from Stalin not only a bundle of domestic ills, but a host of challenging problems of foreign policy as well. In the Far East the most pressing issue was the Korean conflict. Like many issues of the Cold War, that conflict was an unresolved dilemma left over from World War II. Under the terms of the Potsdam Declaration, Korea (an integral part of Japan since 1910) was to emerge as a "free and independent" state. At the time of the Japanese surrender, however, Korea was divided into two parts along the 38th parallel—the northern under control of Soviet forces, and the southern under control of American forces. Soviet-American inability to find a solution for Korea brought the Korean issue before the United Nations. In November, 1947, the United Nations General Assembly approved a resolution calling for free election of an all-Korean government, and set up a Temporary Commission to supervise such an election. Because the Soviets would not allow it to enter North Korea, the Commission performed its task only in South Korea, where a republic was set up with Syngman Rhee as President. In October, 1948, the Soviets announced formation of a government of their own in North Korea.

On June 25, 1950, encouraged by signs of discontent with the Rhee regime, the almost total unpreparedness of South Korean military forces, and an official American declaration that South Korea was outside the United States' defense perimeter, North Korean forces, trained and equipped by the Soviets, attacked South Korea under the absurd pretext that South Korea had attacked first. Well equipped, and having the advantage of surprise, the North Koreans advanced rapidly southwards. Alarmed by this aggression, the United States called an emergency session of the United Nations Security Council, which the USSR decided to boycott. The Security Council appealed to the North Koreans to halt their aggression immediately and withdraw behind the 38th parallel, and asked all United Nations members to "furnish such assistance to the Republic of Korea as may be necessary to repel the armed attack and restore the international peace and security in the area." Because the North Koreans failed to heed the United Nations' request, President Truman committed American land, air, and naval units against the North Korean invasion, and as other United Nations members followed suit, the Korean conflict assumed global significance.

For the first three months of the struggle, the North Koreans pressed the United Nations forces very hard and came perilously close to victory. Fortunes turned in September, 1950, when United Nations forces under General Douglas MacArthur launched a seaborne invasion near Seoul and counter-attacked at Pusan. This action panicked the North Koreans, who either retreated or surrendered in great numbers. By October, all of South Korea was cleared of the invader. With the implicit sanction of the General Assembly, United Nations forces advanced across the 38th parallel to the Yalu River in an effort to unify all of Korea. Many scholars have questioned the wisdom of this decision because it gave Communist China a pretext for entering the Korean conflict with "volunteers," thereby adding new dimensions to the struggle. United Nations forces were overwhelmed by Chinese manpower and were forced to retreat to the south of the 38th parallel. After much bitter fighting, a stalemate developed roughly along the 38th parallel. Convinced that victory was impossible, as well as alarmed by the general Western rearmament effort, the Soviets pressured the North Koreans and the Chinese to enter into truce negotiations. These negotiations began at Panmunjom in July, 1951, and dragged on until July, 1953. The delay was caused by Communist charges that the United States had used "bacteriological warfare" in Korea, and by unprecedented anti-American propaganda, which in its viciousness outdid all Nazi efforts. Negotiations were also delayed by the problem of prisoners of war, thousands of whom decided to resist all efforts of repatriation to North Korea or China. An agreement was finally reached, but to the present day an uneasy truce prevails in Korea.

The Korean conflict was closely tied with the Sino-Soviet relationship. In the previous chapter it was pointed out that Communist victory in China resulted from Soviet direct and indirect aid, from dramatic disintegration of Chiang's authority, and from all-out efforts of Mao's forces. In the long run the Communist victory in China was of great importance in the balance of international forces. Immediately, however, it was a hollow triumph. After some twenty-five years of civil war, accompanied by Japanese occupation, China was a barren land. Its economy was devastated, its communications disrupted, its administration disorganized, its millions hungry and technically backward. To make these conditions even more deplorable, before they allowed Mao's forces to take over Manchuria, the Soviets stripped that region of its modern industry valued at an estimated 858 million dollars, set up various joint Sino-Soviet companies, kept Chinese influence out of North Korea and Outer Mongolia, retained the bases of Port Arthur and Dairen, and in innumerable ways made it clear that they considered Communist China another satellite to be exploited for Soviet interests.

Because they regarded their victory as primarily their own accomplishment, the Chinese did not appreciate Soviet mistreatment of their country. Early in 1950, after some two months of negotiations, Mao succeeded in working out a more satisfactory arrangement with the USSR. By a treaty signed on February 14, 1950, both countries pledged to take joint action against renewed aggression by Japan "or any other state which should unite with Japan directly or indirectly," and promised "in the spirit of friendship and cooperation and in conformity with the principles of equality, mutual interests, and also mutual respect for the state sovereignty and territorial integrity and noninterference in internal affairs," to develop and consolidate economic and cultural ties, "to render each other every possible economic assistance, and to carry out the necessary economic cooperation." In accordance with these high sounding principles, the USSR agreed to transfer gratis to China by the end of 1952 "all its rights in the joint administration of the Chinese Changchun Railway, with all the property belonging to the railway"; to withdraw Soviet forces from the naval base of Port Arthur not later than the end of 1952; to transfer the administration of Dalny to Chinese control; and to grant China 300 million dollars in credits, at 1 per cent annual interest, to pay for Soviet deliveries of industrial equipment. Although the Korean conflict postponed the execution of these commitments, viewed in retrospect the Sino-Soviet treaty of February 14, 1950, was the first major retreat of Soviet influence in the Far East.

Following the signing of that treaty, relations between the two Communist colossi, on the surface at least, appeared satisfactory, as both regimes shared a common ideology as well as hatred for the United States. The USSR, for example, spearheaded the campaign for China's admission to the United Nations, provided some arms and materiel for Chinese "volunteers" fighting in Korea, supported the Chinese in their "bacteriological warfare" charges against the United States, sent thousands of technicians to assist Chinese reconstruction, and admitted thousands of Chinese to Soviet schools and factories for technical training. Underneath the façade of cooperation, however, the Moscow-Peking axis experienced considerable difficulty. The difficulty stemmed from resentment by the proud men of Peking of their secondary status in the Communist movement, Soviet exclusion of Chinese influence in Korea and Mongolia, and the fact that Soviet aid was a pittance compared with Peking's need.

Sino-Soviet relations, though strained, appeared normal as long as Stalin was alive. His death in March, 1953, however, brought changes. The first concrete sign of change came in October, 1954, when Khrushchev, Mikoyan, and Bulganin journeyed to Peking to negotiate a new series of political and economic agreements. What exactly transpired during these negotiations is not known, but the Soviets agreed: (1) to evacuate by May 31, 1955, all of their military units from Port Arthur, and to transfer all the naval base's installations to the Chinese without compensation; (2) to transfer entirely to the Chinese, by January 1, 1955, the Soviet share of four mixed Sino-Soviet companies, which had been set up earlier in Sinkiang and in Dairen; (3) to acknowledge Chinese hegemony in Manchuria; and (4) to assist on a much greater scale than hitherto the Chinese industrialization efforts. The Chinese

China, 1959. Khrushchev, Mao Tse-tung, and Liu Shao-chi.

also extracted from the Soviet visitors a pledge that henceforth Peking's voice would receive more consideration in matters of international Communist strategy in general, and in Asian affairs in particular.

After 1955, signs of existing tensions between Moscow and Peking over the issue of ultimate leadership of the Communist world became more numerous. To weaken Soviet overlordship of the Communist bloc, the Chinese adopted a more liberal policy in 1956, encouraged the Poles to resist Soviet pressures, called upon the Soviet Union to refrain from interfering in the affairs of other Communist countries, criticized Stalin's "tendency toward great-power chauvinism" and his lack of "the spirit of equality," and, following the upheaval in Poland and Hungary in 1956, they tried to mediate between Moscow and its East European satellites. But while they competed with Moscow for leadership in the Communist world, the Chinese emphasized that they acknowledged Moscow as "the center of the international Communist movement," sided with the Kremlin against the West, and constantly sought increased economic aid from the USSR. The Soviets gave the aid (April, 1956, and February, 1959) but gave it reluctantly and in small amounts, aware apparently that any improvement of the military and economic position of China would *ipso facto* endanger the position of the USSR in the Far East.

Underneath the facade of cooperation the two Communist powers experienced growing tensions. The exact nature of this strain is difficult to ascertain because the available information is still inconclusive. The published evidence indicates that while in complete agreement on the final strategic aim—spreading communism throughout the world—the two Communist colossi were unable to agree on whether the present epoch was one of imperialism or revolution; whether world wars were inevitable or avoidable; whether transition from capitalism to socialism must be peaceful or violent; whether peaceful coexistence with the non-Communist world was possible or desirable; whether "revisionism" or "dogmatism" formed the main danger to international communism; and whether bloc leadership should be centered in Moscow under control of *white* men, or in Peking under control of *nonwhites.*

Until June, 1960, the bulk of the Sino-Soviet disagreement was in the main impersonal; that is, on the Soviet side it was directed against unnamed "dogmatists," and on the Chinese side against unnamed "revisionists." This polite form of dispute ended abruptly late in June, 1960, at a conference of Communist leaders in Bucharest. Before the assembled, but selected, delegates, Khrushchev levelled bitter criticism of Chinese policies and attitudes. He accused Mao of Stalinist behavior, called him an "ultra-leftist, an ultra-dogmatist, and a left revisionist," upbraided him for his selfishness, reproached him for his ignorance of modern warfare, and indicted him for his subscription to and mechanical repetition of Leninist theories that were detached from realities of the modern world. The Chinese hit back by accusing Khrushchev of smear tactics, of underhanded dealings aimed at undermining Chinese prestige, and of underestimating the true nature of imperialism. Bitter feelings notwithstanding, for the sake of unity both sides agreed on a joint communiqué and on a full-scale debate of their charges at a meeting of all Communist parties to be held in Moscow in November, 1960.

Between June and November, 1960, Sino-Soviet relations deteriorated further. In part the deterioration resulted from the Soviet decision in August, 1960, to recall many technicians from China and from Soviet suppression of Chinese-Russian journals in the USSR. In part, however, it stemmed from a Chinese circular, sent to all Communist parties, which blamed Khrushchev for the revolts in Poland and Hungary, criticized him for the de-Stalinization policy, questioned his ability to lead an international revolutionary movement, assailed him for alleged unwillingness to support revolutionary struggles all over the world, and reprimanded him for his eagerness to seek an accommodation with the West.

At the November, 1960, Moscow meeting, held in secret for over three weeks, the Chinese renewed their criticism of Khrushchev. They accused him of opportunism and revisionism, reproached him for his lack of knowledge of Marxism, criticized him for his propagation of absurd disarmament ideas, upbraided him for his fear of nuclear war, and denounced him for his support of neutralist leaders. Khrushchev replied to the Chinese charges by accusing them of fractionalism. The end product of the conference was the "Declaration of Representatives of the Communist and Workers' Parties," a temporary compromise between the Soviet and Chinese positions—which the Chinese signed under protest and only on the strict understanding that another meeting would be held within two years to resolve the outstanding differences.

Late in 1961, the Sino-Soviet tension erupted anew at the Twenty-second Congress of the CPSU. The disagreement developed over Khrushchev's bitter denunciation and Chou En-lai's firm defense of Albania's "Stalinist" policies. Apparently the clash between the two men was very bitter, for on October 23, in the midst of the party congress, Chou left Moscow for Peking where he was greeted at the airport by Mao. No reason was given for his sudden departure. Its meaning, however, was obvious. Whether by coincidence or design, a few days after Chou's departure the Soviets set off the world's greatest man-made explosion. Early in December, 1961, the USSR severed its diplomatic ties with Albania. This decision made "the monolithic unity of the socialist camp" a myth.

The outbreak of hostilities in the Sino-Indian border dispute in September, 1962 (in which the Soviet Union assumed a "neutral" position), and Soviet withdrawal of offensive weapons from Cuba in October, 1962 (under pressure from the United States), complicated greatly the precarious nature of relations between Moscow and Peking. During

Moscow, 1961. The Twenty-second Congress of the Communist party in Congress Hall.

and especially after these crises the two Communist colossi hurled increasingly bitter denunciations of each other's policies, and their differences occupied the spotlight at the meetings of Romanian, Bulgarian, Hungarian, Czechoslovak, Italian, Mongolian, and East German Communist party congresses from November, 1962, to January, 1963.

During the first half of 1963, Sino-Soviet relations went from bad to worse. On March 8, 1963, the Chinese introduced the territorial element into the dispute by reminding the Soviets that the Amur Basin and the Maritime Province in the Far East had once belonged to China and that their future would have to be "negotiated." At the same time, in a series of long letters, the Chinese began to press for a meeting with Soviet officials to resolve their "ideological differences." After some maneuvering both sides agreed to a confrontation which took place in July, 1963. Both sides, however, took steps that led to the failure of the meeting. The Chinese, for instance, on June 14 issued a twenty-five point statement as an agenda for discussion, which the Soviets labelled as being "slanderous" and refused to publish. Before the meeting Khrushchev improved his relations with Yugoslavia (China's adversary), and was successful in timing the Chinese-Soviet talks to coincide with the talks with the Western Powers on a partial nuclear test ban. The success of the latter and the failure of the former brought Sino-Soviet relations to their lowest point. In fact, the Chinese labelled the test ban agreement "a capitulation to United States imperialism," and a "dirty fraud" designed "to prevent all the threatened peace-loving countries, including China, from increasing their defense capabilities."

Following the failure of the July, 1963, ideological confrontation, relations between Moscow and Peking continued to deteriorate dramatically. In a series of newspaper editorials the Chinese hurled venomous insults at Soviet leaders in general and at Khrushchev in particular. They referred to him as a "Bible-reading and psalm-singing buffoon" and "the greatest capitulator and splitter of our times." They accused him of supporting Mao's enemies inside China; stigmatized him for his alleged opposition to Mao's ambitious program of communes and rapid industrialization, the renowned "great leap forward" which resulted in a colossal disaster in 1958–59; and denounced him as a more dangerous enemy of communism than Tito or even Trotsky. The Chinese accompanied their verbal challenge to Soviet leadership by a series of direct actions. In December, 1963, for instance, they dispatched Chou En-lai on a two-months' journey through African countries to compete with the Soviets for the allegiance of key African leaders. Early in 1964, they established diplomatic relations with France. And, about the same time, they were also trying to seize control of the African-Asian Solidarity Conference held in Algiers.

For several months Soviet leaders took no official note of Chinese insults, apparently hoping that their silence would induce the Chinese to silence. When this approach proved ineffective, Khrushchev altered his tactics. He referred to Mao on different occasions as "a subversive splitter," "a racist," "a mixture of petty bourgeois adventurist and a great-power chauvinist" and a "worn-out galosh" that should be discarded. He made the Sino-Soviet split a central issue of the February, 1964, meeting of the CC of the CPSU, and officially disclosed the Soviet position on the nature as well as the development of the conflict. Simultaneously with these disclosures Khrushchev and his associates were busily engaged in retaining the allegiance of as many leaders of Communist parties throughout the world as possible. On October 16, 1964, just one day after Khrushchev's sudden removal, the Chinese added a new element to the dispute with their successful detonation of an atomic device. The Sino-Soviet rift—perhaps the most significant political event of the present-day world—dramatically revealed two fundamental things: that the monolithic unity of the Communist world was a myth—not a reality; and that present and future were pregnant with both opportunities and dangers for all mankind.

Whether by coincidence or by design, at the time when they were losing influence in the Far East to the Chinese, the Soviets tried to strengthen their position among the key peoples of underdeveloped areas of Southeast Asia, the Near East, Africa, and Latin America. These areas had long occupied an important place in Soviet ideological pronouncements and long-range political strategy. It was, however, not until after Stalin's death that they made a concentrated effort to penetrate these regions. The immediate Soviet objective and tactics varied considerably from country to country. Everywhere, however, they sought: (1) to exploit dissatisfaction of the less developed countries with their political and economic conditions; (2) to foster the belief among the leaders of those countries that their poverty and weakness stemmed from their previous political status; (3) to establish a measure of good will, especially among politically articulate groups, by supporting their objectives; (4) to portray all Western programs for these countries as merely a disguise for old imperialism intended to maintain the nonindustrial countries in a state of economic subjugation; (5) to present the USSR as a benevolently disinterested brother and champion of underdeveloped countries in their struggle for independence; (6) to identify themselves with national aspirations of new countries and to create the impression that only the USSR was interested in their problems; and (7) to emphasize the superiority of the Soviet type of economy for rapid industrial development.

One of the unique features of Soviet penetration of underdeveloped

Nikolai Bulganin and Nikita Khrushchev with India's President Rajendra Prasad, in India, 1955.

areas was its concentration on key strategic and economically and politically vulnerable countries. In Southeast Asia, India, Burma, and Indonesia were singled out for a concentrated effort. With India the Soviets established close ties in February, 1955, when they took the initiative and agreed, under terms quite favorable to India, to build and equip a steel plant. Late that year Khrushchev and Bulganin made a triumphant and unprecedented tour through India; and in November, 1956, the USSR offered India a $126,000,000 low interest loan, agreed to train Indian technicians, and, while careful not to mix political propaganda with technical assistance and training, the Soviet government flooded India with Soviet books, periodicals, newspapers, and films. In Burma, Soviet penetration started late in 1956 and early in 1957, following the much-publicized visit to that country of Khrushchev and Bulganin in November, 1956, and that of Mikoyan in April, 1957. The Soviet government agreed to build as a "gift" to the Burmese people a series of projects to be completed by 1963. These included a technological institute, hotel, hospital, cultural and sports arena, permanent agricultural and industrial exhibition, theater and conference hall. The Burmese government, in turn, agreed to match the value of this "gift" with surplus rice.

In Indonesia the Soviets were attracted by its resources (rubber, tin, oil), its size, and its critical internal problems. The penetration there began late in 1957, when the Soviet government offered Indonesia a $100,000,000 credit to help its deteriorating economic conditions. They then agreed to survey Indonesian resources and transport facilities, plan industries, train technicians, and supply needed machinery and equipment. They also offered a generous supply of military equipment and sided with Indonesia against the Dutch over the issue of Dutch New Guinea. Following Khrushchev's extended trip through the island nation in February, 1960, the USSR granted Indonesia $250,000,000 in credits; agreed to supply Indonesia with heavy cruisers, long-range jet bombers, ground-to-air missiles, and other sophisticated weapons; assumed responsibility for training of Indonesian economic and military specialists; and contracted to build 410 miles of road, a metallurgical plant, an iron and steel plant, a hydroelectric power station, an aluminum plant, and an atomic reactor. In return for this generous assistance Indonesia opened its doors to Soviet political and cultural penetration and sided with them on all issues in the United Nations.

In the Near East, the main targets of penetration during Khrushchev's years were Egypt and Syria. The Soviets started their offensive towards Egypt in 1955, as a consequence of Egypt's difficulty in marketing its cotton in the West, Egypt's desire for modern arms, and President Gamal Abdel Nasser's "positive neutralism" and his defiance of the Western Powers. The arms deal was made in September, 1955. It was followed by Soviet promises to help Egypt build the High Aswan Dam, and Soviet diplomatic support of Egypt before, during, and following the French-British-Israeli invasion of Egypt in October, 1956. Before it joined Egypt in February, 1958, to form for a brief period the United Arab Republic the Soviets sought to establish a base in Syria. Between 1955 and 1957 the USSR and its satellites offered a $300,000,000 credit to Syria, signed several military and economic agreements, and promised large-scale economic and technical assistance. As a result of Nasser's firm stand against local Communists in the United Arab Republic and his emphasis on Arab unity, the Soviet position in the Near East weakened somewhat between 1958 and 1960. It was revitalized through a series of agreements and official visits. The most significant of these was Khrushchev's tour of Egypt in May, 1964, on which occasion he opened the first stage of the High Aswan Dam Project and offered additional economic and political support.

In Africa, Soviet interest during Khrushchev's rule was at first geared not to any one country but to the rising and ambitious intelligentsia of the Dark Continent. Accordingly they tried to befriend students, labor leaders and politicians, offered them scholarships and awards, received and sent delegations and missions to promote trade and good will, and increased African Studies Programs in Soviet universities. Early in 1960 the Soviets were attracted to the Congo by its strategic location, its resources, its political instability, its military weakness, the continued Western economic influence, and the amenability of one of the Congo spokesmen, Premier Patrice Lumumba, to Soviet suggestions. Overzealousness in the summer of 1960 in the attempt to turn the Congo into a Soviet base in Africa backfired. In September, 1960, anti-Lumumba forces expelled the Soviet ambassador from the Congo and forced Lumumba out of office, and the ensuing chaos brought United Nations intervention. In mid-February, 1961, Soviet interests suffered a further setback with the murder of Lumumba. The Soviet government blamed U.N. Secretary Dag Hammarskjöld for Lumumba's death, demanded the withdrawal of U.N. forces from the Congo, refused to pay its share for the U.N. Congo expedition, recognized the pro-Lumumba rival regime in Stanleyville as the legal Congo government, and threatened to intervene on its behalf.

That threat never materialized. Instead the Soviets stepped up their ideological penetration of African intelligentsia. In February, 1960, they established in Moscow a "University for the Friendship of Peoples," later renamed Patrice Lumumba University, and began to woo African students with free tuition, medical care, and up to $2,500 a year in spending money. The aim of the University was twofold. It sought to train from 3,000 to 4,000 students from Africa (as well as Asia and Latin America [1]) to be good propagandists in their areas for Soviet achievement and power. It also hoped to create a link between Soviet-trained intelligentsia of Africa, Asia, and Latin America to oppose Western influence in all of these regions. In October, 1960, the Soviets created an "Afro-Asian Solidarity Committee," and later they organized machinery for setting up an "All-African Journalists Association." Meanwhile, they also sponsored in the USSR an "African Week" and an "Algerian Week," and in innumerable ways sought to influence the young intelligentsia of the Dark Continent.

In addition to the Congo, Khrushchev's regime tried to establish a base in Guinea, Ghana, and Mali. The Soviets were attracted to these countries by their internal instability and the inclination of the new leaders, dubbed "revolutionary democrats," to applaud Soviet achievements. In 1961 Khrushchev invited delegates of those three countries to attend the Twenty-second Congress of the CPSU and later gave Lenin Peace Prizes to Sékou Touré, Kwame Nkrumah and Modibo Keita. Subsequently, the Soviets joined them in denouncing Western colonialism and white rule, provided them with generous credits, made them grants,

[1] According to some reports, in 1963 there were about 1,000 African students in the countries of the Soviet bloc studying in academic institutions, and about 2,500 studying propaganda and revolutionary tactics. No corresponding figures are available on the number of Asian and Latin American students in the Soviet bloc.

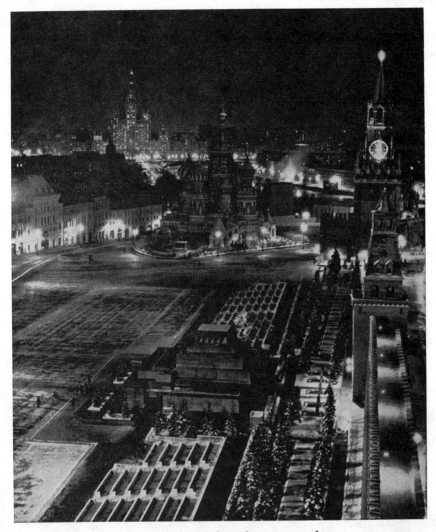

Red Square at night with Lenin's Tomb in the foreground.

offered them low interest loans, pledged to build in their countries such projects as sport arenas, hotels, hospitals, and roads, and supplied them with military hardware.

Soviet efforts to woo the potential and actual leaders of the new African nations received three serious setbacks. Two of these occurred in satellite countries (Bulgaria and Czechoslovakia), where many African students publicly protested alleged racial discrimination, political indoctrination, and inadequate housing conditions. One setback occurred in Moscow, where on December 18, 1963, in Red Square some 500 African students staged the biggest antigovernment protest in forty years. The unprecedented demonstration was triggered by the death under mysterious circumstances of a Ghanian student. The display by the students of such signs as "Moscow, A Second Alabama!" indicated that racial discrimination was a serious, if not the prime, issue behind the protest. The demonstrators surged through Red Square, battled police, and were pacified only after their representatives were received by the Minister of Higher Education, who promised to investigate their complaints. Because of this incident many African students who were financially able left the Soviet Union and either returned home or enrolled in Western universities.

Apparently because the U.N. upset Soviet designs for the Congo (as it earlier did for Korea), late in 1960, the Soviets started an intensive effort to weaken the world body. Speaking as the head of the Soviet delegation to the Sixteenth General Assembly of the U.N. in October, 1960, Khrushchev revealed that he was not content with the present arrangement of the U.N. In formal speeches, and through such antics as removing his shoe to pound his desk in full view of millions of television viewers, he argued that the world organization must reflect the present distribution of world powers, which he believed consisted of the Communist, the Western, and the uncommitted blocs. He demanded that the office of the Secretary General be replaced by a three-man directorate, a *troika*, which would have a built-in Soviet veto power to prevent the world organization from ever acting against Soviet interests. Should the U.N. fail to agree to this suggestion, Khrushchev warned, the USSR would either leave the organization or act outside it. This proposal, coupled with Khrushchev's unruly behavior and his personal attack on Dag Hammarskjöld, created a bad impression and evoked firm opposition. The sudden tragic death of Hammarskjöld in Africa, while on a mission in the Congo in September, 1961, gave the Soviets an opportunity to revive the troika scheme. After lengthy behind-the-scenes negotiations, however, they agreed on a compromise candidate, U Thant of Burma, to fill out Hammarskjöld's term. In November, 1962, U Thant was unanimously elected to a five-year term as Secretary General of the U.N. Early in 1963, in an apparent effort to strengthen their bargaining position in the U.N., the Soviets announced that they would stop payment to the U.N. on some budget items towards which the USSR had hitherto paid its share. This challenge to the U.N., which found itself in acute financial difficulties, apparently was intended to serve as a reminder that unless the world organization behaved in a manner acceptable to the Soviets, the USSR had the power to destroy it.

Under Khrushchev's leadership the Soviets also intensified their interests in Latin America. Until 1956 Argentina was the main center of Soviet attention. In 1953, the two countries signed a trade agreement under which Argentina sent to the Soviet Union its surplus of hides, grain, wool, and other raw materials, and received in return oil products, coal, sheet iron, rails, cement, aluminum ingots, and other industrial materials. In mid-1955 the USSR held a trade exhibit in Buenos Aires featuring a wide variety of industrial equipment—its first such exhibit in Latin America. After 1957, the Soviets sought to expand their influence in Brazil, and other Latin American and Caribbean countries, everywhere insisting on peaceful coexistence and friendship. Following Fidel Castro's seizure of power in Cuba in 1959, the Soviets focused their attention on the island nation. They were attracted to Cuba as a result of the deterioration of United States-Cuban relations, the assumption by the Castro regime of a radical posture, and a hope that the Cuban revolution would set off popular anti-U.S. upheavals throughout Latin America.

Soviet penetration of Cuba began in earnest following Mikoyan's visit to the island country in February, 1960, at which time he signed a trade agreement and granted a loan of $100 million. Later Moscow endorsed all of Castro's nationalization decrees; concluded (in June, 1960) a new trade agreement providing for the delivery of Soviet oil to Cuba and the sale of Cuban sugar to the USSR; agreed to equip the Cuban army with Soviet weapons; promised Cuba all possible help, including rockets, "if the aggressive forces of the Pentagon should dare to start an intervention against Cuba"; and dismissed the Monroe Doctrine as something having no vitality. Following the rupture of diplomatic relations with the United States late in 1960, and especially after the unsuccessful United States-backed attempt early in 1961 (at the Bay of Pigs) to unseat Castro, the Cuban regime threw its lot with Moscow.

Closer ties between Cuba and the USSR developed in the second half of 1962, following the arrival in Moscow of Raul Castro, the Cuban Minister of Armed Forces, and of Che Guevara, the Cuban Minister of Industries. Their visits resulted in an agreement to send Soviet personnel and materiel, including ICBM's to Cuba. This military build-up in turn led directly to the October–November, 1962 United States-Soviet military confrontation, which for a moment threatened mankind with thermonuclear annihilation. Pressed by the United States, Khrushchev withdrew offensive missiles from Cuba. Whether this pullout was complete is not known, for Castro did not allow international inspection to verify it. He continued to maintain close ties with Moscow and made two highly publicized tours of the USSR, one in May, 1963, and one in January, 1964. During the latter journey Castro negotiated a five-year economic agreement under which the Soviets agreed to purchase 24.1 million tons of Cuban sugar, and pledged to assist Castro militarily if

Cuba were either attacked or invaded by the United States. In return for these gains Castro sided with Khrushchev in his ideological quarrel with the Chinese, and cautiously endorsed, but did not become a signatory to, the limited nuclear test ban treaty.

In Europe Khrushchev pursued a policy of "peaceful coexistence" and "relaxation of tensions." The aim of this policy was simple. It sought in return for Soviet adherence to normal behavior in international relations to gain a great deal of good will and thereby to weaken the effectiveness of various anti-Soviet defensive alliances that had emerged after 1948. Among the most notable manifestations of this policy were: (1) Soviet renunciation on May 30, 1953, in a note to Turkey, of Stalin's program of territorial claims against Turkey along the Georgian and Armenian frontiers, on condition that Turkey be willing to work out in the Straits "conditions equally acceptable both for the USSR and for Turkey," and that Turkey withdraw from NATO and other containment pacts; (2) the Soviet decision, after ten years of delaying tactics, to sign on May 15, 1955, a treaty with Austria, which terminated the Four Power occupation of that country, in return for Austria's pledge to follow a neutralist policy and its agreement to pay, over a six-year period, $150,000,000 for the return of enterprises the Soviets had seized at the close of World War II, and Austrian agreement to enter into close economic ties with the USSR; (3) Soviet willingness to participate in the Geneva Summit Meeting (July 18–23, 1955), to discuss disarmament, the German problem, foreign bases, "competitive coexistence" with the West in the underdeveloped areas, and increased trade (but not to discuss the question of East European satellites, the activities of international communism, or President Eisenhower's "open skies" proposal); (4) the Soviet decision in September, 1955, to return to Finland the Porkkala Naval Base with all of its installations and without compensation, in return for a renewed Finnish pledge to maintain with the USSR the close economic ties which stemmed from the April 6, 1948, Treaty of Friendship, Cooperation, and Mutual Assistance; and (5) the Soviet leaders' (Khrushchev and Bulganin, preceded by Malenkov) visit to England in April, 1956, where they mixed their pronouncements on peaceful coexistence and increased Soviet-British trade possibilities with criticism of British postwar policies, warnings against British military action in the Near East, threats to make a deal with the West Germans, and brandishment of the hydrogen bomb. Following the upheavals in Poland and Hungary in 1956, the Soviets abandoned the policy of "relaxation of tensions" in favor of "increased vigilance" and "military preparedness."

In Germany, Khrushchev adhered to a policy set by Stalin—a policy which sought to bring all of Germany under Soviet control. Until mid-1953 the Soviets hoped to achieve this goal by posing East Germany as an example for West Germans to follow, by concentrated appeals "to all the peace-loving peoples of Europe" to protest against West German participation in European recovery and in the European Defense Community, and by veto power, stemming from their control of East Germany, over any program for all of Germany which they found unacceptable. Their efforts to win over the West Germans received a severe setback in June, 1953, as a consequence of the East Berlin uprising. That upheaval, followed by a mass exodus of East Germans to West Germany, destroyed the Soviet belief that East Germany exerted a magnetic influence upon West Germany. It also revealed the unpopularity of the East German regime with the people, and its utter dependence on the Soviet military for its very existence. Soviet efforts to prevent West Germany from joining Western Europe fared no better. In spite of Soviet protests, West Germany experienced extraordinary economic reconstruction and recovery under the Marshall and Schuman Plans, rose rapidly into a respectable free and equal member of the community of nations, and emerged as a vital link in NATO defenses.

In 1954 and 1955 the manner of German unification emerged as the thorniest issue of the German problem. It was the focal point of debates at the Berlin Conference of Foreign Ministers (January 25–February 18, 1954), and it also figured prominently on the agenda at the July, 1955, Summit Meeting in Geneva. On that occasion the four heads of state agreed that as victors in World War II it was their common responsibility to settle the German question and the problem of German unification "by means of free elections . . . [to be] carried out in conformity with the national interests of the German people and the interests of European security." The Foreign Ministers were to work out arrangements for this. Late in October, 1955, the Foreign Ministers met in Geneva, but from the outset it was clear that their views were far apart. The controversy centered over the meaning of "the national interests of the German people." The West understood national interests as reunification in accordance with the rights of peoples and liberty of individuals, and proposed that Germany be reunified by a free election to be carried out in 1956. To dispel Soviet fears, the West also offered a treaty of assurance, which would give the USSR far-reaching safeguards against German aggression. The Soviets refused this offer. They took the position that they too favored German unification, but only under the condition that this unification would extend the benefits of the Soviet system to all of Germany. Needless to say these diametrically opposed positions made a deadlock in negotiations inevitable.

Following the evaporation of the so-called "Geneva Spirit," Germany developed along two vastly different economic, social, political, and cultural lines relatively undisturbed until November 27, 1958, when the

Soviets introduced a new element. In an identical note to the United States, Great Britain, France, and West Germany, Khrushchev proposed that the Western Powers negotiate to end the occupation status of Berlin. These negotiations were to be completed within six months, after which Berlin would be turned into a free city. The note stated that the Soviet Union was willing to assume full responsibility for the employment of West Berliners, and that it would not interfere in the internal affairs of Berlin. Khrushchev also stated that he was even willing to have this document "recorded in a resolution of the United Nations." On January 10, 1959, the Soviet government followed up its six-months' time limit with a proposal to convene a twenty-eight nation peace conference to draw up a German peace treaty. That proposal called, among other things, for withdrawal of all foreign troops from Germany, denial to Germany of the right to join any political or military bloc that did not include all signatory nations, German renunciation of all claims to territories east of the Oder-Neisse Rivers, and assumption by the two German states of the main burden of negotiating German unification.

The West interpreted Khrushchev's six-months' time limit to negotiate the question of Berlin as an ultimatum and responded firmly. It also rejected his proposal on a German peace treaty, which in essence was that which had been offered by Molotov at the Berlin Conference in 1954. Western firmness made the Berlin situation a major international crisis. A new meeting of Foreign Ministers was arranged for Geneva for June, 1959, to solve the problem, but despite some Western concessions the problem remained. It got worse on August 13, 1961, when, to stop East German exodus to the West, Khrushchev ordered East German authorities to build a concrete wall across Berlin and began to tamper with Allied traffic within the city. This challenge, plus frequent provocations along the border, made Berlin the most explosive spot in the world. The danger was increased by lack among the Western Powers of a unified approach on Berlin, and by resumption of Soviet thermonuclear test explosions in the atmosphere. This action, designed, in Khrushchev's own words, to act as the "Sword of Damocles," both shocked and unified world public opinion. Many questioned Khrushchev's sanity, and some even made hasty preparations for what looked like the approaching holocaust.

Relations with the United States during Khrushchev's rule were erratic, alternating between military confrontations, diplomatic conferences, limited exchanges, and top level meetings. This, of course, was to be expected (especially in the early stages) in view of the deep-rooted suspicion generated by Stalin's Cold War, the power struggle within the Kremlin leadership, and the inexperience of the Eisenhower administration. The two giants, therefore, moved cautiously. The breakthrough came in the late spring of 1954 with a coast-to-coast tour of the United States by a group of Soviet journalists headed by Khrushchev's son-in-law Alexei I. Adzhubei. Late that year Soviet authorities allowed several American journalists, agricultural experts, and a number of ordinary citizens to visit selected points in the USSR. Throughout 1955 both sides expanded these contacts, agreed to resume distribution of monthly official information magazines (*Amerika* and *Soviet Life*), in their respective countries, and in December, Soviet officials allowed an American production of *Porgy and Bess* to be performed in Leningrad. Relations between the two powers improved further during the Suez crisis of 1956, when in the U.N. both condemned the British-French-Israeli invasion of Egypt. They parted company, however, following brutal Soviet suppression of the Hungarian quest for freedom.

The chill was brief. In the course of 1958 both countries took appropriate steps designed to renew the disrupted dialogue. In addition to numerous diplomatic notes concerning disarmament, nuclear tests, and other problems, Khrushchev granted extensive interviews to influential American opinion makers and authorized an agreement (signed January 27, 1958) calling for substantial cultural contacts between the two countries. It provided for: (1) the establishment of a direct New York to Moscow air link; (2) regular radio and television exchanges of news and of cultural and political programs; (3) exchanges of scientific, industrial, business, and agricultural experts; (4) visits by authors, film personalities, performers, legislators, educators, and representatives of

Moscow University.

women's and youth organizations; (5) exchanges of qualified faculty and students between Moscow and Columbia and Leningrad and Harvard Universities; and (6) exchanges of athletes. In accordance with the spirit of these steps, late in December both governments signed an agreement calling for construction of an American scientific-cultural exhibit in Moscow and of a similar Soviet exhibit in New York in 1959.

During 1958, and especially 1959, these and other measures enabled thousands of Americans to visit the USSR, including Vice President Richard M. Nixon who engaged Khrushchev in the celebrated "kitchen debate." Unfortunately, only a handful of Soviet citizens came to the United States. Among the most conspicuous were Mikoyan (in January, 1959), Frol R. Kozlov, First Deputy Chairman of the Council of Ministers (in July), and Khrushchev (September 15 to 27). During his stay and trip across the country Khrushchev conferred with political, business, industrial, and labor leaders, and met many performers, journalists, farmers, and ordinary citizens. Though his visit was marred by several annoying incidents, it was, on the whole, a major triumph culminating in Eisenhower-Khrushchev talks at the presidential retreat, "Camp David," where the two leaders, behind closed doors, exchanged views on a variety of critical issues (including China), and where they impressed each other with the need to pursue a calm policy. Events soon proved that the "Spirit of Camp David" was to be a short-lived affair.

The deterioration of Soviet-American relations stemmed from Soviet challenge of the United States position in underdeveloped areas, from their renewal of extreme anti-American propaganda, which pictured the United States as a country of unemployment, starvation, racial injustice, warmongers, and imperialist designs, and from increased Soviet efforts to dislodge the Western position in Germany. The tension between Washington and Moscow increased late in April, 1960, following Khrushchev's angry speech in Baku, in which he warned the Soviet people not to expect too much from the forthcoming summit meeting in Paris designed to work out an agreement on Berlin and disarmament. Then on May 1, 1960, came the ill-fated flight of an American U-2 reconnaissance plane, which the Soviets brought down over Sverdlovsk deep inside the USSR. The United States government maneuvered itself into a trap by first claiming that the U-2 was an unarmed weather plane. To the amazement of the entire world, Khrushchev forced United States admission that the U-2 was not a weather plane but a high-flying craft on a photographic espionage mission, by producing the captured pilot, Francis G. Powers.[1]

[1] On February 11, 1962, the Soviet government released Francis G. Powers in exchange for Soviet agent Colonel Rudolf Abel who had been imprisoned in the United States.

The suspension of the summit meeting created an unprecedented uproar. Almost overnight, there poured forth a vast stream of literature on the subject, full of contradictory statements, charges, and counter-charges, each side trying to find a scapegoat. As expected, the Communists unanimously accused President Eisenhower for the failure of the summit, in view of his admission of his knowledge of air reconnaissance over the USSR and his unwillingness to apologize for it as Khrushchev had insisted. As expected, too, Western observers held Khrushchev fully responsible for wrecking the summit meeting, in view of his ill-tempered outbursts and his unrealistic demands that the President publicly acknowledge that the United States had committed an aggression against the USSR, apologize for it, and punish all those responsible.

The U-2 incident, the failure of the summit, and the Soviet shooting down in June, 1960, of an American RB-47 plane in the Arctic Ocean brought about a frigid atmosphere in Soviet-American relations. This atmosphere continued until the outcome of the presidential election became known. Following the Democratic victory, Khrushchev sent President-Elect John F. Kennedy a congratulatory message, and in January, 1961, as a gesture of "friendship," the Soviets released the imprisoned flyers of the RB-47 plane. Early in June, 1961, the two leaders met in Vienna to feel out each other's position on world problems. During the meeting Khrushchev handed to Kennedy an eight-point *aide mémoire* outlining the Soviet view of the German situation. On June 17, the Western Powers handed Moscow a detailed outline of their position. As neither side made any concessions, the stalemate over Germany continued.

Relations between the United States and the USSR continued to deteriorate throughout 1962, and reached the critical point in the thermo-nuclear confrontation of October, 1962. Kennedy's skillful, daring, and decisive handling of the Cuban crisis was a major turning point in the relations between the two colossi. The importance of the crisis centered not so much in the dismantlement of Soviet missile bases, as in exploding the myth, which had been the basis of Soviet atomic blackmail, that the USSR was prepared to run greater risks than was the United States. The removal of this blackmail, which Soviet leaders had skillfully exploited in the past, led to an improved atmosphere in Soviet-American relations. On June 20, 1963, the two powers, aware of the slowness of diplomatic channels of communication in time of crisis, agreed to establish a direct communication link between the White House and the Kremlin; and on July 25, 1963, the USSR, the United States, and the United Kingdom negotiated successfully a treaty on a partial nuclear test ban.

The latter agreement consisted of a preamble and five articles. In it the three powers solemnly pledged to stop test explosions of nuclear weapons in the atmosphere, in outer space and under water (but not under ground), in order "to put an end to the contamination of man's substances." They invited all other powers to join the ban (many states immediately expressed their readiness to be a party to the treaty). They each reserved the right to propose amendments to the treaty, as well as the right to withdraw from its obligations should any one of them feel that its national interests had been jeopardized. A power which withdraws from the treaty is required to give three months' notice of its intended action. While this agreement did not solve all the issues of the troubled world, it was nevertheless a major breakthrough in the Cold War, or mutual suspicion to which the world had been subjected since 1945.

Following the signing of the partial test ban treaty, Soviet-United States relations (and, in fact, Soviet relations with other Western Powers) continued to improve. Soviet leaders, for instance, officially expressed grief at President Kennedy's assassination, dispatched Mikoyan to Washington to attend the funeral, and offered information to United States authorities on the accused assassin, Lee H. Oswald, a self-proclaimed Marxist who had spent two years in the Soviet Union. Early in 1964 American and Soviet officials began negotiations aimed at establishing consular relations, and on April 21, 1964, in an attempt to break the stalemate in the disarmament negotiations, President Lyndon B. Johnson and Khrushchev simultaneously announced a "substantial reduction" in the production of enriched uranium. The United States' overall cutback was to amount to about 40 per cent. The Soviet action promised discontinuation of construction of two large new atomic reactors for the production of plutonium, "substantial reduction over the next several years" of production of uranium for nuclear weapons, and allocation of more fissionable material for peaceful uses. These cutbacks were not formal agreements and provided neither inspection nor policing, but they did, however, represent bold moves by both powers toward controlling armaments by mutual example in the atmosphere engendered by the partial test ban treaty of 1963.

KHRUSHCHEV'S DEMISE AND HIS LEGACY

On October 15, 1964, an official communiqué announced that a plenary meeting of the CC of the CPSU had granted Khrushchev's request "to be relieved of his duties as the First Secretary of the CC of the CPSU, membership of the Presidium of the CC of the CPSU, and Chairman of the Council of Ministers of the U.S.S.R. in view of his advanced age and deterioration of his health." This explanation, like many similar official

Soviet pronouncements, was pure falsehood. There was nothing wrong with Khrushchev's health. He was vacationing at his Black Sea residence at Sochi. And he did not ask to be relieved of his duties. He was removed by a conspiracy masterminded by an inner clique of his close associates on the Presidium of the CC of the CPSU. It is not known how the conspiracy was born or who was its chief architect. Only one thing is certain. The conspirators prepared the entire affair very carefully, executed it skillfully, and divided Khrushchev's power among themselves. Leonid I. Brezhnev, a long-time protégé of Khrushchev emerged as First Secretary of the CC of the CPSU, and Alexei N. Kosygin, Khrushchev's first deputy, became Chairman of the Council of Ministers of the USSR.

So successful and unexpected indeed was the coup, and so phony was the official announcement about Khrushchev's health, that the conspirators were forced to produce an indictment of their deposed comrade to placate public curiosity at home and abroad. The published and the unpublished versions of the indictment accused Khrushchev of undignified behavior, of creating a new "personality cult," of violating Leninist norms of "collective leadership," of "subjectivism and drifting in Communist construction," of "harebrained scheming, immature conclusions and hasty decisions and actions divorced from reality," of "bragging and bluster," of "attraction to rule by fiat," of causing disorganization in Soviet industry and agriculture, of making serious errors in foreign policy, of causing a split with China, of nepotism, and of an infallibility complex.

These charges were a bit more credible than the earlier ploy that Khrushchev was relieved of his duties on account of his advanced age and poor health, and they have become a permanent official fixture of anti-Khrushchevism. Chinese and Albanians rejoiced over Khrushchev's ouster. East Europeans (Poles, Hungarians, Czechoslovaks, Bulgarians and East Germans) expressed some apprehension but subsequently all accepted the *fait accompli* and the Brezhnev-Kosygin leadership. By year's end all other Communist parties, except the Italian, expressed satisfaction with the official explanation. Non-Communists remained skeptical but, like it or not, they too accepted Khrushchev's ouster and accommodated themselves to his successors. The task was quite painless since the new leadership assured everyone that the change in personnel did not imply a change in Soviet policy.

After they stripped him of all powers, his former lieutenants insulated Khrushchev and his wife in a modest *dacha* outside Moscow. Though officially he became an "unperson" he was allowed to move about and even to receive selected visitors, both Soviet and foreign. During his confinement Khrushchev performed one valuable service: he recorded for posterity his reminiscences, which were secretly smuggled out and then published in the United States in two volumes—*Khrushchev Remembers* and *The Last Testament*. These works attracted wide interest and were generally accepted as authentic in spite of the fact that both contain many omissions and other imperfections. Khrushchev died on September 11, 1971, and was buried quietly.

Though his former comrades-in-arms relegated him to obscurity and in fact assigned him to the gallery of "unpersons," Khrushchev left behind an impressive legacy. A good portion of that legacy was positive. His greatest achievement was the official exposure of Stalin's crimes, the partial dismantling of the reign of terror, and the rehabilitation of many innocent victims of that terror. He promised Soviet citizens a better life on condition that they work hard and produce and sacrifice more. Khrushchev allowed a limited degree of literary and artistic expression at home, and he encouraged scientific, cultural, and sports contacts with the non-Soviet world. In search of greater efficiency and productivity in the party, the government, and the economy, Khrushchev also introduced various reorganizations. Unfortunately for him these measures disturbed the daily do-nothing routine of many bureaucrats who eventually united against him and forced his ouster. Last, but by no means least, Khrushchev opened a dialogue with Tito, and with the influential leaders of the West (Adenauer, Eisenhower, de Gaulle and Macmillan), endorsed fully Soviet space efforts, and inaugurated Soviet economic, military, and ideological assistance in the Third World.

A good portion of Khrushchev's legacy was negative. He brutally suppressed the Hungarian bid for freedom in 1956, approved the construction of the imprisoning wall in Berlin in 1961, and, to secure an advantage over the United States, late in 1962 he authorized the placing of Soviet missiles in Cuba. Khrushchev also tried to force the Western Powers to accept his solution of the crucial German problem, and by his intransigence he accelerated the Sino-Soviet rift. Khrushchev also ostracized many intellectuals for their criticism of the Soviet system, alienated many collective farmers with his insistence that they give up their private plots, and antagonized party and government bureaucrats with endless reorganization schemes. Finally, as a talented demagogue, Khrushchev made too many promises he could not keep. That would be detrimental to any politician; for Khrushchev it was fatal, given the nature of domestic and foreign policy problems he inherited from Stalin.

SUGGESTED READINGS

ALLILUYEVA, SVETLANA. *Only One Year*. New York: Harper & Row, 1969.
———. *Twenty Letters to a Friend*. New York: Harper & Row, 1967.

ANDREWS, W. G. *Soviet Institutions and Policies: Inside View*. Princeton: Princeton University Press, 1966.

The Anti-Stalin Campaign and International Communism. New York: Columbia University Press, 1956.

ARMSTRONG, JOHN A. *The Politics of Totalitarianism: The Communist Party of the Soviet Union*. New York: Random House, 1961.

BARING, ARNULF M. *Uprising in East Germany, June 17, 1953*. Ithaca: Cornell University Press, 1980.

BASS, ROBERT H., and ELIZABETH MARBURY, eds. *The Soviet-Yugoslav Controversy: A Documentary Record, 1948–1958*. New York: Prospect Books, 1958.

BEREDAY, G., and J. PENNAR, eds. *The Politics of Soviet Education*. New York: Praeger, 1960.

BIALER, SEWERYN. *Stalin's Successors: Leadership, Stability and Change in the Soviet Union*. Cambridge: Cambridge University Press, 1980.

BOFFA, GIUSEPPE. *Inside the Khrushchev Era*. New York: Marzani & Munsell, 1963.

BRANT, STEFAN. *The East German Rising*. New York: Praeger, 1957.

BRESLAUER, GEORGE W. *Khrushchev and Brezhnev as Leaders: Building Authority in Soviet Politics*. Winchester: Allen & Unwin, 1982.

BRODERSEN, ARVID. *The Soviet Worker. Labor and Government in Soviet Society*. New York: Random House, 1966.

BROMKE, ADAM, ed. *The Communist States at the Crossroads Between Moscow and Peking*. New York: Praeger, 1965.

BROWN, DEMING. *Soviet Russian Literature Since Stalin*. New York: Cambridge University Press, 1978.

BROWN, EDWARD J. *Russian Literature Since the Revolution*. Revised and enlarged edition. Cambridge: Harvard University Press, 1982.

BROWN, J. F. *The New Eastern Europe: The Khrushchev Era and After*. New York: Praeger, 1966.

BRUMBERG, ABRAHAM, ed. *Russia Under Khrushchev*. New York: Praeger, 1962.

BRZEZINSKI, ZBIGNIEW K., ed. *Africa and the Communist World*. Stanford: Stanford University Press, 1963.

CONQUEST, ROBERT. *Power and Policy in the USSR*. New York: St. Martin's Press, 1961.

CRANKSAW, EDWARD. *Khrushchev: A Career*. New York: Viking, 1966.

———. *Khrushchev's Russia*. Baltimore: Penguin, 1959.

———. *The New Cold War: Moscow Vs. Peking*. Baltimore: Penguin, 1963.

DALLIN, ALEXANDER, ed. *Diversity in International Communism: A Documentary Record, 1961–1963*. New York: Columbia University Press, 1963.

DALLIN, DAVID J. *Soviet Foreign Policy After Stalin*. Philadelphia: Lippincott, 1961.

EMBREE, G. D. *The Soviet Union Between the 19th and 20th Party Congresses, 1952–1956*. The Hague: Nijhoff, 1959.

FEIFER, GEORGE. *Justice in Moscow*. New York: Dell, 1964.

FLOYD, DAVID. *Mao Against Khrushchev: A Short History of the Sino-Soviet Conflict*. New York: Praeger, 1964.

GIBNEY, FRANK. *The Frozen Revolution: Poland A Case Study in Communist Decay*. New York: Farrar, Strauss & Cudahy, 1959.

GRIFFITH, WILLIAM E. *Sino-Soviet Relations 1964–1965*. Cambridge: The MIT Press, 1967.

HALLOWELL, JOHN N., ed. *Soviet Satellite Nations*. Gainesville: University of Florida Press, 1958.

HYLAND, WILLIAM, and RICHARD W. SHRYLOCK. *The Fall of Khrushchev*. New York: Funk & Wagnalls, 1969.

JASNY, NAUM. *Khrushchev's Crop Policy*. Glasgow: Outram, 1965.

JOHNSON, PRISCILLA, and LEOPOLD LABEDZ, eds. *Khrushchev and the Arts: The Politics of Soviet Culture, 1962–1964.* Cambridge: The MIT Press, 1965.

KANET, ROGER E., ed. *The Soviet Union and the Developing Nations.* Baltimore: The Johns Hopkins Press, 1974.

KASER, MICHAEL. *Comecon: Integration Problems of the Planned Economy.* London: Oxford University Press, 1965.

KHRUSHCHEV, NIKITA S. *For Victory in Peaceful Competition with Capitalism.* New York: Dutton, 1960.

———. *Khrushchev Remembers.* Boston: Little, Brown, 1970.

———. *Khrushchev Remembers: The Last Testament.* Boston: Little, Brown, 1974.

KOCHAN, LIONEL, ed. *The Jews in Soviet Russia Since 1917.* New York: Oxford University Press, 1978.

KOREY, WILLIAM. *The Soviet Cage: Anti-Semitism in Russia.* New York: Viking, 1973.

LAQUEUR, WALTER, and LEOPOLD LABEDZ, eds. *Polycentrism.* New York: Praeger, 1962.

LASKY, MELVIN J., ed. *The Hungarian Revolution: A White Book.* New York: Praeger, 1957.

LEONARD, W. *The Kremlin Since Stalin.* New York: Praeger, 1962.

LIBRACH, JAN. *The Rise of the Soviet Empire. A Study of Soviet Foreign Policy.* Revised edition. New York: Praeger, 1965.

LINDEN, CARL A. *Khrushchev and the Soviet Leadership, 1957–1964.* Baltimore: The Johns Hopkins Press, 1966.

LONDON, KURT, ed. *Eastern Europe in Transition.* Baltimore: The Johns Hopkins Press, 1966.

MACKINTOSH, J. M. *Strategy and Tactics of Soviet Foreign Policy.* New York: Oxford University Press, 1963.

MCCAULEY, MARTIN. *Khrushchev and the Development of Soviet Agriculture: The Virgin Land Programme, 1953–1964.* New York: Holmes & Meier, 1976.

MEDVEDEV, ROY A., and ZHORES A. MEDVEDEV. *Khrushchev: The Years in Power.* New York: Columbia University Press, 1977.

MORRISON, DAVID. *The USSR and Africa.* London: Oxford University Press, 1964.

PENKOVSKY, OLEG. *The Penkovsky Papers.* New York: Doubleday, 1965.

PETHYBRIDGE, ROGER, ed. *The Development of the Communist Bloc.* Boston: Heath, 1965.

PISTRAK, LAZAR. *The Great Tactician. Khrushchev's Rise to Power.* New York: Praeger, 1961.

PLOSS, SIDNEY. *Conflict and Decision-Making Process in Soviet Russia: A Case Study of Agricultural Policy, 1953–1963.* Princeton: Princeton University Press, 1965.

ROTHENBERG, ABRAHAM. *The Heirs of Stalin: Dissidence and the Soviet Regime, 1953–1970.* Ithaca: Cornell University Press, 1972.

RUSH, MYRON. *Political Succession in the USSR.* New York: Columbia University Press, 1965.

SLUSSER, ROBERT M. *The Berlin Crisis of 1961.* Baltimore: The Johns Hopkins Press, 1972.

SMOLANSKY, OLES. *The Soviet Union and the Arab East Under Khrushchev.* Lewisburg: Bucknell University Press, 1974.

SWEARER, HOWARD R. *The Politics of Succession in the USSR.* Boston: Little, Brown, 1964.

TATU, MICHAEL. *Power in the Kremlin: From Khrushchev to Kosygin.* New York: Viking, 1969.

VARDYS, V. STANLEY, ed. *Lithuania Under the Soviets: Portrait of a Nation, 1940–1965.* New York: Praeger, 1965.

VUCINICH, WAYNE S., and IVO J. LEDERER, eds. *The Soviet Union and the Middle East: The Post World War II Era.* Stanford: Hoover Institution Press, 1974.

WOLFE, BERTRAM D. *Khrushchev and Stalin's Ghost*. New York: Praeger, 1957.
WOLFE, THOMAS W. *Soviet Power and Europe, 1945–1970*. Baltimore: The Johns Hopkins Press, 1970.
ZAGORIA, DONALD. *The Sino-Soviet Conflict, 1955–1961*. Princeton: Princeton University Press, 1962.
ZINNER, PAUL E., ed. *National Communism and Popular Revolt in Eastern Europe*. New York: Columbia University Press, 1956.

✂ IX

USSR UNDER BREZHNEV

The mid-October, 1964, coup that unceremoniously terminated Khrushchev's power vaulted Brezhnev into the stewardship of the USSR. Brezhnev's leadership produced no outstanding or spectacular imprint on Soviet or international life. It was, however, fairly stable, free of major crises, and it perpetuated Khrushchevism without Khrushchev and Stalinism without Stalin. Apparently for that reason, in conjunction with Brezhnev's seventieth birthday (December 19, 1976), the Soviet press and communications media headlined his accomplishments at considerable length. In fact, one of his close associates publicly referred to Brezhnev as "*vozhd* of our Party and of all the peoples of our motherland"—a description that in the past was reserved only for Lenin and Stalin. This elevation, to some extent, influenced some Western observers who labelled Brezhnev's tenure as "The Brezhnev Era"—an era that lasted for eighteen years, until his death on November 10, 1982.

Like Khrushchev and Stalin before him, Brezhnev reached the pinnacle of power primarily because of his position as the First and later General Secretary of the CC and the CPSU. This command post enabled him to gain control over the CC, over the party apparatus, and over all other institutions of the regime throughout the country, and to replace his potential opponents and incompetents in party and government positions with reliable and trusted friends. Brezhnev accomplished this task with great skill and patience and without making a mockery of the "collective leadership" concept.

Brezhnev made his first major public pronouncement as leader on November 6, 1964. In an address commemorating the forty-seventh anniversary of the Bolshevik seizure of power, he listed old, unresolved, and new problems and shortcomings of the Soviet Union and suggested a number of "scientific" approaches to correct them. The first repair attempt came at the November, 1964, meeting of the CC which, at Brezhnev's suggestion, abolished Khrushchev's 1962 division of the party into agricultural and industrial sections. This scrapping accomplished two important goals. It terminated uncertainty among party and government bureaucrats whose ill-defined jurisdictions had created chaos and bitterness. And it revealed Brezhnev as reasonable, conciliatory, capable, effective, and, if need should require, a Machiavellian prince.

Leonid Brezhnev signing the Helsinki agreement, August, 1975.

Brezhnev enhanced his leadership role at the March, 1965, meeting of the CC where he unveiled a new agricultural program. Intended to pacify collective farm peasants, the new program fixed annual grain delivery quotas until 1970, raised prices for grain and other farm products, and reduced the prices collective farms had to pay the government for industrial goods and services. In addition, Brezhnev's program offered Soviet peasants an old-age pension, guaranteed a minimum monthly income, eased restrictions and reduced taxes on private peasant plots and private livestock holdings, and pledged increased investment in agriculture, irrigation, reclamation, fertilizers, and agricultural machinery. Since the program also promised to provide the urban population with an adequate food supply, the new Brezhnev scheme appeased a good portion of the urban population.

Concurrently with his appeasement of party and government bureaucrats and pacification of collective farm peasants and some urban dwellers, Brezhnev mollified the Stalinists. Within a few weeks after Khrushchev's downfall Brezhnev and his associates terminated Khrushchev's de-Stalinization program and reintroduced a number of features associated with Stalin's regime. Moreover, on May 8, 1965, at a rally commemorating the twentieth anniversary of German surrender in World War II, Brezhnev described Stalin's leadership as beyond reproach, and five months later *Pravda* editorially hailed Stalin's period as "one of the most brilliant in the history of the party and of the Soviet state." The climax came in June, 1970, when authorities unveiled a ten-foot bust of Stalin over his grave. Those who questioned the wisdom of the creeping rehabilitation of Stalin—and there were many—were branded as enemies of the Soviet state and were punished accordingly.

While he placated potentially dangerous groups, from the beginning Brezhnev also quietly promoted his own interests and ambition. Using his position in the Secretariat he either demoted, dismissed, isolated, or reassigned potential adversaries and upgraded and promoted his supporters to key posts. One significant reshuffling took place at the December, 1965, meeting of the CC when Brezhnev obtained a decisive majority in the Secretariat and on the Presidium of the CC. Another occurred at the Twenty-third Congress of the CPSU (March–April, 1966) where Brezhnev advanced his supporters to the CC and subsequently to various key secretaryships throughout the country. The Congress, whose delegates he helped to select, designated Brezhnev as General Secretary and renamed the Presidium of the CC the Politbureau. Because both names were associated with Stalin's rule, many observers interpreted these changes as yet another evidence of neo-Stalinism.

Using his new title and the consolidated position, Brezhnev began to sharpen his profile and enhance his public image in crucial matters of domestic and foreign policy. Though he held no official post in the Soviet government (except membership on the Presidium of the Supreme Soviet), Brezhnev served as the principal host and negotiator during President Charles de Gaulle's official visit to the Soviet Union in June, 1966. Subsequently he played the leading role in all negotiations with world leaders during their visits to the USSR, and to promote Soviet interests he also travelled abroad quite extensively. On all of these occasions he was received with honors normally reserved for heads of state. For example, he personally conducted key negotiations leading to the rapprochement with West Germany; the first phase of the Strategic Arms Limitation Treaty and the détente agreements with the United States; and the Helsinki Agreement on European Security and Cooperation. In others words Brezhnev emerged as the chief spokesman of Soviet foreign policy and the architect of "the Brezhnev Doctrine" seeking to justify Soviet military intervention whenever and wherever "interests of socialism" were threatened.

Brezhnev's activity on vital matters of Soviet domestic policy also were impressive. As General Secretary of the CC he presided over four party congresses (in 1966, 1971, 1976 and 1981) and dismantled some of the most objectionable features of Khrushchevism. He dealt very harshly with dissenters and critics of Soviet reality, and during his tenure in power he allocated massive funds to Soviet defenses and small amounts to the improvement of living standards of the Soviet people. Since he skillfully relegated into obscurity alleged challengers and individuals with liabilities (Alexander Shelepin, Piotr Shelest, Dmitrii Polansky and others), those he advanced built "the Brezhnev cult." The cult seems to have originated on his sixtieth birthday (December 19, 1966) when he was awarded a Hero of the Soviet Union medal and acclaimed as an outstanding leader. Thereafter Brezhnev's name appeared on all major documents, his picture on all billboards, and his statements in all newspapers and even in scholarly works. In May, 1976, Brezhnev was named Marshal of the Soviet Union and accordingly was selected as Chairman of the all-powerful Committee on State Security.

On the eve of his seventieth birthday (December, 1976) his life was depicted in a documentary film, his collected speeches were issued in a new edition, and, as noted before, in a public ceremony he was acclaimed "*vozhd* of our party and of all peoples of our motherland." In the new capacity (in May, 1977) Brezhnev ousted Podgorny from the Politburo and the chairmanship of the Presidium of the Supreme Soviet (which he himself assumed in mid-June, 1977); released a draft of a new Soviet Constitution for nationwide discussion prior to adoption; paid an official visit to France (July, 1977); entertained Tito (August, 1977) during the latter's stopover on his trip to North Korea and China; guided preparations to celebrate the sixtieth anniversary of the Bolshevik seizure of power; and demonstrated that he was a worthy successor to Khrushchev, Stalin, and Lenin.

SOVIET ECONOMY UNDER BREZHNEV

When he replaced Khrushchev, Brezhnev and his co-conspirators inherited not only power but a host of pressing domestic problems. Among the most challenging was the country's economy which was beset by calamities. The central cause of these was the declining rate of growth, brought on by the defective structure of the Soviet economic system and by poor political policies of the past. These were further aggravated by the drying up of resources, waste, mismanagement, lack of incentives, excessive centralization, the continued preoccupation with quantitative increases and the overfulfillment mania, and defective and often counterproductive economic decisions. The net result was a shocking paradox. The USSR was a great industrial power and abounded in natural wealth. Its people, however, enjoyed a very low standard of living, had an acute housing shortage, and suffered constantly from inadequate food supplies and scarce and poor quality consumer goods.

To solve the economic problems he inherited from Khrushchev, Brezhnev adopted a dual approach. He continued some policies of his predecessor and modified others. The continuity aspect was perhaps best illustrated by the performance of Soviet space, defense, and defense-related industries. Between January 1, 1965, and January 1, 1977, Soviet scientists and technicians launched hundreds of artificial satellites (in the Cosmos series); placed into orbit and later recovered several space stations (in the Proton and Zond series); orbited numerous communication and weather satellites (in the Molniia series); sent a score of space ships (in the Soiuz and Voskhod series) into Earth orbit; and launched several probes to the planet Venus (in the Venera series) to the planet Mars (in the Proton series), and to the Moon (in the Luna series). From the technological point of view the most spectacular of these efforts were the first successful "soft-landing" of Luna IX on the moon on February 4, 1966, which resulted in several pictures of the Moon's surface; the first soft-landing and return, on September 12, 1970, of a robot craft (Luna XVI) that brought back three and one-half ounces of dust from the Moon, followed by the November 17, 1970, soft-landing of an eight-wheeled moonrover, Lunakhod, the first self-propelled vehicle to maneuver on the Moon's surface; and the first soft-landing on Venus (early in 1971) and on Mars (late in 1971).

What was the true scientific achievement of these and many other Soviet space probes (both under Brezhnev and under Khrushchev) is difficult to assess because their space work has been very secretive. This much is certain, however. Because the Soviet space program is defense oriented, it received from Brezhnev (as it also did under Khrushchev) all required forces, resources, and financial support. That support, in turn, enabled Soviet scientists to test the latest equipment and techniques, such as manual spaceship control, stabilization systems, the welding of metal in vacuum and weightlessness, space rendezvous, and remote-controlled soft-landing. Two of the Soviet experiments are known to have ended in tragedies. The first was on April 24, 1967, with the flaming crash of a spaceship, Soiuz I, that killed its pilot, V. M. Komarov. The second took place on June 30, 1971, when the three-man crew of the spaceship Soiuz XI, after setting a new endurance record (eighteen days in orbit), died when their reentry craft lost cabin pressure. Soviet space efforts, however spectacular and extensive, failed to capture the imagination and the enthusiasm of the casual observer in the same way as the historic, July 20, 1969, landing, walk about, and safe return from the Moon's surface by the United States astronauts Neil A. Armstrong and Edwin E. Aldrin, followed by several additional safe landings and returns by other astronauts, and by the successful launching of the U.S. space shuttle program. Careful scrutiny of the Soviet space efforts to date, however, indicates that they have very sophisticated space hardware with an extensive, second-to-none backup system, and that they possess the same knowledge and ability as the Americans.

Initially the Soviets were extremely secretive about their space research and refused to share their knowledge with anyone. The spectacular American achievements in space altered that position, however. The partial breakthrough came during private visits by American astronauts to the Soviet Union, where they received a warm reception. A real thaw took place at the end of May, 1972, during President Richard M. Nixon's historic visit to the Soviet Union, when the two governments signed an agreement calling for stepped-up cooperation in the peaceful exploration of outer space and committed themselves to an historic Apollo-Soiuz rendezvous in space, which was accomplished in July, 1975. Another Soviet historic first was the brief space voyage, with Soviet crews, of cosmonauts from all East European countries and Cuba, Vietnam, and France. Still another historic first came on July 1, 1983, when two Soviet cosmonauts successfully boarded the twenty-ton Saliut VII space station and the twenty-ton module, Cosmos 1443, that had been linked in March, 1983. Soviet media gave wide publicity to this achievement and described the Cosmos 1443 module as a prototype of units to house astrophysical, technological, biological and other laboratories in space.

While Soviet space achievements made many valuable contributions to science, because they were defense-oriented they also had a direct bearing on their military capability. That capability increased substantially during Brezhnev's rule, thanks to heavy budgetary allocations for defense. According to official reports, between 1966 and 1977 the Soviet defense budget rose from about 13 billion rubles to over 20 billion rubles. These official figures are inconclusive because historically the published defense expenditures have reflected only a portion of the Soviet allocation to defense. The actual figure (for defense, space, and nuclear energy programs) was much higher and, in all probability, was about 20 per cent of the country's GNP. As a result of these continuous allocations to defense and defense-oriented industries under Brezhnev, the Soviets greatly increased their stockpiles of intercontinental ballistic missiles, built up their conventional land and air forces into the world's largest standing army, transformed the USSR into a mighty sea power with modern fleets (conventional and nuclear) in all the oceans and major seas of the world, equipped their satellites in Eastern Europe with sophisticated weapons, and generously supplied their willing followers in Asia, Africa, the Near East, and Latin America with the latest in military hardware.

No one knows for certain the actual strength of the Soviet military establishment because Soviet authorities historically have kept such information secret. According to an official American estimate the Soviet armed forces numbered about 5,000,000 men at the end of 1982. They consisted of the following units: 1) The Ground Forces of the Army (more than 180 motorized, rifle, tank and airborne divisions stationed in Eastern Europe, within the USSR, along the Chinese frontier, in Afghanistan, and in Cuba); 2) Four Fleets (Baltic, Black Sea, Pacific and Northern) with 1,300 surface combatants, 380 submarines, 760 auxiliary craft, and 1,400 naval aviation units; 3) Air Force with 10,000 surface-to-air missiles, 5,000 front-aviation craft, 2,500 interceptors, 900 long-range bombers, and 40 anti-ballistic missiles; and 4) Strategic Nuclear Forces with 1,400 intercontinental ballistic missiles, 1,000 submarine-launched ballistic missiles and 700 intermediate-range ballistic missiles. It should be pointed out that these numbers do not include the armed forces of such current Soviet client states as: Poland, Czechoslovakia, East Germany, Bulgaria, Hungary, Romania, Cuba, Ethiopia, South Yemen, Syria, Libya, Mongolia, North Korea, Vietnam, and Afghanistan.

During Brezhnev's rule the Soviet military-industrial establishment annually received an unusually large amount of the available funds to expand and improve the readiness and capabilities of the country's armed forces. These funds were allocated to the numerous centers for military research and development; to the military production industry; to clandestine efforts aimed at securing the secrets of Western technology; and to the improved appearance and living standards of enlisted personnel. Because Brezhnev gave these defense needs top priority, the military build-up exerted profound influence on the Soviet economy in general and on consumer goods in particular. The militarization of Soviet life

Astronaut Thomas Stafford and Cosmonaut Alexei Leonov during the Apollo-Soiuz *rendezvous in space, July, 1975.*

also exerted strong influence on Soviet politics. For the first time in Soviet history, professional military men became prominent figures in the Politburo, in the Committee for State Security and in the CC of the CPSU. Finally, during Brezhnev's rule men in military uniform emerged as permanent fixtures not only at important party gatherings and parades commemorating national holidays, but also in practically all daily routines of Soviet public life.

Soviet commitment to space, defense, and heavy industry under Brezhnev can best be illustrated by examining the allocation of resources to and the expected results from three five year plans that went into effect during his rule. The Eighth Five Year Plan (1966–1970), for example, assigned 152 billion rubles (or about 49 per cent of the total allocation) to heavy industry and expected the volume of industrial output to increase by 47 to 50 per cent. In actual figures the Plan called for steel output to increase from 91 to 129 million tons; pig iron from 66.2 to 97 million tons; rolled metal from 70.9 to 99 million tons; coal from 578 to

675 million tons; oil from 243 to 355 million tons; gas from 129 to 240 billion cubic meters; electricity from 507 to 850 billion kw hours; and plastic and synthetic resin from 821,000 to 2,300,000 tons.

The Ninth Five Year Plan (1971–1975), called by some the consumer-oriented Plan because its officially declared chief task was "to ensure a significant upsurge in the material and cultural level of people's life," also provided for a sizable upsurge in production of heavy, war-related industry and a substantial rise (about 40 percent) in labor productivity. By 1975 Soviet steel production was to reach 150,000,000 tons; coal 695,000,000 tons; oil 500,000,000 tons; chemical fibers 1,100,000 tons; finished rolled metal 105,000,000; gas 320 billion cubic meters; and electric power 1,070,000,000,000 kw hours. The Plan also called for construction of several thousand miles of new railway and pipe lines, and allocated funds for the completion of the single power system throughout the USSR. During these two five year plans, the Soviet Union experienced four major crop failures (1965, 1967, 1972, and 1975), which of course diverted huge sums of money from industry to the purchase of large quantities of food abroad, so that in spite of substantial progress, the economy failed to attain the assigned targets for heavy industry.

Guidelines for the development of Soviet economy for 1976–1980, which the Twenty-fifth Congress of the CPSU approved in March, 1976, while calling for increased attention to consumer needs, continued to emphasize heavy, war-related industry. By 1980, Soviet steel output was expected to reach 170,000,000 tons; rolled ferrous metals 120,000,000 tons; chemical fibers 1,500,000 tons; synthetic resin and plastics 5,964,000 tons; oil 640,000,000 tons; coal 810,000,000 tons; and electricity 1,380,000,000,-000 kw hours. These guidelines also called for an increased number of atomic reactors, continued expansion of the railway system (especially in the Baikal-Amur region), and a substantial expansion of hard-surface roads and of air and sea transport. The fulfillment of these ambitious goals was predicated on mechanization and automation of production; on a 27 per cent increase in labor productivity; on close cooperation with the COMECON countries; and on generous infusion of funds and the necessary know-how from such "developed capitalist countries" as the United States, Japan, West Germany, France, Italy, and England.

Apparently the industrial sector of the Soviet economy failed to achieve these goals, because the guidelines for the Eleventh Five Year Plan (1981–1986), which the Twenty-sixth Congress of the CPSU approved in March, 1981, were less pretentious. According to official figures, by 1985 Soviet output of electric power was to reach 1.55 to 1.6 trillion kwh.; 620,000,000 to 645,000,000 tons of petroleum (including gas condensate); between 600 and 640 billion cubic meters of gas; between 117,000,000 and 120,000,000 tons of finished rolled ferrous metal; between 150,000,000 and 155,000,000 tons of mineral fertilizers; between

6,000,000 and 6,250,000 tons of synthetic resins and plastics; 140,000,000 to 142,000,000 tons of cement; 1,600,000 tons of chemical fibers and threads; and 250 billion rubles worth of machine building and metals. As its predecessor had, this Plan too predicated the fulfillment of these fairly modest goals on the mechanization and automation of production, on increased labor productivity, on close cooperation with the COMECON countries, and on generous infusion of funds and the necessary know-how from "the developed capitalist countries."

While Soviet science and technology were making history in space, and while Soviet heavy industry was transforming the country into a major industrial, naval, and military power, Soviet agriculture under Brezhnev was setting records. The latter, however, were not ones of progress or achievement but of dismal failure, caused, as in the past, partly by climatic conditions and partly by bureaucratic mismanagement. To help the rural population and to halt the deterioration of the national diet, immediately after he assumed power Brezhnev and his associates restored private plots of collective farmers to their former size; repealed the tax on cattle owned by city dwellers; pledged to assist collective farmers in acquiring livestock, feed, and pasture; and decreed that in all state farms which Khrushchev had converted from collective farms, the former members who had passed retirement age were to keep or be given back their original plots, unaltered in size.

In March, 1965, a special meeting of the CC of the CPSU approved a doubling of state investments in agriculture, decreed that state purchases and delivery quotas (which in the past had changed from year to year) would remain stable from 1965 to 1970, and ordered a sizable increase in prices for state purchases from collective farms. Later, to ease the burden of the rural population, the new leaders removed the rural surcharges from many items of clothing, footwear, and other necessities; granted collective farmers a guaranteed monthly wage (similar to that of state farm workers) to replace the old exploitative system of deferring payment until crop deliveries had been made to the state; and tabled the Khrushchev-initiated campaign to transform all collective farms into state farms—a scheme that generated a great deal of popular discontent between 1961 and 1964 and that indirectly contributed to Khrushchev's downfall.

In accordance with the new trend, the Eighth Five Year Plan (1966–1970) allocated 71 billion rubles for agriculture. By 1970, the Plan promised to deliver to Soviet farms 1,790,000 tractors and 900,000 tractor trailers; 1,100,000 trucks and 275,000 truck trailers; and 550,000 grain harvesting combines. In also pledged to expand the agricultural base along the lower reaches of the Syr and Daria Rivers in Central Asia, in northern Caucasus, and in southern UkSSR; and to undertake extensive reclamation projects in the UkSSR and the Belorussian SSR and irrigation projects in Central Asia. In addition, the Plan vowed to improve the management of Soviet agriculture; urged diversification of animal husbandry; pleaded for an average annual increase of agricultural output by 25 per cent; promised to expand rural electrification; and pressed for a 40 to 45 per cent increase in productivity of agricultural labor. To spur everyone to greater effort, the Plan offered collective farmers a 35 to 40 per cent increase in remuneration and promised to introduce gradually monthly guaranteed wages for them similar to those of state farm workers.

In an apparent effort to demonstrate that all was well and that collective farms would remain intact, early in 1966 the government announced that the Third All-Union Congress of Collective Farms would convene later that year to draw up a new Model Collective Farm Charter to replace Stalin's Charter of 1935. For unexplained reasons, the meeting was postponed until November, 1969. When at last it was adopted, the new Charter contained only two insignificant innovations. It extended to the collective farmers a unified social security scheme, and it set up a system of collective farm councils at all levels. All other changes in the new Charter were either nebulous or devoid of any real safeguards for the collective farmers. Thus, every member of the collective farm was guaranteed a wage, but the amount of that wage was not indicated. Similarly, the collective farm was adjured to assist its members in tending their private plots and livestock, but it left that assistance to the whim of local bureaucrats. The result was that in spite of a number of changes Brezhnev had introduced between 1965 and 1970, Soviet agriculture remained, as it had always been, the Achilles heel of Soviet economy.

Perhaps for that reason, the Ninth Five Year Plan (1971–1975) was quite generous to agriculture. It allocated to it over 82 billion rubles. This sum was to pay for the delivery of 1,700,000 tractors, 1,100,000 trucks, 547,000 grain harvesting combines, 87,000 excavators, and 82,000 bulldozers. It was also to pay for the expanded irrigation system designed to bring new land under cultivation, for expansion of livestock in Central Asia, for the construction of feed storage facilities, and for extracting mineral fertilizers. The Plan promised a 35 per cent increase in wages of collective farmers, and in return anticipated a 20 to 22 per cent increase in agricultural output. All of these expectations went down the drain as a result of two disastrous crop failures, one in 1972 and one in 1975. So great indeed was the calamity that to feed its people, the Soviet government bought over 700 million bushels of grain (25 per cent of that year's American harvest) in 1972, purchased an additional 45 million bushels in 1974, and in 1975 negotiated a long-term agreement calling for an annual purchase of some 8 million tons of grain from the United States. During the same period, the Soviets also purchased grain and other food stuffs from Canada, Australia, and other countries.

Guidelines set forth for Soviet agriculture for 1976–1980 were modest. They called only for an 18 to 23 per cent investment, the delivery of an unspecified number of self-propelled harvesters, equipment for feed storage, and 143,000,000 tons of mineral fertilizers. By 1980, Soviet agriculture was expected to produce 220,000,000 tons of grain, 7,600,000 tons of sunflower seeds, 98,000,000 tons of sugar beets, 8,500,000 tons of raw cotton, 15,600,000 tons of meat, and 96,000,000 tons of milk. Apparently some of these goals were not realized because, judged by the guidelines set forth by the Twenty-sixth Congress of the CPSU in March, 1981, Soviet agriculture was to reach the following average annual production between 1981 and 1985: 238,000,000 to 243,000,000 tons of grain; 100,000,000 to 103,000,000 tons of sugar beets; 6,800,000 million tons of sunflower seeds; between 9,200,000 and 9,300,000 tons of raw cotton; between 17,000,000 and 17,500,000 tons of meat; between 94,000,000 and 95,000,000 tons of milk; 29,400,000 tons of vegetables; 11,500,000 tons of fruits and berries; between 470,000 and 480,000 tons of wool; and 72 billion eggs. It should be noted that in many instances the official guidelines supplied information only of percentages of Soviet industrial and agricultural outputs in relation to past performances—a practice that historically has always signalled a failure.

Both guidelines for Soviet agriculture, for 1976 to 1980 and 1981 to 1986, made it perfectly clear that they could be achieved only if they were accompanied by intensive production, by proper use of equipment, by the elimination of waste, by improvement in the standards of technical and agro-chemical services, and by the reduction of consumption of agricultural raw materials for technical purposes. To spur collective and state farmers to greater efforts, the guidelines tantalized them with promises of substantial percentage increases in their income. Apparently the improvement was minimal because in May, 1982, the CC of the CPSU launched a massive "Food Program" to solve the country's critical food shortages. Judged by similar past efforts, it is doubtful that Soviet agriculture will attain the assigned goals, because the official guidelines said nothing about the removal of constant political interference and other built-in inefficiencies.

As it had been in the past, the Soviet agricultural crisis under Brezhnev was closely linked with the pervasive shortages of consumer goods and services; with the poor quality of available goods and services; with repressed inflation; and with the low quality of life in general and such serious problems as widespread drunkenness in particular. While officials have blamed the continued existence of these problems on the ravages of World War II, these problems have essentially been caused by the long official neglect of investment in the consumer sector of the economy. The Eighth Five Year Plan (1966–1970) addressed itself partially to this problem when it allocated 75 billion rubles for housing and "cultural construction"; and when it called for a modest increase in the production of textiles, shoes, clothing, radios, television sets, refrigerators; better quality housing; and a five-day week.

The Ninth Five Year Plan offered Soviet consumers additional promises. By 1975 their personal income was to rise by 30 per cent; there were to be available 11 billion square meters of fabrics and some 830 million pairs of footwear; an 80 per cent increase in everyday household goods and utensils; better housing and improved public services; and an improved quality and nutritional value of processed food and an adequate supply of vegetables, fruits, and dairy products. However, as noted earlier, the two devastating crop failures created havoc with these promises. Except for a modest increase in housing and a slightly improved quality of clothing, these promises remained only promises.

There was one ambitious undertaking of the Ninth Five Year Plan that did rather well. This was the Fiat-designed-and-constructed automobile factory designed to mass produce the small *Zhguli* cars. According to preliminary official statements, by 1975 there were to be over 3 million cars in private hands in the USSR. Because this mammoth undertaking encountered many "bugs," the intended goal was not reached. But many cars were produced. And to service them, the Plan provided for a substantial increase of service and repair stations (which in 1971 numbered only 688 for the entire USSR!), and paved roads which in 1970 totaled about 130,000 miles, compared with 1,666,000 miles in the United States. Because these cars were very expensive, only the most affluent could afford to buy them. For most Soviet citizens, the dream of owning a car remained a dream.

However, to keep that dream alive, guidelines for the development of Soviet economy for 1976–1980 included some tantalizing provisions for Soviet consumers. There was, for example, the promise of a 16 to 18 per cent rise in wages and salaries for workers and other state employees. By 1980, they were expected to receive 180 rubles per month. There also was to be a 28 to 30 per cent increase in benefits for pensioners, disabled persons and women with infants. There was to be an unspecified increase in consumer durables and in new housing; improved and expanded medical service and technical and vocational training; and a reduction of prices on some basic necessities. The plan clearly stipulated that these, like all other promises of the past, could be realized only if there were a substantial increase in labor productivity, if all sectors of the economy would eliminate waste, and if the Soviet economy would receive the required infusion of funds and resources from the COMECON countries and above all from the industrial giants of the capitalist world.

When he resolved to cater to Soviet consumers, Brezhnev inadvertently opened the door to consumer dissatisfaction and complaints. Judged by the ever-increasing volume of complaints in the press about unfulfilled promises and the poor quality of products, Soviet consumers became quite vocal. These complaints also revealed strengths and weaknesses of the Soviet economy and clearly pointed out that official assurances notwithstanding, it failed, during the Brezhnev rule, to attain the modest objectives the authorities assigned to it. This failure, of course, was aggravated by four droughts (1965, 1967, 1972 and 1975) and by three consecutive poor harvests (1980, 1981 and 1982). Actually, however, it was caused by arbitrary changes in production plans by political leaders; by widespread indifference to doing a job well; by high rates of absenteeism, labor turnover, and pervasive drunkenness; and above all because the authorities, except for making constant promises, were unwilling to alter the traditional investment priorities. Consequently, while the USSR abounded in resources and emerged as a major industrial power, its people had not only poorer housing but by far the lowest standards of living of any major industrial country.

Brezhnev's last major domestic (as well as international) achievement was the hosting of the 1980 summer Olympic games in Moscow. In some ways the staging of this sport spectacle in Moscow was proper because over the past 25 years Soviet athletes had demonstrated excellence both in Olympic and other international competitions. Because the Soviets consider sports competition an extention of ideological competition with "capitalism," they invested much effort and money to make the 1980 summer Olympics in Moscow a resounding success. They built modern sports facilities and new hotels to accommodate the anticipated millions of foreign visitors. They also repainted many historic buildings, provided appropriate decorations of the entire city, stocked all stores with goods, and made arrangements with an American television network to broadcast the events to all corners of the globe. All of these efforts and expenses proved futile, though, because in the wake of Soviet invasion of Afghanistan in late December 1979, American authorities barred their athletes from the 1980 summer games and urged other countries to do the same. As a result of this boycott the Soviet government suffered embarrassment and a substantial financial loss. The absence of American and many other athletes from the games, however, enabled Soviet athletes to win many medals.

RUSSIAN, NON-RUSSIAN, AND RELIGIOUS DISSENT UNDER BREZHNEV

One of the most remarkable developments within the USSR during Brezhnev's rule was the growing demand by an increasing number of Soviet citizens (both Russian and non-Russian) for individual freedom and social justice. This phenomenon—known in historical literature as dissent—was born, as noted in the preceding chapter, under Khrushchev, following his exposure not only of Stalin's crimes and violations of elementary human rights, but, inadvertently, also of the fact that Leninist ideology is riddled with hypocrisy and duplicity. These shocking revelations and the subsequent posthumous purge of Stalin and the rehabilitation of thousands of innocent victims of his terror resulted in reforms and promises as well as in bitterness and skepticism. The sudden removal of Khrushchev, the principal architect of de-Stalinization, and the partial return to discredited Stalinist tactics and methods by Khrushchev's successors created not only fear and cynicism but restlessness, open defiance, and dissent.

The first prominent dissenters under Brezhnev's rule were: Andrei D. Siniavsky, a literary historian and critic, a lecturer at the Gorky Institute of World Literature in Moscow, and author of such widely acclaimed works as *The Trial Begins, The Icicle, The Makepeace Experiment*, and *The Poetry of the Early Revolutionary Days, 1917–1920*; and Yuli M. Daniel, a poet-translator. The two were arrested on September 13, 1965, for allowing some of their works to be published abroad under the pseudonyms of Abram Tertz (Siniavsky) and Nikolai Arzhak (Daniel). During their pre-trial detention the official media denounced both men as traitors to and slanderers of the Soviet state—charges which made the outcome of their trial in February, 1966, a foregone conclusion. Authorities packed the courtroom with carefully selected spectators and surrounded the court building with tough *komsomol* members who prevented even non-Soviet Communist reporters from attending the burlesque. Both men were accused of violating Article 70 of the RSFSR Criminal Code which prohibits "agitation or propaganda carried out with the purpose of subverting or weakening Soviet authority or of committing certain especially dangerous crimes against the state, or circulating for the same purpose slanderous fabrications which defame the Soviet state and social system." Both Siniavsky and Daniel were found guilty and were sentenced to a labor camp for seven- and five-year terms respectively.

The pre-trial publicity, the staged trial, and the unusually harsh sentences shocked world public opinion and thousands of protests were sent to Soviet officials by Communists and non-Communists alike. In the USSR the Siniavsky-Daniel spectacle produced a shock followed by a nationwide wave of antigovernment demonstrations and protests by students, members of the intelligentsia, workers, and even ordinary housewives. It also caused an outpouring of mimeographed resolutions, statements, and articles by clandestine presses. The most remarkable document dealing with the Siniavsky-Daniel affair was *The White Book* by Alexander I. Ginzburg that provided the most comprehensive account of the trial. The unusually sympathetic consideration the two received from their fellow citizens was not only because they had received harsh punishment, but because for the first time in Soviet history the defendants had refused to confess and to acknowledge their guilt.

The dignified and courageous stand of the two had an electrifying effect on many Soviet citizens. Agitation on behalf of Siniavsky's and Daniel's freedom and for repeal of the notorious Article 70 led to the arrest early in 1967 of Vladimir Bukosky, Yurii T. Galanskov, Ginzburg, and several others. Their trial a year later resembled that of Siniavsky and Daniel. The defendants were accused of publishing illegal journals, of maintaining a link with Russian émigré groups, of violating currency regulations, and of possessing copies of two anti-Soviet songs. As expected, they were found guilty and were sentenced to long years of hard labor. Some of the defendants were placed in mental institutions. Like their two predecessors, these defendants also refused to cooperate with officials, rejected the charges against them, and openly challenged the court's procedures, unconstitutional decrees, and the verdict. Because the whole atmosphere of this trial was vindictive and the charges and procedures absurd, they generated a new wave of protests and petitions. The most remarkable aspect of these petitions was that they were signed by people from all walks of life.

Soviet invasion and occupation of Czechoslovakia on August 21, 1968, aroused a new wave of antigovernment protests, including one in Moscow's Red Square. This time security forces beat several of the protesters and arrested and brought to trial the rest. The most prominent of the protesters against Soviet action in Czechoslovakia was former Major-General Piotr G. Grigorenko, once a lecturer at the Frunze Military Academy in Moscow, who for his earlier protest in 1964 against restraints on freedom in the Soviet Union had been demoted in rank and confined for over a year to an insane asylum. In February, 1969, Grigorenko circulated an appeal to the citizens of the USSR in which he denounced Soviet action in Czechoslovakia and pleaded for the withdrawal of Soviet occupation forces. For his effort he was recommitted to the insane asylum. Perhaps because of his military background, Soviet authorities remained deaf to all appeals on his behalf.

While from 1967 to 1970 authorities dealt firmly with all dissenters and sent many to prisons or insane asylums, many new ones appeared on the scene to take their places. The most outstanding and the most forceful were: Solzhenitsyn, author of such celebrated works exposing the Stalinist system as *One Day in the Life of Ivan Denisovich, The First Circle*, and *The Cancer Ward* (the last two were published abroad) for which he was awarded the Nobel Prize for Literature in 1970; and Andrei D. Sakharov, father of Soviet controlled thermonuclear reaction, author of a thought-provoking document entitled *Thoughts on Progress, Peaceful Coexistence and Intellectual Freedom* (1968), Chairman of the Human Rights Committee (formed late in 1970), whose declared aim

Alexander Solzhenitsyn   *Andrei Sakharov*

was to give consultative aid to the organs of power in applying guarantees of the rights of man, and the 1975 recipient of the Nobel Peace
Prize. For his open defiance of Soviet authorities Solzhenitsyn was expelled first from the Writers' Union and later from the country and thus
deprived of the possibility of publishing his works in the USSR. Sakharov
was denied access to research facilities, but as a member of the prestigious
Academy of Sciences of the USSR and a world-renowned scientist, he
temporarily was allowed to keep his office and living quarters in Moscow. In 1981 authorities changed their approach, dispatched Sakharov
to the town of Gorky, and refused to respond to all pleas in his behalf.

The open commitment of the giant of Soviet literature and the giant
of Soviet science to the cause of freedom and human dignity resulted in
the crystallization of two distinct yet closely interrelated oppositions:
the Scientific and the Literary. The Scientific Opposition attracted followers from the academic world, the technological intelligentsia, and
even scientists from the armed forces. Its members advocated the
establishment of a genuine freedom of thought and discussion to solve
the pressing problems facing Soviet society. They pleaded for the end
to bureaucratic despotism and censorship. They favored a liberal democratic reform of the Soviet system based on a multi-party political order.

They criticized the monopoly of the CPSU, dominated and staffed, in Sakharov's words, by "hypocrites and demagogues." They opposed the continued preaching by the party of class struggle and hatred. And they considered as madness and crime the Marxist-Leninist premise that world ideologies and nations must remain incompatible. The relative isolation of the members of the Scientific Opposition from the citizenry at large, and the lack of a free press and an open political forum in which to propagate and disseminate their ideas, prevented the Scientific Opposition from emerging into a meaningful anti-establishment force in the USSR.

Officials dealt quite firmly with members of the Scientific Opposition. They isolated Sakharov; stripped some of Soviet citizenship, including biochemists Zhores A. Medvedev and Valery N. Chalidze; placed many in insane asylums, including mathematician Leonid Pliushch; and dismissed thousands from their jobs. But they also allowed many Jewish scientists to leave the USSR. What impact this harassment of the scientific community and the mass exodus of scientists had on Soviet research and economy is difficult to ascertain at this point. Based on historical examples in other parts of the world one must conclude that it was quite severe, indeed perhaps even crippling.

The Literary Opposition attracted into its midst artists, poets, writers, teachers, musicians, translators, students, and even ordinary workers. Its members sought to expose all inequities and contradictions of the Soviet system. They called for an end to the officially-sponsored reign of terror against all dissenters (Russian and non-Russian) and persecution of ethnic and religious minorities. They also pleaded for the establishment in the USSR of a philosophy and system based on a universal moral law that would be binding on everyone and that would express the eternally valid human values. The Literary Opposition tried to diffuse its goals and ideas in a variety of ways, ranging from protest demonstrations and clandestine publications to smuggling of literary works abroad and defection of its members. The boldest effort of the Literary Opposition was a bimonthly publication entitled *The Chronicle of Current Events*. Until its suppression in 1973, it carried information on the latest arrests, police interrogations, trials, prison conditions, texts of vital documents, letters of protest against official persecution of ethnic and religious minorities, and similar material. In addition, the Literary Opposition published a whole galaxy of the underground *samizdat* (or self-publication) works. Until his deportation from the USSR in late 1973 as a result of writing *The Gulag Archipelago*, a most devastating indictment of the Soviet system, Solzhenitsyn was the spiritual head of the Literary Opposition. Other prominent figures were: Andrei Amalrik, author of an interesting book entitled *Will the Soviet Union Survive Until 1984?*; Pavel Litvinov, grandson of the late Commissar of Foreign

Affairs Maxim Litvinov, who was allowed to leave the USSR; and the courageous Bukovsky who, after many years of imprisonment and isolation, was deported to Switzerland in December, 1976, in exchange for the imprisoned leader of the Chilean Communist Party.

Because it was more vocal, demanding, and annoying than the Scientific Opposition, officials treated members of the Literary Opposition with great brutality. Thousands of its members were dismissed from their jobs and ostracized as enemies of the Soviet state. Many were placed in correctional labor camps—a euphemistic term for concentration camps—some with and some without benefit of trial. The most puzzling and foreboding of such trials occurred in August, 1973, and involved Piotr Yakir, son of one of Stalin's victims of the 1930's, and Victor Krasin. After lengthy confinements and psychological tortures both defendants were tried for violating Article 70 of the RSFSR Criminal Code. To the dismay of most observers both men pleaded guilty and later confessed in a public news conference. For this cooperation both received "mild" sentences—three years' deprivation of freedom plus three years of exile.

After 1973 official treatment of dissenters alternated between threats, warnings, and silent but continuous surveillance. This approach was caused partly by outside pressure and protests, partly by the spirit of détente, and partly by internal pressures. For reasons that are not clear, early in 1977 the CC of the CPSU adopted a tough approach against Soviet domestic dissenters and foreign Communist deviators from the Moscow-dictated tenets. Many dissenters were given "last warnings." Those connected with the Soviet branch of Amnesty International were advised to stop their activities immediately because they were allegedly damaging the interests of the Soviet state. Late in January, 1977, the Soviets imposed the same hard-line Stalinists tenets also on their East European client-states. This toughness of Soviet bureaucratic mind was responsible for a major explosion in Poland in 1980.

In addition to dealing with Russian dissenters, Brezhnev and his associates were forced to cope with an increasing assertive new nationalism among major non-Russian nations and nationalities who, according to the 1979 census, comprised about 53 per cent of the total population in the USSR. The non-Russian nationalism reasserted itself because of pressure from external as well as internal forces. Of the external the most significant seem to have been the rise of a number of new independent states in Asia and Africa out of the ashes of Western colonial empires, and the active encouragement the Chinese in recent years have voiced in behalf of non-Russian minorities. Of the internal forces the most influential seem to have been: (1) the monopoly enjoyed by Great Russians on all top party and government positions; (2) the uninterrupted official pressure to impose Great Russian culture on non-Russian peoples under the guise of spreading Marxism-Leninism; (3) the unwillingness of Moscow's leadership to live up to many promises to non-Russian minorities; and (4) the rise of young educated, articulate, ambitious, but frustrated and hence restless, non-Russian intellectual elites.

The pressure of the new nationalism varied from area to area. Its presence, however, manifested itself in all union republics. Its spokesmen worked for broader political autonomy and greater allocation of investment for local projects. They sought a greater voice in appointments and promotions of local people to local decision-making bodies in order to bring greater response to local needs. They evaded, failed to comply with, or even sabotaged directives of central authorities which they believed were contrary to local interests. They consciously tried to promote local national cultures in order to create for themselves a power base vis-à-vis Moscow and Great Russian nationalism. Finally, they resisted all Russian efforts aimed at linguistic and cultural assimilation.

Because Moscow officials viewed the demands and tactics of non-Russian dissenters as dangerously disruptive, they branded the spokesmen "bourgeois nationalists" and, as in the past, they treated them extremely harshly. During Brezhnev's rule, major purges took place in the following union republics: Estonian, Latvian, Lithuanian, Ukrainian, Armenian, Georgian, Azerbaidzhan, and Kazakh. As they had done in the past, authorities singled out Ukrainians for Draconian oppression. A major wave of arrests swept the country from mid-1965 to early 1966. Most of those arrested were young intellectuals. The subsequent "trials" of some of the arrested became a *cause célèbre* when Viacheslav Chornovil, a journalist and critic officially appointed to cover one of the trials, refused to testify for the prosecution and subsequently wrote a devastating indictment of illegal practices and procedures in the UkSSR. For his exposure Chornovil was arrested in 1967 and sentenced to three years of hard labor.

The Chornovil case brought to light three new prominent Ukrainian dissenters: Sviatoslav Karavansky, who spent over thirty years in Soviet prisons for protesting Russification policy in the Ukraine; Valentyn Moroz, a young historian, who in his *Report From the Beria Reserve* exposed the physical and moral brutality of Soviet labor camps; and Ivan Dziuba, a literary critic and author of a work entitled *Internationalism or Russification?* which argues that the discontent in the Ukraine stemmed primarily from the Russification policies of the Soviet regime. There is evidence that Moscow officials feared Ukrainian unrest during their invasion of Czechoslovakia in August, 1968, and that they also expressed deep concern in 1972 during President Nixon's visit to Moscow and later to Kiev. Apparently because he was unable to control the Ukrainians to Brezhnev's satisfaction, Piotr E. Shelest, First Secretary of the Communist

Party of the UkSSR and member of the Politbureau of the CC of the CPSU, was dismissed in 1973. He was replaced by Vladimir V. Shcherbitsky who immediately put a lid on Ukrainian activity.

Next to restlessness among the Ukrainians, Brezhnev faced serious discontent among the peoples of the Baltic area—the Lithuanians, Latvians, and Estonians. The most celebrated case of protest was in 1971 when Simas Kudirka, a Lithuianian sailor, jumped from a Soviet vessel at sea and was rescued by a United States Coast Guard boat, only to be returned to his ship as a result of cowardly decisions by United States authorities. Kudirka was tried by a Lithuanian court and sentenced to a labor camp but was released in 1974. Later he was allowed to emigrate to the United States after it was established that he had legitimate claims through his mother, who had been a U.S. citizen. A less happy-ending drama took place in May, 1972, when a young Lithuanian, Roman Kalanta, immolated himself in Kaunas in protest against Soviet suppression of national and religious freedom in Lithuania. At about the same time thousands of Lithuanians, Latvians, and Estonians signed petitions condemning Russification and appealed for Western help against Soviet persecution. For obvious reasons no one acted on their appeals.

The best known and the most successful non-Russian dissenters during Brezhnev's rule were the Jews. Until late 1967 Jewish discontent in the USSR was closely linked with the general effervescence among the Soviet intelligentsia. The turning point came at the end of 1967 when, following the Arab-Israeli war, thousands of young and old Soviet Jews suddenly became proud of their heritage and began to demand the right to emigrate to Israel. This request stunned Soviet officialdom, and those who expressed the desire to leave the USSR were immediately dismissed from their jobs and some were even arrested. Nevertheless by early 1977 Soviet authorities had allowed some 125,000 Jews to leave the USSR. Three basic factors assisted this Jewish exodus: their good organization and connections within the USSR; massive support, both official and unofficial, from foreign powers; and the fact that Soviet Jews were the only ethnic group in the USSR that had a country—Israel—willing and eager to receive them. Except for two incidents, exodus of Soviet Jews was quiet. One occurred late in 1970 when a group of Jewish activists tried to "hijack" a Soviet airliner. All eleven involved in this plot were apprehended and brought to trial. Two were sentenced to death, the rest to long years of confinement. The world-wide outcry at this punishment forced Soviet authorities to commute the death sentences to fifteen years of hard labor.

The other incident affecting the Jewish exodus was at the end of 1974 when the Senate of the United States attached the "Jackson Amendment" calling for liberalization of Soviet emigration policy to a bill authorizing credits for the USSR. The Soviets interpreted the Senate's action as an interference in Soviet domestic affairs, rejected American conditional credits, and tightened their restrictions on Jewish emigration. Subsequently the restrictions were modified and the exodus resumed, although on a somewhat smaller scale. But while Brezhnev and his associates placed a damper on non-Russian dissidents through such measures as imprisonment, dismissals, and exodus, they failed to solve the problem. Indeed it appears that as a result of these steps the problem of non-Russian dissent emerged as a major confrontation issue in Soviet domestic politics and only the future will tell the ultimate outcome.

During Brezhnev's rule a number of prominent Soviet citizens defected from the Soviet Union and sought and received political asylum in the West. Without doubt the most celebrated defector was Svetliana Allilueva, Stalin's only daughter, who after settling in the United States in April 1967, published several critically revealing accounts of her life and times in the USSR. Other prominent defectors included: Natalia Makarova, the prima ballerina of the famed Leningrad Kirov Ballet, who was first granted asylum in Great Britain in September, 1970, and who later came to the United States; Mikhail Baryshnikov, the sensational young dancer of the Kirov Ballet who sought and received asylum in Canada in the spring of 1974; and Lieutenant Victor J. Belenko who in September, 1976, flew his MIG25 supersonic fighter plane to Japan and later received political asylum in the United States. While none of these defectors was an active dissenter, their flights nevertheless confirmed the charge that there were many people in the USSR who were dissatisfied with official Soviet policies.

Last, but by no means an insignificant dissent during Brezhnev's rule was religious. The real impact of the religious dissent is difficult to assess because of its close link with the ethnic dissent (Russian-Orthodox, Jewish-Hebrew, Lithuanian-Catholic, Ukrainian-Uniate, and Turkic-Moslem), and because no figures are available on religious dissenters. Yet judged by the fact that about one-third of the *samizdat* publications were of religious material, one must conclude that religious dissent was a major concern for the Brezhnev regime. All evidence indicates that the religious dissent attracted the disillusioned young people who sought to discover truth, moral values, justice, honesty, and civil rights. The first to voice concern about the lack of religious freedom in the USSR were Soviet Baptists. The credit for articulating religious concerns, however, belongs to two Orthodox priests of Moscow, who in late 1965 wrote letters to Patriarch Alexei and Chairman of the Presidium of the Supreme Soviet, Podgorny. In them they criticized official interference in religious matters; deplored the closing of churches and monasteries; and condemned numerous restrictions on the freedom of religious worship and religious practices; complained about government restrictions on religious education; and lamented the submission of the patriarchate to the wishes of the government. Subsequently the leadership of the Orthodox Church received petitions from numerous dissenters, including Solzhenitsyn and Sakharov, asking that it involve itself in the civil rights movement and above all that it speak out against government persecution of religious and civil rights defenders in the USSR. It is sad to report that to date (December, 1983) the response of the leadership of the Orthodox Church has been very insignificant.

Generally speaking, until early 1977 dissent in the USSR remained largely an internal affair and, except for periodic Israeli protests on behalf of Soviet Jews, no foreign statesmen voiced any concern about it in public. That condition changed with the inauguration of Jimmy E. Carter as President of the United States. Carter, who campaigned on moral and humane approaches to domestic and international politics, formally announced that continued Soviet harassment of dissidents conflicted both with the spirit and the letter of the 1975 Helsinki Agreement, as well as with the accepted international standards of human rights. The Soviets immediately responded with the arrest of Ginzburg and the expulsion of a Russian-speaking AP reporter, George Krimsky. Carter expressed deep regret over Soviet actions, reconfirmed his commitment to the humane approach to politics, separated that issue from all other pressing problems troubling Soviet-American relations, and, to emphasize his deep concern about the plight of Soviet dissidents, in mid-February 1977, sent a personal letter to Sakharov. That unprecedented action brought an instant Soviet protest and it also resulted in increased vigilance in the Soviet Union and throughout Soviet-dominated Eastern Europe. The sudden transformation of the dissident problem into a *cause célèbre* did not put the two superpowers on a military collision course. It only indicated that the scheduled thirty-five nation review of the Helsinki Agreement in Belgrade in 1977 and in Madrid in 1982–3 would be emotion packed events.

BASIC PROVISIONS OF THE 1977 CONSTITUTION

On June 4, 1977, Soviet authorities published a draft text of a new constitution for nationwide public comment. The document (designed to replace the "Stalin Constitution" of 1936) was prepared by a special commission that had worked on it since 1962, and it was formally adopted by a special session of the Supreme Soviet on October 7, 1977. The fact that it took so long to complete suggests that before its release the final document had gone through many changes and compromises to satisfy various interest groups of Soviet politics.

The new constitution (the fourth since the Bolshevik seizure of power in Russia in 1917) consists of a lengthy preamble and 174 articles grouped into 21 chapters. Generally speaking, it is a fairly moderate document; that is, it is neither Stalinist nor anti-Stalinist. Its preamble emphasizes continuity, stability and accomplishments of the Soviet regime, both at home and abroad. It stresses that the USSR has achieved "a society of true democracy" and a society of the entire Soviet people. The new constitution defines the USSR as "a socialist state of the entire people," who possess all power, which they exercise through "the Soviet Peoples' Deputies" (Article 2). At the same time it singles out the CPSU as the leading and guiding force of Soviet society and the nucleus of its political system, of all state and public organizations, and as the principal formulator of Soviet domestic and foreign policies (Article 6).

The new constitution recognizes three types of property ownership in the USSR: 1) *state or socialist ownership*, which includes land, minerals, waters, forests, the basic means of production, means of transport and communication, banks, public utilities, most urban housing and the property of state-run trade organizations; 2) *property of collective farms and other cooperatives*, which they can use wisely and thriftily in perpetuity; and 3) *personal or private property:* articles of daily use, a house, earned savings, and small plots of land, provided they are used rationally and do not produce unearned income. The state controls and determines the work, compensation, and taxes of every individual in the USSR "in accordance with the principle of socialism: 'From each according to his ability, to each according to his work.'" This task is not too difficult to realize since the economy is managed and directed on the basis of state plans (Articles 10–18).

Like its predecessor, the new constitution identifies three social groups living in an "unbreakable alliance": workers, peasants and intelligentsia "of all the nations and nationalities of the USSR." It also declares that in accordance with the communist ideal—"The free development of each is the condition of the free development of all"—the state works at various levels to enhance the "social homogeneity of society," working conditions, educational opportunities, and to improve income, social security, medical facilities, communal services, cultural institutions, vocational training, uniform system of public education, sport, scientific research and professional, and amateur and folk arts (Articles 19–27).

The new constitution lists numerous basic rights and freedoms which, in theory, Soviet citizens enjoy. These can be grouped into three categories: 1) *Economic rights:* the right to work and hence guaranteed employment, rest and leisure, housing, health protection, maintenance in old age, sickness or disability, elementary and secondary education, the right to choose a profession or trade, and guaranteed freedom of scientific, technical and artistic work; 2) *Civil liberties:* the right of free speech, press, association, assembly, public meetings, demonstrations, religious and anti-religious beliefs, inviolability of person and home, privacy of correspondence and telephone and telegraphic communications, and equal rights before the law without distinction of origin, social or property status, race or nationality, sex, education, language, occupation, domicile or other status; 3) *Participatory rights:* the right to vote and be elected, the right to praise and criticize the activity of public officials, and the right to lodge complaints and even to sue government agencies and officials for illegal actions that resulted in damage and to expect compensation (Articles 33–58).

The current constitution makes it abundantly clear that the enjoyment of all these rights and freedoms is based on two conditions: First, that they are in no way detrimental to the interests of Soviet society or the state, or that they do not infringe on the rights of other citizens. But what is detrimental is decided not by the recipient, but by the benefactor of these rights and freedoms. Since the CPSU enjoys an absolute monopoly of power and controls and determines everything, the party then decides what the interests, needs, desires and aspirations of the people are. In actual practice, therefore, this means that Soviet citizens have the right to vote for party-sponsored candidates, to glorify party policies, to participate in party-controlled meetings, and to acclaim the party leaders. In other words, now, as in the past, they have the right to say "yes" to everything the CPSU says or does, but they are not allowed to say "no."

Second, to enjoy these constitutional rights and freedoms all Soviet citizens also have numerous constitutional duties and obligations. These include the duty to "comply with the standards of socialist conduct"; to work conscientiously and to observe labor discipline strictly; to preserve and protect socialist property and to combat its misappropriation and squandering; to safeguard the interests of the USSR and to enhance its power and prestige (the constitution views "betrayal of the motherland" as the gravest of crimes); to serve in the armed forces of the USSR; to strengthen friendship among Soviet nations and nationalities; to respect the rights of other Soviet citizens; to help maintain public order and combat anti-social behavior of others; to raise their children for socially useful work; to have concern for the ecology, conservation of natural resources and the preservation of historical and cultural monuments; and to work with citizens of other countries in promoting friendship and world peace (Articles 59–69).

Almost all of the highest bodies of state power and administration have retained the same names under the new constitution. Thus, the highest legislative body in the USSR is the Supreme Soviet, composed of two co-equal chambers: the *Soviet of the Union,* whose members are "elected by constituencies with equal populations"; and the *Soviet of Nationalities,* whose members represent the following nationality units: 32 deputies from each union republic, 11 deputies from each autonomous republic, 5 deputies from each autonomous region, and 1 deputy from each autonomous area (Articles 108–110). Under the provisions of the current constitution, all members of the Supreme Soviet are elected for a period of five years. In reality, however, presently as well as previously, all are selected by the leadership of the CPSU on the basis of loyalty to the current leadership as well as efficiency in their place of work.

The current constitution specifies that the Supreme Soviet of the USSR "shall be convened twice a year," as well as in special sessions. The infrequency of its meetings, the enormous size of its membership, and the short length of its sessions are clear indicators that the competence of this highest Soviet legislative body remains very limited. It seems, indeed, that the 1977 constitution stripped the Supreme Soviet of many of its former powers and delegated them to the Presidium of the Supreme Soviet, which currently consists of a Chairman, First Vice-Chairman, 15 Vice-Chairmen (one from each Union Republic), a Secretary, and 21 members—all of whom are high-ranking members of the CPSU.

Under the present constitution the Presidium of the Supreme Soviet has the following powers: to set the date of elections and to convene sessions of the Supreme Soviet; to coordinate the work of all committees of the Supreme Soviet; to interpret the laws of the USSR; to ratify and abrogate international treaties; to revoke all decisions of the Council of Ministers of the USSR; to institute military and diplomatic ranks and honorary titles; to grant and remove citizenship; to grant asylum, amnesty and pardons; to appoint and recall all Soviet diplomatic representatives; to receive and expel all foreign diplomats; to appoint and dismiss the high command of the Armed Forces of the USSR; to proclaim martial law and to order general or partial mobilization; and to exercise all "other powers vested in it by the constitution and laws of the USSR" (Articles 120–122).

Another very important body of state power in the USSR under the current constitution is the Council of Ministers. This highest executive and administrative agency currently consists of the Chairman of the Council of Ministers, several First- and Vice-Chairmen, Ministers and Chairmen of various state committees. In theory, all of these officials are responsible and accountable either to the Supreme Soviet or to its Presidium. Actually, however, since all are members of the CPSU, they are accountable to the leadership of the CPSU. The constitutional competence of this body is very broad. Among other things it encompasses: the direction of economic, social, and cultural development; the promotion of the well-being of the people; the development of education; the insurance of rational utilization of the country's natural resources; the control of the monetary and credit system, uniform prices, wages, social security and insurance; the organization and management of industrial, agricultural and communications enterprises; the development of current and long-term economic plans and budgets; the protection of socialist property; the maintenance of public order and state security; the protection of citizens' rights and freedoms; the general direction of the Armed Forces of the USSR; the control of foreign trade; and Soviet economic, scientific, technical and cultural ties with other countries (Articles 128–136).

Although the 1977 constitution describes the USSR as an "integral, federal, multinational state formed on the principle of socialist federalism," Article 73 has delegated the following functions and jurisdictions to central authorities: admission of new republics to the USSR and endorsement of the formation of new autonomous republics and regions; establishment of the general principles, organization and functioning of local units of authority; maintenance of the uniformity of law throughout the USSR, as well as a uniform social and economic policy, the main directions of education, utilization of natural resources and conservation; the drafting and approval of state plans for economic, social and cultural development; the drafting and approval of uniform budget, credit system, taxes, prices and wages; the direction of all sections of the economy; the issues of war and peace, defense of the USSR; representation of the USSR in international relations; and control over the observance and the interpretation of the constitution of the USSR. So comprehensive, indeed, is the jurisdiction of the USSR that it excludes the possibility of any independent action by a union or autonomous republic or by any national administrative unit. The elimination of all possible attributes of sovereignty of any state has not prevented the current constitution from proclaiming that each union republic "shall have the right to secede freely from the USSR" and that each "has the right to enter into relations with other states, conclude treaties with them, exchange diplomatic and consular representatives, and take part in the work of international organizations" (Articles 72 and 80).

SOVIET MISADVENTURE IN CZECHOSLOVAKIA IN 1968

Khrushchev had his Hungary in 1956; Brezhnev had his Czechoslovakia in 1968. Although the two crises were separated by twelve years they had a number of interesting similarities. Both were brought on by Soviet policies that were carried out by incompetent but arrogant native leaders; both sought to introduce a progressive and humane element into the Communist way of life; both were brutally suppressed by Soviet military might while the rest of the civilized world watched helplessly; and both were forced to accept Soviet-appointed satraps—Janos Kadar in Hungary, and Gustav Husak in Czechoslovakia.

The architect of the Czechoslovak crisis of 1968 was Antonin Novotny, an orthodox Stalinist, who, as First Secretary of the Czechoslovak Communist Party and President of the republic, had supervised Soviet interests in Czechoslovakia since 1953. He and a handful of his incompetent bureaucrats created economic chaos, paralyzed all efforts to rehabilitate victims of Stalinist terror, set aside all pleas for reform, rejected all complaints against shortcomings and bureaucratic indifference and arrogance, and refused to consider Slovak demands for more effective self-government. At the end of 1967 anti-Novotny forces within the party's central committee united, and early in January, 1968, forced him to resign as the party's First Secretary. This all-important post went to Alexander Dubček, Soviet-educated but reform-minded First Secretary of the Slovak Communist Party.

For the record at least, Soviet leaders remained "neutral" during this phase of the Czechoslovak crisis, even though Brezhnev came to Prague in early December, 1967, at Novotny's invitation. Initially, too, the change in leadership in Prague gave the Soviets no great cause for concern, since Dubček had received his political training in the Soviet Union. Moreover, after assuming his new duties Dubček announced that he intended to move gradually and carefully to attain the Czechoslovak style of democratic socialism. But gradualness and modernization became impossible. The change in leadership unleashed powerful pressures throughout Czechoslovakia for reform in all aspects of life. The most urgent plea came for the abolishment of "the centralist model of society," the elimination of "administrative and undemocratic interference in all spheres of social and cultural life," and the removal of Novotny as president of the republic.

The latter was realized on March 30, 1968, when the National Assembly accepted Novotny's resignation request, and by secret ballot selected General Ludvik Svoboda, the much decorated hero of World War II, as the new chief of state. Because other demands were more complex they were treated with caution. Nevertheless the Dubček-Svoboda leadership committed itself to reorganize the Czechoslovak judicial system and the electoral laws, and to examine grievances of the victims of past persecutions. For obvious reasons the Soviets became alarmed by this commitment and to express their displeasure they ordered extensive troop movements along Czechoslovakia's eastern frontiers, and, in violation of a pledge not to interfere in Czechoslovakia's domestic affairs, they induced their East German clients to sound the first alarm.

On April 15, 1968, the new Czechoslovak leadership countered Soviet moves with the adoption of "the Action Program." This document solemnly re-emphasized Czechoslovak determination to develop "an advanced socialist society rid of class antagonisms," to offer an "opportunity for dignified human life, comradely relations of mutual cooperation

Czechoslovak youths protesting the Soviet invasion, August, 1968. The banner they are carrying reads: "Never Again with the Soviet Union."

among people, and free scope for the development of human personality," and to discard the obsolete, discredited, and harsh methods of the past. The Action Program pledged Czechoslovakia's continued, undeviating adherence to the Warsaw Pact, to COMECON, and to close cooperation with the Soviet Union. Soviet leaders, however, refused to accept these assurances. In April and early May, 1968, they sent several military and political delegations demanding that Czechoslovaks drastically alter their liberal direction and that they allow the Soviets the right to station troops in Czechoslovakia.

In an apparent effort to demonstrate the seriousness of their concern, early in June, 1968, Soviet leaders ordered "staff exercises" of Soviet, East German, Polish, Hungarian, and Bulgarian forces on Czechoslovak territory, and they also unleashed a bitter press denunciation of selected associates of Dubček. The Czechoslovaks countered Soviet moves by promulgating on June 26, 1968, a law that formally abolished censorship. This step, which caused the resignation and/or dismissal of many die-hard Czechoslovak Stalinists, created a demand for a thorough unbiased investigation of all past misdeeds by Czechoslovak and Soviet authorities in Czechoslovakia, and especially the mystery surrounding the March 10, 1948, death of former Minister of Foreign Affairs Jan Masaryk.

Faced with Czechoslovak intransigence, Brezhnev and his associates refused to withdraw the "staff exercise" troops from Czechoslovakia and in mid-July invited Dubček and his collaborators to attend an interrogation by Warsaw Pact representatives in Warsaw. Because the Czechoslovaks refused to participate in the inquisition, the Soviets and their East European clients sent them a letter of unparalleled insult. This crude attempt at intimidation instantly unified the Czechoslovak people behind Dubček. Outmaneuvered by their own blunders, the Soviets now requested bilateral talks. The first were held at the end of July at Cierna, a town just two miles from the Soviet-Czechoslovak border, but they brought no solution. The second were staged on August 3, in Bratislava, capital of Slovakia. Here the Soviets produced a broad statement of principles which then was signed by all members of the Warsaw Pact except Romania. This document committed all signatories to defend "the socialist gains," to uphold "democratic centralism," to struggle against antisocialist forces, to cooperate closely with each other, and to respect each others' independence, territorial integrity, and sovereignty. The Czechoslovaks interpreted their own signature of the document as adherence to and full compliance with all Soviet demands. The Soviets considered it a carte blanche for intervention in Czechoslovakia in order to preserve the Soviet style of socialism. The last-minute efforts of Yugoslav and Romanian leaders to mediate the obvious differences failed. The stage was thus set for Soviet military invasion of Czechoslovakia.

The invasion came on August 21, 1968. Soviet forces were accompanied by East German, Polish, Hungarian, and Bulgarian units. Militarily, the entire operation was brilliantly executed. Within hours the invading forces occupied the entire country and arrested and deported to Moscow leading reformist politicians, including Dubček. This action stunned the civilized world, but most of all it dumbfounded the Czechoslovaks, who had for years entertained strong Pan-Slav sentiments and to some extent pro-Soviet views. So complete indeed was their shock and bewilderment that the Soviets were unable to find anyone willing to collaborate with them. On August 23, President Svoboda flew to Moscow where he demanded the release of the imprisoned Czechoslovak leaders and threatened suicide if the Soviets failed to comply with his request. Surprisingly, they complied.

On August 26 the Soviets imposed on the freed Czechoslovaks a new sixteen-point agreement. Under its terms the Soviets promised not to interfere in Czechoslovak internal affairs, pledged to cooperate with Czechoslovakia on the basis of "mutual respect and equality," forced the Czechoslovaks to stop harassment of the pro-Soviet party sympathizers, and committed the Czechoslovaks to sign a new treaty of friendship that would guarantee the stationing of Soviet forces on Czechoslovak territory. On the same day they imposed Carthaginian terms on Czechoslovakia, the Soviets also succeeded in attracting Gustav Husak, a Slovak Communist, to collaborate with them, creating the first cleavage in the hitherto unified Czechoslovak stand.

Husak's willingness to play "Russian roulette," coupled with the presence of Soviet forces in Czechoslovakia, assured Brezhnev that the Dubček leadership would have a brief tenure. Early in October, 1968, the Soviets launched a massive antireformist campaign, and on October 16, Kosygin arrived in Prague to sign the agreement on the stationing of Soviet forces in Czechoslovakia. Under Soviet pressure Dubček now intensified censorship of the press and agreed to appoint pro-Soviet sympathizers to high posts in the party and government. Most alarmed by these changes were university students. Because their protests failed to arouse national concern, Husak and other Czechoslovak Stalinists, supported by the Soviets, slowly regained the upper hand. Early in 1969 they launched an intensified "anti-rightist" drive. They were greatly assisted in their efforts by Dubček's irresoluteness and by the March 28, 1969, jubilant anti-Soviet demonstrations throughout Czechoslovakia following the defeat in Stockholm of the Soviet ice hockey team by the Czechoslovak team. That outburst sealed Dubček's fate. On April 17, 1969, he was forced to relinquish his post of First Secretary of the Czechoslovak Communist Party to Husak, who soon brought Czechoslovakia to the bosom of Brezhnev's neo-Stalinist colonial brotherhood. With Soviet blessing Husak transformed Czechoslovakia into the most reactionary and the most oppressive state of Eastern Europe.

FROM KABUL TO WARSAW

In addition to entanglement in Czechoslovakia in 1968, Brezhnev and his government became deeply involved in Afghanistan in 1979 and in Poland in 1980–81. Both the latter involvements left a very far-reaching imprint on Soviet domestic and foreign policy. The embroilment in Afghanistan commenced on December 28, 1979, when Soviet land and air forces (some 100,000 strong) crossed the Afghani border, seized control of the principal highways linking the USSR with Afghanistan, occupied Kabul (the capital) and other key strategic towns, and imposed on Afghanistan a puppet government headed by an Afghani politician named Karmal Babrak. The available evidence suggests that Soviet invasion of Afghanistan was not a spur-of-the-moment decision. It was well-planned militarily and politically. The Soviets began to concentrate their military forces along the Afghani frontier as early as September, 1979, and also at about that time they approached Babrak (who was in Prague, Czechoslovakia), gained his cooperation, and brought him to Kabul with their invading armies.

What the real designs in Afghanistan were is not clear. Publicly, Soviet officials offered two justifications: 1) that Babrak had requested their military presence in Afghanistan in order to preserve his country for socialism, which allegedly was threatened by the United States and China; and 2) that the threat to Afghanistan was also a threat to the USSR. The Soviets emphasized that they would withdraw their military forces as soon as all external interference in Afghanistan's affairs ceased. Because this justification of Soviet invasion was not very convincing, no one outside, and perhaps very few people inside the USSR accepted it. So shocking indeed was the invasion that the United Nations Assembly condemned it repeatedly during its annual sessions. That invasion exerted a profound influence also on Soviet-American and Soviet-Chinese relations.

There is no quick or easy answer as to what compelled the Soviets to intervene in Afghanistan. Until that time they had had friendly relations with Afghanistan and, in fact, had made a substantial financial and economic investment in the country. It seems that the turning point came in April, 1978, when the government of President Sardar Mohammad Daoud was overthrown in a bloody coup by a pro-Soviet military clique headed by Nur Mohammad Taraki. On December 5, 1978, the USSR signed a twenty-year treaty of friendship and cooperation with the Taraki government, and in September, 1979, they applauded him as one of their spokesmen at the conference of non-aligned nations in Havana. In return for this support and trust, Taraki introduced many Soviet political, economic, social and cultural institutions and the Soviet way of life in Afghanistan.

Because his Sovietization of Afghanistan was too precipitous, Taraki was murdered at the end of September, 1979, by the ambitious Deputy Premier and Foreign Minister Hafizollah Amin. Initially the Soviets accepted Amin as their "man in Kabul." Apparently, however, when he revealed that he was receptive to establishing good relations with China and closer ties with the Islamic revolutionary government of Ayatollah Khomeini in Iran, Soviet advisors murdered Amin. And to safeguard the Soviet economic investment in Afghanistan (as well as to prevent the country from becoming an extension of the hostile Chinese or Iranian revolutionary movement), they invaded the country and imposed a government headed by Babrak. The Afghani, obviously, did not approve Soviet action, and following the entry of Soviet forces, the country was engulfed in a civil as well as an anti-Soviet war that resulted in many human casualties and enormous material damage caused by the indiscriminate Soviet bombardment of villages and towns.

All countries of the non-Soviet world condemned Soviet behavior and activity in Afghanistan. However, efforts to solve the problem (by the United Nations and other interested parties) were fruitless because of Soviet intransigence. They expressed willingness to withdraw their forces only on two conditions: 1) If the rest of the world would accept the Babrak government not only as *de facto* but *de jure* government for Afghanistan; and 2) If all outside interference in Afghanistan (except Soviet) would end. Because no country accepted these harsh conditions, there was no end to Soviet occupation and bombing of Afghanistan and to the suffering and displacement of millions of innocent victims.

Concurrently with the Soviet military invasion of Afghanistan, Brezhnev and his associates faced a critical problem in Poland. Because it had many deep and diverse roots, the crisis there was potentially more dangerous to Soviet interests. It was a historic challenge, pitting Poles against Russians. It was a cultural confrontation between Roman Catholics and Russian Orthodox and Atheists. It was a massive withdrawal by Polish workers from the Soviet-imposed labor unions—hence an "ideological deviation." It was a protest against and an exposé of corruption of top Polish officials loyal to the USSR. It was a resistance to Soviet control and exploitation for Soviet ends of Polish economy, politics and destiny. And, finally, it was a serious problem to the security of the USSR and to its interests throughout Eastern and Central Europe.

While the 1980–81 crisis in Poland had deep and diverse roots, it had begun to gain momentum in the late 1960s. It was precipitated by the following major developments: 1) the growing nationwide disillusionment with the government's policies; 2) the government's failure to introduce genuine and desperately-needed economic reforms that would improve the low and precarious living standard; 3) the growing tension between political and religious leaders, which culminated in the government's refusal to allow Pope Paul VI to visit Poland in 1966 to help commemorate the millennium of Polish Catholicism; 4) the arrest and trial of several young party intellectuals who were critical of the official establishment and its policies; 5) the government's stoppage (at the end of January, 1968) of a theater production of a poetic drama, *Dziady* (Forefathers), by Adam Mickiewicz, a 19th century Polish romanticist, because of its anti-Russian line; and 6) the nationwide student unrest in March, 1968, which authorities put down with excessive force.

The growing discontent accelerated in mid-December, 1970, when, in an effort to bring prices more in line with the real cost of production and to reduce the government's huge subsidies for food, the officials announced a series of steep price increases. Because the announcement was made on the eve of Christmas shopping, it provoked immediate protests, work stoppages and demonstrations. The greatest unrest occurred in the Baltic ports of Gdansk and Szczecin, where the protesters set fire to many public buildings, including party headquarters. In several cities police opened fire on the demonstrators. The resulting casualties aroused great indignation throughout the country and brought Poland close to a nationwide working-class insurrection. These events produced the following two significant developments: 1) a list of twenty-one demands by the Szczecin strikers calling for, among other things, the establishment of "independent trade unions under the authority of the working class"; and 2) the replacement of Wladyslaw Gomulka (in power since 1956) by Edward Gierek, a former coal miner and, at the time, a party secretary in industrial Upper Silesia.

Gierek restored normalcy through unprecedented personal meetings with the protesters in their place of work and through a whole series of innovations and promises. These included: 1) a pledge to improve living standards and official willingness to listen to peoples' complaints and not to interfere in their lives; and 2) a commitment to rapid industrialization of the country. To achieve the first goal Gierek granted large wage increases to workers; rescinded the announced increases in food prices; started a massive housing program; removed many restrictions on travel within and outside the country; reformed local administration; and established good rapport with Polish communities outside Poland (especially in the U.S. and Canada), encouraging them to retire in Poland. In pursuit of the second goal, Gierek tried to decentralize industrial management; sought increased credits, food and raw materials in the USSR; and borrowed huge amounts of money from the West (West Germany, France, England, Sweden, Japan and the United States).

For a time Gierek's scheme worked well. However, by the mid 1970s, signs of trouble became visible. Thanks to world-wide inflation (caused by the rising oil prices in the aftermath of the Arab-Israeli war of 1973), the cost of Poland's industrialization drive (based on and geared to Western industrial imports) climbed almost vertically. In 1975 the debt to the West stood at over 6 billion and in 1979 it reached 18 billion dollars. To cope with this skyrocketing cost of industrialization, on June 24, 1976, the government announced price increases for food and other consumer goods. The public responded by immediate protests, mass demonstrations and, in some places, by looting and vandalism of government enterprises.

To avoid nationwide violence similar to that which had toppled Gomulka from power in 1970, Gierek withdrew the announced price increases for further study. This step was ill-advised, for it exposed the government's weakness and hence emboldened its opponents. There soon emerged numerous unofficial opposition groups that flooded the country with bulletins critical of the regime. Authorities harassed these critics, but they failed to use full repressive force to silence them. Instead, they tried to solve the problem by reducing the country's reliance on imports of Western technology, by switching to the production of consumer goods for the domestic market, and by encouraging "capitalist" farming.

All of these efforts were shattered on October 16, 1978, when Cardinal Karol Wojtyla, Archbishop of Cracow, was elected Pope (John

Paul II). This extraordinary event restored national pride and self-confidence in every Pole, heartened all opposition groups, and put enormous pressure on Polish as well as Soviet authorities. To obvious Soviet displeasure, Polish authorities were forced to send a congratulatory message to the new Pope in Rome and to invite that "son of the Polish nation" to visit his homeland. The visit took place in June, 1979, and it was a resounding success. About one fourth of the country's population turned out in person to greet the Polish Pope. Because the flawless arrangements were made by the church and its allies and supporters, they made the country's political situation very delicate, even though there were no open outbreaks of anti-Soviet or anti-communist sentiments.

John Paul II's visit to Poland in 1979 contributed to events of the summer of 1980. Other factors worked in the same direction. One of these was the October, 1979 release of a report by an officially-appointed panel that was critical of various policies, including censorship and privileges enjoyed by the party elite. The other was the public acknowledgment by Gierek and his associates, at the Eighth Congress of the Polish United Workers' Party (PUWP), in February, 1980, that the country's economy was in a disastrous condition. These revelations prompted many workers to redouble their organizing activity, and they did this in spite of official harassment. On July 1, 1980, when the government announced price increases on food, the simmering discontent began to burgeon. The measure prompted uncoordinated but devastating strikes and work stoppages throughout the country. By August 8, 1980, some 150 plants were affected. Authorities refused to rescind the announced price increases, but at the same time publicly acknowledged that the shortages were growing worse. This revelation heightened tensions and led to a strike at the Lenin Shipyard in Gdansk on August 14, and the appearance on the scene of a charismatic leader named Lech Walesa. Within a few days the strike spread throughout the entire Baltic coast area and was hailed throughout the rest of Poland.

Because it was a massive movement the authorities did not know how to handle it. Some spokesmen urged firmness; others advised some accommodation to the strikers' demands, which included increases in wages, family allowances, earlier retirement, better food, the honoring of those killed by police in 1970, the right to form independent trade unions free from government interference, some access to the communications media and release of influential political prisoners. On August 31, 1980, after considering many drafts and amendments, the two sides signed an agreement in Gdansk that set a precedent for similar agreements in other industrial centers and gave birth to the Solidarity movement.

The sudden appearance of a massive independent trade union movement that began to attract members from the government-controlled-and-manipulated unions alarmed Soviet officials and their close allies in

Poland and Eastern Europe. The first victim of this alarm was Gierek, who suffered a political heart attack in December, 1980, and was replaced by Stanislaw Kania as First Secretary of the PUWP. Kania tried to assure everyone that Poland would reestablish normalcy soon. That was impossible because workers and especially students and intellectuals, fresh from their triumph, turned towards greater radicalism, began to press for higher wages, increased their complaints against and criticism of local authorities and resorted to sporadic uncoordinated strikes. This behavior, of course, aggravated the country's fragile economic situation. In the summer of 1980, the USSR offered Poland credits worth 550 million dollars; West Germany offered about 670 million; and the U.S. recommended 900 million dollars in agricultural credits. By November, 1980, Poland's foreign debt stood at 25 billion dollars.

The growing boldness of Polish workers and their defiance of authorities, coupled with the grave economic situation, caused the Soviets to act again. In late October, 1980, they invited Kania to Moscow for discussions and at about the same time exerted strong pressure on Poland through their East German, Czechoslovak and Bulgarian clients. This brought instant results. The Polish government threatened to draft workers into the army in the event of strikes. They expelled several foreign journalists, and a nationwide TV program showed maneuvers of Soviet tanks. In late November, 1980, *Izvestiia* warned that the USSR would not tolerate any interference with their rail communications with Soviet forces in East Germany, and early in December the Soviets summoned all East European leaders to a summit meeting in Moscow to work out a common policy for dealing with the situation in Poland. They also held a series of discussions with Polish and other East European spokesmen during the Twenty-fifth Congress of the CPSU in March, 1981.

During the spring and summer of 1981, as conditions in Poland continued to deteriorate, Soviet alarm increased. They responded with massive maneuvers of land, air and naval forces along the Polish frontiers and joint exercises with Polish units. They and their two loyal satellites (Czechoslovakia and East Germany) closed their frontiers with Poland. Allegations were made also that Soviet authorities were indirectly involved in the May 13, 1981 assassination attempt on the Pope. NATO governments took notice of these actions and, through official and public channels, advised the Soviets to keep out of Polish internal problems. That was impossible because events in Poland, if allowed to continue, presented a potential threat to existing Soviet control not only of Eastern Europe but of the USSR itself. On June 12, 1981, therefore, the CC of the CPSU sent a long letter to their Polish "comrades" expressing great displeasure with Polish inability to regain control of the country.

Intoxicated by their earlier triumphs, Solidarity disregarded the

Soviet warning, as evidenced by their failure to take precautions. With Soviet approval and assistance the Polish authorities prepared a secret plan of action against Solidarity. The man in charge of the operation was General Wojciech Jaruzelski, the newly-appointed first secretary of the PUWP. Forces under his command (army and militia) executed the secret plan with efficiency and ferocity. Within hours after Jaruzelski declared martial law, not only were most leaders of Solidarity arrested, but thousands of union militants, intellectuals, journalists and active sympathizers found themselves in prisons or in detention camps. Polish authorities also crushed all resistance, suspended all trade unions, occupied all Solidarity offices, confiscated the union's property, and subsequently they formally outlawed the Solidarity movement. To keep the rest of the world in darkness, Jaruzelski severed all communication with the outside world. For his efficiency in the operation, the Soviet Government bestowed the Order of Lenin on Jaruzelski and invited him to be a guest speaker commemorating the 60th anniversary of the formal launching of the USSR. In the course of 1982 and 1983, many detained Solidarity members were freed, including Walesa, and some restrictions were eased. In June, 1983, Jaruzelski allowed Pope John II to visit his homeland again (such a visit was not allowed in 1982) and on July 22, 1983 martial law was formally lifted while many of its provisions were retained. On October 5, 1983, the Polish people were heartened and their masters stunned by the announcement that Walesa was recipient of the 1983 Nobel Peace Prize.

SOVIET FOREIGN POLICY UNDER BREZHNEV

Soviet foreign policy under Brezhnev was to a remarkable degree a continuation of that of Khrushchev. And like Khrushchev's, in its quest for protecting and expanding the interests of the territorial base of the revolution, Brezhnev's foreign policy made some impressive gains and it suffered severe setbacks. In the Far East, China commanded the continuous attention of Brezhnev and his associates. Three basic factors were responsible: the unparalleled intensity of Chinese distaste for Soviet leaders and their policies; the size and nature of China's potential military threat to the USSR; and Soviet insistence that military might be the final arbiter of the destinies of all Communist states.

It was noted in the preceding chapter that Sino-Soviet relations deteriorated dramatically during the last years of Khrushchev's rule. His ouster did not improve the situation. A day after Brezhnev replaced him, the Chinese added a new dimension to their dialogue with the Soviets by successfully detonating their first atomic device. A few weeks later Chou En-lai visited Moscow for "frank" and "comradely" talks. Because to date (October, 1983) neither side has revealed the content of these conversations it is impossible to know what actually was discussed. Subsequent developments indicated that both sides retained their earlier views of each other—a situation that precluded the establishment of any meaningful dialogue between the two great Communist powers. In fact, after 1965 relations between the two giants deteriorated to a breaking point.

Sino-Soviet relations became very strained early in 1965 by the increased military involvement of the United States in South Vietnam and their bombing of selected targets in North Vietnam. To make their own military assistance to North Vietnam effective, in April, 1965, the Soviets asked the Chinese for the right to use some airfields in Southwestern China (and the right to station Soviet forces on them); for a free air corridor, or air transit rights; for permission to send Soviet forces to North Vietnam through China; and for the right to use port facilities in Southern China. While this request was reasonable, it did imply the establishment of a more or less permanent Soviet military presence in China. Some of Mao Tse-tung's associates supported the requests. Others, especially Mao, opposed it. This split within the Chinese leadership over the Soviet request set the stage for Mao's purge of his opponents and critics, and it also unleashed his celebrated "Cultural Revolution" of 1966–1967.

During the "Cultural Revolution" Sino-Soviet relations went from bad to worse. The Chinese, for example, rejected the Soviet invitation to attend the Twenty-third Congress of the CPSU (March 29–April 8, 1966). Both sides soon limited their diplomatic representations to the chargé d'affaires level. Both sides, too, resumed vicious verbal attacks that surpassed in intensity all of their earlier duels. So bitter, indeed, became their polemic that in late November, 1966, *Pravda* announced in a long editorial that Soviet leaders were prepared to do everything possible to overcome Mao's policies. Mao responded to this challenge with a three-week siege early in 1967 of the Soviet embassy in Peking by the Young Red Guards, who subjected Soviet diplomatic personnel to abusive treatment. The Soviets retaliated with their own siege of the Chinese embassy in Moscow, and they also unleashed an aggressive shortwave radio campaign designed to foment unrest inside China. Using various Chinese dialects they incited Chinese peasants and workers to sabotage and armed resistance, and they also encouraged the non-Chinese minorities, especially the Uighurs in Sinkiang, to rebel against Mao's rule.

Simultaneously with these developments, both sides began to mass military forces along their protracted frontiers. According to some estimates, in 1968 the Soviets had fifteen divisions along the Chinese border. In 1974 that figure stood at forty-five, including eight tank divisions. No corresponding figures are available for the Chinese side. The inevitable corollary of the escalating military build-up was the increase of serious border incidents, each more severe than the last. Following the Soviet invasion of Czechoslovakia in August, 1968, and the promulgation of the so-called "Brezhnev Doctrine," under which the Soviets reserved for themselves the right to intervene in any socialist country if they thought there was a threat to socialist or Soviet interests, clashes along the Sino-Soviet border became more intense. In March, 1969, serious fighting erupted along the Ussuri River and later at various other points. Both sides suffered heavy casualties and, as in the past, each held the other responsible for starting the conflict.

To defuse this highly explosive game, in September, 1969, Kosygin met Chou En-lai in Peking where the two agreed to normalize relations along their frontiers, to establish a "hot line" between Moscow and Peking, to appoint new ambassadors, to tone down the volume and bitterness of their propaganda, and to resume talks on the border problem. After this meeting the two sides held many discussions (in Peking and in Moscow), but no concrete results were produced except a record of frustration, threats, and decisions to meet again. On several occasions the Soviets publicly expressed readiness to sign a nonaggression pact with China. The Chinese remained cool to this proposal because the Soviets accompanied their public utterances with increased military preparations (including continued reconnaissance flights over Chinese territory); because they continued to foment discord inside China; because they offered generous military assistance to India—China's adversary; because, using economic aid, they tried to establish a foothold in several countries of Southeast Asia; and because, in spite of Soviet efforts to keep China isolated diplomatically, the Chinese established a dialogue with the United States in mid-1971, gained admission to the United Nations later that year, and soon thereafter normalized relations with Japan.

To counter Chinese gains of 1971, the Soviets intensified their courtship of the United States, Japan, and the key countries of Western Europe. They inundated them with high-ranking officials and tantalized them with prospects of rich economic gains. All, however, refused to play this form of "Russian roulette." Because this ploy did not escape Chinese notice, Sino-Soviet exchanges became quite bitter in the United Nations. Nor were their contacts improved when the Chinese shot down the plane of Mao's heir designate, Lin Piao, in his unsuccessful attempt to flee to the Soviet Union. The deaths of Chou En-lai and Mao Tse-tung in 1976 brought no visible change to Sino-Soviet relations. The Chinese, in fact, refused even to accept Soviet condolences. Early in 1977, however, the two governments resumed the suspended border talks, but as in the past, progress was soon affected by charges and countercharges. Sino-Soviet tensions increased in 1979 as a result of three important developments: 1) The establishment of formal diplomatic relations between China and the United States: 2) The violent clash between Chinese and Vietnamese forces along their frontier; and 3) The Soviet military invasion of Afghanistan. In the early 1980s relations between the two communist colossi improved slightly, thanks, among other reasons, to President Reagan's decision to maintain friendly ties (including military) with Taiwan. Obviously, the Soviets took advantage of this development and tried to repair their ties with China. While prospects for good relations between the USSR and China are poor, history shows that in politics nothing is impossible.

While he encountered considerable difficulties in his relations with the Chinese, Brezhnev and his associates had a fair amount of success in their economic, military, and cultural penetration of key countries of the Third World. In Southeast and South Asia, North Vietnam, Indonesia, and India continued to occupy Soviet attention (though they also voiced interest in Cambodia, Laos, the Philippines, and Thailand). The greatest Soviet involvement was in North Vietnam and it was chiefly military. To counter American entanglement in South Vietnam, Kosygin visited Hanoi in February, 1965, and as a result in the course of that year the USSR alone supplied some $550 million worth of planes, rockets, anti-aircraft artillery, tanks, and other war materiel. The Soviets also trained North Vietnamese pilots, and tank and anti-aircraft crews. In subsequent years of the protracted conflict, the USSR substantially increased the flow of war materiel to North Vietnam, as did also the East European satellites. Between 1965 and 1972 numerous Soviet high-ranking officials visited Hanoi to assess North Vietnamese needs, and various North Vietnamese leaders journeyed to Moscow for consultations. Early in October, 1971, Podgorny signed an agreement pledging long-term Soviet support of economic, commercial, cultural, scientific, and technological assistance to the Hanoi regime. As a result of these commitments, which also figured prominently in the Sino-Soviet dialogue, the Soviets backed fully the North Vietnamese solution of the Vietnam problem, including full and unconditional withdrawal of American forces from all of Indochina, and they did precious little to help the United States government in extricating itself from the quagmire. Soviet influence in Vietnam increased appreciably following the withdrawal of American forces from Vietnam in 1973. It increased further in 1978–79 when Soviet-supplied Vietnamese armies successfully gained control of Cambodia. While the growing ties between the USSR and Vietnam caused some strain in Sino-Soviet relations and in US-Soviet relations, these ties offered the Soviets an important geopolitical and strategic bridgehead in Southeast Asia and placed at their disposal several modern harbor facilities.

In Indonesia, Soviet involvement and investment (which Khrushchev had started in 1957, and which included liberal credits, weapons, and generous economic assistance), came to a sudden halt late in 1965 when a military coup stripped pro-Soviet President Sukarno of his powers and annihilated the powerful Communist Party of Indonesia. The setback was not fatal, for the men who ousted Sukarno agreed in November, 1966, to repay some of the 800 million rubles by 1981, provided the Soviets complete the outstanding projects. Relations between the two countries remained on the whole strained during Brezhnev's rule.

While the Soviets gained some ground in Vietnam and lost some in Indonesia, their position in India improved during Brezhnev's rule. A good portion of that improvement stemmed from U.S. actions. The foremost of these was American refusal to support Pakistan militarily in its war with India, first in 1965 and more decisively in 1971. Equally important was American unwillingness to play an active role in bringing about a peace settlement between India and Pakistan. As a result the Soviets stepped into the power vacuum. In 1966 they brought the two warring nations to a peace parley in Tashkent. Relations between India and the USSR improved greatly following the establishment of contact between the United States and Communist China. On August 9, 1971, India and the Soviet Union signed a twenty-year treaty of peace, friendship, and cooperation, wherein they pledged to work for peace and effective disarmament; condemned colonialism and racism; agreed to support anticolonial struggles; vowed to maintain regular contacts on economic, cultural, and technological matters; promised not to enter into any unfriendly alliance; and bound themselves to coordinate their military strategy in case they were threatened. In accordance with these commitments, later that year the Soviet Union threw its full diplomatic and military support behind India in its war with Pakistan (which was diffidently supported by the United States and China) over the issue of Bangladesh. Soviet support was very effective, thanks to the presence of a powerful Soviet fleet in the Bay of Bengal and the Indian Ocean. After 1971 Brezhnev strengthened his ties with India through generous flattery of Mrs. Indira Gandhi as well as through massive military and economic aid. By befriending India, Brezhnev gained for the Soviet Union a major ally in a possible confrontation with Communist China and/or the United States, and, without undue stress and strain he greatly altered the balance of power in South Asia. The fall of Mrs. Gandhi's dictatorship early in 1977 weakened the Soviet grip on India, since her successors immediately went on record as favoring drastic changes in India's domestic and foreign policy. However, except for the rhetoric these relations experienced no change. The dramatic return of Mrs. Gandhi to power in 1979 solidified Soviet influence in India, but the Soviet invasion of Afghanistan later that year placed some strain on these relations.

In the Near East the focal point of Soviet intentions under Brezhnev continued to be Egypt (until 1972), Syria, Iraq, Iran and South Yemen. And as in the past, throughout this period Soviet commitment to Egypt was economic and military. On the economic side the Soviets completed construction of the Aswan High Dam—the showpiece of the Nile. They revamped the Helvan steel and iron complex near Cairo. They helped in the discovery of high-grade iron ore in the Bahariya Oasis in the Western Desert. And they offered technical assistance in drilling for oil in the Western Desert near the Siwa Oasis. To protect this multibillion ruble investment the Soviets and their East European satellites generously supplied Egypt with all kinds of weapons (tanks, planes, heavy guns, armored cars), and after their large-scale destruction during the Arab-Israeli war of June, 1967, they not only resupplied them, but installed many sophisticated surface-to-air missiles and radar stations, and provided Soviet crews to operate them. According to foreign intelligence estimates, over 20,000 Soviet technicians and military experts were in Egypt in 1970.

The sudden death of President Nasser in September, 1970, did not alter the Soviet entrenched position in Egypt. On the surface, in fact, it even strengthened it, as Nasser's successor, President Anwar Sadat, signed a fifteen-year treaty of friendship and cooperation with the USSR on May 15, 1971. By its terms the two countries pledged to cement their political, economic, scientific, and cultural ties and bound themselves to respect each other's sovereignty and territorial integrity. They also resolved not to interfere in each other's domestic affairs and obligated themselves to hold regular consultations on matters of vital interests. They condemned imperialism, colonialism, Zionism, and racism and agreed to coordinate their actions should war threaten. Additionally, the Soviets promised to train the Egyptian military and to support Egypt against Israel in order to "eliminate the consequences of aggression." Soviet-Egyptian friendship was brief. In July, 1972, Sadat expelled all Soviet military advisors from Egypt (technicians at the Aswan High Dam were not affected). Subsequently Sadat withdrew from the 1971 treaty and cancelled Egypt's multibillion ruble financial and economic debt to the USSR.

While the break in Soviet-Egyptian relations seriously jeopardized Soviet designs in the Near East, the Soviet position in the region did not receive a fatal blow. The Soviets continued to enjoy their close ties with Syria, where they completed the building of the High Euphrates Dam. On October 8, 1980, the Soviets further improved their ties with Syria with the signing of a twenty-year treaty of friendship that transformed that country into the Soviet Union's closest ally in the Arab world. The treaty called for Soviet-Syrian consultation if Syria were attacked by a third party, and it also promised Syria massive Soviet military and economic assistance. In accordance with these pledges the Soviets replaced Syrian weapons the Israelis had destroyed during their 1982 invasion of Lebanon and dispatched some of their units to operate the new equipment.

Iraq was also a major center of Soviet intentions during Brezhnev's rule. In 1972 the two countries signed a treaty of friendship and cooperation and established close ties between the two ruling parties (the CPSU and the Baath Arab Socialist Renaissance Party of Iraq). The Soviets also gave Iraq a substantial amount of military equipment and economic assistance, including the development of Iraqi oilfields at Rumaila and the building of several dams and irrigation projects on the Tigris and Euphrates rivers. The Iraqis put Soviet military assistance to good use in the early stages of their war with Iran, but Soviet failure to replace Iraqi losses put a deep strain on Soviet-Iraqi relations.

Soviet-Iranian relations to some extent resembled Soviet-Iraqi relations. During Brezhnev's rule the Soviets entertained the Shah of Iran during his official visits to the USSR in 1965, 1972 and 1974. In return, the Shah welcomed high Soviet dignitaries in Iran. The two neighbors also negotiated a series of agreements calling for massive Soviet technical, industrial, financial, economic and cultural assistance. In 1978 the Soviets became disturbed by the Shah's overtures to China and therefore applauded his overthrow by the followers of Ayatollah Khomeini, the leader of the Islamic revolution. They also endorsed Khomeini's expulsion of the American presence in Iran and the seizure of the United States embassy in November, 1979. Soviet invasion of Afghanistan in late December, 1979 placed considerable strain on Soviet-Iranian relations and subsequent arrests and executions of Iranian communists by the regime of the Ayatollah put those relations on ice. Soviet support of Iraq in the early stages of Iran's war with Iraq put an additional chill on Soviet-Iranian relations.

Another Soviet stronghold in the Near East during Brezhnev's rule was the People's Democratic Republic of South Yemen. The new state made its official debut in November, 1967, when the British colony of Aden and several small units of the Protectorate of South Arabia joined hands to form a new state under the leadership of radical military officers. The USSR immediately recognized the new state and offered it substantial military, technical, economic, and cultural assistance. Together with their East European allies, the Soviets helped the South Yemeni to launch their first five year plan (1974–79) and, in return, the Yemenis adopted many Soviet institutions and placed their strategically located country (on the Gulf of Aden) at Soviet disposal.

It should be noted that in 1982 the Soviets suffered one major setback in the Near East. The setback resulted from the Israeli invasion of Lebanon, which destroyed the Soviet-backed Palestinian forces and Soviet-supplied (but Syrian-manned) missile bases in South Lebanon. The Soviets, of course, condemned the Israeli actions, but, for reasons that are not very clear, they failed to intervene. This failure placed Soviet commitment to the Arabs to a severe test and only the future will tell the final outcome. Since historically the Soviets have maintained a strong interest in the region it is safe to assume that they will continue it in the future.

In Africa, during Brezhnev's rule, the Soviets followed the policy set by Khrushchev. They continued to expand diplomatic and economic contacts with most nations of Africa and contracted to build a number of worthy projects. They also continued to attract African intelligentsia to the Soviet cause and to the Soviet way of life. And everywhere, but especially in the United Nations, they continued to side with African delegates in condemning colonialism, racism, and Western imperialism. Actually, however, during Brezhnev's years the Soviets entrenched themselves only in Somalia, Libya, Ethiopia, and Angola. They continued to maintain a meaningful dialogue with Algeria, Guinea, Mali, Morocco, Nigeria, and Sudan. They lost their foothold in Ghana following the ouster of Nkrumah.

With Somalia, the Soviets established friendly contacts late in 1969 after a military coup brought to power Major General Muhammad Siyad Barrah, who then projected the country along the "socialist" path of development. As a result they supplied Somalia with economic aid, including food during the 1974–1975 severe drought; agreed to help in the resettlement and retraining of Somalia's nomads; and contracted to build the Juba Valley irrigation project, oil storage tanks, and modern naval installations at the port of Berbera. Additional projects were handled by such Soviet clients as East Germany, Cuba, and North Korea. The Soviets also sent to Somalia technical and military advisors to organize and modernize the country's military forces, and towards that end they provided Somalia with a variety of modern weapons. In return for this generosity, Somalia's dictator granted them the right to use his country's port facilities—a right that at once put the Soviet Union in controlling command of the Straits of Aden and of a large area of the Indian Ocean. The Soviets emphasized the importance of their entrenchment in Somalia by the July, 1974, official visit of Podgorny to sign a new treaty that pledged additional economic and military aid to Somalia. Soviet entrenchment in Somalia ran into serious difficulty in mid-1977 after Brezhnev and his associates committed themselves to support the military dictatorship of Colonel Mengistu Haile Mariam in Ethiopia, Somalia's arch adversary. In mid-November, 1977, the Somalis ordered all Soviet officials to leave Somalia and severed diplomatic ties with Cuba.

Although they had expressed a desire to occupy Libya during the Potsdam Conference in 1945, it was only in the first half of 1970 that a possibility for Soviet entrenchment there developed when the two countries exchanged visits of high-ranking oil experts and when they concluded an agreement calling for economic, scientific, and technical cooperation and for the delivery of Soviet arms. In March, 1972, they agreed to help the Libyans to discover, extract, and refine oil and to train Libyan military forces. Subsequently, the two countries established closer links after President Sadat expelled Soviet forces from Egypt and after he rejected the call of the erratic dictator of Libya, Colonel Mu'ammar Qadhafi, for an Egyptian-Libyan federation. In May, 1974, Libyan and Soviet officials vowed to give every possible aid to the Palestinians, and a year later Kosygin visited Libya to sign an agreement calling for sizable Soviet economic and military assistance. The most visible form of that assistance was military hardware, including tanks and ground-to-ground missiles which the Libyans proudly displayed in September, 1976, during their revolution day parade in Tripoli. Because of the unpredictable behavior of Qadhafi it is impossible to ascertain the solidity of Soviet entrenchment in Libya. Only one thing is certain: In Libya the Soviets compensated for their lost base in Egypt and hence in North Africa and the Mediterranean.

In contrast to the rather peacefully engineered economic and military penetration of Somalia and Libya, Soviet involvement in Angola was covert and violent. They were attracted to Angola by the civil war that accompanied transition from the centuries-old Portuguese rule to independence. In that struggle the Soviets sided with the pro-Marxist Popular Movement for the Liberation of Angola and supplied it with the necessary materiel. This involvement had a dual purpose: to establish a Soviet base in the economically rich but politically empty vacuum, and to prevent a Peking-backed revolutionary group from triumphing there. The Soviets won decisively at the end of 1975. They triumphed in Angola because the Chinese were unable to provide their followers the required weapons; because the Congress of the United States refused to give any assistance to anti-Soviet forces in Angola; and because the Soviets introduced into Angola massive military equipment, advisors, and thousands of Cuban armed forces.

Early in October, 1976, Brezhnev and Dr. Antonio A. Neto, the victorious head of the pro-Soviet forces in Angola, signed in Moscow a twenty-year treaty of friendship and cooperation. In it they pledged to develop political, economic, scientific, technological, and cultural cooperation; promised to respect each other's sovereignty, equality, and territorial integrity; and vowed not to interfere in each other's internal affairs. They also condemned colonialism, racism and apartheid, and resolved to support "the lawful struggle of nations for sovereignty, freedom, independence and social progress." Finally, they agreed to consult each other on vital matters affecting their countries, to work closely in the military field, and to establish firm ties in various areas of activity. Only the future will tell what designs the Soviets have for Angola and perhaps for other countries of Southern Africa.

During Brezhnev's rule the following countries of Latin America commanded Soviet attention: Cuba, Chile (between 1967 and 1973) and Nicaragua (after the pro-Marxist Sandanista revolutionaries overthrew the Samosa regime). The Soviets also maintained lively commercial ties with Brazil. Cooperation between the USSR and Cuba, close since 1960, became very intimate in 1968 following Castro's approval of the Soviet-led occupation of Czechoslovakia. In return for this endorsement, the Soviets stepped up their support of the faltering Cuban economy and persuaded Castro to adopt the Soviet political system and Soviet-type administrative and economic institutions and practices. To help project her economic development along Soviet lines, in July, 1972, Cuba was admitted to COMECON as a full member, and later that year the USSR and Cuba negotiated a long-term economic agreement which deferred until 1986 the estimated $4 billion Cuban debt to the Soviet Union, offered Cuba new credits to cover expected deficits, and called for Soviet purchase of Cuban sugar, nickel, and cobalt. Political sovietization of Cuba commenced in February, 1976, when that country adopted a new constitution closely patterned after the 1936 Soviet constitution.

Meanwhile, Brezhnev and his associates also synchronized Cuba's foreign policy with basic Soviet interests. They used Castro to champion Soviet views among the nations of the Third World. And they also utilized Castro's popularity and close contacts to help expand their influence in Latin America. The most outstanding example of Soviet exploitation of Castro was in late 1975, when he agreed to send several thousand Soviet-equipped Cuban troops to assist the Soviet-backed forces in Angola. Because Castro cooperated with his designs, Brezhnev showered him with great honors at the Twenty-fifth Congress of the CPSU in March, 1976, and at the Twenty-sixth Congress in March, 1981.

The other country that attracted Soviet interest during Brezhnev's rule was Chile. The first sign of that interest came in the mid-1960's after the government of President Eduardo Frei established diplomatic relations with the USSR. For this step and the subsequent Chilean effort to break up the Organization of American States' embargo against Cuba, the Soviets granted Chile $55 million in credits. The cautious approach blossomed into a romance in 1970, when with the support of the Communist Party of Chile, Salvador Allende, leader of the Socialist Party, became president of Chile. The Soviets hailed Allende and his tactics and program as a model for other Communists. They also applauded his support of the Soviet position in the Near East and in Vietnam, his closure of some American military posts in Chile, his nationalization of American investments, and his close cooperation with Castro. At the same time, because Allende was unable to establish internal stability, the Soviets were reluctant to invest heavily in Chile. According to some estimates, between 1970 and 1973, Chile's debt to the USSR and its East European satellites rose from $9 million to $40 million. All that investment was lost in early September, 1973, when a military coup overthrew the Allende regime—action that also resulted in Allende's death.

The cardinal objective of Brezhnev's foreign policy in Europe was the same as that of his predecessors. It sought continued economic, political, and military domination of Eastern Europe and the weakening of NATO's effectiveness. The Soviets maintained their economic control of Eastern Europe, as they had in the past, through COMECON, where they set up several supranational corporations aimed at integrating East European economies with that of the USSR. The most prominent of these were: a ball-bearing corporation with headquarters in Warsaw; a steel corporation with headquarters in Budapest; and a chemical corporation with headquarters in Halle, East Germany. Other vital steps designed to make Eastern Europe dependent on the USSR included construction of the "Friendship Oil Pipe Line," the organization of the International Bank for Economic Cooperation, and the establishment of a joint research center. Soviet pressure to integrate economies of East European countries with that of the USSR encountered several problems, the foremost of which was the inability to resolve satisfactorily the problem of joint investments, prices, currency, and convertibility.

New surface-to-air missiles on view at Revolution Day Parade, Moscow, 1975.

The Soviets accomplished greater military integration of their forces with those of Eastern Europe through the Warsaw Pact. They re-equipped the Pact's forces with modern weapons (anti-aircraft missiles and tanks), motorized all infantry divisions, and supplied them with the latest planes (MIG-21 and MIG-25, and SU-7 fighter bombers) and helicopters. To coordinate their tactical and operational efficiency, and to test the mobility and readiness of men and materiel, the Soviets also introduced massive annual joint maneuvers of ground, air, and naval forces. Some of these exercises were held on Soviet territory; most in Eastern Europe. While the Soviets refused to share nuclear weapons with their junior partners and kept their own officers at all important posts, they succeeded nevertheless in transforming Warsaw Pact forces into a highly mobile and efficient fighting force.

Brezhnev's efforts to integrate more fully the East European countries into the Soviet system encountered several obstacles. Opposition came from Romanian leaders, who refused to participate in a number of meetings of COMECON and in practically all military maneuvers of the Warsaw Pact forces. A different kind of opposition—popular opposition—developed in Poland in 1970 and resulted in the replacement of Gomulka with Edward Gierek. The greatest challenge came in 1968 from the reform-minded leaders of Czechoslovakia who tried to establish a "Czechoslovak way of socialism." Soviet response to these challenges differed. They tolerated Romanian recalcitrance, allowed them to experiment with their brand of socialism, and raised no violent objections to their good relations with China, an independent policy toward Israel, and flirtation with France, West Germany, and the United States. In Poland the Soviets approved Gomulka's downfall, granted the Poles 2 million tons of grain and $100 million in hard currency, and pledged to assist Gierek in solving Poland's economic ills. As noted earlier, they treated Czechoslovakia very harshly.

The Soviets realized their other objective in Europe—that of weakening NATO's effectiveness—thanks to French policy makers, who, suspicious of the erratic United States' leadership in and control of Western Europe, and desirous of establishing a French-dominated Europe "from the Atlantic to the Urals," expressed readiness to cooperate with Soviet designs. The Soviets improved their relations with France in the spring of 1965 during Gromyko's visit to Paris. They strengthened it later that year when Couve de Murville, French Minister for Foreign Affairs, visited Moscow. Relations between the two countries blossomed early in 1966 when President de Gaulle announced his intention to withdraw France from NATO. That announcement assured de Gaulle truly royal treatment during his June, 1966, official visit to the USSR, at which time the two powers signed an agreement on economic cooperation. Brezhnev and his associates maintained friendly relations with de Gaulle's successor, Georges Pompidou, who, during his official visit to the USSR in October, 1970, signed a new set of agreements pledging French help in the construction of a Soviet truck plant in Togliatti on the Kama River; doubling of Franco-Soviet trade by 1974; and consultation on problems of mutual interest. For his generosity Pompidou received a guided tour of the Soviet space center. His successor, Valery Giscard d'Estaing, pursued the established course, though not with de Gaullist enthusiasm. And like his two predecessors, Giscard d'Estaing was warmly entertained in Moscow during his official visit in October, 1975, and reciprocated when Brezhnev came to Paris early in 1976, and again in July, 1977. Thereafter Soviet-French relations deteriorated, primarily because of the increased effort by Soviet intelligence to secure French industrial and defense secrets. So concentrated and widespread was the operation that early in 1983 the government of Socialist President François Mitterand ordered 47 Soviet diplomats to leave France.

One of the most interesting spinoffs of improved Franco-Soviet relations in the late 1960s and in early 1970s was the improved climate in the Soviet-West German relations. The architect of what became known as *Ostpolitik* was Willy Brandt, Minister of Foreign Affairs and from 1969 to 1973 Chancellor of West Germany. Brandt's *Ostpolitik* was more complex and at the same time more realistic than the grand design of de Gaulle. And it was also handled with greater skill and finesse. When fully realized it produced four far-reaching documents. The first was the August 12, 1970, treaty between the USSR and West Germany in which the two bitter adversaries of World War II renounced the use of force in their relations, pledged to develop close economic, scientific, and technological cooperation, and acknowledged the Oder-Neisse frontier as the permanent boundary between East Germany and Poland. The second was the December 7, 1970, treaty between West Germany and Poland in which, in addition to restating the main provisions of the Soviet-West German accord, the two powers renounced future territorial claims against one another. The third was the September 3, 1971, four power agreement on the status of West Berlin which bound the United States, Great Britain, France, and the USSR to reduce tensions in that troubled spot, and promised to improve communications between the two Berlins and the two Germanies. And the fourth was the December 22, 1972, treaty between East and West Germany. The chief victor in all of these arrangements was the USSR. It secured stability in the heart of Europe at the time when its relations with China were extremely tense. It also demonstrated to all concerned that it alone had the right to negotiate on behalf of other East European governments. And it obtained access to West German capital, resources, and technological know-how. The principal loser was Brandt. His political career came to a sudden end in 1973 when it was discovered that one of his trusted advisers on

Ostpolitik was a Soviet agent who had been carefully planted on Brandt's staff.

Soviet relations with West Germany under Chancellor Helmut Schmidt, Brandt's successor, were on the whole friendly. This was evident in the exchange of official visits and by increased economic ties. West Germany, in fact, became the most important Soviet trade partner and the principal supplier of sophisticated technology for numerous undertakings, including the ambitious gas pipeline project from the Urals to Western Europe which put considerable strain on West German-American relations. Helmut Kohl, who replaced Schmidt as Chancellor of West Germany at the end of 1982, tried to improve those relations without jeopardizing West German economic ties with the USSR. He did this in spite of substantial Soviet interference in West German elections in early 1983. In July, 1983, Kohl visited Moscow but failed to persuade Soviet leaders to modify their stand on disarmament and on their relations with NATO.

Next to making peace with West Germany and helping to settle the Berlin issue, Brezhnev's most far-reaching move in Europe was the convening of a European Security Conference in Helsinki in the summer of 1975. He had broached the idea of such a conference to de Gaulle in 1966 but nothing came of it because originally the conference was intended to include only European countries and everyone knew that as the strongest power the USSR was bound to have the dominant voice in such an arrangement. The deadlock was broken when the United States established contact with China. The Soviets immediately dropped their insistence on the all-European membership of such a conference and agreed to include the United States and Canada. After many months of preparatory work, in July, 1975, leading spokesmen of thirty-five states met in Helsinki for the ceremony of signing the final document.

In this vital (106 pages long) policy declaration, all signatories pledged to expand their relations among themselves and to make détente their lasting policy. They vowed to respect each other's territorial integrity and renounced threat or the use of force in settling their disputes. They promised to refrain from giving direct or indirect assistance to terrorists or to subversive activities. They also contracted to respect "fundamental freedoms, including the freedom of thought, conscience, religion or belief." They bound themselves to respect international treaties and agreements, and, to avert misunderstanding or accidental attack, they agreed to give advance notice of sizable troop maneuvers. They also resolved to create a good climate for business contacts and obligated themselves to facilitate family visits and reunions. Finally, they pledged to create opportunities for a freer flow of information, tourism, and educational, cultural, and sport exchanges, and agreed to review the performance of these undertakings in June, 1977, in Belgrade.

Because each side (*i.e.*, Soviet and Western) interpreted the Helsinki Accord to suit its own needs, the scheduled review of these provisions in Belgrade (1977–78) was a stormy propaganda affair that reverberated with charges and countercharges between Soviet and Western delegates. The only positive result of the Belgrade meeting was the decision to review the same problems at a meeting in Madrid (1982–83). Because it convened shortly after Polish authorities (under strong Soviet pressure) imposed martial law in Poland and arrested thousands of Solidarity members, the gathering in Madrid was anything but amicable. Both meetings (in Belgrade and in Madrid) were markedly complicated by the harassment and arrests of many citizens inside the USSR who, as self-appointed members of special committees, tried to monitor Soviet compliance with the Helsinki Accord.

It is not surprising that the Helsinki agreement had critics. Some labelled it as a sell-out of Eastern Europe similar to that at Yalta in 1945. Others pointed out that it was a great triumph of Soviet diplomacy because it assured the Soviets security in Europe and accordingly granted them a free hand to deal with the Chinese. More rational observers noted that the agreement merely acknowledged the existing status quo. Only very few regarded it as a covenant that forced all signatories into a predetermined line of conduct both in their domestic and foreign policies— hence as a source of potential embarrassment for violators, including the USSR, the chief sponsor and promoter of the Helsinki agreement. Indeed the Helsinki agreement may yet turn out to be the proverbial Pandora's box for Brezhnev and his successors. To date the greatest annoyance about it has come from Soviet dissidents who set up committees in various parts of the USSR to monitor Soviet official compliance with various provisions (but chiefly human rights) in the 1975 Helsinki historic accord.

Concurrently with his efforts to bring about a conference of European states, Brezhnev launched a campaign designed to impose unity among European Communists. And like the gathering of states, the conference of Communists misfired. The first session was held in April, 1967, in Karlové Vary, Czechoslovakia. The meeting was a failure because several Communist parties, including the Yugoslav, Romanian, Dutch, Icelandic and Norwegian, boycotted the affair. They, and later others, objected to Soviet insistence that all European Communists must acknowledge the CPSU as *primus inter pares*, and that they must synchronize their actions and ideologies with that of the CPSU. To overcome their resistance between November, 1973, and March, 1976, the Soviets organized several consultative group meetings (in Warsaw, Budapest, East Berlin, and Moscow), and they also held a number of bilateral talks. But these meetings produced no desired results. In fact, the more they tried, the more dissidents they produced. Among the new dissidents were the Italian, French, and Spanish Communist parties. The growing numerical strength of this minority, now labelled Eurocommunist, compelled Brezhnev and his associates to modify their stand. This they did sometime in May, 1976, thus setting the stage for the June 29–30 conference in East Berlin.

The conference, attended by all leading Communists of Europe, including Brezhnev and Tito, produced a lengthy document that was remarkable not so much for what it said, but for what it did not say. It did not, for example, condemn China, and it did not praise the USSR. The participants instead pledged to develop "comradely and voluntary cooperation" among themselves, vowed to adhere to "the principles of equality and the sovereign independence of each party," agreed not to interfere in each other's internal affairs, and acknowledged that each party was free to follow its own road "in the struggle for social change" and "for socialism." The conferees also recognized the importance of nonaligned countries, approved collaboration with democratic forces, and agreed that each party had the right to disagree with policies and actions of other parties. Shortly after the conference ended it became evident that beneath the façade of unity there was a continuing disagreement among European Communists. Or to put it differently, Soviet leaders revealed that they were willing and eager, as they had been in the past, to criticize everybody, but they insisted that no one had the right to criticize them. It follows that this formulation produced the usual charges and countercharges.

In his relations with the United States Brezhnev followed closely the outline of Khrushchev's approach to Soviet-American relations; namely, he sought to find an accommodation with the United States without sacrificing any basic Soviet interests. Until early 1972, relations with the United States were cautious because the two superpowers confronted each other directly and indirectly: (1) in a war in Vietnam, where the United States supported South Vietnam, while the USSR assisted North Vietnam; (2) in the Near East, where the United States backed Israel, while the USSR defended the Arab cause; and (3) in Western Europe, where the Soviets tried to dismantle NATO and terminate the American military presence in Europe.

This period, however, was not sterile. In July, 1967, during his brief trip to the United States for an appearance before the United Nations to condemn Israel for the June, 1967 war, Kosygin met briefly with President Johnson at Glassboro, New Jersey, where the two exchanged views on a variety of problems facing them. In August, 1967, after years of negotiations, the two governments signed a treaty to check the spread of nuclear weapons, and in July, 1968, the Soviets endorsed a long-standing American proposal to restrict the missile race. The Soviet-led invasion and occupation of Czechoslovakia in August, 1968, put a chill on Soviet-American relations, but signs of improvement became visible early in 1969 when the Soviets greeted Nixon's inauguration with a call to ratify the nuclear nonproliferation treaty and a proposal that the two powers commence discussions on a strategic arms limitation treaty (SALT). The Soviets also proposed the opening of consulates in cities other than the capitals of their respective countries (consulates were later opened in San Francisco and Leningrad), and continued friendly cooperation in Antarctica. They hailed the landing of the United States astronauts on the Moon, extended a cordial welcome to the astronauts in the Soviet Union, and, following the explosion aboard *Apollo XIII* deep in space, offered all possible assistance to the endangered Americans. Finally, as noted earlier, in September, 1971, the Soviets helped to defuse the ever-explosive Berlin problem. These and many other friendly gestures and contacts demonstrated that although the two powers were governed by different ideologies and confronted each other in several tense areas of the world, they nevertheless had many common interests.

Soviet-American relations entered a new phase during the historic visit of President Nixon to the Soviet Union in May, 1972. Described in the West as "détente" and in the USSR as "peaceful coexistence," the new phase resulted from many pressures. The Soviets adopted peaceful coexistence chiefly because they feared improved American-Chinese relations might jeopardize their security; because they wished either to slow the pace of American military preparedness or keep it at the level of the Vietnam War; and because by behaving correctly they hoped to secure from the United States massive financial and technological assistance to rescue the Soviet economy (especially its consumer and agricultural sector) from its difficulties without slowing the pace of Soviet military preparedness. The Americans wanted the détente in order to improve their balance of payments, to reduce their military expenditures and global commitments, and to offset some of the domestic failures of the Republican administration.

Regardless of what actual motives lay behind the new phase of Soviet-American relations, that phase produced a number of positive results. The most significant of these was the signing on May 29, 1972, during Nixon's historic visit to the USSR, of a document called "Basic Principles of Relations Between the USA and the USSR." In it the two governments agreed to develop normal relations "based on the principle of sovereignty, equality, non-interference in internal affairs, and mutual advantage"; pledged to exercise restraint in order to avoid military confrontations; promised to cooperate in defusing dangerous situations or tensions; vowed to exchange views on problems of mutual interest; contracted to limit their armaments and to develop close economic relations; and promised to cooperate in scientific, technological, and cultural fields.

Richard Nixon with Aleksei Kosygin, Moscow, 1972.

In accordance with the letter and spirit of these principles, the two powers then signed several vital agreements. The most important of these was the Treaty on the Limitation of Anti-Ballistic Missiles Systems (SALT I), and the Interim Agreement on Certain Measures with Respect to Limitations of Strategic Offensive Arms. Under the terms of these complex documents (which subsequently received a fair amount of criticism in the United States), the Soviets secured numerical advantage over the United States in ICBMs (1,618 to 1,054), in missile launching submarines (62 to 44), and in submarine launched ballistic missiles (950 to 710). Other vital measures signed in Moscow on May 30, 1972, included an agreement for a joint space rendezvous (which took place in July, 1975); an agreement calling for a joint effort in attacking various diseases and environmental issues; an agreement settling the problem of the Lend-Lease debt, most favored nation treatment, and long-term credits; and an agreement calling for the creation of a joint Soviet-American commercial commission to plan long-term commercial and economic ties between the two countries.

Soviet-American relations improved in 1973 and 1974. During Brezhnev's visit to the United States in June, 1973, the two governments signed or approved the following important measures: Agreement on the Prevention of Nuclear War; Agreement on Commercial Navigation; the protocol augmenting civil air communication between Washington and Moscow; and the agreement calling for establishment of joint Soviet-American committees for the peaceful uses of atomic energy, agricultural cooperation, oceanographic studies, and transportation. These measures were further strengthened by Nixon's June, 1974, visit to the USSR, and, following his historic resignation from the Presidency, by President Gerald R. Ford's meeting with Brezhnev in Vladivostok in November, 1974.

At the end of 1974, however, the Senate of the United States put a chill on Soviet-American relations by refusing to approve huge credits to the Soviet Union (which had been agreed to by Nixon) and by attaching to the trade agreement (which Nixon had negotiated) the "Jackson Amendment" which called for liberalization of Soviet emigration policy. The Soviets interpreted the Senate's action as flagrant interference in Soviet domestic affairs and accordingly rejected American credits, cancelled their Lend-Lease obligations, terminated several trade deals, assumed a tough line in the SALT II negotiations, turned to other industrial countries for economic and technological assistance (Japan, Great Britain, West Germany, and France), and tightened their vigilance at home. Because they did not cancel all other agreements they had negotiated with the Americans since 1972, and because in 1975 they negotiated a long-term agreement to purchase American grain, many observers felt that relations between the two superpowers were reasonably sound. Cynics, however, described their relations as a stalemated armistice.

In the initial stages of the Carter administration the Soviets received some good and some bad news. On the positive side they applauded Carter's resolve to move forcefully and realistically on the deadlocked SALT II negotiations. The applause soon turned to anger when the new president unveiled his disarmament program calling for a substantial reduction of American and Soviet weapons. The Soviets interpreted Carter's proposal as a ploy to undermine their defense capabilities and refused to consider it seriously. The two sides met at various places (Moscow, Geneva, and Washington) but failed to break the deadlocked SALT II negotiations. The Soviets likewise were disturbed when the new President announced his intention to improve relations between the United States and Communist China. They were also greatly annoyed when he condemned Soviet mistreatment of some dissidents. And they officially protested when he communicated with Andrei Sakharov and when he received some exiled dissidents in the White House.

Subsequently Soviet-American relations improved slightly and the two powers successfully negotiated the SALT II Treaty, which Carter and Brezhnev signed in Vienna on June 18, 1979. The Soviet military invasion of Afghanistan in late December, 1979, caused a serious setback in relations. That action brought instant protests, prevented the ratification of the SALT II Treaty by the Senate of the United States, and prompted Carter to impose a partial economic embargo against the USSR (including the sale of grain), to cancel some cultural and other exchanges, and to announce an American boycott of the 1980 summer Olympics in Moscow. Although Brezhnev and his associates were annoyed by these measures they did not alter their position in Afghanistan. In fact they toughened their stand and accused the United States of assisting Afghani resistance, and interfering in Poland. They also exerted enormous pressure on Polish authorities to do away with the Solidarity movement and began to make inroads (direct and indirect) in the revolutionary turmoil in Central America. These and many other *quid pro quo* measures brought Soviet-American relations to a new low.

The last two years of Brezhnev's rule in the USSR, which coincided with the first two years of the presidency of Ronald Reagan, witnessed further deterioration of Soviet-American relations. To a considerable degree the prime cause was Reagan's firm resolve to improve American military capability which, as a result of the post-Vietnam "syndrome," had suffered serious neglect. Soviet military strength during the same period experienced enormous growth. Another cause for the deterioration was the President's resolve to replace all obsolete US missiles in Western Europe with more advanced Cruise and Pershing II missiles in order to counter the threat of the Soviet intermediate missiles, known in the West as SS–20. Reagan's stand, which was endorsed by all NATO governments, distinctly complicated Soviet-American disarmament negotiations in Geneva. The Soviets made it officially and publicly known that they would *never* allow any power to gain military superiority over them and refused to consider any compromise proposal or to make any concession. To succeed in their stand the Soviets launched a massive propaganda campaign aimed at publicizing their own and discrediting the American point of view. They also endorsed numerous peace and anti-nuclear movements in the United States and in Western Europe while preventing such movements from spreading to the USSR.

SUGGESTED READINGS

AMALRIK, ANDREI. *Will the Soviet Union Survive Until 1984?* New York: Vintage, 1974.
ASCHERSON, NEIL. *The Polish August.* New York: Penguin Books, 1982.
BARGHOORN, FREDERICK C. *Detente and the Democratic Movement in the USSR.* Riverside, N.J.: The Free Press, 1977.

BRESLAUER, GEORGE W. *Khrushchev and Brezhnev as Leaders: Building Authority in Soviet Politics.* Winchester: Allen & Unwin, 1982.

BROWN, ARCHIE, and MICHAEL KASER, eds. *The Soviet Union Since the Fall of Khrushchev.* Riverside, N.J.: The Free Press, 1977.

BROWNE, MICHAEL, ed. *Ferment in the Ukraine.* London: Macmillan, 1971.

BRUMBERG, ABRAHAM, ed. *In Quest of Justice: Protest and Dissent in the Soviet Union Today.* New York: Praeger, 1970.

CHALIDZE, VALERY. *Criminal Russia: Essays on Crime in the Soviet Union.* New York: Random House, 1977.

CHORNOVIL, VIACHESLAV. *Chornovil Papers.* New York: McGraw-Hill, 1968.

CROZIER, BRIAN. *Soviet Pressure in the Caribbean: The Satellisation of Cuba.* London: Institute for the Study of Conflict, 1973.

DALLIN, ALEXANDER, and THOMAS B. LARSEN, eds. *Soviet Politics Since Khrushchev.* Englewood Cliffs: Prentice-Hall, 1968.

DIBB, PAUL. *Siberia and the Pacific: A Study of Economic Development and Trade Prospects.* New York: Praeger, 1972.

DORNBERG, JOHN. *Brezhnev: The Mask of Power.* New York: Basic Books, 1974.

DZIUBA, IVAN. *Internationalism or Russification?* London: Weidenfield & Nicolson, 1968.

FARMER, KENNETH C. *Ukrainian Nationalism in the Post-Stalin Era.* The Hague: Nijhoff, 1980.

FREEDMAN, ROBERT O. *Economic Warfare in the Communist Bloc.* New York: Praeger, 1974.

GRIGORENKO, PETRO G. *Memoirs.* Translated by Thomas P. Whitney. New York: Norton, 1983.

HAHN, WERNER G. *The Politics of Soviet Agriculture, 1960–1970.* Baltimore: The Johns Hopkins Press, 1972.

HAYWARD, MAX, ed. *On Trial: The Soviet State Versus "Abram Tertz" and "Nikolai Arzak."* New York: Harper & Row, 1966.

———, and WILLIAM C. FLETCHER, eds. *Religion and the Soviet State: A Dilemma of Power.* New York: Praeger, 1969.

HAZAN, BARUCH A. *The Olympic Sports and Propaganda Games.* New Brunswick: Transaction Books, 1982.

JACKSON, D. BRUCE. *Castro, the Kremlin and Communism in Latin America.* Baltimore: The Johns Hopkins Press, 1969.

KAISER, ROBERT G. *Russia: The People and Power.* New York: Atheneum, 1976.

KANET, ROGER E., ed. *The Soviet Union and the Developing Nations.* Baltimore: The Johns Hopkins Press, 1974.

KARPINSKI, JAKUB. *Countdown: The Polish Upheavals of 1956, 1968, 1970, 1976, 1980 . . .* New York: Karz-Cohl, 1982.

KATZ, ABRAHAM. *The Politics of Economic Reform in the Soviet Union.* New York: Praeger, 1972.

KATZ, ZEV, ROSEMARIE ROGERS, and FREDERIC HARNED, eds. *Handbook of Major Soviet Nationalities.* Riverside, N.J.: The Free Press, 1975.

LENCZOWSKI, GEORGE. *Soviet Advances in the Middle East.* Washington: American Enterprise Institute for Public Policy Research, 1972.

LEGVOLD, ROBERT. *Soviet Policy in West Africa.* Cambridge: Harvard University Press, 1970.

LITVINOV, PAVEL, ed. *The Demonstration on Pushkin Square.* Boston: Gambit, 1969.

MEDVEDEV, ZHORES A. *Ten Years After Ivan Denisovich.* New York: Vintage, 1974.

MORTON, HENRY W., and RUDOLF L. TÖKES, eds. *Soviet Politics and Society in the 1970s.* New York: Free Press, 1974.

MURPHY, PAUL J. *Brezhnev: Soviet Politician.* Jefferson, N.C.: McFarland, 1981.

PIPES, RICHARD. *US-Soviet Relations in the Era of Detente.* Boulder: Westview Press, 1981.

REDDAWAY, PETER. *Uncensored Russia.* New York: American Heritage Press, 1972.

REMINGTON, ROBIN A., ed. *Winter in Prague: Documents on Czechoslovak Communism in Crisis.* Cambridge: The MIT Press, 1969.

ROTHENBERG, MORRIS. *The USSR and Africa: New Dimensions of Soviet Global Power.* Coral Gables: University of Miami Press, 1980.

RUBINSTEIN, JOSHUA. *Soviet Dissidents: Their Struggle for Human Rights.* Boston: Beacon Press, 1980.

SAKHAROV, ANDREI D. *Progress, Coexistence and Intellectual Freedom.* New York: Norton, 1968.

———. *My Country and the World.* New York: Vintage, 1975.

———. *Sakharov Speaks.* New York: Vintage, 1974.

SCHAEFFER, H. W. *Comecon and the Politics of Integration.* New York: Praeger, 1972.

SCOTT, HARRIET, and WILLIAM F. SCOTT. *The Armed Forces of the USSR.* 2nd edition. Boulder: Westview Press, 1981.

SIMIS, KONSTANTIN M. *USSR: The Corrupt Society. The Secret World of Soviet Capitalism.* New York: Simon & Schuster, 1982.

SIMMONDS, GEORGE W., ed. *Nationalism in the USSR & Eastern Europe in the Era of Brezhnev and Kosygin.* Detroit: University of Detroit Press, 1977.

SMITH, HEDRICK. *The Russians.* New York: Quadrangle, 1976.

SOLZHENITSYN, ALEKSANDR I. *Detente: Prospects for Democracy and Dictatorship.* 2nd edition. New Brunswick: Transaction Books, 1982.

STOWELL, CHRISTOPHER E. *Soviet Industrial Import Priorities.* New York: Praeger, 1975.

STRONG, JOHN W., ed. *The Soviet Union Under Brezhnev and Kosygin.* New York: Van Nostrand, 1971.

TATU, MICHAEL. *Power in the Kremlin: From Khrushchev to Kosygin.* New York: Viking, 1969.

TÖKES, RUDOLPH L., ed. *Dissent in the USSR: Politics, Ideology and People.* Baltimore: The Johns Hopkins Press, 1975.

TOMA, PETER A., ed. *The Changing Face of Communism in Eastern Europe.* Tucson: University of Arizona Press, 1970.

U. S. CONGRESS, SENATE. COMMITTEE ON AERONAUTICAL AND SPACE SCIENCES. *Soviet Space Program, 1966–1970.* Washington: Government Printing Office, 1971.

VALENTA, JIRI. *Soviet Intervention in Czechoslovakia in 1968.* Baltimore: The Johns Hopkins Press, 1979.

WOLFE, THOMAS W. *Soviet Power in Europe, 1945–1970.* Baltimore: The Johns Hopkins Press, 1970.

ꗢ X

USSR UNDER ANDROPOV

On November 10, 1982, Brezhnev died of apparent heart failure. Two days later the CC selected Yurii V. Andropov (1914–) to replace him as Secretary General of the CC of the CPSU. The speed with which the transition of power was accomplished surprised many observers within and outside the USSR. None envied Andropov's task because he inherited many serious problems from Brezhnev. Perhaps for that very reason Brezhnev's name has faded rapidly into oblivion.

The most serious situation was in the economy. During his eighteen-year rule Brezhnev had shelved Khrushchev's ambitious Twenty Year Plan and promulgated instead four five year plans. Judged by the published results, the projected growth failed to materialize and many goals were unfulfilled. This was true not only in agriculture—the perennial problem—but also in industry, transport, housing, and consumer goods.

Mourners in Red Square on November 1, 1982, prior to the funeral of Leonid Brezhnev.

Shortages of food and other basic daily needs became so critical during the last few years of Brezhnev's rule that in many industrial centers rationing was introduced. Two of the many factors that contributed to the weakness of Soviet economy under Brezhnev stand out prominently. The first was his decision to allocate enormous sums of money to military needs in order to match the combined land, naval and air strength of NATO and China and to be able in addition to keep Soviet military presence in such critical areas as Afghanistan, Syria, Libya, Angola, Ethiopia, Cuba, and other trouble spots around the globe. The second was Brezhnev's decision to allocate large sums for his defense-related pet projects, including a very extensive space program, the construction of the Baikal to Amur railroad, and the mammoth "Friendship Pipeline" to Western Europe. These diversions of funds by Brezhnev for the needs of the Soviet military-industrial establishment transformed the USSR into a powerful military machine. The resulting shortages of funds, however, deprived other sectors of the economy, especially agriculture, housing, consumer goods, and services. They also affected labor productivity, morale, absenteeism, drunkenness, negligence and general dissatisfaction.

Brezhnev also left for his successor an unimpressive record in foreign affairs. By his unprecedented military buildup and adventurism in Southeast Asia, Afghanistan, the Near East, Africa, and the Caribbean region, he achieved the following results. First, he destroyed the spirit of detente with the United States, which earlier he had helped to create. Second, he accelerated the normalization of relations between Peking and Washington. Third, he forced American and NATO governments to increase their military preparedness. Fourth, his actions (especially in Afghanistan and Poland) helped to bring about various Western economic sanctions against the USSR. While those sanctions failed to modify Soviet policy, they did inflict some damage to the Soviet economy. And finally, Brezhnev's foreign policies created a climate of suspicion and apprehension, an atmosphere that abounded in accusations, charges and counter-charges, fears and even possibilities of military confrontations.

ANDROPOV'S DOMESTIC POLICIES

The selection of Andropov as General Secretary of the CC of the CPSU and Chairman of the Politburo (thus de facto leader of the USSR) was at once surprising and logical. It was a surprise because it was the first time in Soviet history that a former head of the dreaded secret police, the KGB (Andropov held that post from 1967 to 1982), had become the principal spokesman of the CPSU and of the USSR. His selection, however, was logical, for as a veteran Stalinist aparatchik Andropov was well experienced and ideally equipped to deal with the complex problems facing the party and the government. In addition, as former head of the KGB, he was extremely knowledgeable in gathering and interpreting intelligence. No doubt, in a period of existing tensions between the USSR and its adversaries, this single asset worked in Andropov's favor, but there is no way to substantiate it, for his selection took place at a secret session of the CC. Rumor had it, however, that the military leadership supported Andropov's candidacy over that of Brezhnev's "old protégé" Constantin U. Chernenko in spite of the fact that the sixty-eight-year-old Andropov was suffering from various ailments.

Few observers envied Andropov the problems of his new position. To manage the many pressing problems in domestic and foreign policy he inherited from Brezhnev, Andropov was obliged first to consolidate his own power. First, he appointed former loyal colleagues from the KGB to key party and government posts. The most prominent of these appointees were: Geidar Aliev, a former chief of the Azerbaidzhan KGB and Secretary of the CC of the Communist party of that republic (also an alternate member of the Politburo of the CPSU), who became a full member of the Politburo of the CPSU and a Deputy Chairman of the CM of the USSR; and Vitalii Fedorchuk, a general in the Ukrainian KGB organization, who became Minister of Interior. These and similar top changes were apparently intended to accomplish three objectives: 1) to place "Andropov's men" in key posts so as to enable the new leader to carry out his policies; 2) to dismiss "Brezhnev's men" from these posts for alleged and real corruption; and 3) to instill fear and respect in the rest of the party and government bureaucracy and through them in the entire population of the USSR.

With the aid of "his men" and other principal supporters, especially those in the military-industrial complex, Andropov became chairman of the all-powerful Committee of State Defense. Minister of Defense Dmitrii F. Ustinov disclosed Andropov's appointment to the new post early in May, 1983, at which time he praised Andropov's partisan activity in World War II and said that he enjoyed great respect and authority among military men. In mid-June, 1983, the Supreme Soviet appointed Andropov Chairman of its Presidium, that is, titular head of the USSR. Thus, within seven months of Brezhnev's death, Andropov gained the three most important posts in Soviet politics: control of the party, control of the military and control of the state. The speed with which he consolidated his authority surprised many observers. All agreed that Andropov was a cold, longtime master of Leninist-Stalinist power politics, and some even suggested that his analysis and approach to problems was extraordinarily devoid of passion and human warmth.

Simultaneously with consolidation of his own power Andropov also made numerous innovations in Soviet domestic policies. The most highly publicized concerned his efforts to increase the productivity of industrial labor by controlling or eliminating the perennial and widespread absenteeism, theft of state property, alcoholism, corruption of officials, and black marketeering. To solve these closely-intertwined problems Andropov launched a program that operated on several levels. He dismissed, reassigned and imprisoned many corrupt officials (a few were even executed) as a warning to millions of other bureaucrats and managers that the new government would not tolerate the "business-as-usual" approach. In January, 1983, he ordered police forces throughout the country to comb theaters, bars, public baths and stores in order to identify truant workers and order them back to their jobs. Later, their names (as well as the names of those who were late for work) were prominently posted in factories. And, to dramatize his determination to rid the country of these deficiencies, he made an unprecedented surprise visit to a factory in Moscow in February, 1983, where he urged the startled workers to improve their working habits and the quality of their products.

It is impossible to gauge with any degree of precision the success of Andropov's "get-tough" attempt to revive the flagging economy of the USSR. The immediate effect was that he scared many workers and forced them to come to work on time until they could devise more ingenious ways of going back to the old routine. It seems that in the long run Andropov met the same failures as his predecessors. He at-

Soviet leader Yuri Andropov at the Kremlin, June, 1983.

tacked the symptoms of the problem but neglected the deeply-rooted causes, such as centralized bureaucratic planning, excessive red tape, inefficient management, declining birthrate, lack of incentives, under-utilization of the available working force, cramped housing, laziness and apathy of workers, alcoholism, non-availability of quality consumer goods, poor pay, and limited mobility of the labor force. It should be pointed out that many of these ills affected primarily consumer and non-priority industries. Soviet oil production, for example, was doing well, as is evident in its output, which reached 614 million tons or 12.28 million barrels per day in 1982. The same was true of the output of Soviet armament and space-related industries, whose workers received high wages plus bonuses. And while there were no easy answers or quick solutions to these woes, neither were there signs that Soviet economy or the political system were on the verge of collapse.

In late July, 1983, the Soviet leadership announced a major experimental economic reform intended to relax tight bureaucratic central controls. Beginning January 1, 1984, plant managers in selected industries—heavy and transportation machinery, electrical equipment, food processing, and light industry—were to have wider authority over their budgets, with discretion in matters of investment, wages, bonuses, and the power to reward innovative engineers and workers. The new measure also sought to simplify the criteria for gauging the performance of industrial enterprises. Henceforth the emphasis was to be on the production of better quality goods that would sell at home and abroad, rather than on the fulfillment of the planned quota of poor quality goods that no one wanted to buy. The new measure resembled Liberman's ideas, which the Soviet leadership tried but rejected in the late 1950s.

Andropov's other major headache was agriculture, *i.e.*, failure to produce enough food to satisfy the needs of the expanding urban population. Two new elements aggravated Soviet food shortages: 1) a severe drought that affected the 1980, 1981 and 1982 harvests; and 2) a U.S. grain embargo imposed by President Carter in the aftermath of the Soviet invasion of Afghanistan. To cope with the critical food shortages, the authorities instituted rationing of some foods, purchased some grain in Argentina, Canada and Australia, and tried to develop, on paper at least, a crash program to deal with "the Achilles heel" of Soviet economy. Between March, 1982 and April, 1983, the CC of the CPSU devoted three meetings to this perennial problem. At the last gathering, attended by top party functionaries from throughout the country, Andropov acknowledged in a tough-sounding address that adverse weather had inflicted considerable harm to Soviet agriculture. He urged all those present to overcome the dilemma through upgrading of party, state, and labor discipline and through increased food deliveries. He scolded local party officials for failing to adopt modern techniques in agriculture and rejected all suggestions that insufficient funds had been provided for agriculture. He promised, however, to allocate more money to build rural schools and cultural centers, but insisted that that task belonged to local initiative. Now as in the past the officially-recommended steps did not solve food shortages in the USSR. These were ameliorated by improved weather conditions in 1983 and by the availability of cheap grain from Canada and from the United States after President Reagan lifted the grain embargo.

In late July, 1983, Soviet officials were gratified by two new developments: 1) weather conditions assured the prospect of a good 1983 harvest that they expected would reach about 200 million tons (as compared with 150 million tons for 1981 and 180 million tons for 1982); and 2) a Soviet trade delegation headed by Deputy Trade Minister Boris Gordeev negotiated a favorable agreement in Vienna with a United States counterpart, under which the USSR agreed to purchase from the United States 9 million tons of grain in each of the next 5 years. That arrangement, coupled with the possibility of additional purchases from the United States, Canada, Argentina and Australia, assured Soviet consumers an adequate supply of bread at least until 1989.

Andropov's treatment of critics of Soviet policies varied little from the policy he had pursued while in charge of the KGB. That policy alternated between formal warnings, harassment, intimidation, beatings, imprisonment, hard labor, exile, and expulsion from the USSR of nonconformists or critics of official actions. Some of these measures were handled through legally constituted channels, *i.e.*, courts and police. Others were dealt with by the officially approved "volunteer" vigilante groups recruited from among Komsomol members. Numbering in the millions, these vigilantes helped uniformed police "to struggle against parasites, loafers, drunkards and criminals," prevented Western reporters from attending trials of dissidents, monitored the work of labor brigades, helped to regulate the flow of traffic and crowds, kept a vigil on "socialist legality" and performed other tasks when called upon. As before, because they insisted on their constitutional rights, Jewish, Ukrainian, Lithuanian and Estonian critics of official policies were singled out for harsh treatment.

It is impossible to ascertain how strong or widespread the Soviet dissident movement was under Andropov. Its presence was both irrefutable and well-documented. That fact troubled top party officials, as may be seen from speeches they delivered and resolutions they adopted during the June, 1983 meeting of the CC of the CPSU. Resolutions called, among other things, for improved training of party cadres at all levels and for intensified vigil and ideological work among Soviet citizens. Teachers, writers, artists, historians, economists, journalists, indeed all members of the Soviet intelligentsia, were reminded that the party and the nation expected them to be not only propagandists but warriors in an intensified war of ideas with capitalism.

At the same time he was tightening political and ideological controls, Andropov showed some signs of relaxation. In July, 1983, he allowed a number of Pentacostalists (some of whom had found refuge in the U.S. Embassy for several years) to emigrate. What prompted this action is difficult to say. One thing is certain: it was not Andropov's liberalism. In all likelihood it was a calculated move to accomplish these objectives: 1) to rid Soviet authorities of a nuisance that had gained wide, negative publicity for the USSR in the West; 2) to demonstrate to some segments of the Western public that Soviet authorities were flexible, reasonable, and willing to compromise; 3) to soften criticism of the Soviet record on human rights; and 4) to recruit new individuals in the West, especially among the clergy, to support the Soviet stand on disarmament, thereby exerting greater pressure on Reagan to alter his position.

SOVIET FOREIGN POLICY UNDER ANDROPOV

Soviet foreign policy under Andropov continued basically as under Brezhnev. This was because in both instances the architect of that policy was Minister of Foreign Affairs Andrei Gromyko. Thus, in the Far East the Soviets pursued a tough stand toward Japan's political leaders, who supported United States policies, while at the same time cultivating close economic ties with Japanese industrialists in an effort to gain their support in developing the abundant resources of the Soviet Far East. Some signs of improved atmosphere in Sino-Soviet relations also appeared. A high-ranking Chinese delegation attended Brezhnev's funeral and met with Andropov. Early in 1983 the two powers resumed the suspended talks on their frontier problems. Official statements released at the end of these talks indicated that, except for a decision to meet again at some future date, these discussions produced no visible change in the position of the Soviets on such vital matters of Chinese concern as the Soviet military buildup along China's frontiers, Soviet support of Vietnam's invasion of Kampuchia, and Soviet occupation of Afghanistan. Credit for the improved atmosphere in Sino-Soviet relations belonged not to Andropov or Gromyko, but to Reagan, who insisted on maintaining close ties with Taiwan and who was unable or unwilling fully to live up to the solemn commitments that his predecessors—Nixon, Ford and Carter—had made to the leaders of China.

In Southeast Asia, the Andropov team supported Vietnam both in its adventure in Kampuchia and its frequent armed clashes with China along their protracted frontier. The Soviets also tried to maintain close ties with other countries of this strategically vital region. Their relations with India were cordial in spite of Soviet presence in Afghanistan. They likewise sought to establish a dialogue with the Pakistani leaders. This was natural because after Soviet forces had invaded Afghanistan, Pakistan had accepted millions of Afghani refugees and also provided sanctuary and some assistance to anti-Soviet Afghani fighters.

Another headache for Andropov's men was the chaotic situation in the Middle East. The Soviet position in Iran deteriorated sharply early in 1983, after Khomeini's regime began persecuting Iranian communists. Soon thereafter several Soviet diplomats were expelled on espionage charges and the Iranians accused the Soviets of providing military assistance to Iraq. The latter charge was absurd because the Soviets had provided no assistance to Iraq since the start of the Iraqi-Iranian war in September, 1980—a factor which had caused considerable tension between Baghdad and Moscow.

The situation in Lebanon presented Soviet leaders with an even tougher challenge. There the Soviets supported the Syrian and the Palestine Liberation Organization positions. This worked well until June, 1983, when a serious rift developed between Syria's president, Hafez al-Assad, and Palestinian spokesman Yasir Arafat. That dispute caught the Soviets temporarily off guard. Soon, however, they decided to stand by Syria, whose political position was more stable. Moreover, they had placed not only a substantial economic and military investment in Syria, but also Soviet military units to operate sophisticated weapons.

Soviet interests in Africa, under Andropov as under Brezhnev, were centered around the major client and near-client states including Ethiopia, Angola, Libya, Mozanbique, and Algeria, as well as others. And, as in the past, the Soviets supplied these countries with conventional weapons, some economic aid, a generous dose of propaganda and some educational opportunities. With but one exception Andropov pursued the same policy in Latin America. The exception was Cuba, the USSR's principal ally in Latin America. Here, very close relations at all levels were maintained. With Cuban help the Soviets and their East European satellites increased their presence in Nicaragua and their weapons made their way into the hands of various revolutionary groups that sought to destabilize the hemisphere. By mid-1983, the shrouded Soviet intentions in Central America and in the Caribbean region aroused United States concern and helped to transform this strategic region into a potential powderkeg and a possible arena for superpower confrontation.

Andropov's policy toward Western Europe had two principal objectives: 1) to establish close economic relations with such major industrial powers as West Germany, France, England, Italy and the Benelux countries so as to secure high technology from them in exchange for Soviet raw materials, oil and gas; and 2) to use their tantalizing economic leverage at a time of acute energy crunch, high unemployment and shortages of raw materials, to create good will for the USSR and corresponding doubt and suspicion for the United States among West European politicians and the general public, thereby paralyzing or weakening NATO's effectiveness. In pursuit of the first goal the Soviets negotiated a few lucrative contracts with West European firms and tantalized others with promises of similar or better deals. And, as in the past, whenever they were unable to obtain the desired objective in this way, they tried to obtain it by industrial espionage. In pursuit of the second goal the Soviets launched a massive propaganda drive. They applauded, for instance, every individual and protest group critical of United States policies in Europe and around the globe. They interfered in West German elections in March, 1983, in an effort to prevent Chancellor Kohl (a supporter of U.S. policies) from being reelected. And they threatened West Europeans with massive retaliation if they allowed the scheduled placement of Pershing II and cruise missiles in Europe.

Soviet relations with the U.S. under Andropov were not only cold but hostile. Both superpowers contributed to the persistence of this unfriendly atmosphere. The Soviets did it by their continued occupation of Afghanistan; by their involvement in the imposition of martial law in Poland; by their mistreatment of dissidents in violation of the Helsinki Agreement; by their encouragement and support of revolutionary and anti-American groups in Central America, Africa and throughout the world; by their unprecedented military and naval buildup; by their vocal opposition to the modernization of NATO defenses; and by their increased criticism of all policies of the U.S. government. American officials contributed to the cold atmosphere by their attempts to impose an embargo on the Western high technology desperately needed by the Soviet economy; by their sympathy for and encouragement of the Afghani anti-Soviet resistance; by their exclusion of Soviet involvement in attempts to solve the chaotic problems in the Near and Middle East; by their criticism of Soviet handling of dissidents; and by their determination to go ahead with the development of the MX missile and placement of Pershing II and cruise missiles in Europe.

At the core of their hostility was the fear of the enormous number of nuclear weapons each side had accumulated. Efforts to reduce these numbers at the secret Geneva disarmament talks produced no visible results through mid-October, 1983. This was because: 1) each superpower sought to disarm its adversary without substantially reducing its own arsenal; and 2) because the Soviets insisted that nuclear weapons of England and France (and possibly China) be included in any reduction agreement. Since the British and the French rejected that suggestion, Soviet-US disarmament negotiations went back to square one. In these talks Soviet leaders were able to maintain their intransigence because they were not subjected to any pressure from their "allies"; because they did not have to answer to criticism by their political adversaries at home; and because they did not have to be concerned with domestic anti-nuclear pressure groups, demonstrations, public opinion polls and reelection prospects. These factors kept the negotiating initiative in Soviet hands and kept US leaders on the defensive, forcing them periodically to modify their disarmament proposals. As a result the Soviets refused to negotiate seriously and rejected outright every American proposal submitted for consideration unless it conformed to the Soviet design. This quest to gain absolute nuclear security by imposing absolute insecurity on the United States and everyone else was a very dangerous tactic.

On September 1, 1983 a major incident greatly strained Soviet relations with the United States and with many other countries of the free world. A Soviet fighter plane shot down a South Korean Boeing 747 jumbo passenger jet that inexplicably had strayed into Soviet air space over the Sea of Japan. It is not clear whether the destruction of the commercial airliner with 269 people aboard was ordered by top officials in Moscow or by the commander of the Soviet Far East defense forces. Regardless of who authorized it, this act shocked people throughout the free world, and the resulting wave of protests, boycotts and condemnations compelled the Soviet leadership to admit that a Soviet fighter plane had indeed shot down a commercial airliner. They attempted to justify their action on the grounds that the jetliner was on a spying mission for the United States and they unleashed a venomous anti-American propaganda campaign. Soviet arguments and behavior only reinforced the impression that the current powerful Soviet military establishment was adventuresome, reckless, security-obsessed and trigger-happy, and, therefore, dangerous.

These developments indicated that the road ahead in Soviet-U.S. relations abounded in obstacles. However great these obstacles may be, they must be overcome. There cannot be a return to the discredited tactics and behavior of the past. This course is demanded by the universal yearning for peace and by the limited options the thermonuclear age has imposed on mankind.

Andropov's death on February 9, 1984, after a prolonged illness, which his associates attempted to conceal from the public, has only reinforced that universal demand. The pressure increased because, in the last few months of his inactive leadership of the USSR, relations between the two superpowers deteriorated dramatically at various critical points of their contact. For example, the Soviets withdrew from the secret Geneva disarmament talks on limiting missiles in Europe (after the US began to deploy Pershing II and Cruise missiles to counter Soviet SS-20 missiles); they suspended their separate secret talks on ICBMs; and they expressed little or no interest in conducting serious discussions in Vienna between NATO and Warsaw Pact forces on reducing conventional weapons. These and all other critical matters became the responsibility of Konstantin U. Chernenko, who was selected by the CC of the CPSU on February 13, 1984, to be Andropov's successor. Given the gravity of his responsibility, not only in foreign but in domestic policy, his was not an enviable position.

SUGGESTED READINGS

BEICHMAN, ARNOLD, and M. S. BERNSTAM. *Andropov: New Challenge to the West.* New York: Stein & Day, 1983.

BYRNES, ROBERT F., ed. *After Brezhnev: Sources of Soviet Conduct in the 1980s.* Bloomington, Ind.: Indiana University Press, 1983.

BROWN, ARCHIE, and MICHAEL KASER, eds. *Soviet Policy for the 1980s.* Bloomington, Ind.: Indiana University Press, 1983.

EBON, MARTIN. *The Andropov File.* New York: McGraw-Hill, 1983.

JOHNSON, D. GALE, and KAREN MCCONNELL BROOKS. *Prospects for Soviet Agriculture in the 1980s.* Bloomington, Ind.: Indiana University Press, 1983.

MEDVEDEV, ZHORES A. *Andropov.* New York: Norton, 1983.

ZEMTSOV, ILYA. *Andropov.* Jerusalem: Israel Research Institute of Contemporary Society, 1983.

APPENDICES

Appendix 1 ETHNIC COMPOSITION OF THE POPULATION OF THE USSR, ACCORDING TO THE CENSUSES OF JANUARY 15, 1959 AND JANUARY 17, 1979 [1]

	1959	1979
Russians	114,114,000	137,397,000
Ukrainians	37,253,000	42,347,000
Belorussians	7,913,000	9,463,000
Uzbeks	6,015,000	12,456,000
Tartars	4,968,000	6,317,000
Kazakhs	3,622,000	6,556,000
Azerbaidzhanians	2,940,000	5,477,000
Armenians	2,787,000	4,151,000
Georgians	2,692,000	3,571,000
Lithuanians	2,326,000	2,851,000
Jews	2,268,000	1,811,000
Moldavians	2,214,000	2,968,000
Germans	1,620,000	1,936,000
Chuvash	1,470,000	1,751,000
Latvians	1,400,000	1,439,000
Tadzhiks	1,397,000	2,898,000
Poles	1,380,000	1,151,000
Mordvinians	1,285,000	1,192,000
Turkmenians	1,002,000	2,028,000
Bashkirs	989,000	1,371,000
Estonians	989,000	1,020,000
Kirghiz	969,000	1,906,000
Peoples of Dagestan, including:	947,000	1,657,000
Avars	270,000	
Lezghians	223,000	
Darghins	158,000	
Kumyks	135,000	
Laks	64,000	
Nogais	41,000	
Tabasarans	35,000	
Aguls	7,000	
Rutuls	7,000	
Tsakhurs	7,000	

[1] *Ezhegodnik Bolshoi Sovetskoi Entsiklopedii* (Moscow: 1960), p. 7 and *Ezhegodnik Bolshoi Sovetskoi Entsiklopedii* (Moscow: 1980), p. 11.

	1959	1979
Udmurts	625,000	714,000
Mari	504,000	622,000
Komi and Komi-Permiaks	431,000	478,000
Chechens	419,000	756,000
Ossetians	410,000	
Bulgars	324,000	361,000
Koreans	314,000	389,000
Greeks	309,000	344,000
Buriats	253,000	353,000
Yakuts	237,000	328,000
Kabardians	204,000	322,000
Kara-Kalpaks	173,000	303,000
Karelians	167,000	138,000
Hungarians	155,000	171,000
Gypsies	132,000	209,000
Peoples of the North including:	127,000	158,000
Evenki	24,500	
Nenets	23,000	
Khanty	19,400	
Chukchi	11,700	
Eveny	9,400	
Nanai	8,000	
Mansi	6,400	
Koriaks	6,300	
Selkup	3,800	
Nivki	3,700	
Ulchi	2,100	
Saam	1,800	
Udege	1,400	
Eskimos	1,100	
Itelmen	1,100	
Ket	1,000	
Orochi	800	
Nganasans	700	
Yukagirs	400	
Aleuts	400	
Gagauz	124,000	173,000
Romanians	106,000	129,000
Kalmyks	106,000	147,000
Ingush	106,000	186,000
Tuvinians	100,000	166,000
Uygurs	95,000	211,000
Finns	93,000	77,000
Karachai	81,000	131,000
Adighe	80,000	109,000
Abkhaz	65,000	91,000
Kurds	59,000	116,000

	1959	*1979*
Khakass	57,000	71,000
Altaians	45,000	60,000
Balkars	42,000	66,000
Turks	35,000	93,000
Cherkess	30,000	46,000
Chinese	26,000	
Czechs	25,000	
Aissors	22,000	
Dungans	22,000	52,000
Iranians	21,000	
Abazans	20,000	29,000
Veps	16,000	
Shors	15,000	16,000
Slovaks	15,000	
Tates	11,000	22,000
Arabs	8,000	
Beludzhians	7,800	
Karaimes	5,700	
Yugoslavs	5,000	
Albanians	4,800	
Udins	3,700	
Spaniards	2,400	
Afghans	1,900	
Mongols	1,800	
Italians	1,200	
Izhorans	1,100	
Frenchmen	1,000	
Japanese	1,000	
Vietnamese	800	
Tofalarans	600	
Persians		31,000
Assyrians		25,000
Other nationalities	17,000	
Total	208,826,000	261,949,000

[NOTE: The 1979 Census failed to provide data for numerous nationalities.]

Appendix 2 MEMBERS AND CANDIDATES OF THE
POLITBURO AND SECRETARIES OF THE CC
OF THE CPSU ELECTED BY THE XXVI
PARTY CONGRESS, MARCH, 1981

Politburo Members:
Brezhnev, L. I. (died in 1982)
Andropov, Y. V. (died in 1984)
Aliev, G. A. (appointed in 1982)
Gorbachev, M. S.
Grishin, V. V.
Gromyko, A. A.
Kirilenko, A. P.
Kunaev, D. A.
Pelshe, A. Ia. (died in 1983)
Romanov, G. V.
Suslov, M. A. (died in 1982)
Tikhonov, N. A.
Ustinov, D. F.
Chernenko, K. U.
Shcherbitsky, V. V.
Vorotnikov, V. I. (appointed
   in 1983)
Solomentsev, M. S. (appointed
   in 1983)

Candidates:
Aliev, G. A. (appointed member
   in 1982)
Demichev, P. N.
Kiselev, T. Y.
Kuznetsov, V. V.
Ponomarev, B. N.
Rashidov, Sh. R.
Solomentsov, M. S. (appointed
   member in 1983)
Shevardnadze, E. A.
Chebrikov, V. M. (appointed
   in 1983)

Secretaries:
Brezhnev, L. I. (died in 1982)
Suslov, M. A. (died in 1982)
Kirilenko, P. A.
Chernenko, K. U.
Gorbachev, M. S.
Ponomarev, B. N.
Kapitonov, I. V.
Dolgikh, V. I.
Zimianin, M. V.
Rusakov, K. V.
Romanov, G. V. (appointed
   in 1983)
Ligachev, Y. K. (appointed
   member in 1983)

Appendix 3 [1] ORDER NO. 1, MARCH 14, 1917 [2]

To the garrison of the Petrograd District, to all the soldiers of the guard, army, artillery, and navy, for immediate and strict execution, and to the workers of Petrograd for their information:—

The Soviet of Workers' and Soldiers' Deputies has resolved:

1. In all companies, battalions, regiments, parks, batteries, squadrons, in the special services of the various military administrations, and on the vessels of the navy, committees from the elected representatives of the lower ranks of the above-mentioned military units shall be chosen immediately.

2. In all those military units which have not yet chosen their representatives to the Soviet of Workers' Deputies, one representative from each company shall be selected, to report with written credentials at the building of the State Duma by ten o'clock on the morning of the fifteenth of this March.

3. In all its political actions, the military branch is subordinated to the Soviet of Workers' and Soldiers' Deputies and to its own committees.

4. The orders of the military commission of the State Duma shall be executed only in such cases as do not conflict with the orders and resolutions of the Soviet of Workers' and Soldiers' Deputies.

5. All kinds of arms, such as rifles, machine guns, armored automobiles, and others, must be kept at the disposal and under the control of the company and battalion committees, and in no case be turned over to officers, even at their demand.

6. In the ranks and during their performance of the duties of the service, soldiers must observe the strictest military discipline, but outside the service and the ranks, in their political, general civic, and private life, soldiers cannot in any way be deprived of those rights which all citizens enjoy. In particular, standing at attention and compulsory saluting, when not on duty, is abolished.

7. Also, the addressing of the officers with the title, "Your Excellency," "Your Honor," etc., is abolished, and these titles are replaced by the address of "Mister General," "Mister Colonel," etc. Rudeness towards soldiers of any rank, and, especially, addressing them as "Thou," is prohibited, and soldiers are required to bring to the attention of the company committees every infraction of this rule, as well as all misunderstandings occurring between officers and privates.

The present order is to be read to all companies, battalions, regiments, ships' crews, batteries, and other combatant and non-combatant commands.

[1] The documents appearing in the Appendices have been carefully followed in translation and reprinting. Consequently no effort has been made to regularize spelling, capitalization, or punctuation.

[2] Frank Alfred Golder, ed. *Documents of Russian History, 1914–1917.* Translated by Emanuel Aronsberg. (New York: The Century Co., 1927), pp. 386–387.

Appendix 4 THE PROVISIONAL GOVERNMENT AND WAR AIMS, APRIL, 1917 [1]

Citizens: The Provisional Government, having considered the military situation of the Russian State, and being conscious of its duty to the country, has resolved to tell the people directly and openly the whole truth.

The overthrown government has left the defense of the country in an utterly disorganized condition. By its criminal inactivity and inefficient methods, it disorganized our finances, food supply, transportation, and the supply of the army. It has undermined our economic organization.

The Provisional Government, with the active and vigorous assistance of the whole nation, will make every effort to remove the dire consequences of the old regime. But time does not wait. The blood of large numbers of the sons of our fatherland has been flowing without limit during these two and a half years of war, and still the country remains exposed to the blows of a powerful enemy, who has seized entire provinces of our country, and is now, in the days of the birth of Russian freedom, menacing us with a new, determined assault.

The defense of our own inheritance by every means, and the liberation of our country from the invading enemy, constitute the foremost and most urgent task of our fighters, defending the nation's liberty.

Leaving to the will of the people, in close union with our Allies, the final solution of all problems connected with the World War and its conclusion, the Provisional Government considers it to be its right and its duty to declare at this time that the purpose of free Russia is not domination over other nations, or seizure of their national possessions, or forcible occupation of foreign territories, but the establishment of stable peace on the basis of the self-determination of peoples. The Russian people does not intend to increase its world power at the expense of other nations. It has no desire to enslave or degrade any one. In the name of the loftiest principles of justice, it has removed the shackles from the Polish people. But the Russian people will not permit their fatherland to emerge from this great struggle humiliated and sapped in its vital forces.

These principles will be made the basis of the foreign policy of the Provisional Government, which is unswervingly executing the will of the people and defending the rights of our fatherland, fully observing at the same time all obligations assumed towards our Allies.

The Provisional Government of free Russia has no right to withhold the truth from the people. The State is in danger. Every effort must be made for its salvation. Let the answer of the nation to the truth here revealed

[1] Frank A. Golder, ed. *Documents of Russian History, 1914–1917*. Translated by Emanuel Aronsberg. (New York: The Century Co., 1927), pp. 329–331.

be, not fruitless despair, not discouragement, but a concerted effort to create a single national will. This will give us fresh strength to carry on the fight, and will lead us to salvation.

In this hour of severe trial, let the whole nation find within itself the strength to consolidate the freedom it has won, and work tirelessly for the welfare of free Russia. The Provisional Government, which has taken a solemn oath to serve the people, firmly believes that, with the general and unanimous support of each and every one, it will be enabled to do its duty to the nation to the end.

Prime Minister, PRINCE G. E. LVOV

April 9, 1917

Appendix 5 LENIN'S APRIL THESES, 1917 [1]

1. In our attitude towards the war, which under the new government of Lvov and Co. unquestionably remains on Russia's part a predatory imperialist war owing to the capitalist nature of that government, not the slightest concession to "revolutionary defencism" is permissible.

The class-conscious proletariat can give its consent to a revolutionary war, which would really justify revolutionary defencism, only on condition: (a) that the power pass to the proletariat and the poorest sections of the peasants aligned with the proletariat; (b) that all annexations be renounced in deed and not in word; (c) that a complete break be effected in actual fact with all capitalist interests.

In view of the undoubted honesty of those broad sections of the mass believers in revolutionary defencism who accept the war only as a necessity, and not as a means of conquest, in view of the fact that they are being deceived by the bourgeoisie, it is necessary with particular thoroughness, persistence and patience to explain their error to them, to explain the inseparable connection existing between capital and the imperialist war, and to prove that without overthrowing capital it is *impossible* to end the war by a truly democratic peace, a peace not imposed by violence.

The most widespread campaign for this view must be organised in the army at the front.

Fraternisation.

2. The specific feature of the present situation in Russia is that the country is *passing* from the first stage of the revolution—which, owing to the insufficient class-consciousness and organisation of the proletariat, placed power in the hands of the bourgeoisie—to its *second* stage, which must place power in the hands of the proletariat and the poorest sections of the peasants.

This transition is characterised, on the one hand, by a maximum of legally recognised rights (Russia is *now* the freest of all the belligerent countries in the world); on the other, by the absence of violence towards the masses, and, finally, by their unreasoning trust in the government of capitalists, those worst enemies of peace and socialism.

This peculiar situation demands of us an ability to adapt ourselves to the *special* conditions of Party work among unprecedentedly large masses of proletarians who have just awakened to political life.

3. No support for the Provisional Government; the utter falsity of all its promises should be made clear, particularly of those relating to the renunciation of annexations. Exposure in place of the impermissible, illusion-breed-

[1] V. I. Lenin. *Collected Works*, 4th ed. (Moscow: Progress, 1964) XXIV, pp. 21–24.

ing "demand" that *this* government, a government of capitalists, should *cease* to be an imperialist government.

4. Recognition of the fact that in most of the Soviets of Workers' Deputies our Party is in a minority, so far a small minority, as against a bloc of *all* the petty-bourgeois opportunist elements, from the Popular Socialists and the Socialist-Revolutionaries down to the Organising Committee (Chkheidze, Tsereteli, etc.), Steklov, etc., etc., who have yielded to the influence of the bourgeoisie and spread that influence among the proletariat.

The masses must be made to see that the Soviets of Workers' Deputies are the *only possible* form of revolutionary government, and that therefore our task is, as long as *this* government yields to the influence of the bourgeoisie, to present a patient, systematic and persistent explanation of the errors of their tactics, an explanation especially adapted to the practical needs of the masses.

As long as we are in the minority we carry on the work of criticising and exposing errors and at the same time we preach the necessity of transferring the entire state power to the Soviets of Workers' Deputies, so that the people may overcome their mistakes by experience.

5. Not a parliamentary republic—to return to a parliamentary republic from the Soviets of Workers' Deputies would be a retrograde step—but a republic of Soviets of Workers', Agricultural Labourers' and Peasants' Deputies throughout the country, from top to bottom.

Abolition of the police, the army and the bureaucracy. (The standing army to be replaced by the arming of the whole people.)

The salaries of all officials, all of whom are elective and displaceable at any time, not to exceed the average wage of a competent worker.

6. The weight of emphasis in the agrarian programme to be shifted to the Soviets of Agricultural Labourers' Deputies.

Confiscation of all landed estates.

Nationalisation of *all* lands in the country, the land to be disposed of by the local Soviets of Agricultural Labourers' and Peasants' Deputies. The organisation of separate Soviets of Deputies of Poor Peasants. The setting up of a model farm on each of the large estates (ranging in size from 100 to 300 dessiatines, according to local and other conditions, and to the decisions of the local bodies) under the control of the Soviets of Agricultural Labourers' Deputies and for the public account.

7. The immediate amalgamation of all banks in the country into a single national bank, and the institution of control over it by the Soviet of Workers' Deputies.

8. It is not our *immediate* task to "introduce" socialism, but only to bring social production and the distribution of products at once under the *control* of the Soviets of Workers' Deputies.

9. Party tasks:

a) Immediate convocation of a Party congress;

b) Alteration of the Party Programme, mainly:

    1) On the question of imperialism and the imperialist war;

    2) On our attitude towards the state and *our* demand for a "commune state";

3) Amendment of our out-of-date minimum programme.

c) Change of the party's name. Instead of "Social Democracy," whose official leaders *throughout* the world have betrayed socialism and deserted to the bourgeoisie (the "defencists" and the vacillating "Kautskyites"), we must call ourselves the *Communist Party*

10. A new International.

We must take the initiative in creating a revolutionary International, an International against the *social-chauvinists* and against the "Centre."

Appendix 6   THE SOVIET AND WAR AIMS [1]

I. ON THE WAR

RESOLUTION OF THE ALL-RUSSIAN CONFERENCE OF THE SOVIET OF
WORKERS' AND SOLDIERS' DEPUTIES

In the call to the people of the world on March 27, the Soviet of Workers' and Soldiers' Deputies declared in clear words that in the sphere of foreign policy the Russian democracy intended to bring about the same ideas of freedom and right that it had adopted for domestic life.

Numerous meetings of workers, soldiers, and citizens throughout Russia have approved this stand and have expressed the will of the people, that while defending its personal freedom it would not allow the revolutionary enthusiasm of the nation to be used to oppress other peoples, in the form of either open or concealed seizures of territory, or indemnities.

The Executive Committee of the Soviet of Workers' and Soldiers' Deputies took up the question with the Provisional Government and pointed out that it was necessary for free Russia to make a public statement renouncing the plans of conquest of the tsarist government. On April 10, the Provisional Government published a declaration to the citizens of Russia. It said, "that the purpose of free Russia is not domination over other nations, or seizure of their national possessions, or forcible occupation of foreign territories, but the establishment of stable peace on the basis of self-determination of peoples. The Russian people does not intend to increase its world power at the expense of other nations. It has no desire to enslave or degrade any one."

The Russian democracy attaches tremendous importance to this act of the Provisional Government, and sees in it a step in the direction of the realization of democratic principles in foreign policy. The Soviet of Workers' and Soldiers' Deputies will support with energy all the efforts of the Provisional Government along this line. They [Soviets] call on all the peoples both Allied and enemy, to bring pressure to bear on their Governments to give up their plans of conquests. In addition to this, each nation, in both coalitions, should insist that its Government persuade its allies to make a general renunciation of annexation and indemnity. On its part, the Executive Committee emphasizes the necessity for the Provisional Government to enter into discussion with the Allies for the purpose of working out a general agreement along the line indicated.

Russia's revolutionary people will continue to do its best to bring about,

[1] Frank A. Golder, ed. *Documents of Russian History, 1914–1917.* Translated by Emanuel Aronsberg. (New York: The Century Co., 1927), pp. 331–333.

as soon as possible, peace on the basis of the brotherhood and equality of free nations. An official renunciation of all ideas of conquest by all the governments would be a most powerful means to bring the war to an end on these terms.

As long as these conditions do not exist, as long as the war continues, the Russian democracy realizes that the weakening of the army and a decline in its fighting efficiency would be a most serious blow to the cause of freedom and to the life interests of the country. For the purpose of most energetically protecting revolutionary Russia from all outside attacks and forcefully defending her against all attempts to interrupt the progress of the revolution [on the inside], the Conference of All-Russian Soviets of Workers' and Soldiers' Deputies calls on the democracy of Russia to mobilize all the living force of the country in all branches of the national life in order to strengthen the rear and front. This is the imperative demand of Russia of the moment; this is necessary for the sake of the success of the revolution.

The Conference of All-Russian Soviets of Workers' and Soldiers' Deputies calls on all laborers in factories, mills, railways, mines, post and telegraph, and all other enterprises for the army and the rear, to work with the greatest zeal. The economic conquest by the working classes and the hope for additional reforms require that the workers' efforts should not be lowered, but that production should increase, so as to provide the civilian population and the army with its necessaries.

The Conference of Soviets of Workers' and Soldiers' Deputies calls the attention of all citizens, especially those engaged in agriculture and transportation, to the danger of a food crisis, an inheritance of the old regime, and appeals to them to exert all their energies to ward it off.

The Conference of Soviets of Workers' and Soldiers' Deputies sends its greetings to the revolutionary soldiers and officers who are defending free Russia from its foes at the front and at home.

Appendix 7 DECLARATION OF THE PROVISIONAL GOVERNMENT, JULY, 1917 [1]

CITIZENS:

The terrible hour is here. The forces of the German Emperor have broken through the front of the Russian national revolutionary army. In this they were helped by the light-mindedness and blind fanaticism of some, the treachery and betrayal of others. The former, as well as the latter, have been threatening the very foundations of newly freed Russia with ruin and disintegration. At this critical moment, when the counter-revolutionary forces that have been in hiding are in a position to take advantage of the general turmoil, the reorganized Provisional Government fully realizes the responsibility with all its heavy burden which falls upon its shoulders. But the Government has firm faith in the might of the great Russian people; it believes in the rapid recovery of the political life of the country, now that the contagious disease which has undermined the people's constitution has come to the surface and has ended in an acute crisis. The Provisional Government believes that this crisis will lead to life and not to death.

Believing strongly in this, the Provisional Government is ready to act and will act with all the energy and determination that the extraordinary times require. Its first and fundamental task is to concentrate its forces against the external foe and against the anarchists and counter-revolutionists in their attempts to upset the internal order. The Provisional Government will stop at nothing to bring this about. In regard to its foreign policy, the Government wishes to repeat what it has said again and again: that the revolutionary army can go into the battle with the fullest assurance that not a drop of Russian blood will be shed for aims that are against the ideals of the Russian democracy, as openly expressed before the world in its peace formula.

With these objects in mind, and on the basis of the declaration of its foreign policy made on May 19, the Provisional Government plans to propose to the Allies that they have a conference some time in August to discuss their foreign policies, in the light of the principles put forward by the Russian revolution. At this conference, Russia's spokesmen will be not only the diplomats but the representatives of the Russian democracy.

In other fields of State activity, the Provisional Government will likewise be guided by the declaration of May 19.

The Provisional Government will see to it that the elections for the Constituent Assembly take place on time, September 30, and that the prepara-

[1] Frank A. Golder, ed. *Documents of Russian History, 1914–1917.* Translated by Emanuel Aronsberg. (New York: The Century Co., 1927), pp. 467–469.

tory measures be finished in good season, so as to make it possible to have orderly and free elections.

One of the most important internal undertakings of the Government is to work out and put into force as quickly as possible a system of local self-government on the basis of universal, direct, equal, and secret suffrage. The Provisional Government attaches great importance to the idea that the local self-government bodies should have the confidence of all the population. For that reason it is now inviting public organizations to form local governments by means of uniting the guberniias into larger units, administered by collegiate organs of government.

In its striving to carry out consistently the principles of civic equality, the Provisional Government will abolish in the near future all class distinction, all ranks, orders of merit, except those earned on the field of battle.

For the purpose of fighting the economic disorganization and taking measures for further protection of labor, it is necessary to form, under the Provisional Government, an economic council and main economic committee to proceed at once to work out a general plan for organizing the national economy and labor, to draw up laws for regulating the economic life and industry, and to work out practical plans for carrying out these laws. There is already worked out, and soon will be published, a number of labor laws dealing with the freedom of labor unions, employment bureaus, and arbitration boards. There are being prepared measures on an eight-hour day, all kinds of labor safeguards, all kinds of social insurance for all kinds of hired labor.

The agrarian measures of the Provisional Government are now, as formerly, based on the conviction that the principle underlying land reform should be to hand it over to the toilers, which is in accordance with the fundamental needs of our economic life, the often repeated wishes of the peasants, and the programs of all democratic parties. It is with this in mind that a land reform law is being prepared for the consideration of the Constituent Assembly.

The Provisional Government will in the near future proceed with the following measures:

1. Put a complete stop to the former land policy which disorganized and ruined the villages.

2. Enact measures which will give the Constituent Assembly full freedom in disposing of the land-fund of the country.

3. Regulate the land relations with an eye to the national defense and the food question of the country. This can be done by widening the scope of and strengthening the land committees formed by the State. Their power to settle land questions should be defined by law. They should not touch upon the problem of private land ownership, which the Constituent Assembly alone can solve.

4. To remove by this legal land regulation all serious danger to the State, to land reform, and to the principles of the future State plan of land reform, which reform and plan are threatened by illegal seizures and other lawless acts, to satisfy local needs.

In stating its plans the Provisional Government hopes that all live forces will come to its aid in carrying out its heavy and responsible task. The Government demands a readiness to sacrifice all strength, riches, and even life for the great cause of saving the country, which is no longer a stepmother to the nationalities, but is trying to unite them all on the basis of complete equality and freedom.

Appendix 8   LAWLESS LAND SEIZURES [1]

A. REPORT OF LANDOWNERS

Delegates, representing landowners in the guberniias of Simbirsk, Nizhni-Novgorod, Samara, Saratov, Tver, Kharkov, Poltava, Kursk, Kherson and Ekaterinoslav, submitted the following report to the Provisional Government and the Soviet of Workers' and Soldiers' Deputies:

In the full consciousness of the great moral responsibility before the country, imposed upon us by the Provisional Government, namely, the duty to produce food and fodder for the army and the population, we proceeded to carry out the obligation imposed upon us, totally oblivious to our own interests. However, at the very first steps in this direction, we met with the strongest opposition from village committees and commissars, who are acting illegally and carrying out undisguised propaganda for the abolition by every possible means of private landownership in these guberniias. A situation has thus been created which will compel the above named guberniias, which serve the needs of the largest sugar factories and are for this reason engaged in intensive farming, to cease producing cereals, vegetables, and sugar. The general situation in these guberniias at the present time is as follows:

1. Public organizations and their representatives, contrary to the law, fix the rent on land so low that it does not even cover the necessary payments due on the land.

2. Land is forcibly taken from its owners and handed over to the peasants. In some cases, the land thus seized either remained fallow or was speculated with by being leased to a third party at a higher rate.

3. Wages for labor are arbitrarily set, interfering with freedom of labor and freedom of contract.

4. The sanctity of the home is being violated by searches and by confiscation of movable property. Landowners and their managers are deprived of liberty, without due process of law, for refusing to obey the unlawful demands of the committees and commissars.

5. The committees and their agents usurp the functions of courts, and, contrary to the express provisions of Article I of the Civil Statutes, examine conflicts relating to land and labor.

If the above situation continues, Russia, notwithstanding its rich black earth, will in the very near future become a wilderness covered with weeds, a country with a population poverty-stricken, both morally and materially, with an insignificant amount of low-grade grain, insufficient even for the needs of its cultivators. Her highly efficient agriculture will be ruined, and

[1] Frank A. Golder, ed. *Documents of Russian History, 1914–1917*. Translated by Emanuel Aronsberg. (New York: The Century Co., 1927), pp. 380–381.

there will be a total destruction of the starch, syrup, and sugar-beet production, and pure-bred stock.

Russia's economic ruin is unavoidable. We, the representatives of the guberniias named above, consider it our moral obligation to call this condition to the attention of the Provisional Government and the Soviet of Soldiers' and Workers' Deputies.

Landowners: Lieutenant B. A. Iust, Colonel K. V. Molostov, V. N. Kukol-Iasnopolski.

Appendix 9 DECREE ON PEACE, NOVEMBER, 1917 [1]

The workers' and peasants' government, created by the Revolution of October 24–25 and basing itself on the Soviets of Workers', Soldiers' and Peasants' Deputies, calls upon all the belligerent peoples and their governments to start immediate negotiations for a just, democratic peace.

By a just or democratic peace, for which the overwhelming majority of the working class and other working people of all the belligerent countries, exhausted, tormented and racked by the war, are craving—a peace that has been most definitely and insistently demanded by the Russian workers and peasants ever since the overthrow of the tsarist monarchy—by such a peace the government means an immediate peace without annexations (i.e., without the seizure of foreign lands, without the forcible incorporation of foreign nations) and without indemnities.

The Government of Russia proposes that this kind of peace be immediately concluded by all the belligerent nations, and expresses its readiness to take all the resolute measures now, without the least delay, pending the final ratification of all the terms of such a peace by authoritative assemblies of the people's representatives of all countries and all nations.

In accordance with the sense of justice of democrats in general, and of the working classes in particular, the government conceives the annexation or seizure of foreign lands to mean every incorporation of a small or weak nation into a large or powerful state without the precisely, clearly and voluntarily expressed consent and wish of that nation, irrespective of the time when such forcible incorporation took place, irrespective also of the degree of development or backwardness of the nation forcibly annexed to the given state, or forcibly retained within its borders, and irrespective, finally, of whether this nation is in Europe or in distant, overseas countries.

If any nation whatsoever is forcibly retained within the borders of a given state, if, in spite of its expressed desire—no matter whether expressed in the press, at public meetings, in the decisions of parties, or in protests and uprisings against national oppression—it is not accorded the right to decide the forms of its state existence by a free vote, taken after the complete evacuation of the troops of the incorporating or, generally, of the stronger nation and without the least pressure being brought to bear, such incorporation is annexation, i.e., seizure and violence.

The government considers it the greatest of crimes against humanity to continue this war over the issue of how to divide among the strong and rich nations the weak nationalities they have conquered, and solemnly announces its determination to sign immediately terms of peace to stop this war

[1] V. I. Lenin, *Collected Works*, 4th ed. (Moscow: Progress, 1964), XXVI, pp. 249–253.

422

on the terms indicated, which are equally just for all nationalities without exception.

At the same time the government declares that it does not regard the above-mentioned peace terms as an ultimatum; in other words, it is prepared to consider any other peace terms, and insists only that they be advanced by any of the belligerent countries as speedily as possible, and that in the peace proposals there should be absolute clarity and the complete absence of all ambiguity and secrecy.

The government abolishes secret diplomacy, and, for its part, announces its firm intention to conduct all negotiations quite openly in full view of the whole people. It will proceed immediately with the full publication of the secret treaties endorsed or concluded by the government of landowners and capitalists from February to October 25, 1917. The government proclaims the unconditional and immediate annulment of everything contained in these secret treaties insofar as it is aimed, as is mostly the case, at securing advantages and privileges for the Russian landowners and capitalists and at the retention, or extension, of the annexations made by the Great Russians.

Proposing to the governments and peoples of all countries immediately to begin open negotiations for peace, the government, for its part, expresses its readiness to conduct these negotiations in writing, by telegraph, and by negotiations between representatives of the various countries, or at a conference of such representatives. In order to facilitate such negotiations, the government is appointing its plenipotentiary representative to neutral countries.

The government proposes an immediate armistice to the governments and peoples of all the belligerent countries, and, for its part, considers it desirable that this armistice should be concluded for a period of not less than three months, i.e., a period long enough to permit the completion of negotiations for peace with the participation of the representatives of all peoples or nations, without exception, involved in or compelled to take part in the war, and the summoning of authoritative assemblies of the representatives of the peoples of all countries for the final ratification of the peace terms.

While addressing this proposal for peace to the governments and peoples of all the belligerent countries, the Provisional Workers' and Peasants' Government of Russia appeals in particular also to the class-conscious workers of the three most advanced nations of mankind and the largest states participating in the present war, namely, Great Britain, France and Germany. The workers of these countries have made the greatest contributions to the cause of progress and socialism; they have furnished the great examples of the Chartist movement in England, a number of revolutions of historic importance effected by the French proletariat, and, finally, the heroic struggle against the Anti-Socialist Law in Germany and the prolonged, persistent and disciplined work of creating mass proletarian organisations in Germany, a work which serves as a model to the workers of the whole world. All these examples of proletarian heroism and historical creative work are a pledge that the workers of the countries mentioned will understand the duty that now faces them of saving mankind from the horrors of war and its consequences, that these workers, by comprehensive, determined, and supremely vigorous action, will help us to conclude peace successfully, and at the same time emancipate the labouring and exploited masses of our population from all forms of slavery and all forms of exploitation.

The workers' and peasants' government, created by the Revolution of October 24–25 and basing itself on the support of the Soviets of Workers', Soldiers' and Peasants' Deputies, must start immediate negotiations for peace. Our appeal must be addressed both to the governments and to the peoples. We cannot ignore the governments, for that would delay the possibility of concluding peace, and the people's government dare not do that; but we have no right not to appeal to the peoples at the same time. Everywhere there are differences between the governments and the peoples, and we must therefore help the peoples to intervene in questions of war and peace. We will, of course, insist upon the whole of our programme for a peace without annexations and indemnities. We shall not retreat from it; but we must not give our enemies an opportunity to say that their conditions are different from ours and that therefore it is useless to start negotiations with us. No, we must deprive them of that advantageous position and not present our terms in the form of an ultimatum. Therefore the point is included that we are willing to consider any peace terms and all proposals. We shall consider them, but that does not necessarily mean that we shall accept them. We shall submit them for consideration to the Constituent Assembly which will have the power to decide what concessions can and what cannot be made. We are combating the deception practised by governments which pay lip-service to peace and justice, but in fact wage annexationist and predatory wars. No government will say all it thinks. We, however, are opposed to secret diplomacy and will act openly in full view of the whole people. We do not close our eyes to difficulties and never have done. War cannot be ended by refusal, it cannot be ended by one side. We are proposing an armistice for three months, but shall not reject a shorter period, so that the exhausted army may breathe freely, even if only for a little while; moreover, in all the civilised countries national assemblies must be summoned for the discussion of the terms.

In proposing an immediate armistice, we appeal to the class-conscious workers of the countries that have done so much for the development of the proletarian movement. We appeal to the workers of Britain, where there was the Chartist movement, to the workers of France, who have in repeated uprisings displayed the strength of their class-consciousness, and to the workers of Germany, who waged the fight against the Anti-Socialist Law and have created powerful organisations.

In the Manifesto of March 14, we called for the overthrow of the bankers, but, far from overthrowing our own bankers, we entered into an alliance with them. Now we have overthrown the government of the bankers.

The governments and the bourgeoisie will make every effort to unite their forces and drown the workers' and peasants' revolution in blood. But the three years of war have been a good lesson to the masses—the Soviet movement in other countries and the mutiny in the German navy, which was crushed by the officer cadets of Wilhelm the hangman. Finally, we must remember that we are not living in the depths of Africa, but in Europe, where news can spread quickly.

The workers' movement will triumph and will pave the way to peace and socialism.

Appendix 10   DECREE ON LAND, NOVEMBER, 1917 [1]

1. Landed proprietorship is abolished forthwith without any compensation.

2. The landed estates, as also all crown, monastery, and church lands, with all their livestock, implements, buildings and everything pertaining thereto, shall be placed at the disposal of the volost land committees and the uyezd Soviets of Peasants' Deputies pending the convocation of the Constituent Assembly.

3. All damage to confiscated property, which henceforth belongs to the whole people, is proclaimed a grave crime to be punished by the revolutionary courts. The uyezd Soviets of Peasants' Deputies shall take all necessary measures to assure the observance of the strictest order during the confiscation of the landed estates, to determine the size of estates, and the particular estates subject to confiscation, to draw up exact inventories of all property confiscated and to protect in the strictest revolutionary way all agricultural enterprises transferred to the people, with all buildings, implements, livestock, stocks of produce, etc.

4. The following peasant Mandate, compiled by the newspaper *Izvestia Vserossiiskogo Soveta Krestyanskikh Deputatov* from 242 local peasant mandates and published in No. 88 of that paper (Petrograd, No. 88, August 19, 1917), shall serve everywhere to guide the implementation of the great land reforms until a final decision on the latter is taken by the Constituent Assembly.

PEASANT MANDATE ON THE LAND

"The land question in its full scope can be settled only by the popular Constituent Assembly.

"The most equitable settlement of the land question is to be as follows:

"(1) *Private ownership of land shall be abolished forever;* land shall not be sold, purchased, leased, mortgaged, or otherwise alienated.

"All land, whether *state, crown, monastery, church, factory, entailed, private, public, peasant, etc.,* shall be confiscated *without compensation* and become the property of the whole people, and pass into the use of all those who cultivate it.

"Persons who suffer by this property revolution shall be deemed to be entitled to public support only for the period necessary for adaptation to the new conditions of life.

[1] V. I. Lenin, *Collected Works*, 4th ed. (Moscow: Progress, 1964), XXVI, pp. 258–260.

"(2) All mineral wealth—ore, oil, coal, salt, etc., and also all forests and waters of state importance, shall pass into the exclusive use of the state. All the small streams, lakes, woods, etc., shall pass into the use of the communes, to be administered by the local self-government bodies.

"(3) Lands on which *high-level scientific* farming is practised—orchards, plantations, seed plots, nurseries, hothouses, etc.—*shall not be divided up, but shall be converted into model farms,* to be turned over for exclusive use *to the state or to the communes,* depending on the size and importance of such lands.

"Household land in towns and villages, with orchards and vegetable gardens, shall be reserved for the use of their present owners, the size of the holdings, and the size of tax levied for the use thereof, to be determined by law.

"(4) Stud farms, government and private pedigree stock and poultry farms, etc., shall be confiscated and become the property of the whole people, and pass into the exclusive use of the state or a commune, depending on the size and importance of such farms.

"The question of compensation shall be examined by the Constituent Assembly.

"(5) All livestock and farm implements of the confiscated estates shall pass into the exclusive use of the state or a commune, depending on their size and importance, and no compensation shall be paid for this.

"The farm implements of peasants with little land shall not be subject to confiscation.

"(6) The right to use the land shall be accorded to all citizens of the Russian state (without distinction of sex) desiring to cultivate it by their own labour, with the help of their families, or in partnership, but only as long as they are able to cultivate it. The employment of hired labour is not permitted.

"In the event of the temporary physical disability of any member of a village commune for a period of up to two years, the village commune shall be obliged to assist him for this period by collectively cultivating his land until he is again able to work.

"Peasants who, owing to old age or ill-health, are permanently disabled and unable to cultivate the land personally, shall lose their right to the use of it but, in return, shall receive a pension from the state.

"(7) Land tenure shall be on an equality basis, i.e., the land shall be distributed among the working people in conformity with a labour standard or a subsistence standard, depending on local conditions.

"There shall be absolutely no restriction on the forms of land tenure— household, farm, communal, or co-operative, as shall be decided in each individual village and settlement.

"(8) All land, when alienated, shall become part of the national land fund. Its distribution among the peasants shall be in charge of the local and central self-government bodies, from democratically organised village and city communes, in which there are no distinctions of social rank, to central regional government bodies.

"The land fund shall be subject to periodical redistribution, depending on the growth of population and the increase in the productivity and the scientific level of farming.

"When the boundaries of allotments are altered, the original nucleus of the allotment shall be left intact.

"The land of the members who leave the commune shall revert to the land fund; preferential right to such land shall be given to the near relatives of the members who have left, or to persons designated by the latter.

"The cost of fertilisers and improvements put into the land, to the extent that they have not been fully used up at the time the allotment is returned to the land fund, shall be compensated.

"Should the available land fund in a particular district prove inadequate for the needs of the local population, the surplus population shall be settled elsewhere.

"The state shall take upon itself the organisation of resettlement and shall bear the cost thereof, as well as the cost of supplying implements, etc.

"Resettlement shall be effected in the following order: landless peasants desiring to resettle, then members of the commune who are of vicious habits, deserters, and so on, and, finally, by lot or by agreement."

The entire contents of this Mandate, as expressing the absolute will of the vast majority of the class-conscious peasants of all Russia, is proclaimed a provisional law, which, pending the convocation of the Constituent Assembly, shall be carried into effect as far as possible immediately, and as to certain of its provisions with due gradualness, as shall be determined by the uyezd Soviets of Peasants' Deputies.

5. The land of ordinary peasants and ordinary Cossacks shall not be confiscated.

Appendix 11 DECLARATION OF THE RIGHTS OF THE PEOPLES OF RUSSIA, NOVEMBER, 1917 [1]

The October revolution of the workmen and peasants began under the common banner of emancipation.

The peasants are being emancipated from the power of the landowners, for there is no longer the landowner's property right in the land—it has been abolished. The soldiers and sailors are being emancipated from the power of autocratic generals, for generals will henceforth be elective and subject to recall. The workingmen are being emancipated from the whims and arbitrary will of the capitalists, for henceforth there will be established the control of the workers over mills and factories. Everything living and capable of life is being emancipated from the hateful shackles.

There remain only the peoples of Russia, who have suffered and are suffering oppression and arbitrariness, and whose emancipation must immediately be begun, whose liberation must be effected resolutely and definitely.

During the period of czarism the peoples of Russia were systematically incited against one another. The results of such a policy are known: massacres and pogroms on the one hand, slavery of peoples on the other.

There can be and there must be no return to this disgraceful policy of instigation. Henceforth the policy of a voluntary and honest union of the peoples of Russia must be substituted.

In the period of imperialism, after the February revolution, when the power was transferred to the hands of the Cadet bourgeoisie, the naked policy of instigation gave way to one of cowardly distrust of the peoples of Russia, to a policy of fault-finding and provocation, of "freedom" and "equality" of peoples. The results of such a policy are known: the growth of national enmity, the impairment of mutual trust.

An end must be put to this unworthy policy of falsehood and distrust, of fault-finding and provocation. Henceforth it must be replaced by an open and honest policy which leads to complete mutual trust of the peoples of Russia. Only as the result of such a trust can there be formed an honest and lasting union of the peoples of Russia. Only as the result of such a union can the workmen and peasants of the peoples of Russia be cemented into one revolutionary force able to resist all attempts on the part of the imperialist-annexationist bourgeoisie.

Starting with these assumptions, the first Congress of Soviets, in June of this year, proclaimed the right of the peoples of Russia to free self-determination.

The second Congress of Soviets, in October of this year, reaffirmed this inalienable right of the peoples of Russia more decisively and definitely.

[1] *The Nation,* Vol. 107, No. 2791 (Dec. 28, 1918), p. 81.

The united will of these Congresses, the Council of the People's Commissaries, resolved to base their activity upon the question of the nationalities of Russia, as expressed in the following principles:

1. The equality and sovereignty of the peoples of Russia.

2. The right of the peoples of Russia to free self-determination, even to the point of separation and the formation of an independent state.

3. The abolition of any and all national and national-religious privileges and disabilities.

4. The free development of national minorities and ethnographic groups inhabiting the territory of Russia.

The concrete decrees which follow will be framed immediately upon the formation of a commission for the affairs of nationalities.

Appendix 12 DRAFT DECREE ON THE DISSOLUTION OF THE CONSTITUENT ASSEMBLY, JANUARY, 1918 [1]

At its very inception, the Russian revolution produced the Soviets of Workers', Soldiers' and Peasants' Deputies as the only mass organisation of all the working and exploited classes capable of leading the struggle of these classes for their complete political and economic emancipation.

During the whole of the initial period of the Russian revolution the Soviets multiplied in number, grew and gained strength and were taught by their own experience to discard the illusions of compromise with the bourgeoisie and to realise the deceptive nature of the forms of the bourgeois-democratic parliamentary system; they arrived by practical experience at the conclusion that the emancipation of the oppressed classes was impossible unless they broke with these forms and with every kind of compromise. The break came with the October Revolution, which transferred the entire power to the Soviets.

The Constituent Assembly, elected on the basis of electoral lists drawn up prior to the October Revolution, was an expression of the old relation of political forces which existed when power was held by the compromisers and the Cadets. When the people at that time voted for the candidates of the Socialist-Revolutionary Party, they were not in a position to choose between the Right Socialist-Revolutionaries, the supporters of the bourgeoisie, and the Left Socialist-Revolutionaries, the supporters of socialism. The Constituent Assembly, therefore, which was to have crowned the bourgeois parliamentary republic, was bound to become an obstacle in the path of the October Revolution and Soviet power.

The October Revolution, by giving power to the Soviets, and through the Soviets to the working and exploited classes, aroused the desperate resistance of the exploiters, and in the crushing of this resistance it fully revealed itself as the beginning of the socialist revolution. The working classes learned by experience that the old bourgeois parliamentary system had outlived its purpose and was absolutely incompatible with the aim of achieving socialism, and that not national institutions, but only class institutions (such as the Soviets) were capable of overcoming the resistance of the propertied classes and of laying the foundations of socialist society. To relinquish the sovereign power of the Soviets, to relinquish the Soviet Republic won by the people, for the sake of the bourgeois parliamentary system and the Constituent Assembly, would now be a step backwards and would cause the collapse of the October workers' and peasants' revolution.

[1] V. I. Lenin, *Collected Works*, 4th ed. (Moscow: Progress, 1964), XXVI, pp. 434–436.

431

Owing to the above-mentioned circumstances, the Party of Right Socialist-Revolutionaries, the party of Kerensky, Avksentyev and Chernov, obtained the majority in the Constituent Assembly which met on January 5. Naturally, this party refused to discuss the absolutely clear, precise and unambiguous proposal of the supreme organ of Soviet power, the Central Executive Committee of the Soviets, to recognise the programme of Soviet power, to recognise the Declaration of Rights of the Working and Exploited People, to recognise the October Revolution and Soviet power. By this action the Constituent Assembly severed all ties with the Soviet Republic of Russia. It was inevitable that the Bolshevik group and the Left Socialist-Revolutionary group, who now patently constitute the overwhelming majority in the Soviets and enjoy the confidence of the workers and the majority of the peasants, should withdraw from such a Constituent Assembly.

The Right Socialist-Revolutionary and Menshevik parties are in fact carrying on outside the Constituent Assembly a most desperate struggle against Soviet power, calling openly in their press for its overthrow and describing as arbitrary and unlawful the crushing of the resistance of the exploiters by the forces of the working classes, which is essential in the interests of emancipation from exploitation. They are defending the saboteurs, the servants of capital, and are going as far as undisguised calls to terrorism, which certain "unidentified groups" have already begun. It is obvious that under such circumstances the remaining part of the Constituent Assembly could only serve as a screen for the struggle of the counter-revolutionaries to overthrow Soviet power.

Accordingly, the Central Executive Committee resolves that the Constituent Assembly is hereby dissolved.

Appendix 13 THESES ON THE QUESTION OF THE
IMMEDIATE CONCLUSION OF A SEPARATE
AND ANNEXATIONIST PEACE, JANUARY
20, 1918 [1]

1. The position of the Russian Revolution at the present moment is such that nearly all the workers and the vast majority of the peasants undoubtedly side with Soviet power and the socialist revolution which it has started. To that extent the socialist revolution in Russia is assured.

2. At the same time, the civil war, provoked by the frantic resistance of the wealthy classes, who realise full well that they are faced with the last and decisive fight for the preservation of private ownership of the land and means of production, has not yet reached its climax. The victory of Soviet power in this war is assured, but some time must inevitably elapse, no little exertion of effort will inevitably be required, a certain period of acute economic dislocation and chaos, which accompany all wars, and civil war in particular, is inevitable, before the resistance of the bourgeoisie is crushed.

3. Furthermore, this resistance, in its less active and nonmilitary forms —sabotage, the hire of declassed elements and agents of the bourgeoisie, who worm their way into the ranks of the socialists in order to ruin their cause, and so on and so forth—has proved so stubborn and capable of assuming such diversified forms, that the fight against it will inevitably require some more time, and, in its main forms, is hardly likely to end until several months have passed. And unless this passive and covert resistance of the bourgeoisie and its supporters is definitely crushed the socialist revolution cannot succeed.

4. Lastly, the organisational problems of the socialist transformation of Russia are so immense and difficult that their solution—in view of the numerous petty-bourgeois fellow-travellers of the socialist proletariat, and of the latter's low cultural level—will also require a fairly long time.

5. All these circumstances taken together are such as to make it perfectly clear that for the success of socialism in Russia a certain amount of time, several months at least, will be necessary, during which the hands of the socialist government must be absolutely free to achieve victory over the bourgeoisie first in our own country and to launch far-reaching mass organisational work on a wide scale.

6. The position of the socialist revolution in Russia must form the basis of any definition of the international tasks of our Soviet power, for the international situation in the fourth year of the war is such that it is quite impossible to predict the probable moment of outbreak of revolution and

[1] V. I. Lenin, *Collected Works*, 4th ed. (Moscow: Progress, 1964), XXVI, pp. 442–450.

overthrow of any of the European imperialist governments (including the German). That the socialist revolution in Europe must come, and will come, is beyond doubt. All our hopes for the *final* victory of socialism are founded on this certainty and on this scientific prognosis. Our propaganda activities in general, and the organisation of fraternisation in particular, must be intensified and extended. It would be a mistake, however, to base the tactics of the Russian socialist government on attempts to determine whether or not the European, and especially the German, Socialist revolution will take place in the next six months (or some such brief period). Inasmuch as it is quite impossible to determine this, all such attempts, objectively speaking, would be nothing but a blind gamble.

7. The peace negotiations in Brest-Litovsk have by now—January 7, 1918—made it perfectly clear that the war party has undoubtedly gained the upper hand in the German Government (which has the other governments of the Quadruple Alliance at its beck and call) and has virtually already presented Russia with an ultimatum (and it is to be expected, most certainly to be expected, that any day now it will be presented formally). The ultimatum is as follows: either the continuation of the war, or a peace with annexations, i.e., peace on condition that we surrender all the territory we have occupied, while the Germans retain *all* the territory they have occupied and impose upon us an indemnity (outwardly disguised as payment for the maintenance of prisoners)—an indemnity of about three thousand million *rubles*, payable over a number of years.

8. The socialist government of Russia is faced with the question—a question whose solution brooks no delay—of whether to accept this peace with annexations now, or to immediately wage a revolutionary war. In fact, no middle course is possible. No further postponement can now be achieved, for we have *already* done everything possible and impossible to deliberately protract the negotiations.

9. On examining the arguments in favour of an immediate revolutionary war, the first argument we encounter is that a separate peace at this juncture would, objectively speaking, be an agreement with the German imperialists, an "imperialistic deal" and so forth, and that, consequently, such a peace would mean a complete break with the fundamental principles of proletarian internationalism.

This argument, however, is obviously incorrect. Workers who lose a strike and sign terms for the resumption of work which are unfavourable to them and favourable to the capitalists, do not betray socialism. The only people who betray socialism are those who secure advantages for a section of the workers in exchange for profit to the capitalists; only such agreements are impermissible in principle.

He betrays socialism who calls the war with German imperialism a defensive and just war, but actually receives support from the Anglo-French imperialists, and conceals secret treaties concluded with them from the people. He does not in the least betray socialism who, without concealing anything from the people, and without concluding any secret treaties with the imperialists, agrees to sign terms of peace which are unfavourable to the weak nation and favourable to the imperialists of one group, if at that moment there is no strength to continue the war.

10. Another argument in favour of immediate war is that, by concluding peace, we objectively become agents of German imperialism, for we afford it the opportunity to release troops from our front, we surrender to it millions of prisoners of war, and so on. But this argument too is manifestly incorrect, for a revolutionary war at the present juncture would, objectively speaking, make us agents of Anglo-French imperialism, by providing it with forces which would promote its aims. The British bluntly offered our Commander-in-Chief, Krylenko, one hundred rubles per month for every one of our soldiers provided we continued the war. Even if we did not take a single kopek from the Anglo-French, we nevertheless would be helping them, objectively speaking, by diverting part of the German army.

From that point of view, in neither case would we be entirely escaping some sort of imperialist bond, and it is obvious that it is impossible to escape it completely without overthrowing world imperialism. The correct conclusion from this is that the moment a socialist government triumphed in any one country, questions must be decided, not from the point of view of whether this or that imperialism is preferable, but exclusively from the point of view of the conditions which best make for the development and consolidation of the socialist revolution which has already begun.

In other words, the underlying principle of our tactics must not be, which of the two imperialisms it is more profitable to aid at this juncture, but rather, how the socialist revolution can be most firmly and reliably ensured the possibility of consolidating itself, or, at least, of maintaining itself in one country until it is joined by other countries.

11. It is said that the German Social-Democratic opponents of the war have now become "defeatists" and are requesting us not to yield to German imperialism. But we recognised defeatism only in respect of *one's own* imperialist bourgeoisie, and we always discountenanced victory over an alien imperialism, victory attained in formal or actual alliance with a "friendly" imperialism, as a method impermissible in principle and generally wrong.

This argument is therefore only a modification of the previous one. If the German Left Social-Democrats were proposing that we delay concluding a separate peace for a *definite* period, and guaranteed revolutionary action in Germany within this period, the question *might* assume a different aspect for us. Far from saying this, however, the German Lefts formally declare: "Hold out as long as you can, but decide the question from the point of view of the state of affairs in the *Russian* socialist revolution, for we cannot promise you anything positive regarding the German revolution."

12. It is said that in a number of Party statements we actually "promised" a revolutionary war, and that by concluding a separate peace we would be going back on our word.

That is not true. We said that in the era of imperialism a socialist government *had* to "*prepare for and wage*" a revolutionary war; we said this in order to combat abstract pacifism and the theory that "defence of the fatherland" must be completely rejected in the era of imperialism, and, lastly to combat the purely selfish instincts of a part of the soldiers, but we never gave any pledge to start a revolutionary war without considering whether it is possible to wage it at a given moment.

Unquestionably, even at this juncture we must *prepare for* a revolutionary war. We are carrying out this promise, as we have, in general, carried out all our promises that could be carried out at once: we annulled the secret treaties, offered all peoples a fair peace, and several times did our best to drag out peace negotiations so as to give other peoples a chance to join us.

But the question whether it is possible to carry on a revolutionary war *now, immediately,* must be decided exclusively from the point of view of whether material conditions permit it, and of the interests of the socialist revolution which has already begun.

13. Summing up the arguments in favour of an immediate revolutionary war, we have to conclude that such a policy might perhaps answer the human yearning for the beautiful, dramatic and striking, but that it would totally disregard the objective balance of class forces and material factors at the present stage of the socialist revolution now under way.

14. There can be no doubt that our army is absolutely in no condition at the present moment, and will not be for the next few weeks (and probably for the next few months), to beat back a German offensive successfully; firstly, owing to the extreme fatigue and exhaustion of the majority of the soldiers, coupled with the incredible chaos in the matter of food supply, replacement of the overfatigued, etc.; secondly, owing to the utter unfitness of the horses and the consequent inevitable ruin of our artillery; and, thirdly, owing to the absolute impossibility of defending the coastline from Riga to Revel, which affords the enemy a very certain chance of seizing the rest of Lifland, and then Estland, and of outflanking a large part of our forces, and finally, of capturing Petrograd.

15. Further, there is not the slightest doubt that the peasant majority of our army would at the present juncture unreservedly declare in favour of a peace with annexations and not in favour of an immediate revolutionary war; the socialist reorganisation of the army, the merging of the Red Guard detachments with it, and so on, have only just begun.

With the army completely democratised, to carry on war in defiance of the wishes of the majority of the soldiers would be a reckless gamble, while to create a really staunch and ideologically stable socialist workers' and peasants' army will, at the very least, require months and months.

16. The poor peasants in Russia are capable of supporting the socialist revolution led by the working class, but they are not capable of agreeing to fight a serious revolutionary war immediately, at the present juncture. To ignore the objective balance of class forces on this issue would be a fatal error.

17. Consequently, the situation at present with regard to a revolutionary war is as follows:

If the German revolution were to break out and triumph in the coming three or four months, the tactics of an immediate revolutionary war might perhaps not ruin our socialist revolution.

If, however, the German revolution does not occur in the next few months, the course of events, if the war is continued, will inevitably be such that grave defeats will compel Russia to conclude an even more disadvantageous separate peace, a peace, moreover, which would be concluded, not by a socialist government, but by some other (for example, a bloc of the bourgeois Rada and Chernov's followers, or something similar). For the peasant army, which is exhausted to the limit by the war, will after the very first defeats—and very likely within a matter of weeks, and not of months—overthrow the socialist workers' government.

18. This being the state of affairs, it would be absolutely impermissible tactics to stake the fate of the socialist revolution, which has already begun in Russia, merely on the chance that the German revolution may begin in the immediate future, within a matter of weeks. Such tactics would be a reckless gamble. We have no right to take such risks.

19. The German revolution will by no means be made more difficult of accomplishment as far as its objective premises are concerned, if we conclude a separate peace. Probably chauvinist intoxication will weaken it for a time, but Germany's position will remain extremely grave, the war with Britain and America will be a protracted one, and aggressive imperialism will be fully and completely exposed on both sides. A socialist Soviet Republic in Russia will stand as a living example to the peoples of all countries, and the propaganda and revolutionising effect of this example will be immense. There—the bourgeois system and a fully exposed predatory war between two groups of marauders. Here—peace and a socialist Soviet Republic.

20. In concluding a separate peace we free ourselves *as much as is possible at the present moment* from both hostile imperialist groups, we take advantage of their mutual enmity and warfare which hamper concerted action on their part against us, and for a certain period have our hands free to advance and to consolidate the socialist revolution. The reorganisation of Russia on the basis of the dictatorship of the proletariat, and the nationalisation of the banks and large-scale industry, coupled with *exchange of products* in kind between the towns and the small-peasant consumers' societies, is quite feasible economically, provided we are assured a few months in which to work in peace. And such a reorganisation will render socialism invincible both in Russia and all over the world, and at the same time will create a solid economic basis for a mighty workers' and peasants' Red Army.

21. A really revolutionary war at this juncture would be a war waged by a socialist republic against the bourgeois countries, with the aim—an aim clearly defined and fully approved by the socialist army—of overthrowing the bourgeoisie in other countries. However, we *obviously* cannot set ourselves this aim at the *present* moment. Objectively, we would be fighting now for the liberation of Poland, Lifland and Courland. But no Marxist, without renouncing the principles of Marxism and of socialism generally, can deny that the interests of socialism are higher than the interests of the right of nations to self-determination. Our socialist republic has done all it could, and continues to do all it can to give effect to the right to self-determination of Finland, the Ukraine, etc. But if the concrete situation is such that the existence of the socialist republic is being imperilled at the present moment

on account of the violation of the right to self-determination of several nations (Poland, Lifland, Courland, etc.), naturally the preservation of the socialist republic has the higher claim.

Consequently, whoever says, "We cannot sign a humiliating, atrocious, etc., peace, betray Poland, and so forth," does not realise that by concluding peace on the condition that Poland is liberated, he would only be strengthening German imperialism against Britain, Belgium, Serbia and other countries *still further*. Peace on the condition of the liberation of Poland, Lifland and Courland would be a "patriotic" peace *from the point of view of Russia*, but would by no means cease to be a peace *with the annexationists*, with the German imperialists.

January 21, 1918. The following should be added to the above theses:

22. The mass strikes in Austria and Germany, and, subsequently, the formation of the Soviets of Workers' Deputies in Berlin and Vienna, and, lastly, beginning from January 18–20, armed clashes and street fighting in Berlin—all this should be regarded as evidence of the fact that the revolution in Germany has begun.

This fact offers us the opportunity, for the time being, of further delaying and dragging out the peace negotiations.

Appendix 14 AN APPEAL OF THE GOVERNMENT OF
THE RSFSR TO THE CHINESE PEOPLE
AND TO THE GOVERNMENTS OF SOUTH
AND NORTH CHINA, JULY 25, 1919 [1]

At a time when the Soviet forces, having defeated the army of the counter-revolutionary despot Kolchak, supported by foreign bayonets and foreign gold, have triumphantly entered Siberia and are marching to join with the revolutionary people of Siberia, the Council of People's Commissars addresses the following brotherly words to all the peoples of China:

After two years of struggle and incredible efforts, Soviet Russia and the Soviet Red Army are marching across the Urals to the East, not to coerce, not to enslave, not to conquer. Every Siberian peasant and every Siberian worker already knows this. We bring to the peoples liberation from the yoke of foreign bayonet and the yoke of foreign gold, which are stifling the enslaved peoples of the East, including, and particularly, the Chinese people. We bring help not only to our own working classes, but to the Chinese people too, and we once more remind them of what they have been told ever since the Great October Revolution of 1917, but which was perhaps concealed from them by the corrupt press of America, Europe, and Japan.

As soon as the Workers' and Peasants' Government took power into its own hands in October, 1917, it addressed all the peoples of the world, in the name of the Russian people, with the proposal to establish a firm and lasting peace. The foundation on which this peace was to be established was the renunciation of any seizure of foreign territory, the renunciation of any coercive annexation of foreign nationalities, and of any indemnities. Every people, whether great or small, wherever it dwelt, whether up to then it had lived an independent life or was included against its will as a constituent part of another state, should be free in its internal life, and no government was to keep it by force within its frontiers.

Immediately after this the Workers' and Peasants' Government proclaimed that all the secret treaties concluded with Japan, China, and the former Allies were annulled; these were treaties by which the Tsarist Government, jointly with its Allies, by force and bribery enslaved the peoples of the East, and in the first place the people of China, in order to provide profits for Russian capitalists, Russian landlords, and Russian generals. The Soviet Government then proposed to the Chinese Government that they start negotiations to annul the treaty of 1896, the Peking protocol of 1901, and all agreements concluded with Japan between 1907 and 1916; that is,

[1] USSR Ministry for Foreign Affairs. *Dokumenty vneshnei politiki SSSR.* (Moscow: Gospolitizdat, 1958), II, pp. 221–222. Translation by Basil Dmytryshyn.

439

to return to the Chinese people everything that was taken from them by the Tsarist Government independently, or jointly with the Japanese and the Allies. Negotiations on this question were continued up to March, 1918. Suddenly, the Allies seized the Peking Government by the throat, showered gold on the Peking mandarins and the Chinese press, and forced the Chinese Government to refuse to have any relations with the Russian Workers' and Peasants' Government. Anticipating the return to the Chinese people of the Manchurian Railway, Japan and its allies seized it themselves, invaded Siberia, and even forced Chinese forces to help them in this criminal and unparalleled robbery. And the Chinese people, the Chinese workers and peasants, could not even learn the truth, could not find out the reason for the invasion of Manchuria and Siberia by the American, European, and Japanese robbers.

Now we again address the Chinese people, in order to open their eyes.

The Soviet Government has renounced the conquests made by the Tsarist Government, which deprived China of Manchuria and other areas. Let the peoples living in those areas themselves decide within the frontiers of which state they wish to dwell, and what form of government they wish to establish in their own countries.

The Soviet Government renounces the receipt from China of the 1900 Boxer Rebellion indemnity, and it is obliged to repeat this a third time because, according to the information reaching us, this indemnity, despite our renunciation, is being exacted by the Allies to pay the salaries and to satisfy the whims of the former Tsarist ambassador to Peking and the former Tsarist consuls in China. All these Tsarist slaves have long been deprived of their powers, but they continue at their posts and deceive the Chinese people with the help of Japan and the Allies. The Chinese people should know of this and should expel them from their country as imposters and rogues.

The Soviet Government abolishes all special privileges and gives up all factories owned by Russian merchants on Chinese soil. Not one Russian official, priest, or missionary shall be able to interfere in Chinese affairs, and if he commits a crime, he should be subject to the justice of the local court. In China there should be no authority and no court except the authority and court of the Chinese people. In addition to these principal points, the Soviet Government is ready to discuss all other questions with the Chinese people represented by their plenipotentiaries, and to remove once and for all the acts of coercion and injustice committed in regard to China by former Russian Governments jointly with Japan and the Allies.

The Soviet Government is well aware that the Allies and Japan will again do everything possible to prevent the voice of the Russian workers and peasants from reaching the Chinese people, that the return to the Chinese people of what was taken from them requires first of all putting an end to the robber invasion of Manchuria and Siberia. Therefore it is now sending the news to the Chinese people, together with its Red Army, which is marching across the Urals to the East to help the Siberian peasants and workers, to liberate them from the bandit Kolchak and his ally, Japan.

If the Chinese people wish, like the Russian people, to become free and to avoid the fate which the Allies prepared for them at Versailles, a fate designed to turn China into a second Korea or a second India, they must understand that their only ally and brother in the struggle for freedom is the Russian worker and peasant and their Red Army.

The Soviet Government proposes to the Chinese people, in the person of their government, that they enter now into official relations with us and send their representatives to meet our army.

Deputy People's Commissar for Foreign Affairs [L. Karakhan]

Appendix 15 CONDITIONS FOR ADMISSION TO THE COMMUNIST INTERNATIONAL, 1920 [1]

The first congress of the Communist International did not draw up any precise conditions for the admission of parties to the Third International. When the first congress was convened there were in the majority of countries only communist *trends* and *groups*.

The second congress of the Communist International is meeting in different circumstances. At the present time there are in most countries not only communist trends and tendencies, but communist *parties* and *organizations*.

Application for admission to the Communist International is now frequently made by parties and groups which up to a short time ago still belonged to the Second International, but which have not in fact become communist. The Second International has finally broken down. The inbetween parties and the centrist groups, seeing the utter hopelessness of the Second International, are trying to find a support in the Communist International, which is growing steadily stronger. But in doing so they hope to retain enough "autonomy" to enable them to continue their former opportunist or "centrist" policy. The Communist International is becoming, to some extent, fashionable.

The desire of some leading "centrist" groups to join the Communist International indirectly confirms that it has won the sympathies of the overwhelming majority of the class-conscious workers of the entire world and that with every day it is becoming a more powerful force.

The Communist International is threatened by the danger of dilution by unstable and irresolute elements which have not yet completely discarded the ideology of the Second International.

Moreover, in some of the larger parties (Italy, Sweden, Norway, Yugoslavia, etc.) where the majority adhere to the communist standpoint, there still remains even today a reformist and social-pacifist wing which is only waiting a favourable moment to raise its head again and start active sabotage of the proletarian revolution and so help the bourgeoisie and the Second International.

No communist should forget the lessons of the Hungarian revolution. The Hungarian proletariat paid a high price for the fusion of the Hungarian communists with the so-called "left" social-democrats.

Consequently the second congress of the Communist International thinks

[1] From *The Communist International, 1919–1943. Documents.* Edited by Jane Degras and published by Oxford University Press under the auspices of the Royal Institute of International Affairs. (London: Oxford University Press, 1956), I, pp. 168–172.

442

it necessary to lay down quite precisely the conditions of admission of new parties, and to point out to those parties which have already joined, the duties imposed on them.

The second congress of the Communist International puts forward the following conditions of adherence to the Communist International:

1. *All propaganda and agitation* must be of a genuinely communist character and in conformity with the programme and decisions of the Communist International. The entire party press must be run by reliable communists who have proved their devotion to the cause of the proletariat. The dictatorship of the proletariat is to be treated not simply as a current formula learnt by rote; it must be advocated in a way which makes its necessity comprehensible to every ordinary working man and woman, every soldier and peasant, from the facts of their daily life, which must be systematically noted in our press and made use of every day.

The periodical press and other publications, and all party publishing houses, must be completely subordinated to the party presidium, regardless of whether the party as a whole is at the given moment legal or illegal. Publishing houses must not be allowed to abuse their independence and pursue a policy which is not wholly in accordance with the policy of the party.

In the columns of the press, at popular meetings, in the trade unions and co-operatives, wherever the adherents of the Communist International have an entry, it is necessary to denounce, systematically and unrelentingly, not only the bourgeoisie, but also their assistants, the reformists of all shades.

2. Every organization which wishes to join the Communist International must, in an orderly and planned fashion, remove reformists and centrists from all responsible positions in the workers' movement (party organizations, editorial boards, trade unions, parliamentary fractions, co-operatives, local government bodies) and replace them by tried communists, even if, particularly at the beginning, "experienced" opportunists have to be replaced by ordinary rank and file workers.

3. In practically every country of Europe and America the class struggle is entering the phase of civil war. In these circumstances communists can have no confidence in bourgeois legality. They are obliged everywhere to create a parallel illegal organization which at the decisive moment will help the party to do its duty to the revolution. In all those countries where, because of a state of siege or of emergency laws, communists are unable to do all their work legally, it is absolutely essential to combine legal and illegal work.

4. The obligation to spread communist ideas includes the special obligation to carry on systematic and energetic propaganda in the army. Where such agitation is prevented by emergency laws, it must be carried on illegally. Refusal to undertake such work would be tantamount to a dereliction of revolutionary duty and is incompatible with membership of the Communist International.

5. Systematic and well-planned agitation must be carried on in the countryside. The working class cannot consolidate its victory if it has not by its policy assured itself of the support of at least part of the rural pro-

letariat and the poorest peasants, and of the neutrality of part of the rest of the rural population. At the present time communist work in rural areas is acquiring first-rate importance. It should be conducted primarily with the help of revolutionary communist urban and rural workers who have close connexions with the countryside. To neglect this work or to leave it in unreliable semi-reformist hands, is tantamount to renouncing the proletarian revolution.

6. Every party which wishes to join the Communist International is obliged to expose not only avowed social-patriotism, but also the insincerity and hypocrisy of social-pacifism; to bring home to the workers systematically that without the revolutionary overthrow of capitalism no international court of arbitration, no agreement to limit armaments, no "democratic" reorganization of the League of Nations, will be able to prevent new imperialist wars.

7. Parties which wish to join the Communist International are obliged to recognize the necessity for a complete and absolute break with reformism and with the policy of the "centre," and to advocate this break as widely as possible among their members. Without that no consistent communist policy is possible.

The Communist International demands unconditionally and categorically that this break be effected as quickly as possible. The Communist International is unable to agree that notorious opportunists, such as Turati, Modigliani, Kautsky, Hilferding, Hilquit, Longuet, MacDonald, etc., shall have the right to appear as members of the Communist International. That could only lead to the Communist International becoming in many respects similar to the Second International, which has gone to pieces.

8. A particularly explicit and clear attitude on the question of the colonies and the oppressed peoples is necessary for the parties in those countries where the bourgeoisie possess colonies and oppress other nations. Every party which wishes to join the Communist International is obliged to expose the tricks and dodges of "its" imperialists in the colonies, to support every colonial liberation movement not merely in words but in deeds, to demand the expulsion of their own imperialists from these colonies, to inculcate among the workers of their country a genuinely fraternal attitude to the working people of the colonies and the oppressed nations, and to carry on systematic agitation among the troops of their country against any oppression of the colonial peoples.

9. Every party which wishes to join the Communist International must carry on systematic and persistent communist activity inside the trade unions, the workers' councils and factory committees, the co-operatives, and other mass workers' organizations. Within these organizations communist cells must be organized which shall by persistent and unflagging work win the trade unions, etc., for the communist cause. In their daily work the cells must everywhere expose the treachery of the social-patriots and the instability of the "centre." The communist cells must be completely subordinate to the party as a whole.

10. Every party belonging to the Communist International is obliged to wage an unyielding struggle against the Amsterdam "International" of the yellow trade unions. It must conduct the most vigorous propaganda

among trade unionists for the necessity of a break with the yellow Amsterdam International. It must do all it can to support the international association of red trade unions, adhering to the Communist International, which is being formed.

11. Parties which wish to join the Communist International are obliged to review the personnel of their parliamentary fractions and remove all unreliable elements, to make these fractions not only verbally but in fact subordinate to the party presidium, requiring of each individual communist member of parliament that he subordinate his entire activity to the interests of genuinely revolutionary propaganda and agitation.

12. Parties belonging to the Communist International must be based on the principle of *democratic centralism*. In the present epoch of acute civil war the communist party will be able to fulfil its duty only if its organization is as centralized as possible, if iron discipline prevails, and if the party centre, upheld by the confidence of the party membership, has strength and authority and is equipped with the most comprehensive powers.

13. Communist parties in those countries where communists carry on their work legally must from time to time undertake cleansing (re-registration) of the membership of the party in order to get rid of any petty-bourgeois elements which have crept in.

14. Every party which wishes to join the Communist International is obliged to give unconditional support to any Soviet republic in its struggle against counter-revolutionary forces. Communist parties must carry on unambiguous propaganda to prevent the dispatch of munitions transports to the enemies of the Soviet republics; they must also carry on propaganda by every means, legal or illegal, among the troops sent to strangle workers' republics.

15. Parties which still retain their old social-democratic programmes are obliged to revise them as quickly as possible, and to draw up, in accordance with the special conditions of their country, a new communist programme in conformity with the decisions of the Communist International. As a rule the programme of every party belonging to the Communist International must be ratified by the regular congress of the Communist International or by the Executive Committee. Should the programme of a party not be ratified by the ECCI, the party concerned has the right to appeal to the Congress of the Communist International.

16. All the decisions of the congresses of the Communist International, as well as the decisions of its Executive Committee, are binding on all parties belonging to the Communist International. The Communist International, working in conditions of acute civil war, must be far more centralized in its structure than was the Second International. Consideration must of course be given by the Communist International and its Executive Committee in all their activities to the varying conditions in which the individual parties have to fight and work, and they must take decisions of general validity only when such decisions are possible.

17. In this connexion, all parties which wish to join the Communist International must change their names. Every party which wishes to join the Communist International must be called: *Communist* party of such and such

a country (section of the Communist International). This question of name is not merely a formal matter, but essentially a political question of great importance. The Communist International has declared war on the entire bourgeois world and on all yellow social-democratic parties. The difference between the communist parties and the old official "social-democratic" or "socialist" parties, which have betrayed the banner of the working class, must be brought home to every ordinary worker.

18. All leading party press organs in all countries are obliged to publish all important official documents of the Executive Committee of the Communist International.

19. All parties belonging to the Communist International and those which have applied for admission, are obliged to convene an extraordinary congress as soon as possible, and in any case not later than four months after the second congress of the Communist International, to examine all these conditions of admission. In this connexion all party centres must see that the decisions of the second congress of the Communist International are made known to all local organizations.

20. Those parties which now wish to join the Communist International, but which have not radically changed their former tactics, must see to it that, before entering the Communist International, not less than two-thirds of the members of their central committee and of all their leading central bodies consist of comrades who publicly and unambiguously advocated the entry of their party into the Communist International before its second congress. Exceptions can be made with the consent of the Executive Committee of the Communist International. The ECCI also has the right to make exceptions in the case of representatives of the centre mentioned in paragraph 7.

21. Those members of the party who reject in principle the conditions and theses put forward by the Communist International are to be expelled from the party.

The same applies in particular to delegates to the extraordinary congresses.

Appendix 16 PRELIMINARY DRAFT RESOLUTION OF THE TENTH CONGRESS OF THE R.C.P. ON PARTY UNITY, MARCH, 1921 [1]

1. The Congress calls the attention of all members of the Party to the fact that the unity and cohesion of the ranks of the Party, the guarantee of complete mutual confidence among Party members and genuine team-work that really embodies the unanimity of will of the vanguard of the proletariat, are particularly essential at the present time, when a number of circumstances are increasing the vacillation among the petty-bourgeois population of the country.

2. Notwithstanding this, even before the general Party discussion on the trade unions, certain signs of factionalism had been apparent in the Party—the formation of groups with separate platforms, striving to a certain degree to segregate and create their own group discipline. Such symptoms of factionalism were manifested, for example, at a Party conference in Moscow (November, 1920) and at a Party conference in Kharkov, by the so-called Workers' Opposition group, and partly by the so-called Democratic Centralism group.

All class-conscious workers must clearly realise that factionalism of any kind is harmful and impermissible, for no matter how members of individual groups may desire to safeguard Party unity, factionalism in practice inevitably leads to the weakening of team-work and to intensified and repeated attempts by the enemies of the governing Party, who have wormed their way into it, to widen the cleavage and to use it for counter-revolutionary purposes.

The way the enemies of the proletariat take advantage of every deviation from a thoroughly consistent communist line was perhaps most strikingly shown in the case of the Kronstadt mutiny, when the bourgeois counter-revolutionaries and whiteguards in all countries of the world immediately expressed their readiness to accept the slogans of the Soviet system, if only they might thereby secure the overthrow of the dictatorship of the proletariat in Russia, and when the Socialist-Revolutionaries and the bourgeois counter-revolutionaries in general resorted in Kronstadt to slogans calling for an insurrection against the Soviet Government of Russia ostensibly in the interest of the Soviet power. These facts fully prove that the whiteguards strive, and are able, to disguise themselves as Communists, and even as the most Left-wing Communists, solely for the purpose of weakening and destroying the bulwark of the proletarian revolution in Russia. Menshevik

[1] V. I. Lenin. *Collected Works*, 4th ed. (Moscow: Progress, 1965), XXXII, pp. 241–244.

leaflets distributed in Petrograd on the eve of the Kronstadt mutiny likewise show how the Mensheviks took advantage of the disagreements and certain rudiments of factionalism in the Russian Communist Party actually in order to egg on and support the Kronstadt mutineers, the Socialist-Revolutionaries and the whiteguards, while claiming to be opponents of mutiny and supporters of the Soviet power, only with supposedly slight modifications.

3. In this question, propaganda should consist, on the one hand, in a comprehensive explanation of the harmfulness and danger of factionalism from the standpoint of Party unity and of achieving unanimity of will among the vanguard of the proletariat as the fundamental condition for the success of the dictatorship of the proletariat; and, on the other hand, in an explanation of the peculiar features of the latest tactical devices of the enemies of the Soviet power. These enemies, having realised the hopelessness of counter-revolution under an openly whiteguard flag, are now doing their utmost to utilise the disagreements within the Russian Communist Party and to further the counter-revolution in one way or another by transferring power to a political group which is outwardly closest to recognition of the Soviet power.

Propaganda must also teach the lessons of preceding revolutions, in which the counter-revolution made a point of supporting the opposition to the extreme revolutionary party which stood closest to the latter, in order to undermine and overthrow the revolutionary dictatorship and thus pave the way for the subsequent complete victory of the counter-revolution, of the capitalists and landowners.

4. In the practical struggle against factionalism, every organisation of the Party must take strict measures to prevent all factional actions. Criticism of the Party's shortcomings, which is absolutely necessary, must be conducted in such a way that every practical proposal shall be submitted immediately, without any delay, in the most precise form possible, for consideration and decision to the leading local and central bodies of the Party. Moreover, every critic must see to it that the form of his criticism takes account of the position of the Party, surrounded as it is by a ring of enemies, and that the content of his criticism is such that, by directly participating in Soviet and Party work, he can test the rectification of the errors of the Party or of individual Party members in practice. Analyses of the Party's general line, estimates of its practical experience, check-ups of the fulfilment of its decisions, studies of methods of rectifying errors, etc., must under no circumstances be submitted for preliminary discussion to groups formed on the basis of "platforms," etc., but must in all cases be submitted for discussion directly to all the members of the Party. For this purpose, the Congress orders a more regular publication of *Diskussionny Listok* and special symposiums to promote unceasing efforts to ensure that criticism shall be concentrated on essentials and shall not assume a form capable of assisting the class enemies of the proletariat.

5. Rejecting in principle the deviation towards syndicalism and anarchism, which is examined in a special resolution, and instructing the Central Committee to secure the complete elimination of all factionalism, the Congress at the same time declares that every practical proposal concerning

questions to which the so-called Workers' Opposition group, for example, has devoted special attention, such as purging the Party of non-proletarian and unreliable elements, combating bureaucratic practices, developing democracy and workers' initiative, etc., must be examined with the greatest care and tested in practice. The Party must know that we have not taken all the necessary measures in regard to these questions because of various obstacles, but that, while ruthlessly rejecting impractical and factional pseudo-criticism, the Party will unceasingly continue—trying out new methods—to fight with all the means at its disposal against the evils of bureaucracy, for the extension of democracy and initiative, for detecting, exposing and expelling from the Party elements that have wormed their way into its ranks, etc.

6. The Congress, therefore, hereby declares dissolved and orders the immediate dissolution of all groups without exception formed on the basis of one platform or another (such as the Workers' Opposition group, the Democratic Centralism group, etc.). Non-observance of this decision of the Congress shall entail unconditional and instant expulsion from the Party.

7. In order to ensure strict discipline within the Party and in all Soviet work and to secure the maximum unanimity in eliminating all factionalism, the Congress authorises the Central Committee, in cases of breach of discipline or of a revival or toleration of factionalism, to apply all Party penalties, including expulsion, and in regard to members of the Central Committee, reduction to the status of alternate members and, as an extreme measure, expulsion from the Party. A necessary condition for the application of such an extreme measure to members of the Central Committee, alternate members of the Central Committee and members of the Control Commission is the convocation of a Plenary Meeting of the Central Committee, to which all alternate members of the Central Committee and all members of the Control Commission shall be invited. If such a general assembly of the most responsible leaders of the Party deems it necessary by a two-thirds majority to reduce a member of the Central Committee to the status of alternate member, or to expel him from the Party, this measure shall be put into effect immediately.

Appendix 17 APPEAL OF THE EXECUTIVE
COMMITTEE OF THE COMMUNIST
INTERNATIONAL FOR HELP FOR THE
FAMINE-STRICKEN AREAS OF RUSSIA,
DECEMBER 4, 1921 [1]

PROLETARIANS OF ALL COUNTRIES! TO THE AID OF THE RUSSIAN
PROLETARIAT

Workers! Over the whole world capitalism is moving towards the attack. The more the capitalist world decays, the higher the wave of unemployment and crisis rises, rolling like an avalanche from country to country, the more impudently capital attacks your organizations, the louder it boasts of its strength and its power. But its foremost heralds and trumpeters, ministers and presidents, bankers and kings, are preparing new wars for humanity and are working out new armament programmes, pushing all the countries of the world into a war which will be more destructive, inhuman, and horrible than its predecessor. It will leave nothing standing and will kill and cripple millions of human beings—workers and peasants, the productive population of city and country.

Comrades! All of you, without distinction of party, must realize this. You must all understand that the only guarantee for your victory is your own strength, your own proletarian power. Who at the present time holds in check the insane plans of the capitalists? Who fills them with terror and fear?

Your Soviet Russia! For every capitalist government fears the armed Russian workers. For every capitalist government understands that Soviet Russia is to-day the chief instrument, *the main weapon in the hands of the world proletariat.*

Imagine that Soviet Russia has fallen. Then the wave of bloody reaction would overwhelm the entire world. Capitalism would then stride in a triumphal march over the skulls of the working-class. It would consolidate its position for long, long years.

[1] From *The Communist International, 1919–1943. Documents.* Edited by Jane Degras and published by Oxford University Press under the auspices of the Royal Institute of International Affairs. (London: Oxford University Press, 1956), I, pp. 301–303.

450

THEREFORE HELP SOVIET RUSSIA!

Help its workers who have borne the brunt of the first combined blows of the capitalist governments.

IN YOUR OWN INTERESTS HASTEN TO
THE ASSISTANCE OF THE FIRST SOVIET STATE

The Russian workers have only now won the possibility of building up their economy. Only now is production beginning to rise, are the chimneys of its factories beginning to smoke.

But the drought is clipping the wings of the Russian proletariat. In the rich Volga region the grain has completely withered. Millions of human beings are dying in horrible agony. Sickness and starvation are mowing down old and young, and little children are dying with a cry for help on their lips. The situation is serious. The misfortune is great.

PROLETARIANS, HURRY TO THE AID OF SOVIET RUSSIA!

A number of workers' organizations have already given their mite for the Russian workers and peasants. The communists have collected 100,000,000 marks. Other workers' organizations have also given much help. This enables us to feed about 50,000 persons.

BUT THAT IS NOT ENOUGH! HASTEN, FRIENDS OF THE WORKING CLASS

Especially you, workers of North and South America, Australia, and South Africa. You have not yet gone through the bloody battle with capital. You have not yet been drawn into the final conflict. But the capitalist monster is already grasping you by the throat. It is already throwing millions of workers into the streets. It is ready to deal you too the final blow.

HURRY TO THE ASSISTANCE OF YOUR CHIEF FORTRESS, SOVIET RUSSIA!

Help it to grow strong and to consolidate. You will be repaid a hundred-fold. Together, in serried battle ranks, enter the struggle against the famine in Russia.

Long live the solidarity of the workers who will not let down their brothers in distress and misery!

Appendix 18   TREATY OF RAPALLO, APRIL 16, 1922 [1]

The German Government, represented by Reichsminister Dr. Walther Rathenau, and the Government of the Russian Socialist Federal Soviet Republic, represented by People's Commissary Tchitcherin, have agreed upon the following provisions:

ARTICLE I

The two governments agree that all questions resulting from the state of war between Germany and Russia shall be settled in the following manner:

A. Both governments mutually renounce repayment for their war expenses and for damages arising out of the war, that is to say, damages caused to them and their nationals in the zone of war operations by military measures, including all requisitions effected in a hostile country. They renounce in the same way repayment for civil damages inflicted on civilians, that is to say, damages caused to the nationals of the two countries by exceptional war legislation or by violent measures taken by any authority of the state of either side.

B. All legal relations concerning questions of public or private law resulting from the state of war, including the question of the treatment of merchant ships which fell into the hands of the one side or the other during the war, shall be settled on the basis of reciprocity.

C. Germany and Russia mutually renounce repayment of expenses incurred for prisoners of war. The German Government also renounces repayment of expenses for soldiers of the Red Army interned in Germany. The Russian Government, for its part, renounces repayment of the sums Germany has derived from the sale of Russian Army material brought into Germany by these interned troops.

ARTICLE II

Germany renounces all claims resulting from the enforcement of the laws and measures of the Soviet Republic as it has affected German nationals or their private rights or the rights of the German State itself, as well as claims resulting from measures taken by the Soviet Republic or its authorities in any other way against subjects of the German State or their

[1] *The American Journal of International Law.* Supplement XX (1926), pp. 116–117.

private rights, provided that the Soviet Republic shall not satisfy similar claims made by any third state.

ARTICLE III

Consular and diplomatic relations between Germany and the Federal Soviet Republic shall be resumed immediately. The admission of consuls to both countries shall be arranged by special agreement.

ARTICLE IV

Both governments agree, further, that the rights of the nationals of either of the two parties on the other's territory as well as the regulation of commercial relations shall be based on the most-favored-nation principle. This principle does not include rights and facilities granted by the Soviet Government to another Soviet State or to any State that formerly formed part of the Russian Empire.

ARTICLE V

The two governments undertake to give each other mutual assistance for the alleviation of their economic difficulties in the most benevolent spirit. In the event of a general settlement of this question on an international basis, they undertake to have a preliminary exchange of views. The German Government declares itself ready to facilitate, as far as possible, the conclusion and the execution of economic contracts between private enterprises in the two countries.

ARTICLE VI

Article I, paragraph B, and Article IV of this agreement will come into force after the ratification of this document. The other articles will come into force immediately.

Done in duplicate at Rapallo, April 16, 1922.

(Signed) Rathenau   (Signed) Tchitcherin

Appendix 19 LENIN'S "TESTAMENT," DECEMBER 24, 1922 [1]

By stability of the Central Committee, of which I spoke above, I mean measures against a split, as far as such measures can at all be taken. For, of course, the whiteguard in *Russkaya Mysl* (it seems to have been S. S. Oldenburg) was right when, first, in the whiteguards' game against Soviet Russia he banked on a split in our Party, and when, secondly, he banked on grave differences in our Party to cause that split.

Our Party relies on two classes and therefore its instability would be possible and its downfall inevitable if there were no agreement between those two classes. In that event this or that measure, and generally all talk about the stability of our C.C., would be futile. No measures of any kind could prevent a split in such a case. But I hope that this is too remote a future and too improbable an event to talk about.

I have in mind stability as a guarantee against a split in the immediate future, and I intend to deal here with a few ideas concerning personal qualities.

I think that from this standpoint the prime factors in the question of stability are such members of the C.C. as Stalin and Trotsky. I think relations between them make up the greater part of the danger of a split, which could be avoided, and this purpose, in my opinion, would be served, among other things, by increasing the number of C.C. members to 50 or 100.

Comrade Stalin, having become Secretary-General, has unlimited authority concentrated in his hands, and I am not sure whether he will always be capable of using that authority with sufficient caution. Comrade Trotsky, on the other hand, as his struggle against the C.C. on the question of the People's Commissariat for Communications has already proved, is distinguished not only by outstanding ability. He is personally perhaps the most capable man in the present C.C., but he has displayed excessive self-assurance and shown excessive preoccupation with the purely administrative side of the work.

These two qualities of the two outstanding leaders of the present C.C. can inadvertently lead to a split, and if our Party does not take steps to avert this, the split may come unexpectedly.

I shall not give any further appraisals of the personal qualities of other members of the C.C. I shall just recall that the October episode with Zinoviev and Kamenev was, of course, no accident, but neither can the blame for it be laid upon them personally, any more than non-Bolshevism can upon Trotsky.

[1] V. I. Lenin. *Collected Works.* (Moscow: Progress, 1966), XXXVI, pp. 594–596.

Speaking of the young C.C. members, I wish to say a few words about Bukharin and Pyatakov. They are, in my opinion, the most outstanding figures (among the youngest ones), and the following must be borne in mind about them: Bukharin is not only a most valuable and major theorist of the Party; he is also rightly considered the favourite of the whole Party, but his theoretical views can be classified as fully Marxist only with great reserve, for there is something scholastic about him (he has never made a study of dialectics, and, I think, never fully understood it).

December 25. As for Pyatakov, he is unquestionably a man of outstanding will and outstanding ability, but shows too much zeal for administrating and the administrative side of the work to be relied upon in a serious political matter.

Both of these remarks, of course, are made only for the present, on the assumption that both these outstanding and devoted Party workers fail to find an occasion to enhance their knowledge and amend their one-sidedness.

Lenin

December 25, 1922
Taken down by M. V.

ADDITION TO THE LETTER OF DECEMBER 24, 1922

Stalin is too rude and this defect, although quite tolerable in our midst and in dealings among us Communists, becomes intolerable in a Secretary-General. That is why I suggest that the comrades think about a way of removing Stalin from that post and appointing another man in his stead who in all other respects differs from Comrade Stalin in having only one advantage, namely, that of being more tolerant, more loyal, more polite and more considerate to the comrades, less capricious, etc. This circumstance may appear to be a negligible detail. But I think that from the standpoint of safeguards against a split and from the standpoint of what I wrote above about the relationship between Stalin and Trotsky it is not a detail, or it is a detail which can assume decisive importance.

Lenin

January 4, 1923
Taken down by L. F.

Appendix 20 CONSTITUTION AND RULES OF THE COMMUNIST INTERNATIONAL [1]

I. NAME AND OBJECTS

1. The Communist International—the International Worker's Association—is a union of Communist Parties in various countries; it is a World Communist Party. As the leader and organizer of the world revolutionary movement of the proletariat and the bearer of the principles and aims of Communism, the Communist International strives to win over the majority of the working class and the broad strata of the property-less peasantry, fights for the establishment of the world dictatorship of the proletariat, for the establishment of a World Union of Socialist Soviet Republics, for the complete abolition of classes and for the achievement of Socialism—the first stage of Communist society.

2. The various Parties affiliated to the Communist International are called the Communist Party of, . . . name of country (Section of the Communist International). In any given country there can be only one Communist Party affiliated to the Communist International and representing its Section in that country.

3. Membership of the Communist Party and of the Communist International is open to all those who accept the programme and rules of the given Communist party and of the Communist International, who join one of the basic units of a Party, actively work in it, abide by all the decisions of the Party and of the Communist International, and regularly pay Party dues.

4. The basic unit of the Communist Party organisation is the nucleus in the place of employment (factory, workshop, mine, office, store, farm, etc.) which unites all the Party members employed in the given enterprise.

5. The Communist International and its Sections are built up on the basis of democratic centralism, the fundamental principles of which are: (a) election of all the leading committees of the Party, subordinate and superior, (by general meetings of Party members, conferences, congresses and international congresses); (b) periodical reports by leading Party committees to their constituents; (c) decisions of superior Party committees to be obligatory for subordinate committees, strict Party discipline and prompt execution of the decisions of the Communist International, of its leading committees and of the leading Party organs.

Party questions may be discussed by the members of the Party and by Party organisations until such time as a decision is taken upon them by the competent Party committees. After a decision has been taken by the Congress of the Communist International, by the Congress of the respective Sections, or by leading committees of the Comintern, and of its various Sections, these deci-

---

[1] *International Press Correspondence*, No. 84 (1928), pp. 1600–1601.

sions must be unreservedly carried out even if a Section of the Party membership or of the local Party organisations are in disagreement with it.

In cases where a Party exists illegally, the superior Party committees may appoint the subordinate committees and coopt members on their own committees, subject to subsequent endorsement by the competent superior Party committees.

6. In all non-Party, workers' and peasants' mass organisations and in their leading committees (trade unions, co-operative societies, sport organisations, ex-service men's organisations, [and at their congresses and conferences] and also on) municipal bodies and in parliament, even if there are only two Party members in such organisations and bodies, Communist fractions must be formed for the purpose of strengthening the Party's influence and for carrying out its policy in these organisations and bodies.

7. The Communist fractions are subordinated to the competent Party bodies.

Note:

1. Communist fractions in international organisations (Red International of Labour Unions, International Class War Prisoners Aid Society, International Workers Relief, etc.) are subordinate to the Executive Committee of the Communist International.

2. The organisational structure of the Communist fractions and the manner in which their work is guided are determined by special instructions from the Executive Committee of the Communist International and from the Central Committees of the given Sections of the Comintern.

II. THE WORLD CONGRESS OF THE COMMUNIST INTERNATIONAL

8. The supreme body of the Communist International is the World Congress of representatives of all Parties (Sections) and organisations affiliated to the Communist International.

The World Congress discusses and decides programme, tactical and organisational questions connected with the activities of the Communist International and of its various sections. Power to alter the programme and rules of the Communist International lies exclusively with the World Congress of the Communist International.

The World Congress shall be convened once every two years. The date of the Congress and the number of representatives from the various Sections to the Congress to be determined by the Executive Committee of the Communist International.

The number of decisive votes to be allocated to each Section at the World Congress shall be determined by a special decision of the Congress itself, in accordance with the membership of the given Party and the political importance of the given country. Delegates to the Congress must have a free mandate; no imperative mandate can be recognised.

9. Special Congresses of the Communist International shall be convened on the demand of Parties which, at the preceding World Congress had an aggregate of not less than one half of the decisive votes.

10. The World Congress elects the Executive Committee of the Communist International (E.C.C.I.) and the International Control Commission (I.C.C.).

11. The headquarters of the Executive Committee is decided on by the World Congress.

III. THE EXECUTIVE COMMITTEE OF THE COMMUNIST INTERNATIONAL AND ITS SUBSIDIARY BODIES

12. The leading body of the Communist International in the period between Congresses is the Executive Committee, which gives instructions to all the Sections of the Communist International and controls their activity.

The E.C.C.I. publishes the Central Organ of the Communist International, in not less than four languages.

13. The decisions of the E.C.C.I. are obligatory for all the Sections of the Communist International and must be promptly carried out. The Sections have the right to appeal against decisions of the E.C.C.I. to the World Congress, but must continue to carry out such decisions pending the decision of the World Congress.

14. The Central Committees of the various Sections of the Communist International are responsible to their respective Party Congress and to the E.C.C.I. The latter has the right to annul or amend decisions of Party Congresses and of Central Committees of Parties and also to make decisions which are obligatory for them. (Cf. Par. 13).

15. The E.C.C.I. has the right to expel from the Communist International, entire Sections, groups and individual members who violate the programme and rules of the Communist International or the decisions of the World Congress and of the E.C.C.I. Persons and bodies expelled have the right of appeal to the World Congress.

16. The programmes of the various Sections of the Communist International must be endorsed by the E.C.C.I. In the event of the E.C.C.I. refusing to endorse a programme, the Section concerned has the right to appeal to the World Congress of the Communist International.

17. The leading organs of the press of the various Sections of the Communist International must publish all the decisions and official documents of the E.C.C.I. These decisions must, as far as possible, be published also in the other organs of the Party press.

18. The E.C.C.I. has the right to accept affiliation to the Communist International of organisations and Parties sympathetic to Communism, such organisations to have an advisory vote.

19. The E.C.C.I. elects a Presidium responsible to the E.C.C.I., which acts as the permanent body carrying out all the business of the E.C.C.I. in the interval between the meetings of the latter.

20. The E.C.C.I. and its Presidium has the right to establish Permanent Bureaus (Western European, South American, Eastern and other Bureaus of

the E.C.C.I.) for the purpose of establishing closer contact with the various Sections of the Communist International and in order to be better able to guide their work.

Note:

The scope of the activities of the permanent bureaus of the E.C.C.I. shall be determined by the E.C.C.I. or by its Presidium. The Sections of the Communist International which come within the scope of activities of the permanent bureaus of the E.C.C.I. must be informed by the powers conferred on these bureaus.

21. The Sections must carry out instructions of the permanent bureaus of the E.C.C.I. Sections may appeal against the instructions of the permanent bureaus to the E.C.C.I. or to its Presidium, but must continue to carry out such instructions pending the decision of E.C.C.I. or of its Presidium.

22. The E.C.C.I. and its Presidium have the right to send their representatives to the various Sections of the Communist International. Such representatives receive their instructions from the E.C.C.I. or from its Presidium, and are responsible to them for their activities. Representatives of the E.C.C.I. have the right to participate in meetings of the central Party bodies as well as of the local organisations of the sections to which they are sent. Representatives of the E.C.C.I. must carry out their commission in close contact with the Central Committee of the Section to which they are sent. They may, however, speak in opposition to the Central Committee of the given Section, at Congresses and Conferences of that Section, if the line of the Central Committee in question diverges from the instructions of the E.C.C.I. Respresentatives of the E.C.C.I. are especially obliged to supervise the carrying out of the decisions of the World Congresses and of the Executive Committee of the Communist International.

The E.C.C.I. and its Presidium also have the right to send instructors to the various Sections of the Communist International. The powers and duties of instructors are determined by the E.C.C.I., to whom the instructors are responsible in their work.

23. Meetings of the E.C.C.I. must take place not less than once every six months. A quorum must consist of not less than one half of the membership of the E.C.C.I.

24. Meetings of the Presidium of the E.C.C.I. must take place not less than once a fortnight. A quorum must consist of not less than one half of the membership of the Presidium.

25. The Presidium elects the Political Secretariat, which is empowered to take decisions, and which also prepares questions for the meetings of the E.C.C.I. and of its Presidium, and acts as their executive body.

26. The Presidium appoints the editorial committees of the periodical and other publications of the Communist International.

27. The Presidium of the E.C.C.I. sets up a Department for Work Among Women Toilers, permanent committees for guiding the work of definite groups of Sections of the Communist International (Lander Secretariats) and other departments necessary for its work.

IV. THE INTERNATIONAL CONTROL COMMISSION

28. The International Control Commission investigates matters concerning the unity of the Sections affiliated to the Communist International and also matters connected with the Communist conduct of individual members of the various Sections.

For this purpose the I.C.C.:

(a) Examines complaints against the actions of Central Committees of Communist Parties lodged by Party members who have been subjected to disciplinary measures for political differences;

(b) Examines such analogous matters concerning members of central bodies of Communist Parties and of individual Party members as it deems necessary, or which are submitted to it by the deciding bodies of the E.C.C.I.;

(c) Audits the accounts of the Communist International.

The International Control Commission must not intervene in the political differences or in organisational and administrative conflicts in the Communist Parties.

The headquarters of the I.C.C. are fixed by the I.C.C., in agreement with the E.C.C.I.

V. THE RELATIONSHIPS BETWEEN THE SECTIONS OF THE COMMUNIST INTERNATIONAL AND THE E.C.C.I.

29. The Central Committees of Sections affiliated to the Communist International and the Central Committees of affiliated sympathising organisations must send to the E.C.C.I. the Minutes of their meetings and reports of their work.

30. Resignation from office by individual members or groups of members of Central Committees of the various Sections are regarded as disruption of the Communist movement. Leading posts in the Party do not belong to the occupant of that post, but to the Communist International as a whole. Elected members of the Central leading bodies of the various Sections may resign before their time of office expires, only with the consent of the E.C.C.I. Resignations accepted by Central Committees of Sections without the consent of the E.C.C.I. are invalid.

31. The Sections affiliated to the Communist International must maintain close organisational and informational contact with each other, arrange for mutual representation at each others conferences and congresses, and, with the consent of the E.C.C.I., exchange leading comrades. This applies particularly to the Sections in imperial countries and their colonies, and to the Sections in countries adjacent to each other.

32. Two or more Sections of the Communist International which, (like the Sections in the Scandinavian countries and in the Balkans) are politically connected with each other by common conditions of struggle, may, with the consent of the E.C.C.I., form federations for the purpose of co-ordinating their

activities, such federations to work under the guidance and control of the E.C.C.I.

33. The Sections of the Comintern must regularly pay affiliation dues to the E.C.C.I.; the amount of such dues to be determined by the E.C.C.I.

34. Congresses of the various Sections, ordinary and special, can be convened only with the consent of the E.C.C.I.

In the event of a Section failing to convene a Party Congress prior to the convening of a World Congress, that Section, before electing delegates to the World Congress, must convene a Party conference, or Plenum of its Central Committee, for the purpose of preparing the questions for the World Congress.

35. The Young Communist International is a Section of the Communist International with full rights and is subordinate to the E.C.C.I.

36. The Communist Parties must be prepared for transition to illegal conditions. The E.C.C.I. must render the Parties concerned assistance in their preparations for transition to illegal conditions.

37. Individual members of Sections of the Communist International may pass from one country to another only with the consent of the Central Committee of the Section of which they are members.

Communists changing their domicile must join the Section in the country of their new domicile. Communists leaving their country without the consent of the Central Committee of their Section, must not be accepted into other Sections of the Communist International.

Appendix 21 STALIN'S THOUGHTS ON 'SOCIALISM IN ONE COUNTRY', DECEMBER, 1924 [1]

. . . There are two specific features of the October Revolution which must be understood first of all if we are to comprehend the inner meaning and the historical significance of that revolution.

What are these features?

Firstly, the fact that the dictatorship of the proletariat was born in our country as a power which came into existence on the basis of an alliance between the proletariat and the labouring masses of the peasantry. Secondly, the fact that the dictatorship of the proletariat became established in our country as a result of the victory of socialism in one country—a country in which capitalism was little developed—while capitalism was preserved in other countries where capitalism was more highly developed. This does not mean, of course, that the October Revolution has no other specific features. But it is precisely these two specific features that are important for us at the present moment, not only because they distinctly express the essence of the October Revolution, but also because they brilliantly reveal the opportunist nature of the theory of "permanent revolution." . . .

The October Revolution was victorious because it was able to deprive the bourgeoisie of its peasant reserves, because it was able to win these reserves to the side of the proletariat, and because in this revolution the proletariat proved to be the only guiding force for the vast masses of the labouring people of town and country.

He who has not understood this will never understand either the character of the October Revolution, or the nature of the dictatorship of the proletariat, or the specific characteristics of the internal policy of our proletarian power.

The dictatorship of the proletariat is not simply a governmental stratum "skilfully" selected" by the careful hand of an "experienced strategist," and "judiciously relying" on the support of one section or another of the population. The dictatorship of the proletariat is the class alliance between the proletariat and the labouring masses of the peasantry for the purpose of overthrowing capital, for achieving the final victory of socialism, on the condition that the guiding force of this alliance is the proletariat.

Thus, it is not a question of "slightly" underestimating or "slightly" overestimating the revolutionary potentialities of the peasant movement, as certain diplomatic advocates of "permanent revolution" are now fond of expressing it. It is a question of the nature of the new proletarian state which arose as a result of the October Revolution. It is a question of the character of the proletarian power, of the foundations of the dictatorship of the proletariat itself. . . .

[1] J. V. Stalin, *Works* (Moscow: Foreign Languages Publishing House, 1953), VI, pp. 378 ff.

462

Some comrades believe that this theory is a purely "Russian" theory, applicable only to Russian conditions. That is wrong. It is absolutely wrong. In speaking of the labouring masses of the non-proletarian classes which are led by the proletariat, Lenin has in mind not only the Russian peasants, but also the labouring elements of the border regions of the Soviet Union, which until recently were colonies of Russia. Lenin constantly reiterated that without an alliance with these masses of other nationalities the proletariat of Russia could not achieve victory. In his articles on the national question and in his speeches at the congresses of the Comintern, Lenin repeatedly said that the victory of the world revolution was impossible without a revolutionary alliance, a revolutionary bloc, between the proletariat of the advanced countries and the oppressed peoples of the enslaved colonies. But what are colonies if not the oppressed labouring masses, and, primarily, the labouring masses of the peasantry? Who does not know that the question of emancipating the colonies is *essentially* a question of emancipating the labouring masses of the non-proletarian classes from the oppression and exploitation of finance capital?

But from this it follows that Lenin's theory of the dictatorship of the proletariat is not a purely "Russian" theory, but a theory which necessarily applies to all countries. Bolshevism is not only a Russian phenomenon. "Bolshevism," says Lenin, is *"a model of tactics for all"* (see Vol. XXIII, p. 386).

Such are the characteristics of the first specific feature of the October Revolution. . . .

According to Lenin, the revolution draws its strength primarily from among the workers and peasants of Russia itself. According to Trotsky, the necessary strength can be found *only* "in the arena of the world proletarian revolution."

But what if the world revolution is fated to arrive with some delay? Is there any ray of hope for our revolution? Trotsky offers no ray of hope, for "the contradictions in the position of a workers' government . . . could be solved *only* . . . in the arena of the world proletarian revolution." According to this plan, there is but one prospect left for our revolution: to vegetate in its own contradictions and rot away while waiting for the world revolution.

What is the dictatorship of the proletariat according to Lenin?

The dictatorship of the proletariat is power which rests on an alliance between the proletariat and the labouring masses of the peasantry for "the complete overthrow of capital" and for "the final establishment and consolidation of socialism."

What is the dictatorship of the proletariat according to Trotsky?

The dictatorship of the proletariat is a power which comes "into hostile collision" with "the broad masses of the peasantry" and seeks the solution of its "contradictions" only "in the arena of the world proletarian revolution."

What difference is there between this "theory of permanent revolution" and the well-known theory of Menshevism which repudiates the concept of dictatorship of the proletariat?

Essentially, there is no difference.

There can be no doubt at all. "Permanent revolution" is not a mere underestimation of the revolutionary potentialities of the peasant movement. "Permanent revolution" is an underestimation of the peasant movement which leads to the *repudiation* of Lenin's theory of the dictatorship of the proletariat.

Trotsky's "permanent revolution" is a variety of Menshevism.

This is how matters stand with regard to the first specific feature of the October Revolution. . . .

The second specific feature of the October Revolution lies in the fact that this revolution represents a model of the practical application of Lenin's theory of the proletarian revolution.

He who has not understood this specific feature of the October Revolution will never understand either the international nature of this revolution, or its colossal international might, or the specific features of its foreign policy. . . .

It is plain that these two views [Trotsky's and Lenin's] are incompatible and cannot in any way be reconciled. Trotsky's "permanent revolution" is the repudiation of Lenin's theory of the proletarian revolution; and conversely, Lenin's theory of the proletarian revolution is the repudiation of the theory of "permanent revolution."

Lack of faith in the strength and capacities of our revolution, lack of faith in the strength and capacity of the Russian proletariat—that is what lies at the root of the theory of "permanent revolution." Hitherto only *one* aspect of the theory of "permanent revolution" has usually been noted—lack of faith in the revolutionary potentialities of the peasant movement. Now, in fairness, this must be supplemented by *another* aspect—lack of faith in the strength and capacity of the proletariat in Russia.

What difference is there between Trotsky's theory and the ordinary Menshevik theory that the victory of socialism in one country, and in a backward country at that, is impossible without the preliminary victory of the proletarian revolution "in the principal countries of Western Europe"?

Essentially, there is no difference.

There can be no doubt at all. Trotsky's theory of "permanent revolution" is a variety of Menshevism.

Appendix 22 STALIN'S "DIZZY WITH SUCCESS" ARTICLE, MARCH 2, 1930 [1]

The Soviet government's successes in the sphere of the collective-farm movement are now being spoken of by everyone. Even our enemies are forced to admit that the successes are substantial. And they really are very great.

It is a fact that by February 20 of this year 50 per cent of the peasant farms throughout the U.S.S.R. had been collectivised. That means that by February 20, 1930, we had *overfulfilled* the five-year plan of collectivisation by more than 100 per cent.

It is a fact that on February 28 of this year the collective farms had *already succeeded* in stocking upwards of 36,000,000 centners, i.e., about 220,000,000 poods of seed for the spring sowing, which is more than 90 per cent of the plan. It must be admitted that the accumulation of 220,000,000 poods of seed by the collective farms alone—after the successful fulfilment of the grain-procurement plan—is a tremendous achievement.

What does all this show?

That a *radical turn of the countryside towards socialism may be considered as already achieved.*

There is no need to prove that these successes are of supreme importance for the fate of our country, for the whole working class, which is the directing force of our country, and, lastly, for the Party itself. To say nothing of the direct practical results, these successes are of immense value for the internal life of the Party itself, for the education of our Party. They imbue our Party with a spirit of cheerfulness and confidence in its strength. They arm the working class with confidence in the victory of our cause. They bring forward additional millions of reserves for our Party.

Hence the Party's task is: to *consolidate* the successes achieved and to *utilise* them systematically for our further advancement.

But successes have their seamy side, especially when they are attained with comparative "ease"—"unexpectedly," so to speak. Such successes sometimes induce a spirit of vanity and conceit: "We can achieve anything!" "There's nothing we can't do!" People not infrequently become intoxicated by such successes; they become dizzy with success, lose all sense of proportion and the capacity to understand realities; they show a tendency to overrate their own strength and to underrate the strength of the enemy; adventurist attempts are made to solve all questions of socialist construc-

[1] J. V. Stalin. *Works.* (Moscow: Foreign Languages Publishing House, 1955), XII, pp. 197–205.

tion "in a trice." In such a case, there is no room for concern to *consolidate* the successes achieved and to *utilise* them systematically for further advancement. Why should we consolidate the successes achieved when, as it is, we can dash to the full victory of socialism "in a trice": "We can achieve anything!" "There's nothing we can't do!"

Hence the Party's task is: to wage a determined struggle against these sentiments, which are dangerous and harmful to our cause, and to drive them out of the Party.

It cannot be said that these dangerous and harmful sentiments are at all widespread in the ranks of our Party. But they do exist in our Party, and there are no grounds for asserting that they will not become stronger. And if they should be allowed free scope, then there can be no doubt that the collective-farm movement will be considerably weakened and the danger of its breaking down may become a reality.

Hence the task of our press is: systematically to denounce these and similar anti-Leninist sentiments.

A few facts.

1. The successes of our collective-farm policy are due, among other things, to the fact that it rests on the *voluntary character* of the collective-farm movement and on *taking into account the diversity of conditions* in the various regions of the U.S.S.R. Collective farms must not be established by force. That would be foolish and reactionary. The collective-farm movement must rest on the active support of the main mass of the peasantry. Examples of the formation of collective farms in the developed areas must not be mechanically transplanted to underdeveloped areas. That would be foolish and reactionary. Such a "policy" would discredit the collectivisation idea at one stroke. In determining the speed and methods of collective-farm development, careful consideration must be given to the diversity of conditions in the various regions of the U.S.S.R.

Our grain-growing areas are ahead of all others in the collective-farm movement. Why is this?

Firstly, because in these areas we have the largest number of already firmly-established state farms and collective farms, thanks to which the peasants have had the opportunity to convince themselves of the power and importance of the new technical equipment, of the power and importance of the new, collective organisation of farming.

Secondly, because these areas have had a two-years' schooling in the fight against the kulaks during the grain-procurement campaigns, and this could not but facilitate the development of the collective-farm movement.

Lastly, because these areas in recent years have been extensively supplied with the best cadres from the industrial centres.

Can it be said that these especially favourable conditions also exist in other areas, the consuming areas, for example, such as our northern regions, or in areas where there are still backward nationalities, such as Turkestan, say?

No, it cannot be said.

Clearly, the principle of taking into account the diversity of conditions in the various regions of the U.S.S.R. is, together with the voluntary principle, one of the most important prerequisites for a sound collective-farm movement.

But what actually happens sometimes? Can it be said that the voluntary principle and the principle of taking local peculiarities into account are not violated in a number of areas? No, that cannot be said, unfortunately. We know, for example, that in a number of the northern areas of the consuming zone, where conditions for the immediate organisation of collective farms are comparatively less favourable than in the grain-growing areas, attempts are not infrequently made to *replace* preparatory work for the organisation of collective farms by bureaucratic decreeing of the collective-farm movement, paper resolutions on the growth of collective farms, organisation of collective farms on paper—collective farms which have as yet no reality, but whose "existence" is proclaimed in a heap of boastful resolutions.

Or take certain areas of Turkestan, where conditions for the immediate organisation of collective farms are even less favourable than in the northern regions of the consuming zone. We know that in a number of areas of Turkestan there have already been attempts to "overtake and outstrip" the advanced areas of the U.S.S.R. by threatening to use armed force, by threatening that peasants who are not yet ready to join the collective farms will be deprived of irrigation water and manufactured goods.

What can there be in common between this Sergeant Prishibeyev "policy" and the Party's policy of relying on the voluntary principle and of taking local peculiarities into account in collective-farm development? Clearly, there is not and cannot be anything in common between them.

Who benefits by these distortions, this bureaucratic decreeing of the collective-farm movement, these unworthy threats against the peasants? Nobody, except our enemies!

What may these distortions lead to? To strengthening our enemies and to discrediting the idea of the collective-farm movement.

Is it not clear that the authors of these distortions, who imagine themselves to be "Lefts," are in reality bringing grist to the mill of Right opportunism?

2. One of the greatest merits of our Party's political strategy is that it is able at any given moment to pick out the *main link* in the movement, by grasping which the Party draws the whole chain towards one common goal in order to achieve the solution of the problem. Can it be said that the Party has already picked out the main link of the collective-farm movement in the system of collective-farm development? Yes, this can and should be said.

What is this chief link?

Is it, perhaps, *association for joint cultivation* of the land? No, it is not that. Associations for joint cultivation of the land, in which the means of production are not yet socialised, are already a past stage of the collective-farm movement.

Is it, perhaps, the *agricultural commune*? No, it is not that. Communes are still of isolated occurrence in the collective-farm movement. The conditions are not yet ripe for agricultural communes—in which not only production, but also distribution is socialised—to be the *predominant* form.

The main link of the collective-farm movement, its *predominant* form at the present moment, the link which has to be grasped now, is the *agricultural artel.*

In the *agricultural artel,* the basic means of production, primarily for grain-farming—labour, use of the land, machines and other implements, draught animals and farm buildings—are socialised. In the artel, the household plots (small vegetable gardens, small orchards), the dwelling houses, a part of the dairy cattle, small livestock, poultry, etc., are *not socialised.*

The artel is the *main link of the collective-farm movement* because it is the form best adapted for solving the grain problem. And the grain problem is the *main link in the whole system of agriculture* because, if it is not solved, it will be impossible to solve either the problem of stock-breeding (small and large), or the problem of the industrial and special crops that provide the principal raw materials for industry. That is why the agricultural artel is the main link in the system of the collective-farm movement at the present moment.

That is the point of departure of the "Model Rules" for collective farms, the final text of which is published today.[1]

And that should be the point of departure of our Party and Soviet workers, one of whose duties it is to make a thorough study of these Rules and to carry them out down to the last detail.

Such is the line of the Party at the present moment.

Can it be said that this line of the Party is being carried out without violation or distortion? No, it cannot, unfortunately. We know that in a number of areas of the U.S.S.R., where the struggle for the existence of the collective farms is still far from over, and where artels are not yet consolidated, attempts are being made to skip the artel framework and to leap straight away into the agricultural commune. The artel is still not consolidated, but they are already "socialising" dwelling houses, small livestock and poultry; moreover, this "socialisation" is degenerating into bureaucratic decreeing on paper, because the conditions which would make such socialisation necessary do not yet exist. One might think that the grain problem has already been solved in the collective farms, that it is already a past stage, that the principal task at the present moment is not solution of the grain problem, but solution of the problem of livestock- and poultry-breeding. Who, we may ask, benefits from this blockheaded "work" of lumping together different forms of the collective-farm movement? Who benefits from this running too far ahead, which is stupid and harmful to our cause? Irritating the collective-farm peasant by "socialising" dwelling houses, all dairy cattle, all small livestock and poultry, when the grain problem is still *unsolved,* when the artel form of collective farming is *not yet consolidated*— is it not obvious that such a "policy" can be to the satisfaction and advantage only of our sworn enemies?

One such overzealous "socialiser" even goes so far as to issue an order to an artel containing the following instructions: "within three days, register all the poultry of every household," establish posts of special "commanders" for registration and supervision; "occupy the key positions in the artel";

[1] *Pravda,* March 2, 1930.

"command the socialist battle without quitting your posts" and—of course— get a tight grip on the whole life of the artel.

What is this—a policy of directing the collective farms, or a policy of *disrupting* and *discrediting* them?

I say nothing of those "revolutionaries"—save the mark!—who *begin* the work of organising artels by removing the bells from the churches. Just imagine, removing the church bells—how r-r-revolutionary!

How could there have arisen in our midst such blockheaded exercises in "socialisation," such ludicrous attempts to overleap oneself, attempts which aim at bypassing classes and the class struggle, and which in fact bring grist to the mill of our class enemies?

They could have arisen only in the atmosphere of our "easy" and "unexpected" successes on the front of collective-farm development.

They could have arisen only as a result of the blockheaded belief of a section of our Party: "We can achieve anything!" "There's nothing we can't do!"

They could have arisen only because some of our comrades have become dizzy with success and for the moment have lost clearness of mind and sobriety of vision.

To correct the line of our work in the sphere of collective-farm development, *we must put an end to these sentiments.*

That is now one of the immediate tasks of the Party.

The art of leadership is a serious matter. One must not lag behind the movement, because to do so is to lose contact with the masses. But neither must one run too far ahead, because to run too far ahead is to lose the masses and to isolate oneself. He who wants to lead a movement and at the same time keep in touch with the vast masses must wage a fight on two fronts—against those who lag behind and against those who run too far ahead.

Our Party is strong and invincible because, when leading a movement, it is able to preserve and multiply its contacts with the vast masses of the workers and peasants.

Appendix 23 STALIN'S COMMENTS ON THE DRAFT OF THE 1936 CONSTITUTION [1]

I.

COMRADES!

The Constitutional Commission, whose draft has been submitted for consideration to the present Congress, was formed, as you know, by a special decision of the VIIth Congress of Soviets of the USSR. This decision was adopted on February 6, 1935. . . .

The day after this decision was adopted . . . the First Session of the Central Executive Committee of the Council of the USSR met and, in pursuance of the decisions of the VIIth Congress of Soviets of the USSR, set up a Constitutional Commission, consisting of 31 individuals. It instructed the Constitutional Commission to prepare a draft of an amended Constitution of the USSR. . . .

II.

CHANGES IN THE LIFE OF THE USSR IN THE PERIOD FROM 1924 TO 1936

What are the changes in the life of the USSR that have occurred between 1924 and 1936 and which the Constitutional Commission reflected in its Draft Constitution?

What is the essence of these changes?

What kind of situation did we have in 1924? . . .

If at that time we were in the first stages of the NEP, the beginning of the NEP, in the period of slight revival of capitalism, then presently we are in the last stages of the NEP, the end of the NEP, in the period of complete liquidation of capitalism in all spheres of the national economy. . . .

This means that a complete triumph of the socialist system in all spheres of the national economy is now an established fact.

And what does this mean?

It means that the exploitation of man by man has been abolished and eliminated, and the socialist ownership of the implements and means of production has been established as the unshakable foundation of our Soviet society. (Prolonged applause).

As a result of all these changes in the sphere of the national economy of the USSR we now have a new, socialist economy, which knows neither crises nor unemployment, which knows neither poverty nor ruin and which offers our citizens every opportunity to enjoy a prosperous and cultured life. . . .

[1] *Pravda,* November 26, 1936. Translation by Basil Dmytryshyn.

470

In conformity with these changes in the economic life of the USSR the class structure of our society has also changed.

As you know, the landlord class had already been liquidated as a result of the victorious conclusion of the civil war. As for the other exploiting classes, they have shared the fate of the landlord class. In the sphere of industry the capitalist class has ceased to exist. In the sphere of agriculture the kulak class has ceased to exist. And the merchants and speculators in the sphere of trade have ceased to exist. Thus all the exploiting classes have now been liquidated.

There remains the working class.

There remains the peasant class.

There remains the intelligentsia.

It would be a mistake though to think that these social groups have not undergone any changes during this period, that they have remained the same as they were, say, in the period of capitalism.

Take, for instance, the working class of the USSR. By force of habit it is often called proletariat. But what is proletariat? The proletariat is a class bereaved of the instruments and means of production in an economic system where the means and instruments of production are owned by the capitalists and where a capitalist class exploits the proletariat. Proletariat, therefore, is a class that is exploited by the capitalists. But we do not have a class of capitalists. It is well known that that class has been liquidated and their instruments and means of production have been expropriated and transferred to the state, whose leading force is the working class. . . . This being the case, can our working class be called the proletariat? Clearly, it cannot. . . . And what does this mean? This means that the proletariat of the USSR has been transformed into an entirely new class, the working class of the USSR, which has abolished the capitalist economic system, has established the socialist ownership of the instruments and means of production and is guiding Soviet society along the path of communism. . . .

Let us move now to the problem of the peasantry. By force of habit they say that peasants represent a class of small proprietors whose members are atomized, dispersed throughout the country, who work individually their petty farms using backward technology, who are slaves of private property and who are exploited with impunity by landlords, kulaks, merchants, speculators, usurers, etc. . . . Is it possible to say that our present peasants, Soviet peasants, resemble those peasants? No, it cannot be said. We do not have such peasants. Our Soviet peasants are completely new peasants. We do not have any landlords or kulaks, merchants or usurers who could exploit our peasants. Our peasantry is a peasantry that has been emancipated from exploitation. Moreover, in its overwhelming majority, our Soviet peasantry is a collective farm peasantry, i.e., it bases its work and property not on individual labor and backward technology, but on collective labor and advanced technology. Finally, the economy of our peasantry is based not on private but on collective property, which has emerged on the foundation of collective labor. . . .

Finally, let us move on to the question of the intelligentsia, to the question of engineers and technicians, to the workers on the cultural front, to the employees in general, etc. The intelligentsia, too, has undergone great changes during this period. It is no longer the old stagnant intelligentsia which tried to place itself above classes, but which actually served the landlords and the capitalists.

Our Soviet intelligentsia is an entirely new intelligentsia, bound by all of its roots with the working class and the peasantry. The composition of the intelligentsia has also changed. Those with aristocratic and bourgeois background constitute but a small percentage of our Soviet intelligentsia. Between 80 and 90 percent of Soviet intelligentsia are people who have come from the working class, the peasantry and other layers of the working population. The very nature of the activities of the intelligentsia has also changed. Formerly it had to serve the wealthy classes, because it had no alternative. Now it must serve the people, because there are no longer exploiting classes. And that is precisely why it is now an equal member of Soviet society, in which, side by side with the workers and peasants, in a joint effort, it is engaged in building the new classless, socialist society. . . .

The picture of changes in the social life of the USSR would be incomplete if we would fail to say a few words about the changes in one additional area. I have in view the area of nationality relations in the USSR. As you know there are 60 nations, national groups and nationalities in the Soviet Union. The Soviet state is a multinational state. It is obvious, therefore, that for us relations among the peoples of the USSR are very important.

The USSR came into existence in 1922 during the meeting of the First Congress of Soviets of the USSR. It was founded on the principles of equality and free choice of the peoples of the USSR. The present constitution, which was adopted in 1924, is the first constitution of the USSR. . . . Fourteen years have elapsed. It is a sufficient time to examine the experiment. What are the results? This period has demonstrated definitely that the experiment of a multinational state, based on socialism, has been a complete success. This represents the complete triumph of the Leninist nationality policy. (Prolonged applause). . . .

III.

THE BASIC SPECIFIC FEATURES OF THE DRAFT CONSTITUTION

. . . In drafting the new constitution, the Constitutional Commission proceeded from the proposition that a constitution must not be confused with a program. . . . Whereas a program speaks of that which does not yet exist and which has to be achieved and won in the future, a constitution, in contrast, must speak of that which already exists, of that which has already been achieved and won now, at the present time. A program deals mainly with the future, a constitution with the present.

Two examples by way of illustration.

Our Soviet society has in the main succeeded in achieving socialism, it has created a socialist system, i.e., it has achieved what Marxists call the first, or lower stage of communism. This means that we already have achieved the first phase of communism: socialism. (Prolonged applause). The basic principle of this phase of communism is, as you know, the formula: "From each according to his abilities, to each according to his work." Should our constitution reflect this fact, the fact that socialism has been achieved? Should it be based on this achievement? Unquestionably, it should. It should because for the USSR socialism is something that has already been achieved and won.

But Soviet society has not yet reached the higher phase of communism, in which the guiding principle will be the formula: "From each according to his abilities, to each according to his needs", even though it aims at achieving the higher phase of communism in the future. Can our constitution be based on the higher phase of communism, which does not yet exist and which has yet to be achieved? No, it cannot, because for the USSR the higher phase of communism is something that has not been realized, and which has to be realized in the future. . . .

Furthermore. The constitutions of bourgeois countries usually proceed from the conviction that the capitalist system is immutable. Principles of capitalism form the basic foundation of these constitutions. . . . Unlike these, the draft of the new constitution of the USSR proceeds from the fact that the capitalist system has been liquidated and that the socialist system has triumphed in the USSR. The basic foundation of the draft of the new constitution of the USSR is the principles of socialism. Its main pillars have already been won and realized. These include: the socialist ownership of the land, forests, factories, industrial enterprises and other instruments and means of production; the liquidation of exploitation and of exploiting classes; the elimination of poverty for the majority and of luxury for the minority; the elimination of unemployment; work as an obligation and an honorable duty for every able-bodied citizen in accordance with the formula: "He who does not work, neither shall he eat". The right to work, *i.e.*, the right of every citizen to receive guaranteed employment; the right to rest and leisure; the right to education; etc. . . .

Furthermore. Bourgeois constitutions tacitly proceed from the premise that society consists of antagonistic classes, of classes which own wealth and classes which do not own wealth; that no matter which party comes to power, the state guidance of society (the dictatorship) must be in the hands of the bourgeoisie; and that the constitution is needed only to consolidate a social order desired by and beneficial to the propertied classes.

Unlike bourgeois constitutions, the draft of the new constitution of the USSR proceeds from the fact that there are no longer any antagonistic classes in [Soviet] society; that our society consists of two friendly classes, of workers and peasants; that it is these working classes that are in power; that the state guidance of society (the dictatorship) is in the hands of the working class, the leading class of society; and that a constitution is needed in order to consolidate a social order desired by and beneficial to the working people. . . .

Furthermore. Bourgeois constitutions tacitly proceed from the premise that nations and races cannot have equal rights; that there are nations with full rights and nations without full rights. In addition, there is a third category of nations or races, for instance in the colonies, which have even fewer rights than nations without full rights. Essentially this means that all these constitutions are nationalistic, *i.e*, constitutions of ruling nations.

Unlike these constitutions, the draft of the new constitution of the USSR is, in contrast, profoundly internationalistic. It proceeds from the premise that all nations and races have equal rights. It proceeds from the fact that neither difference in color nor language, cultural level or level of political development, nor any other difference between nations and races, can serve as grounds for justifying national inequality of rights. It proceeds from the premise that irrespective of their past and present position, irrespective of their strength or weakness, all nations and races should enjoy equal rights in all spheres of economic, social, political and cultural life of society. . . .

The fifth unique feature of the draft of the new constitution is its consistent and steadfast democratism. . . . What distinguishes the draft of the new constitution of the USSR is the fact that it is free from [bourgeois-type] reservations and restrictions. For it, there exist neither active nor passive citizens. For it all citizens are active. It does not recognize any difference in rights as between men and women, "residents" and "non-residents", propertied and propertyless, educated and uneducated. For it all citizens are equal and have equal rights. It is not property status, not national origin, not sex, not official position, but personal ability and individual work that determine the position of every citizen in society. . . .

What distinguishes the draft of the new constitution is the fact that it does not confine itself to stating the formal rights of citizens, but emphasizes the guarantees of these rights and the means by which these rights can be exercised. It does not simply proclaim equality of rights of citizens, but ensures through a legislative enactment the fact that the regime of exploitation has been abolished and the fact that the citizens have been emancipated from all forms of exploitation. It does not merely proclaim the right to work, but ensures through a legislative enactment the fact that there are no crises in Soviet society and that unemployment has been solved. It does not simply proclaim democratic liberties, but through legislation ensures these liberties by providing concrete material resources. . . .

IV.

BOURGEOIS CRITICISM OF THE DRAFT CONSTITUTION

A few words about bourgeois criticism of the draft constitution. . . .

The first signs of response to the draft constitution by the foreign press manifested themselves in silence. I have in view here the most reactionary fascist press. This group of critics thought that the best way to treat the matter is to say nothing about the draft constitution and pretend that such a draft never existed and does not exist now. Someone may say that silence is not criticism. That is not true. Silence, as a special way of ignoring, is a form of criticism, stupid and ridiculous, to be sure, but nevertheless it is a form of criticism. . . .

The second group of critics acknowledges that the draft constitution actually exists, but it maintains that the draft does not represent any major interest because it allegedly is not a genuine draft of a constitution but simply empty paper and an empty promise designed to execute a specific maneuver in order to deceive people. . . .

The third group of critics, while willing to acknowledge some merits of the draft constitution, and viewing it as a positive phenomenon, nevertheless is quite skeptical as to whether a number of its proposals can be realized. This group believes that these proposals are unrealizable and that they should remain on paper only. This is the position of skeptics, and skeptics are found in all countries. . . .

The fourth group of critics has attacked the draft of the new constitution and has described it as a "move to the right", as "an abandonment of the dictatorship of the proletariat", and as "a liquidation of the Bolshevik regime." . . . Finally, there is one more group of critics. If the previous group accuses the draft of the constitution of abandoning the dictatorship of the working class, then this group argues the opposite. It says that the draft does not change anything in the USSR; that it leaves unaltered the dictatorship of the working class; that it does not permit any freedom for other political parties; and that it preserves intact the present leading position of the party of communists in the USSR. Moreover, this group of critics maintains that the absence of freedom for other parties to exist in the USSR is actually a sign of the violation of the bases of democratism.

I must acknowledge that the draft of the constitution does preserve the regime of the dictatorship of the working class, just as it also preserves unaltered the present leading position of the Communist Party of the USSR. (Loud applause). If the esteemed critics regard this as a flaw in the draft of the constitution, that is only to be regretted. We Bolsheviks regard it as a merit of the draft. (Loud applause).

As to freedom for various political parties, we adhere to somewhat different views. A party is a part of a class, its most advanced part. Several parties and, consequently, freedom for parties, can exist only in a society where exist antagonistic classes whose interests are mutually hostile and irreconcilable; where, let us say, exist capitalists and workers, landlords and peasants, kulaks and poor peasants, etc. But in the USSR there are no longer such classes as capitalists, landlords, kulaks, etc. In the USSR there are only two classes: workers and peasants whose interests, far from being hostile, are on the contrary friendly. Consequently, there is no basis in the USSR for the existence of several parties and, therefore, for freedom for these parties. In the USSR there is room for only one party, the Communist Party. . . .

They talk of democracy. But what is democracy? Democracy in capitalist countries, where exist antagonistic classes, is, in the final analysis, democracy for the strong, democracy for the propertied minority. In contrast, democracy in the USSR is democracy of the working people, i.e., democracy for all. This means, therefore, that the principles of democratism are violated not by the draft of the new constitution of the USSR, but by the bourgeois constitutions. That is why I think that the Constitution of the USSR is the only fully democratic constitution in the world. . . .

Appendix 24 OFFICIAL VERDICT AGAINST
Y. L. PYATAKOV AND ASSOCIATES IN
THE PURGE TRIAL, JANUARY 30, 1937 [1]

[The Military Collegium of the Supreme Court of the U.S.S.R.] in an
open Court session, in the city of Moscow, on January 23–30, 1937, heard
the case against:

1. *Pyatakov*, Yuri (Georgi) Leonidovich, born 1890, employee;
2. *Sokolnikov*, Grigori Yakovlevich, born 1888, employee;
3. *Radek*, Karl Berngardovich, born 1885, journalist;
4. *Serebryakov*, Leonid Petrovich, born 1888, employee;
5. *Livshitz*, Yakov Abramovich, born 1896, employee;
6. *Muralov*, Nikolai Ivanovich, born 1877, employee;
7. *Drobnis*, Yakov Naumovich, born 1891, employee;
8. *Boguslavsky*, Mikhail Solomonovich, born 1886, employee;
9. *Knyazev*, Ivan Alexandrovich, born 1893, employee;
10. *Rataichak*, Stanislav Antonovich, born 1894, employee;
11. *Norkin*, Boris Osipovich, born 1895, employee;
12. *Shestov*, Alexei Alexandrovich, born 1896, employee;
13. *Stroilov*, Mikhail Stepanovich, born 1899, employee;
14. *Turok*, Yosif Dmitrievich, born 1900, employee;
15. *Hrasche*, Ivan Yosifovich, born 1886, employee;
16. *Pushin*, Gavriil Yefremovich, born 1896, employee;
17. *Arnold*, Valentin Volfridovich, alias Vasilyev Valentin Vasilyevich,
    born 1894, employee;

all being charged with having committed crimes covered by Articles 58[1a],
58[8], 58[9] and 58[11] of the Criminal Code of the R.S.F.S.R.

The preliminary and Court investigations have established that:

In 1933, in accordance with direct instructions given by the enemy of
the people, L. Trotsky, who was deported from the U.S.S.R. in 1929, there
was formed in Moscow, apart from the so-called "united Trotskyite-Zinovievite terrorist centre," consisting of Zinoviev, Kamenev, Smirnov and others,
an underground parallel anti-Soviet, Trotskyite centre, members of which
were the accused in the present case, Y. L. Pyatakov, K. B. Radek, G. Y. Sokolnikov and L. P. Serebryakov.

In accordance with instructions received from the enemy of the people,
L. Trotsky, the principal aim of the parallel anti-Soviet Trotskyite centre
was to overthrow the Soviet power in the U.S.S.R. and to restore capitalism
and the power of the bourgeoisie by means of wrecking, diversive, espionage

[1] U.S.S.R. Peoples Commissariat of Justice. *Report of Court Proceedings in the
Case of the Anti-Soviet Trotskyite Centre* . . . (Moscow: 1937), pp. 574–580.

476

and terrorist activities designed to undermine the economic and military power of the Soviet Union, to expedite the armed attack on the U.S.S.R., to assist foreign aggressors and to bring about the defeat of the U.S.S.R.

In full conformity with this principal aim, the enemy of the people L. Trotsky, abroad, and the parallel anti-Soviet Trotskyite centre, represented by Radek and Sokolnikov, in Moscow, entered into negotiations with certain representatives of Germany and Japan. During the course of negotiation with one of the leaders of the National-Socialist Party of Germany, Rudolph Hess, the enemy of the people, L. Trotsky, promised in the event of a Trotskyite government coming to power as a result of the defeat of the Soviet Union, to make a number of political, economic and territorial concessions to Germany and Japan at the expense of the U.S.S.R., including the cession of the Ukraine to Germany and of the Maritime Provinces and the Amur region to Japan. At the same time, the enemy of the people, L. Trotsky, undertook in the event of seizing power to liquidate the state farms, to dissolve the collective farms, to renounce the policy of industrialization of the country and to restore on the territory of the Soviet Union social relations of capitalist society. Furthermore, the enemy of the people L. Trotsky undertook to render all possible help to aggressors by developing defeatist propaganda and wrecking, diversive and espionage activities, both in time of peace and, in particular, in time of an armed attack on the Soviet Union.

In fulfilment of the instructions of the enemy of the people L. Trotsky, several times received by Radek, and also personally by Pyatakov during a meeting with the enemy of the people L. Trotsky, in December 1935 in the neighbourhood of the city of Oslo, members of the anti-Soviet Trotskyite parallel centre, Pyatakov, Radek, Sokolnikov and Serebryakov developed wrecking, diversive, espionage and terrorist activities.

Local Trotskyite centres were set up in certain large cities in the Soviet Union to exercise direct guidance of anti-Soviet activities in the provinces. In particular, a West-Siberian anti-Soviet Trotskyite centre consisting of N. I. Muralov, M. S. Boguslavsky and Y. N. Drobnis, accused in the present case, was set up in Novosibirsk on the direct instructions of Pyatakov.

Diversive and wrecking work in industry, chiefly in enterprises of importance for defence purposes, and also on the railways, was performed by the accused in the present case at the behest of the enemy of the people Trotsky, and on the instructions and with the direct participation of agents of the German and Japanese intelligence services, and consisted in disrupting plans of production, lowering the quality of product, organizing fires and explosions at factories or factory departments and mines, organizing train wrecks and damaging rolling stock and railway track.

In organizing diversive activities, the accused were guided by the instructions of the enemy of the people Trotsky "to strike palpable blows at the most sensitive places," supplemented by directions from Pyatakov, Livshitz and Drobnis not to shrink before loss of human life, because, "the more victims, the better, since this will rouse the anger of the workers."

In the chemical industry, the accused Rataichak and Pushin, on the instructions of Pyatakov, performed wrecking work with the object of disrupting the State production plan, delaying the construction of new factories and enterprises and spoiling the quality of the construction work on new enterprises.

In addition, in 1934–1935, the accused Rataichak and Pushin organized three diversive acts at the Gorlovka Nitrogen Fertilizer Works, and two of them were accompanied by explosions which caused the death of workers and heavy material loss.

Diversive acts were also organized at the instigation of the accused Rataichak at the Voskressensk Combined Chemical Works and the Nevsky Plant.

In the coal and chemical industries of the Kuznetsk Basin, the accused Drobnis, Norkin, Shestov and Stroilov, on the instructions of Pyatakov and Muralov, carried on wrecking and diversive works with the object of disrupting the output of coal, delaying the building and development of new mines and chemical works, to create conditions of work harmful and dangerous to the workers by allowing gas to accumulate in the galleries and pits, while on September 23, 1936, on the instructions of Drobnis, members of the local Trotskyite organization caused an explosion at the Tsentralnaya Pit in the Kemerovo mine, as a result of which ten workers lost their lives and 14 workers received grave injuries.

On the railways, the diversive and wrecking activities carried on by the accused Serebryakov, Boguslavsky, Livshitz, Knyazev and Turok in accordance with the stand of the anti-Soviet Trotskyite centre, aimed to disrupt the State plan of freight loading, especially for the most important freight (coal, ore, grain), to damage the rolling stock (cars and locomotives) and the railway track, and to organize the wrecking of trains, especially of troop trains.

At the instructions of Livshitz, and being commissioned therefore by an agent of the Japanese intelligence service, Mr. H———, the accused Knyazev in 1935–1936 organized and brought about the wrecking of a number of freight trains, passenger trains and troop trains involving loss of life; as a result of the wreck of a troop train at the Shumikha Station on October 27, 1935, 29 Red Army men were killed and 29 Red Army men injured.

On the direct instructions of the enemy of the people Trotsky, Pyatakov and Serebryakov, members of the anti-Soviet Trotskyite centre, made preparations, in the event of an armed attack on the U.S.S.R., to carry out a number of diversive acts in industries of importance for defense purposes and also on important railway trunk lines.

On the instructions of Pyatakov, the accused Norkin made preparations to set fire to the Kemerovo Chemical Works upon the outbreak of war.

On the instructions of Livshitz, the accused Knyazev proceeded to carry out the commission given him by Mr. H———, an agent of the Japanese intelligence service, to organize during war time the blowing up of railway structures, the burning of military stores and army provision bases, the wreck of troop trains, and also the deliberate infection of trains designed for the transportation of troops, provision supply depots and sanitary centres of the Workers' and Peasants' Red Army with highly virulent bacilli.

In addition to diversive and wrecking activities, the accused Livshitz, Knyazev, Turok, Stroilov, Shestov, Rataichak, Pushin and Hrasche, at the orders of the Trotskyite anti-Soviet centre, engaged in securing and handing over secret information of utmost State importance to agents of the German and Japanese intelligence services.

The accused Rataichak, Pushin and Hrasche were connected with agents of the German intelligence service, Meyerowitz and Lenz, to whom, in 1935–1936, they handed over strictly secret material relating to the condition and operation of chemical plants; Pushin in 1935 handed over to Lenz, agent of the German intelligence service, secret information on the output of products by all the chemical plants of the Soviet Union in 1934, the program of work of all the chemical plants in 1935 and the plan for the construction of nitrogen works, while the accused Rataichak handed over to the same Lenz absolutely secret material on the output in 1934 and the program of the work of chemical enterprises supplying the army for 1935.

The accused Shestov and Stroilov were connected with agents of the German intelligence service Schebesto, Flessa, Floren, Sommeregger and others, and handed over to them secret information about the coal and chemical industries of the Kuznetsk Basin.

The accused Livshitz, Knyazev and Turok regularly transmitted to Mr. H———, agent of the Japanese intelligence service, strictly secret information regarding the technical condition and mobilization capacity of the railways of the U.S.S.R., and also regarding transportation of troops.

At the direct behest of the enemy of the people L. Trotsky, the anti-Soviet Trotskyite centre formed several terrorist groups in Moscow, Leningrad, Kiev, Rostov, Novosibirsk, Sochi and other cities of the U.S.S.R., which engaged in making preparations for terrorist acts against the leaders of the Communist Party of the Soviet Union and the Soviet government, Comrades Stalin, Molotov, Kaganovich, Voroshilov, Orjonikidze, Yezhov, Zhdanov, Kossior, Eiche, Postyshev and Beria; certain terrorist groups (in Moscow, Novosibirsk, in the Ukraine and in Transcaucasia) were under the personal direction of the accused Pyatakov and Serebryakov, members of the anti-Soviet Trotskyite centre.

In organizing terrorist acts, the anti-Soviet Trotskyite centre endeavoured to take advantage of visits paid to the provinces by leaders of the Communist Party of the Soviet Union and the Soviet government.

Thus in the autumn of 1934, Shestov, at the behest of Muralov, endeavoured to carry out a terrorist act against V. M. Molotov, Chairman of the Council of People's Commissars of the U.S.S.R., during his visit to the Kuznetsk Basin, for which purpose a member of the local Trotskyite terrorist group, the accused Arnold, attempted to cause an accident to the automobile in which Comrade V. M. Molotov rode.

Furthermore, on the instructions of Pyatakov and Muralov, the accused Shestov made preparations for a terrorist act against R. I. Eiche, Secretary af the West-Siberian Territory Committee of the C.P.S.U., while the accused Arnold at the instigation of Shestov made preparations for a terrorist act against G. K. Orjonikidze.

Thus the Military Collegium of the Supreme Court of the U.S.S.R. has established that:

I. Pyatakov, Serebryakov, Radek and Sokolnikov were members of the anti-Soviet Trotskyite centre and, at the direct behest of the enemy of the people L. Trotsky, now abroad, with the object of expediting an armed attack on the Soviet Union, assisting foreign aggressors in seizing territory of the Soviet Union, overthrowing the Soviet power and restoring capitalism and the power of the bourgeoisie, directed the treacherous, diversive, wrecking, espionage and terrorist activities of the anti-Soviet Trotskyite organization in the Soviet Union—*i.e.*, have committed crimes covered by Articles 58^{1a}, 58^8, 58^9 and 58^{11} of the Criminal Code of the R.S.F.S.R.

II. Pyatakov and Serebryakov, mentioned in clause I, as well as Muralov, Drobnis, Livshitz and Boguslavsky, members of an anti-Soviet Trotskyite organization, organized and personally directed the treasonable, espionage, diversive and terrorist activities of the members of the anti-Soviet Trotskyite organization—*i.e.*, have committed crimes covered by Articles 58^{1a}, 58^8, 58^9 and 58^{11} of the Criminal Code of the R.S.F.S.R.

III. Knyazev, Rataichak, Norkin, Shestov, Turok, Pushin and Hrasche, while members of an anti-Soviet Trotskyite organization, carried out the instructions of the anti-Soviet Trotskyite centre concerning treasonable, espionage, undermining, wrecking and terrorist activities—*i.e.*, have committed crimes covered by Articles 58^{1a}, 58^8, 58^9 and 58^{11} of the Criminal Code of the R.S.F.S.R.

IV. Arnold, while a member of an anti-Soviet Trotskyite organization, at the instigation of the accused Muralov and Shestov, attempted to carry out terrorist acts against Comrades Molotov and Orjonikidze—*i.e.*, has committed crimes covered by Articles 19, 58^8 and 58^{11} of the Criminal Code of the R.S.F.S.R.

V. Stroilov partially carried out certain individual commissions for espionage and wrecking work—*i.e.*, has committed crimes covered by Articles 58^6 and 58^7 of the Criminal Code of the R.S.F.S.R.

On the basis of the above, and guided by Articles 319 and 320 of the Code of Criminal Procedure of the R.S.F.S.R., *The Military Collegium of the Supreme Court of the U.S.S.R.*

SENTENCES:

1. *Pyatakov,* Yuri (Georgi) Leonidovich, and
2. *Serebryakov,* Leonid Petrovich,

as members of the anti-Soviet Trotskyite centre who organized and directly guided treasonable, espionage, undermining, wrecking and terrorist activities, to the supreme penalty—to be shot.

3. *Muralov,* Nikolai Ivanovich,
4. *Drobnis,* Yakov Naumovich,
5. *Livshitz,* Yakov Abramovich,
6. *Boguslavsky,* Mikhail Solomonovich,
7. *Knyazev,* Ivan Alexandrovich,
8. *Rataichak,* Stanislav Antonovich,
9. *Norkin,* Boris Osipovich,
10. *Shestov,* Alexei Alexandrovich,

11. *Turok*, Yosif Dmitrievich,

12. *Pushin*, Gavriil Yefremovich, and

13. *Hrasche*, Ivan Yosifovich,

as organizers and direct executors of the above-mentioned crimes, to the supreme penalty—to be shot.

14. *Sokolnikov*, Grigori Yakovlevich, and

15. *Radek*, Karl Berngardovich,

as members of the anti-Soviet Trotskyite centre, responsible for its criminal activities, but not directly participating in the organization and execution of acts of a diversive, wrecking, espionage and terrorist nature each to imprisonment for a term of ten years.

16. *Arnold*, Valentin Volfridovich, alias Vasilyev, Valentin Vasilyevich, to imprisonment for a term of ten years.

17. *Stroilov*, Mikhail Stepanovich,

in view of the facts mentioned in point V of the defining section of the present verdict—to imprisonment for a term of eight years.

Sokolnikov, Radek, Arnold and *Stroilov*, who are condemned to imprisonment, shall be deprived of political rights for a period of five years each.

The personal property of all the condemned shall be confiscated.

Enemies of the people, Lev Davidovich Trotsky, and his son, Lev Lvovich Sedov, who were in 1929 deported from the U.S.S.R. and by the decision of the Central Executive Committee of the U.S.S.R. of February 20, 1932, were deprived of citizenship of the U.S.S.R., having been convicted by the testimony of the accused Y. L. Pyatakov, K. B. Radek, A. A. Shestov and N. I. Muralov, and by the evidence of V. G. Romm and D. P. Bukhartsev, who were examined as witnesses at the trial, as well as by the materials in the present case, of personally directing the treacherous activities of the Trotskyite anti-Soviet centre, in the event of their being discovered on the territory of the U.S.S.R., are liable to immediate arrest and trial by the Military Collegium of the Supreme Court of the U.S.S.R.

Appendix 25 TREATY OF NON-AGGRESSION BETWEEN GERMANY AND THE UNION OF SOVIET SOCIALIST REPUBLICS, AUGUST 23, 1939 [1]

The Government of the German Reich and the Government of the Union of Soviet Socialist Republics, desirous of strengthening the cause of peace between Germany and the U.S.S.R., and proceeding from the fundamental provisions of the Treaty of Neutrality, which was concluded between Germany and the U.S.S.R. in April 1926, have reached the following agreement:

ARTICLE I

The two Contracting Parties undertake to refrain from any act of violence, any aggressive action and any attack on each other either severally or jointly with other Powers.

ARTICLE II

Should one of the Contracting Parties become the object of belligerent action by a third Power, the other Contracting Party shall in no manner lend its support to this third Power.

ARTICLE III

The Governments of the two Contracting Parties will in future maintain continual contact with one another for the purpose of consultation in order to exchange information on problems affecting their common interests.

ARTICLE IV

Neither of the two Contracting Parties will join any grouping of Powers whatsoever which is aimed directly or indirectly at the other Party.

ARTICLE V

Should disputes or conflicts arise between the Contracting Parties over questions of one kind or another, both parties will settle these disputes or

[1] U.S. Department of State. *Documents on German Foreign Policy, 1918–1945.* Series D (1937–1945). (Washington: Government Printing Office, 1956), VII, 245–7.

conflicts exclusively by means of a friendly exchange of views or if necessary by the appointment of arbitration commissions.

ARTICLE VI

The present Treaty shall be concluded for a period of ten years with the proviso that, in so far as one of the Contracting Parties does not denounce it one year before the expiry of this period, the validity of this Treaty shall be deemed to be automatically prolonged for another five years.

ARTICLE VII

The present Treaty shall be ratified within the shortest possible time. The instruments of ratification will be exchanged in Berlin. The Treaty shall enter into force immediately upon signature.

Done in duplicate in the German and Russian languages.

Moscow, August 23, 1939.

For the Government of the German Reich: v. Ribbentrop	With full power of the Government of the U.S.S.R.: V. Molotov

Secret Additional Protocol

On the occasion of the signature of the Non-Aggression Treaty between the German Reich and the Union of Soviet Socialist Republics, the undersigned plenipotentiaries of the two Parties discussed in strictly confidential conversations the question of the delimitation of their respective spheres of interest in Eastern Europe. These conversations led to the following result:

1. In the event of a territorial and political transformation in the territories belonging to the Baltic States (Finland, Estonia, Latvia, Lithuania), the northern frontier of Lithuania shall represent the frontier of the spheres of interest both of Germany and the U.S.S.R. In this connection the interest of Lithuania in the Vilna territory is recognized by both Parties.

2. In the event of a territorial and political transformation of the territories belonging to the Polish State, the spheres of interest of both Germany and the U.S.S.R. shall be bounded approximately by the line of the rivers Narev, Vistula, and San.

The question whether the interests of both Parties make the maintenance of an independent Polish State appear desirable and how the frontiers of this State should be drawn can be definitely determined only in the course of further political developments.

In any case both Governments will resolve this question by means of a friendly understanding.

3. With regard to South-Eastern Europe, the Soviet side emphasizes its interest in Bessarabia. The German side declares complete political *désintéressement* in these territories.

4. This Protocol will be treated by both parties as strictly secret.

Moscow, August 23, 1939.

For the Government of
the German Reich:
v. Ribbentrop

With full power of the
Government of the U.S.S.R.:
V. Molotov

Appendix 26 STALIN'S NATION-WIDE RADIO ADDRESS FOLLOWING GERMAN INVASION OF THE USSR, JULY 3, 1941 [1]

Comrades! Citizens! Brothers and sisters! Men of our army and navy! I am addressing you my friends!

The perfidious military attack on our fatherland, begun on June 22 by Hitler Germany, is continuing.

In spite of the heroic resistance of the Red Army, and although the enemy's finest divisions and finest airforce units have already been smashed and have met their doom on the field of battle, the enemy continues to push forward, hurling fresh forces into the attack.

Hitler's troops have succeeded in capturing Lithuania, a considerable part of Latvia, the western part of Byelorussia, part of Western Ukraine. The fascist air force is extending the range of operations of its bombers, and is bombing Murmansk, Orcha, Mogilev, Smolensk, Kiev, Odessa and Sevastopol.

A grave danger hangs over our country.

How could it have happened that our glorious Red Army surrendered a number of our cities and districts to fascist armies? Is it really true that German fascist troops are invincible, as is ceaselessly trumpeted by the boastful fascist propagandists?

Of course not

History shows that there are no invincible armies and never have been. Napoleon's army was considered invincible but it was beaten successively by Russian, English and German armies. Kaiser Wilhelm's German army in the period of the first imperialist war was also considered invincible but it was beaten several times by the Russian and Anglo-French forces and was finally smashed by the Anglo-French forces.

The same must be said of Hitler's German fascist army today. This army had not yet met with serious resistance on the continent of Europe. Only on our territory has it met serious resistance. And if, as a result of this resistance, the finest divisions of Hitler's German fascist army have been defeated by our Red Army, it means that this army too can be smashed and will be smashed as were the armies of Napoleon and Wilhelm.

As to part of our territory having nevertheless been seized by German fascist troops, this is chiefly due to the fact that the war of fascist Germany on the USSR began under conditions favorable for the German forces and unfavorable for Soviet forces. The fact of the matter is that the troops of Germany, as a country at war, were already fully mobilized, and the one hundred and seventy divisions hurled by Germany against the USSR and brought up to the Soviet

[1] Joseph Stalin. *The Great Patriotic War of the Soviet Union.* New York: International Publishers, 1945, pp. 9–17.

frontiers were in a state of complete readiness, only waiting the signal to move into action, whereas Soviet troops had still to effect mobilization and move up to the frontier.

Of no little importance in this respect is that fact that fascist Germany suddenly and treacherously violated the Non-Aggression Pact she had concluded in 1939 with the USSR, disregarding the fact that she would be regarded as the aggressor by the whole world.

Naturally, our peace-loving country, not wishing to take the initiative of breaking the pact, could not resort to perfidy.

It may be asked how could the Soviet government have consented to conclude a non-aggression pact with such treacherous friends as Hitler and Ribbentrop? Was this not an error on the part of the Soviet government? Of course not. Non-aggression pacts are pacts of peace between states. It was such a pact that Germany proposed to us in 1939.

Could the Soviet government have declined such a proposal? I think that not a single peace-loving state could decline a peace treaty with a neighboring state, even though the latter was headed by such fiends and cannibals as Hitler and Ribbentrop. Of course only on one indispensable condition, namely, that this peace treaty does not infringe either directly or indirectly on the territorial integrity, independence, and honor of the peace-loving state. As is well known, the Non-Aggression Pact between Germany and the USSR was precisely such a pact.

What did we gain by concluding the Non-Aggression Pact with Germany? We secured our country peace for a year and a half, and the opportunity of preparing its forces to repulse fascist Germany should she risk an attack on our country despite the pact. This was a definite advantage for us and a disadvantage for fascist Germany.

What has fascist Germany gained and what has she lost by treacherously tearing up the pact and attacking the USSR?

She has gained a certain advantageous position for her troops for a short period, but she has lost politically by exposing herself in the eyes of the entire world as a blood-thirsty aggressor.

There can be no doubt that this short-lived military gain for Germany is only an episode, while the tremendous political gain for the USSR is a serious and lasting factor that is bound to form the basis for the development of decisive military successes of the Red Army in the war with fascist Germany.

That is why our whole valiant Red Army, our whole valiant Navy, all our falcons of the air, all the peoples of our country, all the finest men and women of Europe, America and Asia, finally, all the finest men and women of Germany —condemn the treacherous acts of the German fascists and sympathize with the Soviet government, approve the conduct of the Soviet government, and see that ours is a just cause, that the enemy will be defeated, that we are bound to win.

By virtue of this war which has been forced upon us, our country has come to death-grips with its most malicious and most perfidious enemy—German fascism.

Our troops are fighting heroically against an enemy armed to the teeth with tanks and aircraft. Overcoming innumerable difficulties, the Red Army and Red Navy are self-sacrificingly disputing every inch of Soviet soil. The main forces of the Red Army are coming into action armed with thousands of tanks and airplanes. The men of the Red Army are displaying unexampled valor. Our resistance to the enemy is growing in strength and power.

Side by side with the Red Army, the entire Soviet people are rising in defense of our native land.

What is required to put an end to the danger hovering over our country, and what measures must be taken to smash the enemy?

Above all, it is essential that our people, the Soviet people, should understand the full immensity of the danger that threatens our country and should abandon all complacency, all heedlessness, all those moods of peaceful constructive work which were so natural before the war, but which are fatal today when war has fundamentally changed everything.

The enemy is cruel and implacable. He is out to seize our lands, watered with our sweat, to seize our grain and oil secured by our labor. He is out to restore the rule of landlords, to restore tsarism, to destroy national culture and the national existence of the Russians, Ukrainians, Byelorussians, Lithuanians, Letts, Estonians, Uzbeks, Tatars, Moldavians, Georgians, Armenians, Azerbaidjanians and the other free peoples of the Soviet Union, to Germanize them, to convert them into slaves of German princes and barons.

Thus the issue is one of life or death for the Soviet state, for the peoples of the USSR; the issue is whether the peoples of the Soviet Union shall remain free or fall into slavery.

The Soviet people must realize this and abandon all heedlessness, they must mobilize themselves and reorganize all their work on new, wartime bases, when there can be no mercy to the enemy.

Further, there must be no room in our ranks for whimperers and cowards, for panic-mongers and deserters. Our people must know no fear in fight and must selflessly join our patriotic war of liberation, our war against the fascist enslavers.

Lenin, the great founder of our state, used to say that the chief virtue of the Bolshevik must be courage, valor, fearlessness in struggle, readiness to fight, together with the people, against the enemies of our country.

This splended virtue of the Bolshevik must become the virtue of the millions of the Red Army, of the Red Navy, of all peoples of the Soviet Union.

All our work must be immediately reconstructed on a war footing, everything must be subordinated to the interests of the front and the task of organizing the demolition of the enemy.

The peoples of the Soviet Union now see that there is no taming of German fascism in its savage fury and hatred of our country, which has ensured all working people labor in freedom and prosperity.

The peoples of the Soviet Union must rise against the enemy and defend their rights and their land. The Red Army, Red Navy, and all citizens of the Soviet Union must defend every inch of Soviet soil, must fight to the last drop of blood for our towns and villages, must display the daring initiative and intelligence that are inherent in our people.

We must organize all-round assistance for the Red Army, ensure powerful reinforcements for its ranks and the supply of everything it requires, we must organize the rapid transport of troops and military freight and extensive aid to the wounded.

We must strengthen the Red Army's rear, subordinating all our work to this cause. All our industries must be got to work with greater intensity to produce more rifles, machine guns, artillery, bullets, shells, airplanes. We must organize the guarding of factories, power-stations, telephonic and telegraphic communications, and arrange effective air raid precautions in all localities.

We must wage a ruthless fight against all disorganizers of the rear, deserters, panic-mongers, we must exterminate spies, diversionists, and enemy parachutists, rendering rapid aid in all this to our destroyer battalions.

We must bear in mind that the enemy is crafty, unscrupulous, experienced in deception and the dissemination of false rumors. We must reckon with all this and not fall victim to provocation.

All who by their panic-mongering and cowardice hinder the work of defense, no matter who they are, must be immediately hauled before the military tribunal. In case of forced retreat of Red Army units, all rolling stock must be evacuated, the enemy must not be left a single engine, a single railway car, not a single pound of grain, or a gallon of fuel.

The collective farmers must drive off all their cattle, and turn over their grain to the safe-keeping of state authorities for transportation to the rear. All valuable property, including non-ferrous metal, grain, and fuel which cannot be withdrawn, must be destroyed without fail.

In areas occupied by the enemy, guerrilla units, mounted and on foot, must be formed, diversionist groups must be organized to combat the enemy troops, to foment guerrilla warfare everywhere, to blow up bridges and roads, damage telephone and telegraph lines, set fires to forests, stores, transports. In the occupied regions conditions must be made unbearable for the enemy and all his accomplices. They must be hounded and annihilated at every step, and all their measures frustrated.

This war with fascist Germany cannot be considered an ordinary war. It is not only a war between two armies, it is also a great war of the entire Soviet people against the German fascist forces.

The aim of this national war in defense of our country against the fascist oppressors is not only elimination of the danger hanging over our country, but also aid to all European peoples groaning under the yoke of German fascism.

In this war of liberation we shall not be alone. In this great war we shall have loyal allies in the peoples of Europe and America, including the German people who are enslaved by the Hitlerite despots.

Our war for the freedom of our country will merge with the struggle of the peoples of Europe and America for their independence, for democratic liberties.

It will be a united front of peoples standing for freedom and against enslavement by Hitler's fascist armies.

In this connection the historic utterance of the British Prime Minister Churchill regarding aid to the Soviet Union and the declaration of the United States government signifying its readiness to render aid to our country, which can only evoke a feeling of gratitude in the hearts of the peoples of the Soviet Union, are fully comprehensible and symptomatic.

Comrades, our forces are numberless. The overweening enemy will soon learn this to his cost. Side by side with the Red Army many thousands of workers, collective farmers, intellectuals are rising to fight the enemy aggressor. The masses of our people will rise up in their millions.

The working people of Moscow and Leningrad have already commenced to form vast popular levies in support of the Red Army. Such popular levies must be raised in every city which is in danger of enemy invasion, all working people must be roused to defend our freedom, our honor, our country—in our patriotic war against German fascism.

In order to ensure the rapid mobilization of all forces of the peoples of the USSR and to repulse the enemy who treacherously attacked our country, a State Committee of Defense has been formed in whose hands the entire power of the state has been vested.

The State Committee of Defense has entered upon its functions and calls upon all our people to rally around the party of Lenin-Stalin and around the Soviet government, so as self-denyingly to support the Red Army and Navy, demolish the enemy, and secure victory.

All our forces for support of our heroic Red Army and our glorious Red Navy!

All forces of the people—for the demolition of the enemy!

Forward to our victory!

Appendix 27   YALTA CONFERENCE, 1945: ENTRY OF SOVIETS INTO WAR AGAINST JAPAN [1]

AGREEMENT

The leaders of the three Great Powers—the Soviet Union, the United States of America and Great Britain—have agreed that in two or three months after Germany has surrendered and the war in Europe has terminated the Soviet Union shall enter into the war against Japan on the side of the Allies on condition that:

1. The status quo in Outer-Mongolia (The Mongolian People's Republic) shall be preserved;

2. The former rights of Russia violated by the treacherous attack of Japan in 1904 shall be restored, viz.:

    (a) the southern part of Sakhalin as well as all the islands adjacent to it shall be returned to the Soviet Union,

    (b) the commercial port of Dairen shall be internationalized, the pre-eminent interests of the Soviet Union in this port being safe-guarded and the lease of Port Arthur as a naval base of the U.S.S.R. restored,

    (c) the Chinese-Eastern Railroad and the South-Manchurian Railroad which provides an outlet to Dairen shall be jointly operated by the establishment of a joint Soviet-Chinese Company, it being understood that the preeminent interests of the Soviet Union shall be safeguarded and that China shall retain full sovereignty in Manchuria;

3. The Kuril islands shall be handed over to the Soviet Union.

It is understood, that the agreement concerning Outer-Mongolia and the ports and railroads referred to above will require concurrence of Generalissimo Chiang Kai-Shek. The President will take measures in order to obtain this concurrence on advice from Marshal Stalin.

The Heads of the three Great Powers have agreed that these claims of the Soviet Union shall be unquestionably fulfilled after Japan has been defeated.

For its part the Soviet Union expresses its readiness to conclude with the National Government of China a pact of friendship and alliance between the U.S.S.R. and China in order to render assistance to China with its armed forces for the purpose of liberating China from the Japanese yoke.

J. Stalin
Franklin D. Roosevelt
Winston S. Churchill

February 11, 1945

[1] U.S. Department of State. *Treaties and Other International Agreements of the United States of America 1776–1949.* Compiled under the direction of Charles I. Bevans. (Washington, D.C.: Government Printing Office, 1969), pp. 1022–1023.

Appendix 28 STALIN'S "ELECTION" SPEECH, FEBRUARY 9, 1946 [1]

COMRADES!

Eight years have elapsed since the last election to the Supreme Soviet. This was a period abounding in events of decisive moment. The first four years passed in intensive effort on the part of Soviet people to fulfill the Third Five-Year Plan. The second four years embrace the events of the war against the German and Japanese aggressors, the events of the Second World War. There is no doubt that the war was the principal event in the past period.

It would be wrong to think that the Second World War was a casual occurrence or the result of mistakes of any particular statesmen, though mistakes undoubtedly were made. Actually, the war was the inevitable result of the development of world economic and political forces on the basis of modern monopoly capitalism. Marxists have declared more than once that the capitalist system of world economy harbours elements of general crises and armed conflicts and that, hence, the development of world capitalism in our time proceeds not in the form of smooth and balanced progress but through crises and military catastrophes.

The fact is, that the unevenness of development of the capitalist countries usually leads in time to violent disturbance of equilibrium in the world system of capitalism. Moreover that group of capitalist countries which considers itself less adequately provided than others with raw materials and markets usually makes attempts to alter the situation and repartition the "spheres of influences" in its favor by armed force. The result is a splitting of the capitalist world into two hostile camps and war between them.

Perhaps military catastrophes could be avoided if it were possible for raw materials and markets to be periodically redistributed among the various countries in accordance with their economic importance, by agreement and peaceable settlement. But that is impossible to do under present capitalist conditions of the development of world economy.

Thus the First World War was the result of the first crisis of the capitalist system of world economy, and the Second World War was the result of the second crisis.

That does not mean of course that the Second World War is a copy of the First. On the contrary, the Second World War differs essentially from the First in its nature. It must be borne in mind that before attacking the Allied countries the principal fascist states—Germany, Japan and Italy—destroyed the last vestiges of bourgeois democratic liberties at home, established a brutal terrorist regime in their own countries, rode roughshod over the

---

[1] *Bolshevik*, No. 3 (March, 1946), pp. 1–11. Translation by Basil Dmytryshyn.

principles of sovereignty and free development of small countries, proclaimed a policy of seizure of foreign territories as their own policy and declared for all to hear that they were striving for world domination and the establishment of a fascist regime throughout the world.

Moreover, by the seizure of Czechoslovakia and of the central regions of China, the Axis states showed that they were prepared to carry out their threat of enslaving all freedom-loving nations. In view of this, unlike the First World War, the Second World War against the Axis states from the very outset assumed the character of an anti-fascist war, a war of liberation, one the aim of which was also the restoration of democratic liberties. The entry of the Soviet Union into the war against the Axis states could only enhance, and indeed did enhance, the anti-fascist and liberation character of the Second World War.

Thus was organized the anti-fascist coalition consisting of the Soviet Union, the United States of America, Great Britain, and other freedom loving states which played the decisive role in destroying the armed forces of the Axis powers.

That is how matters stand as regards the origin and character of the Second World War.

By now I should think everyone admits that the war really was not and could not have been an accident in the life of nations, that actually this war became the war of nations for their existence, and that for this reason it could not be a quick lightning affair.

As regards our country, for it this war was the most bitter and arduous of all wars in the history of our Motherland.

But the war was not only a curse. It was at the same time a great school that tried and tested all the forces of the people. The war laid bare all facts and events in the rear and at the front; it pitilessly tore off all veils and coverings which had concealed the true faces of the states, governments, and parties and exposed them to view without a mask or embellishment, with all their shortcomings and merits.

The war was something like an examination for our Soviet system, for our state, for our government, for our Communist Party. It summed up the results of their work, saying to us as it were: "Here they are, your people and organizations, their deeds and their days. Look at them well and reward them according to their deeds."

This was one of the positive aspects of the war.

For us, for the voters, this circumstance is of great importance, for it helps us to make a speedy and objective appraisal of the work of the Party and its members and to draw correct conclusions. At another time we would need to study the speeches and reports of representatives of the Party, analyze them, compare their words with their deeds, sum up, and so forth. This involves complex and difficult work and there is no guarantee that mistakes will not be made. It is a different matter now when the war is over and when the war itself has tested the work of our organizations and leaders and summarized its results. Today, it is much easier for us to see how things stand and to arrive at correct conclusions.

And so, what are the results of the war?

There is one basic result in which all other results have their source. This result is that in the upshot of the war our enemies were defeated and we, together with our Allies, emerged the victors. We concluded the war with complete victory over the enemies. That is the basic result of war. But that result is too general and we cannot stop at that. Of course, to crush an enemy in a war like the Second World War, for which the history of mankind knew no parallel, meant to achieve a world historic victory. All that is true. But still, it is only a general result and we cannot rest content with that. In order to grasp the great historic importance of our victory we must examine the thing more concretely.

And so, how is our victory over our enemies to be understood? What is the significance of this victory as regards the development of the internal forces of our country?

Our victory means, first of all, that our Soviet *social* system has triumphed, that the Soviet social system has successfully passed the ordeal in the fire of war and has proved its unquestionable vitality.

As you know, it was claimed more than once in the foreign press that the Soviet social system was a "risky experiment" doomed to failure, that the Soviet system was a "house of cards" which has no roots in real life and had been imposed upon the people by the Cheka, and that a slight push from without was enough for the "house of cards" to collapse.

Now we can say that the war refuted all these assertions of the foreign press as groundless. The war showed that the Soviet social system is a truly popular system springing from the depths of the people and enjoying their mighty support, that the Soviet social system is a form of organization of society which is perfectly stable and capable of enduring.

More than that. There is no longer any question today whether the Soviet social system is or is not capable of enduring, for after the object lessons of war none of the skeptics ventures any longer to voice doubts as to the vitality of the Soviet social system. The point now is that the Soviet social system has shown itself more stable and capable of enduring than a non-Soviet social system, that the Soviet social system is a form of organization, a society superior to any non-Soviet social system.

Second, our victory means that our Soviet *state* system has triumphed, that our multinational Soviet state has stood all the trials of war and has proved its vitality.

As you know, prominent foreign press men have more than once gone on record to the effect that the Soviet multinational state was an "artificial, non-viable structure," that in event of any complications, the disintegration of the Soviet Union would be inevitable, and that the fate of Austria-Hungary awaited the Soviet Union.

Today we can say that the war refuted these assertions of the foreign press as totally unfounded. The war showed that the Soviet multinational state system passed the test successfully, that it grew even stronger during the war and proved itself as the state system perfectly capable of enduring. These gentlemen did not understand that the parallel with Austria-Hungary did not apply, for our multinational state has not grown up on a bourgeois foundation which stimulates sentiments of national distrust and national animosity, but on the Soviet foundation which on the contrary cultivates the sentiments of friendship and fraternal collaboration among the peoples of our state.

As a matter of fact, after the lessons of the war, these gentlemen no longer venture to deny that the Soviet state system is capable of enduring. Today it is no longer a question of the vitality of the Soviet state system, for that vitality can no longer be doubted. The point now is that the Soviet state system has proved itself a model for a multinational state, has proved that the Soviet state system is a system of state organization in which the national question and the problem of collaboration among nations has been settled better than in any other multinational state.

Third, our victory means that the Soviet armed forces have triumphed, that our Red Army has triumphed, that the Red Army bore up heroically under all the trials of war, utterly routed the armies of our enemies and came out of the war as a victor. [Voice from floor: "Under the leadership of Comrade Stalin!" All rise—stormy, prolonged applause, rising to an ovation.]

Now everyone, friend as well as foe, admits that the Red Army proved equal to its great tasks. But this was not the case some six years ago during the prewar period. As you know, prominent men from the foreign press and many recognized military authorities abroad declared more than once that the condition of the Red Army gave rise to grave doubts, that the Red Army was poorly armed and had no proper commanding personnel, that its morale was beneath all criticism, that while it might be of some use in defense, it was useless for an offensive, and that if the German forces should strike the Red Army was bound to crumble like a "colossus with feet of clay." Statements like these were made not only in Germany, but in France, Great Britain and in America as well.

Today we can say that the war has refuted all such statements as unfounded and absurd. The war showed that the Red Army is not a "colossus with feet of clay," but a first-class contemporary army with fully modern armaments, highly experienced commanding personnel and high morale and fighting qualities. It must not be forgotten that the Red Army is the army that utterly routed the German army which but yesterday was striking terror into the armies of the European states.

It should be noted that the "critics" of the Red Army are growing fewer and fewer. What is more, the foreign press now more and more frequently contains items which note the fine qualities of the Red Army, the skill of its fighting men and commanders and the flawlessness of its strategy and tactics. That is but natural. After the brilliant Red Army victories at Moscow and Stalingrad, at Kursk and at Belgorod, at Kiev and Kirovograd, at Minsk and Bobruisk, at Leningrad and Tallinn, at Jassy and Lvov, on the Vistula and the Niemen, on the Danube and the Oder, at Vienna and Berlin, it cannot be but admitted that the Red Army is a first-class army from which much could be learned. [Stormy applause.]

Such is our concrete understanding of our country's victory over its enemies.

Such in the main are the results of the war.

It would be a mistake to think that such a historic victory could have been won if the whole country had not prepared beforehand for active defense. It would be no less mistaken to imagine that such preparations could be carried through in a short time—in the space of some three or four years. It would be a still greater mistake to say that we won only owing to the gallantry of our troops. Of course, victory cannot be achieved without gallantry. But gallantry alone is not enough to vanquish an enemy who has a large army, first-class armaments, well-trained officer cadres, and a fairly good organization of supplies. To meet the blow of such an enemy, to repulse him and then to inflict utter defeat upon him required, in addition to the matchless gallantry of our troops, fully up-to-date armaments and adequate quantities of them as well as well-organized supplies in sufficient quantities. But that, in turn, necessitated having—and in adequate amounts—such elementary things as *metal* for the manufacture of armaments, equipment and machinery for factories, *fuel* to keep the factories and transport going, *cotton* for the manufacture of uniforms and *grain* for supplying the Army.

Can it be claimed that before entering the Second World War our country already commanded the necessary minimum material potentialities for satisfying all these requirements in the main? I think it can. In order to prepare for this tremendous job we had to carry out three Five-Year Plans of national economic development. It was precisely these three Five-Year Plans that helped us to create these material potentialities. At any rate, our country's position in this respect before the Second World War, in 1940, was several times better than it was before the First World War, in 1913.

What material potentialities did our country command before the Second World War?

To help you examine this point, I shall have to report briefly on the work of the Communist Party in preparing our country for active defense.

If we take the figures of 1940, the eve of the Second World War, and compare them with the figures for 1913—the eve of the First World War—we get the following picture.

In 1913 our country produced 4,220,000 tons of *pig iron,* 4,230,000 tons of *steel,* 29,000,000 tons of *coal,* 9,000,000 tons of *oil,* 21,600,000 tons of *marketable grain* and 740,000 tons of *raw cotton.*

Those were the material potentialities with which our country entered the First World War.

Such was the economic base of old Russia which could be drawn upon for prosecution of the war.

Now as regards 1940. In the course of that year our country produced 15,000,000 tons of *pig iron,* or nearly four times as much as in 1913; 18,300,000 tons of *steel,* or nearly four and one-half times as much as in 1913; 166,000,000 tons of *coal,* or more than five and one-half times as much as in 1913; 31,000,000 tons of *oil,* or nearly three and one-half times as much as in 1913; 38,300,000 tons of *marketable grain,* or nearly 17,000,000 tons more than in 1913; 2,700,000 tons of *raw cotton,* or more than three and one-half times as much as in 1913.

Those were the material potentialities with which our country entered the Second World War.

Such was the economic base of the Soviet Union which could be drawn upon for prosecution of the war.

The difference as you see is tremendous.

Such an unprecedented increase in production cannot be regarded as the simple and usual development of a country from backwardness to progress. It was a leap by which our Motherland was transformed from a backward into an advanced country, from an agrarian into an industrial country.

This historic transformation was accomplished in the course of three Five-Year Plan periods, beginning with 1928, the first year of the First Five-Year Plan. Up to that time we had to concern ourselves with rehabilitating our ravaged industry and healing the wounds received in the First World War and the Civil War. Moreover, if we bear in mind that the First Five-Year Plan was fulfilled in four years, and that the fulfillment of the Third Five-Year Plan was interrupted by war in its fourth year, we find that it took only about 13 years to transform our country from an agrarian into an industrial one.

It cannot but be admitted that 13 years is an incredibly short period for the accomplishment of such an immense task.

This fact also explains the storm of conflicting comment which the publication of these figures produced at the time in the foreign press. Our friends decided that a "miracle" took place. Our ill-wishers declared that the Five-Year Plans were "Bolshevik propaganda" and "the tricks of the Cheka." But since miracles do not happen, and the Cheka is not so powerful as to abolish the laws of social development, "public opinion" abroad had to accept facts.

By what policy did the Communist Party succeed in providing material potentialities in the country in such a short time?

First of all, by the Soviet policy of industrializing the country.

The Soviet method of industrializing the country differs radically from the capitalist method of industrialization. In capitalist countries industrialization usually begins with light industry. Since in light industry smaller investments are required and there is more rapid turnover of capital and since, furthermore, it is easier to make a profit there than in heavy industry, light industry serves as the first object of industrialization in these countries. Only after a lapse of much time, in the course of which light industry accumulates profits and concentrates them in banks, does the turn of heavy industry arrive and accumulated capital begins to be transferred gradually to heavy industry in order to create conditions for its development. But that is a lengthy process requiring an extensive period of several decades, in the course of which these countries have to wait until light industry has developed and must make shift without heavy industry. Naturally, the Communist Party could not take this course. The Party knew that war was looming, that the country could not be defended without heavy industry, that the development of heavy industry must be undertaken as soon as possible, that to be behind with this would mean to lose out. The Party remembered Lenin's words to the effect that without heavy industry it would be impossible to uphold the country's independence, that without it the Soviet system might perish. Accordingly, the Communist Party of our country rejected the "usual" course of industrialization and began the work of industrializing the country by developing heavy industry. It was very difficult, but not impossible. A valuable aid in this work was the nationalization of industry, and banking, which made possible the rapid accumulation and transfer of funds to heavy industry.

There can be no doubt that without this it would have been impossible to secure our country's transformation into an industrial country in such a short time.

Second, by a policy of collectivization of agriculture.

In order to do away with our backwardness in agriculture and to provide the country with greater quantities of marketable grain, cotton, and so forth, it was essential to pass from small-scale peasant farming to large-scale farming, for only large-scale farming can make use of new technology, apply all the achievements of agronomical science and yield greater quantities of marketable produce. There are, however, two kinds of large farms—capitalist and collective. The Communist Party could not adopt the capitalist path of development of agriculture, and not as a matter of principle alone but also because it implies too prolonged a development and involves preliminary ruin of the peasants and their transformation into farm hands. Therefore, the Communist Party took the path of the collectivization of agriculture, the path of creating large-scale farming by uniting peasant farms into collective farms. The method of collectivization proved a highly progressive method not only because it did not cause the ruin of the peasants but especially because it permitted, within a few years, to cover the entire country with large collective farms which are able to use new technology, take advantage of all the achievements of agronomic science and give the country greater quantities of marketable produce.

There is no doubt that without a collectivization policy we could not in such a short time have done away with the age-old backwardness of our agriculture.

It cannot be said that the Party's policy encountered no resistance. Not only backward people, who always decry everything new, but many prominent members of the Party as well, systematically dragged the Party backward and tried by every possible means to divert it on the "usual" capitalist path of development. All the anti-Party machinations of the Trotskyites and the Rightists, all their "activities" in sabotaging the measures of our government, had one single aim: to frustrate the Party's policy and to obstruct the work of industralization and collectivization. But the Party did not yield either to the threats from one side or the wails from the other and advanced forward confidently regardless of everything. It is to the Party's credit that it did not pander to the backward, was not afraid to go against the tide and always retained its position as the leading force. There can be no doubt that without such firmness and tenacity the Communist Party could not have upheld the policy of industrializing the country and collectivizing agriculture.

Was the Communist Party able to make proper use of the material potentialities thus created in order to develop war production and provide the Red Army with the weapons it needed?

I think that it was able to do so and with maximum success.

If we leave out of account the first year of war, when the evacuation of industry to the East held up the development of war production, we see that in the remaining three years of the war the Party scored such successes that allowed it not only to furnish the front with sufficient quantities of artillery, machine guns, rifles, aircraft, tanks and ammunition, but to accumulate reserves. Moreover, it is known that the quality of our weapons was not only not inferior to the German but, taken on the whole, was actually superior to them.

It is known that during the last three years of war our tank industry produced an annual average of more than 30,000 tanks, self-propelled guns and armored cars. [Storm of applause.]

Further, it is known that our aircraft industry produced during the same period up to 40,000 planes per year. [Storm of applause.]

It is also known that our ordnance industry, during this period, produced annually up to 120,000 guns of all calibers [stormy applause], up to 450,000 light and heavy machine guns [stormy applause], over 3,000,000 rifles [applause], about 2,000,000 submachine guns [applause]. It is known, finally, that between 1942–1944 our mortar industry produced annually on the average 100,000 mortars [stormy applause].

It must be remembered that at the same time we produced a corresponding quantity of artillery shells, all kinds of mines, aircraft bombs and rifle and machine gun ammunition.

It is known, that over 240,000,000 shells, bombs and mortar shells, and 7,400,000,000 rounds of small arms ammunition were manufactured in 1944 alone. [Thunderous applause.]

Such, in general, is the picture of the supply of arms and ammunition to the Red Army.

As you see, it does not resemble the picture which our army supplies presented during the First World War when the front experienced a chronic shortage of artillery and shells, when the army was fighting without tanks and aircraft, and only one rifle was issued to every three men.

As regards the supply of the Red Army with provisions and uniforms, it is known to all that far from experiencing any shortage in this respect, the front actually had surplus.

That is how matters stand with regard to the work of the Communist Party of our country in the period up to the outbreak of war and during the war itself.

Now a few words about the Communist Party's plans of work for the immediate future. As is known these plans are set forth in the new Five-Year Plan which is shortly to be approved. The principal aims of the new Five-Year Plan are to rehabilitate the ravaged areas of the country, to restore the prewar level in industry and agriculture, and then to surpass this level in more or less substantial measure. To say nothing of the fact that the rationing system will shortly be abolished [stormy, prolonged applause], special attention will be devoted to extending the production of consumer goods, to raising the living standard of the working people by steadily lowering the prices of all goods [stormy, prolonged applause], and to the widespread construction of all manner of scientific research institutions [applause] that can give science the opportunity to develop its potentialities. [Stormy applause.]

I have no doubt that if we give our scientists proper assistance they will be able in the near future not only to overtake but to surpass the achievements of science beyond the boundaries of our country. [Prolonged applause.]

As regards the plans for a longer period ahead, the Party intends to organize a new mighty upsurge in the national economy, which would allow us to increase our industrial production, for example, three times over as compared with the prewar period. We must achieve a situation where our industry can produce annually up to 50,000,000 tons of pig iron [prolonged applause], up to 60,000,000 tons of steel [prolonged applause], up to 500,000,000 tons of coal [prolonged applause], and up to 60,000,000 tons of oil [prolonged applause]. Only under such conditions can we consider that our Motherland will be safeguarded against all possible eventualities. [Stormy applause.] That will take three Five-Year Plans, I should think, if not more. But it can be done and we must do it. [Stormy applause.]

Such is my brief report on the Communist Party's work in the recent past and its plans of work for the future.

It is for you to judge how correctly the Party has been working and whether it could not have worked better. [Laughter, applause].

There is a saying that victors are not judged [laughter, applause], that they should not be criticized and checked upon. That is incorrect. Victors should and must be judged [laughter, applause]; they should and must be criticized and checked upon. This is essential not only for the process but for the victors themselves. [Laughter, applause.] There will be less conceitedness and more modesty. [Laughter, applause.] I consider that in the election campaign the electors are sitting in judgment on the Communist Party as the ruling party. And the election returns will constitute the electors' verdict. [Laughter, applause.] The Communist Party of our country would not be worth much if it feared to be criticized and checked upon. The Communist Party is prepared to accept the electors' verdict. [Stormy applause.]

The Communist Party is not alone in the election struggle. It goes to the polls in a bloc with non-Party people. In by-gone days the Communists treated non-Party people and non-Party status with some mistrust. This was due to the fact that the non-Party flag was not infrequently used as a camouflage by various bourgeois groups for whom it was not advantageous to face the electorate without a mask. That was the case in the past. But now we have different times. Our non-Party people are now divided from the bourgeoisie by a barrier known as the Soviet social system. This same barrier unites non-Party people with the Communists in a single community of Soviet people. Living in this single community they struggled together to build up the might of our country, fought and shed their blood together on the battle fronts for the sake of freedom and greatness of our Motherland and together they forged and hammered out a victory over the enemies of our country. The only difference between them is that some belong to the Party, while others do not. But that is a formal difference. The important thing is that both are furthering the same common cause. Therefore, the block of Communists and non-Party people is a natural and living thing. [Stormy, prolonged applause.]

In conclusion, allow me to thank you for the confidence you have shown me [prolonged, unabating applause. Shout from the audience: "Hurrah for the great leader of all victories, Comrade Stalin!"] in nominating me to the Supreme Soviet. You need not doubt that I shall do my best to justify your trust. [All rise. Prolonged, unabating applause turning into an ovation. From all parts of the hall come cheers: "Long live our great Stalin!" "Hurrah!" "Hurrah for the great leader of the peoples!" "Glory to the great Stalin!" "Long live Comrade Stalin, the candidate of the entire nation! Glory to Comrade Stalin, the Creator of all victories!"]

Appendix 29 A RESOLUTION OF THE INFORMATION
BUREAU ON EXPULSION OF TITO FROM
THE COMINFORM, JUNE 28, 1948 [1]

The Information Bureau, composed of the representatives of the Bulgarian Workers' Party (communists), Rumanian Workers' Party, Hungarian Workers' Party, Polish Workers' Party, All-Union Communist Party (bolshevik), Communist Party of France, Communist Party of Czechoslovakia, and Communist Party of Italy, having considered the problem of the situation within the Communist Party of Yugoslavia and having taken note of the fact that the representatives of the Communist Party of Yugoslavia had refused to attend the meeting of the Information Bureau, unanimously reached the following conclusions:

1. The Information Bureau notes that the leadership of the Communist Party of Yugoslavia has in the recent past pursued an incorrect line on the main questions of domestic and foreign policy, [a line] which represents a departure from Marxism-Leninism. The Information Bureau, in this connection, approves the actions of the CC of the VKP (b), [All-Union Communist Party (bolshevik)], which assumed the initiative in exposing the incorrect policy of the CC of the Communist Party of Yugoslavia, and especially the incorrect policies of Comrades Tito, Kardelj, Djilas, [and] Rankovic.

2. The Information Bureau declares that the leadership of the Yugoslav Communist Party is pursuing an unfriendly policy towards the Soviet Union and the VKP(b). There has developed in Yugoslavia an undignified policy aimed at defaming Soviet military specialists and discrediting the Soviet Army. A special regime was established in Yugoslavia for Soviet civilian specialists, who were placed under the surveillance of the Yugoslav state security organs and were followed constantly. Comrade Yudin, the representative of the VKP(b) in the Information Bureau, and a number of official representatives of the USSR in Yugoslavia, were followed and kept under observation by Yugoslav state security organs.

All these and similar facts reveal that the leaders of the Communist Party of Yugoslavia have assumed a position unworthy of communists, have compared foreign policy of the USSR with the foreign policy of the imperialist powers, and have conducted themselves in their relations to the USSR similarly as in their relations with bourgeois states. Because of this anti-Soviet stand, there developed within the CC of the Communist Party of Yugoslavia slanderous propaganda about the "degeneration" of the VKP(b), "degeneration" of the USSR, etc., borrowed from the arsenal of counterrevolutionary Trotskyism.

The Information Bureau denounces these anti-Soviet attitudes of the leaders of the CPY [Communist Party of Yugoslavia] as being incompatible with Marxism-Leninism and appropriate only to nationalists.

3. In their domestic policy the leaders of the CPY are departing from the positions of the working class, and breaking with the Marxist theory of classes

[1] *Pravda*, June 29, 1948, p. 2.

and of the class struggle. They deny the existence of the growth of capitalist elements in their country, and the accompanied increase of the class struggle in the Yugoslav village. This denial stems from the opportunist tenet, which maintains that in the period of transition from capitalism to socialism the class struggle is not intensified, as Marxism-Leninism teaches, but dies down, as was maintained by opportunists of the Bukharin type, who propagated the theory of peaceful incorporation of capitalism into socialism.

The Yugoslav leaders are pursuing an incorrect policy in the village by ignoring the class differentiation in the village and considering the individual peasantry as a single entity, contrary to Marxist-Leninist teaching about classes and the class struggle, and contrary to the well known thesis of Lenin that small individual farming gives birth to capitalism and the bourgeoisie constantly, daily, hourly, spontaneously and on a mass scale. Moreover, the political situation in the Yugoslav village provides no basis for self-satisfaction and complacency. As long as conditions in Yugoslavia permit individual peasant farming, prevent nationalization of land, allow private property in land to exist, and [as long as Yugoslavia is a place] where much of the land is concentrated in the hands of *kulaks*, where hired labor is employed, etc., so long it is inappropriate to educate the party in the spirit of glossing over the class struggle and of reconciling class contradictions, without at the same time disarming the party itself in the face of the difficulties connected with the construction of socialism.

Leaders of the Yugoslav Communist Party, by maintaining that peasants are "the very foundation of the Yugoslav state," are deviating from the Marxist-Leninist path and are taking the path of the populist *kulak* party regarding the leading role of the working class. Lenin teaches that the proletariat "as the only revolutionary-to-the-end class of contemporary society . . . must be the leader and the master in the struggle of the entire people for a thorough democratic transformation in the struggle of all the working and exploited people against the oppressors and exploiters."

The Yugoslav leaders are violating this thesis of Marxism-Leninism.

As far as the peasantry is concerned, its majority, *i.e.*, poor and medium peasants, can be or already is allied with the working class, with the working class possessing the leading role in that alliance.

The attitude of the Yugoslav leaders mentioned above violates these theses of Marxism-Leninism.

As is evident, this attitude reflects such views as are appropriate for petty-bourgeois nationalists, but not for Marxists-Leninists.

4. The Information Bureau believes that the leadership of the YCP is revising the Marxist-Leninist teaching on the party. According to the Marxist-Leninist theory, the party is the chief leading and guiding force in the country, has its own specific programme, and does not dissolve itself within the non-party masses. The party is the highest form of organization and the most important weapon of the working class. In Yugoslavia, however, the chief leading force in the country is not the communist party, but the People's Front. The Yugoslav leaders have belittled the role of the communist party, and actually have dissolved the party in the non-party People's Front, which includes very diverse class elements (workers, toiling peasantry, individual peasants, *kulaks*,

merchants, small manufacturers, bourgeois intelligentsia, etc.) as well as diverse political groups, including some bourgeois parties. The Yugoslav leaders stubbornly refuse to acknowledge the error of their premise that the Communist Party of Yugoslavia allegedly cannot have its own programme and must be satisfied with the programme of the People's Front.

The very fact that the People's Front alone figures in the political arena in Yugoslavia, while the party and its organizations do not appear openly before the people in their own right, lowers the role of the party in the political life of the country, and undermines the party as an independent political force called upon to win the increasing confidence of the people and to influence the great masses of toilers through open political activity, and open propagation of its views and of its programme. The leaders of the Yugoslav Communist Party are repeating the errors of the Russian Mensheviks regarding the dissolution of the Marxist party into a non-party mass organization. All this testifies to the presence of liquidation tendencies within the Communist Party of Yugoslavia.

The Information Bureau believes that such a policy of the CC of the CPY threatens the very existence of the communist party, and, in the final analysis, carries with it a danger of the degeneration of the Yugoslav People's Republic.

5. The Information Bureau believes that the bureaucratic regime established within the party by the Yugoslav leaders is disastrous for the life and development of the Yugoslav Communist Party. The party has neither intraparty democracy, nor elections, nor criticism and self-criticism. The CC of the CPY, contrary to the unfounded assurances of Comrades Tito and Kardelj, consists not of elected but of co-opted members. The communist party actually is in a semilegal situation. Party meetings are either not held at all or are held in secret, a fact which undermines the influence of the party among the masses. This type of organization of the Yugoslav Communist Party cannot be described as anything but a sectarian-bureaucratic organization. Such [organization] leads to the liquidation of the party as an active, creative organism and cultivates in the party military methods of leadership, similar to the methods which Trotsky advocated in his day.

It is absolutely nonpermissible when the most elementary rights of party members are violated in the Yugoslav Communist Party, and when the slightest criticism of incorrect measures in the party is brutally repressed.

The Information Bureau considers as disgraceful such acts as the expulsion from the party and arrest of members of the CC of the CPY, Comrades Zhuyovic and Hebrang, because they dared to criticize the anti-Soviet attitudes of the leaders of the Yugoslav Communist Party and because they called for friendship between Yugoslavia and the USSR.

The Information Bureau believes that such a disgraceful, purely Turkish, terrorist regime cannot be tolerated within the communist party. The interests and the very existence and development of the Yugoslav Communist Party demand that an end be put to such a regime.

6. The Information Bureau believes that the criticism of the errors of the CC of the CPY by the CC of the VKP(b) and by the CC's of other communist parties, being brotherly help for the Yugoslav Communist Party, should have created for the leadership of the CPY the necessary prerequisites for the speedy

correction of their errors. However, instead of accepting this criticism honestly and adopting the Bolshevik path of correcting their errors, leaders of the YCP, who suffer from boundless ambition, arrogance, and conceit, met this criticism with belligerence and hostility, adopted an anti-party path of indiscriminate denial of their errors, of their violation of the Marxist-Leninist teaching on the attitude of a political party to its mistakes, and thereby they have aggravated their anti-party errors.

Unable to face the criticism of the CC of the VKP(b) and of other CC's of other fraternal parties, Yugoslav leaders assumed a path of direct deceit of their party and of the people, by concealing from the Yugoslav Communist Party the criticism of the erroneous policy of the CC of the YCP, and by concealing also from the party and the people the real cause for the mistreatment of Comrades Zhuyovic and Hebrang.

During the recent past, already after the criticism by the CC of the VKP(b) and by the fraternal parties of the errors of the Yugoslav leaders, the latter tried to introduce a number of new leftist laws. The Yugoslav leaders hastily decreed the nationalization of small industry and trade. The complete unpreparedness for such action, in view of the haste, will only hamper the supply of goods for the Yugoslav population. They also hurriedly promulgated a new law on peasant grain tax, which, because of unpreparedness, will only dislocate grain supplies to the urban population. Finally, the Yugoslav leaders recently announced in loud but unexpected declarations their love of and devotion to the Soviet Union, even though it is well known that in practice they are pursuing to the very present an unfriendly policy towards the USSR.

But this is not all. Leaders of the CPY have lately announced with great fanfare the liquidation of capitalist elements in Yugoslavia. In a letter to the CC of the VKP(b) dated April 13, 1948, Tito and Kardelj wrote that "the plenum of the CC approved the measures proposed by the Politbureau of the CC to liquidate the remnants of capitalism in the country." In accordance with this line, speaking in the Skupshchina on April 25, Kardelj declared: "The days of the last remnants of the exploitation of man by man are numbered in our country." Such a proposal by the leaders of the YCP to liquidate capitalist elements under the prevailing conditions in Yugoslavia, and accordingly of the *kulaks* as a class, cannot be called other than adventurous and un-Marxist. It is impossible to resolve this problem as long as individual peasant farming, which inevitably gives rise to capitalism, prevails in the country, as long as conditions have not been prepared for the massive collectivization of agriculture, and as long as the majority of the toiling peasantry is not convinced of the advantages of collective methods of farming. The experience of the VKP(b) testifies that the liquidation of the last and the most numerous exploiting class—the *kulak* class—is possible only through a mass collectivization of agriculture, and that the liquidation of the *kulaks* as a class is an organic and integral part of the collectivization of agriculture.

To carry out successfully the liquidation of the *kulaks* as a class, and accordingly to liquidate capitalist elements in the village, the party must prepare a detailed plan aimed at restricting capitalist elements in the village, must strengthen the alliance between the working class and the peasantry under the leadership of the working class, and must develop socialist industry capable of producing machinery for the collective administration of agriculture. Haste in this matter can only lead to irreparable harm.

Only on the basis of such measures, carefully prepared and consistently carried out, is it possible to move from the restriction of capitalist elements in the village to their liquidation.

All attempts of Yugoslav leaders to solve this task hastily or by means of bureaucratic decrees signify either that the venture is foredoomed to failure or that it is a boastful and empty demagogic declaration.

The Information Bureau believes that the Yugoslav leaders are trying to demonstrate, by means of such false and demagogic tactics, that they not only firmly support the class struggle, but that they go even further beyond those demands which, in view of the real possibilities, the Yugoslav Communist Party could have used in limiting capitalist elements.

The Information Bureau believes that since these leftist decrees and declarations of the Yugoslav leadership are demagogic and impracticable in the present conditions, they can but compromise the socialist construction in Yugoslavia.

Therefore the Information Bureau considers such adventurist tactics as an undignified maneuver and a nonpermissible political gamble.

As is evident, these leftist demagogic measures and declarations of the Yugoslav leaders are designed to cover up their refusal to recognize and to correct their own errors.

7. Taking into account the situation in the YCP, and seeking to give the leaders of the Yugoslav Communist Party an opportunity to get out of this situation, the CC of the VKP(b) and the CC's of other fraternal parties sought to examine the situation in the Yugoslav Communist Party at a meeting of the Information Bureau on a similar party basis as that on which the Information Bureau examined the activities of other parties at its first meeting. However, the Yugoslav leaders rejected the repeated proposals of fraternal parties to discuss the situation in the Yugoslav Communist Party at a meeting of the Information Bureau.

To avoid the just criticism of the fraternal parties in the Information Bureau, the Yugoslav leaders invented the fable of their allegedly "unequal position." This story contains not a grain of truth. Everyone knows that when the Information Bureau was organized the communist parties agreed that every party should account for its activity before the Information Bureau and that every party has the right to criticize other parties. The Yugoslav Communist Party took full advantage of this right at the first meeting of the nine communist parties. The refusal of the Yugoslavs to report on their activities to the Information Bureau and to listen to criticism of other communist parties represents a violation of the equality of communist parties and is tantamount to a demand for a privileged position for the YCP in the Information Bureau.

8. In view of the above arguments, the Information Bureau expresses its complete accord with the estimation of the situation in the Yugoslav Communist Party, and with the criticism of the errors of the CC of the CPY and the political analysis of these errors, contained in letters from the CC of the VKP(b) to the CC of the CPY between March and May, 1948.

The Information Bureau unanimously concludes that by their anti-party and anti-Soviet views, incompatible with Marxism-Leninism, by their whole conduct, and by their refusal to attend the meeting of the Information Bureau, the leaders of the CPY have placed themselves in opposition to the communist parties affiliated with the Information Bureau, have assumed a path of secession from the united socialist front against imperialism, have assumed a path of betrayal of the cause of the international solidarity of the workers, and have assumed a position of nationalism.

The Information Bureau condemns this anti-party policy and conduct of the CC of the CPY.

The Information Bureau believes that because of all this the CC of the CPY has placed itself and the Yugoslav Communist Party outside the united communist front, and, consequently, outside the ranks of the Information Bureau.

The Information Bureau believes that the basis of all the errors of the leadership of the CPY centers in the undoubted fact that the nationalist elements, which previously existed in a disguised form, have, during the past five or six months, triumphed in the leadership of the CPY, and that the leadership of the CPY has broken with the internationalist traditions of the Yugoslav Communist Party and has taken the path of nationalism.

The Yugoslav leaders strongly overestimate the internal national forces and possibilities, and think that they can preserve the independence of Yugoslavia and build socialism without the support of communist parties of other countries, without the support of the countries of people's democracies, without the support of the USSR. They think that the new Yugoslavia can do without the aid of these revolutionary forces.

Yugoslav leaders, who reveal their poor understanding of the international situation and who are afraid of the blackmailing threats of imperialists, believe that by making concessions to imperialist states they will gain the favor of these states, will be able to reach an agreement with them on Yugoslavia's independence, and will gradually impose on the Yugoslav people orientation on these states, i.e., orientation on capitalism. In this they proceed tacitly from a well-known bourgeois-nationalist thesis that "capitalist states are a lesser danger to the independence of Yugoslavia than is the USSR."

The Yugoslav leaders evidently do not understand, or perhaps pretend they do not understand, that such a nationalist attitude can only lead to the transformation of Yugoslavia into an ordinary bourgeois republic, to the loss of Yugoslav independence, and to the transformation of Yugoslavia into a colony of the imperialist countries.

The Information Bureau does not doubt that within the Communist Party of Yugoslavia there are many healthy elements loyal to Marxism-Leninism, loyal to the internationalist traditions of the Yugoslav Communist Party, and loyal to the united socialist front.

The task of these healthy elements in the CPY is to force their present leaders to recognize openly their errors and to correct them; to break with nationalism; to return to internationalism; and to strengthen in every possible way the united socialist front against imperialism. Should the present leaders of the CPY be incapable of doing this, they should be replaced and new internationalist leadership in the CPY be chosen.

The Information Bureau does not doubt that the Communist Party of Yugoslavia will be able to fulfill this honorable task.

Dear friend, fighting comrade, teacher and leader:

On your 70th birthday, the Central Committee of the Communist Party of the Soviet Union (Bolsheviks), and the Council of Ministers of the U.S.S.R. warmly salute you, the great companion-in-arms and friend of Lenin, the brilliant continuator of his immortal cause, the indefatigable builder of Communism, our wise teacher and leader.

Together with Lenin, you, Comrade Stalin, built the Bolshevik Party, in close co-operation with Lenin, elaborated the ideological, organisational, tactical and theoretical principles of Bolshevism; tempered the Party in severe battles for the liberation of the working people, and transformed it into the most powerful revolutionary Party in the world.

A fearless revolutionary, brilliant theoretician and splendid organiser, you, together with Lenin, confidently, boldly, firmly and carefully led the Party, the working class to armed uprising, to the Socialist Revolution.

Together with Lenin, you, Comrade Stalin, were the inspirer and leader of the Great October Socialist Revolution, the founder of the first Soviet Socialist State of workers and peasants in the world.

During the years of Civil War and foreign intervention, your genius as organiser and commander led the Soviet people and its heroic Red Army to victory over the enemies of the Fatherland.

Under your direct leadership, Comrade Stalin, vast work was accomplished in establishing the national Soviet Republics, in uniting them into one union—the U.S.S.R.

When death cut short the life of the great Lenin, you, Comrade Stalin, raised aloft the glorious banner of Lenin, and once again boldly and resolutely led our Party along the Lenin path.

The Bolshevik Party, strong in its loyalty to Leninism, blazed the path of Socialist construction, hitherto unknown in history, in a country encircled by capitalist States.

Of the greatest significance for the victory of Socialism was the Lenin theory about the possibility of the victory of Socialism in our country; a theory further developed and enriched by you.

The enemies of Socialism, the enemies of the Soviet people and of the Communist Party tried in vain to divert our Party from the Lenin-Stalin path, to split it from within, to deprive the working class of confidence in their strength, in the possibility of building socialism.

[1] *For a Lasting Peace, for a People's Democracy*, No. 32 (59), December 21, 1949, p. 1.

You ruthlessly exposed the dastardly, criminal attempts of the enemies of the people to disarm the Party ideologically, to smash its unity, to destroy Soviet power and the Socialist Revolution.

In the bitter struggle against the traitors to the cause of Socialism—against the trotskyites, bukharinites, bourgeois nationalists and other enemies—there was welded around you, Comrade Stalin, the leading core of our Party, which upheld the invincible banner of Lenin, consolidated the Communist Party and led the Soviet people on to the high road of Socialist construction.

Carrying out the gigantic programme of Socialist industrialisation of our country elaborated by you, the Soviet people, in an historically short space of time, transformed Russia from a technically and economically backward country into an advanced industrial power.

Your name is associated with the mighty Socialist construction of the Five-Year Plans, with the giants of industry, with new branches of industry, all of which have played a decisive role in strengthening the defence capacity of the State.

Under your wise leadership, Comrade Stalin, an historic turning point was effected in the countryside in 1929, the consequences of which are equal only to the revolutionary upheaval of October 1917.

The Communist Party carried out the complete collectivisation of agriculture, and, on this basis, the liquidation of the kulaks as a class.

As a result of the victories of the collective-farm system and the mechanisation of agriculture, the new Socialist life took root in the Soviet countryside, delivering the working peasantry from bondage, ruin and impoverishment.

Under the leadership of our Party, headed by the beloved Stalin, the Soviet Union became a mighty industrial and collective-farm power; a country of victorious Socialism.

Having built Socialism, the Soviet people once and for all destroyed the exploitation of man by man, created a new social and State order, free of crises and unemployment and ensured a steady rise in the material and cultural level of the working people.

The Constitution of the U.S.S.R., justly called by the people the Stalin Constitution, consolidated the magnificent victories of Socialism, became a magnetic force, a beacon light for the whole of working mankind.

On the basis of the rich experience of the land of Soviets, you, Comrade Stalin, elaborated a complete and all-round teaching on the Socialist State.

In further developing Leninism you reached the brilliant conclusion regarding the possibility of building Communism in our country, and the need to preserve the State under Communism should capitalist encirclement remain.

This conclusion gave the Party and the people a clear perspective of the struggle for the victory of Communism.

The solution of one of the most important questions of the Revolution—the National Question—is linked with your name, Comrade Stalin.

In the fraternal family of Soviet peoples, the formerly oppressed nations have attained unprecedented political, economic, and cultural flowering.

Inspired by you, the friendship between the peoples of the U.S.S.R. was a great gain of the Revolution, one of the sources of the might of our Socialist Fatherland.

With the victory of Socialism, the moral-political unity of the Soviet people, closely consolidated around the Party of Lenin-Stalin, has become invincible.

Our People are imbued with warm and creative Soviet patriotism. Under your leadership, the Bolshevik Party carried out a real cultural revolution in the U.S.S.R.

Your wisdom, indomitable energy and iron will are to be found in every change effected, large or small; changes that are raising our country to ever higher levels.

It is our happiness, the happiness of our people, that the Great Stalin, as leader of the Party and the State, guides and inspires the creative, constructive work of the Soviet people for the flowering of our glorious Fatherland.

Under your leadership, Comrade Stalin, the Soviet Union has become a mighty and invincible force.

When Hitler's Germany forced war on the Soviet Union and mortal danger threatened our Fatherland, you, Comrade Stalin, headed the armed struggle of the Soviet people against fascism—the worst enemy of mankind; rallied all Soviet peoples in the Great Patriotic War; inspired the Soviet people and its Armed Forces to legendary deeds and exploits.

The Party of Lenin and Stalin united the efforts of the front and rear.

Your military and organisational genius brought us victory over fascist Germany and imperialist Japan.

Great commander and organiser of victory, you, Comrade Stalin, created an advanced Soviet military science. The battles directed by you are outstanding examples of military, operational and strategic art.

The first-class military cadres, trained and educated by you carried out with honour the Stalin plans to rout the enemy.

All honest people in the world, and future generations will sing the glory of the Soviet Union, of your name, Comrade Stalin, as the saviour of world civilisation from the fascist pogrom-makers.

In post-war conditions, the whole Soviet people, guided by your counsels, devoted their creative initiative to heal rapidly the aftermath of the war; to carry out the gigantic plans for the further development of national economy and culture in the land of Socialism; to improve the welfare of the working people.

The Lenin-Stalin idea of Socialist emulation, inspiring Soviet patriots to new labour exploits, released the powerful energy of millions of Soviet people to realise the great aim—the victory of Communism.

You, Comrade Stalin, are guiding the foreign policy of the Soviet Union with great firmness and foresight, fighting for peace and security of large and small nations.

The international prestige of the U.S.S.R. as the bulwark of peace and democracy has grown immeasurably.

The working people of the capitalist and colonial countries see in you a true and staunch champion of peace and defender of the vital interests of the people of all countries.

You have kindled in the hearts of all ordinary people of the world an unshakable confidence in the just cause of the struggle for world peace, for the national independence of peoples, for friendship between peoples.

Under your leadership, Comrade Stalin, the Soviet Union played a decisive role in liberating the working people of the New Democracies from the fascist enslavers, from the yoke of capitalists and landlords.

The peoples of these countries are filled with gratitude to you for the disinterested fraternal aid the Soviet Union is rendering them in their economic and cultural development.

Great coryphaeus of science! Your classical works, which developed Marxist-Leninist theory in accordance with the new epoch, the epoch of imperialism and proletarian revolutions, the epoch of the victory of Socialism in our country, are the greatest achievement of mankind, an encyclopaedia of revolutionary Marxism.

Soviet people and the progressive representatives of the working people of all countries draw from these works knowledge, confidence, new strength in the struggle for the victory of the working class and find there the answers to the most burning problems of present-day struggle for Communism.

Like a bright torch your works on the National and Colonial Questions illuminate the path of the national-liberation movement of the peoples of the colonial and dependent countries.

The colossal successes of the forces of peace, democracy and Socialism are illumined by Lenin-Stalin revolutionary thought.

Great architect of Communism! You teach all Bolsheviks to be most exacting towards themselves and others, to criticise shortcomings boldly, and you warn them not to rest on their laurels, not to get bloated with success. You teach us that criticism and self-criticism is an effective weapon in the struggle for Communism, that the integral qualities of Party and Soviet cadres must be Bolshevik modesty, a solicitous and attentive approach to the needs of the people, to be steadfast and principled in the struggle against all manifestations of bourgeois ideology.

Dear Comrade Stalin. You always taught us and still teach us Bolsheviks, to be as the great Lenin was; not to spare our efforts in the service of our people, in every way to contribute to the further blossoming of our beloved Fatherland, to do everything for the victory of Communism.

The Bolshevik Party and Soviet people, all progressive mankind, see in you a teacher and leader, the brilliant continuator of Lenin's immortal work.

The name of Stalin is the name dearest to our people, to the ordinary people of the world. The name of Stalin is the symbol of the coming victory of Communism.

The hearts of Soviet people and millions of working people throughout the world are filled with warm love for you, the Great Stalin.

It is a great happiness to live and create in our Soviet land, to belong to the Party of Lenin-Stalin, to the heroic generation of Soviet people who are fighting in the Stalin epoch for the triumph of Communism under the leadership of Stalin.

Teacher and leader, best friend and fighting comrade, accept our heartfelt wishes to you for many years of health and creative work for the good of the Bolshevik Party, Soviet people and for the happiness of the working people of the world.

Long live our own Stalin!

Central Committee, Communist Party   Council of Ministers
of the Soviet Union (Bolsheviks)   of the U.S.S.R.

Appendix 31 STALIN'S LAST SPEECH, OCTOBER 17, 1952 [1]

[Comrade Stalin's appearance on the rostrum is greeted by the delegates with tumultuous prolonged applause developing into ovation. All rise. Cheers: "Hurrah for Comrade Stalin!" "Long live Comrade Stalin!" "Glory to the great Stalin!"]

Comrades,

Allow me on behalf of our Congress to express thanks to all the fraternal Parties and groups, whose representatives honoured our Congress with their presence or who sent messages of greetings to the Congress,—for their friendly greetings, wishes of success and for their trust. [Tumultuous, prolonged applause growing into ovation.]

Of special value for us is this trust which signifies readiness to support our Party in the struggle for the radiant future for the peoples, in its struggle against war, in its struggle for the preservation of peace. [Tumultuous, prolonged applause.]

It would be a mistake to think that our Party, having become a powerful force, no longer needs support. This is not correct. Our Party and our country have always needed and shall need the trust, sympathy and support of the fraternal peoples abroad.

A peculiarity of this support is that all support for the peace-loving aspirations of our Party on the part of any fraternal Party signifies at the same time support of its own people in their struggle for the preservation of peace. When the British workers in 1918–19, at the time of the armed attack of the British bourgeoisie on the Soviet Union, organised the struggle against war under the slogan "Hands off Russia," this was support, first of all support of the struggle of their people for peace, and then support of the Soviet Union. When Comrade Thorez or Comrade Togliatti declare that their peoples will not fight against the peoples of the Soviet Union [tumultuous applause] this is support, first of all support of the workers and peasants of France and Italy fighting for peace, and then support of the peace-loving strivings of the Soviet Union. This peculiarity of the mutual support is explained by the fact that the interests of our Party not only do not contradict, but, on the contrary, merge with the interests of the peace-loving peoples. [Tumultuous applause.] As for the Soviet Union its interests in general are inseparable from the cause of world peace.

Naturally, our Party cannot remain in debt to the fraternal parties and it must in turn support them and also their people in their struggle for liberation, in their struggle for the preservation of peace. As is known, that is

[1] *For a Lasting Peace, for a People's Democracy,* No. 42 (206), October 17, 1952, p. 1.

precisely what it does. [Tumultuous applause.] After our Party took power in 1917 and after the Party took real measures to do away with capitalist and landlord oppression, representatives of the fraternal Parties, admiring the valour and successes of our Party, named it the "Shock-brigade" of the world revolutionary and working-class movement. In this way they expressed the hope that the successes of the "Shock-brigade" would facilitate the position of the peoples groaning under the yoke of capitalism. I think that our party justified these hopes, especially in the period of the second world war when the Soviet Union, by smashing German and Japanese fascist tyranny, delivered the peoples of Europe and Asia from the menace of fascist slavery. [Tumultuous applause.]

Of course, it was very difficult to fulfill this honourable role, so long as the "Shock-brigade" was all alone and had to carry out this leading role practically single-handed. But this belongs to the past. Now things are altogether different. Now, when from China and Korea to Czechoslovakia and Hungary new "Shock-brigades" have appeared in the shape of the people's democratic countries,—now it has become easier for our Party to fight, and indeed work is going with a swing. [Tumultuous, prolonged applause.]

Those Communist, democratic or worker-peasant Parties which have not yet come to power and which are still working under the heel of the draconic laws of the bourgeoisie, deserve special attention. For them, of course, the work is more difficult. But it is not as difficult for them as it was for us, the Russian Communists, at the time of tsarism, when the slightest forward movement was proclaimed a heinous crime. However, the Russian Communists stood firm, were not afraid of the difficulties and won victory. The same thing will take place with these Parties.

Why, then, will it be less difficult for these Parties to work than was the case with the Russian Communists at the time of tsarism?

Firstly, because they have before their eyes examples of struggle and successes such as we have in the Soviet Union and in the people's democratic countries. Consequently, they can learn from the mistakes and successes of these countries and in this way make their work easier.

Secondly, because the bourgeoisie itself—the main enemy of the liberation movement—has changed, changed substantially, has become more reactionary, has lost contact with the people and by so doing has weakened itself. Obviously, this circumstance too, is bound to make the work of the revolutionary and democratic Parties easier. [Tumultuous applause.]

Formerly the bourgeoisie permitted itself to be liberal, championed bourgeois-democratic freedoms and in doing so created for itself popularity among the people. Now, not even a trace of liberalism remains. Gone is the so-called "freedom of the individual,"—the rights of the individual now are recognised only in the case of those who have capital while all other citizens are regarded as human raw material fit only for exploitation. The principle of equality of people and nations has been trampled underfoot; it has been replaced by the principle of full rights for the exploiting minority and no rights for the exploited majority of citizens. The banner of the bourgeois-democratic freedoms has been thrown overboard. I think that you, representatives of the Communist and democratic Parties, will have to pick up this banner and carry it forward if you wish to rally around yourselves the majority of the people. There is no one else to pick it up. [Tumultuous applause.]

Formerly the bourgeoisie was considered the head of the nation, it championed the rights and independence of the nation, placing them "above everything." Now, not a trace remains of the "national principle." Now the bourgeoisie sells the rights and independence of the nation for dollars. The banner of national independence and national sovereignty has been thrown overboard. There is no doubt that you, representatives of the Communist and democratic Parties, will have to pick up this banner and carry it forward if you wish to be patriots of your country, if you wish to become the leading force of the nation. There is no one else to pick it up. [Tumultuous applause.]

That is how matters stand at present.

Clearly all these circumstances are bound to facilitate the work of the Communist and democratic Parties which have not yet come to power.

Consequently, there is every reason to count on success and victory for the fraternal parties in the countries dominated by capital. [Tumultuous applause.]

Long live our fraternal Parties! [Prolonged applause.]

Long life and good health to the leaders of the fraternal Parties! [Prolonged applause.]

Long live peace among the nations! [Prolonged applause.]

Down with the warmongers! [All rise. Tumultuous, prolonged applause growing into ovations. Cries: "Long live Comrade Stalin!" "Hurrah for Comrade Stalin!" "Long live Comrade Stalin, great leader of the working people of the world!" "Hurrah for the great Stalin!" "Long live peace among the nations!" Cries: "Hurrah!"]

Appendix 32 OFFICIAL CHARGES AGAINST L. P. BERIA
AND HIS ASSOCIATES, DECEMBER, 1953 [1]

The Presidium of the Supreme Soviet of the USSR, having reviewed the report of the Council of Ministers of the USSR on the criminal activities of L. P. Beria, as an agent of foreign capital, directed toward the subversion of the Soviet state, decreed on June 26, 1953: to remove L. P. Beria from the post of First Deputy Chairman of the Council of Ministers of the USSR and from the post of Minister of Internal Affairs of the USSR, and to bring Beria to trial. On August 8, 1953, the Supreme Soviet of the USSR confirmed the June 26 decree of the Presidium of the Supreme Soviet of the USSR.

The Office of Procurator of the USSR has now completed the investigation in the case of the traitor to the Motherland, L. P. Beria.

The investigation has established that Beria, using his position, organized a treacherous group of conspirators hostile to the Soviet state, which made it its criminal aim to use organs of the Ministry of Internal Affairs, both centrally and locally, against the Communist Party and the government of the USSR in the interests of foreign capital, striving in their treacherous intents to place the Ministry of Internal Affairs above the Party and government, to seize power and to liquidate the Soviet worker-peasant system, with a view to restoring capitalism and securing the revival of the domination of the bourgeoisie.

Active participants in the treacherous group of conspirators connected with Beria for a period of many years by joint criminal activity in the organs of the NKVD and MVD were: the former Minister of State Security of the USSR and lately Minister of State Control of the USSR, V. N. Merkulov; the former head of one of the administrations of the NKVD of the USSR and lately Minister of Internal Affairs of the Georgian SSR, V. G. Dekanozov; the former Deputy People's Commissar of Internal Affairs of the Georgian SSR, later Deputy Minister of State Security of the USSR, and more recently Deputy Minister of Internal Affairs of the USSR, B. Z. Kobulov; the former People's Commissar of Internal Affairs of the Georgian SSR and lately head of one of the administrations of the MVD of the USSR, S. A. Goglidze; the former head of one of the administrations of the NKVD of the USSR and lately Minister of Internal Affairs of the Ukrainian SSR, P. Ia. Meshik; and the former head of the Investigation Department, for particularly important matters, of the MVD of the USSR, L. E. Vlodzimirskii.

For a period of many years Beria and his accomplices carefully camouflaged and concealed their hostile treacherous activity. After the demise of J. V. Stalin, when imperialist reactionary forces increased their subversive activities against the Soviet state, Beria intensified his actions in order to

[1] *Izvestiia*, December 17, 1953. Translation by Basil Dmytryshyn.

attain his criminal aims, primarily by utilizing organs of the MVD to seize power, which made it possible in a short period of time to lay bare the true face of the traitor of the Motherland and to take decisive measures to put an end to his hostile activity.

Having become Minister of Internal Affairs of the USSR in March, 1953, Beria began more intensively to elevate members of the conspirators' group into a number of leading posts in the Ministry of Internal Affairs. The conspirators subjected to persecution and victimization honest workers of the MVD who had refused to carry out Beria's criminal instructions.

In order to subvert the collective farm system and to create food difficulties in our country, Beria sabotaged and interfered in every possible way with the implementation of most important measures of the Party and the government which were directed toward an upsurge of the economy of collective and state farms and toward steady improvement of the well-being of the Soviet people.

It has also been established that Beria and his accomplices carried out criminal measures aimed at reviving remnants of bourgeois nationalist elements in the Union Republics, sowing hatred and discord between the peoples of the USSR, and primarily at undermining the friendship of the peoples of the USSR with the Great Russian people.

Deprived of any social support whatsoever within the USSR, Beria and his accomplices sought to build their criminal activity on support for their conspiracy from reactionary imperialist forces from abroad.

As has now been established by the investigation, Beria had established links with foreign intelligence services as far back as the Civil War. In 1919, when he was in Baku, Beria committed a betrayal, having become a secret agent in the intelligence service of the counter-revolutionary Mussavat Government in Azerbaidzhan, which operated under the control of British intelligence organs. In 1920 Beria, then in Georgia, again committed an act of betrayal, having established secret contact with the Georgian Menshevik secret police, which was a branch of British intelligence.

The investigation has established that during subsequent years as well Beria maintained and extended his secret criminal contacts with foreign intelligence services through planted spies, whom he was sometimes able to protect from exposure and the punishment they deserved.

Acting as a traitor and a spy to the Motherland, who had sold himself to foreign intelligence services, Beria, throughout the entire length of his criminal activities, with the aid of his accomplices also maintained secret contacts with counter-revolutionary Georgian Menshevik emigrants and with the agents of a number of foreign intelligence services.

Diligently concealing his criminal past and inimical contacts with intelligence services of foreign states, Beria selected as his basic method slander, intrigues, and various provocations against honest Party and Soviet workers, who stood in the path of his hostile intentions toward the Soviet state, and who interfered with his efforts to gain power.

Having managed, with the aid of these criminal methods, to get responsible posts in Trans-Caucasia and Georgia, and then in the MVD of the USSR, and having conceived treacherous aims and plans for seizing power, Beria and his accomplices dealt arbitrarily with people who did not suit them, not shrinking from acts of arbitrariness and lawlessness, basely deceiving the Party and the state.

The investigation has established a number of Beria's criminal machinations directed toward the attaining of careerist aims and designed to prevent the exposure of his hostile nature. The investigation has established that, in order to attain his treacherous aims, Beria—with the aid of his accomplices—waged a campaign of criminal intrigue over a period of years against the outstanding leader of the Communist Party and the Soviet state, Sergo Ordzhonikidze, seeing in him a man who was an obstacle to his further ambition and the fulfillment of his hostile intentions. As has now been established Sergo Ordzhonikidze felt that Beria could not be trusted politically. After the demise of Sergo Ordzhonikidze, the conspirators continued to wreak severe vengeance on members of his family.

The investigation has also established that the conspirators committed terrorist murders of persons from whom they feared exposure. Thus Beria and his accomplices put to death M. S. Kedrov—a member of the Communist Party from 1902, a former member of the Presidium of the All-Russian CHEKA and the Collegium of the OGPU under F. E. Dzerzhinskii. The conspirators had reasons to suspect Kedrov of having at his disposal evidence of the criminal past of Beria. Other facts have also been established relating to terrorist murders committed by the conspirators, with the criminal intent of exterminating honest cadres devoted to the cause of the Communist Party and the Soviet regime.

As established by the investigation, Beria and his accomplices committed a number of treacherous acts, designed to weaken the defense capability of the Soviet Union.

Material brought to light by the investigation has established that members of the conspiratorial group—the accused Merkulov, Dekanozov, Kobulov, Goglidze, Meshik, and Vlodzimirskii—who were linked to Beria through joint criminal activity over many years, carried out criminal assignments set by Beria, helped him to conceal his treasonous past, and committed a number of grave state crimes which have been referred to above.

Thus it has been established that the accused Beria, Merkulov, Dekanozov, Kobulov, Goglidze, Meshik, and Vlodzimirskii, having betrayed the Motherland, acted as agents of international imperialism, as the worst enemies of the Soviet people.

The investigation has also established other evidence regarding crimes committed by Beria, that testify to his deep moral depravity and also evidence regarding his criminal, mercenary activity and his abuse of power.

Having been exposed during the investigation by testimonies of numerous witnesses and indisputable documentary evidence, the accused admitted their guilt of committing a number of grave crimes against the state.

Beria has been committed for trial on the charge of high treason to the Motherland, of organizing an anti-Soviet conspiracy, of committing acts of terrorism, of active struggle against the working class and the revolutionary workers' movement, of acting as a secret agent in the intelligence services of the counter-revolutionary Mussavat Government during the Civil

War period; that is, crimes provided for by Articles 58-1 (b), 58-8, 58-13, 58-11 of the Criminal Code of the RSFSR.

Merkulov, Dekanozov, Kobulov, Goglidze, Meshik, and Vlodzimirskii have been committed for trial on a charge of high treason against the Motherland, of committing acts of terrorism, and of participating in a counter-revolutionary treasonous group of conspirators; that is, crimes provided for by Articles 58-1 (b), 58-8, 58-11 of the Criminal Code of the RSFSR.

In accordance with the decree of the Presidium of the Supreme Soviet of the USSR, the case against Beria, Merkulov, Dekanozov, Kobulov, Goglidze, Meshik, and Vlodzimirskii is subject to a special review of the Supreme Court of the USSR, in accordance with the procedure established by the law of December 1, 1934.

Appendix 33 THE TEXT OF MALENKOV'S "RESIGNATION," FEBRUARY 8, 1955 [1]

To the Chairman of the Joint Session of the Soviet of the Union and the Soviet of Nationalities:

I ask you to bring to the attention of the Supreme Soviet of the USSR my request to be relieved from the post of Chairman of the Council of Ministers of the USSR.

My request is motivated by practical considerations on the necessity of strengthening the leadership of the Council of Ministers and by the need to have at the post of Chairman of the Council of Ministers another comrade with greater experience in state work. I clearly see that the carrying out of the complex and responsible duties of Chairman of the Council of Ministers is being negatively affected by my insufficient experience in local work, and the fact that I did not have occasion, in a ministry or some economic organ, to direct guidance of individual branches of national economy.

I also consider myself bound to say in the present statement that now, when the Communist Party of the Soviet Union and the workers of our country are concentrating special efforts for the most rapid development of agriculture, I see particularly clearly my guilt and responsibility for the unsatisfactory state of affairs that has arisen in agriculture, because for several years past I have been entrusted with the duty of controlling and guiding the work of central agricultural organs and the work of local party and administrative organizations in the sphere of agriculture. The Communist Party, on the initiative and under the guidance of the Central Committee of the Communist Party of the Soviet Union, has already worked out and is implementing a series of broad measures for overcoming the lagging in agriculture. Among such important measures is, undoubtedly, the reform of agricultural taxation, regarding which I think it opportune to say that it was carried out on the initiative of and in accordance with the proposals of the Central Committee of the Communist Party of the Soviet Union. It is now evident what important role this reform played in the task of developing agriculture. Now, as is known, on the initiative and under the guidance of the Central Committee of the Communist Party of the Soviet Union, a general program has been worked out to overcome the lagging in agriculture and for its most rapid development. This program is based on the only correct foundation: The further development by every means of heavy industry, and only its implementation will create the necessary conditions for a real upsurge in the production of all essential commodities for popular consumption.

It is to be expected that various bourgeois hysterical viragos will busy

[1] *Izvestiia,* February 9, 1955, p. 1. Translation by Basil Dmytryshyn.

themselves with slanderous inventions in connection with my present statement, and the fact itself of my release from the post of Chairman of the USSR Council of Ministers, but we, Communists and Soviet people, will ignore this lying and slander. For every one of us the interests of the motherland, the people, and of the Communist Party stand above everything else.

Expressing the request for my release from the post of Chairman of the Council of Ministers of the USSR, I wish to assure the Supreme Soviet of the USSR that, in the new sphere entrusted to me, under the guidance of the Central Committee of the Communist Party of the Soviet Union and the Soviet Government, monolithic in its unity and solidarity, I will perform in the most conscientious manner my duty and the functions which will be entrusted to me.

> G. MALENKOV
> Chairman of the Council of
> Ministers of the USSR

Appendix 34 THE WARSAW SECURITY PACT, MAY 14, 1955 [1]

The Contracting Parties,

reaffirming their desire for the establishment of a system of European collective security based on the participation of all European states irrespective of their social and political systems, which would make it possible to unite their efforts in safeguarding the peace of Europe;

mindful, at the same time, of the situation created in Europe by the ratification of the Paris agreements, which envisage the formation of a new military alignment in the shape of "Western European Union," with the participation of a remilitarized Western Germany and the integration of the latter in the North-Atlantic bloc, which increased the danger of another war and constitutes a threat to the national security of the peaceable states;

being persuaded that in these circumstances the peaceable European states must take the necessary measures to safeguard their security and in the interests of preserving peace in Europe;

guided by the objects and principles of the Charter of the United Nations Organization;

being desirous of further promoting and developing friendship, cooperation and mutual assistance in accordance with the principles of respect for the independence and sovereignty of states and of noninterference in their internal affairs,

have decided to conclude the present Treaty of Friendship, Cooperation and Mutual Assistance and have for that purpose appointed as their plenipotentiaries:

[names follow]

who, having presented their full powers, found in good and due form, have agreed as follows:

ARTICLE I

The Contracting Parties undertake, in accordance with the Charter of the United Nations Organization, to refrain in their international relations from the threat or use of force, and to settle their international disputes peacefully and in such manner as will not jeopardize international peace and security.

[1] U.S. Department of State, *American Foreign Policy 1950–1955.* (Washington: Government Printing Office, 1957), I, pp. 1239–1242.

ARTICLE II

The Contracting Parties declare their readiness to participate in a spirit of sincere cooperation in all international actions designed to safeguard international peace and security, and will fully devote their energies to the attainment of this end.

The Contracting Parties will furthermore strive for the adoption, in agreement with other states which may desire to cooperate in this, of effective measures for universal reduction of armaments and prohibition of atomic, hydrogen and other weapons of mass destruction.

ARTICLE III

The Contracting Parties shall consult with one another on all important international issues affecting their common interests, guided by the desire to strengthen international peace and security.

They shall immediately consult with one another whenever, in the opinion of any one of them, a threat of armed attack on one or more of the Parties to the Treaty has arisen, in order to ensure joint defence and the maintenance of peace and security.

ARTICLE IV

In the event of armed attack in Europe on one or more of the Parties to the Treaty by any state or group of states, each of the Parties to the Treaty, in the exercise of its right to individual or collective self-defence in accordance with Article 51 of the Charter of the United Nations Organization, shall immediately, either individually or in agreement with other Parties to the Treaty, come to the assistance of the state or states attacked with all such means as it deems necessary, including armed force. The Parties to the Treaty shall immediately consult concerning the necessary measures to be taken by them jointly in order to restore and maintain international peace and security.

Measures taken on the basis of this Article shall be reported to the Security Council in conformity with the provisions of the Charter of the United Nations Organization. These measures shall be discontinued immediately the Security Council adopts the necessary measures to restore and maintain international peace and security.

ARTICLE V

The Contracting Parties have agreed to establish a Joint Command of the armed forces that by agreement among the Parties shall be assigned to the Command, which shall function on the basis of jointly established principles. They shall likewise adopt other agreed measures necessary to strengthen their defensive power, in order to protect the peaceful labours of their peoples, guarantee the inviolability of their frontiers and territories, and provide defence against possible aggression.

ARTICLE VI

For the purpose of the consultations among the Parties envisaged in the present Treaty, and also for the purpose of examining questions which may arise in the operation of the Treaty, a Political Consultative Committee shall be set up, in which each of the Parties to the Treaty shall be represented by a member of its Government or by another specifically appointed representative.

The Committee may set up such auxiliary bodies as may prove necessary.

ARTICLE VII

The Contracting Parties undertake not to participate in any coalitions or alliances and not to conclude any agreements whose objects conflict with the objects of the present Treaty.

ARTICLE VIII

The Contracting Parties declare that they will act in a spirit of friendship and cooperation with a view to further developing and fostering economic and cultural intercourse with one another, each adhering to the principle of respect for the independence and sovereignty of the others and non-interference in their internal affairs.

ARTICLE IX

The present Treaty is open to the accession of other states, irrespective of their social and political systems, which express their readiness by participation in the present Treaty to assist in uniting the efforts of the peaceable states in safeguarding the peace and security of the peoples. Such accession shall enter into force with the agreement of the Parties to the Treaty after the declaration of accession has been deposited with the Government of the Polish People's Republic.

ARTICLE X

The present Treaty is subject to ratification, and the instruments of ratification shall be deposited with the Government of the Polish People's Republic.

The Treaty shall enter into force on the day the last instrument of ratification has been deposited. The Government of the Polish People's Republic shall notify the other Parties to the Treaty as each instrument of ratification is deposited.

ARTICLE XI

The present Treaty shall remain in force for twenty years. For such Contracting Parties as do not at least one year before the expiration of this period present to the Government of the Polish People's Republic a statement of denunciation of the Treaty, it shall remain in force for the next ten years.

Should a system of collective security be established in Europe, and a General European Treaty of Collective Security concluded for this purpose, for which the Contracting Parties will unswervingly strive, the present Treaty shall cease to be operative from the day the General European Treaty enters into force.

Done in Warsaw on May 14, 1955, in one copy each in the Russian, Polish, Czech and German languages, all texts being equally authentic. Certified copies of the present Treaty shall be sent by the Government of the Polish People's Republic to all the Parties to the Treaty.

In witness whereof the plenipotentiaries have signed the present Treaty and affixed their seals.

Mehmet Shehu	Jozef Cyrankiewicz
Vylko Chervenkov	Gheorghe Gheorghiu-Dej
Andras Hegedus	Nikolai A. Bulganin
Otto Grotewohl	Viliam Siroky

Appendix 35 KHRUSHCHEV'S DE-STALINIZATION SPEECH, FEBRUARY 24–25, 1956 [1]

Comrades, in the report of the Central Committee of the party at the 20th Congress, in a number of speeches by delegates to the Congress, as also formerly during the plenary CC/CPSU [Central Committee of the Communist Party of the Soviet Union] sessions, quite a lot has been said about the cult of the individual and about its harmful consequences.

After Stalin's death the Central Committee of the party began to implement a policy of explaining concisely and consistently that it is impermissible and foreign to the spirit of Marxism-Leninism to elevate one person, to transform him into superman possessing supernatural characteristics akin to those of a god. Such a man supposedly knows everything, sees everything, thinks for everyone, can do anything, is infallible in his behavior.

Such a belief about a man, and specifically about Stalin, was cultivated among us for many years.

The objective of the present report is not a thorough evaluation of Stalin's life and activity. Concerning Stalin's merits, an entirely sufficient number of books, pamphlets and studies had already been written in his lifetime. The role of Stalin in the preparation and execution of the Socialist revolution, in the civil-war, and in the fight for the construction of socialism in our country, is universally known. Everyone knows this well. At present, we are concerned with a question which has immense importance for the party now and for the future —(we are concerned) with how the cult of the person of Stalin has been gradually growing, the cult which became at a certain specific stage the source of a whole series of exceedingly serious and grave perversions of party principles, of party democracy, of revolutionary legality.

Because of the fact that not all as yet realize fully the practical consequences resulting from the cult of the individual, the great harm caused by the violation of the principle of collective direction of the party and because of the accumulation of immense and limitless power in the hands of one person—the Central Committee of the party considers it absolutely necessary to make the material pertaining to this matter available to the 20th Congress of the Communist Party of the Soviet Union.

Allow me first of all to remind you how severely the classics of Marxism-Leninism denounced every manifestation of the cult of the individual. In a letter to the German political worker, Wilhelm Bloss, Marx stated: "From my antipathy to any cult of the individual, I never made public during the existence of the International the numerous addresses from various countries which recognized my merits and which annoyed me. I did not even reply to them, except sometimes to rebuke their authors. Engels and I first joined the secret society of Communists on the condition that everything making for supersti-

---

[1] U.S. Congress. *Congressional Record*, 84th Congress, 2nd Session, vol. 102, part 7, pp. 9389–9402.

tious worship of authority would be deleted from its statute. Lassalle subsequently did quite the opposite."

Sometime later Engels wrote: "Both Marx and I have always been against any public manifestation with regard to individuals, with the exception of cases when it had an important purpose; and we most strongly opposed such manifestations which during our lifetime concerned us personally."

The great modesty of the genius of the Revolution, Vladimir Ilyich Lenin, is known. Lenin had always stressed the role of the people as the creator of history, the directing and organizational role of the party as a living and creative organism, and also the role of the Central Committee.

Marxism does not negate the role of the leaders of the workers' class in directing the revolutionary liberation movement.

While ascribing great importance to the role of the leaders and organizers of the masses, Lenin at the same time mercilessly stigmatized every manifestation of the cult of the individual, inexorably combated the foreign-to-Marxism views about a "hero" and a "crowd," and countered all efforts to oppose a "hero" to the masses and to the people.

Lenin taught that the party's strength depends on its indissoluble unity with the masses, on the fact that behind the party follow the people—workers, peasants and intelligentsia. "Only he will win and retain the power," said Lenin, "who believes in the people, who submerges himself in the fountain of the living creativeness of the people."

Lenin spoke with pride about the Bolshevik Communist Party as the leader and teacher of the people; he called for the presentation of all the most important questions before the opinion of knowledgeable workers, before the opinion of their party; he said: "We believe in it, we see in it the wisdom, the honor, and the conscience of our epoch."

Lenin resolutely stood against every attempt aimed at belittling or weakening the directing role of the party in the structure of the Soviet state. He worked out Bolshevik principles of party direction and norms of party life, stressing that the guiding principle of party leadership is its collegiality. Already during the prerevolutionary years, Lenin called the central committee of the party a collective of leaders and the guardian and interpreter of party principles. "During the period between congresses," pointed out Lenin, "the central committee guards and interprets the principles of the party."

Underlining the role of the central committee of the party and its authority, Vladimir Ilyich pointed out: "Our central committee constituted itself as a closely centralized and highly authoritative group."

During Lenin's life the central committee of the party was a real expression of collective leadership of the party and of the nation. Being a militant Marxist-revolutionist, always unyielding in matters of principle, Lenin never imposed by force his views upon his co-workers. He tried to convince; he patiently explained his opinions to others. Lenin always diligently observed that the norms of party life were realized, that the party statute was enforced, that the party congresses and the plenary sessions of the central committee took place at the proper intervals.

In addition to the great accomplishments of V. I. Lenin for the victory of the working class and of the working peasants, for the victory of our party and for the application of the ideas of scientific communism to life, his acute mind expressed itself also in this that he detected in Stalin in time those negative characteristics which resulted later in grave consequences. Fearing the future fate of the party and of the Soviet nation, V. I. Lenin made a completely correct characterization of Stalin, pointing out that it was necessary to consider the question of transferring Stalin from the position of Secretary General because of the fact that Stalin is excessively rude, that he does not have a proper attitude toward his comrades, that he is capricious and abuses his power.

In December 1922, in a letter to the party congress, Vladimir Ilyich wrote: "After taking over the position of Secretary General, Comrade Stalin accumulated in his hands immeasurable power and I am not certain whether he will be always able to use this power with the required care."

This letter—a political document of tremendous importance, known in the party history as Lenin's testament—was distributed among the delegates to the Twentieth Party Congress. You have read it and will undoubtedly read it again more than once. You might reflect on Lenin's plain words, in which expression is given to Vladimir Ilyich's anxiety concerning the party, the people, the state, and the future direction of party policy.

Vladimir Ilyich said: "Stalin is excessively rude, and this defect, which can be freely tolerated in our midst and in contacts among us Communists, becomes a defect which cannot be tolerated in one holding the position of the Secretary General. Because of this, I propose that the comrades consider the method by which Stalin would be removed from this position and by which another man would be selected for it, a man, who above all, would differ from Stalin in only one quality, namely, greater tolerance, greater loyalty, greater kindness, and more considerate attitude toward the comrades, a less capricious temper, etc."

This document of Lenin's was made known to the delegates at the 13th Party Congress, who discussed the question of transferring Stalin from the position of Secretary General. The delegates declared themselves in favor of retaining Stalin in this post, hoping that he would heed the critical remarks of Vladimir Ilyich and would be able to overcome the defects which caused Lenin serious anxiety.

Comrades, the party congress should become acquainted with two new documents, which confirm Stalin's character as already outlined by Vladimir Ilyich Lenin in his testament. These documents are a letter from Nadezhda Konstantinovna Krupskaya to [Lev B.] Kamenev, who was at that time head of the Political Bureau, and a personal letter from Vladimir Ilyich Lenin to Stalin.

1. I will now read these documents:

"*Lev Borisovich:*

"Because of a short letter which I had written in words dictated to me by Vladimir Ilyich by permission of the doctors, Stalin allowed himself yesterday an unusually rude outburst directed at me. This is not my first day in the party. During all these 30 years I have never heard from any comrade one word of rudeness. The business of the party and of Ilyich are not less dear to me than to Stalin. I need at present the maximum of self-control. What one can and what one cannot discuss with Ilyich—I know better than any doctor, because I know what makes him nervous and what does not, in any case I know better than Stalin. I am turning to you and to Grigory [E. Zinoviev] as much closer comrades of V. I. and I beg you to protect me from rude interference with my private life and from vile invectives and threats. I have no doubt as to what will be the unanimous decision of the Control Commission, with which Stalin sees fit to threaten me; however, I have neither the strength nor the time to waste on this foolish quarrel. And I am a living person and my nerves are strained to the utmost.

N. Krupskaya"

Nadezhda Konstantinovna wrote this letter on December 23, 1922. After two and a half months, in March 1923, Vladimir Ilyich Lenin sent Stalin the following letter:

2. The Letter of V. I. Lenin
"To Comrade Stalin:
(Copies For: Kamenev and Zinoviev.)
"Dear Comrade Stalin:
You permitted yourself a rude summons of my wife to the telephone and a rude reprimand of her. Despite the fact that she told you that she agreed to forget what was said, nevertheless Zinoviev and Kamenev heard about it from her. I have no intention to forget so easily that which is being done against me, and I need not stress here that I consider as directed against me that which is being done against my wife. I ask you, therefore, that you weigh carefully whether you are agreeable to retracting your words and apologizing or whether you prefer the severance of relations between us. [Commotion in the hall]

Sincerely, *Lenin*

March 5, 1923

Comrades, I will not comment on these documents. They speak eloquently for themselves. Since Stalin could behave in this manner during Lenin's life, could thus behave toward Nadezhda Konstantinovna Krupskaya, whom the party knows well and values highly as a loyal friend of Lenin and as an active fighter for the cause of the party since its creation—we can easily imagine how Stalin treated other people. These negative characteristics of his developed steadily and during the last years acquired an absolutely insufferable character.

As later events have proven, Lenin's anxiety was justified; in the first period after Lenin's death Stalin still paid attention to his (i.e. Lenin's) advice, but, later he began to disregard the serious admonitions of Vladimir Ilyich.

When we analyze the practice of Stalin in regard to the direction of the party and of the country, when we pause to consider everything which Stalin perpetrated, we must be convinced that Lenin's fears were justified. The negative characteristics of Stalin, which, in Lenin's time, were only incipient, transformed themselves during the last years into a grave abuse of power by Stalin, which caused untold harm to our party.

We have to consider seriously and analyze correctly this matter in order that we may preclude any possibility of a repetition in any form whatever of what took place during the life of Stalin, who absolutely did not tolerate collegiality in leadership and in work, and who practiced brutal violence, not only toward everything which opposed him, but also toward that which seemed, to his capricious and despotic character, contrary to his concepts.

Stalin acted not through persuasion, explanation, and patient cooperation with people, but by imposing his concepts and demanding absolute submission to his opinion. Whoever opposed this concept or tried to prove his viewpoint, and the correctness of his position-was doomed to removal from the leading collective and to subsequent moral and physical annihilation. This was especially true during the period following the 17th party congress, when many prominent party leaders and rank-and-file party workers, honest and dedicated to the cause of communism, fell victim to Stalin's despotism.

We must affirm that the party had fought a serious fight against the Trotskyites, rightists and bourgeois nationalists, and that it disarmed ideologically all the enemies of Leninism. This ideological fight was carried on successfully as a result of which the party became strengthened and tempered. Here Stalin played a positive role.

The party led a great political-ideological struggle against those in its own ranks who proposed anti-Leninist theses, who represented a political line hostile to the party and to the cause of socialism. This was a stubborn and a difficult fight but a necessary one, because the political line of both the Trotskyite-Zinovievite bloc and of the Bukharinites led actually toward the restoration of capitalism and capitulation to the world bourgeoisie. Let us consider for a moment what would have happened if in 1928–1929 the political line of right deviation had prevailed among us, or orientation toward "cotton-dress industrialization," or toward the kulak, etc. We would not now have a powerful heavy industry, we would not have the Kolkhozes, we would find ourselves disarmed and weak in a capitalist encirclement.

It was for this reason that the party led an inexorable ideological fight and explained to all party members and to the non-party masses the harm and the danger of the anti-Leninist proposals of the Trotskyite opposition and the rightist opportunists. And this great work of explaining the party line bore fruit; both Trotskyites and the rightist opportunists were politically isolated; the overwhelming party majority supported the Leninist line and the party was able to awaken and organize the working masses to apply the Leninist party line and to build socialism.

Worth noting is the fact that even during the progress of the furious ideological fight against the Trotskyites, the Zinovievites, the Bukharinites and others, extreme repressive measures were not used against them. The fight was on ideological grounds. But some years later when socialism in our country was fundamentally constructed, when the exploiting classes were generally liquidated, when the Soviet social structure had radically changed, when the social basis for political movements and groups hostile to the party had violently contracted, when the ideological opponents of the party were long since defeated politically—then the repression directed against them began.

It was precisely during this period (1935, 1937, and 1938) that the practice of mass repression through the government apparatus was born, first against the enemies of Leninism—Trotskyites, Zinovievites, Bukharinites, long since politically defeated by the party, and subsequently also against many honest Communists, against those party cadres who had borne the heavy load of the Civil War and the first and most difficult years of industrialization and collectivization, who actively fought against the Trotskyites and the rightists for the Leninist party line.

Stalin originated the concept enemy of the people. This term automatically rendered it unnecessary that the ideological errors of a man or men engaged in a controversy be proven; this term made possible the usage of the most cruel repression, violating all norms of revolutionary legality, against anyone who in any way disagreed with Stalin, against those who were only suspected of hostile intent, against those who had bad reputations. This concept, enemy of the people, actually eliminated the possibility of any kind of ideological fight or the making of one's views known on this or that issue even those of a practical character. In the main, and in actuality, the only proof of guilt used, against all norms of current legal science, was the confession of the accused himself, and, as subsequent probing proved, confessions were acquired through physical pressures against the accused.

This led to glaring violations of revolutionary legality, and to the fact that many entirely innocent persons, who in the past had defended the party line, became victims.

We must assert that in regard to those persons who in their time had opposed the party line, there were often no sufficiently serious reasons for their physical annihilation. The formula "enemy of the people" was specifically introduced for the purpose of physically annihilating such individuals.

It is a fact that many persons who were later annihilated as enemies of the party and people had worked with Lenin during his life. Some of these persons had made errors during Lenin's life, but, despite this, Lenin benefited by their work, he corrected them, and he did everything possible to retain them in the ranks of the party; he induced them to follow him.

In this connection the delegates to the party congress should familiarize themselves with an unpublished note by V. I. Lenin directed to the central committee's political bureau in October 1920. Outlining the duties of the control commission, Lenin wrote that the commission should be transformed into a real organ of party and proletarian conscience.

"As a special duty of the control commission there is recommended a deep, individualized relationship with, and sometimes even a type of therapy for, the representatives of the so-called opposition—those who have experienced a psychological crisis because of failure in their soviet or party career. An effort should be made to quiet them, to explain the matter to them in a way used among comrades, to find for them (avoiding the method of issuing orders) a task for which they are psychologically fitted. Advice and rules relating to this matter are to be formulated by the central committee's organizational bureau, etc."

Everyone knows how irreconcilable Lenin was with the ideological enemies of Marxism, with those who deviated from the correct party line. At the same time, however, Lenin, as is evident from the given document, in his practice of directing the party demanded the most intimate party contact with people who have shown indecision or temporary nonconformity with the party line, but whom it was possible to return to the party path. Lenin advised that such people should be patiently educated without the application of extreme methods.

Lenin's wisdom in dealing with people was evident in his work with cadres.

An entirely different relationship with people characterized Stalin. Lenin's traits—patient work with people, stubborn and painstaking education of them; the ability to induce people to follow him without using compulsion, but rather through the ideological influence on them of the whole collective—were entirely foreign to Stalin. He (Stalin) discarded the Leninist method of convincing and educating; he abandoned the method of ideological struggle for that of administrative violence, mass repressions, and terror. He acted on an increasingly larger scale and more stubbornly through punitive organs, at the same time often violating all existing norms of morality and of Soviet laws.

Arbitrary behavior by one person encouraged and permitted arbitrariness in others. Mass arrests and deportations of many thousands of people, execution without trial and without normal investigation created conditions of insecurity, fear, and even desperation.

This, of course, did not contribute toward unity of the party ranks and of all strata of working people, but on the contrary brought about annihilation and the expulsion from the party of workers who were loyal but inconvenient to Stalin.

Our party fought for the implementation of Lenin's plans for the construction of socialism. This was an ideological fight. Had Leninist principles been observed during the course of this fight, had the party's devotion to principles been skillfully combined with a keen and solicitous concern for people, had they not been repelled and wasted but rather drawn to our side—we certainly would not have had such a brutal violation of revolutionary legality and many thousands of people would not have fallen victim of the method of terror. Extraordinary methods would then have been resorted to only against those people who had in fact committed criminal acts against the Soviet system.

Let us recall some historical facts.

In the days before the October Revolution, two members of the central committee of the Bolshevik Party—Kamenev and Zinoviev—declared themselves against Lenin's plan for an armed uprising. In addition, on October 18 they published in the Menshevik newspaper, *Novaya Zhizn*, a statement declaring that the Bolsheviks were making preparations for an uprising and that they considered it adventuristic. Kamenev and Zinoviev thus disclosed to the enemy the decision of the central committee to stage the uprising, and that the uprising had been organized to take place within the very near future.

This was treason against the party and against the revolution. In this connection, V. I. Lenin wrote: "Kamenev and Zinoviev revealed the decision of the central committee of their party on the armed uprising to Rodzyanko and Kerensky . . ." He put before the central committee the question of Zinoviev's and Kamenev's expulsion from the party.

However, after the great Socialist October revolution, as is known, Zinoviev and Kamenev were given leading positions. Lenin put them in positions in which they carried out most responsible party tasks and participated actively in the work of the leading party and Soviet organs. It is known that

Zinoviev and Kamenev committed a number of other serious errors during Lenin's life. In his testament Lenin warned that "Zinoviev's and Kamenev's October episode was of course not an accident." But Lenin did not pose the question of their arrest and certainly not of their shooting.

Or, let us take the example of the Trotskyites. At present, after a sufficiently long historical period, we can speak about the fight with the Trotskyites with complete calm and can analyze this matter with sufficient objectivity. After all, around Trotsky were people whose origin cannot by any means be traced to bourgeois society. Part of them belonged to the party intelligentsia and a certain part were recruited from among the workers. We can name many individuals who in their time joined the Trotskyites; however, these same individuals took an active part in the workers' movement before the Revolution, during the Socialist October revolution itself, and also in the consolidation of the victory of this greatest of revolutions. Many of them broke with Trotskyism and returned to Leninist positions. Was it necessary to annihilate such people? We are deeply convinced that had Lenin lived such an extreme method would not have been used against many of them.

Such are only a few historical facts. But can it be said that Lenin did not decide to use even the most severe means against enemies of the revolution when this was actually necessary? No, no one can say this. Vladimir Ilyich demanded uncompromising dealings with the enemies of the revolution and of the working class and when necessary resorted ruthlessly to such methods. You will recall only V. I. Lenin's fight with the Socialist Revolutionary organizers of the anti-Soviet uprising, with the counterrevolutionary kulaks in 1918 and with others, when Lenin without hesitation used the most extreme methods against the enemies. Lenin used such methods, however, only against actual class enemies and not against those who blunder, who err, and whom it was possible to lead through ideological influence and even retain in the leadership. Lenin used severe methods only in the most necessary cases, when the exploiting classes were still in existence and were vigorously opposing the revolution, when the struggle for survival was decidedly assuming the sharpest forms, even including a civil war.

Stalin, on the other hand, used extreme methods and mass repressions at a time when the revolution was already victorious, when the Soviet state was strengthened, when the exploiting classes were already liquidated, and socialist relations were rooted solidly in all phases of national economy, when our party was politically consolidated and had strengthened itself both numerically and ideologically. It is clear that here Stalin showed in a whole series of cases his intolerance, his brutality and his abuse of power. Instead of proving his political correctness and mobilizing the masses, he often chose the path of repression and physical annihilation, not only against actual enemies, but also against individuals who had not committed any crimes against the party and the Soviet Government. Here we see no wisdom but only a demonstration of the brutal force which had once so alarmed V. I. Lenin.

Lately, especially after the unmasking of the Beria gang, the Central Committee looked into a series of matters fabricated by this gang. This revealed a very ugly picture of brutal willfulness connected with the incorrect behavior of Stalin. As facts prove, Stalin, using his unlimited power, allowed himself many abuses, acting in the name of the Central Committee, not asking for the opinion of the Committee members nor even of the members of the Central Committee's Political Bureau; often he did not inform them about his personal decisions concerning very important party and government matters.

Considering the question of the cult of an individual, we must first of all show everyone what harm this caused to the interests of our party.

Vladimir Ilyich Lenin had always stressed the party's role and significance in the direction of the Socialist government of workers and peasants; he saw in this the chief precondition for a successful building of socialism in our country. Pointing to the great responsibility of the Bolshevik Party, as ruling party of the Soviet state, Lenin called for the most meticulous observance of all norms of party life; he called for the realization of the principles of collegiality in the direction of the party and the state.

Collegiality of leadership flows from the very nature of our party, a party built on the principles of democratic centralism. "This means," said Lenin, "that all party matters are accomplished by all party members—directly or through representatives—who without any exceptions are subject to the same rules; in addition, all administrative members, all directing collegia, all holders of party positions are elective, they must account for their activities and are recallable."

It is known that Lenin himself offered an example of the most careful observance of these principles. There was no matter so important that Lenin himself decided it without asking for advice and approval of the majority of the Central Committee members or of the members of the Central Committee's Political Bureau. In the most difficult period for our party and our country, Lenin considered it necessary regularly to convoke congresses, party conferences, and plenary sessions of the Central Committee at which all the most important questions were discussed and where resolutions, carefully worked out by the collective of leaders, were approved.

We can recall, for example, the year 1918 when the country was threatened by the attack of the imperialistic interventionists. In this situation the 7th party congress was convened in order to discuss a vitally important matter which could not be postponed—the matter of peace. In 1919, while the civil war was raging, the 8th party congress convened which adopted a new party program, decided such important matters as the relationship with the peasant masses, the organization of the Red Army, the leading role of the party in the work of the Soviets, the correction of the social composition of the party, and other matters. In 1920 the 9th party congress was convened which laid down guiding principles pertaining to the party's work in the sphere of economic construction. In 1921 the 10th party congress accepted Lenin's New Economic Policy and the historical resolution called "About Party Unity."

During Lenin's life, party congresses were convened regularly; always when a radical turn in the development of the party and the country took place, Lenin considered it absolutely necessary that the party discuss at length all the basic matters pertaining to internal and foreign policy and to questions bearing on the development of party and government.

It is very characteristic that Lenin addressed to the party congress as the highest party organ his last articles, letters and remarks. During the period between congresses, the central committee of the party, acting as the most authoritative leading collective, meticulously observed the principles of the party and carried out its policy.

So it was during Lenin's life. Were our party's holy Leninist principles observed after the death of Vladimir Ilyich?

Whereas, during the first few years after Lenin's death, party congresses and central committee plenums took place more or less regularly; later, when Stalin began increasingly to abuse his power, these principles were brutally violated. This was especially evident during the last 15 years of his life. Was it a normal situation when 13 years elapsed between the 18th and 19th party congresses, years during which our party and our country had experienced so many important events? These events demanded categorically that the party should have passed resolutions pertaining to the country's defense during the Patriotic War [World War II] and to peacetime construction after the war. Even after the end of the war a congress was not convened for over seven years. Central committee plenums were hardly ever called. It should be sufficient to mention that during all the years of the Patriotic War not a single central committee plenum took place. It is true that there was an attempt to call a central committee plenum in October 1941, when central committee members from the whole country were called to Moscow. They waited two days for the opening of the plenum, but in vain. Stalin did not even want to meet and talk to the Central Committee members. This fact shows how demoralized Stalin was in the first months of the war and how haughtily and disdainfully he treated the Central Committee members.

In practice, Stalin ignored the norms of party life and trampled on the Leninist principle of collective party leadership.

Stalin's willfulness vis-à-vis the party and its central committee became fully evident after the 17th party congress which took place in 1934.

Having at its disposal numerous data showing brutal willfulness toward party cadres, the central committee has created a party commission under the control of the central committee presidium; it was charged with investigating what made possible the mass repressions against the majority of the central committee members and candidates elected at the 17th Congress of the All-Union Communist Party (Bolsheviks).

The commission has become acquainted with a large quantity of materials in the NKVD archives and with other documents and has established many facts pertaining to the fabrication of cases against Communists, to false accusations, to glaring abuses of socialist legality, which resulted in the death of innocent people. It became apparent that many party, Soviet and economic activists, who were branded in 1937–1938 as "enemies," were actually never enemies, spies, wreckers, etc., but were always honest Communists; they were only so stigmatized and, often, no longer able to bear barbaric tortures, they charged themselves (at the order of the investigative judges—falsifiers) with all kinds of grave and unlikely crimes. The commission has presented to the central committee presidium lengthy and documented materials pertaining to mass repressions against the delegates to the 17th party congress and against members of the central committee elected at that congress. These materials have been studied by the presidium of the central committee.

It was determined that of the 139 members and candidates of the party's Central Committee who were elected at the 17th congress, 98 persons, i.e., 70 per cent, were arrested and shot (mostly in 1937–1938). [Indignation in the Hall.] What was the composition of the delegates to the 17th Congress? It is known that 80 per cent of the voting participants of the 17th Congress joined the party during the years of conspiracy before the revolution and during the civil war; this means before 1921. By social origin the basic mass of the delegates to the congress were workers (60 per cent of the voting members).

For this reason, it was inconceivable that a congress so composed would have elected a central committee a majority of whom would prove to be enemies of the party. The only reason why 70 per cent of central committee members and candidates elected at the 17th Congress were branded as enemies of the party and of the people was because honest Communists were slandered, accusations against them were fabricated, and revolutionary legality was gravely undermined.

The same fate met not only the central committee members but also the majority of the delegates to the 17th party congress. Of 1,966 delegates with either voting or advisory rights, 1,108 persons were arrested on charges of antirevolutionary crimes, i.e., decidedly more than a majority. This very fact shows how absurd, wild and contrary to common sense were the charges of counterrevolutionary crimes made out, as we now see, against a majority of participants at the 17th party congress. [Indignation in the hall.]

We should recall that the 17th party congress is historically known as the Congress of Victors. Delegates to the congress were active participants in the building of our socialist state; many of them suffered and fought for party interests during the pre-Revolutionary years in the conspiracy and at the civil-war fronts; they fought their enemies valiantly and often nervelessly looked into the face of death. How then can we believe that such people could prove to be "two-faced" and had joined the camps of the enemies of socialism during the era after the political liquidation of Zinovievites, Trotskyites and rightists and after the great accomplishments of socialist construction? This was the result of the abuse of power by Stalin, who began to use mass terror against the party cadres.

What is the reason that mass repressions against activists increased more and more after the 17th party congress? It was because at that time Stalin had so elevated himself above the party and above the nation that he ceased to consider either the central committee or the party. While he still reckoned with the opinion of the collective before the 17th congress, after the complete political liquidation of the Trotskyites, Zinovievites and Bukharinites, when as a result of that fight and socialist victories the party achieved unity, Stalin ceased to an ever greater degree to consider the members of the party's central committee and even the members of the Political Bureau. Stalin thought that now he could decide all things alone and all he needed were statisticians; he treated all others in such a way that they could only listen to and praise him.

After the criminal murder of S[ergei] M. Kirov, mass repressions and brutal acts of violation of socialist legality began. On the evening of December 1, 1934, on Stalin's initiative (without the approval of the Political Bureau—which was passed two days later, casually), the Secretary of the Presidium of the Central Executive Committee, Yenukidze, signed the following directive:

"1. Investigative agencies are directed to speed up the cases of those accused of the preparation or execution of acts of terror.

"2. Judicial organs are directed not to hold up the execution of death sentences pertaining to crimes of this category in order to consider the possibility of pardon, because the Presidium of the Central Executive Committee [of the] U.S.S.R. does not consider as possible the receiving of petitions of this sort.

"3. The organs of the Commissariat of Internal Affairs are directed to execute the death sentences against criminals of the above-mentioned category immediately after the passage of sentences."

This directive became the basis for mass acts of abuse against socialist legality. During many of the fabricated court cases the accused were charged with "the preparation" of terroristic acts; this deprived them of any possibility that their cases might be re-examined, even when they stated before the court that their confessions were secured by force, and when, in a convincing manner, they disproved the accusations against them.

It must be asserted that to this day the circumstances surrounding Kirov's murder hide many things which are inexplicable and mysterious and demand a most careful examination. There are reasons for the suspicion that the killer of Kirov, Nikolayev, was assisted by someone from among the people whose duty it was to protect the person of Kirov.

A month and a half before the killing, Nikolayev was arrested on the grounds of suspicious behavior but he was released and not even searched. It is an unusually suspicious circumstance that when the Chekist assigned to protect Kirov was being brought for an interrogation, on December 2, 1934, he was killed in a car accident in which no other occupants of the car were harmed. After the murder of Kirov, top functionaries of the Leningrad NKVD were given very light sentences, but in 1937 they were shot. We can assume that they were shot in order to cover the traces of the organizers of Kirov's killing. [Movement in the hall.]

Mass repressions grew tremendously from the end of 1936 after a telegram from Stalin and [Andrei] Zhdanov, dated from Sochi on September 25, 1936, was addressed to Kaganovich, Molotov and other members of the Political Bureau. The content of the telegram was as follows:

"We deem it absolutely necessary and urgent that Comrade Yezhov be nominated to the post of People's Commissar for Internal Affairs. Yagoda has definitely proved himself to be incapable of unmasking the Trotskyite-Zinovievite bloc. The OGPU is four years behind in this matter. This is noted by all party workers and by the majority of the representatives of the NKVD."

Strictly speaking we should stress that Stalin did not meet with and, therefore, could not know the opinion of party workers.

This Stalinist formulation that the "NKVD is four years behind" in applying mass repression and that there is a necessity for catching up with the neglected work directly pushed the NKVD workers on the path of mass arrests and executions.

We should state that this formulation was also forced on the February-March plenary session of the central committee of the All-Union Communist Party (Bolsheviks) in 1937. The plenary resolution approved it on the basis of

Yezhov's report, "Lessons flowing from the harmful activity, diversion and espionage of the Japanese-German-Trotskyite agents," stating: "The plenum of the central committee of the All-Union Communist Party (Bolsheviks) considers that all facts revealed during the investigation into the matter of an anti-Soviet Trotskyite center and of its followers in the provinces show that the People's Commissariat of Internal Affairs has fallen behind at least four years in the attempt to unmask these most inexorable enemies of the people."

The mass repressions at this time were made under the slogan of a fight against the Trotskyites. Did the Trotskyites at this time actually constitute such a danger to our party and to the Soviet state? We should recall that in 1927, on the eve of the 15th party congress, only some 4,000 votes were cast for the Trotskyite-Zinovievite opposition while there were 724,000 for the party line. During the 10 years which passed between the 15th party congress and the February-March central committee plenum, Trotskyism was completely disarmed; many former Trotskyites had changed their former views and worked in the various sectors building socialism. It is clear that in the situation of socialist victory there was no basis for mass terror in the country.

Stalin's report at the February-March central committee plenum in 1937, "Deficiencies of party work and methods for the liquidation of the Trotskyites and of other two-facers," contained an attempt at theoretical justification of the mass terror policy under the pretext that as we march forward toward socialism class war must allegedly sharpen. Stalin asserted that both history and Lenin taught him this.

Actually Lenin taught that the application of revolutionary violence is necessitated by the resistance of the exploiting classes, and this referred to the era when the exploiting classes existed and were powerful. As soon as the nation's political situation had improved, when in January 1920 the Red Army took Rostov and thus won a most important victory over [White General Anton] Denikin, Lenin instructed [Cheka chief Felix] Dzerzhinsky to stop mass terror and to abolish the death penalty. Lenin justified this important political move of the Soviet state in the following manner in his report at the session of the All-Union Central Executive Committee on February 2, 1920:

"We were forced to use terror because of the terror practiced by the Entente, when strong world powers threw their hordes against us, not avoiding any type of conduct. We would not have lasted two days had we not answered these attempts of officers and White Guardists in a merciless fashion; this meant the use of terror, but this was forced upon us by the terrorist methods of the Entente.

"But as soon as we attained a decisive victory, even before the end of the war, immediately after taking Rostov, we gave up the use of the death penalty and thus proved that we intend to execute our own program in the manner that we promised. We say that the application of violence flows out of the decision to smother the exploiters, the big landowners and the capitalists; as soon as this was accomplished we gave up the use of all extraordinary methods. We have proved this in practice."

Stalin deviated from these clear and plain precepts of Lenin. Stalin put the party and the NKVD up to the use of mass terror when the exploiting classes had been liquidated in our country and when there were no serious reasons for the use of extraordinary mass terror.

This terror was actually directed not at the remnants of the defeated exploiting classes but against the honest workers of the party and of the Soviet state; against them were made lying, slanderous and absurd accusations concerning "two-facedness," "espionage," "sabotage," preparation of fictitious "plots," etc.

At the February-March central committee plenum in 1937 many members actually questioned the rightness of the established course regarding mass repressions under the pretext of combating "two-facedness."

Comrade Postyshev most ably expressed these doubts. He said:

"I have philosophized that the severe years have passed, party members who have lost their backbones have broken down or have joined the camp of the enemy; healthy elements have fought for the party. These were the years of industrialization and collectivization. I never thought it possible that after this severe era had passed Karpov and people like him would find themselves in the camp of the enemy. (Karpov was a worker in the Ukrainian Central Committee whom Postyshev knew well.) And now, according to the testimony, it appears that Karpov was recruited in 1934 by the Trotskyites. I personally do not believe that in 1934 an honest party member who had trod the long road of unrelenting fight against enemies for the party and for socialism would now be in the camp of the enemies. I do not believe it. . . . I cannot imagine how it would be possible to travel with the party during the difficult years and then, in 1934, join the Trotskyites. It is an odd thing. . . ." [Movement in the hall.]

Using Stalin's formulation, namely, that the closer we are to socialism the more enemies we will have, and using the resolution of the February-March Central Committee plenum passed on the basis of Yezhov's report—the *provocateurs* who had infiltrated the state-security organs together with conscienceless careerists began to protect with the party name the mass terror against party cadres, cadres of the Soviet state and the ordinary Soviet citizens. It should suffice to say that the number of arrests based on charges of counterrevolutionary crimes had grown ten times between 1936 and 1937.

It is known that brutal willfulness was practiced against leading party workers. The party statute, approved at the 17th party congress, was based on Leninist principles expressed at the 10th party congress. It stated that, in order to apply an extreme method such as exclusion from the party against a central committee member, against a central committee candidate and against a member of the party control commission, "it is necessary to call a Central Committee plenum and to invite to the plenum all Central Committee candidate members and all members of the Party Control Commission"; only if two-thirds of the members of such a general assembly of responsible party leaders find it necessary, only then can a central committee member or candidate be expelled.

The majority of the Central Committee members and candidates elected at the 17th congress and arrested in 1937–1938 were expelled from the party illegally through the brutal abuse of the party statute, because the question of their expulsion was never studied at the Central Committee plenum.

Now when the cases of some of these so-called "spies" and "saboteurs" were examined it was found that all their cases were fabricated. Confessions of guilt of many arrested and charged with enemy activity were gained with the help of cruel and inhuman tortures.

At the same time Stalin, as we have been informed by members of the Political Bureau of that time, did not show them the statements of many accused political activists when they retracted their confessions before the military tribunal and asked for an objective examination of their cases. There were many such declarations, and Stalin doubtless knew of them.

The central committee considers it absolutely necessary to inform the congress of many such fabricated "cases" against the members of the party's central committee elected at the 17th party congress.

An example of the vile provocation, of odious falsification and of criminal violation of revolutionary legality is the case of the former candidate for the Central Committee Political Bureau, one of the most eminent workers of the party and of the Soviet Government, Comrade Eikhe, who was a party member since 1905. [Commotion in the hall.]

Comrade Eikhe was arrested on April 29, 1938 on the basis of slanderous materials, without the sanction of the Prosecutor of the USSR, which was finally received 15 months after the arrest.

Investigation of Eikhe's case was made in a manner which most brutally violated Soviet legality and was accompanied by willfulness and falsification.

Eikhe was forced under torture to sign ahead of time a protocol of his confession prepared by the investigative judges, in which he and several other eminent party workers were accused of anti-Soviet activity.

On October 1, 1939 Eikhe sent his declaration to Stalin in which he categorically denied his guilt and asked for an examination of his case. In the declaration he wrote: "There is no more bitter misery than to sit in the jail of a government for which I have always fought."

A second declaration of Eikhe has been preserved which he sent to Stalin on October 27, 1939; in it he cited facts very convincingly and countered the slanderous accusations made against him, arguing that this provocatory accusation was on the one hand the work of real Trotskyites whose arrests he had sanctioned as First Secretary of the West Siberian Krai [Territory] Party Committee and who conspired in order to take revenge on him, and, on the other hand, the result of the base falsification of materials by the investigative judges.

Eikhe wrote in his declaration: ". . . On October 25 of this year I was informed that the investigation in my case has been concluded and I was given access to the materials of this investigation. Had I been guilty of only one hundredth of the crimes with which I am charged, I would not have dared to send you this pre-execution declaration; however, I have not been guilty of even one of the things with which I am charged and my heart is clean of even the shadow of baseness. I have never in my life told you a word of falsehood, and now, finding my two feet in the grave, I am also not lying. My whole case is a typical example of provocation, slander and violation of the elementary basis of revolutionary legality. . . .

". . . The confessions which were made part of my file are not only absurd but contain some slander toward the Central Committee of the All-Union Communist Party (Bolsheviks) and toward the Council of People's

Commissars, because correct resolutions of the Central Committee of the All-Union Communist Party (Bolsheviks) and of the Council of People's Commissars which were not made on my initiative and without my participation are presented as hostile acts of counterrevolutionary organizations made at my suggestion. . . .

"I am now alluding to the most disgraceful part of my life and to my really grave guilt against the party and against you. This is my confession of counterrevolutionary activity. . . . The case is as follows: Not being able to suffer the tortures to which I was submitted by Ushakov and Nikolayev—and especially by the first one—who utilized the knowledge that my broken ribs have not properly mended and have caused me great pain—I have been forced to accuse myself and others.

"The majority of my confession has been suggested or dictated by Ushakov, and the remainder is my reconstruction of NKVD materials from Western Siberia for which I assumed all responsibility. If some part of the story which Ushakov fabricated and which I signed did not properly hang together, I was forced to sign another variation. The same thing was done to Rukhimovich, who was at first designated as a member of the reserve net and whose name later was removed without telling me anything about it; the same was also done with the leader of the reserve net, supposedly created by Bukharin in 1935. At first I wrote my name in, and then I was instructed to insert Mezhlauk. There were other similar incidents.

"I am asking and begging you that you again examine my case, and this not for the purpose of sparing me but in order to unmask the vile provocation which, like a snake, wound itself around many persons in a great degree due to my meanness and criminal slander. I have never betrayed you or the party. I know that I perish because of vile and mean work of the enemies of the party and of the people, who fabricated the provocation against me."

It would appear that such an important declaration was worth an examination by the Central Committee. This, however, was not done, and the declaration was transmitted to Beria while the terrible maltreatment of the Political Bureau candidate, Comrade Eikhe, continued.

On February 2, 1940 Eikhe was brought before the court. Here he did not confess any guilt and said as follows:

"In all the so-called confessions of mine there is not one letter written by me with the exception of my signatures under the protocols, which were forced from me. I have made my confession under pressure from the investigative judge, who from the time of my arrest tormented me. After that I began to write all this nonsense. The most important thing for me is to tell the court, the party and Stalin that I am not guilty. I have never been guilty of any conspiracy. I will die believing in the truth of party policy as I have believed in it during my whole life."

On February 4 Eikhe was shot. [Indignation in the hall.]

It has been definitely established now that Eikhe's case was fabricated; he has been posthumously rehabilitated.

Comrade Rudzutak, candidate-member of the Political Bureau, member of the party since 1905, who spent 10 years in a Tsarist hard-labor camp, completely retracted in court the confession which was forced from him. The protocol of the session of the Collegium of the Supreme Military Court contains the following statement by Rudzutak:

"The only plea which he places before the court is that the Central Committee of the All-Union Communist Party (Bolsheviks) be informed that there is in the NKVD an as yet not liquidated center which is craftily manufacturing cases, which forces innocent persons to confess; there is no opportunity to prove one's non-participation in crimes to which the confessions of various persons testify. The investigative methods are such that they force people to lie and to slander entirely innocent persons in addition to those who already stand accused. He asks the Court that he be allowed to inform the Central Committee of the All-Union Communist Party (Bolsheviks) about all this in writing. He assures the Court that he personally never had any evil designs in regard to the policy of our party because he had always agreed with the party policy pertaining to all spheres of economic and cultural activity."

This declaration of Rudzutak was ignored, despite the fact that Rudzutak was in his time the chief of the Central Control Commission, which was called into being in accordance with Lenin's concept for the purpose of fighting for party unity. In this manner fell the chief of this highly authoritative party organ, a victim of brutal willfulness; he was not even called before the Central Committee's Political Bureau because Stalin did not want to talk to him. Sentence was pronounced on him in 20 minutes and he was shot. [Indignation in the hall.]

After careful examination of the case in 1955, it was established that the accusation against Rudzutak was false and that it was based on slanderous materials. Rudzutak has been rehabilitated posthumously.

The way in which the former NKVD workers manufactured various fictitious "anti-Soviet centers" and "blocs" with the help of provocatory methods is seen from the confession of Comrade Rozenblum, party member since 1906, who was arrested in 1937 by the Leningrad NKVD.

During the examination in 1955 of the Komarov case Rozenblum revealed the following fact: When Rozenblum was arrested in 1937, he was subjected to terrible torture during which he was ordered to confess false information concerning himself and other persons. He was then brought to the office of Zakovsky, who offered him freedom on condition that he make before the court a false confession fabricated in 1937 by the NKVD concerning "sabotage, espionage and diversion in a terroristic center in Leningrad." [Movement in the hall.] With unbelievable cynicism, Zakovsky told about the vile "mechanism" for the crafty creation of fabricated "anti-Soviet plots."

"In order to illustrate it to me," stated Rozenblum, "Zakovsky gave me several possible variants of the organization of this center and of its branches. After he detailed the organization to me, Zakovsky told me that the NKVD would prepare the case of this center, remarking that the trial would be public. Before the court were to be brought 4 or 5 members of this center: Chudov, Ugarov, Smorodin, Pozern, Shaposhnikova (Chudov's wife) and others together with 2 or 3 members from the branches of this center. . . .

". . . The case of the Leningrad center has to be built solidly, and for this reason witnesses are needed. Social origin (of course, in the past) and the party standing of the witness will play more than a small role.

" 'You, yourself,' said Zakovsky, 'will not need to invent anything. The NKVD will prepare for you a ready outline for every branch of the center; you will have to study it carefully and to remember well all questions and answers which the Court might ask. This case will be ready in four-five months, or perhaps a half year. During all this time you will be preparing yourself so that you will not compromise the investigation and yourself. Your future will depend on how the trial goes and on its results. If you begin to lie and to testify falsely, blame yourself. If you manage to endure it, you will save your head and we will feed and clothe you at the Government's cost until your death.' "

This is the kind of vile things which were then practiced. [Movement in the hall.]

Even more widely was the falsification of cases practiced in the provinces. The NKVD headquarters of the Sverdlov Oblast discovered the so-called Ural uprising staff—and organ of the bloc of rightists, Trotskyites, Socialist Revolutionaries, church leaders—whose chief supposedly was the Secretary of the Sverdlov Oblast Party Committee and a member of the Central Committee, All-Union Communist Party (Bolsheviks), Kabakov, who had been a party member since 1914. The investigative materials of that time show that in almost all *krais, oblasts* [provinces] and republics there supposedly existed rightist Trotskyite, espionage-terror and diversionary-sabotage organizations and centers and that the heads of such organizations as a rule—for no known reason—were first secretaries of *oblast* or republic Communist party committees or central committees. [Movement in the hall.]

Many thousands of honest and innocent Communists have died as a result of this monstrous falsification of such "cases," as a result of the fact that all kinds of slanderous "confessions" were accepted, and as a result of the practice of forcing accusations against oneself and others. In the same manner were fabricated the "cases" against eminent party and state workers—Kossior, Chubar, Postyshev, Kosarev and others.

In those years repressions on a mass scale were applied which were based on nothing tangible and which resulted in heavy cadre losses to the party.

The vicious practice was condoned of having the NKVD prepare lists of persons whose cases were under the jurisdiction of the Military Collegium and whose sentences were prepared in advance. Yezhov would send these lists to Stalin personally for his approval of the proposed punishment. In 1937–1938, 383 such lists containing the names of many thousands of party, Soviet, Komsomol, army and economic workers were sent to Stalin. He approved these lists.

A large part of these cases are being reviewed now and a great part of them are being voided because they were baseless and falsified. Suffice it to say that from 1954 to the present time the Military Collegium of the Supreme Court has rehabilitated 7,679 persons, many of whom were rehabilitated posthumously.

Mass arrests of party, Soviet, economic and military workers caused tremendous harm to our country and to the cause of socialist advancement.

Mass repressions had a negative influence on the moral-political condition of the party, created a situation of uncertainty, contributed to the spreading of unhealthy suspicion, and sowed distrust among Communists. All sorts of slanderers and careerists were active.

Resolutions of the January plenum of the Central Committee, All-Union Communist Party (Bolsheviks), in 1938 had brought some measure of improvement to the party organizations. However, widespread repression also existed in 1938.

Only because our party has at its disposal such great moral-political strength was it possible for it to survive the difficult events in 1937–1938 and to educate new cadres. There is, however, no doubt that our march forward toward socialism and toward the preparation of the country's defense would have been much more successful were it not for the tremendous loss in the cadres suffered as a result of the baseless and false mass repressions in 1937 –1938.

We are justly accusing Yezhov for the degenerate practices of 1937. But we have to answer these questions: Could Yezhov have arrested Kossior, for instance, without the knowledge of Stalin? Was there an exchange of opinions or a Political Bureau decision concerning this? No, there was not, as there was none regarding other cases of this type. Could Yezhov have decided such important matters as the fate of such eminent party figures? No, it would be a display of naivete to consider this the work of Yezhov alone. It is clear that these matters were decided by Stalin, and that without his orders and his sanction Yezhov could not have done this.

We have examined the cases and have rehabilitated Kossior, Rudzutak, Postyshev, Kosarev and others. For what causes were they arrested and sentenced? The review of evidence shows that there was no reason for this. They, like many others, were arrested without the prosecutor's knowledge.

In such a situation, there is no need for any sanction, for what sort of a sanction could there be when Stalin decided everything? He was the chief prosecutor in these cases. Stalin not only agreed to, but on his own initiative issued, arrest orders. We must say this so that the delegates to the congress can clearly undertake and themselves assess this and draw the proper conclusions.

Facts prove that many abuses were made on Stalin's orders without reckoning with any norms of party and Soviet legality. Stalin was a very distrustful man, sickly suspicious; we knew this from our work with him. He could look at a man and say: "Why are your eyes so shifty today?" or "Why are you turning so much today and avoiding to look me directly in the eyes?" The sickly suspicion created in him a general distrust even toward eminent party workers whom he had known for years. Everywhere and in everything he saw "enemies," "two-facers" and "spies." Possessing unlimited power he indulged in great willfulness and choked a person morally and physically. A situation was created where one could not express one's own will.

When Stalin said that one or another should be arrested, it was necessary to accept on faith that he was an "enemy of the people." Meanwhile, Beria's gang, which ran the organs of state security, outdid itself in proving the guilt of the arrested and the truth of materials which it falsified. And what proofs were offered? The confessions of the arrested, and the investigative judges accepted these "confessions." And how is it possible that a person confesses to crimes which he has not committed? Only in one way—because of application of physical methods of pressuring him, tortures bringing him to a state of unconsciousness, deprivation of his judgment, taking away of his human dignity. In this manner were "confessions" acquired.

When the wave of mass arrests began to recede in 1939, and the leaders of territorial party organizations began to accuse the NKVD workers of using methods of physical pressure on the arrested. Stalin dispatched a coded telegram on January 20, 1939 to the committee secretaries of *oblasts* and *krais*, to the central committees of republic Communist parties, to the People's Commissars of Internal Affairs and to the heads of NKVD organizations. This telegram stated:

"The Central Committee of the All-Union Communist Party (Bolsheviks) explains that the application of methods of physical pressure in NKVD practice is permissible from 1937 on in accordance with permission of the Central Committee of the All-Union Communist Party (Bolsheviks) . . . It is known that all bourgeois intelligence services use methods of physical influence against the representatives of the socialist proletariat and that they use them in their most scandalous forms. The question arises as to why the socialist intelligence service should be more humanitarian against the mad agents of the bourgeoisie, against the deadly enemies of the working class and of the *kolkhoz* workers. The Central Committee of the All-Union Communist Party (Bolsheviks) considers that physical pressure should still be used obligatorily, as an exception applicable to known and obstinate enemies of the people, as a method both justifiable and appropriate."

Thus, Stalin had sanctioned in the name of the Central Committee of the All-Union Communist Party (Bolsheviks) the most brutal violation of socialist legality, torture and oppression, which led as we have seen to the slandering and self-accusation of innocent people.

Not long ago—only several days before the present Congress—we called to the Central Committee Presidium session and interrogated the investigative judge Rodos, who in his time investigated and interrogated Kossior, Chubar and Kosarev. He is a vile person, with the brain of a bird, and morally completely degenerate. And it was this man who was deciding the fate of prominent party workers; he was making judgments also concerning the politics in these matters, because having established their "crime," he provided therewith materials from which important political implications could be drawn.

The question arises whether a man with such an intellect could alone make the investigation in a manner to prove the guilt of people such as Kossior and others. No; he could not have done it without proper directives. At the Central Committee Presidium session he told us: "I was told that Kossior and Chubar were people's enemies and for this reason I, as an investigative judge, had to make them confess that they are enemies." [Indignation in the hall.]

He could do this only through long tortures, which he did, receiving detailed instructions from Beria. We must say that at the Central Committee Presidium session he cynically declared: "I thought that I was executing the orders of the party." In this manner, Stalin's orders concerning the use of methods of physical pressure against the arrested were in practice executed.

These and many other facts show that all norms of correct party solution of problems were invalidated and everything was dependent upon the willfulness of one man.

The power accumulated in the hands of one person, Stalin, led to serious consequences during the Great Patriotic War.

When we look at many of our novels, films and historical "scientific studies," the role of Stalin in the Patriotic War appears to be entirely improbable. Stalin had foreseen everything. The Soviet Army, on the basis of a strategic plan prepared by Stalin long before, used the tactics of so-called "active defense," i.e., tactics which, as we know, allowed the Germans to come up to Moscow and Stalingrad. Using such tactics, the Soviet Army, supposedly thanks only to Stalin's genius, turned to the offensive and subdued the enemy. The epic victory gained through the armed might of the land of the Soviets, through our heroic people, is ascribed in this type of novel, film and "scientific study" as being completely due to the strategic genius of Stalin.

We have to analyze this matter carefully because it has a tremendous significance not only from the historical, but especially from the political, educational and practical point of view. What are the facts of this matter?

Before the war, our press and all our political-educational work was characterized by its bragging tone: When an enemy violates the holy Soviet soil, then for every blow of the enemy we will answer with three blows, and we will battle the enemy on his soil and we will win without much harm to ourselves. But these positive statements were not based in all areas on concrete facts, which would actually guarantee the immunity of our borders.

During the war and after the war, Stalin put forward the thesis that the tragedy which our nation experienced in the first part of the war was the result of the "unexpected" attack of the Germans against the Soviet Union. But, comrades, this is completely untrue. As soon as Hitler came to power in Germany he assigned to himself the task of liquidating Communism. The fascists were saying this openly; they did not hide their plans. In order to attain this aggressive end, all sorts of pacts and blocs were created, such as the famous Berlin-Rome-Tokyo Axis. Many facts from the prewar period clearly showed that Hitler was going all out to begin a war against the Soviet state, and that he had concentrated large armed units, together with armored units, near the Soviet borders.

Documents which have now been published show that by April 3, 1941 Churchill, through his ambassador to the USSR, Cripps, personally warned Stalin that the Germans had begun regrouping their armed units with the intent of attacking the Soviet Union. It is self-evident that Churchill did not do this at all because of his friendly feeling toward the Soviet nation. He had in this his own imperialistic goals—to bring Germany and the USSR into a bloody war and thereby to strengthen the position of the British Empire. Just the same, Churchill affirmed in his writings that he sought to warn Stalin and call his attention to the danger which threatened him. Churchill stressed this repeatedly in his dispatches of April 18 and in the following days. However, Stalin took no heed of these warnings. What is more, Stalin ordered that no credence be given to information of this sort, in order not to provoke the initiation of military operations.

We must assert that information of this sort concerning the threat of

German armed invasion of Soviet territory was coming in also from our own military and diplomatic sources; however, because the leadership was conditioned against such information, such data was dispatched with fear and assessed with reservation.

Thus, for instance, information sent from Berlin on May 6, 1941 by the Soviet military attache, Captain Vorontsov, stated: "Soviet citizen Bozer . . . communicated to the deputy naval attache that, according to a statement of a certain German officer from Hitler's headquarters, Germany is preparing to invade the USSR on May 14 through Finland, the Baltic countries and Latvia. At the same time Moscow and Leningrad will be heavily raided and paratroopers landed in border cities . . ."

In his report of May 22, 1941, the deputy military attache in Berlin, Khlopov, communicated that ". . . the attack of the German Army is reportedly scheduled for June 15, but it is possible that it may begin in the first days of June . . ."

A cable from our London Embassy dated June 18, 1941 stated: "As of now Cripps is deeply convinced of the inevitability of armed conflict between Germany and the USSR, which will begin not later than the middle of June. According to Cripps, the Germans have presently concentrated 147 divisions (including air force and service units) along the Soviet borders."

Despite these particularly grave warnings, the necessary steps were not taken to prepare the country properly for defense and to prevent it from being caught unaware.

Did we have time and the capabilities for such preparations? Yes; we had the time and capabilities. Our industry was already so developed that it was capable of supplying fully the Soviet Army with everything that it needed. This is proven by the fact that, although during the war we lost almost half of our industry and important industrial and food-production areas as the result of enemy occupation of the Ukraine, Northern Caucasus and other western parts of the country, the Soviet nation was still able to organize the production of military equipment in the eastern parts of the country, install there equipment taken from the western industrial areas, and to supply our armed forces with everything which was necessary to destroy the enemy.

Had our industry been mobilized properly and in time to supply the Army with the necessary materiel, our wartime losses would have been decidedly smaller. Such mobilization had not been, however, started in time. And already in the first days of the war it became evident that our Army was badly armed, that we did not have enough artillery, tanks and planes to throw the enemy back.

Soviet science and technology produced excellent models of tanks and artillery pieces before the war. But mass production of all this was not organized, and, as a matter of fact, we started to modernize our military equipment only on the eve of the war. As a result, at the time of the enemy's invasion of the Soviet land we did not have sufficient quantities either of old machinery which was no longer used for armament production or of new machinery which we had planned to introduce into armament production. The situation with anti-aircraft artillery was especially bad; we did not organize the production of anti-tank ammunition. Many fortified regions had proven to be indefensible as soon as they were attacked, because the old arms had been withdrawn and new ones were not yet available there.

This pertained, alas, not only to tanks, artillery and planes. At the outbreak of the war we did not even have sufficient numbers of rifles to arm the mobilized manpower. I recall that in those days I telephoned Comrade Malenkov from Kiev and told him, "People have volunteered for the new Army and demand arms. You must send us arms."

Malenkov answered me, "We cannot send you arms. We are sending all our rifles to Leningrad and you have to arm yourselves." [Movement in the hall.]

Such was the armament situation.

In this connection we cannot forget, for instance, the following fact. Shortly before the invasion of the Soviet Union by the Hitlerite army, Korponos, who was chief of the Kiev Special Military District (he was later killed at the front), wrote to Stalin that the German armies were at the Bug River, were preparing for an attack and in the very near future would probably start their offensive. In this connection, Korponos proposed that a strong defense be organized, that 300,000 people be evacuated from the border areas and that several strong points be organized there: anti-tank ditches, trenches for the soldiers, etc.

Moscow answered this proposition with the assertion that this would be a provocation, that no preparatory defensive work should be undertaken at the borders, that the Germans were not to be given any pretext for the initiation of military action against us. Thus, our borders were insufficiently prepared to repel the enemy.

When the fascist armies had actually invaded Soviet territory and military operations began, Moscow issued the order that the German fire was not to be returned. Why? It was because Stalin, despite evident facts, thought that the war had not yet started, that this was only a provocative action, on the part of several undisciplined sections of the German Army, and that our reaction might serve as a reason for the Germans to begin the war.

The following fact is also known. On the eve of the invasion of the territory of the Soviet Union by the Hitlerite army, a certain German citizen crossed our border and stated that the German armies had received orders to start the offensive against the Soviet Union on the night of June 22 at 3 o'clock. Stalin was informed about this immediately, but even this warning was ignored.

As you see, everything was ignored; warnings of certain Army commanders, declarations of deserters from the enemy army, and even the open hostility of the enemy. Is this an example of the alertness of the chief of the party and of the state at this particularly significant historical moment?

And what were the results of this carefree attitude, this disregard of clear facts? The result was that already in the first hours and days the enemy had destroyed in our border regions a large part of our Air Force, artillery and other military equipment; he annihilated large numbers of our military cadres and disorganized our military leadership; consequently we could not prevent the enemy from marching deep into the country.

Very grievous consequences, especially in reference to the beginning of the war, followed Stalin's annihilation of many military commanders and political workers during 1937–1941 because of his suspiciousness and through slanderous accusations. During these years repressions were instituted against certain parts of military cadres beginning literally at the company and battalion commander level and extending to the higher military centers; during this time the cadre of leaders who had gained military experience in Spain and in the Far East was almost completely liquidated.

The policy of large-scale repression against the military cadres led also to undermined military discipline, because for several years officers of all ranks and even soldiers in the party and Komsomol cells were taught to unmask their superiors as hidden enemies. [Movement in the hall.] It is natural that this caused a negative influence on the state of military discipline in the first war period.

And, as you know, we had before the war excellent military cadres which were unquestionably loyal to the party and to the fatherland. Suffice it to say that those of them who managed to survive, despite severe tortures to which they were subjected in the prisons, have from the first war days shown themselves real patriots and heroically fought for the glory of the fatherland; I have here in mind such comrades as Rokossovsky (who, as you know, had been jailed), Gorbatov, Maretskov (who is a delegate at the present Congress), Podlas (he was an excellent commander who perished at the front), and many, many others. However, many such commanders perished in camps and jails and the Army saw them no more.

All this brought about the situation which existed at the beginning of the war and which was the great threat to our Fatherland.

It would be incorrect to forget that, after the first severe disaster and defeats at the front, Stalin thought that this was the end. In one of his speeches in those days he said: "All that which Lenin created we have lost forever."

After this Stalin for a long time actually did not direct the military operations and ceased to do anything whatever. He returned to active leadership only when some members of the Political Bureau visited him and told him that it was necessary to take certain steps immediately in order to improve the situation at the front.

Therefore, the threatening danger which hung over our fatherland in the first period of the war was largely due to the faulty methods of directing the nation and the party by Stalin himself.

However, we speak not only about the moment when the war began, which led to serious disorganization of our Army and brought us severe losses. Even after the war began, the nervousness and hysteria which Stalin demonstrated, interfering with actual military operation, caused our Army serious damage.

Stalin was very far from an understanding of the real situation which was developing at the front. This was natural because, during the whole Patriotic War, he never visited any section of the front or any liberated city except for one short ride on the Mozhaisk highway during a stabilized situation at the front. To this incident were dedicated many literary works full of fantasies of all sorts and so many paintings. Simultaneously, Stalin was interfering with operations and issuing orders which did not take into consideration the real situation at a given section of the front and which could not help but result in huge personnel losses.

I will allow myself in this connection to bring out one characteristic fact which illustrates how Stalin directed operations at the fronts. There is present at this Congress Marshal Bagramian, who was once the chief of operations in the headquarters of the southwestern front and who can corroborate what I will tell you.

When there developed an exceptionally serious situation for our Army in 1942 in the Kharkov region, we had correctly decided to drop an operation whose objective was to encircle Kharkov, because the real situation at that time would have threatened our Army with fatal consequences if this operation were continued.

We communicated this to Stalin, stating that the situation demanded changes in operational plans so that the enemy would be prevented from liquidating a sizable concentration of our Army.

Contrary to common sense, Stalin rejected our suggestion and issued the order to continue the operation aimed at the encirclement of Kharkov, despite the fact that at this time many Army concentrations were themselves actually threatened with encirclement and liquidation.

I telephoned to Vasilevsky and begged him—"Alexander Mikhailovich, take a map (Vasilevsky is present here) and show Comrade Stalin the situation which has developed." We should note that Stalin planned operations on a globe. [Animation in the hall.] Yes, comrades, he used to take the globe and trace the front line on it. I said to Comrade Vasilevsky: "Show him the situation on a map; in the present situation we cannot continue the operation which was planned. The old decision must be changed for the good of the cause."

Vasilevsky replied, saying that Stalin had already studied this problem and that he, Vasilevsky, would not see Stalin further concerning this matter, because the latter didn't want to hear any arguments on the subject of this operation.

After my talk with Vasilevsky, I telephoned to Stalin at his villa. But Stalin did not answer the telephone and Malenkov was at the receiver. I told Comrade Malenkov that I was calling from the front and that I wanted to speak personally to Stalin. Stalin informed me through Malenkov that I should speak with Malenkov. I stated for the second time that I wished to inform Stalin personally about the grave situation which had arisen for us at the front. But Stalin did not consider it convenient to raise the phone and again stated that I should speak to him through Malenkov, although he was only a few steps from the telephone.

After "listening" in this manner to our plea, Stalin said: "Let everything remain as it is !"

And what was the result of this? The worst that we had expected. The Germans surrounded our Army concentrations and consequently we lost hundreds of thousands of our soldiers. This is Stalin's military "genius"; this is what it cost us. [Movement in the hall.]

On one occasion after the war, during a meeting of Stalin with members of the Political Bureau, Anastas Ivanovich Mikoyan mentioned that Khrushchev must have been right when he telephoned concerning the Kharkov operation and that it was unfortunate that his suggestion had not been accepted.

You should have seen Stalin's fury. How could it be admitted that he, Stalin, had not been right. He is after all a "genius," and a genius cannot help but be right! Everyone can err, but Stalin considered that he never erred, that he was always right. He never acknowledged to anyone that he made any mistake, large or small, despite the fact that he made not a few mistakes in the matter of theory and in his practical activity. After the Party Congress we shall probably have to re-evaluate many wartime military operations and to present them in their true light.

The tactics on which Stalin insisted without knowing the essence of the conduct of battle operations cost us much blood until we succeeded in stopping the opponent and going over to the offensive.

The military know that already by the end of 1941, instead of great operational maneuvers flanking the opponent and penetrating behind his back, Stalin demanded incessant frontal attacks and the capture of one village after another. Because of this, we paid with great losses until our generals, on whose shoulders rested the whole weight of conducting the war, succeeded in changing the situation and shifting to flexible-maneuver operations, which immediately brought serious changes at the front favorable to us.

All the more shameful was the fact that, after our great victory over the enemy which cost us so much, Stalin began to downgrade many of the commanders who contributed so much to the victory over the enemy, because Stalin excluded every possibility that services rendered at the front should be credited to anyone but himself.

Stalin was very much interested in the assessment of Comrade Zhukov as a military leader. He asked me often for my opinion of Zhukov. I told him then, "I have known Zhukov for a long time; he is a good general and a good military leader."

After the war Stalin began to tell all kinds of nonsense about Zhukov, among others the following, "You praised Zhukov, but he does not deserve it. It is said that before each operation at the front Zhukov used to behave as follows: He used to take a handful of earth, smell it and say, 'We can begin the attack,' or the opposite, 'The planned operation cannot be carried out.'" I stated at that time, "Comrade Stalin, I do not know who invented this, but it is not true."

It is possible that Stalin himself invented these things for the purpose of minimizing the role and military talents of Marshal Zhukov.

In this connection, Stalin very energetically popularized himself as a great leader; in various ways he tried to inculcate in the people the version that all victories gained by the Soviet nation during the Great Patriotic War were due to the courage, daring and genius of Stalin and of no one else. Exactly like Kuzma Kryuchkov he put one dress on seven people at the same time. [Animation in the hall.]

In the same vein, let us take, for instance, our historical and military films and some literary creations; they make us feel sick. Their true objective is the propagation of the theme of praising Stalin as a military genius. Let us recall the film, *The Fall of Berlin*. Here only Stalin acts; he issues orders in the hall in which there are many empty chairs and only one man approached him and reports something to him—that is Poskrebyshev, his loyal shield-bearer. [Laughter in the hall.]

And where is the military command? Where is the Political Bureau? Where is the Government? What are they doing and with what are they engaged? There is nothing about them in the film. Stalin acts for everybody; he does not reckon with anyone; he asks no one for advice. Everything is shown to the nation in this false light. Why? In order to surround Stalin with glory, contrary to the facts and contrary to historical truth.

The question arises: And where are the military, on whose shoulders rested the burden of the war? They are not in the film; with Stalin in, no room was left for them.

Not Stalin, but the party as a whole, the Soviet Government, our heroic Army, its talented leaders and brave soldiers, the whole Soviet nation—these are the ones who assured the victory in the Great Patriotic War. [Tempestuous and prolonged applause.]

The Central Committee members, ministers, our economic leaders, leaders of Soviet culture, directors of territorial-party and Soviet organizations, engineers, and technicians—every one of them in his own place of work generously gave of his strength and knowledge toward ensuring victory over the enemy.

Exceptional heroism was shown by our hard core—surrounded by glory is our whole working class, our *kolkhoz* peasantry, the Soviet intelligentsia, who under the leadership of party organizations overcame untold hardships, and, bearing the hardships of war, devoted all their strength to the cause of the defense of the fatherland.

Great and brave deeds during the war were accomplished by our Soviet women who bore on their backs the heavy load of production work in the factories, on the *kolkhozes*, and in various economic and cultural sectors; many women participated directly in the Great Patriotic War at the fronts; our brave youth contributed immeasurably at the front and at home to the defense of the Soviet fatherland and to the annihilation of the enemy.

Immortal are the services of the Soviet soldiers, of our commanders and political workers of all ranks; after the loss of a considerable part of the Army in the first war months they did not lose their heads and were able to reorganize during the progress of combat; they created and toughened during the progress of the war a strong and heroic Army and not only stood off pressure of the strong and cunning enemy but also smashed him.

The magnificent and heroic deeds of hundreds of millions of people of the East and of the West during the fight against the threat of fascist subjugation which loomed before us will live centuries and millennia in the memory of thankful humanity. [Thunderous applause.]

The main role and the main credit for the victorious ending of the war belongs to our Communist Party, to the armed forces of the Soviet Union, and to the tens of millions of Soviet people raised by the party. [Thunderous and prolonged applause.]

Comrades, let us reach for some other facts. The Soviet Union is justly considered as a model of a multinational state because we have in practice assured the equality and friendship of all nations which live in our great fatherland.

All the more monstrous are the acts whose initiator was Stalin and which are rude violations of the basic Leninist principles of the nationality policy of the Soviet state. We refer to the mass deportations from their native places of whole nations, together with all Communists and Komsomols without any exception; this deportation action was not dictated by any military considerations.

Thus, already at the end of 1943, when there occurred a permanent breakthrough at the fronts of the Great Patriotic War benefiting the Soviet Union, a decision was taken and executed concerning the deportation of all the Karachai from the lands on which they lived.

In the same period, at the end of December 1943, the same lot befell the whole population of the Autonomous Kalmyk Republic. In March 1944, all the Chechen and Ingush peoples were deported and the Chechen-Ingush Autonomous Republic was liquidated. In April 1944, all Balkars were deported to faraway places from the territory of the Kabardino-Balkar Autonomous Republic and the Republic itself was renamed the Autonomous Kabardian Republic.

The Ukrainians avoided meeting this fate only because there were too many of them and there was no place to which to deport them. Otherwise, he would have deported them also. [Laughter and animation in the hall.]

Not only a Marxist-Leninist but also no man of common sense can grasp how it is possible to make whole nations responsible for inimical activity, including women, children, old people, Communists and Komsosols, to use mass repression against them, and to expose them to misery and suffering for the hostile acts of individual persons or groups of persons.

After the conclusion of the Patriotic War, the Soviet nation stressed with pride the magnificent victories gained through great sacrifices and tremendous efforts. The country experienced a period of political enthusiasm. The party came out of the war even more united; in the fire of the war, party cadres were tempered and hardened. Under such conditions nobody could have even thought of the possibility of some plot in the party.

And it was precisely at this time that the so-called "Leningrad affair" was born. As we have now proven, this case was fabricated. Those who innocently lost their lives included Comrades Voznesensky, Kuznetsov, Rodionov, Popkov, and others.

As is known, Voznesensky and Kuznetsov were talented and eminent leaders. Once they stood very close to Stalin. It is sufficient to mention that Stalin made Voznesensky first deputy to the chairman of the Council of Ministers and Kuznetsov was elected Secretary of the Central Committee. The very fact that Stalin entrusted Kuznetsov with the supervision of the state-security organs shows the trust which he enjoyed.

How did it happen that these persons were branded as enemies of the people and liquidated?

Facts prove that the "Leningrad affair" is also the result of willfulness which Stalin exercised against party cadres. Had a normal situation existed in the party's Central Committee and in the Central Committee Political Bureau, affairs of this nature would have been examined there in accordance with party practice, and all pertinent facts assessed; as a result, such an affair as well as others would not have happened.

We must state that, after the war, the situation became even more complicated. Stalin became even more capricious, irritable and brutal; in particular his suspicion grew. His persecution mania reached unbelievable dimensions. Many workers were becoming enemies before his very eyes. After the war, Stalin separated himself from the collective even more. Everything was decided by him alone without any consideration for anyone or anything.

This unbelievable suspicion was cleverly taken advantage of by the abject *provocateur* and vile enemy, Beria, who had murdered thousands of Communists and loyal Soviet people. The elevation of Voznesensky and Kuznetsov alarmed Beria. As we have now proven, it had been precisely Beria who had "suggested" to Stalin the fabrication by him and by his confidants of materials in the form of declarations and anonymous letters, and in the form of various rumors and talks.

The party's central committee has examined this so-called "Leningrad affair"; persons who innocently suffered are now rehabilitated and honor has been restored to the glorious Leningrad party organization. Abakumov and others who had fabricated this affair were brought before a court; their trial took place in Leningrad and they received what they deserved.

The question arises: Why is it that we see the truth of this affair only now, and why did we not do something earlier, during Stalin's life, in order to prevent the loss of innocent lives? It was because Stalin personally supervised the "Leningrad affair," and the majority of the Political Bureau members did not, at that time, know all of the circumstances in these matters and could not therefore intervene.

When Stalin received certain material from Beria and Abakumov, without examining these slanderous materials he ordered an investigation of the "affair" of Voznesensky and Kuznetsov. With this, their fate was sealed.

Instructive in the same way is the case of the Mingrelian nationalist organization which supposedly existed in Georgia. As is known, resolutions by the Central Committee, Communist Party of the Soviet Union, were made concerning this case in November 1951 and in March 1952. These resolutions were made without prior discussion with the Political Bureau. Stalin had personally dictated them. They made serious accusations against many loyal Communists. On the basis of falsified documents, it was proven that there existed in Georgia a supposedly nationalistic organization whose objective was the liquidation of the Soviet power in that republic with the help of imperialist powers.

In this connection, a number of responsible party and Soviet workers were arrested in Georgia. As was later proven, this was a slander directed against the Georgian party organization.

We know that there have been at times manifestations of local bourgeois nationalism in Georgia as in several other republics. The question arises: Could it be possible that, in the period during which the resolutions referred to above were made, nationalist tendencies grew so much that there was a danger of Georgia's leaving the Soviet Union and joining Turkey? [Animation in the hall, laughter.]

This is, of course, nonsense. It is impossible to imagine how such assumptions could enter anyone's mind. Everyone knows how Georgia has developed economically and culturally under Soviet rule.

Industrial production of the Georgia Republic is 27 times greater than it was before the revolution. Many new industries have arisen in Georgia which did not exist there before the revolution: iron smelting, an oil industry, a machine-construction industry, etc. Illiteracy has long since been liquidated, which, in pre-Revolutionary Georgia, included 78 per cent of the population.

Could the Georgians, comparing the situation in their republic with the hard situation of the working masses in Turkey, be aspiring to join Turkey? In 1955, Georgia produced 18 times as much steel per person as Turkey. Georgia produces 9 times as much electrical energy per person as Turkey. According to the available 1950 census, 65 per cent of Turkey's total population are illiterate, and, of the women, 80 per cent are illiterate. Georgia has 19 institutions of higher learning which have about 39,000 students; this is 8 times more than in Turkey (for each 1,000 inhabitants). The prosperity of the working people has grown tremendously in Georgia under Soviet rule.

It is clear that, as the economy and culture develop, and as the socialist consciousness of the working masses in Georgia grows, the source from which bourgeois nationalism draws its strength evaporates.

As it developed, there was no nationalistic organization in Georgia. Thousands of innocent people fell victim of willfulness and lawlessness. All of this happened under the "genial" leadership of Stalin, "the great son of the Georgian nation," as Georgians like to refer to Stalin. [Animation in the hall.]

The willfulness of Stalin showed itself not only in decisions concerning the internal life of the country but also in the international relations of the Soviet Union.

The July plenum of the Central Committee studied in detail the reasons for the development of conflict with Yugoslavia. It was a shameful role which Stalin played here. The "Yugoslav affair" contained no problems which could not have been solved through party discussions among comrades. There was no significant basis for the development of this "affair"; it was completely possible to have prevented the rupture of relations with that country. This does not mean, however, that the Yugoslav leaders did not make mistakes or did not have shortcomings. But these mistakes and shortcomings were magnified in a monstrous manner by Stalin, which resulted in a break of relations with a friendly country.

I recall the first days when the conflict between the Soviet Union and Yugoslavia began artificially to be blown up. Once, when I came from Kiev to Moscow, I was invited to visit Stalin, who, pointing to the copy of a letter lately sent to Tito, asked me, "Have you read this?"

Not waiting for my reply, he answered, "I will shake my little finger and there will be no more Tito. He will fall."

We have dearly paid for this "shaking of the little finger." This statement reflected Stalin's mania for greatness, but he acted just that way: "I will shake my little finger—and there will be no Kossior"; "I will shake my little finger once more and Postyshev and Chubar will be no more"; "I will shake my little finger again—and Voznesensky, Kuznetsov and many others will disappear."

But this did not happen to Tito. No matter how much or how little Stalin shook, not only his little finger but everything else that he could shake, Tito did not fall. Why? The reason was that, in this case of disagreement with the Yugoslav comrades, Tito had behind him a state and a people who had gone through a severe school of fighting for liberty and independence, a people which gave support to its leaders.

You see to what Stalin's mania for greatness led. He had completely lost consciousness of reality; he demonstrated his suspicion and haughtiness not only in relation to individuals in the USSR, but in relation to whole parties and nations.

We have carefully examined the case of Yugoslavia and have found a proper solution which is approved by the peoples of the Soviet Union and of Yugoslavia as well as by the working masses of all the people's democracies and by all progressive humanity. The liquidation of the abnormal relationship with Yugoslavia was done in the interest of the whole camp of socialism, in the interest of strengthening peace in the whole world.

Let us also recall the affair of the doctor-plotters. [Animation in the hall.] Actually there was no affair outside of the declaration of the woman doctor Timashuk, who was probably influenced or ordered by someone (after all, she was an unofficial collaborator of the organs of state security) to write Stalin a letter in which she declared that doctors were applying supposedly improper methods of medical treatment.

Such a letter was sufficient for Stalin to reach an immediate conclusion that there are doctor-plotters in the Soviet Union. He issued orders to arrest a group of eminent Soviet medical specialists. He personally issued advice on the conduct of the investigation and the method of interrogation of the arrested persons. He said that the academician Vinogradov should be put in chains, another one should be beaten. Present at this Congress as a delegate is the former Minister of State Security, Comrade Ignatiev. Stalin told him curtly, "If you do not obtain confessions from the doctors we will shorten you by a head." [Tumult in the hall.]

Stalin personally called the investigative judge, gave him instructions, advised him on which investigative methods should be used; these methods were simple—beat, beat and, once again, beat.

Shortly after the doctors were arrested, we members of the Political Bureau received protocols with the doctors' confessions of guilt. After distributing these protocols, Stalin told us, "You are blind like young kittens; what will happen without me? The country will perish because you do not know how to recognize enemies."

The case was so presented that no one could verify the facts on which the investigation was based. There was no possibility of trying to verify facts by contacting those who had made the confessions of guilt.

We felt, however, that the case of the arrested doctors was questionable. We knew some of these people personally because they had once treated us. When we examined this case after Stalin's death, we found it to be fabricated from beginning to end.

This ignominious case was set up by Stalin; he did not, however, have the time in which to bring it to an end (as he conceived that end), and for this reason the doctors are still alive. Now all have been rehabilitated; they are working in the same places they were working before; they treat top individuals, not excluding members of the Government; they have our full confidence; and they execute their duties honestly, as they did before.

In organizing the various dirty and shameful cases, a very base role was played by the rabid enemy of our party, an agent of a foreign intelligence service—Beria, who had stolen into Stalin's confidence. In what way could this *provocateur* gain such a position in the party and in the state, so as to become the First Deputy Chairman of the Council of Ministers of the Soviet Union and a member of the Central Committee Political Bureau? It has now been established that this villain had climbed up the Government ladder over an untold number of corpses.

Were there any signs that Beria was an enemy of the party? Yes, there were. Already in 1937, at a Central Committee plenum, former People's Commissar of Health Protection Kaminsky said that Beria worked for the Mussavat intelligence service. But the Central Committee plenum had barely concluded when Kaminsky was arrested and then shot. Had Stalin examined Kaminsky's statement? No, because Stalin believed in Beria, and that was enough for him. And when Stalin believed in anyone or anything, then no one could say anything which was contrary to his opinion; anyone who would dare to express opposition would have met the same fate as Kaminsky.

There were other signs, also. The declaration which Comrade Snegov made at the party's Central Committee is interesting. (Parenthetically speaking, he was also rehabilitated not long ago, after 17 years in prison camps.) In this declaration, Snegov writes:

"In connection with the proposed rehabilitation of the former Central Committee member, Kartvelishvili-Lavrentiev, I have entrusted to the hands of the representative of the Committee of State Security a detailed deposition concerning Beria's role in the disposition of the Kartvelishvili case and concerning the criminal motives by which Beria was guided."

In my opinion, it is indispensable to recall an important fact pertaining to this case and to communicate it to the Central Committee, because I did not consider it as proper to include in the investigation documents.

On October 30, 1931, at the session of the Organizational Bureau of the Central Committee, All-Union Communist Party (Bolsheviks), Kartvelishvili, secretary of the Transcaucasian Krai Committee, made a report. All members of the executive of the Krai Committee were present; of them I alone am alive.

During this session, J. V. Stalin made a motion at the end of his speech concerning the organization of the secretariat of the Transcaucasian Krai Committee composed of the following: first secretary, Kartvelishvili; second secretary, Beria (it was then, for the first time in the party's history, that Beria's name was mentioned as a candidate for a party position). Kartvelishvili answered that he knew Beria well and for that reason refused categorically to work together with him. Stalin proposed then that this matter be left open and that it be solved in the process of the work itself. Two days later a decision was arrived at that Beria would receive the party post and that Kartvelishvili would be deported from the Transcaucasus.

This fact can be confirmed by Comrades Mikoyan and Kaganovich, who were present at that session.

The long, unfriendly relations between Kartvelishvili and Beria were widely known; they date back to the time when Comrade Sergo [Ordzhonikidze] was active in the Transcaucasus: Kartvelishvili was the closest assistant of Sergo. The unfriendly relationship impelled Beria to fabricate a case against Kartvelishvili.

It is a characteristic thing that in this case Kartvelishvili was charged with a terroristic act against Beria.

The indictment in the Beria case contains a discussion of his crimes. Some things should, however, be recalled, especially since it is possible that not all delegates to the Congress have read this document. I wish to recall Beria's bestial disposition of the cases of Kedrov, Golubev, and Golubev's adopted mother, Baturina—persons who wished to inform the Central Committee concerning Beria's treacherous activity. They were shot without any trial and the sentence was passed *ex post facto,* after the execution.

Here is what the old Communist, Comrade Kedrov, wrote to the Central Committee through Comrade Andreyev (Comrade Andreyev was then a Central Committee secretary):

"I am calling to you for help from a gloomy cell of the Lefortovsky prison. Let my cry of horror reach your ears; do not remain deaf; take me under your protection; please, help remove the nightmare of interrogations and show that this is all a mistake.

"I suffer innocently. Please believe me. Time will testify to the truth. I am not an *agent provocateur* of the Tsarist Okhrana; I am not a spy; I am not a member of an anti-Soviet organization of which I am being accused on the basis of denunciations. I am also not guilty of any other crimes against the party and the Government. I am an old Bolshevik, free of any stain; I have honestly fought for almost 40 years in the ranks of the party for the good and prosperity of the nation. . . .

"Today I, a 62-year-old man, am being threatened by the investigative judges with more severe, cruel and degrading methods of physical pressure. They (the judges) are no longer capable of becoming aware of their error and of recognizing that their handling of my case is illegal and impermissible. They try to justify their actions by picturing me as a hardened and raving enemy and are demanding increased repressions. But let the party know that I am innocent and that there is nothing which can turn a loyal son of the party into an enemy, even right up to his last dying breath.

"But I have no way out. I cannot divert from myself the hastily approaching new and powerful blows.

"Everything, however, has its limits. My torture has reached the extreme. My health is broken, my strength and my energy are waning, the end is drawing near. To die in a Soviet prison, branded as a vile traitor to the fatherland—what can be more monstrous for an honest man? And how monstrous all this is! Unsurpassed bitterness and pain grips my heart. No! No! This will not happen; this cannot be, I cry. Neither the party, nor the Soviet Government, nor the People's Commissar, L. P. Beria, will permit this cruel, irreparable injustice. I am firmly certain that, given a quiet, objective examination, without any foul rantings, without any anger and without the fearful tortures, it would be easy to prove the baselessness of the charges. I believe deeply that truth and justice will triumph. I believe. I believe."

The old Bolshevik, Comrade Kedrov, was found innocent by the Military Collegium. But despite this, he was shot at Beria's order. [Indignation in the hall.]

Beria also handled cruelly the family of Comrade Ordzhonikidze. Why? Because Ordzhonikidze had tried to prevent Beria from realizing his shameful plans. Beria had cleared from his way all persons who could possibly interfere with him. Ordzhonikidze was always an opponent of Beria, which he told to Stalin. Instead of examining this affair and taking appropriate steps, Stalin allowed the liquidation of Ordzhonikidze's brother and brought Ordzhonikidze himself to such a state that he was forced to shoot himself. [Indignation in the hall.] Such was Beria.

Beria was unmasked by the party's Central Committee shortly after Stalin's death. As a result of the particularly detailed legal proceedings, it was established that Beria had committed monstrous crimes and Beria was shot.

The question arises why Beria, who had liquidated tens of thousands of the party and Soviet workers, was not unmasked during Stalin's life. He was not unmasked earlier because he had utilized very skillfully Stalin's weaknesses; feeding him with suspicions, he assisted Stalin in everything and acted with his support.

Comrades, the cult of the individual acquired such monstrous size chiefly because Stalin himself, using all conceivable methods, supported the glorification of his own person. This is supported by numerous facts. One of the most characteristic examples of Stalin's self-glorification and of his lack of even elementary modesty is the edition of his *Short Biography*, which was published in 1948.

This book is an expression of the most dissolute flattery, an example of making a man into a godhead, of transforming him into an infallible sage, "the greatest leader, sublime strategist of all times and nations." Finally, no other words could be found with which to lift Stalin up to the heavens.

We need not give here examples of the loathesome adulation filling this book. All we need to add is that they all were approved and edited by Stalin personally and some of them were added in his own handwriting to the draft text of the book.

What did Stalin consider essential to write into this book? Did he want to cool the ardor of his flatterers who were composing his *Short Biography*? No! He marked the very places where he thought that the praise of his services was insufficient. Here are some examples characterizing Stalin's activity, added in Stalin's own hand:

"In this fight against the skeptics and capitulators, the Trotskyites, Zinovievites, Bukharinites and Kamenevites, there was definitely welded together, after Lenin's death, that leading core of the party . . . that upheld the great banner of Lenin, rallied the party behind Lenin's behests, and brought the Soviet people into the broad road of industrializing the country and collectivizing the rural economy. The leader of this core and the guiding force of the party and the state was Comrade Stalin."

Thus writes Stalin himself! Then he adds:

"Although he performed his task as leader of the party and the people with consummate skill and enjoyed the unreserved support of the entire Soviet people, Stalin never allowed his work to be marred by the slightest hint of vanity, conceit or self-adulation."

Where and when could a leader so praise himself? Is this worthy of a leader of the Marxist-Leninist type? No. Precisely against this did Marx and Engels take such a strong position. This also was always sharply condemned by Vladimir Ilyich Lenin.

In the draft text of his book appeared the following sentence: "Stalin is the Lenin of today." This sentence appeared to Stalin to be too weak, so, in his own handwriting, he changed it to read: "Stalin is the worthy continuer of Lenin's work, or, as it is said in our party, Stalin is the Lenin of today." You see how well it is said, not by the nation but by Stalin himself.

It is possible to give many such self-praising appraisals written into the draft text of that book in Stalin's hand. Especially generously does he endow himself with praises pertaining to his military genius, to his talent for strategy.

I will cite one more insertion made by Stalin concerning the theme of the Stalinist military genius. "The advanced Soviet science of war received further development," he writes, "at Comrade Stalin's hands. Comrade Stalin elaborated the theory of the permanently operating factors that decide the issue of wars, of active defense and the laws of counteroffensive and offensive, of the cooperation of all services and arms in modern warfare, of the role of big tank masses and air forces in modern war, and of the artillery as the most formidable of the armed services. At the various stages of the war Stalin's genius found the correct solutions that took account of all the circumstances of the situation." [Movement in the hall.]

And, further, writes Stalin: "Stalin's military mastership was displayed both in defense and offense. Comrade Stalin's genius enabled him to divine the enemy's plans and defeat them. The battles in which Comrade Stalin directed the Soviet armies are brilliant examples of operational military skill."

In this manner was Stalin praised as a strategist. Who did this? Stalin himself, not in his role as a strategist but in the role of an author-editor, one of the main creators of his self-adulatory biography. Such, comrades, are the facts. We should rather say shameful facts.

And one additional fact from the same *Short Biography* of Stalin. As is known, *The Short Course of the History of the All-Union Communist Party (Bolsheviks)* was written by a commission of the party Central Committee.

This book, parenthetically, was also permeated with the cult of the individual and was written by a designated group of authors. This fact was reflected in the following formulation on the proof copy of the *Short Biography* of Stalin: "A commission of the Central Committee, All-Union Communist Party (Bolsheviks), under the direction of Comrade Stalin and with his most active personal participation, has prepared a *Short Course of the History of the All-Union Communist Party (Bolsheviks).*"

But even this phrase did not satisfy Stalin: The following sentence replaced it in the final version of the *Short Biography:* "In 1938 appeared the book, *History of the All-Union Communist Party (Bolsheviks), Short Course,* written by Comrade Stalin and approved by a commission of the Central Committee, All-Union Communist Party (Bolsheviks)." Can one add anything more? [Animation in the hall.]

As you see, a surprising metamorphosis changed the work created by a group into a book written by Stalin. It is not necessary to state how and why this metamorphosis took place.

A pertinent question comes to our mind: If Stalin is the author of this book, why did he need to praise the person of Stalin so much and to transform the whole post-October historical period of our glorious Communist party solely into an action of "the Stalin genuis"?

Did this book properly reflect the efforts of the party in the socialist transformation of the country, in the construction of socialist society, in the industrialization and collectivization of the country, and also other steps taken by the party which undeviatingly traveled the path outlined by Lenin? This book speaks principally about Stalin, about his speeches, about his reports. Everything without the smallest exception is tied to his name.

And when Stalin himself asserts that he himself wrote the *Short Course of the History of the All-Union Communist Party (Bolsheviks),* this calls at least for amazement. Can a Marxist-Leninist thus write about himself, praising his own person to the heavens?

Or let us take the matter of the Stalin Prizes. [Movement in the hall.] Not even the Tsars created prizes which they named after themselves.

Stalin recognized as the best a text of the national anthem of the Soviet Union which contains not a word about the Communist party; it contains, however, the following unprecedented praise of Stalin: "Stalin brought us up in loyalty to the people. He inspired us to great toil and acts."

In these lines of the anthem is the whole educational, directional and inspirational activity of the great Leninist party ascribed to Stalin. This is, of course, a clear deviation from Marxism-Leninism, a clear debasing and belittling of the role of the party. We should add for your information that the Presidium of the Central Committee has already passed a resolution concerning the composition of a new text of the anthem, which will reflect the role of the people and the role of the party. [Loud, prolonged applause.]

And was it without Stalin's knowledge that many of the largest enterprises and towns were named after him? Was it without his knowledge that Stalin monuments were erected in the whole country—these memorials to the living? It is a fact that Stalin himself had signed on July 2, 1951 a resolution of the USSR Council of Ministers concerning the erection on the Volga-Don Canal of an impressive monument to Stalin; on September 4 of the same year he issued an order making 33 tons of copper available for the construction of this impressive monument.

Anyone who has visited the Stalingrad area must have seen the huge statue which is being built there, and that on a site which hardly any people frequent. Huge sums were spent to build it at a time when people of this area had lived since the war in huts. Consider, yourself, was Stalin right when he wrote in his biography that ". . . he did not allow in himself . . . even a shadow of conceit, pride, or self-adoration"?

At the same time Stalin gave proofs of his lack of respect for Lenin's memory. It is not a coincidence that, despite the decision taken over 30 years ago to build a Palace of Soviets as a monument to Vladimir Ilyich, this palace was not built, its construction was always postponed and the project allowed to lapse.

We cannot forget to recall the Soviet Government resolution of August 14, 1925 concerning "the founding of Lenin prizes for educational work." This resolution was published in the press, but until this day there are no Lenin prizes. This, too, should be corrected. [Tumultuous, prolonged applause.]

During Stalin's life—thanks to known methods which I have mentioned, and quoting facts, for instance, from the *Short Biography of Stalin*—all events were explained as if Lenin played only a secondary role, even during the October Socialist Revolution. In many films and in many literary works the figure of Lenin was incorrectly presented and inadmissibly depreciated.

Stalin loved to see the film, *The Unforgettable Year of 1919*, in which he was shown on the steps of an armored train and where he was practically vanquishing the foe with his own saber. Let Kliment Yefremovich [Voroshilov], our dear friend, find the necessary courage and write the truth about Stalin; after all, he knows how Stalin had fought. It will be difficult for Comrade Voroshilov to undertake this, but it would be good if he did it. Everyone will approve of it, both the people and the party. Even his grandsons will thank him. [Prolonged applause.]

In speaking about the events of the October Revolution and about the Civil War, the impression was created that Stalin always played the main role, as if everywhere and always Stalin had suggested to Lenin what to do and how to do it. However, this is slander of Lenin. [Prolonged applause.]

I will probably not sin against the truth when I say that 99 per cent of the persons present here heard and knew very little about Stalin before the year 1924, while Lenin was known to all; he was known to the whole party, to the whole nation, from the children up to the graybeards. [Tumultuous, prolonged applause.]

All this has to be thoroughly revised so that history, literature and the fine arts properly reflect V. I. Lenin's role and the great deeds of our Communist party and of the Soviet people—the creative people. [Applause.]

Comrades, the cult of the individual has caused the employment of faulty principles in party work and in economic activity; it brought about rude violation of internal party and Soviet democracy, sterile administration, deviations of all sorts, covering up the shortcomings and varnishing of reality. Our nation gave birth to many flatterers and specialists in false optimism and deceit.

We should also not forget that, due to the numerous arrests of party, Soviet and economic leaders, many workers began to work uncertainly, showed overcautiousness, feared all which was new, feared their own shadows and began to show less initiative in their work.

Take, for instance, party and Soviet resolutions. They were prepared in a routine manner, often without considering the concrete situation. This went so far that party workers, even during the smallest sessions, read their speeches. All this produced the danger of formalizing the party and Soviet work and of bureaucratizing the whole apparatus.

Stalin's reluctance to consider life's realities and the fact that he was not aware of the real state of affairs in the provinces can be illustrated by his direction of agriculture.

All those who interested themselves even a little in the national situation saw the difficult situation in agriculture, but Stalin never even noted it. Did we tell Stalin about this? Yes, we told him, but he did not support us. Why? Because Stalin never traveled anywhere, did not meet city and *kolkhoz* workers; he did not know the actual situation in the provinces.

He knew the country and agriculture only from films. And these films had dressed up and beautified the existing situation in agriculture. Many films so pictured *kolkhoz* life that the tables were bending from the weight of turkeys and geese. Evidently, Stalin thought that it was actually so.

Vladimir Ilyich Lenin looked at life differently; he was always close to the people; he used to receive peasant delegates and often spoke at factory gatherings; he used to visit villages and talk with the peasants.

Stalin separated himself from the people and never went anywhere. This lasted ten years. The last time he visited a village was in January 1928, when he visited Siberia in connection with grain deliveries. How then could he have known the situation in the provinces?

And when he was once told during a discussion that our situation on the land was a difficult one and that the situation of cattle breeding and meat production was especially bad, a commission was formed which was charged with the preparation of a resolution called "Means toward further development of animal breeding in *kolkhozes* and *sovkhozes*." We worked out this project.

Of course, our propositions of that time did not contain all possibilities but we did chart ways in which animal breeding on *kolkhozes* and *sovkhozes* would be raised. We had proposed then to raise the prices of such products in order to create material incentives for the *kolkhoz*, MTS [Machine-Tractor Station] and *sovkhoz* workers in the development of cattle breeding. But our project was not accepted and in February 1953 was laid aside entirely.

What is more, while reviewing this project Stalin proposed that the taxes paid by the *kolkhozes* and by the *kolkhoz* workers should be raised by 40 billion rubles; according to him the peasants are well off and the *kolkhoz* worker would need to sell only one more chicken to pay his tax in full.

Imagine what this meant. Certainly, 40 billion rubles is a sum which the *kolkhoz* workers did not realize for all the products which they sold to the Government. In 1952, for instance, the *kolkhozes* and the *kolkhoz* workers received 26,280,000,000 rubles for all their products delivered and sold to the Government.

Did Stalin's position, then, rest on data of any sort whatever? Of course not. In such cases facts and figures did not interest him. If Stalin said anything, it meant it was so—after all, he was a "genius," and a genius does not need to count, he only needs to look and can immediately tell how it should be. When he expresses his opinion, everyone has to repeat it and to admire his wisdom.

But how much wisdom was contained in the proposal to raise the agricultural tax by 40 billion rubles? None, absolutely none, because the proposal was not based on an actual assessment of the situation but on the fantastic ideas of a person divorced from reality.

We are currently beginning slowly to work our way out of a difficult agricultural situation. The speeches of the delegates to the Twentieth Congress please us all; we are glad that many delegates deliver speeches, that there are conditions for the fulfillment of the sixth Five-Year Plan for animal husbandry, not during the period of five years, but within two to three years. We are certain that the commitments of the new Five-Year Plan will be accomplished successfully. [Prolonged applause.]

Comrades, if we sharply criticize today the cult of the individual which was so widespread during Stalin's life and if we speak about the many negative phenomena generated by this cult which is so alien to the spirit of Marxism-Leninism, various persons may ask: How could it be? Stalin headed the party and the country for 30 years and many victories were gained during his lifetime. Can we deny this? In my opinion, the question can be asked in this manner only by those who are blinded and hopelessly hypnotized by the cult of the individual, only by those who do not understand the essence of the revolution and of the Soviet state, only by those who do not understand, in a Leninist manner, the role of the party and of the nation in the development of the Soviet society.

The Socialist Revolution was attained by the working class and by the poor peasantry with the partial support of middle-class peasants. It was attained by the people under the leadership of the Bolshevik Party. Lenin's great service consisted of the fact that he created a militant party of the working class, but he was armed with Marxist understanding of the laws of social development and with the science of proletarian victory in the fight with capitalism, and he steeled this party in the crucible of revolutionary struggle of the masses of the people.

During this fight the party consistently defended the interests of the people, became its experienced leader, and led the working masses to power, to the creation of the first socialist state. You remember well the wise words of Lenin that the Soviet state is strong because of the awareness of the masses that history is created by the millions and tens of millions of people.

Our historical victories were attained thanks to the organizational work of the party, to the many provincial organizations, and to the self-sacrificing work of our great nation. These victories are the result of the great drive and activity of the nation and of the party as a whole; they are not at all the fruit of the leadership of Stalin, as the situation was pictured during the period of the cult of the individual.

If we are to consider this matter as Marxists and as Leninists, then we have to state unequivocally that the leadership practice which came into being during the last years of Stalin's life became a serious obstacle in the path of Soviet social development. Stalin often failed for months to take up some unusually important problems, concerning the life of the party and of the state, whose solution could not be postponed. During Stalin's leadership our peaceful relations with other nations were often threatened, because one-man decisions could cause, and often did cause, great complications.

In the last years, when we managed to free ourselves of the harmful practice of the cult of the individual and took several proper steps in the sphere of internal and external policies, everyone saw how activity grew before their very eyes, how the creative activity of the broad working masses developed, how favorably all this acted upon the development of economy and of culture. [Applause.]

Some comrades may ask us: Where were the members of the Political Bureau of the Central Committee? Why did they not assert themselves against the cult of the individual in time? And why is this being done only now?

First of all, we have to consider the fact that the members of the Political Bureau viewed these matters in a different way at different times. Initially, many of them backed Stalin actively because Stalin was one of the strongest Marxists and his logic, his strength and his will greatly influenced the cadres and party work.

It is known that Stalin, after Lenin's death, especially during the first years, actively fought for Leninism against the enemies of Leninist theory and against those who deviated. Beginning with Leninist theory, the party, with its Central Committee at the head, started on a great scale the work of socialist industrialization of the country, agricultural collectivization and the cultural revolution.

At that time Stalin gained great popularity, sympathy and support. The party had to fight those who attempted to lead the country away from the correct Leninist path; it had to fight Trotskyites, Zinovievites and rightists, and the bourgeois nationalists. This fight was indispensable.

Later, however, [Stalin,] abusing his power more and more, began to fight eminent party and Government leaders and to use terroristic methods against honest Soviet people. As we have already shown, Stalin thus handled such eminent party and Government leaders as Kossior, Rudzutak, Eikhe, Postyshev and many others.

Attempts to oppose groundless suspicions and charges resulted in the opponent falling victim of the repression. This characterized the fall of Comrade Postyshev.

In one of his speeches Stalin expressed his dissatisfaction with Postyshev and asked him, "What are you actually?"

Postyshev answered clearly, "I am a Bolshevik, Comrade Stalin, a Bolshevik."

This assertion was at first considered to show a lack of respect for Stalin; later it was considered a harmful act and consequently resulted in Postyshev's annihilation and branding without any reason as a "people's enemy."

In the situation which then prevailed I have talked often with Nikolai Alexandrovich Bulganin; once when we two were traveling in a car, he said, "It has happened sometimes that a man goes to Stalin on his invitation as a friend. And, when he sits with Stalin, he does not know where he will be sent next—home or to jail."

It is clear that such conditions put every member of the Political Bureau in a very difficult situation. And, when we also consider the fact that in the last years the Central Committee plenary sessions were not convened and that the sessions of the Political Bureau occurred only occasionally, from time to time, then we will understand how difficult it was for any member of the Political Bureau to take a stand against one or another unjust or improper procedure, against serious errors and shortcomings in the practices of leadership.

As we have already shown, many decisions were taken either by one person or in a roundabout way, without collective discussion. The sad fate of Political Bureau member Comrade Voznesensky, who fell victim to Stalin's repressions, is known to all. It is a characteristic thing that the decision to remove him from the Political Bureau was never discussed but was reached in a devious fashion. In the same way came the decision concerning the removal of Kuznetsov and Rodionov from their posts.

The importance of the Central Committee's Political Bureau was reduced and its work was disorganized by the creation within the Political Bureau of various commissions—the so-called "quintets," "sextets," "septets" and "novenaries." Here is, for instance, a resolution of the Political Bureau of October 3, 1946:

"Stalin's Proposal:

"1. The Political Bureau Commission for Foreign Affairs ("Sextet") is to concern itself in the future, in addition to foreign affairs, also with matters of internal construction and domestic policy.

"2. The Sextet is to add to its roster the Chairman of the State Commission of Economic Planning of the USSR, Comrade Voznesensky, and is to be known as a Septet.

"Signed: Secretary of the Central Committee, J. Stalin."

What a terminology of a card player! [Laughter in the hall.] It is clear that the creation within the Political Bureau of this type of commissions—"quintets," "sextets," "septets" and "novenaries"—was against the principle of collective leadership. The result of this was that some members of the Political Bureau were in this way kept away from participation in reaching the most important state matters.

One of the oldest members of our party, Kliment Yefremovich Voroshilov, found himself in an almost impossible situation. For several years he was actually deprived of the right of participation in Political Bureau sessions. Stalin forbade him to attend the Political Bureau sessions and to receive documents. When the Political Bureau was in session and Comrade Voroshilov heard about it, he telephoned each time and asked whether he would be allowed to attend. Sometimes Stalin permitted it, but always showed his dissatisfaction.

Because of his extreme suspicion, Stalin toyed also with the absurd and ridiculous suspicion that Voroshilov was an English agent. [Laughter in the hall.] It's true—an English agent. A special tapping device was installed in his home to listen to what was said there. [Indignation in the hall.]

By unilateral decision, Stalin had also separated one other man from the work of the Political Bureau—Andrei Andreyevich Andreyev. This was one of the most unbridled acts of willfulness.

Let us consider the first Central Committee plenum after the 19th Party Congress when Stalin, in his talk at the plenum, characterized Vyacheslav Mikhailovich Molotov and Anastas Ivanovich Mikoyan and suggested that these old workers of our party were guilty of some baseless charges. It is not excluded that had Stalin remained at the helm for another several months, Comrades Molotov and Mikoyan would probably have not delivered any speeches at this Congress.

Stalin evidently had plans to finish off the old members of the Political Bureau. He often stated that Political Bureau members should be replaced by new ones.

His proposal, after the 19th Congress, concerning the election of 25 persons to the Central Committee Presidium, was aimed at the removal of the old Political Bureau members and the bringing in of less experienced persons so that these would extol him in all sorts of ways.

We can assume that this was also a design for the future annihilation of the old Political Bureau members and, in this way, a cover for all shameful acts of Stalin, acts which we are now considering.

Comrades, in order not to repeat errors of the past, the Central Committee has declared itself resolutely against the cult of the individual. We consider that Stalin was excessively extolled. However, in the past Stalin doubtless performed great services to the party, to the working class and to the international workers' movement.

This question is complicated by the fact that all this which we have just discussed was done during Stalin's life under his leadership and with his concurrence; here Stalin was convinced that this was necessary for the defense of the interests of the working classes against the plotting of enemies and against the attack of the imperialist camp. He saw this from the position of the interest of the working class, of the interest of the laboring people, of the interest of the victory of socialism and communism. We cannot say that these were the deeds of a giddy despot. He considered that this should be done in the interest of the party, of the working masses, in the name of the defense of the revolution's gains. In this lies the whole tragedy!

Comrades, Lenin had often stressed that modesty is an absolutely integral part of a real Bolshevik. Lenin himself was the living personification of the greatest modesty. We cannot say that we have been following this Leninist example in all respects. It is enough to point out that many towns, factories and industrial enterprises, *kolkhozes* and *sovkhozes*, Soviet institutions and cultural institutions have been referred to by us with a title—if I may express it so—of private property of the names of these or those Government or party leaders who were still active and in good health. Many of us participated in the action of assigning our names to various towns, *rayons*, undertakings and *kolkhozes*. We must correct this. [Applause.]

But this should be done calmly and slowly. The Central Committee will discuss this matter and consider it carefully in order to prevent errors and excesses. I can remember how the Ukraine learned about Kossior's arrest. The Kiev radio used to start its programs thus: "This is Radio (in the name of) Kossior." When one day the programs began without naming Kossior, everyone was quite certain that something had happened to Kossior, that he probably had been arrested.

Thus, if today we begin to remove the signs everywhere and to change names, people will think that these comrades in whose honor the given enterprises, *kolkhozes* or cities are named also met some bad fate and that they have also been arrested. [Animation in the hall.]

How is the authority and the importance of this or that leader judged? On the basis of how many towns, industrial enterprises and factories, *kolkhozes* and *sovkhozes* carry his name. Is it not about time that we eliminate this "private property" and "nationalize" the factories, the industrial enterprises, the *kolkhozes* and the *sovkhozes?* [Laughter, applause, voices: "That is right."] This will benefit our cause. After all, the cult of the individual is manifested also in this way.

We should, in all seriousness, consider the question of the cult of the individual. We cannot let this matter get out of the party, especially not to the press. It is for this reason that we are considering it here at a closed Congress session. We should know the limits; we should not give ammunition to the enemy; we should not wash our dirty linen before their eyes. I think that the delegates to the Congress will understand and assess properly all these proposals. [Tumultuous applause.]

Comrades, we must abolish the cult of the individual decisively, once and for all; we must draw the proper conclusions concerning both ideological-theoretical and practical work. It is necessary for this purpose:

First, in a Bolshevik manner to condemn and to eradicate the cult of the individual as alien to Marxism-Leninism and not consonant with the principles of party leadership and the norms of party life, and to fight inexorably all attempts at bringing back this practice in one form or another.

To return to and actually practice in all our ideological work the most important theses of Marxist-Leninist science about the people as the creator of history and as the creator of all material and spiritual good of humanity, about the decisive role of the Marxist party in the revolutionary fight for the transformation of society, about the victory of communism.

In this connection we will be forced to do much work in order to examine critically from the Marxist-Leninist viewpoint and to correct the widely spread erroneous views connected with the cult of the individual in the sphere of history, philosophy, economy and of other sciences, as well as in literature and the fine arts. It is especially necessary that in the immediate future we compile a serious textbook of the history of our party which will be edited in accordance with scientific Marxist objectivism, a textbook of the history of Soviet society, a book pertaining to the events of the Civil War and the Great Patriotic War.

Secondly, to continue systematically and consistently the work done by the party's Central Committee during the last years, a work characterized by minute observation in all party organizations, from the bottom to the top, of the Leninist principles of party leadership, characterized, above all, by the main principle of collective leadership, characterized by the observation of the norms of party life described in the statutes of our party, and, finally, characterized by the wide practice of criticism and self-criticism.

Thirdly, to restore completely the Leninist principles of Soviet socialist democracy, expressed in the Constitution of the Soviet Union, to fight willfulness of individuals abusing their power. The evil caused by acts violating revolutionary socialist legality which have accumulated during a long time as a result of the negative influence of the cult of the individual has to be completely corrected.

Comrades, the 20th Congress of the Communist Party of the Soviet Union has manifested with a new strength the unshakable unity of our party, its cohesiveness around the Central Committee, its resolute will to accomplish the great task of building communism. [Tumultuous applause.] And the fact that we present in all their ramifications the basic problems of overcoming the cult of the individual which is alien to Marxism-Leninism, as well as the problem of liquidating its burdensome consequences, is an evidence of the great moral and political strength of our party. [Prolonged applause.]

We are absolutely certain that our party, armed with the historical resolutions of the 20th Congress, will lead the Soviet people along the Leninist path to new successes, to new victories. [Tumultuous, prolonged applause.]

Long live the victorious banner of our party—Leninism! [Tumultuous, prolonged applause ending in ovation. All rise.]

Appendix 36 STATUTE OF THE COMMUNIST PARTY
OF THE SOVIET UNION ADOPTED BY
THE TWENTY-SECOND PARTY CONGRESS,
OCTOBER, 1961 [1]

The Communist Party of the Soviet Union (CPSU) is the tried and tested militant vanguard of the Soviet people, which unites, on a voluntary basis, the more advanced, the politically more conscious section of the working class, collective-farm peasantry and intelligentsia of the USSR.

Founded by V. I. Lenin as the vanguard of the working class, the Communist party has travelled a glorious road of struggle, and has brought the working class and the working peasantry to the victory of the Great October Socialist Revolution and to the establishment of the dictatorship of the proletariat in the USSR. Under the leadership of the Communist party, the exploiting classes were abolished in the Soviet Union, and the moral and political unity of Soviet society has taken shape and grown in strength. Socialism has triumphed completely and finally. The Communist party, the party of the working class, has now become the party of the Soviet people as a whole.

The party exists for, and serves, the people. It is the highest form of socio-political organization, and is the leading and guiding force of Soviet society. It directs the great creative activity of the Soviet people, and imparts an organized, planned and scientifically-based character to their struggle to achieve the ultimate goal, the victory of communism.

The CPSU bases its work on the unswerving adherence to the Leninist standards of party life—the principle of collective leadership, the comprehensive development of inner-party democracy, the activity and initiative of the communists, criticism and self-criticism.

Ideological and organizational unity, monolithic cohesion of its ranks, and a high degree of conscious discipline on the part of all communists are an inviolable law of the CPSU. All manifestations of factionalism and clique activity are incompatible with Marxist-Leninist party principles, and with party membership.

In all its activities, the CPSU is guided by Marxist-Leninist theory and the Program based on it, which defines the fundamental tasks of the party for the period of the construction of communist society.

In creatively developing Marxism-Leninism, the CPSU vigorously combats all manifestations of revisionism and dogmatism, which are profoundly alien to revolutionary theory.

The CPSU is an integral part of the international communist and working-class movement. It firmly adheres to the tried and tested Marxist-Leninist principles of proletarian internationalism; it actively promotes the unity of the entire international communist and workers' movement, and of the fraternal ties with the great army of communists of all countries.

[1] *Pravda*, November 3, 1961, pp. 1–3.

I. PARTY MEMBERS, THEIR DUTIES AND RIGHTS

1. Membership in the CPSU is open to any citizen of the Soviet Union who accepts the Program and Statute of the Party, takes an active part in communist construction, works in one of the party organizations, carries out all party decisions, and pays membership dues.

2. It is the duty of a party member:

A. to work for the creation of the material and technical base of communism; to serve as an example of the communist attitude toward labor; to raise labor productivity; to take the initiative in all that is new and progressive; to support and propagate advanced methods; to master techniques; to improve his skills; to protect and increase socialist property, the mainstay of the might and prosperity of the Soviet country;

B. to put party decisions firmly and steadfastly into effect; to explain the policy of the party to the masses; to help strengthen and broaden the party's ties with the people; to be considerate and attentive to people; to respond promptly to the needs and requirements of the working people;

C. to take an active part in the political affairs of the country, in the administration of state affairs, and in economic and cultural development; to set an example in the fulfillment of his public duty; to assist in developing and strengthening communist social relations;

D. to master Marxist-Leninist theory, to improve his ideological knowledge, and to contribute to the molding and education of the man of communist society; to combat decisively all manifestations of bourgeois ideology, remnants of a private-property psychology, religious prejudices, and other survivals of the past; to observe the rules of communist morality, and to give public interest precedence over his own;

E. to be an active proponent of the ideas of socialist internationalism and Soviet patriotism among the masses of the working people; to combat survivals of nationalism and chauvinism; to contribute by word and by deed to the consolidation of the friendship of the peoples of the USSR and the fraternal bonds linking the Soviet people with the peoples of the socialist countries, with the proletarians and other working people in all countries;

F. to strengthen vigorously the ideological and organizational unity of the party; to safeguard the party against the infiltration of people unworthy of the lofty name of communist; to be truthful and honest with the party and people; to display vigilance, to guard party and state secrets;

G. to develop criticism and self-criticism, boldly to lay bare shortcomings and strive for their removal; to combat ostentation, conceit, complacency and parochial tendencies; firmly to rebuff all attempts at suppressing criticism; to resist all actions injurious to the party and the state, and to give information about them to party bodies, up to and including the Central Committee of the Communist Party of the Soviet Union (CC CPSU);

H. to implement undeviatingly the party's policy with regard to the proper selection of personnel according to their political and professional qualifications; to be uncompromising whenever the Leninist principles of the selection and education of personnel are infringed on;

I. to observe party and state discipline, which is equally binding on all party members. The party has one discipline, one law, for all communists, irrespective of their past services or the positions they occupy;

J. to assist vigorously in the strengthening of the defensive might of the USSR in order that the USSR may lead the tireless struggle for peace and friendship among nations.

3. A party member has the right:

A. to elect and be elected to party bodies;

B. to discuss freely questions of the party's policies and practical activities at party meetings, conferences and congresses, at the meetings of party committees and in the party press; to table motions; openly to express and uphold his opinion as long as the organization concerned has not adopted a decision;

C. to criticize any communist, irrespective of the position he holds, at party meetings, conferences, and congresses, and at the plenary meetings of party committees. Those who commit the offense of suppressing criticism or victimizing anyone for criticism are responsible to and will be penalized by the party, to the point of expulsion from the CPSU;

D. to attend in person all party meetings and all bureau and committee meetings that discuss his activities or conduct;

E. to address any question, statement or proposal to any party body, up to and including the CC CPSU, and to demand an answer on the substance of his address.

4. Applicants are admitted to party membership only individually. Membership in the party is open to politically conscious and active workers, peasants, and members of the intelligentsia devoted to the communist cause. New members are admitted from among the candidate members who have passed through the established probationary period. Persons may join the party on attaining the age of eighteen. Young people up to the age of twenty may join the party only through the Young Communist League (YCL).

The procedure for the admission of candidate members to full party membership is as follows:

A. applicants for party membership must submit recommendations from three party members who have a party standing of not less than three years and who know the applicants from having worked with them, professionally and socially, for not less than one year.

Note 1. In the case of members of the YCL applying for membership in the party, the recommendation of a district or city committee of the YCL is equivalent to the recommendation of one party member.

Note 2. Members and alternate members of the CC CPSU shall refrain from giving recommendations.

B. Applications for party membership are discussed and a decision is taken by the general meeting of the primary party organization; the decision of the latter takes effect after endorsement by the district party committee, or by the city party committee in cities with no district divisions.

The presence of those who have recommended an applicant for party membership at the discussion of the application concerned is optional.

C. Citizens of the USSR who formerly belonged to the Communist or Workers' Party of another country are admitted to membership of the CPSU in conformity with the rules established by the CC CPSU.

Former members of other parties are admitted to membership of the CPSU in conformity with the regular procedure, except that their admission must be endorsed by a regional or territorial committee or the CC of the Communist party of a union republic.

5. Communists recommending applicants for party membership are responsible to party organizations for the impartiality of their description of the political, professional, and moral qualifications of those they recommend.

6. The party standing of those admitted to membership dates from the day when the general meeting of the primary party organization decides to accept them as full members.

7. The procedure of registering members and candidate members of the party, and their transfer from one organization to another is determined by the appropriate instructions of the CC CPSU.

8. If a party member or candidate member fails to pay membership dues for three months in succession without sufficient reason, the matter shall be discussed by the primary party organization. If it is established, as a result, that the party member or candidate member in question has virtually lost contact with the party organization, he shall be regarded as having ceased to be a member of the party; the primary party organization shall pass a decision thereon and submit it to the district or city committee of the party for endorsement.

9. A party member who fails to fulfill his duties as laid down in the Statute or commits other offenses, shall be called to account, and may be subjected to the penalty of admonition, reprimand (or severe reprimand), with entry in the registration card. The highest party penalty is expulsion from the party.

Should the necessity arise, a party organization may, as a party penalty, reduce a party member to the status of candidate member for a period of up to one year. The decision of the primary party organization reducing a party member to candidate membership is subject to endorsement by the district or city party committee. On the expiration of his period of reduction to candidate membership, his readmission to full membership of the party will follow the regular procedure, with retention of his former party standing.

In the case of insignificant offenses, measures of party education and influence should be applied—in the form of comradely criticism, party censure, warning, or reproof.

When the question of expelling a communist member from the party is discussed, the maximum prudence and attention must be shown, and the grounds for the charges preferred against him must be thoroughly investigated.

10. The decision to expel a communist from the party is made by the general meeting of a primary party organization. The decision of the primary party organization expelling a member is regarded as adopted if not less than two-thirds of the party members attending the meeting have voted for it, and is endorsed by a district or city party committee. The decision of the district or city party committee expelling a member from the party takes effect after

endorsement by a regional or territorial committee or the CC of the Communist party of a union republic.

Until such time as the decision to expel him is endorsed by a regional or territorial party committee or the CC of the Communist Party of a union republic, the party member retains his membership or candidate membership card and is entitled to attend closed party meetings.

An expelled party member retains the right to appeal, within the period of two months, to the higher party bodies, up to and including the CC CPSU.

11. The question of calling a member or alternate member of the CC of the Communist party of a union republic, of a territorial, regional, area, city or district party committee, or of an inspection commission, to account before the party is discussed by primary party organizations.

Party organizations pass decisions imposing penalties on members or alternate members of the said party committees, or on members of inspection commissions, in conformity with the regular procedure.

A party organization which proposes expelling a communist from the CPSU communicates its proposal to the party committee of which he is a member. A decision to expel from the party a member or alternate member of the CC of the Communist party of a union republic or a territorial, regional, area, city or district party committee, or a member of an inspection commission, is taken at the plenary meeting of the committee concerned by a majority of two-thirds of the membership.

The decision to expel from the party a member or alternate member of the CC CPSU, or a member of the Central Inspection Commission (CIC), is made by the party congress, and in the interval between two congresses, by a plenary meeting of the CC, by a majority of two-thirds of the membership.

12. Should a party member commit an indictable offense, he shall be expelled from the party and prosecuted in conformity with the law.

13. Appeals against expulsion from the party or against the imposition of a penalty, as well as the decisions of party organizations on expulsion from the party shall be examined by the appropriate party bodies within not more than one month from the date of their receipt.

II. CANDIDATE MEMBERS

14. Those joining the party must pass through a probationary period as candidate members in order to familiarize themselves with the Program and Statute of the CPSU and prepare for admission to full membership of the party. Party organizations must assist candidates to prepare for admission to full membership of the party, and test their personal qualities. Probationary membership shall be one year.

15. The procedure for the admission of candidate members (individual admission, submission of recommendations, decision of the primary organization as to admission, and its endorsement) is identical with the procedure for the admission of party members.

16. On the expiration of a candidate member's probationary period the

primary party organization discusses and passes a decision on his application for admission to full membership. Should a candidate member fail, in the course of his probationary period, to show his worthiness, and should he prove, by his personal qualities, that he cannot be admitted to membership in the CPSU, the party organization shall pass a decision rejecting his admission to membership in the party; after endorsement of that decision by the district or city party committee, he shall cease to be considered a candidate member of the CPSU.

17. Candidate members of the party must participate in all the activities of their party organizations; they shall have a consultative voice at party meetings. They may not be elected to any leading party body, nor may they be elected delegates to a party conference or congress.

18. Candidate members of the CPSU pay membership dues at the same rate as full members.

III. ORGANIZATIONAL STRUCTURE OF THE PARTY. INNER-PARTY DEMOCRACY

19. The guiding principle of the organizational structure of the party is democratic centralism, which signifies:

A. election of all leading party bodies, from the lowest to the highest;

B. periodic reports of party bodies to their party organizations and to higher bodies;

C. strict party discipline and subordination of the minority to the majority;

D. the unconditionally binding nature of the decisions of the higher bodies upon lower ones.

20. The party is built on the territorial-industrial principle: Primary organizations are established wherever communists are employed, and are associated territorially in district, city, etc., organizations. An organization serving a given area is higher than any party organization serving part of that area.

21. All party organizations are autonomous in the decisions of local questions, unless their decisions conflict with party policy.

22. The highest leading body of a party organization is the general meeting (in the case of primary organizations); the conference (in the case of district, city, area, regional or territorial organizations); or the congress (in the case of the Communist Parties of union republics and the CPSU).

23. The general meeting, conference or congress elects a bureau or committee which acts as its executive body and directs all the current work of the party organization.

24. The election of party bodies shall be effected by secret ballot. In an election, all party members have the unlimited right to challenge candidates and to criticize them. Each candidate shall be voted upon separately. A candidate is considered elected if more than one-half of those attending the meeting, conference, or congress has voted for him.

25. The principle of systematic renewal of the composition of party bodies and of continuity of leadership shall be observed in the election of those bodies.

At each regular election, not less than one-quarter of the composition of the CC CPSU and its Presidium shall be renewed. Members of the Presidium shall not, as a rule, be elected for more than three successive terms. Particular party officials may, by virtue of their generally recognized prestige and high political, organizational and other qualities, be successively elected to leading bodies for a longer period. In that case, a candidate is considered elected if not less than three-quarters of the votes are cast for him by secret ballot.

The composition of the CC of the Communist parties of the union republics, and of the territorial and regional party committees shall be renewed by not less than one-third at each regular election; the composition of the area, city and district party committees and of the committees or bureaus of primary party organizations, by one-half. Furthermore, members of these leading party bodies may be elected successively for not more than three terms, and the secretaries of primary party organizations, for not more than two terms.

A meeting, conference, or congress may, in consideration of the political and professional qualities of a person, elect him to a leading body for a longer period. In such cases a candidate is considered elected if not less than three-quarters of the communists attending vote for him.

Party members not re-elected to a leading party body on the expiration of their term may be re-elected at subsequent elections.

26. A member or alternate member of the CC CPSU must by his entire activity justify the great trust placed in him by the party. A member or alternate member of the CC CPSU who does not uphold his honor and dignity may not remain a member of the CC. The question of the removal of a member or alternate member of the CC CPSU from that body shall be decided by a plenary meeting of the CC by secret ballot. The decision is regarded as adopted if not less than two-thirds of the membership of the CC CPSU vote for it.

The question of the removal of a member or alternate member of the CC of the Communist party of a union republic, or of a territorial, regional, area, city or district party committee from the party body concerned is decided by a plenary meeting of that body. The decision is regarded as adopted if not less than two-thirds of the membership of the committee in question vote for it by secret ballot.

A member of the CIC who does not justify the great trust placed in him by the party shall be removed from the Commission. This question shall be decided by a meeting of the CIC. The decision is regarded as adopted if not less than two-thirds of the membership of the CIC have voted by a secret ballot for the removal from that body of the member or alternate member concerned.

The question of the removal of a member from the inspection commission of a republican, territorial, regional, area, city or district party organization shall be decided by a meeting of the appropriate commission according to the procedure established for members and alternate members of party committees.

27. The free and business-like discussion of questions of party policy in individual party organizations or in the party as a whole is the inalienable right of every party member and is an important principle of inner-party democracy. Only on the basis of inner-party democracy is it possible to develop criticism

and self-criticism and to strengthen party discipline, which must be conscious and not mechanical.

Discussion of controversial or insufficiently clear issues may be held within the framework of individual organizations or the party as a whole.

Party-wide discussion is necessary:

A. if the necessity is recognized by several party organizations at regional or republican level;

B. if there is not a sufficiently solid majority in the CC on major questions of party policy;

C. if the CC CPSU considers it necessary to consult the party as a whole on any particular questions of policy.

Wide discussion, especially discussion on a countrywide scale, of questions of party policy must be held so as to insure for party members the free expression of their views and preclude attempts to form factional groupings destroying party unity, attempts to split the party.

28. The highest principle of party leadership is collectivism, which is an absolute requisite for the normal functioning of party organizations, the proper education of personnel, and the promotion of the activity and initiative of communists. The cult of the individual and the violations of inner-party democracy resulting from it must not be tolerated in the party; they are incompatible with the Leninist principles of party life.

Collective leadership does not exempt persons in office from their responsibility for the job entrusted to them.

29. The CC of the Communist Parties of union republics, and territorial, regional, area, city and district party committees shall in the period between congresses and conferences, systematically inform party organizations of their work.

30. Meetings of the most active members of districts, city, area, regional and territorial party organizations and of the Communist Parties of union republics shall be held to discuss major decisions of the party and to work out practical measures for their execution, as well as to examine questions of local significance.

IV. HIGHER PARTY ORGANS

31. The supreme organ of the CPSU is the party congress. Congresses are convened at least once in four years. The convocation of a party congress shall be announced at least six weeks before the congress. Extraordinary congresses are convened by the CC of the party on its own initiative or on the demand of not less than one-third of the total membership represented at the preceding party congress. Extraordinary congresses shall be convened within two months. A congress is considered properly constituted if not less than one-half of the total party membership is represented at it.

The norms of representation at a party congress are determined by the CC.

32. Should the CC of the party fail to convene an extraordinary congress within the period specified in article 31, the organizations which demanded it

have the right to form an organizing committee which shall enjoy the powers of the CC of the party with respect to the convocation of the extraordinary congress.

33. The congress:

A. hears and approves the reports of the CC, of the CIC, and of the other central organizations;

B. reviews, amends and endorses the Program and the Statute of the party;

C. determines the line of the party in matters of domestic and foreign policy, and examines and decides the most important questions of communist construction;

D. elects the CC and the CIC.

34. The number of members to be elected to the CC and to the CIC is determined by the congress. In the event of vacancies occurring in the CC, they are filled from among the alternate members of the CC CPSU elected by the congress.

35. Between congresses the CC CPSU directs the activities of the party and the local party bodies; selects and appoints leading functionaries; directs the work of central government bodies and social organizations of working poeple through the party groups in them; sets up various party organs, institutions, and enterprises and directs their activities; appoints the editors of the central newspapers and journals operating under its control; and distributes the funds of the party budget and controls its execution.

The CC represents the CPSU in its relations with other parties.

36. The CC CPSU shall keep the party organizations regularly informed of its work.

37. The CIC supervises the expeditious and proper handling of business by the central bodies of the party, and audits the accounts of the treasury, and the enterprises of the CC CPSU.

38. The CC CPSU shall hold not less than one plenary meeting every six months. Alternate members of the CC shall attend its plenary meetings with consultative voice.

39. The CC CPSU elects a Presidium to direct the work of the CC between plenary meetings and a Secretariat to direct current work, chiefly the selection of personnel and the verification of the fulfillment of party decisions, and sets up a Bureau of the CC CPSU for the Russian Soviet Federated Socialist Republic (RSFSR).

40. The CC CPSU organizes the Party Control Committee of the CC.

The Party Control Committee of the CC of the CPSU:

A. verifies the observance of party discipline by members and candidate members of the CPSU, and takes action against communists who violate the Program and the Statute of the Party, and party or state discipline, and against violators of party ethics;

B. considers appeals against decisions of CC's of the Communist Parties of union republics or of territorial and regional Party committees to expel members from the party or impose party penalties upon them.

V. REPUBLICAN, TERRITORIAL, REGIONAL, AREA, CITY AND DISTRICT ORGANIZATIONS OF THE PARTY

41. The republican, territorial, regional, area, city and district party organizations and their committees take guidance in their activities from the Program and the Statute of the CPSU, conduct all work for the implementation of party policy, and organize the fulfillment of the directives of the CC CPSU within the republics, territories, regions, areas, cities and districts concerned.

42. The basic duties of republican, territorial, regional, area, city and district party organizations, and of their leading bodies, are:

A. political and organizational work among the masses; mobilization of the masses for the fulfillment of the tasks of communist construction, for the maximum development of industrial and agricultural production, for the fulfillment and over-fulfillment of state plans; solicitude for the steady improvement of the material and cultural standards of the working people;

B. organization of ideological work; propaganda of Marxism-Leninism; promotion of the communist awareness of the working people, guidance of the local press, radio and television; and control over the activities of cultural and educational institutions;

C. guidance of Soviets, trade unions, the YCL, the cooperatives and other public organizations through the party groups in them, and increasingly broader enlistment of working people in the activities of these organizations; development of the initiative and activity of the masses as an essential condition for the gradual transition from socialist statehood to public self-government under communism.

Party organizations must not act in place of government, trade union, cooperative or other public organizations of the working people; they must not allow either the merging of the functions of party and other bodies or undue parallelism in work;

D. selection and appointment of leading personnel, their education in the spirit of communist ideas, honesty and truthfulness, and a high sense of responsibility to the party and the people for the work entrusted to them;

E. large-scale enlistment of communists in the conduct of party activities as non-staff workers, as a form of social work;

F. organization of various institutions and enterprises of the party within the bounds of the respective republic, territory, region, area, city or district, and guidance of their activities; distribution of party funds within the given organization; systematic information of the higher party body and accountability to it for their work.

LEADING BODIES OF REPUBLICAN, TERRITORIAL AND REGIONAL PARTY ORGANIZATIONS

43. The highest body of regional, territorial and republican party organizations is the respective regional or territorial party conference or the congress of the communist party of the union republic, and in the interim between their

meetings the regional committee, territorial committee, or the CC of the communist party of the union republic.

44. Regional and territorial party conferences, and congresses of the communist parties of union republics, are convened by the respective regional or territorial committees or the CC of the communist parties of union republics once every two years, and extraordinary conferences and congresses are convened by decision of regional or territorial committees, or the CC of the Communist Parties of union republics, or on the demand of one-third of the total membership of the organizations belonging to the regional, territorial or republican party organization. Congresses of communist parties of those union republics divided into regions (the Ukraine, Belorussia, Kazakhstan and Uzbekistan) may be convened once in four years.

The norms of representation at regional and territorial conferences and at congresses of communist parties of union republics are determined by the respective party committees.

Regional and territorial conferences and congresses of the communist parties of union republics hear and act upon the reports of the respective regional or territorial committee, or the CC of the Communist Party of the union republic, and of the Inspection Commission; discuss at their own discretion other matters of party, economic and cultural development, and elect the regional or territorial committee, the CC of the union republic, the Inspection Commission and the delegates to the congress of the CPSU.

45. The regional and territorial committees, and the CC of the Communist Parties of union republics elect bureaus, which also include secretaries of the committees. The secretaries must have a party standing of not less than five years. The plenary meetings of the committees also confirm the chairmen of party commissions, heads of departments of these committees, editors of party newspapers and journals.

Regional and territorial committees and the CC of the Communist Parties of union republics may set up secretariats to examine current business and verify the execution of decisions.

46. The plenary meetings of regional and territorial committees and the CC of the Communist Parties of union republics shall be convened at least once every four months.

47. The regional and territorial committees and the CC of the Communist Parties of union republics direct the activities of area, city and district party organizations, inspect their work, and regularly hear reports of area, city and district party committees.

Party organizations in autonomous republics, and in autonomous and other regions forming part of a territory or union republic, function under the guidance of the respective territorial committees or CC of the Communist Parties of union republics.

LEADING BODIES OF AREA, CITY AND DISTRICT (URBAN AND RURAL) PARTY ORGANIZATIONS

48. The highest body of an area, city or district party organization is the area, city and district party conference or the general meeting of communists

convened by the area, city or district committee at least once in two years, and the extraordinary conference convened by decision of the respective committee or on the demand of one-third of the total membership of the party organization concerned.

The area, city or district conference (general meeting) hears reports of the committee and inspection commission, discusses at its own discretion other questions of party, economic and cultural development, and elects the area, city and district committee, the inspection commission and delegates to the regional and territorial conference or the congress of the communist party of the union republic.

The norms of representation at area, city and district conferences are determined by the respective party committees.

49. The area, city or district committee elects a bureau, which includes the secretaries of the committee, and confirms the appointment of heads of committee departments and newspaper editors. The secretaries of the area, city and district committees must have a party standing of at least three years. The committee secretaries are confirmed by the respective regional or territorial committee, or the CC of the Communist Party of the union republic.

50. The area, city and district committee organizes and confirms the primary party organizations, directs their work, regularly hears reports concerning the work of party organizations, and keeps a register of communists.

51. The plenary meeting of the area, city and district committee is convened at least once in three months.

52. The area, city and district committee has non-staff instructors, sets up permanent or *ad hoc* commissions on various aspects of party work and uses other ways to draw communists into the activities of the party committee on social lines.

VI. PRIMARY PARTY ORGANIZATIONS

53. The primary party organizations are the basis of the party.

Primary party organizations are formed at the places of work of party members—in factories, on state farms and at other enterprises, collective farms, units of the Soviet Army, offices, educational establishments, etc., wherever there are not less than three party members. Primary party organizations may also be organized on the residential principle in villages and at house administrations.

54. Shop, sectional, farm, team, departmental, etc., party organizations may be formed at units of the general primary party organization, with the sanction of the area, city or district committee, at enterprises, collective farms and institutions with over 50 Party members and candidate members.

Within shop, sectional, etc., organizations, and also within primary party organizations having less than 50 members and candidate members, party groups may be formed in the teams and other production units.

55. The highest organ of the primary party organization is the party meeting, which is convened at least once a month.

In large party organizations with a membership of more than 300 Communists a general party meeting is convened when necessary at times fixed by the party committee or on the demand of a number of shop or departmental party organizations.

56. For the conduct of current business the primary, shop or departmental party organization elects a bureau for the term of one year.

The number of its members is fixed by the party meeting. Primary, shop and departmental party organizations with less than 15 party members do not elect a bureau. Instead, they elect a secretary and deputy secretary of the party organization.

Secretaries of primary, shop and departmental party organizations must have a party standing of at least one year.

Primary party organizations with less than 150 party members shall have, as a rule, no salaried functionaries released from their regular work.

57. In large factories and offices with more than 300 members and candidate members of the party, and in exceptional cases in factories and offices with over 100 communists by virtue of special production conditions and territorial dispersion, subject to the approval of the regional committee, territorial committee or CC of the Communist Party of the union republic, party committees may be formed, the shop and departmental party organizations at these factories and offices being granted the status of primary party organizations.

The party organizations of collective farms may set up party committees if they have a minimum of 50 communists.

The party committees are elected for the term of one year. Their numerical composition is determined by the general party meeting or conference.

58. In its activities the primary party organization takes guidance from the Program and the Statute of the CPSU. It conducts its work directly among the working people, rallies them around the CPSU, organizes the masses to carry out the party policy and to work for the building of communism.

The primary party organization:

A. enrolls new members to the CPSU;

B. educates communists in a spirit of loyalty to the party cause, ideological staunchness and communist ethics;

C. organizes the study by communists of Marxist-Leninist theory in close connection with the practice of communist construction and opposes all attempts to introduce revisionist distortions into Marxism-Leninism and its dogmatic interpretation;

D. insures the vanguard role of communists in the sphere of labor and in the socio-political and economic activities of enterprises, collective farms, institutions, educational establishments, etc.;

E. acts as the organizer of the working people for the performance of the current tasks of communist construction; heads the socialist emulation movement for the fulfillment of state plans and undertakings of the working people; rallies the masses to disclose and make the best use of untapped resources at enterprises and collective farms, and on a broad scale to apply in production the achievements of science, engineering and the experience of front-rankers; works for the strengthening of labor discipline, the steady increase of labor productivity and improvement of the quality of production, and shows concern for the protection and increase of social wealth at enterprises, state farms and collective farms;

F. conducts agitational and propaganda work among the masses, educates them in the communist spirit, helps the working people to acquire proficiency in administering state and social affairs;

G. on the basis of extensive criticism and self-criticism, combats cases of bureaucracy, parochialism, and violations of state discipline, thwarts attempts to deceive the state, acts against negligence, waste and extravagance at enterprises, collective farms and offices;

H. assists the area, city and district committees in their activities and is accountable to them for its work.

The party organization must see to it that every communist observes in his own life and cultivates among working people the moral principles set forth in the Program of the CPSU—the moral code of a builder of communism:

—loyalty to the communist cause, love of his own socialist country, and of other socialist countries;

—conscientious labor for the benefit of society: He who does not work, neither shall he eat;

—concern on everyone's part for the protection and increase of social wealth;

—a lofty sense of public duty, intolerance of violations of public interests;

—collectivism and comradely mutual assistance: one for all, and all for one;

—humane relations and mutual respect among people: Man is to man a friend, comrade and brother;

—honesty and truthfulness, moral purity, unpretentiousness and modesty in public and personal life;

—mutual respect in the family circle and concern for the upbringing of children;

—intolerance of injustice, parasitism, dishonesty, careerism, and profiteering;

—friendship and fraternity among all peoples of the USSR, intolerance of national and racial hostility;

—intolerance of the enemies of communism, the enemies of peace and those who oppose the freedom of the peoples;

—fraternal solidarity with the working people of all countries, with all peoples.

59. Primary party organizations of industrial enterprises and trading establishments; state farms, collective farms; and design organizations, drafting offices and research institutes directly related to production enjoy the right to control the work of the administration.

The party organizations at ministries, state committees, economic councils and other central and local government or economic agencies and departments, whose function is not that of controlling the administration, must actively promote the improvement of the apparatus, cultivate among the personnel a high sense of responsibility for work entrusted to them, work for the strengthening of state discipline and for the better servicing of the population, firmly combat bureaucracy and red tape, inform the appropriate party bodies in good time of shortcomings in the work of the respective offices and individuals, regardless of what posts the latter may occupy.

VII. THE PARTY AND THE YCL

60. The Leninist YCL of the Soviet Union is a voluntary social organization of young people, an active helper and reserve of the party. The YCL helps the party educate the youth in the communist spirit, draws it into the work of building a new society, trains a rising generation of harmoniously developed people who will live and work and administer public affairs under communism.

61. YCL organizations enjoy the right of broad initiative in discussing and submitting to the appropriate party organizations questions related to the work of enterprises, collective farms and offices. They must be really active in the implementation of party directives in all spheres of communist construction, especially where there are no primary party organizations.

62. The YCL conducts its activities under the guidance of the CPSU. The work of the local YCL organizations is directed and controlled by the appropriate republican, territorial, regional, area, city and district party organizations.

63. Members of the YCL, admitted to the CPSU, cease to belong to the YCL the moment they join the party, provided they do not hold leading posts in YCL organizations.

VIII. PARTY ORGANIZATIONS IN THE SOVIET ARMY

64. Party organizations in the Soviet Army take guidance in their work from the Program and the Statute of the CPSU and operate on the basis of instructions issued by the CC.

The party organizations of the Soviet Army carry out the policy of the party in the Armed Forces; rally servicemen around the Communist party; educate them in the spirit of Marxism-Leninism and boundless loyalty to the socialist homeland; actively further the unity of the army and the people; work for the strengthening of discipline; rally servicemen to carry out the tasks of military and political training and acquire skill in the use of new techniques and weapons, and irreproachably to perform their military duty and the orders and instructions of the command.

65. The guidance of party work in the Armed Forces is exercised by the CC of the CPSU through the Chief Political Administration of the Soviet Army and Navy, which functions as a department of the CC CPSU.

The chiefs of the political administrations of military areas and fleets, and chiefs of the political administrations of armies must be party members of five-years' standing, and the chiefs of political departments of military formations must be party members of three years' standing.

66. The party organizations and political bodies of the Soviet Army maintain close contact with local party committees, and keep them informed about

political work in the military units. The secretaries of military party organizations and chiefs of political bodies participate in the work of local party committees.

IX. PARTY GROUPS IN NON-PARTY ORGANIZATIONS

67. At congresses, conferences and meetings and in the elective bodies of Soviets, trade unions, cooperatives and other mass organizations of the working people, having at least three party members, party groups are formed for the purpose of strengthening the influence of the party in every way and carrying out party policy among non-party people, strengthening party and state discipline, combatting bureaucracy and verifying the fulfillment of party and government.

68. The party groups are subordinate to the appropriate party bodies: CC CPSU, the CC of the Communist parties of union republics, territorial, regional, area, city or district party committees.

In all matters the groups must strictly and unswervingly abide by decisions of the leading party bodies.

X. PARTY FUNDS

69. The funds of the party and its organizations are derived from membership dues, income from party enterprises and other revenue.

70. The monthly membership dues for party members and candidate members are as follows:

Monthly Earnings	Dues	
up to 50 rubles	10 kopeks	
from 51 to 100 rubles	0.5 per cent	
from 101 to 150 rubles	1.0 per cent	
from 151 to 200 rubles	1.5 per cent	of the
from 201 to 250 rubles	2.0 per cent	monthly
from 251 to 300 rubles	2.5 per cent	earnings
over 300 rubles	3.0 per cent	

71. An entrance fee of 2 per cent of monthly earnings is paid on acceptance into the party as a candidate member.

Appendix 37 OFFICIAL ANNOUNCEMENTS OF THE
OUSTER OF N. S. KHRUSHCHEV AND
THE APPOINTMENT OF L. I. BREZHNEV
AND A. N. KOSYGIN, OCTOBER 14, 1964 [1]

1. *Communique on the Plenary Session of the Central Committee of the CPSU.*

A plenary session of the Central Committee of the CPSU was held on October 14, 1964.

The plenary session of the CC of the CPSU granted the request of C[omrade] N. S. Khrushchev that he be released from the duties of First Secretary of the CC of the CPSU, member of the Presidium of the CC of the CPSU and Chairman of the Council of Ministers of the USSR, in view of his advanced age and deterioration of his health.

The plenary session of the CC of the CPSU elected C[omrade] L. I. Brezhnev First Secretary of the CC of the CPSU.

2. *In the Presidium of the Supreme Soviet of the USSR.*

A session of the Presidium of the Supreme Soviet of the USSR was held on October 15, 1964 under the chairmanship of Comrade A. I. Mikoyan, Chairman of the Presidium of the Supreme Soviet of the USSR.

The Presidium of the Supreme Soviet of the USSR discussed the matter of of the Chairman of the Council of Ministers of the USSR.

The Presidium of the Supreme Soviet of the USSR granted the request of Comrade Nikita Sergeevich Khrushchev that he be released from the duties of Chairman of the Council of Ministers of the USSR, in view of his advanced age and deterioration in the state of his health.

The Presidium of the Council of Ministers of the USSR appointed Comrade Alexei Nikolaevich Kosygin Chairman of the Council of Ministers of the USSR, and released him from the duties of First Vice Chairman of the Council of Ministers of the USSR.

The decrees of the Presidium of the Supreme Soviet of the USSR on releasing Comrade N. S. Khrushchev from the duties of Chairman of the Council of Ministers of the USSR and on appointing Comrade N. S. Kosygin Chairman of the Council of Ministers of the USSR were adopted unanimously by the members of the Presidium of the Supreme Soviet of the USSR.

Members of the Presidium of the Supreme Soviet of the USSR warmly congratulated Comrade A. N. Kosygin on his appointment to the post of Chairman of the Council of Ministers of the USSR.

Comrade A. N. Kosygin heartily thanked the Central Committee of the Communist Party of the Soviet Union and the Presidium of the Supreme Soviet of the USSR for the confidence shown in him and pledged to exert every effort to perform the duties entrusted to him.

[1] *Pravada*, October 16, 1964, p. 1. Translation by Basil Dmytryshyn.

3. *Decree of the Presidium of the Supreme Soviet of the USSR Appointing Comrade N. S. Kosygin Chairman of the Council of Ministers of the USSR.*

Comrade Alexei Nikolaevich Kosygin is appointed Chairman of the Council of Ministers of the USSR and is released from the duties of First Vice Chairman of the Council of Ministers of the USSR.

> A. Mikoyan, Chairman of the Presidium
> of the Supreme Soviet of the USSR
> M. Georgadze, Secretary of the
> Presidium of the Supreme Soviet of
> the USSR

4. *Decree of the Presidium of the Supreme Soviet of the USSR Releasing Comrade N. S. Khrushchev from the Duties of Chairman of the Council of Ministers of the USSR.*

The request of Comrade Nikita Sergeevich Khrushchev that he be released from the duties of Chairman of the Council of Ministers of the USSR in view of his advanced age and deterioration of the state of his health is granted.

> A. Mikoyan, Chairman of the Presidium
> of the Supreme Soviet of the USSR
> M. Georgadze, Secretary of the
> Presidium of the Supreme Soviet of
> the USSR

Moscow, The Kremlin, October 15, 1964

Appendix 38 SOVIET WARNING TO CZECHOSLOVAKIA, JULY 15, 1968 [1]

TO THE CENTRAL COMMITTEE
OF THE COMMUNIST PARTY
OF CZECHOSLOVAKIA

Dear comrades!

On behalf of the Central Committees of the Communist and Workers' Parties of Bulgaria, Hungary, the German Democratic Republic, Poland and the Soviet Union, we address ourselves to you with this letter, prompted by a feeling of sincere friendship based on the principles of Marxism-Leninism and proletarian internationalism and by the concern for our common affairs, for strengthening the positions of socialism and the security of the socialist community of nations.

The development of events in your country evokes in us deep anxiety. It is our firm conviction that the offensive of the reactionary forces, backed by imperialism, against your Party and the foundations of the social system in the Czechoslovak Socialist Republic, threatens to push your country off the road of socialism and that consequently it jeopardises the interests of the entire socialist system.

We expressed these apprehensions at the meeting in Dresden, during repeated bilateral meetings, as well as in letters which our Parties sent in the recent period to the Presidium of the Central Committee of the Communist Party of Czechoslovakia.

Recently we offered the Presidium of the Central Committee of the Communist Party of Czechoslovakia to hold a new joint meeting on July 14th this year so as to exchange information and opinions on the state of affairs in our countries, including the development of events in Czechoslovakia. Unfortunately, the CPC Central Committee Presidium did not take part in this meeting and did not use the opportunity for a collective comradely discussion of the situation that has developed. That is why we thought it necessary to state for you in this letter, with complete sincerity and frankness, our common opinion. We want you to understand us well and assess our intentions correctly.

We neither had nor have any intention of interfering in such affairs as are strictly the internal business of your Party and your state, nor of violating the principles of respect, independence and equality in the relations among the Communist Parties and socialist countries.

We are not coming before you as representatives of the past, who would like to interfere in the correction of mistakes and shortcomings, including the violations of socialist law which have taken place.

[1] *Moscow News*, Supplement to No. 30 (917), 1968, pp. 3–6.

We are not interfering in the methods of planning and management of the socialist national economy of Czechoslovakia, and in your actions aimed at improving the structure of the economy and developing socialist democracy.

We shall hail the settlement of relations between Czechs and Slovaks on healthy foundations of friendly cooperation within the framework of the Czechoslovak Socialist Republic.

At the same time we cannot agree to have hostile forces push your country from the road of socialism and create a threat of severing Czechoslovakia from the socialist community. This is no longer only your cause. It is the common cause of all the Communist and Workers' Parties and states united by alliance, cooperation and friendship. This is the common cause of our countries, which have joined in the Warsaw Treaty to ensure independence, peace and security in Europe, and to set up an insurmountable barrier against the intrigues of the imperialist forces, against aggression and revenge.

At the price of tremendous losses the peoples of our countries gained the victory over hitlerite fascism, won freedom and independence and an opportunity to follow the road of progress and socialism. The frontiers of the socialist world have moved to the centre of Europe, to the Elbe and Sumava mountains. And we shall never agree to have these historical gains of socialism, independence and security of all our peoples being put to threat. We shall never agree to have imperialism, using peaceful or non-peaceful methods, making a gap from the inside or from the outside in the socialist system, and changing in imperialism's favour the correlation of forces in Europe.

The might and firmness of our alliances depend on the inner strength of the socialist system in each of our brother countries, on the Marxist-Leninist policy of our Parties who discharge the leading role in the political and social life of their respective nations and states. Hamstringing of the leading role of the Communist Party leads to the liquidation of socialist democracy and the socialist system. That in itself constitutes a threat to the foundations of our alliance and the safety of the community of our countries.

You are aware of the understanding with which the fraternal Parties treated the decisions of the January Plenary Meeting of the Central Committee of the Communist Party of Czechoslovakia, as they believed that your Party, firmly controlling the levers of power, would direct the entire process in the interests of socialism, and not let anti-communist reaction exploit it to its own ends. We shared the conviction that you would protect the Leninist principle of democratic centralism as the apple of your eye. For the flouting of any aspect of this principle, democracy or centralism, inevitably serves to weaken the Party and its guiding role, by transforming the Party into either a bureaucratic organisation or a debating club. We discussed all these matters time and again at the meetings we had, and received from you assurances that you are aware of all the dangers and are fully resolved to repulse them.

Unfortunately events have taken another course.

Capitalising on the weakening of Party leadership of the country, and demagogically abusing the slogan of "democratisation," the forces of reaction unleashed a campaign against the Communist Party of Czechoslovakia and its honest and devoted cadres, clearly seeking to abolish the Party's leading role, subvert the socialist system, and place Czechoslovakia in opposition to the other socialist countries.

The political organisations and clubs that have emerged of late outside the framework of the National Front have become, in effect, headquarters of the forces of reaction. The Social Democrats are doggedly striving to establish their own party, are organising underground committees, and are seeking to split the working class movement in Czechoslovakia, and to take over the leadership of the country in order to effect a bourgeois restoration. Anti-socialist and revisionist forces have laid hand on the press, radio and television, making of them a rostrum for attacking the Communist Party, disorientating the working class and all working folk, for unbridled anti-socialist demagogy, and for undermining the friendly relations between the Czechoslovak Socialist Republic and the other socialist countries. Some mass communication media are carrying on a systematic campaign of real moral terror against people opposing the forces of reaction or voicing anxiety over the trend of developments.

Despite the decisions of the May Plenary Meeting of the Central Committee of the Communist Party of Czechoslovakia, which indicated the threat emanating from right-wing and anti-communist forces as the main danger, the increasing attacks that reaction has mounted have not met with any rebuff. This is precisely why reaction has been able to publicly address the entire country and to print its political platform under the title of "The 2,000 Words" which contain an outright call for struggle against the Communist Party and constitutional authority, for strikes and disorders. This call represents a serious danger to the Party, the National Front and the socialist state and is an attempt to introduce anarchy. In essence this statement is the organisational and political platform of counter-revolution. The claims made by its writers that they do not seek to overthrow the socialist system, operate without the Communists or rupture alliances with the socialist countries, should kid nobody. This is empty talk, the purpose of which is to legalise the platform of counter-revolution and hoodwink the vigilance of the Party, the working class and all the working folk.

Far from being repudiated, this platform, being so extensively circulated at a responsible moment, on the eve of the extraordinary Congress of the Communist Party of Czechoslovakia, has, on the contrary, also found obvious advocates in the Party rank-and-file and leadership, who support the anti-socialist calls.

Anti-socialist and revisionist forces smear all the activities of the Communist Party, wage a slander campaign against its cadres, and discredit Communists honest and loyal to the Party.

A situation has thus arisen which is absolutely unacceptable for a socialist country.

It is in this atmosphere that attacks are also being made on the CSSR socialist foreign policy, attacks are being undertaken on the alliance and friendship with socialist countries. Voices are heard demanding a revision of our common coordinated policy as regards the FRG, despite the fact that the West German Government invariably pursues a policy hostile to the interests of the security of our countries. The attempts at flirtation of the FRG authorities and revenge-seekers meet with a response among leading circles of your country.

The entire course of events in your country in recent months shows that the forces of counter-revolution, supported by imperialist centres, have developed a broad offensive on the socialist system without meeting due resistance on the part of the Party and the people's power. There is no doubt that the centres of international imperialist reaction are also involved in these events in Czechoslovakia, and are doing everything to inflame and aggravate the situation, and inspiring anti-socialist forces to act in this direction. The bourgeois press under the pretext of praising "democratisation" and "liberalisation" in the CSSR is waging an instigative campaign against the fraternal socialist countries. FRG ruling quarters are especially active, attempting to use the events in Czechoslovakia to sow discord between the socialist countries, to isolate the GDR and carry out their revenge-seeking designs.

Don't you, comrades, see these dangers? Is it possible under such conditions to remain passive, to limit oneself to mere declarations and assurances of loyalty to the cause of socialism and allied obligations? Don't you see that counter-revolution is wresting from you one position after another, that the Party is losing control over the course of events and is further retreating under the pressure of anti-communist forces?

Is it not for the purpose of sowing distrust and enmity towards the Soviet Union and other socialist countries that the press, radio and television of your country unleashed a campaign in connection with the staff exercises of the Armed Forces of the Warsaw Treaty Organisation? Matters went as far as this, that the joint staff exercises of our troops with the participation of several units of the Soviet Army, customary for military cooperation, are being used for groundless accusations of violating the sovereignty of the CSSR. And this is taking place in Czechoslovakia, whose people sacredly honour the memory of Soviet servicemen who gave their lives for the freedom and sovereignty of that country. At the same time near the western borders of your country exercises of military forces of the NATO aggressive bloc are being conducted with the participation of the army of revenge-seeking Western Germany. But not a single word is mentioned about this.

The inspirers of this unfriendly campaign apparently wish to confuse the minds of the Czechoslovak people, disorient them and undermine this truth that Czechoslovakia can retain her independence and sovereignty only as a socialist country, as a member of the socialist community. And only the enemies of socialism can today speculate on the slogan of "defending the sovereignty" of the CSSR from the socialist countries, from those countries with whom alliance and fraternal cooperation create a most reliable foundation of the independence and free development of each of our peoples.

It is our conviction that a situation has arisen, in which the threat to the foundations of socialism in Czechoslovakia jeopardises the common vital interests of other socialist countries. The peoples of our states would never forgive us for being indifferent and careless in the face of such a danger.

We are living in such a time when peace, security and the freedom of peoples more than ever demand the unity of the forces of socialism. The international tension is not relaxing. American imperialism has not rejected its policy of force and open intervention against the peoples fighting for freedom. It continues its criminal war in Vietnam, supports Israeli aggressors in the Near East, and hampers a peaceful settlement of the conflict. The arms race has not been slowed down. The Federal Republic of Germany, in which the neo-fascist forces are growing, is attacking the status quo, demanding the revision of the borders, does not want to give up its aspirations either for seizing the GDR or for getting access to nuclear weapons, and opposes the disarmament proposals. In Europe, where tremendous means of mass destruction have been accumulated, the peace and security of peoples are maintained first of all thanks to the power, unity and peace-loving policy of the socialist states. All of us are responsible for this power and unity of the socialist countries, and for the destiny of peace.

Our countries are linked with one another by treaties and agreements. These important mutual obligations of states and peoples are based on the general aspiration to defend socialism and ensure collective security of the socialist countries. Historic responsibility rests on our parties and peoples, that the revolutionary gains should not be lost.

Each of our Parties is responsible not only to its working class and its people, but also to the international working class, and the world communist movement, and cannot evade the obligations following from this. Therefore, we must be solid and united in defending the gains of socialism, our security and the international positions of the whole of the socialist community.

That is why we believe that a decisive rebuff to the anti-communist forces, and decisive efforts for the preservation of the socialist system in Czechoslovakia are not only your task but ours as well.

The cause of defending the power of the working class and all working people, of the socialist gains in Czechoslovakia demands a decisive and bold offensive against the right-wing and anti-socialist forces, and the mobilisation of all means of defence created by the socialist state; the stopping of the activity of all political organisations coming out against socialism; the mastery by the Party of the means of mass information— press, radio, television—and the use of them in the interests of the working class, all working people and socialism; the closing of the ranks of the Party itself on the principled basis of Marxism-Leninism, undeviating observation of the principle of democratic centralism, and the struggle against those who help the inimical forces by their activity.

We are aware that forces exist in Czechoslovakia which are capable of defending the socialist system and inflicting defeat on the anti-socialist elements. The working class, the toiling peasantry, the front-rank intelligentsia —the overwhelming majority of the working people of the Republic are ready to do everything necessary for the sake of the further development of the socialist society. The task today is to provide these healthy forces with a clear-cut perspective, to stir them to action, to mobilise their energy for the struggle against the forces of counter-revolution in order to safeguard and consolidate socialism in Czechoslovakia.

In the face of the danger of counter-revolution and in response to the appeal of the Communist Party, the voice of the working class should ring out in full might. The working class, together with the toiling peasantry, exerted the greatest effort for the sake of the triumph of the socialist revolution. It is precisely they who cherish most of all the safeguarding of the gains of socialism.

We express the conviction that the Communist Party of Czechoslovakia, conscious of its responsibility, will take the necessary steps to block the path of reaction. In this struggle you can count on the solidarity and all-round assistance of the fraternal socialist countries.

Signed by: Todor Zhivkov   Wladyslaw Gomulka
Stanko Todorov   Marian Spychalski
Boris Velchev   Jozef Cyrankiewicz
Pencho Kubadinsky Zenon Kliszko
Janos Kadar   L. I. Brezhnev
Jenö Fock   N. V. Podgorny
Walter Ulbricht   A. N. Kosygin
Willi Stoph   P. E. Shelest
Herman Axen   K. F. Katushev

Warsaw, July 15, 1968

Appendix 39 PETITION ON CZECHOSLOVAKIA BY
P. G. GRIGORENKO AND I. YAKHIMOVICH,
FEBRUARY, 1969 [1]

To the Citizens of the Soviet Union:

The campaign of self-immolation started by Prague student Jan Palach on January 16, 1969, as a protest against interference in the internal affairs of the CzSSR is not abating. One more live torch, the latest so far, burned in St. Wenceslas Square in Prague on February 21.

This protest, which has taken so horrible a form, is addressed primarily to us, the Soviet people. It is the unsolicited and completely unjustified presence of our troops that brings forth such anger and despair, among the Czechoslovak people. Not in vain has Jan Palach's death aroused the entire working people of Czechoslovakia.

We all bear some part of the guilt for his death and for the deaths of other Czechoslovak brothers who have committed suicide. By approving the armed forces' intervention, by justifying it, or by simply remaining silent, we contribute to the continued burning of live torches in the squares of Prague and other cities. The Czechs and the Slovaks have always considered us their brothers. How, then, can we permit the word "Soviet" to become for them synonymous with the word "enemy"?

Citizens of our great country!

The greatness of a country lies not in the might of its armed forces brought down upon a numerically small, freedom-loving nation, but in its moral strength.

Shall we then continue to look on in silence while our brothers perish?

It is now clear to all that the presence of our troops on the territory of the CzSSR is based neither on the defense of our fatherland nor on the interests of the countries of the socialist community.

Is it possible that we lack the courage to admit that a tragic mistake has been made and to do everything in our power to correct it?! It is our right and our duty!

We call on all the Soviet people to use every legal means, without taking hasty and ill-considered action, to bring about the withdrawal of Soviet troops from Czechoslovakia and the renunciation of interference in her internal affairs! Only thus can the friendship between our peoples be restored.

[1] U.S. Congress. 91st Congress, 1st Session. Committee on Government Operations. *Czechoslovakia and the Brezhnev Doctrine.* (Washington: Government Printing Office, 1969), pp. 58–59.

594

Long live the heroic Czechoslovak people!
Long live Soviet-Czechoslovak friendship!

Piotr Grigorenko
Ivan Yakhimovich

Moscow
February, 1969

Appendix 40 SINO-SOVIET VERSIONS OF THEIR 1969 TERRITORIAL DISPUTE

A. NOTE OF THE MINISTRY OF FOREIGN AFFAIRS OF THE PEOPLE'S
REPUBLIC OF CHINA TO THE SOVIET EMBASSY IN CHINA, MARCH 2, 1969

On the morning of March 2, 1969, Soviet frontier guards intruded into the area of Chenpao Island, Heilunkiang Province, China, and killed and wounded many Chinese frontier guards by opening fire on them, thus creating an extremely grave border armed conflict. Against this, the Ministry of Foreign Affairs of the People's Republic of China is instructed to lodge the strongest protest with the Soviet Government.

At 09:17 hours on March 2, large numbers of fully armed soldiers, together with four armoured vehicles and cars, sent out by the Soviet frontier authorities, flagrantly intruded into the area of Chenpao Island which is indisputable Chinese territory, carried out blatant provocations against the Chinese frontier guards on normal patrol duty and were first to open cannon and gun fire, killing and wounding many Chinese frontier guards. The Chinese frontier guards were compelled to fight back in self-defence when they reached the end of their forbearance after their repeated warnings to the Soviet frontier guards had produced no effect. This grave incident of bloodshed was entirely and solely created by the Soviet authorities. It is another grave new crime perpetrated by the Soviet authorities which have long been deliberately encroaching upon China's territory, carrying out armed provocations and creating ceaseless incidents of bloodshed.

The Chinese Government firmly demands that the Soviet Government punish the culprits of this incident and immediately stop its encroachment upon China's territory and its armed provocations, and reserves the right to demand compensation from the Soviet side for all the losses suffered by the Chinese side. The Chinese Government once again sternly warns the Soviet Government: China's sacred territory brooks no violation; if you should wilfully cling to your reckless course and continue to provoke armed conflicts along the Sino-Soviet border, you will certainly receive resolute counterblows from the Chinese people; and it is the Soviet Government that must bear full responsibility for all the grave consequences arising therefrom.

[1] *Peking Review*, No. 10, March 7, 1969, pp. 5–7; No. 11, March 14, 1969, p. 5; and No. 33, August 15, 1969, p. 3.

B. TO: THE MINISTRY OF FOREIGN AFFAIRS OF THE U.S.S.R.

After creating the grave incident of armed provocation on Chinese territory of Chenpao Island, the Soviet authorities went still farther and organized a despicable anti-China demonstration before the Embassy of the People's Republic of China at 13:30 hours on March 7. The Soviet authorities collected a group of ruffians who grossly insulted and abused the great leader of the Chinese people Chairman Mao Tse-tung and the Chinese people, barbarously damaged the buildings of the Chinese Embassy, wrecked its newsphoto display cases and threw iron objects and fired air-guns at embassy personnel, thus seriously hampering the normal functioning of the Embassy and seriously menacing the personal safety of its personnel. The Embassy of the People's Republic of China hereby lodges a strong protest against the new anti-China provocation made by the Soviet authorities before the Chinese Embassy and demands that they immediately stop this anti-China farce solely stage-managed by them and compensate for all the losses of the Chinese Embassy caused by the ruffians' sabotaging activities.

It must be pointed out that the above grave new anti-China provocation engineered by the Soviet authorities is a continuation of the armed provocation against China on the Sino-Soviet border which they plotted single-handedly. The Soviet authorities must be held fully responsible for their anti-China crime which has further worsened Sino-Soviet relations.

The Embassy of the People's Republic of China
in the Soviet Union

Moscow
March 7, 1969

C. TO: EMBASSY OF THE U.S.S.R. IN CHINA

On the morning of August 13, 1969, the Soviet side sent two helicopters, dozens of tanks and armoured vehicles and several hundred armed troops to intrude into the Tiehliekti area in Yumin County of the Sinkiang Uighur Autonomous Region, China, who penetrated a depth of two kilometers, unwarrantedly fired at the Chinese frontier guards on normal patrol duty, killing and wounding many of them on the spot, and closed in on them. Driven beyond the limits of forbearance, the Chinese frontier guards were compelled to fight back in self-defence. At present, the Soviet side is continuing to amass large numbers of troops and tanks in an attempt to provoke still larger armed conflicts; the situation is developing.

The Chinese Government hereby lodges a strong protest with the Soviet Government against its deliberate intrusion into Chinese territory and provocation of a fresh incident of bloodshed, and demands that the Soviet Government immediately withdraw all its intruding troops from Chinese territory and immediately stop its firing. Otherwise, the Soviet Government must be held fully responsible for all the grave consequences arising therefrom.

Ministry of Foreign Affairs of the
People's Republic of China

Peking
August 13, 1969

D. A STATEMENT BY THE SOVIET GOVERNMENT ON BORDER CLASHES, MARCH 29, 1969 [1]

Armed border incidents provoked by the Chinese side have taken place lately in the area of Damansky Island on the Ussuri River. The Chinese authorities did not and could not have any justification for organizing such incidents, for clashes and bloodshed. Such events can please only those who would like by any means to dig a chasm of hostility between the Soviet Union and the Chinese People's Republic. They have nothing in common with the fundamental interests of the Soviet and Chinese peoples.

I.-The circumstances of the armed attacks on the Soviet border guards on the Ussuri River are well known. These were premeditated actions planned in advance.

On the morning of March 2, 1969, an observation post discovered that the Soviet border at Damansky Island had been violated by about 30 Chinese servicemen. A group of Soviet border guards headed by an officer set out to meet the intruders with the intention of lodging a protest and demanding that they leave Soviet territory, as had been done on previous occasions. The Chinese servicemen let the Soviet border guards approach within a few meters of them and then suddenly, with no warning whatever, opened fire at them at point-blank range.

Simultaneously, from an ambush on Damansky Island—to which the Chinese soldiers had secretly advanced beforehand under cover of darkness—and from the Chinese bank, fire was opened from artillery, mortar, and automatic weapons on another group of Soviet border guards near the Soviet bank, who returned the fire and, with the support of a neighboring border post, drove the intruders from Soviet territory. This treacherous attack resulted in dead and wounded on both sides.

Despite a warning by the Soviet government and an appeal to refrain from such provocations, on March 14 and 15 the Chinese side made new attempts at an armed incursion into the Soviet Union in the same area. Regular Chinese army groups supported by artillery and mortar fire attacked the Soviet border

---

[1] *Izvestia*, March 30, 1969. Translation copyright 1969 by *The Current Digest of the Soviet Press*, published weekly at The Ohio State University by The American Association for the Advancement of Slavic Studies; reprinted by permission of the Digest.

troops guarding Damansky Island. The attack was resolutely repulsed, and the intruders were thrown off Soviet territory. This provocation by the Chinese side brought new casualties.

In their statements the Chinese authorities are now trying to divest themselves of responsibility for the armed clashes. They allege that it was not Chinese, but Soviet border guards who violated the state frontier and that the island does not belong to the Soviet Union. The Chinese side does not deny that its military personnel acted in accordance with a prepared plan, although by resorting to a false allegation, it seeks to present the Chinese intruders' use of arms as a "measure of necessity."

The Chinese statements imply that the question of Damansky Island is just part of a still-unsolved territorial problem supposedly inherited from the past and involving the redemarcation of the state borders. At the same time the Chinese government refuses to take into account the existing treaties between China and the U.S.S.R., ignores the long-standing practice of Soviet-Chinese interstate relations and garbles history to suit its own territorial claims.

Obviously, all this stems from the fundamental change that has taken place in recent years in the C.P.R.'s policy toward the Soviet Union and the Soviet people.

As we know, Chinese official propaganda in general questions the present borders of China's neighboring states, within which an historical communality took shape long ago among the peoples inhabiting them. Claims to adjacent territories are advanced under the pretext that there was once a dispute over them among some feudal lords, Chinese emperors, and tsars, or that Chinese conquerors or merchants had once been there.

History is full of examples of those who laid claim to the territories of others and proclaimed some feudal conquerors of the past to be "just" and others "unjust". Such an approach to invaders, to oppressors of the people, is alien to Leninist policy.

II.-The Soviet-Chinese border in the Far East, as it now exists, took shape many generations ago and runs along natural frontiers dividing the territories of the Soviet Union and China. This border was given legal status in the Treaties of Aigun (1858), Tientsin (1858) and Peking (1860). In 1861 the two sides signed and affixed their state seals to a map showing the line of demarcation in the Ussuri region. In the area of Damansky Island this line passes directly along the Chinese bank of the Ussuri River. The originals of the abovementioned documents are in the possession of both the Soviet and Chinese states.

The provisions on territorial questions set down in these treaties, as well as in protocols, maps and descriptions, are still fully valid today. The Soviet government takes a position of strict and unswerving fulfillment of these provisions by the two sides. If the C.P.R. government takes the same position on this question, then there is no basis for friction and conflicts on the Soviet-Chinese border.

After the victory of the great October Socialist Revolution in Russia, the Republic of the Soviets solemnly renounced the unequal and secret treaties with China, Tsarist Russia's spheres of influence in China and extraterritorial and consular jurisdiction rights. It took the Russian share of the tribute exacted from China by the imperialist states after the suppression of the so-called Boxer rebellion and earmarked it for educational needs in China, liquidated the former Russian concessions in China and returned the right of way of the Chinese Eastern Railroad to China. The annulment of the above-mentioned treaties was legally formalized in the May 31, 1924, agreement on general principles for the settlement of issues between the Soviet Union and China. This agreement did not say that the Russian-Chinese treaties defining the state border were unequal or secret. No mention was made of annulling or revising them.

The great Chinese democratic revolutionary Sun Yat-sen stressed repeatedly that the Soviet government had voluntarily annulled all unequal treaties and had renounced all of the Tsarist government's unjust claims and rights in China. In Sun Yat-sen's political testament of March 12, 1925, he expressed the hope regarding the Soviet and Chinese peoples that the U.S.S.R. and a free China would unite in a mighty alliance and that they would move hand in hand toward victory in the great struggle for the liberation of oppressed peoples.

It is appropriate to recall here that the leaders of the Communist Party of China, and later the C.P.R. government, repeatedly emphasized that since the October Revolution the Soviet state had based its relations with China on principles of equality and respect for the sovereign rights of the Chinese people. At the Seventh C.P.C. Congress in 1945 Mao Tse-tung observed that "the Soviet Union was the first to renounce unequal treaties and to conclude new, equal treaties with China." Mao Tse-tung said this again in Moscow on Dec. 16, 1949.

And so, the question of some sort of unequal treaties in Soviet-Chinese relations—a question that Chinese propaganda importunately harps on over and over—is a fabrication from beginning to end. Propaganda coming out of Peking has a single purpose—to sow enmity and hostility among the Chinese people toward our country and the Soviet people.

The historical picture would be incomplete if we neglected to mention the Soviet people's heroic struggle under the leadership of the Communist Party and V. I. Lenin personally to liberate the Soviet Far East from the foreign interventionists in 1918–1922, who tried to wrest Maritime Territory, Khabarovsk Territory and Eastern Siberia from the young Soviet republic. Soviet people defended their Far Eastern lands at the cost of immense efforts and sacrifices.

In subsequent years the Japanese militarists and their accomplices also attempted more than once to test the firmness of the Soviet frontiers in the Far East. After occupying Manchuria, they tried to seize the islands belonging to the Soviet Union on the Amur and Ussuri Rivers. At times these islands were the sites of serious armed clashes in which the Japanese aggressors were crushingly rebuffed.

Of course, the point was not the islands but the Japanese imperialists' more serious claims on the sacred and inviolable frontiers of the Soviet Union and its ally, the Mongolian People's Republic. The end result of all this is common knowledge: First near Khasan, then near Khalkhin-Gol, the aggressors were utterly defeated and driven out.

After the Soviet Army defeated militarist Japan in 1945, a peaceful atmosphere was established on the Ussuri and Amur Rivers for the first time in many years.

The victory of the Chinese Revolution and the formation of the Chinese People's Republic created all the preconditions for the development of good-neighbor relations and lasting peace on Soviet-Chinese borders. In accordance with the Treaty of Friendship, Alliance and Mutual Aid between the U.S.S.R. and the C.P.R., which was concluded in 1950, the two sides structured their relations on the principles of "mutual respect for state sovereignty and territorial integrity." At the Chinese side's request, in the early 1950's the Soviet Union gave the C.P.R. complete sets of topographic maps showing the demarcation line. At the time the Chinese authorities made no objections to the boundary as drawn on the maps, and this line was observed in practice.

Taking into account the national-economic needs of both countries, in 1951 a Soviet-Chinese agreement was signed on navigation procedure along the Amur, Ussuri, Argun and Sungacha border rivers and Lake Khanka, as well as the establishment of conditions for navigating these waterways. The agreement on this specific economic question is based completely on the aforementioned treaties that established the borders between the two countries. On the basis of this agreement, normal shipping was conducted along these waterways in a spirit of cooperation.

The population living on the two sides of the border maintained friendly relations among themselves and developed border trade and cultural and other ties. In a businesslike manner Soviet and Chinese border guards settled the issues that arose, and there were no misunderstandings requiring the intervention of central bodies.

The Chinese authorities displayed interest in using some of the Soviet islands on the Ussuri and Amur Rivers for economic and industrial purposes (haymaking, logging, etc.) and in enabling Chinese fishermen to fish in the Soviet sections of the rivers. They applied to the competent Soviet bodies to obtain permission to this effect. These requests received favorable consideration and were granted by the Soviet side. This procedure of asking permission to use Soviet islands and the Soviet river sections—a procedure the Chinese authorities followed for many years—is part of the evidence that the Chinese side did not question the fact that the islands, including Damansky Island, belong to the Soviet Union.

III.-The Soviet government, faithful to Lenin's behests, has done everything in its power to strengthen Soviet-Chinese friendship and cooperation.

The foundation of this friendship was laid back in the years when the Soviet Union was rendering broad and all-around assistance to the Chinese people in their struggle for national and social liberation. The Soviet Republic's assistance to the revolutionary forces of China in 1923–1927 and the political, economic and military support the Soviet Union gave to China in repulsing the Japanese imperialists' aggression in 1937–1945 are striking pages in the history of Soviet-Chinese relations and the fraternal ties between the working people of our two countries. It was the Soviet Army that dealt a crushing defeat to the Japanese militarists' crack Kwantung grouping and thereby made an outstanding contribution to the liberation of China from Japanese occupation.

The Soviet Union's broad and comprehensive assistance to the people of China and the Chinese Communists in winning the victory of the people's revolution, which resulted in the formation of the Chinese People's Republic, was a genuine manifestation of proletarian internationalism. In December, 1949, Mao Tse-tung stated: "For almost 30 years the Soviet people and the Soviet government have time and again aided the cause of liberating the Chinese people. This fraternal friendship that the Soviet people and the Soviet government proffered to the Chinese people during the grim ordeals will never be forgotten."

It can be said without exaggeration that the Soviet Union—its loans, shipments of the latest industrial equipment and the sharing, at the Chinese government's request, of a vast amount of scientific and technical experience free of charge—helped China to create a modern industrial base and to lay the economic foundations for socialism. Thousands of Soviet specialists labored in China itself, hand in hand with Chinese workers and engineers, to establish a number of industries that were completely new to China—aircraft construction, the motor vehicle industry, radio engineering and many others. Thousands of Chinese citizens received vocational training in the Soviet Union's educational institutions and in Soviet plants and laboratories. Jenmin Jihpao, the newspaper of the C.P.C. Central Committee, stressed in February, 1959, when it was still writing the truth about our country, that Soviet aid to China "is unprecedented in scope. The Chinese people have always believed that Soviet aid has been among the most important factors in achieving rapid progress in our country."

During that period Soviet-Chinese trade was developing on a very broad scale; by 1959 its annual volume had reached almost 2,000,000,000 rubles. This was equitable and mutually advantageous cooperation. Had it not been for the Chinese side's position, trade, economic and scientific-technical cooperation between our countries could undoubtedly have developed further. This still holds true today.

In the international arena the Soviet Union and China struggled together against imperialism and for the consolidation of international security. Whenever the C.P.R.'s security was threatened, the Soviet Union, true to its obligations under the Treaty of Friendship, Alliance and Mutual Aid, unfailingly supported people's China and together with it thwarted the imperialist circles' aggressive plans.

IV.-This good-neighbor cooperation, which embodied the principles of socialist internationalism, was upset as a result of the changes in the Chinese government's domestic and foreign policies in the early 1960s. The border situation also began to deteriorate at that time. At first these were small, minor violations of existing border regulations and were as a rule committed by the civilian population or, at any rate, by people not wearing military uniform. In certain areas Chinese servicemen attempted an ostentatious violation of the Soviet Union's state border. Concurrently, in regions bordering on the U.S.S.R., construction was begun on airfields, access roads, barracks and military supply depots.

Official Chinese propaganda began openly to sing the praises of the expansionist campaigns against the peoples of Asia and Europe waged by Genghis Khan, who has been declared the "emperor of China"; the Manchu emperor Kang-Hsi; and Chinese emperors and feudal lords who pursued aggressive policies. In the same vein school textbooks and other C.P.R. publications were rewritten, and maps were published on which vast territories of the Soviet Union were shown as Chinese. On some maps depicting China "during the period of its greatest power," the border was drawn in such a way as to incorporate within China lands now inhabited by almost all peoples of Asia and even many European peoples.

During this period the Soviet government took a good many constructive steps to avert the spread of border frictions and to ease their acuteness. To this end, on May 17, 1963, the Soviet government proposed to the C.P.R. government that bilateral consultations be held between our states. These consultations began in February, 1964, in Peking. The Soviet delegation was headed by P. I. Zyryanov, a U.S.S.R. plenipotentiary with the rank of Deputy Minister, and the Chinese delegation was headed by Deputy Foreign Minister Tseng Yung-chuan.

The Soviet side presented proposals whose adoption permitted (sic) clarification through mutual agreement, in the shortest possible time, of the Soviet-Chinese state boundary line at some sectors. The Soviet delegation was guided by the consideration that successful conclusion of the consultations would be an important contribution to the cause of maintaining friendly relations between our peoples and states.

The conduct of the Chinese representatives at the 1964 consultations showed, however, that reaching an agreement did not enter into the Chinese side's plans. The C.P.R. delegation attempted to question the state border, which had been established historically and consolidated by treaties. The Chinese side considered that the point of the consultations was the artificial creation of a "territorial problem," which was to complicate relations between our peoples and countries for many years to come.

The consultations in Peking were not concluded. An agreement was reached, in principle, to continue them in Moscow on Oct. 15, 1964. However, despite repeated reminders from the Soviet side during this period and in subsequent years, the C.P.R. government avoided bringing these consultations to a conclusion.

Yet it would not have been much trouble to reach agreement and rule out misinterpretations and misunderstandings in the future. It required only that the Chinese side display goodwill and that the Chinese representatives act in the same spirit as Premier Chou En-lai showed, for example, when he spoke on April 28, 1960, at a press conference in Katmandu, capital of Nepal. In answering a correspondent's question about whether there were "areas where the borders between the U.S.S.R. and the C.P.R. were not fixed," he emphasized: "There are minor differences on the maps. It is very easy to settle this peacefully." Nonetheless, this statement was not backed by practical actions.

Not only did border violations by the Chinese side continue, but these violations also increased in number.

V.-Thus, the Chinese authorities' armed provocations on the Ussuri River in the area of Damansky Island are not fortuitous incidents. These actions, like the overall creation of tension on the Soviet-Chinese border, do serious damage to the cause of socialism and peace, to the common front of the anti-imperialist struggle and to the friendship between the Soviet and Chinese peoples.

Guided by an unswerving desire to ensure a stable peace and security and maintain friendship and cooperation with the Chinese people, the Soviet government believes it is imperative to take immediate practical measures to normalize the situation on the Soviet-Chinese border. It calls on the C.P.R. government to refrain from actions on the border that could cause complications and urges the settlement of disagreements, if they arise, in a calm atmosphere and through negotiations.

The Soviet government also advocates that Soviet and Chinese official representatives resume in the immediate future the consultations started in Peking in 1964.

The Soviet government is firmly convinced that in the final analysis the fundamental interests of the Soviet and Chinese peoples will make it possible to eliminate and overcome the difficulties in Soviet-Chinese relations.

The U.S.S.R. government has stated and deems it necessary to state again that it resolutely rejects any encroachments by anyone on Soviet lands. And attempts to talk with the Soviet Union and the Soviet people in the language of weapons will meet with a firm rebuff.

The Soviet people unanimously support the Leninist foreign policy of the Communist Party of the Soviet Union and the U.S.S.R. government and the measures taken to ensure the inviolability and security of our socialist homeland's sacred frontiers.

March 29, 1969

❊   ❊   ❊

The above statement by the U.S.S.R. government was officially transmitted to the C.P.R. government on March 29, 1969, through the Chinese Embassy in Moscow.

Appendix 41 BASIC PRINCIPLES OF RELATIONS
BETWEEN THE UNITED STATES OF
AMERICA AND THE UNION OF SOVIET
SOCIALIST REPUBLICS, MAY 29, 1972 [1]

The United States of America and the Union of Soviet Socialist Republics,

Guided by their obligations under the Charter of the United Nations and by a desire to strengthen peaceful relations with each other and to place these relations on the firmest possible basis,

Aware of the need to make every effort to remove the threat of war and to create conditions which promote the reduction of tensions in the world and the strengthening of universal security and international cooperation,

Believing that the improvement of US-Soviet relations and their mutually advantageous development in such areas as economics, science and culture, will meet these objectives and contribute to better mutual understanding and business-like cooperation, without in any way prejudicing the interests of third countries,

Conscious that these objectives reflect the interests of the peoples of both countries,

Have agreed as follows:

First. They will proceed from the common determination that in the nuclear age there is no alternative to conducting their mutual relations on the basis of peaceful coexistence. Differences in ideology and in the social systems of the USA and the USSR are not obstacles to the bilateral development of normal relations based on the principles of sovereignty, equality, non-interference in internal affairs and mutual advantage.

Second. The USA and the USSR attach major importance to preventing the development of situations capable of causing a dangerous exacerbation of their relations. Therefore, they will do their utmost to avoid military confrontations and to prevent the outbreak of nuclear war. They will always exercise restraint in their mutual relations, and will be prepared to negotiate and settle differences by peaceful means. Discussions and negotiations on outstanding issues will be conducted in a spirit of reciprocity, mutual accommodation and mutual benefit.

Both sides recognize that efforts to obtain unilateral advantage at the expense of the other, directly or indirectly, are inconsistent with these objectives. The prerequisites for maintaining and strengthening peaceful relations between the USA and the USSR are the recognition of the security interests of the Parties based on the principle of equality and the renunciation of the use or threat of force.

[1] *Weekly Compilation of Presidential Documents* (Washington D.C.: Office of the Federal Register, GSA., 1972), vol. 8, No. 23, pp. 943–44.

Third. The USA and the USSR have a special responsibility, as do other countries which are permanent members of the United Nations Security Council, to do everything in their power so that conflicts or situations will not arise which would serve to increase international tensions. Accordingly, they will seek to promote conditions in which all countries will live in peace and security and will not be subject to outside interference in their internal affairs.

Fourth. The USA and the USSR intend to widen the juridical basis of their mutual relations and to exert the necessary efforts so that bilateral agreements which they have concluded and multilateral treaties and agreements to which they are jointly parties are faithfully implemented.

Fifth. The USA and the USSR reaffirm their readiness to continue the practice of exchanging views on problems of mutual interest and, when necessary, to conduct such exchanges at the highest level, including meetings between leaders of the two countries.

The two governments welcome and will facilitate an increase in productive contacts between representatives of the legislative bodies of the two countries.

Sixth. The Parties will continue their efforts to limit armaments on a bilateral as well as on a multilateral basis. They will continue to make special efforts to limit strategic armaments. Whenever possible, they will conclude concrete agreements aimed at achieving these purposes.

The USA and the USSR regard as the ultimate objective of their efforts the achievement of general and complete disarmament and the establishment of an effective system of international security in accordance with the purposes and principles of the United Nations.

Seventh. The USA and the USSR regard commercial and economic ties as an important and necessary element in the strengthening of their bilateral relations and thus will actively promote the growth of such ties. They will facilitate cooperation between the relevant organizations and enterprises of the two countries and the conclusion of appropriate agreements and contracts, including long-term ones.

The two countries will contribute to the improvement of maritime and air communications between them.

Eighth. The two sides consider it timely and useful to develop mutual contacts and cooperation in the fields of science and technology. Where suitable, the USA and the USSR will conclude appropriate agreements dealing with concrete cooperation in these fields.

Ninth. The two sides reaffirm their intention to deepen cultural ties with one another and to encourage fuller familiarization with each other's cultural values. They will promote improved conditions for cultural exchanges and tourism.

Tenth. The USA and the USSR will seek to ensure that their ties and cooperation in all the above-mentioned fields and in any others in their mutual interest are built on a firm and long-term basis. To give a permanent character to these efforts, they will establish in all fields where this is feasible joint commissions or other joint bodies.

Eleventh. The USA and the USSR make no claim for themselves and would not recognize the claims of anyone else to any special rights or advantages in world affairs. They recognize the sovereign equality of all states.

The development of U.S.-Soviet relations is not directed against third countries and their interests.

Twelfth. The basic principles set forth in this document do not affect any obligations with respect to other countries earlier assumed by the USA and the USSR.

Moscow, May 29, 1972

For the United States of America
   Richard Nixon
      President of the United States of America

For the Union of Soviet Socialist Republics
   Leonid I. Brezhnev
      General Secretary of the Central Committee, CPSU

Appendix 42 SOVIET BLUEPRINT FOR A PEACE SETTLEMENT IN THE MIDDLE EAST, APRIL 29, 1976 [1]

The Soviet Government finds it necessary to again draw the attention of the Governments of all states the world over to the situation in the Middle East and the events taking place there. It is prompted to this action by the anxiety caused by the lengthy absence of a settlement of the Middle East conflict, by the Soviet Union's awareness of its international responsibility as a permanent member of the United Nations Security Council, and by a striving to facilitate a further relaxation of international tensions and the consolidation of universal peace.

1. For many years now Israel's armed forces have been occupying vast territories belonging to independent Arab states. A policy of racial discrimination and oppression is being conducted against the Arab population in these territories. The native inhabitants of the occupied lands are being driven from their homes, their dwellings being razed to clear ground for the establishment of settlements for citizens of an alien state—Israel. Those who resist this cruel occupation policy are subjected to arrests, deportation and other repressions. Step by step, the captured territories are being incorporated into the state of Israel. All this creates in the Middle East an atmosphere of a drawn-out and dangerous crisis.

Israel's ruling circles obstruct the implementation of the inalienable right of the Arab people of Palestine to create their own state. The three million Palestinian Arabs, who have the same right to such a course as any other people in the Middle East, or any other people anywhere in the world, continue to remain in the position of an exiled people. And all this despite the fact that their right to create their own state on the territory of Palestine was confirmed by the United Nations Organization and that the Palestine Liberation Organization is widely recognized as the lawful representative of this people and has the support of the popular masses in Israeli-occupied territories.

Israel's armaments are being further built up on a huge scale, with the United States sending over various modern arms, including rockets capable of carrying both conventional and nuclear warheads. Alarming in this respect are reports that Israel is producing or has already produced its own nuclear weapons. It is not difficult to see what a potential danger to peace this presents.

While last year's separate deals concerning some small sections of Israeli-occupied territories did create in some quarters the illusion of a calming down

[1] *Izvestiia,* April 29, 1976, as reproduced in *Reprints From the Soviet Press,* vol. 22, No. 11 (June 15, 1976), pp. 14–20.

in the Middle East, today everybody sees that these deals, which side-stepped cardinal questions of a Middle East settlement, have not only failed to defuse the situation but have even further aggravated it. Nothing demonstrates this as convincingly as the tragic and bloody events in and around Lebanon. These events have once again confirmed that unless resolute efforts are taken toward an all-embracing political settlement in the Middle East, the situation there can worsen still further, and every new day brings fresh evidence of this.

2. The situation in the Middle East conflict, so long as it remains unsettled, is fraught with the danger of a new military explosion. The obtaining situation means that the aggressor continues with impunity to reap the fruits of its criminal policy while the lawful interests and rights of the victims of aggression are further flouted. It is clear that there can be no stability and no tranquility in the Middle East on such a basis. The absence of a settlement of the conflict has already, within a comparatively short period of time, resulted in four separate military clashes between Israel and the Arab states. It would be naive to proceed from the assumption that this could not happen a fifth time. Meanwhile the potential consequences of a new war in the Middle East, including its consequences for the international situation as a whole, are obvious to all.

What gives even more grounds for alarm is that some states strive to put further and further off the solution of the main questions of the Middle East settlement and use wholly spurious arguments to justify this. First they say it is necessary to wait for the Presidential elections in the United States to be over, then that conditions for a Middle East settlement are simply not ripe at all.

The real aims of those who would like to put off the solution of the problem of a Middle East settlement indefinitely should be clear to any objectively minded person. The preservation of the status quo in the Middle East fully accords with their long-term plans for establishing their control over the Middle East area, over its tremendous oil resources and important strategic positions.

It is precisely for this reason that those who pursue aims which have nothing in common with the true interests of the peoples of the Middle East would like to weaken the Arab states to the maximum, push them off the road of progressive social development, range them against one another and compel them to act in disunity.

Who does not know that until recently the arsenal of imperialist policy in the Middle East included one main weapon—Israel's Zionist ruling circles, which are pursuing a policy of territorial expansion at the expense of the Arabs? Now, however, the aggressors and their patrons hope also to rely in their policy on some Arab states. But one can express confidence that in the final count the peoples of the Arab East will frustrate this plan, so hostile to the cause for which the Arabs are struggling, the cause of their independence and freedom.

Obvious attempts are being made to strike a blow at the forces of the Palestine Resistance Movement and draw Arabs into a fratricidal war against Arabs. This is the real meaning of the events in Lebanon. It is even more clearly emphasized by such provocative actions as the concentration of Israeli troops on Lebanon's southern borders and the sending of US naval ships to Lebanese shores although they have no business there.

Such is imperialism's Middle East policy, a policy of encouraging and supporting aggression, of weakening the positions of national progressive forces, of undermining their unity and asserting on this basis its domination in that area.

3. The Soviet Union is promoting a fundamentally different policy in questions related to the Middle East. It proceeds from the premise that the peoples of that area should be full masters of their destiny, should have the opportunity to live in conditions of independence, freedom and peace. That is precisely why the Soviet Union stands firmly for a radical political settlement of the Middle East conflict and believes that such a goal is attainable. The discussion in recent years of questions of the situation in the Middle East and the relevant decisions of the United Nations Security Council and General Assembly determined the basis on which such a settlement can and must be achieved. This basis consists of three organically interconnected elements:

—First, withdrawal of Israeli troops from all Arab territories occupied as a result of Israel's aggression in 1967;
—Second, satisfaction of the legitimate national demands of the Arab people of Palestine, including their inalienable right to establish their own state;
—Third, international guarantees for the security and inviolability of the frontiers of all Middle East states, and their right to independent existence and development.

These basic and interconnected aspects of a Middle East settlement take due account of the legitimate rights of all the sides directly concerned and create a just and realistic basis for settlement.

This is a just basis for the Arab states, victims of Israel's aggression, for it provides for returning to them the territories belonging to them, restores their sovereignty over these territories, and does away with the danger of a new aggression.

The peoples of the Arab countries would thus get an opportunity of concentrating their energies and resources on the solution of problems of economic and social development, and on eliminating the backwardness they inherited from colonialism. The Arab states will also be able to play a more important role in international affairs.

This is a just basis for settlement because it takes into account the right of the Palestinian Arab people to establish their own independent state. The Arab people of Palestine will at last leave the refugee camps, gain freedom from oppression by the invaders, and build their own state in their homeland.

This basis for a political settlement is also just to Israel because it ensures for it peace and security within its recognized frontiers. Its young people will no longer be sacrificed on the altar of war. The Israeli working people, the entire people of the state of Israel, will be able to live in conditions of confidence in the morrow. The state of Israel will get an opportunity to normalize its position among the other world states.

An overall and radical political settlement in the Middle East will bring peace and a chance of prosperity to all the peoples of the area. It will create a firm foundation for peace in the future, particularly considering the fact that within the framework of such a settlement it will be possible to find a solution to the problem of stopping the arms race in the Middle East, as is advocated by the Soviet Union.

Only those circles which cannot abandon the dangerous policy of brinkmanship in the Middle East can object to such a basis for a political settlement.

4. Not only is there a just and realistic basis for a settlement of the Middle East conflict. There is also an international mechanism for working out appropriate accords, namely, the Geneva Peace Conference on the Middle East.

No one denies that given the desire of the states concerned, the Geneva Peace Conference could lead to agreement on all aspects of settlement. Nor is this denied by the United States. What is more, an identity of view on this matter was several years ago made the basis of agreement on the convocation of the Geneva Conference. What is lacking now? The desire is lacking. This and this alone accounts for the fact that changing moods, determined by transient considerations, have been the dominant attitudes at the Geneva Conference in recent years. This refers, first of all, to the position of the USA and Israel with regard to the role of this Conference.

Hence the crux of the matter is not that the Geneva Peace Conference is not a suitable mechanism for a settlement of the conflict but that some elements are unwilling to put this mechanism into operation. This is exactly how matters stand if the entire question of the Geneva Conference and its role is stripped of falsity.

The Soviet Union comes out for the resumption of the Geneva Peace Conference with the participation of all the sides directly concerned, including the Palestine Liberation Organization as a representative of the Arab people of Palestine.

True, this calls for certain preparatory work. The Soviet Government understands this. It believes that the work of the Conference could be arranged in two stages. In the initial stage, it would solve all the organizational questions that may arise, including the procedure of considering the concrete aspects of settlement, the possibility of establishing appropriate working bodies, etc.

This stage would evidently not be a long one, and in the next phase the Conference could take up its basic task, that of finding solutions concerning the substance of the settlement problems. It goes without saying that representatives of the Palestine Liberation Organization should take part in the work of both stages of the Conference.

The Soviet Union is prepared without delay to appoint its representatives to attend both the preparatory and the basic phases of the Geneva Conference. The Soviet Government would like to hope that all the other sides concerned will adopt the same position. If, however, some Governments continue to obstruct the resumption of the Geneva Conference, they will naturally be assuming a serious responsibility for the consequences of such a policy.

5. Setting forth its considerations on the need for more active efforts toward a settlement of the Middle East conflict, the Soviet Government considers it necessary to stress that the Soviet Union does not seek any gains or advantages for itself in the Middle East. Neither in the Middle East nor in any other area of the world does it demand military bases or any rights to develop local natural

resources, nor an opportunity for itself to influence the internal development of the states concerned. The Soviet Union, loyal as it is to the ideal of solidarity with the peoples fighting for freedom and social progress, firmly supports, and intends to continue its firm support, for the just position of the Arab states, the Arab peoples.

Peace and tranquility in the Middle East are the goal of Soviet policy in the area. The Soviet Union is also interested in creating the conditions for the development of relations with all states of the Middle East. There are not, nor can there be, any prejudices against any of these states, including Israel, provided the latter drops its policy of aggression and takes the road of peace and good-neighbor relations with the Arabs.

Elimination of the dangerous source of tensions that remains in the Middle East is one of the top-priority tasks in the efforts to strengthen international peace and security. It is the duty of all states to contribute to the solution of this task. The Soviet Government urges the Governments of all states in the world to discharge this duty and to facilitate efforts to achieve a just and lasting political settlement in the Middle East.

Appendix 43 CONSTITUTION (FUNDAMENTAL LAW) OF THE UNION OF SOVIET SOCIALIST REPUBLICS [1]

PREAMBLE

The Great October Socialist Revolution, accomplished by the workers and peasants of Russia under the leadership of the Communist Party headed by Lenin, overthrew capitalist and landowner rule, broke the chains of oppression, established the dictatorship of the proletariat, and created the Soviet state, a new type of state, the basic instrument for defending the gains of the revolution and for building socialism and communism. Humanity thereby began the epoch-making turn from captialism to socialism.

After achieving victory in the Civil War and repulsing imperialist intervention, the Soviet Government carried through far-reaching social and economic transformations, and put an end once and for all to exploitation of man by man, antagonisms between classes, and strife between nationalities. The unification of the Soviet Republics into the Union of Soviet Socialist Republics multiplied the forces and opportunities of the peoples of the country in the building of socialism. Social ownership of the means of production and genuine democracy for the working masses were established. For the first time in the history of mankind a socialist society was created.

The strength of socialism was vividly demonstrated by the never-to-be forgotten feat of the Soviet people and their Armed Forces in achieving their historic victory in the Great Patriotic War. This victory consolidated the influence and international standing of the Soviet Union and created new opportunities for the growth of the forces of socialism, national liberation, democracy, and peace throughout the world.

Continuing their creative efforts, the working people of the Soviet Union have ensured the rapid, all-around development of the country and the steady improvement of the socialist system. They have consolidated the alliance of the working class, the collective-farm peasantry and the people's intelligentsia, and the friendship of the nations and nationalities of the USSR. The sociopolitical and ideological unity of Soviet society, in which the working class is the leading force, has now been achieved. The aims of the dictatorship of the proletariat having been fulfilled, the Soviet state has become a state of the whole people. The leading role of the Communist Party, the vanguard of all the people, has grown.

A developed socialist society has now been built in the USSR. At this stage, when socialism is developing on its own foundations, the creative forces of the

[1] *Pravda*, October 8, 1977, as reproduced in *Reprints From the Soviet Press,* vol. XXV, Nos. 8–9 (October 31–November 15, 1977), pp. 34–78.

new system and the advantages of the socialist way of life are becoming increasingly evident, and the working people are more and more widely enjoying the fruits of their great revolutionary gains.

It is a society wherein powerful productive forces, advanced science and a high culture have been created, where the well-being of the people is constantly rising, and more and more favorable conditions are being provided for the all-around development of the individual.

It is a society of mature socialist social relations, where, on the basis of the drawing together of all classes and social strata, and of the juridical and factual equality of all its nations and nationalities and their fraternal cooperation, a new historical community of people has been formed—the Soviet people.

It is a society where high organizational capacity, high ideological commitment and consciousness characterizes the working people, who are patriots and internationalists.

It is a society where the concern of all for the good of each and the concern of each for the good of all is the law of life.

It is a society of true democracy, the political system of which ensures effective management of all public affairs, ever more active participation by the working people in running the state, and the combining of citizens' real rights and freedoms with their obligations and responsibility to society.

Developed socialist society is an objectively necessary, law-governed stage on the road to communism.

The supreme goal of the Soviet state is the building of a classless communist society wherein there will be public, communist self-government. The main aims of the people's socialist state are: to lay the material and technical foundation of communism; to perfect socialist social relations and transform them into communist relations; to mold the citizen of communist society; to raise the people's living and cultural standards; to safeguard the country's security; and to further the consolidation of peace and the development of international cooperation.

The Soviet people,

guided by the ideas of scientific communism and true to their revolutionary traditions;

relying on the great social, economic, and political gains of socialism;

striving for the further development of socialist democracy;

taking into account the international position of the USSR as part of the world system of socialism, and conscious of their internationalist responsibility;

preserving the continuity of ideas and principles of the first Soviet Constitution of 1918, the 1924 Constitution of the USSR and the 1936 Constitution of the USSR;

hereby affirm the principles of the social structure and policy of the USSR, and define the rights, freedoms and obligations of citizens and the principles of the organization of the socialist state of the whole people, and its aims, and proclaim these in this Constitution.

I. PRINCIPLES OF THE SOCIAL STRUCTURE
AND POLICY OF THE USSR

CH. 1. THE POLITICAL SYSTEM

Article 1. The Union of Soviet Socialist Republics is a socialist state of the whole people, expressing the will and interests of the workers, peasants and intelligentsia, the working people of all the nations and nationalities of the country.

Article 2. All power in the USSR belongs to the people.

The people exercise state power through Soviets of People's Deputies, which constitute the political foundation of the USSR.

All other state bodies are under the control of, and accountable to, the Soviets of People's Deputies.

Article 3. The Soviet state is organized and functions on the principle of democratic centralism, namely, the electiveness of all bodies of state authority, from the lowest to the highest, their accountability to the people, and the obligation of lower bodies to carry out the decisions of higher ones. Democratic centralism combines central leadership with local initiative and creative activity and with the responsibility of each state body and each official for the work entrusted to them.

Article 4. The Soviet state and all its bodies function on the basis of socialist law, ensure the maintenance of law and order, and safeguard the interests of society and the rights and freedoms of citizens.

State organizations, public organizations and officials shall obey the Constitution of the USSR and Soviet laws.

Article 5. Major matters of state shall be submitted to nationwide discussion and put to a popular vote (referendum).

Article 6. The leading and guiding force in Soviet society and the nucleus of its political system, of all state organizations and public organizations, is the Communist Party of the Soviet Union. The CPSU exists for the people and serves the people.

The Communist Party, armed with Marxist-Leninist theory, determines the general perspectives of the development of society and the course of the domestic and foreign policy of the USSR, directs the great constructive work of the Soviet people, and imparts a planned, systematic and theoretically substantiated character to their struggle for the victory of communism.

All Party organizations shall function within the framework of the Constitution of the USSR.

Article 7. Trade unions, the All-Union Leninist Young Communist League (Komsomol), cooperatives, and other public organizations, participate, in accordance with the aims laid down in their rules, in managing state and public affairs and in deciding political, economic, and social and cultural matters.

Article 8. Work collectives take part in discussing and deciding state and public affairs, in planning production and social development, in training and placing personnel, and in discussing and deciding matters pertaining to the management of enterprises and institutions, the improvement of working and living conditions, and the use of funds allocated both for developing production and for social and cultural purposes and financial incentives.

Work collectives promote socialist emulation, the spread of advanced methods of work and the strengthening of production discipline, educate their members in the spirit of communist morality, and strive to enhance their political consciousness and raise their cultural level, skills and qualifications.

Article 9.   The principal direction in the development of the political system of Soviet society is the extension of socialist democracy, namely, the ever broader participation by citizens in managing the affairs of society and the state, a continuous improvement of the machinery of state, heightening of the activity of public organizations, strengthening of the system of people's control, consolidation of the legal foundations of the functioning of the state and the life of society, greater openness and publicity, and constant awareness of and responsiveness to public opinion.

CH. 2.   THE ECONOMIC SYSTEM

Article 10.   The foundation of the economic system of the USSR is socialist ownership of the means of production in the form of state property (belonging to all the people), and collective farm-and-cooperative property.

Socialist ownership also embraces the property of trade unions and other public organizations, property they require for carrying out their work under their rules.

The state protects socialist property and provides the conditions for its growth.

No one has the right to use socialist property for personal gain or other selfish ends.

Article 11.   State property, i.e., the common property of the Soviet people, is the principal form of socialist property.

The land, its minerals, waters and forests are the exclusive property of the state. The state owns the basic means of production in industry, construction and agriculture; means of transport and communication; the banks; the property of state-run trade organizations and public utilities, and other state-run undertakings; most urban housing; and other property necessary for state purposes.

Article 12.   The property of collective farms and other cooperative organizations, and of their joint undertakings, comprises the means of production and other assets which they require for the purposes laid down in their rules.

The land held by collective farms is secured to them for their free use in perpetuity.

The state promotes the development of collective farm and cooperative property and its approximation to state property.

Collective farms, like other land users, are under obligation to make effective and thrifty use of the land and to increase its fertility.

Article 13.   Earned income forms the basis of the personal property of Soviet citizens. The personal property of citizens of the USSR may include articles of everyday use, personal consumption and convenience, the implements and other objects of a (subsidiary) small-holding, a house, and earned savings. The personal property of citizens and the right to inherit it are protected by the state.

Citizens may be granted the use of plots of land, in the manner prescribed by law, for a subsidiary small-holding (including the keeping of livestock and poultry), for fruit and vegetable growing or for building an individual dwelling. Citizens are required to make rational use of the land allotted to them. The state and the collective farms provide assistance to citizens in working their small-holdings.

Property owned or used by citizens shall not serve as a means of deriving unearned income or be employed to the detriment of the interests of society.

Article 14. The source of growth of social wealth and of the well-being of the people, and of each individual, is the labor, free from exploitation, of the Soviet people.

The state exercises control over the measure of labor and of consumption in accordance with the principle of socialism: "From each according to his ability, to each according to his work." It fixes the rate of taxation on taxable income.

Socially useful work and its results determine a person's status in society. By combining material and moral incentives and encouraging innovation and a creative attitude toward work, the state helps transform labor into the prime vital need of every Soviet citizen.

Article 15. The supreme goal of social production under socialism is the fullest possible satisfaction of the people's growing material, cultural and intellectual requirements.

By relying on the creative initiative of the working people, socialist emulation and scientific and technological progress, and by improving the forms and methods of economic management, the state ensures the growth of labor productivity, the raising of the efficiency of production and of the quality of work, and the dynamic, planned, proportionate development of the economy.

Article 16. The economy of the USSR makes up an integral economic complex comprising all the elements of social production, distribution, and exchange on its territory.

The economy is managed on the basis of state plans for economic and social development, with due account taken of the sectoral and territorial principles, and by combining centralized direction with the managerial independence and initiative of individual and amalgamated enterprises and other organizations, toward which end active use is made of management accounting, profit, cost, and other economic levers and incentives.

Article 17. In the USSR, the law permits individual labor in handicrafts, farming, the provision of services for the public, and other forms of activity based exclusively on the personal work of individual citizens and members of their families. The state provides regulations for such work to ensure that it serves the interests of society.

Article 18. In the interests of the present and future generations, the necessary steps are being taken in the USSR to protect, and make scientifically substantiated, rational use of, the land and its mineral and water resources and the plant and animal kingdoms, to preserve the purity of air and water, ensure the reproduction of natural wealth, and improve the human environment.

CH. 3. SOCIAL DEVELOPMENT AND CULTURE

Article 19. The social basis of the USSR is the unbreakable alliance of the workers, peasants, and intelligentsia.

The state helps enhance the social homogeneity of society, namely, the elimination of class differences and of the essential distinctions between town and country and between mental and physical labor, and the all-around development and drawing together of all the nations and nationalities of the USSR.

Article 20. In accordance with the communist ideal, "The free development of each is the condition of the free development of all," the state pursues the aim of giving citizens more and more extensive opportunities to apply their creative energies, abilities and talents, and to develop their personalities in every way.

Article 21. The state concerns itself with improving working conditions, safety and labor protection and the scientific organization of work, and with reducing and ultimately eliminating all arduous physical labor through comprehensive mechanization and automation of production processes in all branches of the economy.

Article 22. A program is being consistently implemented in the USSR to convert agricultural work into a variety of industrial work, to extend the network of educational, cultural and medical institutions, as well as of trade, public catering, community service, and public utility facilities in rural localities, and to transform hamlets and villages into well-planned and well-appointed settlements.

Article 23. The state pursues a steady policy of raising the people's pay levels and real incomes through increases in productivity.

In order to satisfy the needs of Soviet people more fully, social consumption funds are being created. The state, with broad participation of public organizations and work collectives, ensures the growth and the fair distribution of these funds.

Article 24. In the USSR, state systems of health protection, social security, trade and public catering, community services and amenities, and public utilities, are operating and being extended.

The state encourages cooperatives and other public organizations to provide all types of services for the population. It encourages the development of physical culture and sports on a mass scale.

Article 25. The USSR has a uniform system of public education which is being constantly improved and which provides general education and vocational training for all citizens, serves the communist education and intellectual and physical development of the youth, and trains them for work and public activity.

Article 26. In accordance with the needs of society, the state provides for the planned development of science and the training of scientific personnel, and organizes the introduction and incorporation of the results of research into the economy and other spheres of life.

Article 27. The state concerns itself with protecting, augmenting and making extensive use of society's cultural wealth for the moral and esthetic education of the Soviet people, for raising their cultural level.

In the USSR the development of the professional amateur and folk arts is encouraged in every way.

CH. 4.   FOREIGN POLICY

Article 28.   The USSR steadfastly pursues a Leninist policy of peace and stands for strengthening the security of nations and broad international cooperation.

The foreign policy of the USSR is aimed at ensuring international conditions favorable for building communism in the USSR, safeguarding the state interests of the Soviet Union, consolidating the positions of world socialism, supporting the struggle of peoples for national liberation and social progress, preventing wars of aggression, achieving universal and complete disarmament, and consistently implementing the principle of the peaceful coexistence of states with different social systems.

In the USSR war propaganda is prohibited by law.

Article 29.   The USSR's relations with other states are based on observance of the following principles: sovereign equality; mutual renunciation of the use of force or threats of force; inviolability of frontiers; the territorial integrity of states; peaceful settlement of disputes; nonintervention in internal affairs; respect for human rights and fundamental freedoms; equal rights for all peoples and their right to decide their own destinies; cooperation among states; and fulfillment in good faith of obligations arising from the generally recognized principles and rules of international law, and from the international treaties signed by the USSR.

Article 30.   The USSR, as part of the world system of socialism and of the socialist community, promotes and strengthens friendship, cooperation and comradely mutual assistance with other socialist countries on the basis of the principle of socialist internationalism, and takes an active part in socialist economic integration and the socialist international division of labor.

CH. 5.   DEFENSE OF THE SOCIALIST MOTHERLAND

Article 31.   Defense of the socialist motherland is one of the most important functions of the state, and is the concern of the whole people.

In order to defend the gains of socialism, the peaceful labor of the Soviet people, and the sovereignty and territorial integrity of the state, the USSR maintains Armed Forces and has instituted universal military service.

The duty of the Armed Forces of the USSR to the people is to provide reliable defense of the socialist motherland and to maintain constant combat readiness, guaranteeing that any aggressor is instantly repulsed.

Article 32.   The state ensures the security and defense capability of the country, and supplies the Armed Forces of the USSR with everything necessary for that purpose.

The duties of state bodies, public organizations, officials and citizens in regard to safeguarding the country's security and strengthening its defense capacity are defined by the legislation of the USSR.

II. THE STATE AND THE INDIVIDUAL

CH. 6.   CITIZENSHIP OF THE USSR. EQUALITY OF CITIZENS' RIGHTS

Article 33.   Uniform federal citizenship is established for the USSR. Every citizen of a Union Republic is a citizen of the USSR.

The grounds and procedure for acquiring or forfeiting Soviet citizenship are defined by the Law on Citizenship of the USSR.

When abroad, citizens of the USSR enjoy the protection and assistance of the Soviet State.

Article 34.   Citizens of the USSR are equal before the law, without regard to origin, social or property status, race or nationality, sex, education, language, attitude toward religion, type and nature of occupation, domicile, or other status.

The equal rights of citizens of the USSR are guaranteed in all fields of economic, political, social, and cultural life.

Article 35.   Women and men have equal rights in the USSR.

Exercise of these rights is ensured by according women equal access with men to education and vocational and professional training; equal opportunities in employment, equal remuneration and promotion; equality in social, political and cultural activity; and via special labor and health protection measures for women; by providing conditions enabling mothers to work; by legal protection, and by material and moral support for mothers and children, including paid leaves and other benefits for mothers and expectant mothers, and a gradual reduction of working time for mothers with small children.

Article 36.   Citizens of the USSR of different races and nationalities have equal rights.

Exercise of these rights is ensured by a policy of all-around development and drawing together of all the nations and nationalities of the USSR, by educating citizens in the spirit of Soviet patriotism and socialist internationalism, and by making it possible for them to use their native language and the languages of other peoples of the USSR.

Any direct or indirect limitation of the rights of citizens or establishment of direct or indirect privileges on grounds of race or nationality, and any advocacy of racial or national exclusiveness, hostility or contempt, are punishable by law.

Article 37.   Citizens of other countries and stateless persons in the USSR are guaranteed the rights and freedoms provided by law, including the right to apply to a court and other state bodies for the protection of their personal property, family, and other rights.

Citizens of other countries and stateless persons, when in the USSR must respect the Constitution of the USSR and observe Soviet laws.

Article 38.   The USSR grants the right of asylum to foreigners persecuted for defending the interests of the working people and the cause of peace, or for participation in the revolutionary and national liberation movement, or for progressive social and political, scientific or other creative activity.

CH. 7. THE BASIC RIGHTS, FREEDOMS, AND DUTIES OF CITIZENS OF THE USSR

Article 39. Citizens of the USSR enjoy in full the social, economic, political and personal rights and freedoms proclaimed and guaranteed by the Constitution of the USSR and by Soviet laws. The socialist system ensures the extension of the rights and freedoms of citizens and a continuous improvement of their living standards as social, economic, and cultural development programs are fulfilled.

Enjoyment by citizens of their rights and freedoms must not prejudice the interests of society or the state, or infringe the rights of other citizens.

Article 40. Citizens of the USSR have the right to work (that is, the right to guaranteed employment and pay in accordance with the quantity and quality of their work, and not below the state-established minimum), including the right to choose their trade or profession, type of job or work, in accordance with their inclinations, abilities, training and education, with due account taken of the needs of society.

This right is ensured by the socialist economic system, the steady growth of the productive forces, free vocational and professional training, improvement of skills, training in new trades or professions, and development of the systems of vocational guidance and job placement.

Article 41. Citizens of the USSR have the right to rest and leisure.

This right is ensured by the establishment of a working week not exceeding 41 hours for workers and other employees, a shorter working day in a number of trades and industries, and shorter hours for night work; by providing paid annual vacations and weekly days of rest, by extending the network of cultural, educational and health-building institutions, and the development on a mass scale of sports, physical culture, and camping and tourism; by making available neighborhood recreational facilities and other opportunities for the rational use of free time.

The length of collective farmers' working and leisure time is established by their collective farms.

Article 42. Citizens of the USSR have the right to health protection.

This right is ensured by qualified free medical care provided by state health institutions; by extending the network of therapeutic and health-building institutions; by the further development and improvement of safety provisions and hygiene in industry; by carrying out broad prophylactic measures; by measures to improve the environment; by special care for the health of the rising generation; including the prohibition of child labor, exclusive of the work done by children as part of the school curriculum; and by developing research to prevent and reduce the incidence of disease and ensure citizens a long and active life.

Article 43. Citizens of the USSR have the right to maintenance in old age, in sickness, and in the event of complete or partial disability or loss of the breadwinner.

This right is guaranteed by social insurance in the case of workers and other employees and collective farmers; by allowances for temporary disability; by the state or the collective farms providing retirement pensions, disability pensions, and pensions for loss of the breadwinner; by providing employment for the partially disabled; by care for the elderly and the disabled; and by other forms of social security.

Article 44. Citizens of the USSR have the right to housing.

This right is ensured by the development and upkeep of state- and socially-owned housing; by assistance for cooperative and individual house-building; by fair distribution, under public control, of the housing that becomes available through fulfillment of the program of building well-appointed dwellings, and by low rents and low charges for utility services. Citizens of the USSR shall take good care of the housing allocated to them.

Article 45. Citizens of the USSR have the right to an education.

This right is ensured by the free provision of all forms of education, by the institution of universal, compulsory secondary education, and the broad development of vocational, specialized secondary, and higher education, in which instruction is oriented toward practical activity and production; by the development of extramural, correspondence and evening courses; by providing state scholarships and grants and privileges for students; by the free issue of school textbooks; by the opportunity to attend a school where teaching is in the student's native language; and by the availability of facilities for self-education.

Article 46. Citizens of the USSR have the right to enjoy cultural benefits.

This right is ensured by broad access to the cultural treasures of their own land and of the world, which are preserved in state and other public collections; by the development and fair distribution of cultural and educational institutions throughout the country; by developing television and radio broadcasting and the publishing of books, newspapers and periodicals, and by extending free library services; by expanding cultural exchanges with other countries.

Article 47. Citizens of the USSR, in accordance with the aims of building communism, are guaranteed freedom of scientific, technical, and artistic work. This freedom is ensured by broadening scientific research, encouraging invention and innovation, and developing literature and the arts. The state provides the necessary material conditions for this and support for voluntary societies and unions of workers in the arts, and organizes the introduction of new inventions and innovations in production and other spheres of activity.

The rights of authors, inventors and innovators are protected by the state.

Article 48. Citizens of the USSR have the right to take part in the management and administration of state and public affairs and in the discussion and adoption of laws and measures of All-Union and local significance.

This right is ensured by the opportunity to vote and to be elected to Soviets of People's Deputies and other elective state bodies, to take part in nationwide discussions and referendums, in people's control, in the work of state bodies, public organizations and local community groups, and in meetings at one's place of work or residence.

Article 49. Every citizen of the USSR has the right to submit proposals to state bodies and public organizations for improving their activity, and to criticize shortcomings in their work.

Officials are under obligation, within established time limits, to examine citizens' proposals and requests, to reply to them, and to take appropriate action.

Persecution for criticism is prohibited. Persons guilty of such persecution shall be called to account.

Article 50. In accordance with the interests of the people and in order to strengthen and develop the socialist system, citizens of the USSR are guaranteed freedom of speech, of the press, and of assembly, open meetings, street processions and demonstrations.

Exercise of these political freedoms is ensured by putting public buildings, streets and public squares at the disposal of the working people and their organizations; by broad dissemination of information; and by the opportunity to make use of the press, television, and radio.

Article 51. In accordance with the aims of building communism, citizens of the USSR have the right to associate in public organizations that promote their political activity and initiative and the satisfaction of their various interests.

Public organizations are guaranteed the necessary conditions for successfully performing the functions defined in their rules.

Article 52. Citizens of the USSR are guaranteed freedom of conscience, that is, the right to profess or not to profess any religion, and to conduct either religious worship or atheistic propaganda. Incitement of hostility or hatred on religious grounds is prohibited.

In the USSR, the church is separated from the state, and the school from the church.

Article 53. The family enjoys the protection of the state.

Marriage is based on the free consent of the woman and the man; the spouses are completely equal in their family relations.

The state helps the family by providing and developing a broad system of child-care institutions, by organizing and improving communal services and public catering, by paying out grants upon the birth of a child, by providing children's allowances and benefits for large families, and other forms of family allowances and assistance.

Article 54. Citizens of the USSR are guaranteed inviolability of the person. No one may be arrested except by court decision or on the warrant of a procurator.

Article 55. Citizens of the USSR are guaranteed inviolability of the home. No one may, without lawful grounds, enter a home against the will of those residing in it.

Article 56. The privacy of citizens, and of their correspondence, telephone conversations, and telegraphic communications is protected by law.

Article 57. Respect for the individual and protection of the rights and freedoms of citizens are the duty of all state bodies, public organizations, and officials.

Citizens of the USSR have the right to protection by the courts against encroachment on their honor and reputation, life and health, and personal freedom and property.

Article 58. Citizens of the USSR have the right to lodge a complaint against the actions of officials, state bodies and public bodies. Complaints shall be examined according to the procedure and within the time limit established by law.

Actions by officials that contravene the law or exceed their powers, and infringe the rights of citizens, may be appealed against in a court in the manner prescribed by law.

Citizens of the USSR have the right to compensation for damages resulting from unlawful actions by both state organizations and public organizations, or by officials in the performance of their duties.

Article 59. Citizens' exercise of their rights and freedoms is inseparable from the performance of their duties and obligations.

Citizens of the USSR are obligated to observe the Constitution of the USSR and Soviet law, comply with the standards of socialist conduct, and uphold the honor and dignity of Soviet citizenship.

Article 60. It is the duty of, and a matter of honor for, every able-bodied citizen of the USSR to work conscientiously in his chosen, socially useful occupation, and strictly to observe labor discipline. Evasion of socially useful work is incompatible with the principles of socialist society.

Article 61. It is the obligation of citizens of the USSR to preserve and protect socialist property. It is the duty of a citizen of the USSR to combat misappropriation and dissipation of state and socially-owned property and to make thrifty use of the people's wealth.

Persons encroaching in any way on socialist property shall be punished according to the law.

Article 62. It is the obligation of citizens of the USSR to safeguard the interests of the Soviet state, and to enhance its power and prestige.

Defense of the socialist motherland is the sacred duty of every citizen of the USSR.

Betrayal of the motherland is the gravest of crimes against the people.

Article 63. Military service in the ranks of the Armed Forces of the USSR is the honorable duty of Soviet citizens.

Article 64. It is the duty of every citizen of the USSR to respect the national dignity of other citizens, and to strengthen friendship among the nations and nationalities of the multinational Soviet state.

Article 65. A citizen of the USSR is obligated to respect the rights and lawful interests of other persons, to be uncompromising toward antisocial behavior, and to help maintain public order.

Article 66. Citizens of the USSR are under obligation to concern themselves with the upbringing of their children, to train them for socially useful work, and to raise them as worthy members of socialist society. Children have a similar obligation to care for their parents and help them.

Article 67. Citizens of the USSR have an obligation to protect nature and safeguard its riches.

Article 68. Concern for the preservation of historical monuments and other cultural values is the duty and obligation of citizens of the USSR.

Article 69. It is the internationalist duty of citizens of the USSR to promote friendship and cooperation with peoples of other lands and help, maintain and strengthen world peace.

III.   THE NATIONAL-STATE STRUCTURE OF THE USSR

CH. 8.   THE USSR—A FEDERAL STATE

Article 70.   The Union of Soviet Socialist Republics is an integral, federal multinational state formed on the principle of socialist federalism as a result of the free self-determination of nations and the voluntary association of equal Soviet Socialist Republics.

The USSR embodies the state unity of the Soviet people and draws all its nations and nationalities together for the purpose of jointly building communism.

Article 71.   The Union of Soviet Socialist Republics unites:

the Russian Soviet Federated Socialist Republic,

the Ukrainian Soviet Socialist Republic,

the Byelorussian Soviet Socialist Republic,

the Uzbek Soviet Socialist Republic,

the Kazakh Soviet Socialist Republic,

the Georgian Soviet Socialist Republic,

the Azerbaijan Soviet Socialist Republic,

the Lithuanian Soviet Socialist Republic,

the Moldavian Soviet Socialist Republic,

the Latvian Soviet Socialist Republic,

the Kirghiz Soviet Socialist Republic,

the Tajik Soviet Socialist Republic,

the Armenian Soviet Socialist Republic,

the Turkmen Soviet Socialist Republic,

the Estonian Soviet Socialist Republic.

Article 72.   Every Union Republic shall retain the right freely to secede from the USSR.

Article 73.   The jurisdiction of the Union of Soviet Socialist Republics, as represented by its highest bodies of state authority and administration, shall cover:

1) the admission of new republics to the USSR; endorsement of the formation of new autonomous republics and autonomous regions within Union Republics;

2) determination of the state boundaries of the USSR and approval of changes in the boundaries between Union Republics;

3) establishment of the general principles for the organization and functioning of Republic and local bodies of state authority and administration;

4) insurance of uniformity of legislative regulations throughout the USSR and establishment of the fundamentals of the legislation of the Union of Soviet Socialist Republics and Union Republics;

5) pursuance of a uniform social and economic policy; administration of the country's economy; determination of the main lines of scientific and technological progress and of general measures for the rational exploitation and conservation of natural resources; the drafting and approval of state plans for the economic and social development of the USSR, and endorsement of reports on their fulfillment;

6) the drafting and approval of the consolidated State Budget of the

USSR, and endorsement of the report on its execution; management of a single monetary and credit system; determination of the taxes and revenues forming the Budget of the USSR; and formulation of the price and wage policy;

7) administration of the sectors of the economy and of enterprises and amalgamations under Union jurisdiction, and general guidance of industries under Union-Republic jurisdiction;

8) issues of war and peace, defense of the sovereignty of the USSR and the safeguarding of its frontiers and territory, and organization of defense; direction of the Armed Forces of the USSR;

9) state security;

10) representation of the USSR in international relations; the USSR's relations with other states and with international organizations; establishment of the general procedure for, and coordination of, the relations of Union Republics with other states and with international organizations; foreign trade and other forms of external economic activity on the basis of state monopoly;

11) control over the observance of the Constitution of the USSR, and insurance of conformity of the Constitutions of Union Republics to the Constitution of the USSR;

12) settlement of other matters of All-Union importance.

Article 74. The laws of the USSR shall have the same force in all Union Republics. In the event of a discrepancy between a Union Republic law and an All-Union law, the law of the USSR shall prevail.

Article 75. The territory of the Union of Soviet Socialist Republics is a single entity and comprises the territories of the Union Republics.

The sovereignty of the USSR extends throughout its territory.

CH. 9.   THE UNION SOVIET SOCIALIST REPUBLIC

Article 76. A Union Republic is a sovereign Soviet socialist state that has united with other Soviet Republics in the Union of Soviet Socialist Republics.

Outside the spheres listed in Article 73 of the Constitution of the USSR, a Union Republic exercises independent authority on its territory.

A Union Republic shall have its own Constitution conforming to the Constitution of the USSR, with the specific features of the Republic taken into account.

Article 77. Union Republics take part in decision-making in the Supreme Soviet of the USSR, the Presidium of the Supreme Soviet of the USSR, the Government of the USSR, and other bodies of the Union of Soviet Socialist Republics in matters that come within the jurisdiction of the Union of Soviet Socialist Republics.

A Union Republic shall ensure comprehensive economic and social development on its territory, facilitate exercise of the powers of the USSR on its territory, and implement the decisions of the highest bodies of state authority and administration of the USSR.

In matters that come within its jurisdiction, a Union Republic shall coordinate and control the activity of enterprises, institutions, and organizations subordinate to the Union.

Article 78. The territory of a Union Republic may not be altered without its consent. The boundaries between Union Republics may be altered by mutual agreement of the Republics concerned, subject to ratification by the Union of Soviet Socialist Republics.

Article 79. A Union Republic shall determine its division into territories, regions, areas and districts, and decide other matters relating to its administrative and territorial structure.

Article 80. A Union Republic has the right to enter into relations with other states, conclude treaties with them, exchange diplomatic and consular representatives, and take part in the work of international organizations.

Article 81. The sovereign rights of Union Republics shall be safeguarded by the USSR.

CH. 10. THE AUTONOMOUS SOVIET SOCIALIST REPUBLIC

Article 82. An Autonomous Republic is a constituent part of a Union Republic.

In spheres not within the jurisdiction of the Union of Soviet Socialist Republics and the Union Republic, an Autonomous Republic shall deal independently with matters within its jurisdiction.

An Autonomous Republic shall have its own Constitution conforming to the Constitutions of the USSR and the Union Republic, with the specific features of the Autonomous Republic being taken into account.

Article 83. An Autonomous Republic takes part in decision-making through the highest bodies of state authority and administration of the USSR and of the Union Republic respectively, in matters that come within the jurisdiction of the USSR and the Union Republic.

An Autonomous Republic shall ensure comprehensive economic and social development on its territory, facilitate exercise of the powers of the USSR and the Union Republic on its territory, and implement the decisions of the highest bodies of state authority and administration of the USSR and the Union Republic.

In matters within its jurisdiction, an Autonomous Republic shall coordinate and control the activity of enterprises, institutions, and organizations subordinate to the Union or the Union Republic.

Article 84. The territory of an Autonomous Republic may not be altered without its consent.

Article 85. The Russian Soviet Federated Socialist Republic includes the Bashkir, Buryat, Daghestan, Kobardin-Balkar, Kalmyk, Karelian, Komi, Mari, Mordovian, North Ossetian, Tatar, Tuva, Udmurt, Chechen-Ingush, Chuvash and Yakut Autonomous Soviet Socialist Republics.

The Uzbek Soviet Socialist Republic includes the Kara-Kalpak Autonomous Soviet Socialist Republic.

The Georgian Soviet Socialist Republic includes the Abkhasian and Adzhar Autonomous Soviet Socialist Republics.

The Azerbaijan Soviet Socialist Republic includes the Nakhichevan Autonomous Soviet Socialist Republic.

Article 86. An Autonomous Region is a constituent part of a Union Republic or Territory. The Law on Autonomous Regions, upon submission by the Soviet of People's Deputies of the Autonomous Region concerned, shall be adopted by the Supreme Soviet of the Union Republic.

Article 87. The Russian Soviet Federated Socialist Republic includes the Adygei, Gorno-Altai, Jewish, Karachai-Circassian, and Khakass Autonomous Regions.

The Georgian Soviet Socialist Republic includes the South Ossetian Autonomous Region.

The Azerbaijan Soviet Socialist Republic includes the Nagorno-Karabakh Autonomous Region.

The Tajik Soviet Socialist Republic includes the Gorno-Badakhshan Autonomous Region.

Article 88. An Autonomous Area is a constituent part of a Territory or Region. The Law on Autonomous Areas shall be adopted by the Supreme Soviet of the Union Republic concerned.

IV. SOVIETS OF PEOPLE'S DEPUTIES AND ELECTORAL PROCEDURES

CH. 12.   THE SYSTEM OF SOVIETS OF PEOPLE'S DEPUTIES
AND THE PRINCIPLES OF THEIR WORK

Article 89. The Soviets of People's Deputies, i.e., the Supreme Soviet of the USSR, the Supreme Soviets of Union Republics, the Supreme Soviets of Autonomous Republics, the Soviets of People's Deputies of Territories and Regions, the Soviets of People's Deputies of Autonomous Regions and Autonomous Areas, and the Soviets of People's Deputies of districts, cities, city districts, settlements and villages shall constitute a single system of bodies of state authority.

Article 90. The term of office for the Supreme Soviet of the USSR, the Supreme Soviets of Union Republics, and the Supreme Soviets of Autonomous Republics shall be five years.

The term of office for local Soviets of People's Deputies shall be two-and-a-half years.

Elections to Soviets of People's Deputies shall be called not later than two months before expiration of the term of office of the Soviet in question.

Article 91. The most important matters within the jurisdiction of the respective Soviets of People's Deputies shall be considered and settled at their sessions.

Soviets of People's Deputies shall elect standing commissions and form executive-administrative bodies, and others accountable to them.

Article 92. Soviets of People's Deputies shall form people's control bodies combining state control with control by the working people at enterprises, collective farms, institutions, and organizations.

People's control bodies shall check on the fulfillment of state plans and assignments, combat breaches of state discipline, parochial tendencies, narrow departmental attitudes, mismanagement, extravagance and waste, red tape and bureaucracy, and help improve the working of the state machinery.

Article 93. Soviets of People's Deputies shall direct all sectors of state, economic and social and cultural development, either directly or through bodies instituted by them; make decisions and ensure their execution; and verify their implementation.

Article 94. Soviets of People's Deputies shall function on the basis of collective, free, constructive, open discussion and decision-making, of systematic accountability to them and the people by their executive-administrative and other bodies, and with the broadest possible involvement of the citizenry in this work.

Soviets of People's Deputies and the bodies set up by them shall systematically inform the public about their work and the decisions adopted by them.

CH. 13.   THE ELECTORAL SYSTEM

Article 95. Deputies to all Soviets shall be elected on the basis of universal, equal and direct suffrage by secret ballot.

Article 96. Elections shall be universal: all citizens of the USSR who have reached the age of 18 shall have the right to vote and to be elected, with the exception of persons who have been legally certified insane.

To be eligible for election to the Supreme Soviet of the USSR, a citizen of the USSR must have reached the age of 21.

Article 97. Elections shall be equal: each citizen shall have one vote; all voters shall exercise the franchise on an equal footing.

Article 98. Elections shall be direct: Deputies to all Soviets of People's Deputies shall be elected by citizens by direct vote.

Article 99. Voting at elections shall be secret: control over voters' exercise of the franchise is inadmissible.

Article 100. The following shall have the right to nominate candidates: branches and organizations of the Communist Party of the Soviet Union, trade unions, and the All-Union Leninist Young Communist League (Komsomol); cooperatives and other public organizations; work collectives; meetings of servicemen in their military units.

Citizens of the USSR and public organizations are guaranteed the right to free and all-around discussion of the political and personal qualities and competence of candidates standing for election, and the right to campaign for them at meetings, in the press, on television and over the radio.

The expenses involved in holding elections to Soviets of People's Deputies shall be met by the state.

Article 101. Deputies to Soviets of People's Deputies shall be elected by constituencies.

A citizen of the USSR may not, as a rule, be elected to more than two Soviets of People's Deputies.

Elections to the Soviets shall be conducted by electoral commissions consisting of representatives of public organizations and work collectives, and of meetings of servicemen in military units.

The procedure for holding elections to Soviets of People's Deputies shall be defined by the laws of the USSR and of Union and Autonomous Republics.

Article 102. Electors give mandates to their Deputies.

The relevant Soviets of People's Deputies shall examine electors' mandates, take them into account in drafting economic and social development plans and in drawing up the budget, organize implementation of the mandates, and inform citizens about it.

CH. 14. PEOPLE'S DEPUTIES

Article 103. Deputies are the plenipotentiary representatives of the people in the Soviets of People's Deputies.

In the Soviets, Deputies deal with matters relating to state, economic and social and cultural development, organize implementation of the decisions of the Soviets, and exercise control over the work of state bodies, enterprises, institutions and organizations.

Deputies shall be guided in their activities by the interests of the state, and shall take the needs of their constituents into account and work to implement the mandates of their electors.

Article 104. Deputies shall exercise their powers without discontinuing their regular employment or duties.

During sessions of the Soviet, and so as to be able to exercise their elective powers in other cases stipulated by law, Deputies shall be released from their regular employment or duties, without loss of their average earnings at their permanent place of work.

Article 105. A Deputy has the right to address inquiries to the appropriate state bodies and officials, who thereupon are obligated to reply to them at a session of the Soviet.

Deputies have the right to approach any state or public body, enterprise, institution or organization on matters arising from their work as Deputies and to take part in considering the questions thus raised. The heads of the state or public bodies, enterprises, institutions or organizations concerned are obliged to receive Deputies without delay and to consider their proposals within the time limit established by law.

Article 106. Deputies shall be assured conditions for the unobstructed and effective exercise of their rights and duties.

The immunity of Deputies, and other guarantees of their activity as Deputies, are defined in the Law on the Status of Deputies and other legislative acts of the USSR and of Union and Autonomous Republics.

Article 107. Deputies shall report on their work and on that of their Soviet to their constituents and to the work collectives and/or public organizations that nominated them.

Deputies who have not justified the confidence of their constituents may be recalled at any time by decision of a majority of the electors, in accordance with the procedure established by law.

V.   HIGHER BODIES OF STATE AUTHORITY
AND ADMINISTRATION OF THE USSR

CH. 15.   THE SUPREME SOVIET OF THE USSR

Article 108.   The highest organ of state authority in the USSR shall be the Supreme Soviet of the USSR.

The Supreme Soviet of the USSR is empowered to deal with all matters within the jurisdiction of the Union of Soviet Socialist Republics, as defined by this Constitution.

The adoption and amendment of the Constitution of the USSR; admission of new Republics to the USSR; endorsement of the formation of new Autonomous Republics and Autonomous Regions; approval of the state plans for economic and social development, of the Budget of the USSR, and of reports on their execution; and the institution of bodies of the USSR accountable to it, are the exclusive prerogative of the Supreme Soviet of the USSR.

Laws of the USSR shall be enacted by the Supreme Soviet of the USSR or by a nationwide vote (referendum) held by decision of the Supreme Soviet of the USSR.

Article 109.   The Supreme Soviet of the USSR shall consist of two chambers: the Soviet of the Union and the Soviet of Nationalities.

The two chambers of the Supreme Soviet of the USSR shall have equal rights.

Article 110.   The Soviet of the Union and the Soviet of Nationalities shall have equal numbers of deputies.

The Soviet of the Union shall be elected by constituencies with equal populations.

The Soviet of Nationalities shall be elected on the basis of the following representation: 32 Deputies from each Union Republic, 11 Deputies from each Autonomous Republic, five Deputies from each Autonomous Region, and one Deputy from each Autonomous Area.

The Soviet of the Union and the Soviet of Nationalities, upon representation by the credentials commissions elected by them, shall decide on the validity of Deputies' credentials, and, in cases where the election law has been violated, shall declare the election of the Deputies concerned null and void.

Article 111.   Each chamber of the Supreme Soviet of the USSR shall elect a Chairman and four Vice-Chairmen.

The Chairmen of the Soviet of the Union and of the Soviet of Nationalities shall preside over the sittings of the respective chambers and conduct their affairs.

Joint sittings of the chambers of the Supreme Soviet of the USSR shall be presided over alternately by the Chairman of the Soviet of the Union and the Chairman of the Soviet of Nationalities.

Article 112.   Sessions of the Supreme Soviet of the USSR shall be convened twice a year.

Extraordinary sessions shall be convened by the Presidium of the Supreme Soviet of the USSR at its discretion, or on the recommendation of a Union Republic, or of not less than one-third of the Deputies of one of the chambers.

A session of the Supreme Soviet of the USSR shall consist of separate and joint sittings of the chambers, and of meetings of the standing commissions of the chambers or commissions of the Supreme Soviet of the USSR held between sittings of the chambers. A session may be opened and closed at either separate or joint sittings of the chambers.

Article 113. The right to initiate legislation in the Supreme Soviet of the USSR is vested in the Soviet of the Union and the Soviet of Nationalities, the Presidium of the Supreme Soviet of the USSR, the Council of Ministers of the USSR, Union Republics through their higher organs of state power, commissions of the Supreme Soviet of the USSR and standing commissions of its chambers, Deputies of the Supreme Soviet of the USSR, the Supreme Court of the USSR, and the Procurator-General of the USSR.

The right to initiate legislation is also vested in public organizations through their All-Union organs.

Article 114. Draft laws and other matters submitted to the Supreme Soviet of the USSR shall be debated by its chambers at separate or joint sittings. Where necessary, a draft law or other matter may be referred to one or more commissions for preliminary or additional consideration.

A law of the USSR shall be deemed adopted when it has been passed in each chamber of the Supreme Soviet of the USSR by a majority of the total number of its Deputies. Decisions and other acts of the Supreme Soviet of the USSR are adopted by a majority of the total number of Deputies of the Supreme Soviet of the USSR.

Draft laws and other highly important matters of state may be submitted for nationwide discussion by decision of the Supreme Soviet of the USSR or its Presidium, taken on their own initiative, or if proposed by a Union Republic.

Article 115. In the event of disagreement between the Soviet of the Union and the Soviet of Nationalities, the matter at issue shall be referred for settlement to a conciliation commission formed by the two chambers on a parity basis, after which it shall be considered for a second time by the Soviet of the Union and the Soviet of Nationalities at a joint sitting. If agreement is again not reached, the matter shall be postponed for debate at the next session of the Supreme Soviet of the USSR or submitted by the Supreme Soviet to a nationwide vote (referendum).

Article 116. Laws of the USSR and decisions and other acts of the Supreme Soviet of the USSR shall be published in the languages of the Union Republics over the signatures of the Chairman and Secretary of the Presidium of the Supreme Soviet of the USSR.

Article 117. A Deputy of the Supreme Soviet of the USSR has the right to address inquiries to the Council of Ministers of the USSR, and to Ministers and heads of other bodies formed by the Supreme Soviet of the USSR. The Council of Ministers of the USSR, or the official to whom the inquiry is addressed, is under obligation to give a verbal or written reply within three days at the relevant session of the Supreme Soviet of the USSR.

Article 118. A Deputy of the Supreme Soviet of the USSR may not be prosecuted, or arrested, or incur a court-imposed penalty, without the sanction of the Supreme Soviet of the USSR or, between sessions, of the Presidium of the Supreme Soviet of the USSR.

Article 119. The Supreme Soviet of the USSR, at a joint sitting of its chambers, shall elect a Presidium of the Supreme Soviet of the USSR, which shall be a standing body of the Supreme Soviet of the USSR, accountable to it for all its work and exercising the functions of the highest organ of state power of the USSR between sessions of the Supreme Soviet, within the limits prescribed by the Constitution.

Article 120. The Presidium of the Supreme Soviet of the USSR shall be elected from among the Deputies and shall consist of a Chairman, First Vice-Chairman, 15 Vice-Chairmen (one from each Union Republic), a Secretary, and 21 members.

Article 121. The Presidium of the Supreme Soviet of the USSR shall:

1) name the date of elections to the Supreme Soviet of the USSR;

2) convene sessions of the Supreme Soviet of the USSR;

3) coordinate the work of the standing commissions of the chambers of the Supreme Soviet of the USSR;

4) ensure observance of the Constitution of the USSR and conformity of the Constitutions and laws of Union Republics to the Constitution and laws of the USSR;

5) interpret the laws of the USSR;

6) ratify and/or denounce international treaties of the USSR;

7) revoke decisions and ordinances of the Council of Ministers of the USSR and of the Councils of Ministers of Union Republics, should they fail to conform to the law;

8) institute military and diplomatic ranks and other special titles; and confer the highest military and diplomatic ranks and other special titles;

9) institute orders and medals of the USSR, and honorary titles of the USSR; award orders and medals of the USSR; and confer honorary titles of the USSR;

10) grant citizenship of the USSR, and rule on matters of the renunciation or deprivation of citizenship of the USSR and of granting asylum;

11) issue All-Union acts of amnesty and exercise the right of pardon;

12) appoint and recall diplomatic representatives of the USSR to other countries and to international organizations;

13) receive the letters of accreditation and recall of diplomatic representatives of foreign states accredited to it;

14) form the Council of Defense of the USSR and confirm its composition; appoint and/or dismiss the high command of the Armed Forces of the USSR;

15) proclaim martial law in particular localities or throughout the country in the interests of the defense of the USSR;

16) order general or partial mobilization;

17) between sessions of the Supreme Soviet of the USSR, proclaim a state of war in the event of armed attack on the USSR, or when it is necessary to meet international treaty obligations relating to mutual defense against aggression;

18) and exercise other powers vested in the Supreme Soviet by the Constitution and laws of the USSR.

Article 122. The Presidium of the Supreme Soviet of the USSR, between sessions of the Supreme Soviet of the USSR and subject to submission for its confirmation at the next session, shall:

1) when necessary, amend existing legislative acts of the USSR;

2) approve changes in the boundaries between Union Republics;

3) form and abolish Ministries and State Committees of the USSR on the recommendations of the Council of Ministers of the USSR;

4) relieve individual members of the Council of Ministers of the USSR of their responsibilities and appoint persons to the Council of Ministers on the recommendation of the Chairman of the Council of Ministers of the USSR.

Article 123.   The Presidium of the Supreme Soviet of the USSR promulgates decrees and adopts decisions.

Article 124.   On expiration of the term of the Supreme Soviet of the USSR, the Presidium of the Supreme Soviet of the USSR shall retain its powers until the newly elected Supreme Soviet of the USSR has formed a new Presidium.

The newly elected Supreme Soviet of the USSR shall be convened by the outgoing Presidium of the Supreme Soviet of the USSR within two months after the elections.

Article 125.   The Soviet of the Union and the Soviet of Nationalities shall elect standing commissions from among the Deputies to make a preliminary review of matters coming within the jurisdiction of the Supreme Soviet of the USSR, to promote execution of the laws of the USSR and other acts of the Supreme Soviet of the USSR and its Presidium, and to check on the work of state bodies and organizations. The chambers of the Supreme Soviet of the USSR may also set up joint commissions on a parity basis.

When it deems it necessary, the Supreme Soviet of the USSR sets up commissions of inquiry and audit, and commissions on any other matters.

All state and public bodies, organizations and officials have the obligation to meet the requests of the commissions of the Supreme Soviet of the USSR and of its chambers, and must submit the requisite materials and documents to them.

The commissions' recommendations shall be subject to consideration by state and public bodies, institutions and organizations. The commissions shall be informed, within the prescribed time limit, of the results of such consideration or of the action taken.

Article 126.   The Supreme Soviet of the USSR shall supervise the work of all state bodies accountable to it.

The Supreme Soviet of the USSR shall form a Committee of People's Control of the USSR to head the system of people's control.

The organization and procedure of people's control bodies are defined by the Law on People's Control in the USSR.

Article 127.   The procedure of the Supreme Soviet of the USSR and of its bodies shall be defined in the Rules and Regulations of the Supreme Soviet of the USSR and other laws of the USSR enacted on the basis of the Constitution of the USSR.

CH. 16.   THE COUNCIL OF MINISTERS OF THE USSR

Article 128.   The Council of Ministers of the USSR, i.e., the Government of the USSR, is the highest executive and administrative organ of state power of the USSR.

Article 129.   The Council of Ministers of the USSR shall be formed by the Supreme Soviet of the USSR at a joint sitting of the Soviet of the Union and the Soviet of Nationalities, and shall consist of the Chairman of the Council of Ministers of the USSR, the First Vice-Chairmen and Vice-Chairmen, the Ministers of the USSR, and Chairmen of State Committees of the USSR.

The Chairmen of the Councils of Ministers of Union Republics shall be *ex officio* members of the Council of Ministers of the USSR.

On the recommendation of the Chairman of the Council of Ministers of the USSR, the Supreme Soviet of the USSR may include in the Government of the USSR the heads of other bodies and organizations of the USSR.

The Council of Ministers of the USSR shall tender its resignation to a newly elected Supreme Soviet of the USSR at its first session.

Article 130.   The Council of Ministers of the USSR shall be responsible and accountable to the Supreme Soviet of the USSR and, between sessions of the Supreme Soviet of the USSR, to the Presidium of the Supreme Soviet of the USSR.

The Council of Ministers of the USSR shall report regularly on its work to the Supreme Soviet of the USSR.

Article 131.   The Council of Ministers of the USSR is empowered to deal with all matters of state administration within the jurisdiction of the Union of Soviet Socialist Republics insofar as, under the Constitution, they do not come within the competence of the Supreme Soviet of the USSR or the Presidium of the Supreme Soviet of the USSR.

Within its powers the Council of Ministers of the USSR shall:

1) ensure guidance of economic, social and cultural development; draft and implement measures to promote the well-being and cultural development of the people, to develop science and technology, to ensure the rational exploitation and conservation of natural resources, to consolidate the monetary and credit system, to pursue a uniform price, wage, and social security policy, and to organize state insurance and a uniform system of accounting and statistics; and organize the management of industrial, building and agricultural enterprises and amalgamations, transport and communications undertakings, banks, and other organizations and institutions of Union subordination;

2) draft current and long-term state plans for the economic and social development of the USSR and the Budget of the USSR, and submit them to the Supreme Soviet of the USSR; take measures to execute the state plans and the Budget; and report to the Supreme Soviet of the USSR on the implementation of the plans and Budget;

3) implement measures to defend the interests of the state, protect socialist property and maintain public order, and guarantee and protect citizens' rights and freedoms;

4) take measures to ensure state security;

5) exercise general guidance over the development of the Armed Forces

of the USSR, and determine the annual contingent of citizens to be called up for active military service;

6) provide general guidance in regard to relations with other states, foreign trade, and economic, scientific, technical, and cultural cooperation between the USSR and other countries; take measures to ensure fulfillment of the USSR's international treaties; and ratify and/or denounce intergovernmental international agreements;

7) when necessary, form committees, central boards and other departments under the Council of Ministers of the USSR to deal with matters of economic, social and cultural development, and defense.

Article 132.   A Presidium of the Council of Ministers of the USSR, consisting of the Chairman, the First Vice-Chairmen, and Vice-Chairmen of the Council of Ministers of the USSR, shall function as a standing body of the Council of Ministers of the USSR to deal with questions relating to guidance of the economy, and with other matters of state administration.

Article 133.   The Council of Ministers of the USSR, on the basis and in pursuance of the laws of the USSR and other decisions of the Supreme Soviet of the USSR and its Presidium, shall issue decisions and ordinances and verify their execution. The decisions and ordinances of the Council of Ministers of the USSR shall be binding throughout the USSR.

Article 134.   The Council of Ministers of the USSR has the right, in matters within the jurisdiction of the Union of Soviet Socialist Republics, to suspend execution of decisions and ordinances of the Councils of Ministers of Union Republics, and to rescind acts of Ministries and state committees of the USSR, and of other bodies subordinate to it.

Article 135.   The Council of Ministers of the USSR shall coordinate and direct the work of All-Union and Union-Republic Ministeries, state committees of the USSR, and other bodies subordinate to it.

All-Union Ministries and state committees of the USSR shall direct the work of the branches of administration entrusted to them, or exercise interbranch administration, throughout the territory of the USSR directly or through bodies set up by them.

Union-Republic Ministries and state committees of the USSR direct the work of the branches of administration entrusted to them, or exercise interbranch administration, as a rule through the corresponding ministries and state committees and other bodies of Union Republics, and directly administer individual enterprises and amalgamations of Union subordination. The procedure for transferring enterprises and amalgamations from Republic or local subordination to Union subordination shall be defined by the Presidium of the Supreme Soviet of the USSR.

Ministries and state committees of the USSR shall be responsible for the condition and development of the spheres of administration entrusted to them; within their competence, they issue orders and other acts on the basis of, and in execution of, the laws of the USSR and other decisions of the Supreme Soviet of the USSR and its Presidium, and of decisions and ordinances of the Council of Ministers of the USSR, and organize and verify their implementation.

Article 136.   The competence of the Council of Ministers of the USSR and its Presidium, the procedures for their work, the relationships between the

Council of Ministers and other state bodies, and the list of All-Union and Union-Republic Ministries and state committees of the USSR are defined, on the basis of the Constitution, in the Law on the Council of Ministers of the USSR.

VI. BASIC PRINCIPLES OF THE STRUCTURE OF THE BODIES OF STATE AUTHORITY AND ADMINISTRATION IN UNION REPUBLICS

CH. 17.   HIGHER BODIES OF STATE AUTHORITY AND ADMINISTRATION OF A UNION REPUBLIC

Article 137. The highest body of state authority of a Union Republic shall be the Supreme Soviet of that Republic.

The Supreme Soviet of a Union Republic is empowered to deal with all matters within the jurisdiction of that Republic under the Constitutions of the USSR and the Republic.

Adoption and amendment of the Constitution of a Union Republic; endorsement of state plans for economic and social development, of the Republic's Budget, and of reports on their fulfillment; and the formation of bodies accountable to the Supreme Soviet of the Union Republic are the exclusive prerogative of that Supreme Soviet.

Laws of a Union Republic shall be enacted by the Supreme Soviet of that Union Republic or by a popular vote (referendum) held by decision of the Republic's Supreme Soviet.

Article 138. The Supreme Soviet of a Union Republic shall elect a Presidium, which is a standing body of that Supreme Soviet and accountable to it for all its work. The composition and powers of the Presidium of the Supreme Soviet of a Union Republic shall be defined in the Constitution of that Union Republic.

Article 139. The Supreme Soviet of a Union Republic shall form a Council of Ministers of the Union Republic, i.e., the Government of that Republic, which shall be the highest executive and administrative organ of state power in the Republic.

The Council of Ministers of a Union Republic shall be responsible and accountable to the Supreme Soviet of that Republic or, between sessions of the Supreme Soviet, to its Presidium.

Article 140. The Council of Ministers of a Union Republic issues decisions and ordinances on the basis of, and in pursuance of, the legislative acts of the USSR and of the Union Republic, and of decisions and ordinances of the Council of Ministers of the USSR, and shall organize and verify their execution.

Article 141. The Council of Ministers of a Union Republic has the right to suspend the execution of decisions and ordinances of the Councils of Ministers of Autonomous Republics, to rescind the decisions and orders of the Executive Committees of Soviets of People's Deputies of Territories, Regions, and cities (i.e., cities under Republic jurisdiction) and of Autonomous Regions, and, in Union Republics not divided into regions, of the Executive Committees of district and corresponding city Soviets of People's Deputies.

Article 142.   The Council of Ministers of a Union Republic shall coordinate and direct the work of the Union-Republic and Republic Ministries and of state committees of the Union Republic, and other bodies under its jurisdiction.

The Union-Republic Ministries and the state committees of a Union Republic shall direct the branches of administration entrusted to them, or exercise inter-branch control, and shall be subordinate to both the Council of Ministers of the Union Republic and the corresponding Union-Republic Ministry or state committee of the USSR.

Republic Ministries and state committees shall direct the branches of administration entrusted to them, or exercise inter-branch control, and shall be subordinate to the Council of Ministers of the Union Republic.

CH. 18.   HIGHER BODIES OF STATE AUTHORITY AND
ADMINISTRATION OF AN AUTONOMOUS REPUBLIC

Article 143.   The highest body of state authority of an Autonomous Republic shall be the Supreme Soviet of that Republic.

Adoption and amendment of the Constitution of an Autonomous Republic; endorsement of state plans for economic and social development, and of the Republic's Budget; and the formation of bodies accountable to the Supreme Soviet of the Autonomous Republic are the exclusive prerogative of that Supreme Soviet.

Laws of an Autonomous Republic shall be enacted by the Supreme Soviet of the Autonomous Republic.

Article 144.   The Supreme Soviet of an Autonomous Republic shall elect a Presidium of the Supreme Soviet of that Autonomous Republic and shall form a Council of Ministers of the Autonomous Republic, i.e., the Government of that Republic.

CH. 19.   LOCAL BODIES OF STATE AUTHORITY AND ADMINISTRATION

Article 145.   The bodies of state authority in Territories, Regions, Autonomous Regions, Autonomous Areas, districts, cities, city districts, settlements, and rural communities shall be the corresponding Soviets of People's Deputies.

Article 146.   Local Soviets of People's Deputies shall deal with all matters of local significance in accordance with the interests of the whole state and of the citizens residing in the area under their jurisdiction; implement decisions of higher bodies of state authority; guide the work of lower Soviets of People's Deputies; take part in the discussions of matters of Republic and All-Union significance, and submit their proposals concerning them.

Local Soviets of People's Deputies shall direct state, economic, social and cultural development within their territory; endorse plans of economic and social development and the local budget; exercise general guidance over state bodies, enterprises, institutions and organizations subordinate to them; ensure observance of the law, maintenance of law and order and protection of citizens' rights, and help strengthen the country's defense capacity.

Article 147. Within their powers, local Soviets of People's Deputies shall ensure the comprehensive, all-around economic and social development of their area; exercise control over the observance of legislation by enterprises, institutions and organizations subordinate to higher authorities and located in their area; and coordinate and supervise their activity as regards land use, nature conservation, building, employment of manpower, production of consumer goods, and social, cultural, communal and other services and amenities for the public.

Article 148. Local Soviets of People's Deputies shall decide matters within the powers accorded them by the legislation of the USSR and of the relevant Union Republic and Autonomous Republic. Their decisions shall be binding on all enterprises, institutions and organizations located in their area and likewise on officials and citizens within their territory.

Article 149. The Executive Committees elected by them from among their Deputies shall be the executive-administrative bodies of the local Soviets.

Executive Committees shall report on their work at least once a year to the Soviets that elected them and to meetings of citizens at their places of work or residence.

Article 150. Executive Committees of local Soviets of People's Deputies shall be directly accountable both to the Soviet that elected them and to the higher executive-administrative body.

VII.   JUSTICE, ARBITRATION, AND PROCURATOR'S SUPERVISION

CH. 20.   COURTS AND ARBITRATION

Article 151. Justice in the USSR is administered solely by the courts.

In the USSR the court system consists of the following: the Supreme Court of the USSR; the Supreme Courts of Union Republics; the Supreme Courts of Autonomous Republics; Territorial, Regional, and city courts; courts of Autonomous Regions, courts of Autonomous Areas, district (city) people's courts, and military tribunals in the Armed Forces.

Article 152. All courts in the USSR shall be formed on the principles of the electiveness of judges and people's assessors.

People's judges of district (city) people's courts shall be elected for a term of five years by the citizens of the district (city) on the basis of universal, equal and direct suffrage by secret ballot. People's assessors of district (city) people's courts shall be elected for a term of two-and-a-half years, at meetings of citizens at their places of work or residence, by a show of hands.

Higher courts shall be elected for a term of five years by the relevant Soviet of People's Deputies.

The judges of military tribunals shall be elected for a term of five years by the Presidium of the Supreme Soviet of the USSR, and people's assessors for a term of two-and-a-half years by meetings of servicemen.

Judges and people's assessors are responsible and accountable to their electors or the bodies that elected them, shall report to them, and may be recalled by them in the manner prescribed by law.

Article 153. The Supreme Court of the USSR is the highest judicial body in the USSR and supervises the administration of justice by the courts of the USSR and Union Republics within the limits established by law.

The Supreme Court of the USSR shall be elected by the Supreme Soviet of the USSR and shall consist of a Chairman, Vice-Chairmen, members, and people's assessors. The Chairmen of the Supreme Courts of Union Republics are *ex officio* members of the Supreme Court of the USSR.

The organization and procedure of the Supreme Court of the USSR are defined in the Law on the Supreme Court of the USSR.

Article 154. The hearing of civil and criminal cases in all courts is by collegium; in courts of first instance, cases are heard with the participation of people's assessors. In the administration of justice people's assessors have all the rights of judges.

Article 155. Judges and people's assessors are independent and subject only to the law.

Article 156. Justice in the USSR is administered on the principle of the equality of citizens before the law and the court.

Article 157. Proceedings in all courts shall be open to the public. Hearings in camera are only allowed in cases provided for by law, with observance of all the rules of judicial procedure.

Article 158. A defendant in a criminal action is guaranteed the right to legal assistance.

Article 159. Judicial proceedings shall be conducted in the language of the Union Republic, Autonomous Republic, Autonomous Region, or Autonomous Area, or in the language spoken by the majority of the people in the locality. Persons participating in court proceedings, who do not know the language in which these proceedings are being conducted, shall be ensured the right to become fully acquainted with the materials in the case, the services of an interpreter during the proceedings, and the right to address the court in their own language.

Article 160. No one may be adjudged guilty of a crime and subjected to punishment as a criminal except by the sentence of a court and in conformity with the law.

Article 161. Collegiums of advocates (lawyers) are available to render legal assistance to citizens and organizations. In cases provided for by legislation, citizens shall be rendered legal assistance free of charge.

The organization and procedures of the bar are determined by the legislation of the USSR and Union Republics.

Article 162. Representatives of public organizations and of work collectives may take part in civil and criminal proceedings.

Article 163. Economic disputes between enterprises, institutions and organizations are settled by state arbitration bodies within the limits of their jurisdiction.

The organization and manner of functioning of state arbitration bodies are defined in the Law on State Arbitration in the USSR.

CH. 21.   THE PROCURATOR'S OFFICE

Article 164.   Supreme supervisory power over the precise and uniform observance of laws by all ministries, state committees and departments, enterprises, institutions and organizations, executive-administrative bodies of local Soviets of People's Deputies, collective farms, cooperatives and other public organizations, officials and citizens is vested in the Procurator General of the USSR and procurators subordinate to him.

Article 165.   The Procurator General of the USSR is appointed by the Supreme Soviet of the USSR and is responsible and accountable to it and, between sessions of the Supreme Soviet, to the Presidium of the Supreme Soviet of the USSR.

Article 166.   The procurators of Union Republics, Autonomous Republics, Territories, Regions and Autonomous Regions are appointed by the Procurator General of the USSR. The procurators of Autonomous Areas, and district and city procurators, are appointed by the procurators of Union Republics, subject to confirmation by the Procurator General of the USSR.

Article 167.   The term of office of the Procurator General of the USSR and all lower-ranking procurators shall be five years.

Article 168.   The agencies of the Procurator's Office exercise their powers independently of any local bodies whatsoever, and are subordinate solely to the Procurator General of the USSR.

The organization and procedure of the agencies of the Procurator's Office are defined in the Law on the Procurator's Office of the USSR.

VIII.   THE EMBLEM, FLAG, ANTHEM,
AND CAPITAL OF THE USSR

Article 169.   The State Emblem of the Union of Soviet Socialist Republics is a hammer and sickle on a globe depicted in the rays of the sun and framed by ears of wheat, with the inscription, "Workers of All Countries, Unite!" in the languages of the Union Republics. At the top of the Emblem is a five-pointed star.

Article 170.   The State Flag of the Union of Soviet Socialist Republics is a rectangle of red cloth with a hammer and sickle depicted in gold in the upper corner next to the staff and with a five-pointed red star edged in gold above them. The ratio of the width of the flag to its length is 1:2.

Article 171.   The State Anthem of the Union of Soviet Socialist Republics is confirmed by the Presidium of the Supreme Soviet of the USSR.

Article 172.   The Capital of the Union of Soviet Socialist Republics is the city of Moscow.

IX. THE LEGAL FORCE OF THE CONSTITUTION
OF THE USSR AND PROCEDURE FOR
AMENDING THE CONSTITUTION

Article 173. The Constitution of the USSR shall have supreme legal force. All laws and other acts of state bodies shall be promulgated on the basis of and in conformity with it.

Article 174. The Constitution of the USSR may be amended by decision of the Supreme Soviet of the USSR, adopted by a majority of not less than two-thirds of the total number of Deputies of each of its chambers.

Appendix 44 BREZHNEV'S COMMENTS ON AFGHANISTAN, JANUARY 13, 1980 [1]

. . . Today the opponents of peace and detente are trying to speculate on the events in Afghanistan. Mountains of lies are being built up around these events, and a shameless anti-Soviet campaign is being mounted. What has really happened in Afghanistan?

A revolution took place there in April 1978. The Afghani people took their destiny into their own hands and embarked on the road of independence and freedom. As always in history, the forces representing the past ganged up against the revolution. The people of Afghanistan, of course, could have coped with these internal forces themselves. But from the very beginning the revolution also faced external aggression and blatant interference from the outside in their internal affairs.

Thousands and tens of thousands of insurgents, armed and trained abroad, and whole armed units were sent into the territory of Afghanistan. In effect imperialism, together with its accomplices, launched an undeclared war against Afghanistan.

Afghanistan insistently demanded an end to the aggression and that it be left to build its new life in peace. Resisting the external aggression, the Afghani leadership, during the lifetime of President [Nur Mohammad] Taraki and again later on, repeatedly asked the Soviet Union for assistance. On our part, we warned those concerned that if the aggression did not stop, we would not abandon the Afghani people in a time of trial. And as is known, we stand by what we say.

The actions of the aggressors against Afghanistan were assisted by H[afizollah] Amin who, upon seizing power, launched cruel repressions against broad segments of Afghani society, against party and military cadres, against representatives of the intelligentsia and the Moslem clergy, that is, against precisely those segments on which the April Revolution relied. And the people under the leadership of the People's Democratic Party headed by Babrak Karmal rose against this Amin tyranny and put an end to it. Now in Washington and certain other capitals they are mourning Amin. This exposes their hypocrisy with particular clarity. Where were these mourners when Amin was engaging in conducting his mass repressions, when he forcibly and unlawfully removed, then murdered Taraki, the founder of the new Afghani state.

The unceasing armed intervention, the far advanced plotting of the forces of external reaction, created a real danger that Afghanistan would lose its independence and be turned into an imperialist military bridgehead on our country's southern border. In other words, the time came when we could no longer fail to respond to the request of the Government of friendly Afghanistan. To have

---

[1] *Pravda*, January 13, 1980, as reproduced in *Reprints From the Soviet Press*, vol. XXX, No. 2 (January 31, 1980), pp. 13–18.

acted otherwise would have meant leaving Afghanistan prey to imperialism and allowing the aggressive forces to repeat in that country what they had succeeded in doing, for instance, in Chile, where the people's freedom was drowned in blood. To act otherwise would also have meant to watch passively while a seat of serious danger to the security of the Soviet state originated on our southern border.

When making its request to us, Afganistan proceeded from clear-cut provisions of the Treaty of Friendship, Good-neighborliness and Cooperation, concluded between Afghanistan and the USSR in December 1978, on the right of each of the two states, in accordance with the United Nations Charter, to individual or collective self-defense, a right that other states have exercised more than once.

It was no simple decision for us to send Soviet military contingents to Afghanistan. But the Party's Central Committee and the Soviet Government acted in full awareness of their responsibility and took into account the sum total of circumstances. The only task given to the Soviet contingents is to assist the Afghanis in repulsing the aggression from the outside. These contingents will be fully withdrawn from Afghanistan once the causes that forced Afghanistan's leadership to request their introduction have disappeared.

It is deliberately and unscrupulously that the imperialist and also the Peking propaganda channels distort the Soviet Union's role in Afghanistan's affairs.

It goes without saying that there has been no Soviet "intervention" or "aggression" at all. And another thing: We are helping the new Afghanistan, at the request of its Government, to defend the national independence, freedom and honor of its country against armed aggressive actions from the outside.

Neither the national interests nor the security of the United States of America and other states are affected in any way by the events in Afghanistan. All attempts to portray matters otherwise are sheer nonsense. They are deliberately ill-intentioned and aimed at simplifying the fulfillment of the United States Government's own imperialist plans.

Also absolutely false are the allegations that the Soviet Union has some sort of expansionist plans in respect to Pakistan, Iran or other countries of that area. Both the policy and the psychology of colonialism are alien to us. We are not coveting the lands or the wealth of others. It is the colonialists who are attracted by the smell of oil.

Plainly hypocritical, too, are all attempts to talk at length about a "Soviet threat to peace" and to pose as strict observers of international morality on the part of those whose record includes the "dirty war" against Vietnam, those who did not lift a finger when the Chinese aggressors staged their armed intrusion into Socialist Vietnam, those who for decades have kept a military base on Cuban soil contrary to the will of Cuba's people and Government, who are engaged in saber rattling, who are threatening to impose a blockade and are exerting open military pressure on the revolutionary Iranian people by sending to the shores of Iran a naval armada armed with atomic weapons and including a considerable part of the US carrier force.

In this connection one last point must be made. Interference in the internal affairs of Afghanistan is truly taking place, and even so august and respected an institution as the United Nations Organization is being used for this purpose.

Indeed, can the discussion of the so-called Afghani question at the United Nations, contrary to objections by the Government of Afghanistan, be described in any other way than as a gross flouting of the sovereign rights of the Afghani state?

For the Afghani Government and its responsible representatives in the United Nations Organizations are stating for all to hear: Leave us alone; the Soviet military contingents were brought in at our own request and in accordance with the Soviet-Afghani Treaty and Article 51 of the United Nations Charter.

Meantime, under cover of the clamor, assistance is being increased to those elements that are intruding into Afghanistan and committing aggressive actions against its legitimate government. The White House recently openly announced its decision to expand the supply to these elements of military equipment and everything necessary for hostile activities. The Western press reports that during his talks in Peking, the US Secretary of Defense colluded with the Chinese leadership on the coordination of such actions.

In conclusion, it must be said on the Afghani theme that there is nothing surprising in the hostile reaction of imperialist forces to the events in Afghanistan. The crux of the matter is that the card on which the imperialists and their accomplices so firmly counted has been trumped.

In short, the sum total of the American Administration's steps in connection with the events in Afghanistan; the freezing of the SALT-II Treaty; refusal to deliver to the USSR a number of commodities, including grain, in accordance with already concluded contracts; the termination of talks with the Soviet Union on a number of questions of bilateral relations, and so on, shows that Washington once again, as decades ago, is trying to talk to us in the language of cold war. In this the Carter Administration is showing contempt for important interstate documents and disrupting established ties in the fields of science, culture and human contacts.

It is difficult even to enumerate all the various treaties, intergovernmental agreements, accords and understandings reached between our two countries on questions of mutual relations in various fields which have recently been arbitrarily and unilaterally violated by the Government of President Carter. Of course, we can manage without these ties with the United States. Moreover, we have never sought such ties as any sort of special favor to ourselves, but saw the whole matter of reciprocal trade and similar relations as meeting the interests of the peoples of both our countries, primarily in the context of strengthening peace.

But the arrogation by Washington of some sort of "right" to "reward" or "punish" independent sovereign states raises a question of a principled character. In effect, by such actions the US Government is dealing a blow at the orderly international system of legal relations among states.

As a result of the Carter Administration's actions the impression is increasingly forming in the world that the United States is a wholly unreliable partner in interstate ties, a state whose leadership, prompted either by whims, caprice or emotional outbursts, or by considerations of narrowly understood immediate advantage, is capable at any moment of violating its international obligations and cancelling treaties and agreements it has signed. Is there any need to explain what a dangerous destabilizing impact this has on the entire international situation, the more so since this is the behavior of the leadership of a major influential power from which the peoples have the right to expect a well-considered and responsible policy?

It goes without saying that these actions of the US Administration will not inflict on us the damage obviously hoped for by their initiators. The cynical estimates concerning a worsening of the food situation in the Soviet Union as a result of US refusal to sell us grain are based on nonsensical notions about our economic potential. The Soviet people have sufficient possibilities to continue living and working calmly, fulfilling our plans and raising living standards. In particular, I can assure you that the plans to provide the Soviet people with bread and bakery products will not be cut back by a single kilogram.

We cannot interpret the actions of the American Administration otherwise than as a poorly weighed attempt to use the events in Afghanistan for blocking the international effort to lessen the military danger, strengthen peace and restrict the arms race—in short, for blocking the attainment of arms in which humankind is vitally interested.

The unilateral measures taken by the United States are tantamount to serious political miscalculations. Like a boomerang, they will hit back at their initiators, if not today, then tomorrow.

Now if all these sallies against our policy are intended to test our mettle, it means that the experience of history is being totally ignored. When the world's first socialist state was born in 1917, our people did not ask anyone's permission. Today, too, they themselves decide what their way of life is to be. Imperialism tried to put us to the test long ago, at the dawn of Soviet government, and everyone remembers what came of this. Later the fascist aggressors tried to break us in the bloodiest war ever experienced by humankind. They suffered defeat. We were subjected to trials in the years of the cold war, when the world was being pushed to the brink of the precipice, when one international crisis was engineered after another. But then, too, nobody succeeded in making us waver. It is very useful to remember all this today.

Appendix 45   OPEN LETTER TO THE CENTRAL COMMITTEE OF THE POLISH UNITED WORKERS' PARTY FROM THE CENTRAL COMMITTEE OF THE CPSU [1]

Dear Comrades,

The Central Committee of the Communist Party of the Soviet Union addresses this letter to you because it is deeply worried about the destinies of socialism in Poland and about Poland as a free, independent state.

Our letter is motivated by our comradely interest in the affairs of the Party of Polish Communists, in the entire fraternal Polish people, in socialist Poland as a member of the Warsaw Treaty Organization and the Council of Mutual Economic Assistance. Soviet and Polish Communists fought shoulder to shoulder in the battle against Nazism; they continued to stand side by side throughout the postwar years. Our Party and the whole Soviet people helped their Polish comrades to build a new life, and we cannot but be alarmed by the mortal danger which today threatens the revolutionary gains of the Polish people.

We say this frankly: some trends in the development of the Polish People's Republic, especially in the field of ideology and the economic policy of its former leadership, have been a source of concern to us over a number of years. In full conformity with the spirit of the relations that have taken shape between the CPSU and PUWP, the Polish leaders were told of this in the course of talks at summit level and during other meetings. Regrettably, our friendly warnings, just as various sharply critical statements made within the PUWP itself, were not taken into consideration and were even ignored. As a result, a deep crisis has broken out in Poland and has by now enveloped the entire political and economic life of the country.

We responded with complete understanding to the change of leadership in the PUWP, to their striving to rectify the gross mistakes of the past connected with the violation of the laws of building socialism and to restore the confidence of the masses—primarily that of the working class—in the Party, and to strengthen socialist democracy. From the very first days of the crisis, we considered it important that the Polish Party resolutely repulse the attempts of the enemies of socialism to take advantage of the difficulties that were arising and which they were using to further their own far-reaching aims. However, this was not followed up. Instead, endless concessions to the anti-socialist forces and to their demands brought about a situation in which the PUWP began retreating step by step under the onslaught of international counterrevolution which relies on the support of imperialist subversive centers abroad.

Today the situation is not merely dangerous: it has brought the country to

[1] *Pravda*, June 12, 1981, as reproduced in *Reprints From the Soviet Press,* vol. XXXIII, No. 1, July 15, 1981, pp. 22–7.

the brink of crisis—no other assessment of it is possible. The enemies of socialist Poland are not even making any particular effort to conceal their intentions. They are engaged in a struggle for power, and are already capturing it. They are gaining control over one position after another. The counterrevolution uses as its strike force the extremist wing of Solidarity, using deception to draw the workers who joined that trade union association into a criminal conspiracy against the people's power. The wave of anti-communism and anti-Sovietism is mounting. The imperialist forces are making ever more brazen attempts to interfere in Poland's affairs.

The extremely serious danger hanging over socialism in Poland is also a threat to the very existence of the independent Polish state. Had the worst happened, had the enemies of socialism seized power, had Poland been deprived of defense by the socialist community, the greedy hands of the imperialists would have immediately reached out, and who could then guarantee the independence, sovereignty and borders of Poland as a state?

You all know, comrades, about the meeting of the leaders of the fraternal Parties of the countries of the socialist community held in Moscow on December 5, 1980. On March 4, 1981, talks were held between the Soviet leadership and the PUWP delegation to the 26th Congress of the CPSU. On April 23, 1981, a CPSU delegation met with the entire Polish leadership. During these meetings and other contacts, growing concern was emphasized by our side concerning the intrigues of counterrevolutionary forces in Poland. We spoke of the need to overcome the confusion in the ranks of the PUWP, the need firmly to defend its cadres against enemy attacks, to stand up resolutely in defense of the people's power.

Special attention was drawn to the fact that the enemy had actually gained control of the mass media, which mostly have become a tool of antisocialist activity and are used for undermining socialism, for demoralizing the Party. It was pointed out that it is impossible to win the battle for the Party so long as the press, the radio and television work not for the PUWP, but for its enemies.

The question was pointedly raised of the need to strengthen the prestige in the country of the bodies of public order and the Army, and to protect them from encroachments by the forces of counterrevolution. To permit the success of attempts to defame and demoralize the security organs, the militia, and finally the Army means in effect to disarm the socialist state, to place it at the mercy of the class enemy.

We want to stress that Stanislaw Kania, Wojciech Jaruzelski and other Polish comrades expressed agreement with our views on all the issues that were brought up for discussion. Yet in fact everything remains as it was. No changes or corrections have been made in the policy of concessions and compromises. One position after another is being surrendered. Notwithstanding the fact that the materials of the recent plenary meetings of the PUWP Central Committee recognize the existence of the counterrevolutionary danger, no measures to combat that danger have been taken so far, and the organizers of the counterrevolution are not even being directly named.

Moreover, the situation within the PUWP itself has recently become a cause for special alarm. With only a little over a month remaining until the Congress, the tone in the election campaign is increasingly being set by forces hostile to socialism. The fact that not infrequently total unknowns, who openly advocate opportunist views, assume posts of leadership in local Party organizations and figure among the delegates to conferences and the Congress, cannot but cause concern. Meanwhile, as a result of various manipulations by the enemies of the PUWP, as well as by revisionists and simple opportunists, experienced workers dedicated to the cause of the Party—men and women with unblemished reputations and moral qualities—are being pushed aside.

Also alarming is the fact that among the delegates to the forthcoming Congress the number of Communists from the working class is insignificant. The course of preparations for the Congress is complicated by the so-called movement of horizontal structures—a tool of splitting the Party that is being used by the opportunists to stack the Congress with the people they need and thus to deflect its work into a channel advantageous to them. The possibility cannot be excluded that an attempt may be made at the Congress itself to defeat the Marxist-Leninist forces of the Party in order to eliminate it.

We must also make special mention of the fact that in recent months counterrevolutionary forces have been actively spreading all sorts of anti-Soviet fabrications aimed at eliminating the fruit of all the work done by our Parties, at reviving nationalistic, anti-Soviet sentiments among various sections of Polish society. The slander, the lies, stop short of nothing. The claim is even raised that the Soviet Union is "plundering" Poland. And this is being said in deliberate disregard of the fact that the Soviet Union has given and continues giving enormous additional material aid to Poland at this difficult time. This is being said about a country which, because it sends in supplies of oil, gas, ores and cotton at prices that are from 33 percent to 50 percent lower than the world market price, actually nourishes the main branches of Poland's industry.

Esteemed Comrades! In addressing this letter to you, we proceed not only from our concern over the situation in fraternal Poland, over the conditions and prospects for further Soviet-Polish cooperation. We, and other fraternal Parties with us, are no less concerned over the fact that the offensive of the hostile anti-socialist forces inside the Polish People's Republic threatens the interests of our whole community, its cohesion, its integrity, the security of its borders. Yes, the threat is to our common security. Imperialist reaction, which supports and encourages the Polish counterrevolution, does not conceal its hopes thus sharply to change in their favor the balance of forces in Europe and even the rest of the world.

The crisis in Poland is being actively used by imperialism to slander the socialist system, the ideals and principles of socialism. It is being used for fresh attacks against the international communist movement.

Hence a historical responsibility rests on the PUWP not only for the destiny of its homeland, for its independence and progress, for the cause of socialism in Poland. On your shoulders, comrades, also rests the enormous responsibility for the common interests of the whole socialist community.

We believe that it is still possible to prevent the worst, prevent a national catastrophe. There are many honest and staunch Communists in the PUWP who are ready to do battle for the ideals of Marxism-Leninism, for an independent Poland. There are many people in Poland who are dedicated to the cause of socialism. We believe that the working class, the country's working people, even those who were drawn by deception into the machinations of the enemy, will in the long run follow the Party.

The point is to mobilize all healthy forces of society and thus to repulse the class enemy, to struggle against the counterrevolution. And this requires, first of all, the revolutionary determination of the Party itself, of its activists and its leadership. Yes, leadership is important. And the time is now. The Party can and must find within itself the strength to change the course of events, and even before the 9th Congress of the PUWP direct them into the necessary channel.

We would like to be confident that the Central Committee of the Party of Communists in fraternal Poland will know how to live up to its historical responsibility!

We want to assure you, dear comrades, that in these difficult days, as was always the case in the past, the Central Committee of the CPSU, all Soviet Communists and the entire Soviet people are with you in your struggle. Our stand was clearly expressed in the statement made by Comrade Leonid Brezhnev at the 26th Congress of the CPSU: "We will not abandon fraternal, socialist Poland in its hour of need—we will stand by it!"

Central Committee of the Communist
Party of the Soviet Union

Appendix 46 THE FOOD PROGRAM OF THE USSR FOR THE PERIOD ENDING IN 1990 [1]

The Plenary Meeting of the Central Committee of the CPSU, held on May 24, 1982, has approved the Food Program of the USSR for the Period Ending in 1990. The following is a summary of the Program.

PREAMBLE

The Soviet people, led by the Communist Party, have scored outstanding achievements in creating the material and technical foundations of communism. This country now possesses highly developed productive forces, an extensive, advanced industry, and a large-scale, highly-mechanized system of agriculture. A society of developed socialism has been built in the USSR. The achievements gained provide striking and conclusive evidence of the great advantages and vast potentialities of the socialist system.

Concern for the human being, for creating increasingly favorable conditions for the all-around and well-balanced development of the individual, has been and continues to be in the focus of attention of the Party and the Soviet state.

Far-reaching measures have been carried out in this respect over the past fifteen years. Pay scales have almost doubled. Fringe benefits and allowances paid out to the population from the social consumption funds have increased by 2.8 times; real per capita incomes have doubled, and over 160 million Soviet citizens have had their housing conditions improved. Further headway has been made in education, in the cultural level, in health care, and in the service industries.

The Soviet people have wide-ranging socioeconomic and political rights— the right to work, to rest and recreation, to housing, to free education and health care. They are active in running the affairs of the community and of the state. The rights of the Soviet citizen are guaranteed by the Constitution of the USSR.

The basic factor behind the Soviet people's rising standard of living is their honest work, which ensures continuous national economic growth. In the last 15 years alone, the basic production assets of the national economy have expanded by 3.2 times, while the national income has increased by 2.4 times. There has been a dynamic expansion of industrial and agricultural production, as well as faster scientific and technological progress.

The nation's present economic, scientific and technological potential enables it to resolve effectively new large-scale problems in its effort to build a communist society.

The 26th Congress of the CPSU, in putting forward a wide-ranging pro-

[1] Pravada, May 26, 1982, as reproduced in Reprints From the Soviet Press, vol. XXXV, No. 1 (July 15, 1982), pp. 19–58.

gram for social development and increased well-being, declared that improvement of the food supply was to be a top priority.

The Food Program of the USSR to run until 1990, which is the major component of the Party's economic strategy for the next decade, has been drawn up to this end, upon the initiative of Leonid Brezhnev, General Secretary of the Central Committee of the CPSU and President of the Presidium of the Supreme Soviet of the USSR.

I. MAIN RESULTS AND OBJECTIVES OF THE
DEVELOPMENT OF THE AGRO-INDUSTRIAL COMPLEX

The Communist Party, consistently following the agrarian policy course mapped out by the historic March 1965 Plenary Meeting of the CPSU Central Committee and carried forward at subsequent Plenary Meetings as well as at the 23rd through 26th Congresses of the CPSU, has already done a large amount of work to secure an advance in agricultural production.

The material and technical facilities available to the agro-industrial complex have been considerably expanded through increasing the efficiency of the national economy. There have been substantial improvements in the technical equipment of the farming industry, and productivity has increased on collective farms and state farms. The application of chemicals, land reclamation and other methods of improvement have been intensified. Supplies of mineral fertilizers for the farming community have tripled in the last 15 years, while the total area of irrigated and drained land has expanded by 1.7 times.

Specialized animal-husbandry complexes complete ʌwith industrial technology, as well as large poultry farms, are being put into service, and high-efficiency interfarm and agro-industrial individual and amalgamated units are being developed.

New branches have been set up to service agriculture: machine-building for animal husbandry and fodder production; rural construction and the mixed-feed and microbiological industries; farm-machinery building—all this has made further headway. The productive capacities of the sectors involved in the procurement, storage, and processing of agricultural produce have been expanded. The basic production assets of the food-producing sectors have expanded 2.7 times over the last 15 years.

The latest advances of science are being turned to good account on collective farms and state farms.

There have been some appreciable positive changes in the patterns of providing manpower for collective farms and state farms, which now employ 1.8 million specialists with a higher or specialized secondary education and nearly 4.5 million tractor drivers—machine operators and truck drivers.

Much has been done to improve the social amenities and living conditions in the countryside. Compared with 1965, average monthly wages and salaries for both manual and mental labor on state farms had doubled by 1980, while the pay rates for collective farmers had gone up 2.3 times; the pension system for rural workers had been improved.

Housing accommodations totaling around 500 million square meters of floor space have been turned over for occupancy in the countryside during that period, along with preschool children's institutions to accommodate 2.6 million youngsters, as well as clubhouses and community centers with facilities for 7.7 million persons.

Implementation of the measures to carry through the Party's agrarian policy has—despite certain difficulties caused by adverse weather conditions over the last few years—assured an increase in the average annual gross agricultural output under the 10th Five-Year Plan to 124 billion rubles in value terms—that is, to half as much again as in the five-year period preceding the March 1965 Plenary Meeting.

Our country has substantially increased grain production, bringing the average gross annual harvest up from 130 million tons to 205 million tons. Production of meat (slaughter weight) has gone up from 9.3 million tons to 14.8 million tons, that of milk, from 65 million tons to 93 million tons, and eggs, from 29,000 million to 63,000 million. There has been a substantial expansion of fruit and vegetable production, with vegetable output going up by 1.6 times, fruit crops and berries by 2.6 times, and grapes twofold.

All this has made it possible to step up the rate of food consumption by a substantial margin, even though the country's population has increased by 35 million since 1965. Uninterrupted supplies of bread, bakery and macaroni products, and sugar have been ensured everywhere. The average per capita consumption of meat and meat products has gone up by 41 percent, that of milk and dairy products by 25 percent, eggs by 1.9 times, and vegetables by 35 percent. In terms of calories, the Soviet per capita diet conforms to optimal physiological standards.

Now the Party wants to see stable supplies of all foodstuffs made readily available to the whole population within the shortest possible time limits, using the nation's increased economic potential to achieve this, and the nutritional structure of the Soviet people's diet substantially improved through increased consumption of the nutritionally most valuable foods.

The object to be achieved under the 11th Five-Year Plan, along with meeting the population's demand for a wide range of bread, bakery and macaroni products, potatoes and sugar, is to provide enough groats, confectionery, margarine, eggs, and fish, to meet the existing demand in full, and also to improve the availability of meat, milk, vegetable oil, fruit, and vegetables.

The rate of consumption of meat, vegetable oil, and vegetables is to be appreciably stepped up under the 12th Five-Year Plan through expanding production.

By the end of the 12th Five-Year Plan period, the annual per capita rate of consumption of staple foodstuffs will be roughly as follows: meat and meat products, 70 kg; fish products, 19 kg; milk and dairy products, 330 to 340 kg; eggs, 260 to 266 pieces; vegetable oil, 13.2 kg; vegetables and melons, 126–135 kg; fruit and berries, 66–70 kg; potatoes, 110 kg; sugar, 45.5 kg; bakery products, 135 kg. But this will be merely the average national rate of food consumption—figures will vary for various regions, depending on natural and climatic conditions, native traditions, and other specific features.

The main directions of implementation of the USSR's Food Program are as follows:

—the proportionate and balanced development of the agro-industrial complex; improvement of management, planning and economic incentives in all its sectors; and the fullest possible gearing of production to high end results;

—ensuring high rates of growth of agricultural production on the basis of its steady intensification, the effective use of land, the greatest possible strengthening of its material and technical base, and the accelerated introduction of scientific achievements and progressive know-how;

—the best possible utilization of the production and technical potential of the agro-industrial complex; a considerable increase in returns on capital investments and material inputs; the development of the specialization and concentration of production through broader interfarm and intersectoral ties;

—a drive for economies and rationalization, for reducing losses and increasing the quality of agricultural production through the extensive introduction of advanced technologies for the production, processing and storing of output and shipping it by specialized transport;

—continued further improvement of living conditions in the countryside.

Collective farms and state farms will play a decisive role in increasing agricultural production. Party, Government and economic organizations should concentrate on ensuring the steady growth of labor productivity on all farms, a radical improvement in their performance, and the strengthening of the economies of loss-producing and low-efficiency collective farms and state farms.

To increase our food resources, it is necessary, wherever appropriate conditions exist, to develop the subsidiary farms operated by industrial enterprises and organizations so as to achieve maximal satisfaction of the requirements of public catering, thus meeting the demand of factory and office workers in meat, milk, potatoes and vegetables. To make more extensive use of the possibilities of the personal subsidiary plots of individual citizens and of collective orchards and vegetable gardens.

Economically and politically, the food problem is the central issue of the current decade. An earnest of its successful solution is in the fulfillment and overfulfillment of annual plans and the 11th Five-Year Plan as a whole.

Attainment of the targets set forth in the USSR's Food Program is a national cause, the prime responsibility of all Party, Government and economic bodies, all trade union and YCL organizations, all collective farmers and state farm workers, the personnel of other enterprises within the agro-industrial complex, and, finally, all Soviet citizens.

II. PRODUCTION OF STAPLE FOODS
ORGANIZATION OF THE FOOD TRADE

Production of Grain and Grain Products: The Program stresses that the accelerated and steady growth of grain production is the key issue of agriculture.

The aim is to satisfy in the next few years the growing national requirements in quality food and fodder grain and create the necessary state reserves of grain and resources for grain exports. The main way to increase grain output is to raise crop yields at all enterprises. In the current decade, it is necessary to raise grain yields by 6 to 7 centners to bring them to between 21 and 22 metric centners per hectare by 1990. Annual grain production is to average 238 to 243 million tons under the 11th Five-Year Plan and 250 to 255 million tons under the 12th Five-Year Plan.

To increase fodder grain resources, more fully to use, along with the rise in barley and oats production, the great potentialities of maize. To bring the gross output of maize grain to at least 17 million tons in 1985 and 20 million tons in 1990. To extend the industrial techniques of growing and harvesting maize to the entire area planted to this crop.

To bring the output of leguminous crops to between 12 million and 14 million tons in 1985 and 18 million to 20 million tons in 1990.

While increasing the production of grain in every way possible, it is also necessary to show unflagging concern for the economical and rational consumption of food and fodder grain, bread, and bakery products.

Production of Livestock Products: Our target is to bring the annual average production of meat (slaughter weight) to between 17 million and 17.5 million tons under the 11th Five-Year Plan, and to between 20 million and 20.5 million tons under the 12th Five-Year Plan; the output of milk to between 97 million and 99 million tons, then to between 104 million and 106 million tons respectively; and the production of eggs to 72 billion, then to between 78 billion and 79 billion pieces respectively. To ensure a general changeover to the intensive methods of livestock breeding and a considerable increase in the productivity of all categories of livestock and poultry. To staff livestock farms and complexes with skilled personnel.

To raise the standards of pedigreed stockbreeding. To expand and strengthen the material base of the state veterinary services and of enterprises manufacturing biological preparations.

Acceleration of the rise in beef production should become the main direction of increasing meat resources. The output of beef (slaughter weight) should be brought to at least 7.8 million tons in 1985 and 9.5 million tons in 1990. To continue the gradual transition to industrial cattle-raising and fattening techniques on collective farms and state farms and at interfarm enterprises, and to encourage the provision of fodder mostly locally, through producing it on the farms.

To devote more attention to the further development of pig breeding, which yields output faster than other sectors of animal husbandry. To bring pork output (slaughter weight) to not less than 6.5 million tons in 1985 and to between 7 million and 7.3 million tons in 1990. To raise the efficiency of pig breeding.

Along with organizing intensive pig breeding at industrialized farms and complexes, to make fuller use of the possibilities for increasing pork output on nonspecialized collective farms and state farms, subsidiary farms operated by industrial enterprises and organizations, and the personal subsidiary plots of individual citizens.

To use the possibilities of the steppe, forest-and-steppe, semidesert and mountainous regions of the country more effectively for increasing the production of mutton and bringing its output up to at least 1 million tons (slaughter weight) by 1985 and 1.2 million to 1.3 million tons in 1990. To take measures to increase the population of Romanoff, Tsygaiskaya, and other meat-and-wool sheep breeds in the areas of their traditional breeding.

To bring the output of poultry (slaughter weight) to not less than 2.6 million tons in 1985 and to between 3.4 million and 3.6 million tons in 1990.

To increase the output of rabbit meat; to improve the work of voluntary rabbit-breeding societies, and more fully to satisfy public demand for pedigreed rabbits.

To take measures to increase meat resources through the development of horse and reindeer breeding.

The main direction for increasing the output of milk and dairy products is to raise the productivity of cows. Our task is to increase average annual milk yields per cow on collective farms and state farms by 500 kg to 600 kg by 1990. To bring the average annual milk yield per cow to 4,000 kilograms in the areas of developed dairy livestock breeding.

To work steadily to transfer dairy livestock-breeding methods to an industrial foundation, primarily through enlarging and reconstructing operating farms. To raise the quality of milk.

Measures have been drafted to increase the variety of meat and dairy products and raise their quality.

Development of a Reliable Fodder Base for Livestock Breeding: The Program provides for bringing the output of fodder to 500 million tons of fodder units in 1985 and to between 540 million and 550 million tons by 1990. To bring hay production to between 110 million and 112 million tons, and the output of fodder root crops to between 60 million and 63 million tons by 1990.

To carry out other necessary measures to further intensify the production of field, meadow and pasture fodder crops and raise the productivity of all fodder-producing land, so that every enterprise might fully meet the requirements of animal husbandry in quality coarse, succulent, and pasture fodder.

To impart a specialized sectoral character to the production of various feeds on collective farms and state farms. To pay special attention to ensuring the balanced character of feeds as regards protein content and other components; to improving the quality of feeds, stressing their rational use and reducing their losses.

Widely to introduce the most advanced technology of procurement and the storing of feeds. To put into operation silage and haylage facilities with an aggregate capacity of between 240 million and 245 million cubic meters, hay stores with a total capacity of 60 million to 65 million tons, and root storages with a total capacity of 30 million to 35 million tons during the decade.

Measures have been mapped out for boosting the production of mixed feeds at state and interfarm enterprises, and on collective farms and state farms, with the aim of making rational use of fodder grain.

Targets have been set for increasing the output of adequate protein-vitamin additives to ensure their proper supply to interfarm enterprises and to collective farms and state farms, and for boosting the output of fodder yeast and fodder lysine, fish meal, and feeds of organic origin.

Production of fruit, vegetables and potatoes: The Program provides for implementing large-scale measures to improve the system of supplying the population with fruit, vegetables and potatoes as a result of the further boosting of their output and of improving their quality, as well as of a drastic reduction in the losses of produce on its way from the fields to the consumers.

It is planned to bring the average annual output of vegetables and melons to between 33 million and 34 million tons in the 11th Five-Year Plan period and between 37 and 39 million tons in the 12th Five-Year Plan period, with fruit and berries reaching between 11 million and 12 million tons, then 14 million to 15 million tons, and grapes between 7.5 million and 8 million tons, then between 10 million and 11 million tons respectively. Considerably to increase the production of vegetables in protected ground. To ensure the average annual gross output of potatoes at between 87 million and 89 million tons in the 11th Five-Year Plan period, and at 90 million to 92 million tons in the 12th Five-Year Plan period.

It is planned to set up large specialized farms and agro-industrial enterprises for producing and processing fruit and vegetables in the southern regions of the Russian Federation, in the Ukrainian SSR, the Kazakh SSR, the Central Asian and Transcaucasian republics, and the Moldavian SSR, and to turn these areas into the main base for supplying the urban population of the center and north of the European part of the USSR, the Urals, Siberia and the Far East with warm-climate vegetables, fruit and berries.

To complete the creation of specialized zones for commercial, industrial-basis potato production, primarily in the Byelorussian SSR, in the regions of the Non-Black-Soil Zone of the Russian Federation, and in the Baltic republics. To extend the zones for growing early potatoes in the regions of the Ukrainian SSR and the republics of the Transcaucasus and Central Asia. To develop at an accelerated rate the agricultural base for growing potatoes and vegetables in the areas of Siberia and the Far East, particularly in the zone of the Baikal-Amur railway.

To carry out measures for the rational distribution of fruit, vegetable and potato storages, in order significantly to reduce both losses of such produce and the volume of its transportation in the periods of its massive procurement. To make extensive use of the most up-to-date methods of storing potatoes, fruit and vegetables.

Considerably to increase the picking and procurement of wild-growing fruit, berries and mushrooms.

Measures have been mapped out for an accelerated buildup of capacities for processing and storing fruit and vegetables.

It has been recommended that the setting up of capacities for processing and storing fruit and vegetables directly on collective farms and state farms should be much more widely practiced, so as to preserve, process and sell all the produce the farms grow.

Sugar Production: It is planned to bring the average annual output of sugar beet to between 102 and 103 million tons in the 12th Five-Year Plan period. To this end, it is planned in the main to complete the transition of sugar beet-growing to industrial technology to the 12th Five-Year Plan period.

Plan targets for sugar production have been set, and to prevent losses, measures have been mapped out for reducing the duration of the season of processing sugar beet to 100 or at most 105 days by the year 1990. The production of honey will be considerably increased. It is planned to continue setting up specialized bee-keeping farms and bee gardens on an industrial basis, and to pay more attention to developing bee-keeping on personal small-holdings.

Production of vegetable oil and margarine products: Ensuring considerable growth in the output of seeds of oil-producing crops, improving the organization of their procurement, storing and processing, and reducing losses of oil seeds constitute an important task for the Party, Government and agricultural bodies, collective farms and state farms, and procurement and processing enterprises.

It is planned to bring the average annual production of sunflower seeds to 6.7 million tons in the 11th Five-Year Plan period and to between 7.2 million and 7.5 million tons in the 12th Five-Year Plan period, and of soya, to 1.4 million tons and 2.2 million to 2.3 million tons respectively. To extend the areas sown to soya on irrigated lands in the European part of the USSR, Central Asia and Kazakhstan. To master the growing of rapeseed crops in some areas of the country in the 11th Five-Year Plan period in order to increase vegetable oil resources.

The plan targets set in the Program provide for rapid growth in the output of vegetable oil and margarine products during the 11th and 12th Five-Year Plan periods, and measures have been mapped out for improving their quality.

Production of confectionery, food concentrates, grape wine, beer and soft drinks: It is planned to raise the production of confectionery products to at least 4.4 million tons, while food concentrates will rise to 350,000 tons in 1990. The output of products in heightened demand among the population, such as pastille marmelade and flour confectionery with a lower sugar content, will go up.

It is planned to increase tea-leaf picking to 560,000 tons in 1985, and to between 740,000 and 750,000 tons in 1990, and the production of natural tea, to 230,000 tons and 280,000 to 300,000 tons respectively. Considerably to improve the quality of the tea produced, and to expand its assortment.

Output of fish products: Measures have been mapped out for increasing the output of fish and seafood products, and for raising the productivity of fishing and the efficiency of the use of the fishing industry's fleet.

To increase commercial fish output at fish farms in the next decade, approximately tripling it on the basis of the intensification of pond-fish culture. Ministries and departments should make extensive use for this purpose of industrial water reservoirs belonging to enterprises under their jurisdiction and suitable for fish production. Roughly, to double the output of live and frozen fish in the next two Five-Year Plan periods.

Output of products at subsidiary farms: The Central Committees of the Communist Parties and the Councils of Ministers of the Union Republics, their Ministries and Departments, and Party, Government, economic and trade union bodies should adopt measures for sizably increasing the production of foodstuffs on the subsidiary farms of enterprises and organizations. They should commandeer the land necessary for these farms, and supply them with farm machinery, fertilizers and other material and technical resources on an equal basis with collective and state farms.

A major task for the Councils of Ministers of the Union and autonomous republics, the executive councils of the Soviets of territories, regions and districts, agricultural bodies, managers of farms and enterprises, and trade union organizations is to create conditions that would enable every family living in the countryside to have a plot of land attached to its house and to keep livestock and poultry.

The consumers' cooperative societies must ensure the timely purchase of surplus agricultural produce from the population.

Organization of Trade in Foodstuffs: The Councils of Ministers of the Union Republics and the Ministries and Departments of the USSR which have a trade network must considerably improve the methods of selling goods to the population. They must take measures to expand and rationalize the location of shops, canteens and other trading establishments and improve their working schedules in order to ensure maximum convenience for the population. Every large enterprise, construction project and educational institution must have a canteen.

The network of collective-farm markets must be expanded, the system of trade on the markets should be improved, and their material and technical base should be strengthened.

Everything must be done to promote the development of the consumers' cooperative trade network, expand trade in agricultural products purchased at the personal subsidiary plots of citizens, provide premises for cooperative organizations to set up shops to sell these products in industrial centers, and help them by supplying their needs in transport facilities.

Direct ties between trade and collective farms and state farms and other enterprises within the agro-industrial complex must be developed and improved.

III. THE DEVELOPMENT OF THE MATERIAL AND TECHNICAL BASE OF THE AGRO-INDUSTRIAL COMPLEX

A major condition for the successful implementation of the Food Program of the USSR is the acceleration of scientific and technological progress, effective use of the production capacities and the strengthening of the material and technical base of agriculture and all sectors of the agro-industrial complex through further development of mechanization and chemicalization of production and extensive land improvement.

Comprehensive Mechanization of Agricultural Production and Technical Retooling of the Food Industry: The Program emphasizes that the prime task for the machine-building ministries and all ministries and departments of the agro-industrial complex is to complete, mainly before 1990, comprehensive mechanization of crop-growing and livestock-breeding and the retooling of the food industry on a new technological basis.

During the ten-year period agriculture is to receive: 3,740,000 to 3,780,000 tractors; at least 200,000 excavators; 215,000 bulldozers; 93,000 scrapers; 13,000 road graders; 1,170,000 grain combine harvesters and other farm machinery worth a total of 67 to 70 billion rubles, including 38 to 40 billion rubles' worth of machinery for plant growing and 29 to 30 billion rubles' worth of machinery for livestock breeding and fodder production.

The supply of electricity to agriculture is to be increased: in 1990 it will reach between 210 billion and 235 billion kilowatt-hours.

It has been recommended to the machine-building ministries that they organize the production of spare parts for tractors, trucks, farm machines and technological equipment in accordance with fixed consumption quotas.

The assignment for the tractor and agricultural machine-building industry in the 12th Five-Year Plan period will be to ensure the production of new and modernized models of high-powered tractors. During the 11th Five-Year Plan period it will have to modernize and enhance the dependability of the grain combine harvesters Niva, Kolos and Sibiryak. The production of caterpillar rice combine-harvesters must be increased.

Production capacities must be increased at a fast rate and agriculture adequately supplied with machines for the introduction of soil-protection techniques; combine aggregates, heavy-disc implements, precision seeders, sugar beet loaders and other machinery necessary for industrializing the cultivation of sugar beet, maize, potatoes, vegetables and other agricultural crops; highly efficient machinery and equipment for the transportation, mixing and application of solid mineral and liquid composite fertilizers and also liquid ammonia; machines and equipment for the preparation of working solutions of pesticides and their use in small amounts; wide-cut self-propelled and trailer roll-mill harvesters, conveyor belts and equipment for the processing and storage of agricultural produce after harvesting; small-scale technical equipment to meet both the needs of collective farms and state farms and of the population at large in such equipment.

The building and road-building industry is to produce highly efficient new technology. Machine-building for light industry and the food industry is to produce mainly conveyor belts and complete plants.

The Development of Chemicalization of Agriculture: In 1985, agriculture is to be supplied with 26.5 million tons, and in 1990 with 30 million to 32 million tons of chemical fertilizers (in terms of 100 percent nutrient content), and with 950,000 tons and 1.2 million tons of chemical fodder additives respectively.

Also, in 1985, agriculture is to be supplied with 680,000 tons of chemical plant protection agents and, in 1990, with 750,000 to 790,000 tons. Production of highly effective means of plant protection is to be increased.

The output of fodder preservatives is also to be increased. Using 1985 and 1990 as target dates, collective farms and state farms are to receive at least 110,000 tons, then 380,000 to 400,000 tons of such preservatives respectively. Measures are to be taken to supply agriculture with lime materials and improve their quality.

The application of organic fertilizers on collective farms and state farms in 1985 and 1990 is to increase to 1.2 billion tons and at least 1.5 billion tons respectively. In the 12th Five-Year Plan period the production of peat for compost and farm litter is to come to not less than 170 million tons a year.

Measures have been worked out to create a material and technical base for chemicalization on collective farms and state farms as well as agro-chemical organizations. The agro-chemical service must assume more responsibility for the effective use of mineral fertilizers and other means of chemicalization as well as for the introduction in production of the achievements of science, technology, and advanced know-how.

The Development of Land Improvement: The Program provides for the further enhancement of the role of land improvement in increasing the production of agricultural products. The area of irrigated land is to be increased to 20.8 million hectares in 1985 and 23 million to 25 million hectares in 1990, and the area of drained land to 15.5 million and 18 to 19 million hectares respectively.

Efforts should be focused on the need to ensure comprehensive land improvement and the development of land for agricultural use, and higher projected crop productivity should be achieved on irrigated and drained lands. Guaranteed grain output zones, especially in maize production, should be set up in irrigated farming regions. The production of fodder on reclaimed land should be brought to 63 million tons of fodder units in 1985 and to between 80 million and 82 million tons in 1990. Irrigated fodder-growing areas should be created on livestock-breeding farms.

The creation of zones of guaranteed production of vegetables and spring potatoes on irrigated lands near large cities and industrial centers should be completed. The construction of large rice irrigation systems will continue.

The machine-building ministries must work out and organize large-scale production of new types of highly efficient irrigation machines and mechanisms for land improvement. The Ministry of the Shipbuilding Industry is to produce and supply agriculture in 1982–90 with 32,000 sprinkler machines Fregat and Kuban.

Before the end of 1990, the first stage of the project to transfer part of the flow of northern rivers to the Volga and the Volga-Don, Rostov-Krasnodar and Danube-Dnieper canals must be completed.

Development of the production capacities of the sectors of the agro-industrial complex: To continue the course of the further strengthening of the material and technical base of the country's agro-industrial complex. To ensure during the 11th Five-Year Plan period the use of investments in these sectors amounting to around 233 billion rubles, including 189.6 billion rubles in agriculture.

The Program envisages that investments be made primarily in those capacities which will make is possible to raise the output of foodstuffs within the shortest possible time; that the projects of the agro-industrial complex be regarded as the USSR's major, top-priority projects.

In agriculture, investments will be concentrated on raising the fertility of land, on providing stable fodder resources in livestock farming, and on capacities for the primary processing of products, the construction of storehouses, the modernization and extension of livestock premises, and also the social development of the countryside. Measures have been agreed upon for improving the organization of rural housing construction.

IV. SUPPLYING THE VARIOUS SECTORS OF THE AGRO-INDUSTRIAL COMPLEX
WITH TRANSPORT, CONTAINERS AND PACKING MATERIALS

Providing the agro-industrial complex with transport facilities is one of the major tasks of the food program. The following measures have been mapped out for its solution.

To provide agriculture within the current decade with 3 million to 3.06 million trucks and 3.2 million to 3.3 million tractor trailers. To supply collective farms, state farms and enterprises of the food industry with 110,000 to 116,000 milk carriers and 50,000 to 53,000 semitrailer cattle carriers. To increase the supply of the sectors of the food and fishing industries with specialized motor vehicles for the haulage of granulated sugar and liquid sugar, living fish and other foodstuffs, beer and mineral water; to deliver during the current decade 76,000 to 78,000 refrigerator trucks to the various sectors of the agro-industrial complex and the common transport. To provide the Ministry of Railways with 29,000 to 30,000 refrigerator and isothermal cars.

During the 11th Five-Year Plan period, the Ministry of the Automobile Industry should ensure the creation of capacities for the annual production of 20,000 articulated trucks for agriculture at the Kutaisi Motor Works and of 10,000 trucks of high trafficability with a carrying capacity of seven or eight tons at the Urals Motor Works.

To take appropriate measures in order to meet the requirements of the food sectors of industry, trade, and agriculture for *containers and packing materials*.

By 1990, to bring the output of basic foodstuffs in packaged form to between 60 percent and 70 percent of the overall volume of all food sales.

V.   RAISING THE ROLE OF SCIENCE IN THE IMPLEMENTATION OF THE FOOD PROGRAM

The USSR State Committee for Science and Technology, the USSR Academy of Sciences, the USSR Ministry of Agriculture, the USSR Ministry of Fruit and Vegetable Farming, the All-Union Lenin Academy of Agricultural Sciences and other ministries and departments have been entrusted with taking, in the 1982–1990 period, concrete measures aimed at the further development of research and the accelerated introduction of the achievements of science into the various sectors of the agro-industrial complex.

To develop the network of research-production associations established on the basis of sectoral and zonal research and design organizations.

To make—on the basis of the generalization of all this experience—scientifically grounded recommendations concerning the further improvement of the specialization, concentration and interfarm cooperation of production, and the introduction of advanced forms of labor organization and labor incentives for obtaining optimal end work results.

To intensify the breeding of new varieties and hybrids of farm crops meeting the requirements of industrial technologies used in plant-growing; to breed and introduce varieties resistant to unfavorable environmental factors, with high grain quality and immunity to diseases and pests.

To take measures aimed at improving the pedigree and productive qualities of cattle and poultry, at bettering the existing, and creating new, highly productive breeds, groups, lines, hybrids and crossbreeds adapted to industrial technologies in various sectors of livestock farming.

To ensure the following:

—the development and introduction of power-saving soil-protection and industrial technologies of farm crop cultivation suited to a wide variety of soil and climatic conditions; and

—technologies of producing high-quality fodder on natural grazing grounds and ploughlands, which will make it possible to obtain 10,000 to 15,000 fodder units per hectare on irrigated lands and 5,000 to 6,000 fodder units per hectare on non-irrigated ground, as well as production processes for conserving green fodder, making it possible to preserve at least 90 percent of the nutrients;

—more efficient methods and means of preventing and curing animal diseases; efficient biological and chemotherapeutic veterinary preparations and the technology of their manufacture, instruments and devices for mass surveys and treatment of animals;

—new technologies for storing farm products with the use of active ventilation, artificial freezing, and in a regulated gaseous medium.

To intensify studies of the rational use of water resources and their protection against pollution and depletion; the construction of economical and reliable irrigation systems with mechanized and automated water distribution.

The USSR Academy of Sciences, the Academies of Sciences of the Union Republics and the All-Union Lenin Academy of Agricultural Sciences should concentrate on developing theoretical investigations into the problems of genetic engineering in the selection of plants, microorganisms and animals, the bio-technology of the synthesis of protein, and biologically active substances. They must plan to ensure the development of new, effective means of plant protection against pests, diseases and weeds, concentrate on producing growth regulators and other preparations for agriculture, and work out and introduce the necessary technology for the industrial production of these means.

To ensure the elaboration and implementation of the programs of integrated standardization providing for a mutually coordinated rise in the general demand for improving the quality of farm produce and foodstuffs, mineral fertilizers, plant protection agents, machinery and equipment, containers and packing materials for agricultural production, and also the expansion of the use of modern methods of assessing the quality of these products.

VI. IMPROVEMENT OF LIVING CONDITIONS IN THE COUNTRYSIDE

The Program emphasizes that the consistent implementation of measures for the social development of the countryside, further raising the general level of well-being and the cultural, medical and community services for rural residents, is a highly important task for Party, Soviet, economic and trade union bodies. It is necessary to enhance in every possible way the prestige of rural labor, and to speed up the introduction of a rational work-and-rest pattern for the personnel of state farms and collective farms. The levels of pay for agricultural and industrial work should be brought closer together on the basis of higher labor productivity.

Well-appointed dwellings complete with household structures, preschool centers for children, clubs, libraries, other cultural and service institutions, trade, public-catering and public-service establishments, as well as roads, are to be built on collective farms and state farms and other agricultural projects at accelerated rates.

Dwellings with a total floor space of not less than 176 million square meters should be built on collective farms and state farms as well as at other agricultural projects in the 11th Five-Year Plan period. In the 12th Five-Year Plan period, an additional 15 percent to 18 percent more housing should be added. Communal services to the rural population should also continue to be considerably enhanced.

Individual construction of dwelling houses on collective farms and state farms should be increased. Plans should provide for the allocation of necessary building materials for these purposes. The construction of farmstead-type housing, wood panel housebuildings, and the production of modules for agricultural construction should be intensified.

The amounts of community services provided to rural residents should be increased twofold over the decade. The standards of all services for the population should be raised. More orders for all necessary community services should be taken directly on collective farms and state farms.

The construction of outpatient clinics and pharmacies should be increased. Measures should be taken to improve the staffing of medical institutions in the countryside.

Work on expanding the physical plant of rural schools should continue. Additional general-education schools with accommodations for a student body of 2.3 million must be built in the countryside in the 11th Five-Year Plan period. This figure should be increased by about 14 percent to 17 percent in the 12th Five-Year Plan period.

Reliable transport communications between collective farms and state farms, on the one hand, and district centers on the other, should be established. All-purpose motor roads totaling approximately 130,000 kilometers and intra-farm roads with a total length of 150,000 kilometers should be built. The length of rural bus lines should be steadily extended so that by the year 1990 all the central farmsteads of collective farms and state farms can be connected with district centers, mainly by bus routes.

Ancillary industries and crafts, as well as production cooperation with industrial enterprises, should be developed on farms wherever this is expedient, with a view to ensuring year-round employment for collective farmers and farm workers.

VII.   ENHANCING WORK EFFICIENCY ON COLLECTIVE FARMS AND STATE FARMS
AND AT OTHER ENTERPRISES AND ORGANIZATIONS OF THE
AGRO-INDUSTRIAL COMPLEX

The Food Program of the USSR maps out large-scale measures on the further development of agriculture and related industries, and has earmarked the necessary funds for this.

Fixed assets in agriculture and in the food industry will grow 1.5-fold over the decade. Power generating capacities on collective farms and state farms will increase more than 1.6-fold, and the supply of mineral fertilizer for the countryside will go up 1.7-fold.

Now the center of gravity is being shifted to returns on capital investment, the growth of productivity in agriculture, and the deepening and improvement of its ties with all branches of the agro-industrial complex. As the 26th CPSU Congress noted, this is a distinguishing feature of the agrarian policy in the 1980s.

Labor productivity on collective farms and state farms should be raised over the decade approximately 1.5-fold, while the per-hectare production of agricultural output should be increased by not less than one-third.

The Central Committees of the Communist Parties and Councils of Ministers of Union Republics, ministries and departments of the USSR, local Party, Soviet and economic bodies, collective farms, state farms, enterprises and organizations should ensure a sharp switchover to intensive methods of economic management, improved utilization of land, production capacities, manpower, material and financial resources and all available reserves, thus enhancing all opportunities for increasing the output of food products.

The role of economic accounting principles in achieving the stable profitability of farms as the basis of expanded reproduction should be enhanced. Precise economic estimates of land, water, material and manpower resources should be used more actively in the practice of planning and control of the farms' activity.

Special attention should be paid to improving the economic activity of backward collective farms and state farms so as to help them attain stable and high production growth rates in the near future.

Consumption of materials per unit of agricultural output, as well as all losses of this type, should be substantially reduced.

Measures on comprehensive processing of agricultural raw materials and diminishing their losses should be carried out in the food industry through the introduction of highly efficient technological equipment.

Work in all sections of collective farm and state farm production should be improved through the involvement of well trained executives, specialists, and cadres in the mass-scale trades. Further improvement of the qualifications of this personnel should be ensured, and fluctuations in employment reduced. Special attention should be paid to raising the caliber of workers in the medium echelons.

The latest scientific and technological advances, as well as the scientific organization of labor, should be introduced more actively. It is necessary to work for a considerable increase in the effectiveness of the systems of material and moral incentives.

In the field of planning and management, it is necessary to effect the transition to planning the activity and management of the agro-industrial complex as a single whole at all levels, and to achieve well balanced development and the close interaction of all its branches. The institutional structure of administering the agro-industrial complex should be simplified, and any redundant or duplicating links should be abolished. The managerial staff should be considerably reduced. Petty supervision in respect to collective farms and state farms should not be allowed.

In the field of material incentives in production, encouragement of the highest possible end results should become the main form of stimulating the work of collectives of enterprises and organizations, executives and specialists at all links of the agro-industrial complex.

Incentives for obtaining more growth of agricultural output should be used on a broader scale in organizations and enterprises servicing collective farms and state farms. Payment in kind, primarily in grain, fruits, vegetables and fodder, for the work of collective farmers and state farm employees should be raised.

Measures on the large-scale introduction of improved methods of labor organization and stimulation, ensuring a close connection between the size of wages and the end results of the agricultural year, should be worked out and implemented in all branches of the agro-industrial complex. Experience with team-contract work and the rate-plus-bonus system should be more widely disseminated.

Bonus payments for uninterrupted service on a single farm, plus additional leave, should be introduced as an added incentive during the 11th Five-Year Plan period for workers employed in livestock breeding.

VIII. PRINCIPAL TASKS OF UNION REPUBLICS IN THE IMPLEMENTATION OF THE USSR FOOD PROGRAM

Each Union republic must make a maximum contribution to the fulfillment of the Food Program of the USSR. It is the responsibility of the Central Committees of the Communist Parties and the Councils of Ministers of Union republics to ensure the absolute implementation of plans for the production and purchases of farm produce and its delivery to the all-Union stock reserve.

The Union republics will be assigned the following basic tasks for the period until 1990 as regards the realization of the Food Program of the USSR:

In the Russian Soviet Federated Socialist Republic, to ensure an average annual gathered crop of 134 million to 136 million tons of grain in the 11th, and 140 million to 142 million tons in the 12th Five-Year Plan period; by 1990, as compared with the average annual output in the 10th Five-Year Plan period, to increase the gross average annual output of sugar beet by approximately 30 percent, sunflower seeds by 50 percent, potatoes by 20 percent, vegetables and melon crops by 40 percent, fruit and berries by 40 percent, and grapes by 160 percent. To increase the production of rapeseed to around a million tons in 1990.

To increase the output of all kinds of fodder during the decade by 30 percent to 40 percent.

During these ten years, to raise the average milk yield per cow by 600 to 700 kilograms.

To ensure the average annual production of 8.4 million to 8.7 million tons of meat (slaughter weight) in the 11th, and 9.8 million to 10 million tons in the 12th Five-Year Plan period, and also to produce, respectively, 50 million to 52 million and 53 million to 54 million tons of milk.

In the Non-Black-Soil Zone of the RSFSR, to continue land improvement work and carry out a set of measures for the accelerated growth of output of crop and livestock products.

In areas of Siberia and the Far East, to ensure the higher efficiency of all branches of agriculture for purposes of reliably supplying the population of these regions with food, mainly via local production.

In the Central and Black Soil Area and in the Northern Caucasus, to carry out measures aimed at further intensification of agriculture, animal husbandry and horticulture.

In the Volga Area, through the development of land irrigation, considerably to raise the output of grain, fodder, vegetables, melon crops and livestock products.

In the course of the decade, to bring under cultivation 3.3 million hectares of irrigated land and drain 3.7 million hectares of waterlogged land.

During the ten-year period, to increase the production of granulated sugar from sugar beet by 90 percent to 100 percent, canned vegetables and fruit (those processed from state stocks of raw produce) by 50 percent to 60 percent, vegetable oil by at least 150 percent, meat by 30 percent, cheeses by 50 percent to 60 percent, and potato products to between 100,000 and 110,000 tons.

In the Ukrainian SSR, to ensure an average annual crop of 51 million tons to 52 million tons of grain in the 11th, and 53 million to 54 million tons in the 12th Five-Year Plan period, and of 57 million tons and 60 million tons respectively of sugar beet. To increase, during the ten years, the gross harvests of sunflower seeds, vegetables and berries by not less than 40 percent, and grapes by 80 percent. To secure a further rise in the production of potatoes and vegetables, and to raise the output of rapeseed in 1990 to between 210,000 and 230,000 tons.

To implement measures for a steady rise in the production and purchases of millet, buckwheat, rice, durum and strong wheat, and kidney beans. To establish zones of the guaranteed production of maize grain in areas favorable to the cultivation of this crop.

To increase in the ten years the output of all types of fodder by 30 percent to 40 percent.

By 1990, to raise average milk yields per cow on collective farms and state farms by 600 to 700 kilograms.

To bring the average annual production of meat (slaughter weight) to between 3.9 million and 4.1 million tons in the 11th, and to between 4.6 million and 4.7 million tons in the 12th Five-Year Plan period, with milk, respectively, at between 22.5 million and 23 million, and 24 million to 24.4 million tons.

To bring under cultivation at least 1 million hectares of irrigated and to drain 1.3 million hectares of waterlogged land.

To develop all branches of the food industry at a high rate.

In the Byelorussian SSR, to ensure an average annual grain crop of between 7.8 million and 8.1 million tons in the 11th, and between 8.2 million and 8.6 million tons in the 12th Five-Year Plan period. During the decade, to increase gross harvests of vegetables by approximately 20 percent, fruit and berries by 40 percent, and the output of all types of fodder by 30 percent to 40 percent.

To ensure the average annual production of 1 million tons of meat (slaughter weight) in the 11th, and 1.1 million to 1.2 million tons in the 12th Five-Year Plan period, with the corresponding figures for milk at between 6.5 million to 6.7 million tons and 6.9 million to 7 million tons respectively. To raise the average annual milk yield per cow by 600 to 700 kilograms.

During the ten-year period, to bring under cultivation 10,000 hectares of irrigated land and drain waterlogged and marshy land on an area of 950,000 to 970,000 hectares. To complete the construction of top-priority flood control installations protecting farmlands in the Polesye lowlands.

To continue the buildup of capacities in the meat, dairy and other food industries; to increase production—with the use of state stocks of raw supplies—as follows: meat by 60 percent, cheese by 70 percent, and the output of potato products to between 35,000 and 38,000 tons.

In the Uzbek SSR, to make more effective use of the established land-reclamation complex. Alongside the development of cotton growing, to increase at fast rates the production of livestock products, vegetables and melon crops. To ensure an average annual crop of 2.8 million to 3 million tons of grain in the 11th, and 3.3 million to 3.5 million tons in the 12th Five-Year Plan period. To extend irrigated maize cultivation. To bring the average annual harvests of vegetable and melon crops to 3.6 million tons in the 11th, and between 4.3 million and 4.4 million tons in the 12th Five-Year Plan period.

To ensure in the ten years the growth of production of fruit and berries by about 80 percent and grapes by 200 percent. To give special consideration to increasing the output and deliveries to the trade network of table grapes and raisin grapes as well as lemons.

To secure an 80 percent to 100 percent rise in the production of all types of fodder.

To ensure the average annual production of 400,000 to 410,000 tons of meat (slaughter weight) in the 11th, and 540,000 to 560,000 tons of meat in the 12th Five-Year Plan period, and of 2.6 million and 3.5 million tons of milk respectively.

During the decade, to bring under cultivation not less than 900,000 hectares of irrigated land, and to bring water to 2.6 million hetcares of pasture land.

To develop at a high rate the food industries, especially the production of whole milk products, vegetable oil, canned vegetables and fruit, and fruit and grape juice.

In the Kazakh SSR, to ensure an average annual harvest of 28 million to 29 million tons of grain in the 11th, and 30.5 million to 31.5 million tons in the 12th Five-Year Plan Period. To work for steady growth in the output of durum and strong wheat, maize, buckwheat, millet and rice, legumes, and the seeds of oil-bearing crops.

To ensure a gross output in 1985 of 1.7 million tons, and in 1990 of approximately 2 million tons of vegetables and melon crops; to bring the production of rapeseed in 1990 to between 210,000 and 130,000 tons [sic] and steadily to increase the output of fruit and grapes for table use.

To increase the production of all types of fodder by 50 percent to 60 percent.

To ensure the average annual production of 1.2 million to 1.3 million tons of meat (slaughter weight) in the 11th, and at least 1.4 million tons in the 12th Five-Year Plan period, and of at least 4.9 million, then 5.3 million to 5.4 million tons of milk respectively. To secure a considerable increase in the productivity of dairy and beef cattle. To develop the breeding of sheep, especially fine-fleeced sheep.

In the ten-year period, to bring under cultivation 820,000 hectares of irrigated land and bring water to not less than 22 million hectares of pasture in desert and semidesert regions.

In the next ten years, the production of meat from raw stocks of state reserves should increase by at least 50 percent, that of whole-milk products by 40 percent, and of cheese by 50 percent.

In the Georgian SSR, the production of tea, grapes, lemons, tangerines and early potatoes should develop at a high rate.

The average annual production of grain should reach at least 740,000 tons in the 11th Five-Year Plan period and 750,000 to 780,000 tons in the Twelfth

Five-Year Plan period; vegetables and gourds 700,000 and between 880,000 and 900,000 tons; grapes, 1.1 million and 1.4 million tons; and high-quality tea leaves, at least 488,000 and 635,000 tons respectively.

The production of all types of fodder should be increased by 60 percent to 70 percent.

The average annual production of meat (slaughter weight) should be ensured at a level of 160,000 tons in the 11th Five-Year Plan period and 215,000 to 220,000 tons in the 12th Five-Year Plan period, and the milk yield should reach 710,000 tons and between 830,000 tons and 850,000 tons respectively. It is necessary to work for the further improvement of stock and poultry productivity.

During the ten years, 70,000 hectares of land in the Kolkhida Valley should be reclaimed and developed, 120,000 hectares of land irrigated, and 150,000 hectares of pastureland provided with water.

Production of canned fruit and vegetables is to be increased by 120 percent during the decade. It is necessary to develop the production of quality wines and of fruit and grape juices, to build up at a high rate the capacities for the production of tea, and considerably to improve tea quality.

In the Azerbaijan SSR, along with further development of cotton growing, it is necessary widely to utilize the possibilities for increasing the production of grapes, including table varieties, and of early vegetables and potatoes for delivery to the cities and industrial centers of the country.

The annual production of grapes should average 1.4 million tons in the 11th Five-Year Plan period and from 2.3 million to 2.5 million tons in the 12th Five-Year Plan period, that of grain, 1.1 million and 1.2 million tons, and vegetables and gourds, 950,000 to 970,000 tons and 1.2 million to 1.3 million tons respectively.

The production of all types of fodder is to be increased by 90 percent to 100 percent. The average annual production of meat (slaughter weight) should amount to 150,000 tons in the 11th Five-Year Plan period and between 180,000 and 185,000 tons in the 12th Five-Year Plan period, and that of milk, 850,000 to 860,000 tons and 950,000 to 970,000 tons respectively.

During the ten years, 160,000 hectares of irrigated land should be put under cultivation and water should be brought to 285,000 hectares of pastureland.

In the same period, the production of canned fruits and vegetables processed from state reserves of raw stocks is to grow by 70 percent, and that of vegetable oil by 50 percent. Capacities for the production of canned fruit and vegetables, and fruit and grape juices, as well as for the primary processing of grapes and for the production of champagne, should be developed at accelerated rates.

In the Lithuanian SSR, it is necessary to deepen the specialization of agriculture in the production of meat and dairy products. The annual production of meat (slaughter weight) should average 500,000 to 520,000 tons in the 11th Five-Year Plan period and 590,000 to 600,000 tons in the 12th Five-Year Plan period. Production of milk should average between 2.8 million and 2.9 million tons, and between 3 million and 3.10 million tons, respectively.

Production of all types of fodder is to increase by 30 percent, and the average milk yield per cow by 600 to 700 kg in the ten years.

The average annual grain production figures should reach between 3.2 million and 3.4 million tons in the 11th Five-Year Plan period and 3.6 million to 3.9 million tons in the 12th Five-Year Plan period. Production of potatoes, vegetables and fruit is to be increased.

At least 900,000 hectares of overmoist and waterlogged lands should be reclaimed in the ten years.

Production of meat from state reserves of raw stocks is to be increased by 50 percent in the ten years, that of whole milk products by 30 percent, and cheese by at least 50 percent.

In the Moldavian SSR, it is necessary to deepen the specialization of regions and farms in the production of fruits, especially drupes, and vegetables and grapes, as well as hybrid seeds of maize and sunflower.

The annual gross production of grain should average 3.6 million to 3.8 million tons in the 11th Five-Year Plan period and 3.9 million to 4 million tons in the 12th Five-Year Plan period. It is necessary to achieve considerable further increases in the production of grain maize, as well as to ensure the average annual production of grapes at a level of 1.5 million to 1.6 million tons in the 11th Five-Year Plan period and 1.7 million to 1.8 million tons in the 12th Five-Year Plan period. Production of fruits and berries must be brought up to between 1.4 million and 1.6 million tons, and 2.2 million and 2.5 million tons, respectively. Over the ten years, the production of sugar beet is to increase by 30 percent and that of sunflower and vegetables by 20 percent.

To work for considerable increases in deliveries of fresh vegetables, fruits and grapes to the cities and industrial centers of the country.

To increase the output of all kinds of fodder by 40 percent to 50 percent.

To ensure the average annual production of 300,000 to 310,000 tons of meat (slaughter weight) in the 11th Five-Year Plan period, and 340,000 to 350,000 tons in the 12th Five-Year Plan period, and, correspondingly, 1,250 thousand to 1,350 thousand tons and 1,390 thousand to 1,420 thousand tons of milk.

Over the ten years, to put under cultivation at least 240,000 hectares of irrigated land, which includes the creation of systems with the use of drip or spray irrigation for the watering of orchards and vineyards over an area of 35,000 to 40,000 hectares.

Over the whole ten-year span, to increase the production of granulated sugar from sugar beet by 70 percent, and to raise the output of meat out of the state reserves of raw stocks by 70 percent to 80 percent; canned fruits and vegetables by 100 percent; and vegetable oil by 20 percent. To expand the production of high-quality grape wines and champagne.

In the Latvian SSR, to build up at accelerated rates the output of livestock-farming produce, especially the production of cheese and butter. To provide an average annual output of 300,000 tons to 310,000 tons of meat (slaughter weight) in the 11th Five-Year Plan period and 340,000 to 345,000 tons in the 12th Five-Year Plan period; correspondingly, to process 1.8 million to 1.9 million tons and 1.9 million to 2 million tons of milk, and 2 million to 2.1 million tons, then 2.1 million to 2.3 million tons of grain. To build up the production of potatoes, vegetables, and fruits. Over the decade, to attain increases in the production of all kinds of fodder, amounting to between 30 percent and 40 percent.

To carry out land improvement work over an area of 520,000 hectares of waterlogged land.

By 1990, to increase the output of meat processed from state reserves of raw stocks by not less than 40 percent, and cheese, by 60 percent.

In the Kirghiz SSR, to ensure the average annual production of 170,000 tons of meat (slaughter weight) in the 11th Five-Year Plan period, and of 200,000 tons to 210,000 tons in the 12th Five-Year Plan period, and, correspondingly, 700,000 tons and 770,000 to 800,000 tons of milk. To increase the production of all kinds of fodder by 50 percent to 60 percent. By 1990, to raise the production of vegetables and gourds by 60 percent, of fruits and berries by 50 percent, and grapes by 80 percent.

To expand the production of sugar beet seeds with the nontransplanting technique, and also the seeds of alfalfa, for delivery to the national seed fund.

To put under cultivation over the decade not less than 150,000 hectares of irrigated land, and to irrigate 750,000 hectares of pastureland.

Over the ten-year period, to increase the output of meat from state resources of raw stocks by 50 percent, and of whole milk products by 40 percent.

In the Tajik SSR, simultaneously with a buildup of production of raw cotton, and especially the fine-fiber varieties, to effect measures for a further rise in the output of livestock products.

To ensure the average annual production of 110,000 tons of meat (slaughter weight) in the 11th Five-Year Plan period and 130,000 to 140,000 tons in the 12th Five-Year Plan period, and, correspondingly, 520,000 tons and 580,000 to 600,000 tons of milk, and 315,000 tons and 320,000 to 340,000 tons of grain.

Over the decade, to boost the production of vegetables, gourds and grapes to not less than double the present crops, fruits and berries by 40 percent, and all kinds of fodder by 50 percent to 60 percent. To achieve a rise in the production of citrus fruits, especially lemons.

To ensure over the decade the irrigation of land over an area of 100,000 to 110,000 hectares.

To develop at a rapid pace the sectors engaged in the processing of agricultural produce.

In the Armenian SSR, to ensure the average annual production of 240,000 to 260,000 tons of grapes in the 11th Five-Year Plan period, and 310,000 to 330,000 tons in the 12th Five-Year Plan period, and, correspondingly, 310,000 tons and 320,000 to 340,000 tons of grain.

Over the ten-year span, to raise the production of vegetables and gourds by 20 percent, of fruits and berries by 70 percent, and of all kinds of fodder by 40 percent.

To bring the average annual production of meat up to 95,000 tons (slaughter weight) in the 11th Five-Year Plan period, and to between 120,000 and 122,000 tons in the 12th Five-Year Plan period, and, correspondingly, 520,000 tons and 570,000 to 590,000 tons of milk. To pay special attention to the raising of productivity of stock and poultry.

To put under cultivation over the decade not less than 60,000 hectares of irrigated lands and to irrigate 120,000 hectares of pastureland.

To build up the capacities of the food sectors of industry.

In the Turkmen SSR, consistently to build up the harvest of raw cotton, especially of fine-fiber varieties, and considerably to increase the production and delivery to industrial centers of the country of gourds, currants, table grapes, and lemons.

To provide for the average annual production of 555,000 tons of vegetables and melon crops in the 11th Five-Year Plan period and 790,000 to 850,000 tons in the 12th Five-Year Plan period, and, correspondingly, 100,000 to 110,000 tons and not less than 270,000 tons of grapes, and 380,000 tons and between 450,000 and 480,000 tons of grain. To increase the production of all kinds of fodder over the decade by between 50 percent and 60 percent.

To ensure the average annual production of 90,000 tons of meat (slaughter weight) in the 11th Five-Year Plan period and of 110,000 to 111,000 tons in the 12th Five-Year Plan period, and, correspondingly, 325,000 tons and between 360,000 and 370,000 tons of milk.

To complete the construction of the Kara-Kum Canal. To put under cultivation over the ten-year span 180,000 to 190,000 hectares of irrigated lands and to irrigate 8.4 million hectares of pastureland.

Over the decade, to raise the production of canned fruits and vegetables by 90 percent, and vegetable oil, by 170 percent.

In the Estonian SSR, using the already-created potential of milk production and the accumulated experience in the raising of bacon hogs, to ensure the average annual production of 210,000 to 215,000 tons of meat (slaughter weight) in the 11th Five-Year Plan period, and 235,000 to 240,000 tons in the 12th Five-Year Plan period, and, correspondingly, between 1.2 million to 1.3 million tons and 1.3 million to 1.4 million tons of milk, and 1.4 million to 1.45 million tons and 1.5 million to 1.6 million tons of grain. To increase the gross harvest of potatoes over the decade by 20 percent, and fodder production by 40 percent.

To drain waterlogged lands over an area of 170,000 hectares. To raise the output of meat over the decade, using state reserves of raw stocks, by approximately 30 percent, and cheese by 90 percent.

IX.   THE DEVELOPMENT OF FOREIGN ECONOMIC TIES WITH SOCIALIST COUNTRIES

On the basis of long-term, goal-oriented programs, to deepen cooperation with the CMEA member countries in the field of agricultural production, processing, and the rational use of raw materials.

Consistently to promote cooperation and specialization in the production of mineral fertilizers, means of plant protection and fodder additives, as well as of machinery and equipment, including small-size machines, for the comprehensive mechanization of agricultural production, especially for the procurement and preparation of fodder and for the mechanization of work in orchards and vineyards, and in the harvesting of vegetables.

To promote scientific and technical cooperation in the field of breeding new, highly productive varieties and hybrids of agricultural crops and their introduction into production, in the cultivation of seeds and seeding stock, in the development of new strains and breeds of stock and poultry, and the use of genetic funds of plants and animals.

To expand cooperation in the field of modernization and retooling of food industry enterprises and refrigerator and storage facilities. To make wider use of the existing experience of the CMEA member countries in the production of crop-growing and livestock farming produce, using advanced technologies.

To deepen in every possible way the socialist economic integration of the CMEA member countries, and find additional possibilities for increasing the production of all kinds of foodstuffs in the interests of a further rise in the well-being of the Soviet people and the peoples of the fraternal socialist countries.

The Food Program of the Soviet Union meets the vital interests of the Soviet people. Its fulfillment will ensure a further rise in the living standards of the working people and the steady progress of Soviet society toward communism.

The country now has everything it needs for a radical approach to solving the food problem. For this purpose, it is extremely important to make the most of the vast possibilities latent in the socialist planned economy, and primarily the production potential that has been created in agriculture and other sectors of the agro-industrial complex.

A highly important task for the Party, Government and economic bodies and the trade union and Komsomol organizations is to mobilize the efforts of all work collectives for the successful accomplishment of the task of considerably raising food production.

It is necessary for the Central Committees of the Communist Parties and the Councils of Ministers of the Union Republics and for the Ministries and Departments of the USSR to draw up concrete measures for the increased production of all kinds of foodstuffs, to intensify organizational work in this direction, to launch a nationwide socialist emulation campaign for the fulfillment and overfulfillment of the assignments of the Food Program, and to establish comprehensive and effective control over the course of its implementation.

The CPSU Central Committee expressed confidence that the Soviet people would accept the Food Program as their own vital concern and would exert every effort considerably to raise food production in the shortest possible time.

Appendix 47 Y. V. ANDROPOV'S PUBLIC ASSESSMENT OF SOVIET ACHIEVEMENTS AND CHALLENGES, DECEMBER 21, 1982 [1]

. . . The path traversed by the Soviet Union in sixty years is an epoch in itself. I would say that history has never seen such rapid progress from backwardness, misery and ruin to a mighty, modern great power with an extremely high level of culture and constantly climbing living standards.

What are the most significant results of our development? History has fully borne out the theory of Marx and Lenin that the nationalities question can be settled only on a class basis. National discord and all forms of racial and national inequality and oppression have receded into the past together with social antagonism. It has been compellingly demonstrated that the Communist Party and its scientific policy are the guiding force in the socialist settlement of the nationalities question and the guarantor that this settlement is correct. Backward outlying regions populated by ethnic minorities, in many of which feudal-patriarchal and even clan relations were still dominant, have completely disappeared. An integral unionwide economic complex has formed on the basis of the dynamic economic growth of all the republics, a growth guided by the general state plan.

There has been a qualitative change of the social structure of the republics: a modern working class has emerged in each of them, the peasants are moving along the new road of collective farming, and intelligentsia of its own has been created, and skilled cadres have been trained in all areas of the life of both state and society. A socialist multinational culture has burgeoned on the basis of progressive traditions and of an intensive exchange of cultural values. Socialist nations have formed, and these now comprise a historic community, the Soviet people.

The interests of the republics are intertwining ever more closely, and the mutual assistance and mutual links that direct the creative efforts of the nations and nationalities of the USSR into a single channel are growing more productive. The all-sided development of each of the socialist nations in our country logically brings them ever closer together.

Each of the Union republics—the Russian Federation, the Ukraine and Byelorussia, Uzbekistan and Kazakhstan, Georgia and Azerbaijan, Lithuania and Moldavia, Latvia and Kirghizia, Tajikistan and Armenia, Turkmenia and Estonia —each, I repeat, of the Union republics is making an invaluable contribution to the overall growth of the economy and culture of the Soviet Union. This is not simply an adding together, but a multiplication of our creative capability.

All the nations and nationalities living in the twenty Autonomous Republics and eighteen Autonomous Regions and Areas are successfully unfolding their

[1] *Pravda*, December 22, 1982, as reproduced in *Reprints From the Soviet Press*, vol. XXXVI, No. 1 (January 15, 1983), pp. 8 ff.

potentialities in a fraternal family. The millions of Germans, Poles, Koreans, Kurds, and people of other nationalities, for whom the Soviet Union long ago became the homeland, are full-fledged Soviet citizens.

The peoples of our country address special words of gratitude to the Russian people. None of the republics' present achievements would have been possible without their disinterested fraternal assistance. The Russian language, which has naturally entered the life of millions of people of every nationality, is a factor of exceptional importance in the country's economic, political and cultural life, in the drawing together of all its nations and nationalities, in making the treasures of world civilization accessible to them.

The new Constitution of the USSR is a major landmark in the consolidation of the national-state foundations of Soviet society. This outstanding document not only sums up the results of earlier development but codifies solid and lasting political-legal principles for the further burgeoning and drawing together of all of the country's nations and nationalities.

The tangible qualitative changes that have taken place in the course of sixty years in the relations between nationalities are evidence that the nationalities question, as it was left to us by the exploiting system, has been settled successfully, finally and irreversibly. For the first time in history the multinational character of a country has turned from a source of weakness into a source of strength and prosperity. . . .

Comrades, in summing up what has been accomplished, we naturally give most of our attention to what still remains to be done. Our end goal is clear: it is, to quote Lenin's words, "not only to bring the nations closer together but to fuse them." The Party is well aware that the road to this goal is a long one. On no account must there be either any forestalling of events or any holding back of processes that have already matured.

The successes in settling the nationalities question by no means signify that all the problems generated by the very fact of the life and work of numerous nations and nationalities in a single state have vanished. That would hardly be possible so long as nations exist, so long as there are national distinctions. And those will exist for a long time to come, much longer than class distinctions. . . .

Consider the economy. Modern productive forces demand integration even in the case of different countries. Much more so do they require the close and skillful coordination of the efforts of the various regions and republics of one and the same country. The most judicious utilization of the natural and labor resources and climatic specifics of each republic and the most rational incorporation of this potential into that of the union as a whole is what will yield the greatest benefit to each region, each nation and nationality, and to the state as a whole.

Such is the general fundamental guideline. In order to put it into effect, a great deal will have to be done by our central and local planning and economic agencies. There will have to be further improvements in the distribution of the productive forces, of regional specialization and cooperation, and of the patterns of economic links and transportation. This, of course, is not an easy task. But it is on our agenda, and its fulfillment holds out the promise of considerable benefit.

The whole country is now working on the Food Program, a program that clearly defines concrete aims for all the Union republics. And each of them will have to work hard in order to make tangible contributions—in the immediate future—to the key matter of ensuring an uninterrupted supply of food for all Soviet people.

We know that the Program in its adopted form deals with immediate, urgent tasks. But if we take a long-term view, it becomes obvious that a further development of our agro-industrial complex—and, for that matter, the country's economy as a whole—will require the still more in-depth and more consistent specialization of agriculture on a nationwide scale.

One more point: in a vast country like ours, transport plays a particularly significant role—economic, political and, if you will, psychological. It is very difficult to ensure the accelerated development of all our republics and further intensification of their economic cooperation without a smoothly functioning transport system. But transport is important not only for purely economic reasons. The development of transport, of the road network, will, for example, greatly help to stabilize personnel in rural communities by bringing rural areas closer to urban ones. It will, of course, help to cope with the major social task of securing the more rational and flexible use of manpower. By facilitating everyday personal contacts on a countrywide scale, by facilitating vital ties between all the republics and areas of our country, transport brings the achievements of our socialist civilization, in the broadest sense of the term, within everyone's reach.

Our joining together in a union has become an added source of material, and indeed, spiritual wealth for the Soviet people. Here, too, however, we certainly still aren't using all of our available potentialities. We should persistently look for new methods and forms of work that suit present-day needs and make for a still more fruitful mutual enrichment of cultures, while giving everyone still broader access to all that is best in the culture of each of our peoples. Radio and television—and naturally, other mass media as well—must play a steadily increasing role in this lofty endeavor.

Of course, here we must remember that there are both good and bad, or outdated, elements in the cultural heritage, traditions and customs of each nation. Hence another task—not to conserve these bad elements but to get rid of all that is outdated and that runs counter to the norms of Soviet community life, to socialist morality, and to our communist ideals. . . .

Representation in Party and state bodies of the republics and the Union as a whole is also a highly important question. The reference here, of course, is not to any formal quotas. Arithmetic is not the way to deal with the problem of representation. There should be a consistent effort to ensure proper representation of all nationalities in every republic in the various Party and Government bodies at all levels. Unremitting regard for competence, for moral and political qualities, a caring attitude, attentiveness, and finally great tact in selecting and posting cadres are especially necessary in view of the multinational composition of the Union and Autonomous Republics.

An ever-present and all-important task is to continue instilling in Soviet people a spirit of mutual respect and friendship for all the nations and nationalities of the country, of love for their great Soviet land, of internationalism and solidarity with the working people of other countries. It is up to all Party and

Komsomol organizations, the Soviets, trade unions and our Armed Forces—all of which have always been a good school of internationalism—to work toward this end. It should also be an everyday concern of all educational establishments in our country. . . .

We speak boldly both about the existing problems and the outstanding tasks because we know for certain that we are equal to them, that we can and must solve them. A disposition to action rather than rhetoric is what we need, now as always, to make the great and powerful Union of Soviet Socialist Republics even stronger. . . .

Over these six decades the position of our Soviet state has changed radically; its prestige and influence have grown enormously. Close peaceful cooperation links the Soviet Union with countries on all continents. Its voice commands respect at international forums. The principles of peaceful coexistence—the basis of Soviet foreign policy—have won broad international recognition and have been incorporated into scores of international instruments, including the Final Act of the European Conference in Helsinki. Soviet proposals have been the basis of major UN decisions on strengthening peace and security.

But each step along the road to more stable peace has taken and still takes a lot of effort; it calls for intense struggle against imperialist war hawks. This struggle has become especially acute now that the more warlike factions in the West have become so aggressively active, their class-based hatred of socialism prevailing over considerations of realism and sometimes over plain common sense.

The imperialists have not given up their scheme for economic war against the socialist countries, for interfering in their internal affairs in the hope of eroding their social system, and are trying to win military superiority over the USSR, over all the countries of the socialist community.

Of course, these plans are sure to fail. It is not given to anyone to turn back the course of historical development. Attempts to "strangle" socialism failed even when the Soviet state was still just getting on its feet and was the only socialist country in the world. So too, surely, nothing will come of it now. . . .

No program of a further arms buildup will ever force the Soviet Union to make unilateral concessions. We will be compelled to counter the challenge of the American side by deploying corresponding weapons systems of our own— an analogous missile to counter the MX missile, and our own long-range cruise missile, which we are now testing—to counter the US long-range cruise missile.

These are certainly not threats on our part. We are wholly averse to any such course of events, and are doing everything possible to avoid it. But it is essential that those who shape US policy, as well as the public at large, should be perfectly clear on the true state of affairs. Hence, if the men in Washington really believe that new weapons systems would mean a "trump card" for the Americans at the negotiating table, we want them to know that such "trumps" are false. A policy directed at securing military superiority over the Soviet Union has no future and can only heighten the threat of war. . . .

The Soviet Union is prepared to go very far. As everyone knows, we have suggested an agreement renouncing all types of nuclear weapons—both medium range and tactical ones—designed to strike targets in Europe. But this proposal has come up against a solid wall of silence. Evidently the other side does not want to accept it, yet is afraid to reject it openly. I want to reaffirm again that we have not withdrawn this proposal.

We have also suggested another variant: that the USSR and the NATO countries reduce their medium-range weaponry by more than two-thirds. So far the United States will not consider this. For its part, it has submitted a proposal which, as if mockery, is called the "zero option." It envisages elimination of all Soviet medium-range missiles not only in the European, but also in the Asian part of the Soviet Union, while NATO's nuclear-missile arsenal in Europe is to remain intact and may even be increased. Does anyone really think that the Soviet Union can agree to this? . . .

We, for our part, will continue to work for an agreement on a basis that is fair to both sides. We are prepared, among other things, to agree that the Soviet Union should retain in Europe only as many missiles as are kept there by Britain and France—and not a single one more. This means that the Soviet Union would reduce its missiles by hundreds, including dozens of the latest missiles known in the West as SS-20s. . . . And if later on the number of British and French missiles were scaled down, the number of Soviet ones would be additionally reduced by as many.

Along with this there must also be an accord on reducing to equal levels on both sides the number of medium-range nuclear-delivery aircraft stationed in this region by the USSR and the NATO countries.

We call on the other side to accept these clear and fair terms, to take this opportuinty while it still exists. But let no one delude himself: we will never let our security or the security of our allies be jeopardized. . . .

In conclusion, let me say the following. We are for a broad, fruitful cooperation among all the nations of our planet to their mutual advantage and in the interests of all mankind—cooperation free from diktat and interference in the affairs of other countries. The Soviet Union will do everything in its power to secure a peaceful, untroubled future for the present and future generations. That is the aim of our policy, and we shall not depart from it.

A Note on Dates

Between January 1, 1700, and February 14, 1918, Russia officially followed the Julian Calendar. In the eighteenth century that calendar was eleven days behind the Gregorian Calendar used in the West; in the nineteenth century the lag was twelve days; and in the twentieth it was thirteen days. According to the Julian Calendar the serfs were emancipated on February 19, 1861 (March 3, 1861, by the Gregorian Calendar), the government of Imperial Russia collapsed on February 27, 1917 (March 12, 1917 by the Gregorian Calendar), and the Bolsheviks seized power on October 25, 1917 (November 7, 1917 by the Gregorian Calendar). To avoid chronological confusion, all dates are given here by the Gregorian Calendar.

A Note on Old Russian Measures and Weights

Officially, since September 14, 1918, the USSR has used the metric system. Occasionally, however, the following old units are employed:

Linear Measures

arshin = 71.12 cm. = 28 inches
sazhen = 3 *arshins* = 7 feet = 2.13 meters
verst = 500 *sazhens* = 0.66 mile = 1.0668 km.

Square Measures

desiatina = 2.7 acres = 2,400 square *sazhens*
hectare = 2.471 acres

Weights

funt = 0.41 kg. = 0.903 lb.
pud = 16.38 kg. = 36.113 lbs.
ton = 2,204.6 lbs.

INDEX